EU LAW TODAY

Dr Alina Kaczorowska

Dear David,
Thank you very much for
your help
Alina

OLD BAILEY PRESS

OLD BAILEY PRESS
200 Greyhound Road, London W14 9RY

First published 1998

© Old Bailey Press Ltd 1998

ISBN 1 85836 271 7

British Library Cataloguing-in-Publication.

A CIP Catalogue record for this book is available from the British
Library.

Printed and bound in Great Britain.

Contents

Contents

Acknowledgement

I wish to acknowledge first the indispensable assistance of my research associate and friend, Erving Newton, whose devotion to this book was equal to my own. I thank him for all his research, for his careful reading of the manuscript and for his insightful suggestions on every chapter. I owe a special thanks to Professor Jeremy Cooper, Head of the Law Faculty at the Southampton Institute, who encouraged me throughout, for his support and his consistent warmth. I am grateful to Andrea Dowsett my first editor, more than she will ever know. Without her, this book would never have come into being. I also wish to express a special thanks to Professor Cedric Bell, my editor, for his trust in me and my project and for his encouragement.

I have tried to state Community law as it stood on 1 September 1997.

Alina Kaczorowska
November 1997

Table of Cases

Table of Treaty Articles, Statutes and Other Materials

1 The History of European Unity: from the Roman Empire to the Treaty of Rome

The idea of a peaceful and united Europe did not come suddenly out of the blue. European unity achieved by peaceful means has been the dream of many people for many centuries but as any dream it has rarely come true. Although Europe has only flourished and prospered in peace, its history is one of bloodshed and wars. There are many examples of military conquest: from the Frankish King Charles the Great (or Charlemagne) and his successful expansion at the expense of neighbouring nations which led to the Frankish Empire being almost equal in size to that of the Roman Empire (only Britain and Southern Italy were outside his control), to the attempts of the successive emperors of the Holy Roman Empire that claimed sovereignty over the Christian world, and to Napoleon who was the master of Europe at the beginning of the nineteenth century. Also in the nineteenth century the use of force in the name of 'national security' became a vital part of national policy for many European leaders.[1] The aggressive use of force, even though the supporting ideologies varied, was often the only device for unifying Europe. In the long run, however, the military conquest of Europe brought only poverty, hunger and despair to all Europeans. Thus, it is interesting to examine the few attempts at the unification of Europe in an

---

[1] See M Mandelbaum, *The Fate of Nations: the Search for National Security in the Nineteenth and Twentieth Centuries*, New York: Cambridge University Press, 1988.

historical context when military dominance and the use of force were not involved. In this respect the contributions of the Roman Empire during the *Pax Romana*, the Roman Catholic Church in the Middle Ages, and commercial organisations such as the Hanseatic League in the fourteenth century must be considered.

Furthermore, the idea of European unity cannot be divorced from history and politics of the twentieth century. To do so would be to divorce it from reality although, in general, our century has not been a happy period in the history of Europe. Two wars of unimaginable destruction and two ruthless ideologies – Communism and Nazism – both undermining democratic institutions and the liberal tradition of individual rights, both committed to total victory no matter how high the price, tore apart the very fabric of life in Europe. The darkness which descended on our continent was brightened after World War II by modest attempts by western Europe to shape a better world through a strong, united, prosperous and democratic Europe.

1.1 The Roman Empire

With the end of the Roman Republic the aggressive policy of conquest faded away. Augustus proclaimed in January 27 BC before the Roman Senate the restoration of the Republic. In fact, this date marked the commencement of a new era for Rome, that is, the beginning of the Roman Empire. Under the principate of Augustus (27 BC–14 AD) peace in Rome and the Empire was established, social and moral renewal took place, administration was reorganised and in the provinces the development of local autonomy was encouraged.[2] The policy was to strengthen the Empire internally and, indeed, no major military operation took place in the first century apart from the conquest of Britain in 44 AD. After the death of Augustus, in his testament which was read publicly in the Senate, he advised the Romans to confine the Empire within its natural boundaries. At that time, and until the conquest of Trajan (98–117 AD), the Empire spread from the Atlantic Ocean on the west to the Euphrates on the east, from the Rhine and Danube in the north to the deserts of Arabia and Africa in the south. The wise recommendation of Augustus was adopted, for various reasons, by his successors. As the wars of expansion ceased, for the next two centuries, and especially during the period of *Pax Romana* (98 AD–180 AD), the Empire prospered and its inhabitants became gradually Romanised. For the first time, European unity was a reality. The 41 provinces of the Roman Empire with their 120 million inhabitants remained attached to Rome on a voluntary basis. The vanquished nations abandoned the idea of independence and preferred to stay an integral part of the Empire for many reasons. The most important of these was that Rome ensured lasting peace, political stability and general security within its provinces by pursuing a comprehensive policy of religious tolerance and moderation, and by conferring extensive autonomy on local governments. Furthermore, the Empire had much to offer its provinces: its exquisite literature represented by the works of Virgil, Horace, Ovid, Lucretius, Catullus, and Tacitus, and the speeches, philosophical works and letters of Cicero; and a language which at the time of the Empire became a true *lingua franca* and

---

[2] E Badian, *Roman Imperialism in the Late Republic*, Ithaca, New York: Cornell University Press, 1985; R Duncan-Jones, *The Economy of the Roman Empire*, 2nd ed, New York: Cambridge University Press, 1982.

which survived the fall of Rome and finds uses even now due to its flexibility and exactitude in many areas such as law, medicine, liturgy, natural science, etc. However, the greatest intellectual achievement of all is certainly Roman law. By 450 BC customary law of Rome was codified and written in the Twelve Tables. These rules as developed with the increase of wealth and importance of Rome formed the *ius civile*, a very formalistic set of legal rules, applied only to Roman citizens. As Rome expanded, the necessity arose for regulating legal relations between Roman citizens and foreigners. The pragmatic solution to this problem was the appointment of a special magistrate, the *praetor peregrinus* in 242 BC. He created law acceptable to both Roman citizens and foreigners called the *ius gentium*, the first truly international law as it was based on the commercial law in use in Mediterranean trade, *ius civile*, in its less formalistic version and on principles of equity and *bone fides*. The distinction between *ius civile* and *ius gentium* was obliterated when the Roman citizenship was granted to all inhabitants of the Empire in 212 AD. However, the *ius gentium* did not disappear but become an essential part of Roman law. Under the Emperor Justinian in the sixth century AD Roman law was codified in the *Corpus Juris Civilis* which consists of the *Code* (imperial statutes), the *Digest* (jurisprudence), the *Institutes* (elementary treaties) and the *Novellae*, which were added later and comprised legislation enacted by Justinian and his successors. The definition of law formulated by Celsus and cited by Ulpian in the *Digest* reflects the spirit of Roman law. It states that 'Law is the art of the good and fair' (*ius est ars boni et aequi*) and its main objective is justice which, once again according to the *Digest*, 'is the constant and perpetual will to give each man his rights'. Roman law was inspired by the idea that moral requirements were more important than strict observance of law. Although law had to be enforced as long as it was in force (*dura lex, sed lex*) its blind and strict application may lead to lawlessness (*summum ius summa inuria*), and thus such principles as equity, fairness and humanism (*bonum, aequitas* and *humanitas*) should be taken into consideration in its application and interpretation.[3] For that reason Roman law is eternal and has greatly influenced all European legal systems, including European Union law.

Although the intellectual achievements of the Romans were outstanding, they were essentially very practical people. They built an efficient transportation system based upon 50,000 miles of hard-surface highways (hence the words 'all roads lead to Rome'), and founded many towns according to strict plans which not only specified that in each city, however small it was, baths, theatres and amphitheatres were a necessity but also regulated the height of buildings and set rules for traffic. Each town was supplied with water by underground channels or aqueducts and from storage tanks the water was carried by lead pipes into houses. In Rome itself 14 aqueducts, in length totalling 265 miles, delivered about 50 gallons of water a day per head of population. Also, each town had its sewage disposal system. The practical genius of the Romans resulted in many outstanding innovations such as central heating, new methods in construction following the Romans' invention of concrete, and the building of public baths which were designed not only for cleansing the body but, more importantly, to exercise intellect as they were meeting places endowed with libraries and art exhibits. The list of benefits that the Roman Empire offered to the provinces is long. One of them is that the Romans did not impose their values and civilisation upon conquered nations but absorbed and integrated foreign culture,

---

[3] On Roman law see R W Lee, *The Elements of Roman Law*, 4th ed, London: Sweet & Maxwell, 1990.

particularly that of Greece. Also, they gave conquered nations a wide autonomy and did not interfere in local matters unless Roman interests were endangered. In this respect, it is interesting to mention that when Roman legions stationed in the province of Britain were called to defend Rome against the barbarians, the leaders of the British sent a letter to the Emperor asking for the return of the legions and pleading their allegiance to Rome. They wanted to be a part of the civilised world of the Roman Empire. As Gibbon said:

> '... the obedience of the Roman world was uniform, voluntary and permanent. The vanquished nations, blended into one great people resigned the hope, nay even the wish, of resuming their independence, and scarcely considered their own existence as distinct from the existence of Rome'.[4]

Thus, the moderate and wise policy of Rome toward their colonies made the Empire very popular amongst the conquered nations. As a result, the relationship between Rome and its provinces was based on a voluntary submission to the Roman Empire.

Another important link unifying the Roman Empire was Roman citizenship. In 212 AD Roman citizenship was granted to all free adult males living within the border of the Empire. At that time all discrimination between Roman and non-Roman population was abolished. In addition, in the Roman Empire discrimination based on race was unknown. Also, under the Roman Empire, its inhabitants enjoyed the freedom of travel and trade. Thus, for example, a Roman from Britannia could travel to Jerusalem without any passport or visa in a space of six weeks. In respect to trade, no tariffs were erected between different regions of the Empire and only harbour charges were levied on goods. As the elder Pliny said:

> 'The might of the Roman Empire has made the world the possession of all; human life has profited by the exchange of goods and by partnership in the blessing of peace.'[5]

Under the Roman Empire a highly sophisticated civilisation was created. All nations living under the rule of Rome enjoyed peace, stability and prosperity, especially during the *Pax Romana*.

1.2 The Roman Catholic Church in the Middle Ages

As the Roman Empire in the west declined and eventually fell, Christianity, one of its principal legacies, superseded the Roman Empire as the bearer of the idea of European unity. Indeed, this idea continued down the centuries in the political ambitions of the Roman Church. By the tenth century Roman Catholicism had become the official religion of all European States. Also, the crusading ideal strengthened the unity of Christendom as the military energy of the Europeans was directed toward the Muslims. The success of the first crusade launched in 1095, which captured the city of Jerusalem from the hands of infidels and resulted in the creation of the Kingdom of Jerusalem, enhanced the spiritual unity of Europe and added to the prestige of popes.

---

[4] E Gibbon, *Decline and Fall of the Roman Empire*, abridged version, London: Bison Group, 1993, pp24–25.
[5] R H Barrow, *The Romans*, London: Penguin Books, 1962, p97.

However, the papal leadership in all spiritual and temporal matters in the Christian Empire was not established overnight. In the ninth century German Kings Otto I and Otto III appointed and removed popes as they wished. In 1046, King Henry III of Germany came to Rome in order to be crowned emperor of the Holy Roman Empire and found three different claimants to the title of pope. He deposed all of them (Sylvester III, Gregory IV and Benedict IX) and appointed his own candidate, a German bishop he had brought with him, as Pope Clement. His successors to the papal throne were elected in a similar way but in the next decades the German born popes started to introduce reforms in order to purify the Church. Pope Leon IX was the first to impose his authority upon the Church, considering himself as the vicar of Christ and therefore in possession of full powers (*plenitudo potestas*) over the Church. The confrontation between the papacy and German emperors over the ultimate authority in the Christian empire lasted for centuries. The struggle of the popes to get rid of lay control in the Church started with the Investiture Controversy which questioned the emperor's practice of appointing all German bishops and bestowing them with ring and staff, symbols of the episcopal office, but preceded by an act of homage to the king. Although, the conflict was officially settled by the Concordat of Worms in 1122, and nominally represented a compromise, in fact the spiritual authority of the Church was reaffirmed.

Gregory VII was the greatest reforming pope of the Middle Ages and laid down the foundations for the future of the papacy in Europe. He fought against simony and nicolaitism (clerical marriage and concubinage), confirmed the moral authority of the Church and established its political power. He was so powerful that he deposed and excommunicated the German King and Emperor of the Holy Roman Empire, Henry IV. The excommunication was so effective that Henry IV was forced to come to Italy in 1077 as a penitent and waited outside the castle of Canossa for three cold January nights begging Gregory VII for absolution. In their confrontation, both sides invoked legal arguments based on Roman law and Canon law to bolster their claims. The popes argued that they, as the supreme representatives of God on earth, were entitled to exercise universal sovereignty. Had not Christ said to Peter:

> 'To you I shall give the keys of the kingdom of heaven: and whatsoever you shall bind on earth shall be bound also in heaven, and whatsoever you shall loose upon earth will be loosed also in heaven.'

The benefit of the legal battle between popes and emperors, however, was the revival of legal studies in Italian universities.[6]

By twelfth and thirteenth centuries the papal leadership in all matters was accepted throughout Europe, and the distinction between Church and 'States' as separate entities had disappeared. European kingdoms voluntarily recognised the feudal suzerainty of the papacy.[7] The supreme spiritual authority of the Church, combined with papal primacy and infallibility in all matters, led to their intervention in political affairs. Although Jesus said that 'My kingship is not of this world', all vital political questions of Europe were of concern

---

[6] H Wierussowski, *The Medieval University*, Princeton: Van Nostrand, 1966.
[7] See G Barraclough, *The Medieval Papacy*, New York: W Norton, 1968; H A Oberman, *The Harvest of Medieval Theology*, Cambridge: Labyrinth Press, 1963.

and subject to the interference of the Church. At its height the medieval Church was omnipresent. Furthermore, the Church had developed a system of ecclesiastical courts all over Europe that touched the lives of virtually every person in Christendom. As well as dealing with sacramental matters and the governance of Church property and heresy, the Church's jurisdiction extended into secular areas, including matrimonial causes and legitimacy, wills, sexual crimes, oaths and promises. Appeals went to bishops and through papal legates to Rome, as the pope was the highest judicial authority. By the end of the twelfth century, the papal court was one of the busiest in Europe. To all cases Canon law was applied, which consisted of a compilation of various rules and regulations (canons) together with papal laws and decisions called *decretals*. All this legal material was published in 1500 in Paris in *Corpus Juris Canonici* (Corpus of Canon law). At that time, lawyers were trained in Canon law schools at Bologna and served later as advisors to virtually all the governments in Europe.

The *Republicana Christiana* of the Middle Ages had unified Europe morally and spiritually. It influenced social, political and economic life in Europe. Christianity had created a common culture and similar way of life throughout Europe.

1.3 Economic integration in Europe in the Middle Ages

Also in the Middle Ages another interesting attempt at unifying Europe took place, although economic objectives were placed in the foreground. With the revival of trade in the tenth century merchants started to travel throughout Europe in order to sell, buy and place orders for various goods.[8] These commercial activities required the establishment of a common legal framework. Out of necessity the European merchants created their own rules of conduct and fair dealing which formed the *lex mercatoria*. Furthermore, some merchant organisations became very powerful by monopolising the trade of certain goods in some regions of Europe. The most striking example is provided by the Hanseatic League.

Medieval commercial communities and the lex mercatoria

This pragmatic, universal and uniform law which developed out of the activities of the guilds and the maritime cities was created by practical men engaged in commerce for themselves and administered promptly and efficiently by courts of merchants. This cosmopolitan law would not be workable without such concepts as 'my word is my bond', 'bethink you of my poor honesty' and 'goodwill'.[9] At the centre of these trading activities was the principle of good faith. External factors reinforced the importance of these principles. First, the business practices of merchants were devoid of all legal sanctions. Particularly, at the first stage of formation of the *lex mercatoria*, the royal and feudal courts refused to enforce the newly established rules of conduct invented by merchants. Thus, it was in the interests of merchants, and essential to the development of commerce, to deal with

---

[8] R S Lopez, *The Commercial Revolution of the Middle Ages, 950–1350,* New York: Cambridge University Press, 1971.

[9] A Kadar, K Hoyle and G Whitehead, *Business Law*, 2nd ed, Oxford: Oxford University Press, 1987, p12.

litigation involving members of the merchant community. Special courts were instituted which decided on the basis of commercial expediency what was fair, just and reasonable under the circumstances of the case. Relying on business practices, usages of trade, legal principles of Canon law such as *pacta sunt servanda* and the notion of *bone fides*, the merchant courts settled cases quickly 'between tides' in ports or in the 'piepowder courts' on the last day of a fair. The merchant courts, due to the practical common sense of the judges, themselves merchants and familiar with mercantile practices, achieved excellent solutions for problems regarding international trade. They created a new, flexible and professional body of rules which was truly universal and uniform.

Second, a merchant was closely connected with the community within which he operated. The same group of merchants moved from fair to fair throughout Europe. Everyone knew everyone else or at least could find out easily about the other party. Thus, the reputation of a merchant, his good name, was an essential part of his business. If he wished to earn his living as a merchant, he had to deal in good faith and conduct his affairs honestly. The pressure that could be exercised by the community of merchants made the enforcement of decisions of commercial courts easy, since an undesirable member of the community could be forced out of business if he refused to comply with a judgment rendered by a commercial court.

Also, fairs in the Middle Ages contributed to the development of the *lex mercatoria* as they constituted a meeting place for merchants. The greatest fairs took place in the region of Champagne as it was situated between Flanders and Italy, the two most commercialised areas in Europe, the largest being the 'Hot Fair' at Troyes.[10] During fairs the local authorities ensured safety and honest dealings by appointing 'Keepers of the Fair' who patrolled the market place, kept the master set of measures against which all the merchants' sets of measures had to be calibrated, and protected merchants from unfair competition and the public from defective or underweight goods. Thieves were persecuted and dishonest merchants barred from all future fairs. The truly international fairs, such as the six trade fairs organised in Champagne, attracted merchants from all over Europe and 'these great international exchanges connected the financial and marketing centres of the south with the manufacturing and trading communities of the north, tying the northern world to the south more effectively than had any system since the political institutions of the Roman Empire'.[11]

Finally, French became a *lingua franca* of commercial communities in Europe.

The Hanseatic League

Certain organisations of merchants in the Middle Ages became very powerful. The Hanseatic League, which to some extent can be considered as a forerunner of the European Economic Community, is the best example in this area.[12] The League was formed in the 1280s when

---

[10] J and F Gies, in *Life in a Medieval City*, New York: 1969, describe medieval urban life in the city of Troyes, amid the Champagne fairs.

[11] M Kishlansky, P Geary, P O'Brien, *Civilisation in the West*, Volume A, New York: Harper Collins Publishers, 1991, p275.

[12] See P Dollinger, *The German Hansa*, Stanford: Stanford University Press, 1970.

northern German towns and merchants which mastered trade in the Baltic Sea joined in association with merchants from Cologne and Rhineland who operated in Flanders and England. The northern German towns set up a political alliance to control northern trade in the twelfth and early thirteenth centuries. Lübeck became the major town from which merchants from Westphalia and Saxonia expanded their trade northward and eastward. The northern German merchants established themselves in Visby, Novgrad, Riga, Reval (now Tallinn), Danzing (now Gdansk) and Dorpat (now Tartu), thus monopolising Baltic trade. Once the two powerful associations of merchants united in the Hanseatic League all trade in the Baltic and North Sea was in one hand. The Hanseatic League had mainly commercial objectives: to protect and develop its trading interests; to ensure peace and order in its towns; to protect its ships from pirates and brigands; to ensure safe navigation by building lighthouses and training pilots; to introduce common legislation in all Hanseatic towns (based on the law of Lübeck); to defend merchants and their goods; and to expand its trade by gaining new privileges and monopolies from foreign political leaders and gain access to new markets. Usually, the League was against the use of force and relied heavily on loans, bribes and gifts to local authorities where required. The League did not hesitate to resort to blockades of ports and embargoes if its interests were threatened, on one occasion in 1368 raising an army and crushing the Danes when the Danish King Valdemar IV wanted to deprive the League of its monopoly in the southwestern Baltic. The defeated Danes signed the Treaty of Stralsund in 1370 recognising the League's supremacy in the Baltic by granting it exclusive rights to export Scandinavian fish throughout Europe. The goods that the League shuttled back and forth across Baltic and North Sea included grain, timber, furs, tar, honey, flax, fish, salt, wax and spices, as well as cloth and other finished products. The League had both established ports at various cities and set up permanent commercial enclaves in towns such as Bruges in Flanders, Bergen in Norway and the Steel Yard in London. At its heights in the fourteenth century the Hanseatic League had a membership of about 100 towns. The only permanent body of the League was its assembly (diet) which met from time to time. With the rise of the nation-state the Hanseatic League declined, its last diet being held in 1669.

1.4 The twentieth century

In the first decades of this century, the idea of European unity was very popular in intellectual circles but was not supported by European public opinion. According to Ward '... another of many ironies which pervaded European studies is that the most substantive intellectual fuel for European Union in the immediate post-1918 years was British',[13] and he cites the examples of Lord Milner's Round Table Movement, the work of British economists Lionel Robbins and William Beveridge, as well as the impact of the British federalist movement upon Sir Winston Churchill which culminated in his famous Declaration of Anglo-French Union on 16 June 1940. Due to the German invasion of France the proposed union failed.

In other European countries the federalist idea resulted in the creation of the Pan-

---

[13] I Ward, *A Critical Introduction to European Law*, London: Butterworths, 1996, p3.

European Movement by Count Richard Coudenhove-Kalergi in 1923 aimed at reinforcing European autonomy and shielding Europe from Soviet and American domination. Also, Giovanni Angelli and Attilo Cabiati advocated a federal structure for Europe in order to replace the inefficient League of Nations. However, the one and only attempt at formalising the idea of a federal Europe came from Aristide Briand, the French Minister for Foreign Affairs. Briand in his speech before the Assembly of the League of Nations on 5 September 1929, backed by the German Foreign Minister, Gustav Streseman, declared that the moment had come for 'a kind of federal link' among European nations. A French memorandum based on his speech was transmitted to all European States in 1930 and a special European Committee was set up by the League of Nations in order to study governmental comments on the French project.[14] Nothing came of it, European countries showing a total lack of enthusiasm. Furthermore, the death of Aristide Briand in March 1932 and, most importantly, Hitler's rise to power in 1933 stopped any hope of European unity. Unfortunately, attempts at the unification of Europe by force in the twentieth century have been more popular than peaceful means. Indeed, Europe has witnessesed and survived two powerful ideologies – Communism and Nazism – trying to unify Europe in their own manner.

1.5 Communism

The ideological foundations of Communism emanate from the *Communist Manifesto* of Karl Marx who believed that the class struggle which constitutes the result of the dialectical nature of history would culminate in the world revolution. As Marx wrote in the *Communist Manifesto* of 1848: 'The bourgeoisie produces its own grave-diggers. The fall of the bourgeoisie and the victory of the proletariat are equally inevitable.'[15] However, Marx was unsure whether the old world would perish by a violent revolution or a permanent revolution. When the first Communist world revolution occurred in Russia it was Vladimir Ilich Ulyanov, known as Lenin, who adapted the ideas of Marx to the Russian conditions. In practice, Communism instead of creating a paradise for the working class became an oppressive, totalitarian regime ruthlessly eliminating political adversaries and completely disregarding fundamental human rights.[16]

The aggressive expansion of Communism by use of all possible means had been experienced for the first time during the Soviet-Polish war in 1920. On 25 April 1920, Marshall Jozef Pilsudski, the Polish leader, frightened by the Soviet regime and the sovietisation of eastern Europe, decided to assist Ukraine to became an independent State, and at the same time pursued his dream of restoring the Grand Polish-Lithuanian-Ukrainian Empire, that is, Poland within the frontiers before the partition. At that time civil war in Russia was in full blossom and both fighting factions – the White and the Red – were exhausted by the ferocious struggle. The Polish army took Kiev but the Red Army

---

[14] F Kirgis, Jr, 'The European Communities', in *International Organisations in Their Legal Setting: Documents, Comments, and Questions*, St Paul: West, 1977, p603.

[15] K Marx, *Manifeste Communiste*, Paris: Editions Costes, 1947, p54.

[16] S Fitzpatrick, *The Russian Revolution, 1917–1932*, Oxford: Oxford University Press, 1982.

recaptured the capital of Ukraine and continued to advance to Warsaw itself. The battle of Warsaw was decisive as to the destiny of Europe. The Red Army created by Leon Trotsky had no intention of stopping at the gates of Warsaw but was set to conquer the entire continent. Josef Pilsudski, with advice from French attaché General Maxime Weygard, in what is known as the '18 decisive battles in the history of our civilisation', defeated the Red Army, taking 66,000 prisoners and recapturing vast territories of Byelorussia (now Belarus). Thus, the first attempt at conquering the whole world by the Soviet Russia was a total failure. The Treaty of Riga, signed between the Poles and the Soviet Russia on the humiliating terms for the latter, ended the march of the Red Army 'through the heart of Poland to the conquest of Europe and world conflagration'.[17]

The aggressive policy of the Soviet Union, the centre of world revolution, continued. On 23 August 1939 the Molotov-Ribbentrop Non-aggression Pact between the USSR and Germany was signed. The partition of Poland was decided and Hitler's support for the USSR in overtaking Finland, the Baltic States and Bessarabia was promised to Stalin in return for non-interference in Germany's invasion of Poland.

The next opportunity for the USSR to expand was provided by the end of World War II. The 'liberation' of the eastern part of Europe from German occupation by the Red Army gave the Russians an opportunity for military and political control of these countries. Once the Red Army entered it stayed, and as a result nine countries which before 1939 had been independent became incorporated into the Soviet Union as republics (for example, Latvia, Lithuania and Estonia), or became Soviet satellites. Stalin imposed a police state and terror equal to that of Nazi Germany in the 'liberated territory'. Crimes against humanity, and atrocities and contempt for basic human rights were common in the USSR and all occupied countries. Stalin built a network of concentration camps (gulags) for his own people where millions worked to death in inhuman conditions. His suspicious and paranoid mind saw imperialist plots everywhere. Tens of millions of people were tortured by his political police, the NKVD, to confess imaginary crimes and then were condemned to death or forced labour in gulags. Two of his crimes are particularly appalling. When Ukraine resisted Stalin's collectivisation of agriculture, as a punishment he imposed very high quotas of delivery of agricultural products and confiscated all foodstuffs. These measures resulted in a famine in Ukraine in 1932–33 and a loss of at least five million lives. At that time, Stalin continued to export Russian grain abroad without any consideration for the peasantry of Ukraine dying from hunger. Also, Stalin had no qualms in committing one of the worse war crimes in the history of mankind. He ordered the execution of Polish military officers, prisoners of war of 1939, by the NKVD, who shot and then buried the soldiers in mass graves in the woods of Katyn (only 4,443 bodies were found out of 15,000 missing Polish officers).[18] It was also in the name of Communism that the Hungarian uprising in 1956 was crushed by the Red Army and the Hungarian reformist prime minister, Imre Nagy, was murdered. Subsequent military interventions in Czechoslovakia in 1968, and the invasion of Afghanistan in 1979, etc, were also aimed at achieving the expansion of Communism. Fortunately, the Soviet empire collapsed in 1989 – Michail Gorbachev, the laureate of the Nobel Peace Prize of 1990, accepted the inevitable and set eastern Europe free that year.

---

[17] Quoted by D Lasok, *Law and Institutions of the European Union*, 6th ed, London: Butterworths, 1994, p3.
[18] A Hall, *War Crimes*, London: Blitz Editions, 1993, pp33–41.

1.6 Nazism

As to Nazism, the Third Reich was born on 30 January 1933 when Adolf Hitler was sworn in as Chancellor of the German Republic by its President, Field Marshal Paul von Hindenburg. Adolf Hitler was not imposed upon the Germans but lawfully appointed the Chancellor in accordance with the German constitution as leader of the largest party, the National Socialist German Worker's Party. Hitler in *Mein Kampf* (My Struggle), which constitutes a blueprint for the Third Reich (he wrote it in prison after his unsuccessful putsch of 1923), put forward his ideas of the New Order he intended to build in the conquered Europe. He abandoned the idea of the Hohenzollern Empire to expand Germany in Africa and emphasised that German territorial policy should not be fulfilled in the Cameroons but almost exclusively in Europe. He wanted to create *Volksgemeinschaft*, a racial community where only the true Aryan would enjoy privileges, and people of inferior blood would become slaves or would be eliminated. However, all people of German nationality, the Aryan race that belonged to the master race, needed the living space – *Lebensraum* – which according to Hitler could be found in the east as this territory was inhabited by Slavs, an inferior race (subhumans). According to him the conquest of the Soviet Russia would not pose a major problem for Germany since Russia was under the government of Jewish-Bolsheviks. Hitler hated capitalists, socialists, pacifists and liberals – all of them were associated in his mind with Jews.

Once in power, Hitler established the dictatorship and started to implement his policy of crude Darwinism in both internal and external matters. For the Germans, the 'Lords of the Earth' who followed blindly and with great enthusiasm, a new era had commenced. In 1936 Hitler invaded the Rhineland thus freeing Germany from the shackles of the Versailles Treaty and started a rearmament programme which created jobs for six million unemployed Germans. He incorporated German workers into his programme of *Volksgemeinschaft* by providing subsidised holidays and leisure activities within his 'Strength through Joy' scheme, and an opportunity to acquire an automobile, the Volkswagen, a symbol of wealth and luxury for every German worker. They, as everybody else, paid dearly for their folly and even their Volkswagen never materialised during the Third Reich.[19] Hitler ruthlessly prosecuted his political adversaries, Jews, the mentally ill and handicapped, gypsies, Jehovah's Witnesses and homosexuals. Indeed, not every German was welcomed in his *Volkgemeinschaft* or was worthy of propagation as the Law for the Protection of Hereditary Health of 14 July 1933 made clear. This legislation authorised the sterilisation of about two million people. Hitler had an obsessive hatred of Jews, blaming them for everything, even the war that he had started, a war which resulted in the extinction of six million Jews. From the Nuremberg Laws of September 1935 which stripped all Jews of their German citizenship, prohibited mixed marriages and any sexual intercourse between Jews and

---

[19] This scheme was one of the biggest swindles of the Third Reich. Every worker had to pay a weekly instalment of five marks out of his salary toward the total of 999 marks. The design of the new car was claimed by Hitler, although in fact it was executed under the supervision of Dr Ferdinand Porsche. Not a single car was delivered to its owner during the Third Reich. For the history of Volkswagen and the use of slave labour and prisoners of war during the Third Reich by Volkswagen see H Mommsen and M Grieger, *Das Volkswagenwerk und Seine Arbeiter im Dritten Reich*, Düsseldorf: Econ Verlag, 1996.

Germans, to the *Kristallnacht* (Night of Broken Glass of 9–10 November 1938) when Jews and their property were viciously attacked, the 'final solution' to the Jewish problem was planned. Its execution was entrusted to Adolf Eichmann and consisted of the physical extermination of European Jews in the gas chambers of Auschwitz, Treblinka, Sobibor, Bergen-Belsen and other concentration camps.

The German plan was also to conquer the entire European continent. Initially successful, the Germans introduced Hitler's New Order in Europe, a reign of terror, sadism and madness. But after twelve years, four months and eight days, the Third Reich which was to have lasted for a thousand years collapsed. Germany surrendered unconditionally at 2.45 on the morning of 7 May 1945 to the allied forces. General Jodl who signed the act of capitulation for Germany was authorised to submit a final plea for his country. He said:

> 'With this signature the German people and the German armed forces are, for better or worse, delivered into the hands of the victors … In this hour I can only express the hope that the victor will treat them with generosity.'

No answer came from the allied side.[20]

Indeed, forgiveness and reconciliations were not easy. Some 50 million people lost their lives during the World War II, 60 million across 55 ethnic groups from 27 countries were displaced, 45 million were left homeless, many millions were wounded and only some 670,000 were liberated from the Nazi death camps. The psychological devastation of the survivors was even greater than the physical destruction: holocaust, genocide, slave labour, mass killing, mass rape, concentration camps and other horrors perpetrated during World War II exceeded anything ever experienced. Europe was shocked by the atrocities and lay in ruins; its inhabitants were hungry, sick and without a future.

The rebuilding of Europe posed not only a formidable challenge but was also the catalyst that led to European unity. Many factors have contributed to a new perception of post-war Europe, most important was the United States' vision of the post-war world and reconstruction of Europe.

1.7 The United States' vision of the post-war world

The United States' vision of the post-war world was based on President Woodrow Wilson's Fourteen Point Plan, which was outlined on 8 January 1918 in his speech to the US Congress. He advocated free trade, open negotiations, freedom of the sea to all nations in wartime and peace, reduction of armaments, self-determination for many European nations that were under foreign domination, a reform of the existing colonial system which would take into account the interests of the native people and, above all, establishment of international law and a collective security system which would ensure lasting peace and make World War I the 'war to end war', the last war in the history of mankind. According to Wilson in order to oversee the new system:

> 'a general association of nations must be formed under specific covenants for the purpose of

---

[20] W L Shirer, *The Rise and Fall of the Third Reich*, London: Mandarin, 1991, p1139.

affording mutual guarantees of political independence and territorial integrity to great and small states alike'.[21]

The League of Nations was set up in 1920 on the basis of this proposal.[22]

Wilsonian internationalism, which considered war as an atavism and advocated democracy and freedom, served as an ideological foundation for the United States' new international order after World War II, although some modifications were introduced in order to avoid mistakes that were made after 1918. The first concrete measure in this direction was taken by the US in 1943 with the establishment of the United Nations Relief and Rehabilitation Administration to distribute food and medicine to people suffering in the war-stricken areas. The United States' vision of the post-war world encompassed economic, commercial, financial, and political matters. At the Bretton Woods Conference in summer 1944 the monetary and banking issues were discussed by representatives of 44 countries. As a result, the International Monetary Fund was set up which provided the basis for the international monetary system that prevailed until August 1971. Its main function was to supervise the international exchange market intervention system and supplied supplementary international reserves if needed.[23] Also, the International Bank for Reconstruction and Development (the World Bank) was established at the same time which finances governments and private projects that further the economic development of Member States when private loans are not available on reasonable terms. Moreover, it provides technical assistance in respect of these projects when appropriate.

The liberalisation of international trade was to be conducted by the International Trade Organisation which did not materialise as the US Congress decided against US participation in the proposed organisation, despite the fact that the United States drafted its charter in 1945. Instead, the General Agreement on Tariffs and Trade (GATT, which has recently been renamed the World Trade Organisation (WTO)) has become a device for co-ordination of national policies on international trade.[24] The main purpose of GATT (now the WTO) is to remove trade barriers by eliminating or reducing tariffs and non-tariff barriers to trade, and outlawing discriminatory practices in international trade. The last round of tariff negotiations conducted under the auspices of GATT, known as the Uruguay Round, began in 1986 and was completed in December 1993. It turned out to be a great success. Indeed, the multilateral negotiations resulted in the agreed cut in subsidies for export of agricultural products by 36 per cent in value and domestic farm supports by 20 per cent over six years, while over 40 per cent of manufactured goods would enter foreign markets without tariffs and the remaining tariffs for such goods would be reduced by over one-third. Much stricter

---

[21] See Point XIV in *Selected Literary and Political Papers and Addresses of Woodrow Wilson*, Volume 2, New York: Grosset and Dunlap, 1927.

[22] For a comprehensive study of the League of Nations: F Walters, *A History of the League of Nations*, London: Oxford University Press, 1952.

[23] R M Dunn and J C Ingram, *International Economics*, 4th ed, London: John Wiley & Sons, 1996, pp479–536.

[24] J Jackson, *The World Trading System, Law and Policy of International Economic Relations*, Cambridge: the MIT Press, 1992, pp27–57.

protection for intellectual property and the extension of the GATT powers in the enforcement of dumping, subsidies and other areas were agreed.[25]

In political matters, the Atlantic Charter, drafted by Roosevelt and Churchill at a meeting on the *USS Augusta* off Newfoundland in August 1941, outlined the political future of the post-war world. On 1 January 1942 Soviet Russia, together with 26 other nations, approved the Atlantic Charter by signing the Declaration of the United Nations and thus agreeing on Roosevelt's Four Freedoms – freedom of speech, freedom of worship, freedom from want, freedom from fear everywhere in the world – as necessary requirements of peace, the restoration of independence for all the States that had been invaded by the Germans, as well as the right of all people to determine their own form of government, and the creation of a new international system of general security which would effectively disarm aggressor nations. The idea of creating a successor to the League of Nations was carried out and developed in the 'Declaration of Moscow' and at a conference in Teheran, where Roosevelt, Churchill and Stalin meet in 1943. This was followed by the Dumbarton Oaks Conference where representatives of China, the Soviet Union, the United Kingdom and the United States formulated the main principles of the United Nations. At the meeting of Churchill, Roosevelt and Stalin in Yalta in February 1945 it was decided to call for an international conference in San Francisco in order to draft a charter for the United Nations. Also in Yalta important concessions were made to Stalin concerning the Soviet annexation of a large section of eastern Poland in return for free elections to be held in Poland. Roosevelt was convinced that only co-operation between super powers and their participation in a new international organisation would bring lasting peace. He considered that the failure of the League of Nations was essentially due to the absence of the United States and the Soviet Union within the organisation. The Conference in San Francisco was attended by 260 representatives of 50 States, and on 26 June 1945 the Charter of the United Nations was signed.[26] After the five great powers (the United States, the Soviet Union, China, the United Kingdom and France) and a majority of its signatories ratified the Charter, the United Nations was officially established on 24 October 1945.[27]

---

[25] For the detailed contents of the Uruguay Round Agreement see: *The Economic Report of the President: 1994*, Washington DC: US Governmental Printing Office, 1994, pp205–240; J Schott, *The Uruguay Round: an Assessment*, Washington DC, Institute for International Economics, 1994.

[26] Poland was not represented at the San Francisco Conference but signed the Charter later and thus become one of the 51 original signatories.

[27] The main purposes of the United Nations as described in art 1 of the Charter are:

'1. To maintain international peace and security, and to that end: to take effective measures for the prevention and removal of threats to the peace, and for the suppression of acts of aggression of other breaches of the peace and to bring about by peaceful methods, and in conformity with the principles of justice and international law, adjustment or settlement of international disputes or situation which might lead to a breach of the peace.
2. To develop friendly relations among nations based on respect for the principle of equal rights and self–determination of people, and to take other appropriate measures to strengthen universal peace.
3. To achieve international co-operation in solving international problems of an economic, social, cultural, or humanitarian character, and in promoting and encouraging respect for human rights and for fundamental freedoms for all without distinction as to race, sex, language, or religion.
4. To be a centre for harmonizing the actions of nations in the attainment of these common ends.'

For brief history of the UN and its transformation after the end of Cold War see P R Baehr and L Gordenker, *The United Nations in the 1990s*, 2nd ed, London: Macmillan, 1994.

The United Nations has six principal organs: the General Assembly, the Security Council, the Economic and Social Council, the Trusteeship Council, the International Court of Justice and the Secretariat. The system set up by the Charter can work properly only in an atmosphere of co-operation amongst the major powers since they assigned to themselves the role of an international gendarme which is reflected by their voting rights in the Security Council. Indeed, the big five are permanent members of the Security Council which, under art 24 of the Charter, is the main institution responsible for the maintenance of international peace and security. It is the only organ of the UN that is entitled to pass a binding resolution under Chapter VII and, particularly, arts 41 and 42 which provide for enforcement measures, including the use of force when international peace is in jeopardy. However, a veto by any of the permanent members is sufficient to block all but procedural resolutions of the Council.[28] The veto was one of the major causes of the failure of the Security Council as the relationship between the Soviet Union and the United States steadily deteriorated once the war ended.[29]

Stalin never intended to keep his promises; free elections did not take place in Poland or any other eastern European country under Soviet Union control. Instead pro-Soviet puppet regimes were established, and the US President Truman responded by terminating the Lend-Lease aid to the Soviet Union. On both sides positions were hardening and suspicions were mounting. The Cold War had begun which ended the possibility for establishing a new world order based on the American ideals. As Winston Churchill said in his speech in Missouri in 1946: 'From Stettin in the Baltic to Trieste in the Adriatic an iron curtain has descended across the continent'.[30]

1.8 The United States and European reconstruction

Three factors have determined the policy of the United States towards European reconstruction: political, economic and humanitarian.

As to the political factor, the Cold War and consequently the division of Europe into two blocs prompted the United States to prevent the spread of Communism at all costs. On 12 March 1947 President Truman announced his approach towards the Soviet Union before Congress. He said:

'At the present moment in world history nearly every nation must choose between alternative ways of life. The choice is too often not a free one ... It must be the policy of the United States to support people who are resisting attempted subjugation by armed minorities or by outside pressure.'[31]

His statement is known as the Truman doctrine. Immediately after his speech Truman asked for financial aid of $400 million for Greece and Turkey in order to contain the expansion of Communism in both countries. As the United Kingdom was no longer able to

---

[28] F L Kirgis, 'The Security Council's First Fifty Years' (1995) 89 Am JIL 506–539.
[29] W Lafeber, *America, Russia and the Cold War, 1945–1966*, New York: John Wiley & Sons, 1978.
[30] H Middleton, *Britain and the World since 1750*, Oxford: Basil Blackwell, 1984, p93.
[31] M Kishlansky, P Geary and P O'Brian, *Civilisation in the West, Volume C*, New York: Harper Collins, 1991, p928.

sustain economic and military aid to Greece, where a civil war provoked by Communists had erupted, and to Turkey, which was under pressure from the Soviet Union for setting up bases and allowing naval passage through the Dardanelles, the United States felt it necessary to intervene. From that time the containment of Communism has played an important role in helping European reconstruction.

It was not the only factor that shaped American policy toward Europe. The United States had emerged from the war richer and more powerful than ever. As a main supplier for the allied forces, its industry and business boomed. In 1945–46 the US had accounted for half of the gross world products of goods and services and held two-third of the world's gold. Therefore, for the Americans it was necessary to find new markets. Only a prosperous Europe could became a major market for American goods, and thus American self-interest has contributed to European recovery.

Finally, there were also humanitarian considerations which should not be minimised. Indeed, the chaos facing post-war Europe was an obstacle to any significant progress towards political stability and economic prosperity. From 1945 to 1947 Europe did not make any significant progress in this direction

1.9 The Marshall Plan (formally known as the European Recovery Programme (April 1948 – December 1951))[32]

Against the background outlined in the previous section, Truman's Secretary of State, George C Marshall, at a conference at Harvard University on 5 June 1947, announced the American plan for European reconstruction. In order to eliminate 'hunger, poverty, desperation and chaos', the real enemies of freedom and democracy, and to restore 'the confidence of the European people in the economic future of their own countries', Marshall proposed cash grants to all European nations under two conditions: European States were to co-operate in the distribution of American aid and they had to abolish progressively trade barriers.[33] All European nations were invited to participate in the Marshall Plan; even the Soviet Union if it contributed some of its resources to the cause. Stalin called the plan a capitalist plot and forced all countries under his control which had expressed interests in the Plan, such as Poland and Finland, to withdraw. However, the British Foreign Secretary, Ernest Bevin, informed Parliament that when the Marshall proposals were announced he grabbed them with both hands. So did other European countries. As a result of the Marshall Plan $13.6 billion was transferred to Europe, in addition to $9.5 billion in earlier loans and $500 million in private charities. The Marshall Plan was a huge success as it helped to restore western European trade and production while controlling inflation, and by 1951 western Europe was booming. However, not only the Plan itself but, most importantly, the manner in which it was administered greatly contributed to the European unity. Sixteen

---

[32] It is interesting to mention that in the original draft bill of Marshall Aid which provided that: 'It is further declared to be the policy of the United States should at all times be dependent on the continuity of co-operation among countries taking part in the programme' the word 'co-operation' was replaced by the word 'unification' in its 1949 and 1950 enactments in the US Congress.

[33] S Hoffman and C Maier, *The Marshall Plan: a Retrospective*, Boulder Co, Westview Press, 1984, p6.

European countries participated in the plan: Austria, Belgium, Denmark, France, Greece, Iceland, Ireland, Italy, Luxembourg, The Netherlands, Norway, Portugal, Sweden, Switzerland, Turkey and the United Kingdom. West Germany joined the Plan later and thus through economic co-operation West Germany was reconciled with other European countries. Under the leadership of France and the United Kingdom, the Committee of European Economic Cooperation was set up, to be later replaced by the permanent Organisation for European Economic Co-operation (OEEC) to plan and distribute American aid. The main features of the administration of the plan were: co-operation among its participants in order to stabilise their economies; intensified planning at the inter-governmental level, thus developing a global approach toward economic recovery; limited nationalisation in all member States; and co-operation between private and public sectors in order to free market forces, modernise production and raise productivity. The success of reconstruction through centrally co-ordinated planning and co-operation in Europe made clear that the best way to recover an international position and prestige for Europe was to act as an entity in the world markets. As a result of economic co-operation within the framework of the Marshall Plan, various European organisation began to emerge in order to strengthen inter-governmental integration in political, military and economic matters.

1.10 Western European integration

In the aftermath of World War II, public opinion in many European countries favoured the adoption of a federal approach towards European integration. Winston Churchill delivered a famous speech in September 1946 at the University of Zurich which urged the formation of a United States of Europe.[34] His vision of a United Europe did not include the United Kingdom as he considered that the world peace would be ensured if three powerful democratic groups: the United States of America, the United Kingdom and its Commonwealth and a United States of Europe acted together in areas such as defence and certain aspects of foreign policy. The cornerstone of European unity would be the close co-operation between France and Germany. Winston Churchill as an advocate of European unity was asked to chair a meeting held in The Hague in 1948. This so-called Congress of Europe gathered together representatives of non-governmental federalist movements in Europe.[35] It resulted in the creation of the Council of Europe. Its statute was signed on 5 May 1949 in London and entered into force on 3 August 1949.

---

[34] He declared: 'I am going to say something that will astonish you. The first step in the re-creation of the European family must be a partnership between France and Germany.[...] We must re-create the European family in a regional structure called, it may be, the United States of Europe' in M Charlton, *The Price of Victory*, London: British Broadcasting Corporation, 1983, pp38–39.

[35] Over 700 delegates from 16 countries and observers from ten others attended a 'Congress of Europe' in The Hague which called for a united Europe, especially for a European Assembly, a Charter and a Court of Human Rights. It set up an unofficial organisation, the European Movement, that submitted to the governments of Belgium, France, Luxembourg, The Netherlands and the UK proposals in this respect. In 1948 those countries concluded the Brussels Treaty which provided for military, economic, social and cultural co-operation.

Political integration of Europe: the Council of Europe

The Council of Europe, which has its headquarters in Strasbourg, is one of the most efficient and competent inter-governmental organisations in Europe. At its conception it had only ten members, today it claims a membership of 36 States. Since the collapse of the Soviet Union and the admission of new members from central and eastern European States, including Russia, the Council of Europe encompasses almost the entire continent. Only a democratic country which ensures the protection of human rights may become a member of the Council of Europe.

The main objectives of the Council of Europe are: the promotion of European unity by proposing and encouraging common European action in economic, social, legal, and administrative matters; the protection of both human rights and fundamental freedoms and pluralist democracies; and the development of a European cultural identity. Since the end of the Soviet regime the Council of Europe, within its 'oriental' policy that started with the admission of Finland, provides assistance to central and eastern European countries with their political, legislative and constitutional reforms. In addition, it also supervises the protection of human rights in post-Communist democracies.

The Council of Europe is composed of the Committee of Ministers, the Parliamentary Assembly and the Congress of Local and Regional Authorities of Europe. The Committee of Ministers is made up of the ministers for foreign affairs of the 36 Member States who meet at least twice a year, and their permanent representatives meet at least twice a month in order to examine all matters of mutual interest except defence. It is a decision-making body acting upon proposals from the Parliamentary Assembly and the Congress of Local and Regional Authorities of Europe. The Committee of Ministers takes decisions on submitted proposals by a two-thirds majority or by unanimity (art 20(a)) where its decisions concern the adoption of proposals in the form of recommendations or European conventions or other binding agreements which are to be ratified by Member States. The Committee of Ministers is not a legislative body. It is empowered only to make recommendations for the adoption of approved measures by Member States. The Committee issues declarations and resolutions relating to both political matters and international problems. The Committee of Ministers is neither accountable to the Assembly nor to the Congress of Local and Regional Authorities of Europe.

The Parliamentary Assembly is made up of representatives of the Member States elected or appointed by their national parliaments. The number of representatives is proportional to the population of Member State although it is not a mathematical formula. The Assembly has an advisory role, thus it solely elaborates projects which are later transmitted to the Committee of Ministers for adoption. Since the amendments to the Statute of the Council of Europe were made in May 1951 the Assembly can choose its agenda as opposed to having the agenda imposed on it by the Committee of Ministers.

Finally, the Congress of Local and Regional Authorities of Europe represents the local and regional authorities of the Member States. It is also a consultative body which submits proposals to the Committee of Ministers for adoption. It has two chambers: the Chamber of Local Authorities and the Chamber of Regions. The main function of the Congress is to ensure that regional interests are represented at European level and to promote regional democracy and inter-regional development.

The greatest achievement of the Council is undoubtedly the European Convention for the Protection of Human Rights and Fundamental Freedoms, based on art 3 of the Statute of the Council of Europe, under which Member States 'must accept the principles of the rule of law and of the enjoyment by all persons within its jurisdiction of human rights and fundamental freedoms'.

The Convention was adopted on 4 November 1950 and entered into force in 1953. To date it has been ratified by 31 Member States of the European Council. The European Convention on Human Rights, together with its protocols and procedures for enforcement, constitutes the first and the most efficient regional arrangement for the protection of human rights. Rights protected under the Convention are both civil and political rights such as the right to life, liberty, and security of person, justice, respect for privacy and family life, the right to freedom of expression and opinion, peaceful assembly and association, the right to marry and found a family, freedom from torture, inhuman or degrading treatment and punishment, freedom from slavery and forced labour, etc. The originality of the European Convention lies in its unique enforcement machinery. Two bodies were created under the Convention – the European Commission of Human Rights and the European Court of Human Rights – which are empowered to deal with complaints from both States and private individuals relating to the violation of any rights conferred by the Convention. Member States are placed under a duty to provide effective domestic remedies to uphold these rights. The Court of Human Rights has given over 500 judgments and the European Commission has issued hundreds of reports and thousands of admissibility decisions.[36]

The considerable work of the Council of Europe towards European unity has been to some extent overshadowed by other European organisations, although all important problems relating to Europe are discussed and examined by the Council of Europe. There is no area which the Council has left unattended. Under the auspices of the Council of Europe over 150 conventions have been established and more than 133 are in force in Member States. These include: the European Social Charter of 1961, in operation since 1965, regarding social, economic and cultural rights; the European Code of Social Security; the conventions on the prevention of torture, terrorism, spectator violence, trans-frontier television, etc. Amongst its diverse activities the Council of Europe also funds the College of Europe in Bruges, has adopted a proposal by Swedish minister Berthil Ohlin to reduce customs duties amongst Member States, as well as accepting the proposal of Winston Churchill for the immediate creation of the united European Army on 11 August 1950. However, the attitude of the post-war Labour government in the UK towards the Council of Europe was reluctant, although eventually the UK became a Member State.[37] As to the military integration of Europe, it has occurred essentially under the United States' initiatives (the North Atlantic Treaty Organisation (NATO)) as the Western European Union proved inefficient.

---

[36] On the European Convention on Human Rights see D J Harris, M O'Boyle and C Warbrick, *Law of the European Convention on Human Rights*, London: Butterworths, 1995.

[37] Ernest Bevin had agreed on the participation of the UK in the Council of Europe but was less than enthusiastic. In this respect, he said to Christopher Mayhew, 'Let's give them a talking shop', and to Sir Roderick Barceley of the Foreign Office, 'Open that Pandora's box and you'll never know what Trojan horses will jump out', supra note 34, p124.

Military integration

The Western European Union

The Western European Union (WEU) was founded on 6 May 1955 as an extension of the Brussels Treaty of 1948 between the United Kingdom, France, Belgium, Luxembourg and The Netherlands, which provided for collective defence and co-operation in economic, social and cultural matters when West Germany and Italy were allowed to join the existing structure. Both NATO and the Council of Europe have evolved from the 1948 Treaty of Brussels. The Western European Union was intended to strengthen security co-operation among contracting States and for that reason other activities envisaged by the 1948 Treaty were transferred to the Council of Europe. The WEU, as a result of NATO, lost its importance at European level. At the meeting of foreign and defence ministers of Member States in Rome on 26 and 27 October 1984, the thirtieth anniversary of the WEU, it was decided to re-examine its structure in order to achieve closer co-operation on security and defence and to create a European identity in that area. The WEU has been revitalised by the Treaty of Maastricht. Under the Pillar 2 of the Treaty on European Union the WEU has been made responsible for ensuring a common defence policy.

The North Atlantic Treaty Organisation

The Cold War necessitated the establishment of a common European military defence system to respond to the threat of any Soviet attack on western Europe. However, the initiative in this respect came from the United States. In order to implement the North Atlantic Treaty, signed on 4 April 1949 and in force from 24 August 1949, the North Atlantic Treaty Organisation was established. NATO is based on art 51 of the United Nations Charter, which permits the right of collective self-defence, and art 52, which recognises the existence of regional arrangements dealing with international peace and security consistent with the purposes and principles of the United Nations.[38] Its principal objective is described in art 5 of the North Atlantic Treaty which provides 'that an armed attack against one or more of them in Europe or North America shall be considered an attack against them all', and that in the event of such an attack 'each Member State would take individually and in concert with the other Parties such action as it deems necessary, including the use of armed force'. The news of the production of an atomic bomb by the Soviet Union in September 1949 prompted the American Congress to allocate $1.5 billion to arm NATO. Altogether some $25 billion were transferred to Member States in the first 20 years of its existence.

Until the end of Cold war, the United States' contribution to NATO consisted of the deployment of US tactical nuclear weapons in western Europe and approximately 300,000 conventional forces stationed mostly in Germany, but also in other NATO countries. The future of NATO is under consideration since the end of Cold War in 1990. Indications are that NATO is proposing to change from a military to a political organisation with the objective of maintaining international stability in Europe.

---

[38] The following States are Contracting Parties to NATO: Belgium, Canada, Denmark, France, West Germany (from 1955 and from 1990 the unified Germany), Greece, Iceland, Italy, Luxembourg, The Netherlands, Norway, Portugal, Spain, Turkey, the United Kingdom, the United States of America. In 1966 France formally withdrew from NATO but is still a Party to the Treaty.

Economic integration – the Benelux Union and the Schuman Plan

In political and military matters European integration has taken a classical form. Through various international organisations European countries decided to co-operate and no limitations were imposed on their national soveregnity. However, a change of approach was adopted by the Benelux countries and the creation of the European Steel and Coal Community based on the Robert Schuman plan.

Benelux Union

The idea of a closer co-operation between the Benelux countries (Belgium, The Netherlands and Luxembourg) was not new. In 1851, The Netherlands and Luxembourg were linked by a personal union, and further attempts in this direction took place in 1869, 1886 and 1907. Finally, an economic union between Belgium and Luxembourg was signed on 2 July 1921 which entered into force on 1 May 1922. Thus, it is not surprising that towards the end of the World War II the governments in exile of Belgium, The Netherlands and Luxembourg signed, on 5 September 1944 in London, the Customs Convention as a first step toward the creation of total economic integration. The Customs Convention was aimed at ensuring free circulation of goods, persons, capital and services, establishing a common customs duties' tariff vis-à-vis the external world, and a common policy in the economic, financial and social matters. The London Customs Convention came into force in 1948. By 1956 almost all barriers to internal trade were eliminated. The success of the customs union prompted the three countries to extend their integration. On 3 February 1958 they signed the Treaty of the Benelux Economic Union which became operative on 1 November 1960, and as a result the three countries became one economy and the free movement of goods, labour, capital and services was completed by co-ordination of welfare policies and standardisation of postal and transport rates. Finally, in 1970, all border controls were eliminated.

Common institutions were set up in order to supervise the proper functioning of the Union: the Committee of Ministers as its legislative body; the Inter-parliamentary Consultative Council, which is an emanation of national parliaments; the Council of the Economic Union which is an executive body; the Consultative Economic and Social Council which has advisory functions in relation to all social and economic matters of common interest; and the Arbitral College which is empowered to settle disputes arising out of the Treaty and concerning its application. Awards by the Arbitral College are adopted by the majority of votes and are final.

In order to ensure the uniform application and interpretation of Union law, on 31 March 1965 the Benelux Court of Justice was set up. It is made up of nine judges, three from each Member State Supreme Court and three Advocates-General. The Benelux Court of Justice issues preliminary rulings on matters of interpretation of the Benelux Treaties. When such a question is raised before any court of a Member State, that court may, where it considers it necessary to enable it to give judgment, refer the matter to the Benelux Court of Justice for a preliminary ruling. The Council of Ministers may ask the Benelux Court of Justice for an advisory opinion on a point of law at any time and without following any special procedure.

The Benelux Economic Union has been very successful; internal trade between the Benelux countries increased by 50 per cent, and the increase in external trade placed them in fifth position behind the United States, the United Kingdom, West Germany and Canada.

The Benelux experiment encouraged other European countries to seek new forms of economic integration.

The Schuman Plan

France has also been interested in achieving regional economic arrangements. The first attempt resulted in the signature of the Protocol of Turin on 20 March 1948, which was a blueprint for a customs union between Italy and France. However, the so-called Francital, conceived by Robert Schuman and Count Sforza never materialised. The failure of Francital, and the refusal of the United Kingdom to form a customs union with France to counteract the growing independence and recovery of Germany, prompted Robert Schuman, the French Minister for Foreign Affairs, to seek a different solution.[39] Robert Schuman followed the advice of Winston Churchill who emphasised in his speeches that France should take Germany back into the community of nations. In addition, Robert Schuman, who fought in World War I on the German side, studied in Bonn and was fluent in German, was the right person to make the first step in the normalisation of relations with Germany. Robert Schuman believed that Europe was facing three problems: economic dominance by the United States, military dominance by the Soviet Union and a possible war with a rejuvenated Germany. The Americans supported the idea of political and economic integration in Europe since it would reduce, in the long term, the cost of their obligations and commitments in Europe. Robert Schuman considered that the best way to achieve stability in Europe was to place the production of steel and coal, two commodities essential to conduct a modern conventional war, under international control of a supra-national entity. The creation of a common market for steel and coal meant that interested countries would delegate their powers in those commodities to an independent authority. Robert Schuman announced his plan, based on proposals put forward by Jean Monnet, an eminent French economist and a 'father of European integration', on 9 May 1950.[40] Although in his plan only France and Germany were expressly mentioned, Schuman invited other European States to join and 'in particular, Britain, Italy, and the Benelux countries'.[41]

The Schuman Plan was enthusiastically accepted by Germany as Konrad Adenauer, the German Chancellor, saw it as a breakthrough, the beginning of German statehood and independence. Personally, Adenauer was in favour of closer relations with the West and for the abandonment of the traditional German policy which for centuries had concentrated on the East. Indeed, the Schuman Plan was advantageous to both parties as it offered a way to regain international respectability for Germany, and in the immediate future to gain access to the Saarland, and for France the opportunity to control the German economy. The Schuman Plan attracted attention in many European countries. As a result an international

---

[39] P Gerbet, *La génése du Plan Schuman, dès origines à la Déclaration du 9 mai 1950*, Revue française de science politique, 1956, p525 et seq.

[40] The text of the Schuman Plan was delivered to Ernest Bevin from Rene Massigli, the French ambassador in London and specified that the French wanted: 'To place the French and German production of coal and steel as a whole under a common "Higher Authority" within the framework of an organisation open to the participation of the other countries of Europe ... by pooling basic production and by instituting a new Higher Authority whose decisions will be bind France, Germany and other member countries. This proposal will lead to the realisation of the first concrete foundations of a European federation', supra note 34, p98.

[41] Ibid, p99.

Conference was held in Paris on 20 June 1950 attended by France, Italy, West Germany and the Benelux countries in order to consider the Schuman Plan. Under the Presidency of Jean Monnet, the conference extended its work for ten months, a draft Treaty being produced on 19 March 1951. The Treaty that created the European Coal and Steel Community (ECSC) was signed on 18 April 1951 and entered into force on 25 July 1952. The ECSC was very successful, and by 1954 all barriers to trade in coal, coke, steel, pig iron and scrap iron were eliminated between Member States. Trade in those commodities rose spectacularly and the common pricing policy and production limits set up by the High Authority, as well as common rules on competition, merger controls, etc, rationalised the production of steel and coal within a wholly integrated market.

The ECSC had been envisaged as a first step toward a federal Europe.[42] The European Community of Defence was a next stage towards the Treaty of Rome.

The European Defence Community

In 1950 the tension between the Soviet Union and the United States mounted as the conflict in Korea escalated, and as a result the US commitments in this region increased. The Cold War between the two blocs forced the re-examination of German participation in rearmament and a common European defence. René Plevin, the French Defence Minister, a personal assistant to Jean Monnet in wartime London, and inspired by the Churchill motion carried out by the Council of Europe in April 1950 regarding the creation of an European army, had drafted a common defence plan. The plan was presented before the Council of Europe in 1951 by Robert Schuman and called for the formation of a supra-national European army in which German soldiers would 'be Europeans, in European uniforms, under European command'. The number of German soldiers was reduced to the strict minimum while the financial contribution of Germany was considerable. The idea behind the plan was to let the Germans defend Europe without conferring upon them too much power, a very controversial plan fully endorsed by the US. The plan was transformed into a Treaty, creating the European Defence Community, signed on 27 May 1952 in Paris. However, its fate hinged upon British participation in the plan. The UK response came from two British cabinet ministers supporting diametrically opposed positions in two foreign European cities. Maxwell Fyfe, the Home Secretary, declared in Strasbourg that the UK agreed in principle, but a few hours later, Anthony Eden, then Foreign Secretary, at a press conference in Rome where he was attending a NATO meeting, gave a definitive 'no' to the British participation in the European Defence Community. The President of the Council of Europe, Paul-Henri Spaak, a well known anglophile and a fervent supporter of European federalism, tendered his resignation in protest against the British 'betrayal'. The Council of Europe was outraged and disappointed by the UK answer, and as a result the Plevin plan failed and was formally terminated when the French Assembly refused to ratify the Treaty on 30 August 1954. However, visionaries like Paul-Henri Spaak learnt a precious lesson from this abortive attempt at closer European integration. Only a supra-national organisation requiring surrender of national sovereignty on the part of Member States could achieve

---

[42] As Robert Schuman said while announcing his plan: 'L'Europe ne se fera pas d'un seul coup ni dans une construction d'ensemble: elle se fera par des réalisation concrétes créant d'abord une solidarité de fait', C A Colliard, *Institutions des relations internationales*, 9ème ed, Paris: Dalloz, 1990, p524.

European integration. This idea was examined at the meeting of ministers for foreign affairs of the European Coal and Steel Community in Messina in 1955.

The Messina Conference.
In June 1955 in Messina (Sicily) the foreign ministers of the ECSC decided to 'pursue the establishment of a united Europe through the development of common institutions, a progressive fusion of national economies, the creation of a Common Market and harmonisation of social policies'.[43] They asked Paul-Henri Spaak to preside over committees to be set up in Brussels in the forthcoming months which would prepare a blueprint for a common programme.[44] It took several meetings of foreign ministers, and an enormous amount of work by many experts and governmental officials, to prepare a draft Treaty. Finally, on 25 March 1957 in Rome, two Treaties were signed: the first established the European Economic Community (EEC) and the second the European Atomic Energy Community (Euratom). The Treaties after having been ratified in all six Member States came into force on 1 January 1958.

1.11 The United Kingdom and European integration

After World War II the leadership of the United Kingdom in building a new Europe was badly needed; it was the only country in Europe that had neither surrendered nor had been invaded by the Germans. Not only the prestige of the United Kingdom as a liberator had predisposed it to a great destiny, that is to champion the movement towards European integration, but also the fact that during the war the UK had been a home to many European governments in exile. Close links and the lasting friendship of the European political and intellectual elite were firmly established. France, although on the winning side at the end of the war, had been compromised by the Vichy regime, destroyed by English and American bombing and, like the rest of the continent, was demoralised by years of Nazi occupation. Winston Churchill as early as in 1942 had explained his the vision of post-war Europe:

> 'I must admit that my thoughts rest primarily in Europe, in the revival of the glory of Europe, the parent continent of modern nations and of civilisation. It would be a measureless disaster if Russian barbarism overlaid the culture and independence of the ancient states of Europe. Hard as it is to say now, I trust that the European family may act unitedly as one, under a Council of Europe in which the barriers between nations will be greatly minimised and unrestricted travel will be possible. I hope to see the economy of Europe studied as a whole.'[45]

However, in his speech in 1946 in Zurich Churchill made clear that the United Kingdom had assigned for herself the role of a sponsor and a friend of a United States of Europe and would remain aloof from full participation in plans for European integration. There are

---

[43] *Documents on International Affairs*, 1955, p163.
[44] A summary of Part I of the Spaak Report *The Common Market* was published by Political and Economic Planning in Broadsheet, no 405 of 17 December 1956.
[45] Supra note 34, p13.

three essential reasons for the UK reluctance. First, at that time, the UK was still centre of a great empire with all her colonies intact. As a great sea power with a large empire her interests were not in Europe. As Churchill emphasised: 'If there is a choice for the United Kingdom between Europe and the sea, she will always choose the sea.' Second, the UK based her future on the 'special relationship' with the United States. Already, a common language, culture, law and institutions of parliamentary democracy had built solid foundations for a mutual understanding that was further reinforced by a common vision of the post-war world described in the Atlantic Charter. Moreover, the United States emerged after the war as the greatest economic, commercial and military power in the world. The development of the atomic weapon, in which the British fully participated, was an additional factor in maintaining the 'special relationship'. When on 6 August 1945 the Superfortress Enola Gay dropped an atomic bomb on Hiroshima causing the death of about 78,000 people and injuring around 100,000 more, the entire world recognised US hegemony in international relations. The United Kingdom because of the close link with the US had been a nuclear power from the beginning. Finally, World War II had shown the vulnerability of a nation State and both governments in exile and those subjected to Nazi occupation had lost faith in the concept. The UK, to the contrary, was convinced that her sovereignty should not be undermined and that Britain's insularity had given to its sovereignty an important additional dimension of security.

In April 1949, Jean Monnet, the architect of the European integration, came to London in order to discuss a possible union between France and the United Kingdom, but his proposals were turned down. Ernest Bevin, foreign minister in Attlee's government, was not interested because the British government was convinced that the UK was still a great independent power and saw no reason for surrendering her sovereignty. However, when the Schuman Plan was announced on 9 May 1948, the British government was genuinely surprised at the French initiative, furious at not being consulted, and felt cheated when it learnt that the plan was known and approved by the United States. The French invitation to join the plan was declined, and the UK government also refused to participate in any negotiations regarding the future structure of the steel, iron and coal community, including the issue of competencies of the supra-national entity charged with its functioning. The refusal ran contrary to Winston Churchill's view, when as leader of the opposition he accused the Labour government of 'piling their own prejudice upon French pedantry'. According to Harold Wilson (then a junior minister in the Attlee government), Harold Macmillan, also in opposition, had strongly opposed the Schuman Plan as well, declaring 'he was not having anyone in Europe telling him which pits to close down [and that] we will not allow any supra-national authority to put large numbers of our people out of work in Durham, in the Midlands, in South Wales and Scotland'.[46]

The Labour government at that time did not realise the significance and the implications of the Schuman Plan; the decision not to negotiate over the Plan was taken by the Cabinet when Prime Minister Attlee was on holiday in France and Bevin, the foreign minister, in hospital. Even the change of government did not bring a dramatic chance in the British position on European integration, when in 1951 the Conservatives came to power and Winston Churchill became Prime Minister once more. At that stage it was not too late

[46] Supra note 34, p109.

to join the Schuman Plan as it had not yet been ratified but, contrary to Churchill's federalist speeches in Zurich and Strasbourg and the expectations of all continental western European countries, no shift in UK European policy took place. Churchill's romantic views on Europe did not translate into actions. He confirmed in 1950 what he wrote in 1930 in his article on 'The United States of Europe' which was published in the *Saturday Evening Post* in the United States, that is, the UK wanted to be 'with Europe but not of it, linked but not comprised'. The British refusal to participate in the European Defence Community disappointed the Europeans as well as the Americans. The subsequent decision of the British government, under Anthony Eden as Prime Minister, concerning the Messina Conference, and the refusal to participate in negotiations leading to the Treaty of Rome, finally closed the door for the UK to become an original member of the EEC. More importantly, the UK lost its opportunity to shape European integration. At Messina, Russell Bretherton, an under-secretary at the Board of Trade, and a minor official at that, represented the United Kingdom, while eminent politicians and foreign ministers of the six ECSC countries attended the Conference. Russell Bretherton was instructed before attending the Messina Conference not to commit the UK government to any European initiatives.

The original six did not give up on the UK, and on 7 June 1955 their foreign ministers prompted by the Benelux countries and supported by France sent an invitation to the British government to take part in the preparation of a new agenda for Europe. At this stage even the six were uncertain whether they should form a customs union or a free trade area or a common external tariff, and in what fields the integration should be pursued. For that reason the Benelux memorandum submitted at the Messina Conference which put forward a concept of a Common Market was accepted as a basis for future discussions. Once again, the UK sent Russell Bretherton to Brussels with the same instructions he had been given for the Messina Conference. His presence, short-lived since he was recalled to the UK in November 1955, confirmed the negative attitude of the UK towards European integration.

As the work of 'Spaak committees' focused on plans for a Common Market, in the absence of any British representatives Paul-Henri Spaak decided to come to London in order to personally convince the British to join the negotiations. After meetings with the Chancellor of the Exchequer and the Foreign Secretary, the position of the UK was clear. European projects were not taken seriously in London and the official British position was that co-operation with Europe was approved but no commitments should be made. Other attempts by Brussels to encompass and enrol the UK into a Common Market during the period of gestation of the European Communities were regarded by Anthony Eden, the UK Prime Minister, and Rab Butler, the Chancellor of the Exchequer, the two most influential people in the Cabinet, as 'a bore'.[47] In the meantime, in Brussels, the European integration took concrete form. The Spaak Report and its recommendations favouring the creation of a Common Market in the form of a customs union were adopted by the foreign ministers of the six countries in Venice in May 1956.[48] The biggest surprise was the French adherence to this project. It demonstrated that the French government after suffering humiliating defeats in Indo-China in 1954, growing unrest in North Africa and a very difficult economic

---

[47] Supra note 34, p195.
[48] It was one of the shortest meeting of the Six: in one-and-a-half hours the Conference confirmed the decision to establish the Common Market, supra note 34, p197.

situation at home had made necessary changes to its traditional policy. According to Charlton: 'Britain's orderly transition from Empire to Commonwealth, and the dimension and nature of her overseas relationship, offered no strict analogy and no similar sense of urgency'[49] in making new arrangements and re-assessing traditional foreign policy.

However, the British as a pragmatic nation decided to submit its own proposal concerning European integration. It was the Plan G regarding the Industrial European Free Trade Association (IEFTA) confined exclusively to industrial goods. It is still controversial whether the British Plan G was a genuine British initiative, or a rival to a Common Market, or was designed to sabotage the Common Market. In any event, the British tried to revive the OEEC (see section 1.9) in order to use it as a platform for launching Plan G, and especially in order to associate the concept of IEFTA with the European Common Market. Plan G was rejected by the six when they decided that no association was possible between the 'outer seven' and the Common Market. It was also considered of peripheral importance by the United States that had enthusiastically supported European integration within the Common Market from its conception. Nevertheless, in 1960 Plan G became the foundation of the European Free Trade Association (EFTA) comprising the United Kingdom, Norway, Sweden, Denmark, Austria, Switzerland and Portugal.

During 1960s the attitude of the United Kingdom towards European integration changed dramatically. Many considerations dictated the reappraisal of the UK position, the most important of these were: the end of the British Empire and the Suez conflict in 1957 which demonstrated the fragility of the 'special relationship' with the United States. A common military invasion of Suez by the UK, France and Israel was jointly condemned by the Soviet Union and the US and thus destroyed the illusion that the UK was still a great independent power. This was brought home by: the realisation that the UK was too poor to stay an important nuclear power as it was unable to finance on its own long-range missile, 'Blue Streak'; the change of the Prime Minister as Anthony Eden resigned suffering from a nervous breakdown after the Suez conflict; and the growing feeling in UK political circles that the place of the UK was in Europe. Economic considerations were also important, the success of the Common market was self-evident. In addition, in the 1960s for the first time the UK exported more to Europe than to the Commonwealth. As a result, on 31 July 1961, a formal announcement was made in the House of Commons of the UK's intention to lodge an application for the accession to the Treaty of Rome. However, Harold Macmillan, the Prime Minister of the UK at that time, faced almost an impossible mission: he had to convince General Charles de Gaulle that the British intention regarding accession to the Treaty was genuine.

1.12 The French refusal to the British accession

In order to understand the French refusal, it is necessary to examine French policy under de Gaulle. His foreign policy was based on two principles. He believed in the nation State and that national interests, not ideologies, were the driving force in international relations.

---

[49] Ibid, p205.

Supra-nationality, as diametrically opposed to the concept of nation State, was considered a dangerous illusion. It was an illusion since, in reality, only national interests existed and were pursued even within a supra-national structure – the common consciousness inherent to the concept of nation State could not command allegiance to a supra-national organisation. As a result, the supra-national structure lacked an essential and vital element, namely the common consciousness upon which all national feelings are based and thus could easily serve as a device of American hegemony. The second principle was the policy of 'greatness' (grandeur) for France, that is, independence from any foreign interference. For that reason de Gaulle decided to develop a French nuclear deterrent and thus ended the American nuclear monopoly. France was to play a unique role in world politics as a third force, between the Soviet Union and the United States. De Gaulle's vision of Europe was based upon the 'European Europe' as third neutral force, free of all domination but led by France. As Cerny said, the objective of France was to 'increase [France's] manoeuvrability and to widen her options ... [to] exploit the structural interstices and the margins of the international system' in order to 'escape from the strait-jacket of bi-polar equilibrium' between the Soviet Union and the US.[50]

To emphasise French independence, in 1959 de Gaulle withdrew her Mediterranean fleet from a NATO command. De Gaulle disliked the Treaty of Rome but used its structure to further his ideas.

As to the negotiations between France and the UK, the two leaders, de Gaulle and Macmillan, had known each other very well. Macmillan and de Gaulle were closely associated during the World War II in Algiers, the allied HQ in the Mediterranean. In 1943 de Gaulle moved the French Committee of National Liberation to Algiers and became its joint president with General Henri Giraud. Macmillan, appointed by Churchill, represented the allied interests in this area and supported de Gaulle in his political struggle against Giraud, which resulted in de Gaulle achieving full control of the French Committee of National Liberation and his recognition as the sole leader of Free France. However, the relations between the UK and de Gaulle had never been easy. De Gaulle deeply resented the fact that he was not invited to the Yalta Conference in 1945. Although, Churchill took a hard line against Roosevelt and achieved the recognition of France as one of the powers to participate in the post-war settlement of Germany, de Gaulle was haunted by the Yalta complex and had never shown any gratitude toward the British for their support and assistance during World War II.

On 2 December 1958 de Gaulle was elected president of the Republic and in December 1962 the Gaullists gained a parliamentary majority for the first time. The position of de Gaulle in France had never been stronger; he alone could shape French foreign policy.

On 14 January 1963 de Gaulle made two announcements: he blocked the British entry to the Common Market and rejected the United States' offer regarding the development of Polaris missiles within the framework of NATO. Both issues were interrelated. When the UK cancelled the 'Blue Streak' missile programme as being too expensive, she turned to the US for assistance. In exchange for granting the US a base for nuclear submarines at Holy Loch in Scotland, the US offered the UK the 'Skybolt', a nuclear missile, and in the future the

---

[50] P Cerny, *The Politics of Grandeur: Ideological Aspects of de Gaulle's Foreign Policy*, Cambridge: Cambridge University Press, 1980, p131.

most sophisticated weapon, the Polaris submarine. However, the 'Skybolt' missile was cancelled for technical reasons.

In December 1962, after a meeting between Macmillan and de Gaulle, at which the UK was almost certain that France would reject the British bid for entry into the Common Market, the British Prime Minister went to Nassau to meet the US President Kennedy. The outcome of the Nassau meeting was a triumph for UK diplomacy; the US agreed to assign Polaris to NATO but under independent control of the UK in a moment of 'supreme national interest'. In addition, Macmillan negotiated the same deal for France. The generous offer from the US, a result of British initiative, was an additional argument in favour of the UK accession to the Treaty of Rome as it proved that the UK had still a 'special relationship' with the United States, and that British-French co-operation in the nuclear field, and especially in Polaris, would be beneficial for both countries once the UK was inside the Common Market.

In these circumstances, de Gaulle announced his veto of British entry to the Common Market.

De Gaulle's justifications for blocking the UK accession were that the UK was not ready for membership because of her close links with the Commonwealth, her tradition of free trade, and her agriculture which would fit badly into the protectionist Common Agricultural Policy of the EEC. The main reason, however, was the UK's 'special relationship' with the US, and for de Gaulle the Polaris deal was supreme proof of the British dependence on the United States. He felt that the UK would be an American Trojan horse that would reinforce American hegemony in his 'European Europe'. A more convincing, but unstated, reason for rejecting the UK application was de Gaulle's fear of France losing its dominance within the EEC as he had successfully forced the other Member States to implement an agricultural policy favourable to France and opposed any attempts to increase the powers of the Commission and other European institutions. Furthermore, the Common Market was based on a partnership between France and Germany dominated by France. De Gaulle did not want to share the leadership of Europe or allow a British challenge to French primacy within the Common Market.

The reasons for the French refusal were epitomised in somewhat emotional terms by Macmillan:

> 'He [de Gaulle] also had a real hatred of the Americans, and a kind of love-hate complex about the British. The truth is – I may be cynical, but I fear it is true – if Hitler had danced in the streets of London, we'd have had no trouble with de Gaulle. What they could not forgive us is that we held on, and that we saved France. People can forgive an injury, but they can hardly ever forgive a benefit'.[51]

Macmillan's disappointment and bitterness are easy to understand. After two years of extremely complex negotiations encompassing multilateral discussion with each Member State of EEC, reappraising of the UK policy towards the Commonwealth which required new arrangements in order to find ways to accommodate the Commonwealth, and convincing public and party opinion at home as to the neccesity of the British entry into a Common market, France vetoed the British application.

---

[51] Supra note 34, p262.

The second application for membership of the European Economic Community was submitted in 1967 under the Labour government of Harold Wilson. This time the answer from de Gaulle was immediate; once again he blocked the British entry.[52]

A third attempt was made by Edward Heath in 1970. At that time de Gaulle was no longer the President of France; he had resigned after losing a referendum held in February 1969 concerning the reform of the French Senate and measures regarding regional decentralisation. Although these issues were important they were not vital and the referendum provided de Gaulle with an elegant means of leaving power without being forced out. In these circumstances there was no opposition to the United Kingdom membership. After concluding negotiations with the EEC in January 1972, the UK became a Member State. The European Communities Act 1972 came into force on 1 January 1973.

---

[52] At the press conference on 27 November 1967 he declared that the Common Market '... is incompatible with Britain's economy as it stands, in which the chronic balance of payments deficit is proof of its permanent imbalance and which, as concerning, sources of supply/credit practices and working conditions, involves factors which that country could not alter without modifying its own nature', and thus the UK accession 'means breaking up a Community that was built and operates according to rules which do not tolerate such a monumental exception', Lord Cockfield, *The European Union, Creating the Single Market*, London: Wiley Chancery Law, 1994, p10.

2 The Evolution of the European Communities

In the development of the European Communities, the main changes can be divided into two categories: the geographical expansion of the Communities, from six original Members to fifteen, and up to twenty in the near future; and the inward consolidation of its structure accompanied by extended co-operation among Member States, both as to the subject-matter and methods of the achievement of common objectives.

This chapter focuses on outward expansion and inward consolidation of the European Communities. First, the requirements for admission of new members and practical problems posed by subsequent accession to the European Communities, including the admission of the United Kingdom as well as the challenge of its future enlargement will be examined. Second, fundamental reforms to the structure of the European Communities and their implications upon the process of European integration will be analysed. In this respect, it is quite clear that the vision of Europe presented by the founding fathers more than 40 years ago, with a view of establishing a more market-oriented structure collides with the 'model' of Europe that it is necessary to build now. With the globalisation of economics, the technical innovations of the post-World War II era, and the emergence of worldwide electronic networks, the world has become increasingly interdependent and vulnerable to rapidly changing economic forces. Also, many problems such as the widening gap between the north and the south, the rich and the poor and cross-border issues, such as drug-trafficking, money-laundering, organised crime, control of immigration, etc, which threaten the stability of our society, require regulation at an international level. The need for common policies on a European, or a wider, forum implies that the traditional role of a nation State with classical power politics has ended. Some people, in the United Kingdom and other Member States, have not yet grasped the practical implications of this change. By ignoring the reality, this faction of European public opinion continues to perceive the growing competence of the European Union as a loss of national sovereignty, but the re-definition of common objectives for mankind on a regional as well as the international level constitutes the only answer to the problems of the twenty-first century. As the Belgian Prime Minister, L Tindemans, emphasised in his *Report on the European Union*:

> 'a return to inter-governmental co-operation would not help to solve European problems. Such co-operation tends to underline the differences of power and interest between our countries and does not meet our collective needs'.[1]

---

[1] EC Bull Suppl 1/76; see also J D B Mitchell, 'The Tindemans Report – Retrospect and Prospect' (1976) 13 CMLR 455.

2.1 Membership of the European Union

All Member States of the EU are equal.[2] They enjoy the same privileges and have to fulfil the same obligations vis-à-vis each other and the EU. Contrary to certain international organisations (eg UNESCO) no special status is granted to any Member States of the EU. In this respect it is necessary to emphasise that:

1. Article 131 EC, which allows a Member State to associate with the Community some non-European countries and territories which have a special relationship with that State (overseas territories which are part of a Member State, etc), provides for the territorial extension of the scope of application of the EC Treaty but does not create a genuine association which implies participation in European structures.
2. Even if a State has concluded an association agreement with the EC, for example, on the basis of art 238 EC, it is still outside the EC and therefore cannot be considered as a Member State.[3]

Admission to the European Union

The three Communities have been created by multilateral treaties which were negotiated, signed, ratified and entered into force in accordance with classical rules of the law of treaties by the six original Members: Belgium, France, Germany, Italy, Luxembourg and The Netherlands.

All three Communities were open for future accessions by other European countries. Before the creation of the European Union the procedure for admission was expressly provided by the founding Treaties: arts 98 ECSC, 237 EEC and 205 Euratom. All three Treaties provided that a candidate State had to submit its application for admission to the Council which asked the Commission for an opinion before taking a final decision. That was, however, the only identical part of the admission procedure. A candidate State had to seek admission separately to each Community. The procedure for admission to the ECSC was different from that relating to the two remaining Communities. Under art 98 ECSC the conditions for admission were to be determined by the 'decision' of the Council. It was a purely Communitary matter, and by a unilateral act of the Council a candidate State became a Member State. It had to deposit its accession instrument to the ECSC with the French government, the depository of the Treaty of Paris of 1951.

In practice, however, there was one procedure for admission of a new Member State since it had to accede to all three Communities at the same time.[4] Admission to the ECSC and Euratom was accessory and a direct consequence of the admission to the EEC which posed the most difficult and complex political and economic problems.

An unwritten but necessary condition of admission was also imposed upon the candidate State, that is, its participation in co-operation, mainly in the area of foreign policy. The

---

[2] In this respect it is interesting to note what Jean Monnet said: 'I have always realised that equality is absolutely essential in relations between nations, as it is between people': *Monnet*, Memoirs, London: Collins, 1978, p97.
[3] See the association agreements in Chapter 4.
[4] According to the Resolution on the co-ordination of the three European Communities adopted by the European Parliamentary Assembly (OJ no 9 of 1958, p260 et seq).

(second) meeting of the Heads of State or Government at Bad Godesberg on 18 July 1961, which laid down foundations for political co-operation among Members States, expressly mentioned that new members were required to participate in activities leading to political unification.[5]

The Treaty on European Union (TEU) modified the procedure of admission. Article O of the TEU stipulates that:

'Any European State may apply to become a Member of the Union. It shall address its application to the Council, which shall act unanimously after consulting the Commission and after receiving the assent of the European Parliament, which shall act by an absolute majority of its component members.

The conditions of admission and the adjustments to the Treaties on which the Union is founded which such admission entails shall be the subject of an agreement between the Member States and the applicant State. The agreement shall be submitted for ratification by all the contracting States in accordance with their respective constitutional requirements.'

Therefore, art O TEU simplifies the admission procedure since a candidate State accedes to the European Union which implies adhesion to all three Communities.

Requirements for admission

The conditions for admission are both substantial and formal. As to the substance, certain legal and political requirements must be satisfied by a new Member State. The procedure for admission, itself, is complex and lengthy.

'Legal' requirements imposed upon a candidate State The legal requirements imposed upon a candidate State are specified in the TEU and can be easily verified by the European Court of Justice (ECJ). In this respect an action against a 'decision of admission' issued by the Council can be brought under art 173 EC. However, the ECJ is limited solely to reviewing whether the legal conditions and procedural requirements for admission were fulfilled by the Community institutions. Any decision on the merits of a State's admission remains within the discretion of the Council and escapes the jurisdiction of the Court of Justice. This was confirmed in Case 93/78 *Lothar Mattheus* v *Duego Fruchtimport und Tiefkühlkost*.[6]

The parties had entered into a contract on 1 August 1977. According to their agreement the plaintiff would set up market survey systems in Spain and Portugal, to be operational by the date of the decision of the accession of those States to the Communities. In consideration, the defendant was to pay a half-yearly lump sum to cover the plaintiff's expenses. The contract contained the following clause:

'This agreement is definitively concluded for a period of five years. If the said accession should not in fact or in law prove to be unpracticable, the Principal [Duego] shall have the right to terminate this agreement. The decisive factor in determining whether the said accession is practicable in law shall be a decision of the ECJ. In the event of a justifiable termination the Agent shall lose his right to repayment of expenses.

...The courts in Essen shall have jurisdiction in matters arising out of this agreement.'

---

[5] EC Bull 1961, pp7–8.
[6] [1978] ECR 2203.

On 29 January 1978 Mattheus wrote to the defendants requesting reimbursement of DM 527.85 expenses; the defendants terminated the contract under the above clause and were sued in the local court, Amtsgericht Essen, which made a reference to the ECJ for a preliminary ruling under art 177 asking three questions, namely:

1. whether art 237 EC, standing alone or in conjunction with other articles of the EC Treaty, is to be interpreted as meaning that it imposes substantive legal limits on the accession of third countries over and above the formal conditions laid down in art 237 EC?;
2. what are those limits?; and
3. is the accession of Spain, Portugal and Greece for reasons of Community law not possible in the future?

The ECJ held that art 177 EC empowers it to give preliminary rulings on the interpretation of the Treaty upon reference from any national court or tribunal. The division of powers within the Community is mandatory and it cannot be impeded by arrangements by private persons tending to compel courts to request a preliminary ruling, thus depriving them of the independent exercise of the discretion they are granted by art 177. Article 237 EC lays down a precise procedure encompassed within well-defined limits for the admission of new Member States, during which the conditions for accession are drawn up by the authorities indicated in the article itself. Thus the legal conditions for such accession remain to be defined in the context of that procedure without it being possible to determine the content judicially in advance. The ECJ cannot give a ruling on the form or subject-matter of the conditions that may be applied. The ECJ has no jurisdiction to give a ruling on the question referred to it by the national court.

As to the legal requirements themselves, there are four of them. First, a candidate State must be recognised as a State. In this respect, reference to the rules of public international law will clarify the legal status of the applying entity. In practice, since the Council must reach a unanimous decision regarding the admission of a candidate State, if the latter is not recognised by only one Member State its application for admission will be rejected. So far no problem has arisen in this area, although the candidacy of Cyprus poses delicate problems. The Republic of Cyprus came into being on 16 August 1960 but, due to many factors, the most important being the Turkish invasion of the island in 1974, is now divided into two sectors: Greek and Turkish. In May 1983 the Rauf Denktash movement, which represents Turkish Cypriots, proclaimed the creation of the Turkish Republic of Northern Cyprus, which is not recognised as an independent State by the international community, except by Turkey.

Second, a candidate State must be a European State. This requirement can be explained by the fact that the EU wants to preserve the European identity of the Union. In the Declaration on European Identity of 14 December 1973 the Heads of State or Government described the essential elements of the European identity as 'principles of representative democracy, of the rule of law, of social justice – which is the ultimate goal of economic progress – and of respect for human rights'.[7] The Commission in its report on *Europe and the Challenge of Enlargement* stated that:

---

[7] EC Bull 1973–12–130.

'The term 'European' has not been officially defined. It combines geographical, historical and cultural elements ... and is subject to review. It is neither possible nor opportune to establish now the frontiers of the European Union, whose contours will be shaped over many years to come.'[8]

Presently, there are 45 States in Europe. Some of them have a short existence as States, having become independent as a result of the collapse of the Soviet Union, the Yugoslav Federation and through the division of Czechoslovakia into the Czech Republic and Slovakia. Until now, only one non-European State has submitted an application for admission – Morocco in 1985 – which was rejected in 1987 by the Council as being incompatible with art 237 EC.

Finally, the last two requirements are set out in art F of the TEU. Article F(1) stipulates that: 'The Union shall respect the national identities of its Member States, whose systems of government are founded on the principles of democracy.' The liberal-democratic model of government of a candidate State, which ensures the respect for civil, political, economic and social rights of its citizens, is a vital element of membership of the EU.[9] Furthermore, art F(2) adds that the EU respects fundamental human rights as guaranteed by the European Convention for the Protection of Human Rights and Fundamental Freedoms of 1950 and as they 'result from the constitutional traditions common to the Member States, as general principles of Community law'. Therefore, only democratic States which respect human rights can apply for membership. Those implicit but essential conditions were confirmed in practice in relation to Greece. From 1961 Greece was associated with the European Communities with a view of becoming a Member State in the near future. However, the military coup led by Colonel G Papadopoulos, and the following rule of a ruthless and brutal military junta (1967–1974), stopped the progress towards the membership of Greece. With the restoration of democracy, the relations between Greece and the European Communities were resumed. In 1981 Konstantinos Karamanlis, democratically elected President of the Hellenic Republic, finally accomplished his main political objective, that is, membership of the European Communities for Greece.

With adoption of art F(1) the promotion and protection of human rights has been woven into the structures of the EU. Its concern for the advancement of human rights is vital for obvious reasons. As Andrey Sakharow, a Nobel laureate and Russian dissident, once wrote: 'The defence of human rights is a clear path toward the unification of people in our turbulent world, and a path toward the relief of suffering.'[10]

Economic and political requirements A candidate State may satisfy all legal conditions and still be rejected by the EU. The decision is taken by all Member States having assessed all advantages and disadvantages flowing from the future enlargement. As a result, political and economic criteria play an important role. The level of economic development was crucial in the last enlargement regarding Sweden, Finland, Austria and Norway, all of them wealthy, relatively small and members of the European Economic Area. In the Commission's report

---

[8] EC Bull Suppl 3/92, point 7.
[9] See Frowein, 'The European Community and the Requirement of a Republican Form of Government' (1984) 82 Michigan Law Review 1311 et seq.
[10] *Encyclopedia Britannica*, 20 Macropaedia, 15th ed, p664.

on *Europe and the Challenge of Enlargement* it was stressed that membership 'presupposes a functioning and competitive market economy and an adequate legal and administrative framework in the public and private sectors'.[11]

As to political requirements, the most important is the acceptance by a candidate State of the 'acquis communautaire'[12] which according to the European Parliament constitutes a 'criterion of global integration'.[13] This term means, in the context of accession,[14] the acceptance by a new Member State, without reservation and from the commencement of its formal membership, of the following:

1. The normative 'acquis' such as:
   - the founding Treaties and their amendments;
   - acts enacted by the institutions such as regulations, directives, decisions, recommendations and opinions (arts 189 EC, 14 ECSC, 161 Euratom);
   - other acts whose adoption is provided by the Treaties (eg rules of procedures, etc);
   - measures adopted in the area of the external relations of the Communities, such as agreements entered into by any Community with one or more third State, with international organisations, or with a national of a third State, as well as so-called 'mixed agreements', that is, agreements and international conventions between Member States and any of the Communities, acting jointly;
   - other agreements whose conclusion have been necessary to attain the objectives of the Treaties, such as the Agreement of January 1957 establishing European Schools. This category also includes agreements concluded on the basis of art 220 EC, such as the 1968 Brussels Convention on Jurisdiction and the Enforcement of Judgments in Civil and Commercial Matters, the 1980 Rome Convention on the Law Applicable to Contractual Obligations, etc;
   - the Treaty on European Union (TEU) and measures enacted in relation to Pillars 2 and 3 of the TEU.

2. Political 'acquis' such as declarations, resolutions, principles and guidelines, etc, adopted by the European Council, the Council of Ministers, as well as common agreements of the Member States regarding development and strengthening of the Communities and the Union.

3. The judicial 'acquis', that is case law of the Court of Justice of the European Communities (ECJ) which outlines the essential characteristics of the Community legal order (direct effect, supremacy, unification, co-operation between ECJ and national

---

[11] Supra note 8, point 9.

[12] This term is usually used in French, see the English version of the TEU, although it was translated as 'Community patrimony' in the judgment in Joined Cases 80 and 81/77 *Commissionaires Reunis et Ramel* [1978] ECR 927, para 36. On the 'acquis communautaire' see P Pescatore, *Aspects judiciares de l'acquis communautaire*, RTDE, pp617–651.

[13] In its Resolution on enlargement adopted on 15 July 1993, the European Parliament emphasised that all candidate States must accept the 'acquis communautaire', including the TEU, the objectives of further integration and eliminate the opt-out options such as those obtained by the UK and Denmark (OJ C225/207 20.8.93 p36).

[14] On different aspects of the 'acquis communautaire', C C Gialdino, 'Some Reflections on the Acquis Communautaire' [1995] CMLR 1089–1121.

courts). However, in the Acts of Accession there is no reference to specific case law for two reasons: first, the rulings of the ECJ are 'acts' of the European institutions and thus already part of the 'acquis communautaire'; and, second, it is unnecessary and even dangerous to 'freeze' the case law of the ECJ for new members and, at the same time, allow its further development for old Member States. Indeed, the ECJ is not bound by its own decisions and it may always change the existing case law in order to promote the new and essential objectives of the EU.

The acceptance of the 'acquis communautaire' is a *sine qua non* of the accession as it encompasses rights and obligations attached to the Union and its institutional framework. From a practical point of view, a candidate State is given time to fully accept all rights and obligations deriving from its membership. During an agreed transition period some technical adjustment, derogations and transitional measures will be agreed between the State and the EU in order to ease full acceptance and adherence to the 'acquis communautaire'.

Procedure for admission

The first step consists of submitting a formal application for admission in the form of a letter signed by the minister for foreign affairs of a candidate State to the Presidency of the Council of the European Union. At that stage the Member States decide whether to initiate negotiations with an applicant State. This process can take a considerable time. The Commission also becomes involved and, after investigations, presents a 'preliminary opinion' which either recommends the opening of negotiations (Cyprus, Malta) or advises the Member States to wait until certain requirements are satisfied by a candidate State, or expresses its opposition to the admission (Turkey). This opinion is not binding, but is nevertheless of great influence. This influence is demonstrated by the fact that the Commission convinced the Member States to 'freeze' the enlargement of the EC until the completion of the common market.

The Council may take a position regarding the 'preliminary opinion' of the Commission by adopting the 'conclusion', which in the case of Cyprus and Malta confirmed the favourable opinion of the Commission but was ignored in relation to the Greek accession.[15]

Some negotiations have been lengthy and complex (Spain, Portugal), others swiftly and smoothly concluded (Austria, Finland, Norway and Sweden). Until the conclusion of negotiations admission is uncertain. The negotiations are conducted by the Council acting on proposals submitted by the Commission in which the latter endeavours to establish a common basis for negotiations and then play the role of a broker between Member States and a candidate State. If no major problems arise the negotiations end with a draft Treaty of Accession which has to be signed by the representatives of all Member States and the candidate State. The Treaty of Accession is usually very short, in the case of the UK it consists of three articles stating that the UK accedes to the three Communities and accepts all Community law, but the Act of Accession annexed to the Treaty of Accession is a voluminous document often accompanied by protocols, annexes and declarations. All these

---

[15] The Commission issued a negative opinion which was disregarded by the Council. Solely for political reasons, that is, to support nascent democracy in Greece, the Council decided to accept its application for admission: Opinion on the Greek Application for Membership: EC Bull Suppl 2/76.

documents, apart from declarations which have an interpretative function, are legally binding.

At this stage, the Council has to take a final decision after consultations with the Commission and the European Parliament. The opinion of the Commission is not binding in practice and as the Commission is fully involved in negotiations, its opinion is a pure formality. The European Parliament (EP) for the first time adopted the assent procedure in 1994 regarding the admission of Austria, Finland, Norway and Sweden. By four 'legislative resolutions' on the 4 May 1994, the EP granted its assent to the accession of four new Members. During the proceedings leading to membership of these States, the EP was kept informed by the Council and by the Commission of their progress in negotiations and expressed its comments in several resolutions in this respect.

The last stage concerns the ratification of the Treaty of Accession by the Member States and a candidate State in conformity with their respective national constitutional rules. For example, in 1972 France used the referendum by virtue of art 11 of the French Constitution to ratify the Treaty of Accession with the UK, Denmark, Ireland and Norway. Also, a candidate State often submits the final acceptance of its future membership to its people. In the last enlargement, all candidate States held national referenda.[16]

The Treaty of Accession enters into force only if all Members States ratify it. In case of multiple candidates, non-ratification by any one of them does not affect the membership of others. In the case of Norway, its government notified the EU that it would not ratify the Treaty of Accession as a result of a negative referendum. The Council of the EU, including the three new States, on 1 January 1995 adopted a decision 'adjusting the instruments concerning the accession of new Member States to the European Union'[17] and thus gave a legal effect to the withdrawal of Norway.

From the signature of the Treaty of Accession to the actual accession a future Member State is kept informed, and is consulted at all levels and in all areas as well as involved in the Community decision-making procedures, although it still has no right to vote. Its presence ensures that the existing Member States are fully aware of any difficulties and opposition to new measures, while permitting the new Member State participation in developments which are taking place within the EU.

2.2 Territorial expansion of the Communities

So far, four enlargements have taken place. As a result, the EU covers almost the entire western Europe and is inhabited by 371.9 million people, that is approximately 8 per cent of the world's population.

---

[16] Austria on 12 June 1994 (66.6 per cent in favour); Finland on 16 October 1994 (59.9 per cent in favour); Sweden on 13 November 1994 (52.3 per cent in favour); Norway on 28 November 1994 (52.2 per cent against).
[17] OJ L1 1.1.95 p1. A similar decision was taken by the Council when Norway, following the negative referendum (53.49 per cent against), failed to join the Communities in 1972.

First enlargement

On 1 January 1973, the UK, Denmark and Ireland joined the European Communities. Norway following a negative referendum, was not able to accede. The reasons for accession of the three new Member States were quite different, although the main consideration for Ireland and Denmark was the economic links with the UK.

In Ireland 83 per cent voted in favour of accession. For Ireland membership was very attractive as it provided an opportunity to open up new markets on the continent and thus reduce the traditional dependency upon the UK for Irish exports (70 per cent to the UK). Furthermore, as an agricultural country, the Irish could only gain from being a party to the Common Agricultural Policy (CAP).

Denmark, mainly an agricultural country, would also clearly benefit from the CAP. Its principal commercial partner, Germany, was already a Member State, and the UK, with whom it had strong economic links, was about to join the European Communities. The advantages were carefully weighed by the Danes against disadvantages, mainly the severance of traditional links with other Nordic countries based on inter-governmental rather than supra-national co-operation. In the national referendum, which took place after a negative vote in Norway, 63 per cent of Danes voted in favour of accession.

The most controversial candidate was the UK.[18] After the departure of de Gaulle there was no opposition to the United Kingdom membership. However, the accession negotiations lasted one year and focused on the following issues:

1. The length of the transition period.
2. The question of agriculture. In the UK food was cheap due to imports from the Commonwealth countries. The Heath government had two objectives in this respect: in the short term to slow down the impact of the CAP by phasing it in as slowly as possible; and in the long term to obtain compensation of the negative impact of the CAP by a satisfactory budgetary arrangement.
3. The UK contribution to the Community budget. It was agreed that its contribution would be 8.64 per cent of the Community budget in 1973, increasing to 18.92 per cent in 1977, with limits on further increases in 1978 and 1979. There was no agreement on 1980.
4. New commercial arrangements with Commonwealth countries. They were offered participation in the Yaoundé Convention which was later replaced by the Lomé Convention.[19] In addition, a Community General System of Preferences was extended to those countries. The question of exports of Caribbean sugar and New Zealand dairy products to the UK required special arrangements.
5. Fisheries. The first enlargement offered an opportunity for the EEC to create a Common Fisheries Policy based on free and equal access of the Member States to each other's waters – as a result UK participation in the CFP was examined.

The negotiations were concluded in January 1972 when the Treaty of Accession for the four applying States was signed. The European Communities Act 1972 came into force on 1

---

[18] The attitude of the UK toward European integration is examined in Chapter 1.
[19] See Chapter 4.

January 1973. However, the Labour party opposed the terms of the UK entry and promised in its electoral campaign to 'renegotiate' the Treaty of Accession. Indeed, once in power, the question of the UK membership became a main item on the political agenda of the Labour government.[20] In the end the UK membership was approved by the House of Commons (396 to 170), by the Government (16 to 7), and by the people of the UK in a national referendum (67.2 per cent in favour).

The terms of membership were not favourable to the UK as it has gained almost nothing from the Common Agricultural Policy. Indeed, barely 3 per cent of the population were engaged in agriculture, the lowest in Europe. Furthermore, the competitiveness of British industry in the new markets on the Continent was doubtful. From 1 January 1973 to 31 December 1986, the UK's net contribution to the EC Budget was £7,772 million, which represented a net payment of £1.52 million per day of membership.[21] The main question was not that the UK contribution was too high, as it was similar to other Member States, but the imbalance between its contribution and receipts from the EC budget. The UK reaction was to concentrate all efforts on the renegotiations of the financial contribution, which anyway was marginal compared to the UK budget as a whole, instead of taking advantage of the political role that membership of the Community made possible. This negative attitude contributed to the growing unpopularity of the UK within the Community and, at the same time, to the growing unpopularity of the Community with British people. As one observer noted, the reputation of the UK, and particularly Margaret Thatcher in the 1980s, was appalling. Her strategy was to 'rampage from summit to summit as a sort of fishwife Britannia demanding her money back. Fellow leaders, most notably Chancellor Kohl, adopted the habit of getting up and walking out of Council summits, rather than listen to yet another diatribe on the injustice of financial contributions'. They returned once her speech was finished. The clear and persistent failure of British politicians and British public opinion to objectively analyse British interests, and the optimal means of pursuing them, is one of the main features of British post-war politics. The single-minded preoccupation of the British government with its financial contribution, and thus the continuation of a negative diplomacy without seeing the opportunity to play a leading role in world affairs through the EC, is difficult to justify on rational grounds. The anti-European feeling ignores the basic fact that:

'In 1994 Britain sold more to Ireland than to Canada, Australia, New Zealand and South Africa.
– France buys more from Britain than do all the Commonwealth countries put together.
– in 1994, Britain earned more from selling to The Netherlands [than] to Korea, Taiwan, Singapore, Indonesia, China and the Philippines.
– in 1994 Britain exported more to Sweden than to all of Latin America from Rio Grande to Cape Horn'.[22]

Nowadays, the reluctance to participate in the Economic and Monetary Union (EMU) shows that the emotional approach toward the EU is still a very important factor in the UK decision-making process. Self-exclusion from a single currency will undermine vital and

---

[20] The question of 'renegotiation' is examined in MSO, *Membership of the European Community: Report on Renegotiation*, Cmnd 6003, March 1975.

[21] I Barnes and J Preston, *The European Community*, London and New York: Longman, 1988, p5.

[22] D MacShane, *Left out of Europe?*, Fabian Society, Discussion Paper No 26, London, 1996, p8.

essential national interests, *inter alia*, the decline of the City of London as Europe's major financial centre (already Frankfurt has gained considerable advantages from the absence of the UK in first stages of the EMU).[23]

Second enlargement

The second enlargement concerned the Hellenic Republic. Greece submitted its candidacy on 12 June 1975. The negotiations were opened on 25 June 1975. On 23 May 1979 the Treaty of Accession and the Act of Accession were signed. The Hellenic Republic became a Member State on 1 January 1981.

Greece is the first eastern European country to join the EC. Its heritage resulting from centuries of the Ottoman Turkish Empire rule combined with its Orthodox Christianity, a legacy of the Byzantine Empire, set Greece apart from other Member States. For Greece, with its inefficient agriculture (only 30 per cent of the land is cultivable), low rainfall and based upon mainly smallholdings, its limited natural resources, weak industry and a fragile democracy as it emerged from years of dictatorship, the attraction of being a Member State was obvious. A transition period of five years was agreed for Greece in all areas except tomatoes and peaches, which became included in the CAP at the end of 1987. It has taken many years for Greece to fully benefit from the membership and even today, despite considerable financial aid from the EU (eg ECU 2 billion from the Integrated Mediterranean Programmes introduced in 1985), it is still one of the least-developed Member States.

Third enlargement

Spain and Portugal joined the EC on 1 January 1986. Spain applied on 28 July and Portugal on 28 March 1977. Both signed the Treaty of Accession on 12 June 1985. The end of military dictatorship in both countries that enabled them to submit their applications for accession to the Communities.

The negotiations with Spain were protracted, as its proposed accession posed three major economic problems:

1. Spanish agriculture and its competitiveness, especially against that of France and Italy, made its participation in the CAP very controversial.
2. The Spanish fishing fleet was almost equal in size to that of the entire Community and therefore placed the Common Fisheries Policy under strain.
3. Spanish industry, and especially cotton, woollen textiles, clothing and steel, due to low wages, threatened the position of other Member States and posed a challenge to the EC which had already overcapacity problems in these sectors.

Portugal, a small and relatively poor country, posed no such threats to the economy of existing Member States. Its accession was delayed as a result of applying for membership at the same time as Spain.

Furthermore, the negotiations with Spain and Portugal were halted when France decided that, before a new enlargement, the budgetary matters within the EC should be

---

[23] See 'Should Britain Join or Stay Out' (1995) The European 12–16 June.

settled. As a result, it was after the Fontainebleau Summit in 1984 which reached an agreement on contributions to the EC budget that the accession negotiations with Spain and Portugal were resumed.

Fourth enlargement[24]

On 1 January 1995 Austria, Finland and Sweden joined the European Union. Austria submitted a formal application on 17 July 1989, Sweden on 1 July 1991, Finland on 18 March 1992 and Norway on 25 November 1992. Formal negotiations commenced on 1 February 1993.

All candidate States were EFTA countries and Members of the European Economic Area.[25] As such they already had considerable experience of working with the Community institutions as well as in the interpretation and application of Community law. Also, they had the appropriate 'infrastructure', that is, staff, procedures and material support to adapt to the negotiations with the European Communities. The negotiations went smoothly, although the question of the weighting of votes and the threshold of the qualified majority in the Council of the European Union was subject to much controversy which the 'Ioannina Compromise' settled for a while.[26] It was agreed that once the TEU had entered into force, the negotiations would be transformed automatically with an objective of membership of the Union. The candidate States were formally informed in this respect on 9 November 1993. The Treaty of Accession was signed on 24 June 1994. As Members of EFTA, the candidate States had to renounce their EFTA membership as well as terminate all bilateral agreements between themselves and with the Communities and all other international agreements incompatible with membership of the European Union.

De facto *enlargement: the case of the German Democratic Republic (GDR)*

On 3 October 1990, in conformity with the West German Constitution, the former GDR became an integral part of the Federal Republic of Germany (FRG). On that date, by virtue of art 227 EC, the territorial scope of application of all three Community Treaties was extended to the former East Germany.[27] Indeed, it was not necessary to revise EC Treaties as the FRG, the only legal government of Germany, always considered the GDR as part of its country when signing international treaties. However, Germany, taking into account the importance of the re-unification, and its impact on the German and EU economy, asked other Member States for approval which was formally issued by the Dublin Summit on 28 April 1990. Also, the Dublin summit laid down the transitory measures allowing temporary derogations in the application of EC law to the territory of GDR in certain areas such as competition policy, protection of environment, etc. Furthermore, transitional tariffs were

---

[24] On the fourth enlargement see D Booss and J Forman, 'Enlargement: Legal and Procedural Aspects' (1995) 32 CMLR 95–130.

[25] See S Peers, 'An Even Closer Waiting Room?: the Case for Eastern European Accession to the European Economic Area' (1995) 32 CMLR 187.

[26] Council Decision of 29 March 1994 (OJ C105 13.4.94 p1, amendment in OJ C1 1.1.95 p1).

[27] See C W A Timmermans, 'German Unification and Community Law' (1990) 27 CMLR 437–449; C Tomuschat, 'A United Germany within the European Community' (1990) 27 CMLR 415–436.

introduced for goods coming from other post-Communist countries, members of the Council for Mutual Economic Assistance (COMECON), under agreements previously signed by the GDR government (a period of one year from December 1990 to December 1991 was granted to those countries in order to adjust to the new situation).[28] The Commission was empowered to legislate and apply transitory measures.[29]

The challenge of enlargement

The candidacy of many countries wanting to join the EU are currently being examined by the Community institutions. So far the Commission has linked only six of them to open admission negotiations at the beginning of 1998: Hungary, Poland, Slovenia, the Czech Republic, Estonia and Cyprus. Others are still waiting, among them Turkey, the oldest candidate.

Turkey

Turkey applied on 14 April 1987. The Commission issued a negative opinion on 17 December 1989[30] recommending more effective application of the existing association agreement signed in 1964. It also considered that the next step in Turkey's route to Brussels was a customs union with the Communities. In January 1996 the customs union was agreed, but so far it is of little benefit as a Greek veto blocked aid worth hundreds of millions of ECUs due as compensation for loss of customs income. Turkey, a member of NATO, has threatened to use all necessary means – such as blocking the enlargement of NATO – in order to obtain membership of the EU. There are three main obstacles to the Turkish admission to the EU. First, its poor human rights record, which was also a main reason in the negative opinion of the Commission in 1989. According to the latest report from the US State Department the human rights' situation in 1996 deteriorated compared to 1995. Widespread torture by security forces, death during detention, etc, as well as the imposition of restriction on freedom of expression, are the examples of serious human rights shortcoming in Turkey. Second, Turkey is still fighting a vicious and ruthless war against the Kurdish separatists in the southwest. Turkish governmental sources confirmed that during the last 12 years of fighting, 4,157 members of the security forces, 13,000 Kurdish People Party members and 3,875 civilians were killed.[31] Finally, relations with Greece are still very tense. In 1996 both countries were ready to start a war over two islets in the Aegean. The main problem, however, is the question of Cyprus. Greece will certainly use its veto to block the entry of Turkey until a satisfactory solution is achieved regarding the division of Cyprus. Indeed, the candidacy of Turkey poses a difficult problem for the EU: Turkey half in Europe, half in Asia, with its mostly Muslim population and poor economy, is not ready for membership – but on the other hand, it is a member of NATO and has been patiently waiting for years for admission.

---

[28] EC Bull Suppl 4/90, pp5–27.
[29] On the basis of the Council Regulation 2684/90 (OJ L263 26.9.90 p1) and the Council Directive 90/476/EEC (OJ L266 28.9.90 p1).
[30] *Twenty-second General Report*, 1989, point 801.
[31] I Mather, 'Turkey Talks Tough as Union Shies from Islam' (1997) The European 6–12 February p5.

In order to soften the blow to Ankara of being left out of the first wave of enlargement, the Commission proposed the establishment of closer relations with Turkey, beyond the existing customs union.[32]

Cyprus

Cyprus formally applied for membership on 3 July 1990. Its application was favourably assessed by the Commission. It has been strongly supported by Greece, which warned that it would use its veto regarding the accession of central and eastern European countries if Cyprus's admission was unduly delayed. The division of Cyprus constitutes the main obstacle to its membership, although the EU declared that this division would not prejudice Cyprus's application.[33] The EU agreed to start admission negotiations with Cyprus six months after the conclusion of the Inter-governmental Conference (June 1997). The EU believes that the time is ripe to start the peace process and direct talks between the leaders of the two communities. In reality, the two sides in Cyprus remain as far apart as possible. The situation on this troubled island has deteriorated in recent years, with the reduction of the UN involvement and recent incidents in the buffer zone.

Malta

Malta formally applied on 16 July 1990. As in the case of Cyprus, the Commission is in favour of the admission of Malta.[34] The main hurdle in Malta's path to Brussels is its weak economy necessitating major reforms, although Malta is small enough to be assimilated without posing a particular challenge to the EU.[35]

The Corfu European Council of 24–25 June 1994 confirmed the progress of Malta and Cyprus within the framework of their respective Association Agreements (signed with Cyprus in December 1972 and with Malta in 1973). However, a newly elected government in Malta promised to withdraw Malta's application for membership of the EU.

Central and eastern European countries

Hungary officially applied on 1 April 1994, Poland on 8 April 1994,[36] followed in 1995 by the Czech Republic and Slovakia.

Central and eastern European countries do not form a homogeneous group. The four 'Visegrad'[37] countries – Hungary, Poland, the Czech Republic and Slovakia – are the most advanced in terms of economy, although the average per capita income in the EU is 8.4 times higher than that of those countries. After the collapse of the Soviet Union, the EU granted Generalised System of Preferences (GSP) status to some central and eastern

---

[32] (1997) The European 17–23 July p23.

[33] J Redmond, 'The European Community and the Mediterranean Applicants', in F R Pfetsch (ed), *International Relations and Pan-Europe*, Hamburg: Lit, 1993, p45, although he added that a 'divided Cyprus is unlikely to be welcomed' by the EU.

[34] The Commission issued its opinions concerning Cyprus and Malta simultaneously in 1993 (EC Bull Suppls 4 and 5/93).

[35] Commission of the European Communities, EC Bull Suppl 4/93.

[36] EC Bull 4–1994, point 1.3.18–19.

[37] They are known as Visegrad countries from a co-operation agreement concluded at Visegrad (Hungary) on 15 February 1991 among the Czech Republic, Hungary, Poland and Slovakia.

European countries.[38] GSP status confers preferential rates of duty on imports from these countries into the EU. It covered only manufactured goods and excluded sensitive products such as steel and textiles. GSP was followed by special agreements, so-called 'Europe agreements', with the Visegrad countries as well as two less-developed countries, Bulgaria and Romania. These agreements are in fact association agreements and considered as a first step in those countries' path to Brussels. For Hungary and Poland the full association agreement came into force on 1 February 1994. The Czech Republic and Slovakia, two countries which were established on 1 January 1993 after the division of the former Czechoslovakia, had to renegotiate their agreements. In the meantime, provisory measures were applied[39] to both countries. Until 1992 trade with the Visegrad countries was very successful. It confirmed that central and eastern European countries could successfully compete – in fact, the Visegrad countries' exports to the EC in 1991 were mostly in technology-intensive and high-skilled labour intensive product groups (69–70 per cent) which was unusual for less developed countries.[40]

Since 1992 the trade has declined. This can be explained by the current recession in the EU and particularly in Germany which was a main market for export from central and eastern European countries, and a growing resistance in the EU to imports from these countries, especially in sensitive sectors in which central and eastern Europe are most competitive, namely steel, textiles and clothing.

The Copenhagen European Council in June 1993 recognised the undesirable slowdown in the development of the economic relations between the EU and the associated countries, and especially the growing trade deficit with the EU, as well as imperfections in the association agreements. As a result, some modification were made to the association agreements.[41] The Copenhagen Summit of June 1993 acknowledged the desire of the associated countries to become Member States in the future, but did not set a deadline for their admission. Furthermore, it repeated once again that the admission would be subject to the fulfilment of economic and political requirements by the candidate countries. The Corfu Summit of 24–25 June 1994 accepted the applications for membership submitted by Poland and Hungary and asked the Commission to prepare a report on the strategy concerning the accession of the associated countries. The Commission submitted its conclusions in the communication *The Europe Agreements and Beyond: a Strategy to Prepare the Countries of Central and Eastern Europe for Accession* and a follow-up document in July 1994.[42] The 1997 Inter-governmental Conference issued a Declaration welcoming the enlargement, but it was the Commission's assessment of the applicant's state of readiness issued on 16 July

---

[38] January 1990 (Hungary and Poland), January 1991 (Czechoslovakia, Romania and Bulgaria).

[39] European Parliament Directorate-General for Research. 1994, Facts Sheets on the European Parliament and the Activities of the EU, European Parliament, Luxembourg, p121.

[40] A Inotai, 'Central and Eastern Europe', in *Reviving the European Union*, C R Henning, E Hochreiter, G C Hufbauer (eds), Institute for International Economics and the Austrian National Bank, Washington DC, 1994, p144 et seq.

[41] The modifications concerned: the removal of all tariffs for manufactured products by the end of 1994, and thus the transitional period was reduced from five to three years, but for sensitive sectors such as textiles and steel from five to four years; the increase of exports of some agricultural products such as meat, fruit, dairy products by 10 per cent per annum for five years, etc: (1993) Financial Times 1–2 May.

[42] COM(94)320 final and COM(94)361 final.

1997 called *Agenda 2000* which was crucial for eastern European countries. Six of the 11 applicants have the green light to start negotiations at the beginning of 1998. They are: Hungary, Poland, the Czech Republic, Slovenia, Estonia and Cyprus. The following data relating to the economic status of the applicant countries may be helpful in the assessment of the Commission's report:[43]

Who's next in the EU?				
	Population (m)	Unemployment (%)	GDP ($bn)	Inflation 1996
Czech Republic	10.3	3.5	43.0	8.6
Hungary	10.3	9.0	30.0	20.0
Poland	38.5	13.6	130.0	18.5
Slovenia	2.0	14.0	18.0	8.8
Estonia	1.6	4.0	4.2	15.0
Lithuania	3.7	6.4	7.7	13.0
Latvia	2.6	7.1	5.5	13.0
Romania	22.8	8.9	28.0	57.0
Bulgaria	8.4	13.0	9.7	310.0
Slovakia	5.3	12.0	11.0	5.8

However, no date for their final admission to the EU was fixed. Indeed, as the Amsterdam Summit did not resolve the two key questions, that is, the Commission size and the re-weighting of Council voting, at least two inter-governmental conferences would be necessary before any decision is taken. In any event, the Luxembourg Summit in December 1997 will make its decision on enlargement. The Commission's ambitious *Agenda 2000*[44] may be in jeopardy for many reasons. First, some Member States – Italy, Belgium, The Netherlands and Finland – fiercely oppose any enlargement before the reform of the Union's institutions take place. Second, the poorer Member States are hostile to any enlargement to the east as they would lose the financial help they currently receive from structural funds and the Cohesion Fund. Third, the CAP must be reformed. In this respect, Poland alone with six million dairy farmers, more than in all 15 Member States put together, if incorporated in the CAP price support mechanisms and compensatory payments as it stand now, would make the EU bankrupt.

---

[43] (1997) The European 17–23 July p23.
[44] Ibid.

From the perspective of the central and eastern European countries the EU is considered as a main stabilisation force in terms of economic and political development. Indeed, the EU is prepared and willing to aid these countries. Apart from association agreements, the Phare Programme was set up in July 1989 on the basis of a Commission proposal and with assistance from G7 – the industrialised countries. It provides aid for the reconstruction of the economy of central and eastern European countries, and encompasses such areas as agriculture, industry, investment, environmental protection, trade and services mainly in the private sector (approximately ECU 1 billion in 1993). Also, the European Bank for Reconstruction and Development (EBRD) was set up under the auspices of the G7 in May 1990 in order to facilitate:

> 'the transition towards open market-orientated economies and to promote private and entrepreneurial initiative in the central and eastern European countries committed to ... multi-party democracy, pluralism and market economy'.[45]

In the fields of cultural and educational assistance, the EU sponsors several programmes such as Tempus (Trans-European Mobility Programme for University Students, which also includes the exchange of academics), ACE (economics), COSINE (infrastructure), SIGMA (government and management), TACIS (similar to Phare but applicable to countries of the former Soviet Union), etc. However, the assistance and aid of the EU is still not sufficient.[46] The Visegrad countries' transition to a market economy has been quite successful, although foreign indebtedness, and the necessity to modernise their industry while restructuring agriculture, pose serious problems. In other central and eastern European countries the transition period is very painful and their nascent democracy is still very fragile.

The question of the future enlargement is very important for both the EU and the eastern and central European countries. The EU has certainly a moral obligation to accept these countries and ensure a peaceful change to their political and economic systems. An unstable and unpredictable situation in central and eastern European countries would threaten peace and prosperity in Europe. The expansion of the EU to encompass relatively poor countries means that current Member States will have to make sacrifices and assume collectively the burden of admission. Many authors consider that the EU should not fear enlargement, arguing that the admission of central and eastern European countries would improve those countries real income by an estimated 1.5 per cent to 18.8 per cent, with an annual cost to the EU between zero and $9 billion per year, that is, 0.1 per cent of the EU's total output.[47] The price to the EU for meeting this historic challenge seems relatively low. Indeed, as Wistrich stated the EU:

> 'should offer an assurance to those central and eastern European countries who wish to join that, subject to the necessary economic transformation and the maintenance of political pluralism, they would be admitted to membership of the Community within a specific number of years but not later than by the end of this century. Nothing would contribute more to the confidence of those countries, speed up internal reforms and safeguard their democracies than

---

[45] OJ C241 1990 p33.
[46] See Chapter 5, on the project of the EU to establish a new Marshall Plan for central and eastern European countries.
[47] T Naudin, 'EU Should Not Shrink from the Challenge of Enlargement' (1997) The European 17–23 April p20.

a clear goal within a defined timescale of full membership of the emerging European Union. If further economic adjustments were necessary, those could form part of transitional arrangements of appropriate length after a country joins'.[48]

Withdrawal and expulsion from the EU

The EC and the Euratom Treaties are concluded for an indeterminate period of time; however, the ECSC is limited to 50 years.

The Treaties are silent as to the possibility of withdrawal from the European Communities and the European Union. This omission is not accidental. The Member States wanted to enhance the very serious nature of membership of the Communities. However, in the absence of any provisions in this respect, the question of withdrawal raises many controversies.

It is submitted that the right to withdraw is implicit. The absence of provisions in this respect in the Community Treaties means that the 1969 Vienna Convention on the Law of Treaties will apply. Its art 54 states that where no specific provisions in the treaty provide for its termination, the consent of all contracting parties after consultation will be sufficient to terminate the treaty. In the event that some Member States refuse to give their consent art 56 of the 1969 Vienna Convention may be invoked. It provides that if a treaty contains no provision concerning termination, and does not provide for denunciation or withdrawal specifically, a contracting party may only denounce or withdraw from that treaty if the parties intended to admit such a possibility, or where the right may be implied by the nature of the treaty. Whichever provision of the 1969 Vienna Convention applies, it is clear that a Member State will not be constrained to stay within the EU against its will. First, art F(1) of the TEU underlines the respect of the EU for the national identity of Member States; in the case of flagrant and irreconcilable conflicts between a Member State's interests and EU policies, the former should be free to leave. This solution can also be justified on practical grounds; it is undoubtably preferable to permit a Member State to withdraw than to jeopardise the existence of the EU, as for example when France decided to apply its 'policy of empty chairs'[49] the Communities were paralysed and unable to function properly. Once a Member State decides not to share the EU ideals, refuses to fulfil its obligations arising out of the Treaties and becomes a nuisance, it is difficult to imagine a different solution. Second, the right to withdrawal was implicitly accepted by the Member States in 1974 when the UK asked for renegotiation of its Treaty of Accession and threatened to withdraw from the Communities unless her requirements were satisfied. Neither Member States nor the Community institutions opposed the UK withdrawal or claimed the impossibility of terminating UK membership. The Dublin Summit in May 1975 reduced the previously agreed level of subsequent UK contributions to the EC budget, but neither the Treaty of Accession not the Act of Accession of the UK were modified. Finally, if the people of a particular Member State were unhappy about the membership of the EU, which would be reflected in the result of their parliamentary elections, it is impossible to imagine that the EU will stand against its fundamental principles and oppose the withdrawal.

[48] E Wistrich, *The United States of Europe*, London: Routledge, 1994, p129.
[49] See section 2.3 below.

Until now no Member State has expressed a desire to leave the EU, but the Community has twice dealt with a question of State succession, that is, when a part of an existing territory of a Member State has acquired political sovereignty or large autonomy from that State. In case of Greenland, which is the world's largest island, and was an integral part of the Kingdom of Denmark at the time of its accession to the Communities, no opposition was expressed to the Greenland withdrawal. In 1979 the government of Denmark granted home rule to Greenland; as a result Greenland remains under the Danish crown, its people are still considered as Danish citizens. The island enjoys autonomy in all matters but constitutional affairs, foreign relations and defence. In 1985 the people of Greenland decided in a referendum to withdraw from the European Communities, and negotiations were conducted between the Kingdom of Denmark and other Member States. As a result, the specific provisions for Greenland are set out in the protocol on special arrangements for Greenland, annexed to the EC Treaty. Also, the EC Treaty was modified: Greenland is now mentioned in Annex IV of the EC Treaty concerning countries and territories with a special relationship with a Member State. Furthermore, art 136b EC was added which provides that arts 131–136 EC apply to Greenland, subject to the protocol on special arrangements for Greenland. The ECSC Treaty was also revised. Its art 79 states that the present Treaty does not apply to Greenland.

The second case concerns the St Pierre and Miquelon Islands. Their transformation from an overseas territory into an overseas department was considered as an internal matter of France. The Communities received notification in this respect from the French authorities. As a result, the St Pierre and Miquelon Islands no longer came under the special arrangement for the association of the overseas countries and territories with the Community provided for in Part IV of the EC Treaty and governed by the Council Decision of 29 June 1976,[50] but under the arrangements that apply to all French overseas departments by virtue of art 227(2) EC.

As to expulsion from the EU, at present this possibility is not provided by the Community Treaties.

2.3 Consolidation of the European Communities

The Robert Schuman Plan announced on 9 May 1950, which set up the European Coal and Steel Community, was the first step towards European integration. The idea was very much alive, but its actual application bristled with difficulties and controversies, the most important being the constant struggle between inter-governmentalism and supra-nationality. Indeed, the vision of Europe and the shape of European integration depends upon the form of co-operation chosen by the Member States. Supra-nationality entails important restrictions on national sovereignty and, if successful, leads to the creation of a federal structure. By contrast, inter-governmentalism implies that the Members States competencies are intact unless agreed by them. Its ultimate form is a confederation.

---

[50] OJ L176 1.7.76 p8.

The European Coal and Steel Community

The ECSC is based on supra-nationality. The Treaty creating the ECSC was signed on 18 April 1951 in Paris and entered into force on 25 July 1952 among the six original Members. The Member States unanimously decided to appoint Jean Monnet the first President of the High Authority, but the choice of a seat was more controversial. In the end Luxembourg has become the 'provisory' headquarters of the ECSC. The ECSC Treaty was concluded for a period of 50 years and is due to expire in July 2002. Therefore, the future of the ECSC is uncertain, especially in the light of declining importance of coal and steel.[51] One possibility is to let the Treaty of Paris lapse, while incorporating the most important provisions of that Treaty into the EC Treaty.

The fundamental objective of ECSC is to support production, research, development and the restructuring need of the coal and steel sectors. Article 4 ECSC provides a description of the negative mechanisms leading to a common market for coal and steel, such as the prohibition of import and export duties and measures having an equivalent effect, quantitative restrictions, discriminatory practices and measures between producers, between purchasers or between consumers, subsidies and aids granted by States, and restrictive practices aimed at the sharing or exploiting of markets.

The main innovation introduced by the Treaty of Paris was the creation of the High Authority, made up of representatives of the Member States but acting independently in the interests of the ECSC, in charge of the production and distribution of coal and steel, and entrusted with supra-national competencies, including the power to make legally binding 'decisions' and 'recommendations' directly applicable in Member States. The originality of the institutional structure is also enhanced by the creation of: a Special Council of Ministers, a partly legislative, partly consultative body representing the interests of the Member States; the Common Assembly made up of MPs from Member States which is, however, limited to only supervisory and advisory functions; and the Court of Justice responsible for ensuring 'that in the interpretation and application of this Treaty ... the law is observed'.[52]

There are two important differences between the ECSC Treaty and the EC Treaty: the High Authority/the Commission (under the Merger Treaty of 1965 a single Commission for all three Communities was set up) enjoys greater power under the ECSC Treaty than under the Treaties of Rome; and, second, some provisions of the ECSC Treaty do not have direct effect while similar provisions of EC Treaty are directly effective.[53]

The ECSC has certainly moved European integration forward. Its main achievements were the establishment of a common market for coal and steel within the Member States and the introduction of a common external tariff on these commodities. However, the first major crises regarding the overproduction of coal showed its shortcomings. The High Authority which wanted to deal with the crises by applying Community measures was

---

[51] See Memorandum from the ECSC Consultative Committee on the future of the ECSC Treaty (OJ C14 20.1.93 p5), and Memorandum of the ECSC Consultative Committee on matters connected with the expiry of the ECSC Treaty in 2002 (OJ C206 11.8.95 p7).

[52] Article 31 ECSC.

[53] Case C–128/92 *Banks* [1994] ECR I–1209; Case C–18/94 *Hopkins* [1996] ECR I–2281.

overruled by the Council in 1959. As a result, national rather than Community approaches to the overproduction of coal prevailed.[54]

The European Economic Community (EEC) and the European Atomic Energy Community (Euratom)

On 25 March 1957 in Rome the six original Member States signed two Treaties: one establishing amongst them the European Economic Community (EEC) and the second creating the European Atomic Energy Community (Euratom), both entered into force on 1 January 1958. The main objective of Euratom was to create 'the conditions necessary for the speedy establishment and growth of nuclear industries'.[55] Its tasks are laid down in art 2 Euratom and encompass: the promotion of research and dissemination of technical information regarding atomic energy; the establishment of uniform standards for health and safety; the promotion of investment; the equitable supply of ores and nuclear fuels; the security of nuclear materials; the international promotion of peaceful uses of nuclear energy; and, finally, the creation of a common market in this area. The institutional framework set up by the Euratom Treaty is identical to that of the EEC.

Euratom is another sectorial unification which has not been very successful due mainly to a French reluctance to co-operate from May 1958. The Euratom Treaty has been applied only partially. As a result, both Communities – Euratom and the ECSC – for different reasons have been marginalised. They also demonstrate that a sector-by-sector approach is not the best solution to European integration.

The European Economic Community, now known as the European Community (EC) under the Treaty on European Union, has become the most important Community and the heart of European integration. It mainly concerns the creation of economic co-operation among Member States, including the establishment of a common market, as well as opening the possibility for further co-operation in any area not covered by the Treaty of Rome but chosen by the Member States by common consent.[56] Although the economic objectives are in the forefront, the Treaty of Rome also contains a political agenda. The main feature of the EC is the creation of a common market: involving the abolishment of customs duties and charges having an equivalent effect to customs duties (arts 9–17), while prohibiting discriminatory internal taxation (art 95), and the establishment of a common external tariff (art 9 EC); ensuring the free movement of goods by eliminating quantitative restrictions and measures having an equivalent effect to quantitative restrictions (arts 30–35); while allowing the Member States the imposition of such measures by virtue of art 36, introducing the free movement of labour, both of workers (art 48) and self-employed (arts 52–58), but permitting the Member States to impose important restrictions on the grounds of public policy, public security and public health (art 48(3)), while enacting measures in the area of social security (art 51); abolishing restrictions on the freedom to provide services (arts 59–66); ensuring the free flow of capital; and, finally, submitting market forces to fair

---

[54] On the ECSC see Merry, 'The European Coal and Steel Community: Operations of the High Authority' (1995) 8 Western Political Quarterly 166.
[55] Article 1 Euratom.
[56] Article 235 EC.

competition (arts 85–86), although State monopoly and State aid are permitted, subject to many restrictions. This creative approach was enhanced by the establishment of a common policy in agriculture and transport, and was completed by setting up the European Social Fund, which provides vocational training and employment opportunities, and the European Investment Bank, offering loans to enhance economic expansion. Articles 2 and 3 EC laid down the long terms objectives for the EC, that is, the co-ordination of the economic and monetary policies leading to a union amongst the Member States. However, the EC's uniqueness and originality lies in its institutions:[57]

1. the Commission, a supra-national body, the executive of the Communities and a guardian of the Treaty;
2. the Council represents the interests of the Member States and is the main legislative body;
3. the European Parliament which from a purely advisory body (the Parliamentary Assembly) has evolved into a directly elected parliament endowed with some legislative powers; and
4. the Court of Justice of the European Communities (ECJ) which is entrusted with the interpretation of the Treaty, settlement of disputes between Member States or against the Community institutions, and the enforcement of Community law.

Also, the EC Treaty has created the European Investment Bank, the Court of Auditors and the Economic and Social Committee (ECOSOC), as well as a number of complementary bodies.

The first decade of the EC was exceptional in terms of economic growth, investment and internal integration. Small countries like Belgium, Luxembourg and The Netherlands realised that their membership allowed them to have an influence upon international matters and international trade out of proportion to their size.

The Luxembourg Accord

The first disagreement among the Member States occurred in 1965. It is known as the 'empty chair' crisis as France refused to attend the Council meetings from June 1965 to January 1966. The President of the French Republic, Charles de Gaulle, was in favour of inter-governmentalism and thus against the increasing of powers of the Community. The immediate cause of the crisis was the Commission package of proposals aimed at increasing the competencies of the Commission and the European Parliament (EP). Only the Commission proposal on the adoption of the financing arrangements for the CAP was accepted by France. The two remaining proposals were rejected. The first concerned new methods of financing the Community, aiming to end national contributions towards the budget and replacing it by a system of 'own resources' of the Community mainly provided by the revenue from the common external tariff. This proposal was considered as essential by the Commission. The second proposal concerned increasing the involvement of the EP in decision-making procedures in general, and in budgetary matters in particular. It was supported by the EP and by The Netherlands. The proposals were used by France to express its dissatisfaction in two areas: the role of the Commission, which under the Presidency of

---

[57] See Chapter 6.

Walter Hallstein was accused by France of exceeding its competence by acting more like a supra-national rather than inter-governmental body; and France was hostile to the major change in decision-making within the Council by replacing unanimity with qualified majority voting. The EC Treaty provided that at the beginning of the final stage of the transitional period, which was approaching, the new voting system should apply.

In order to dramatise the situation, France decided not to attend the Council meetings (hence the empty chair), but under pressure from French farmers de Gaulle decided to negotiate with other Member States (the Commission was not invited). In January 1966 an informal agreement was reached known as Luxembourg Accord which provided that:

> 'Where, in the case of decision which may be taken by majority vote ... the Council will endeavour ... to reach solutions which can be adopted by all the Members of the Council ... the French delegation considers that where very important interests are at stake the discussion must be continued until unanimous agreement is reached.'[58]

It meant that the unanimous vote was the main way of adopting EC legislation.

The Luxembourg Accord marked a clear return to inter-governmental co-operation and thus constituted a serious blow to supra-nationality. It was the main reason for years of stagnation of the Community as it paralysed progress towards further integration by giving priority to national interests of the Member States, although the Luxembourg Accord has never been recognised as binding under Community law. In Case 68/86 *United Kingdom* v *Council* the ECJ made clear that the decision-making procedures set up by the Treaty 'are not at the disposal of the Member States or the institutions themselves'.[59] The role of the Luxembourg Accord has steadily diminished: the first time a reference to the Luxembourg Accord was ignored by the Council was in 1982 when the UK tried to prevent the adoption of the agriculture price package in order to obtain a reduction of the British contribution to the Community budget. Furthermore, when Germany in 1985 successfully invoked the Luxembourg Accord to block a decision on the reduction of cereal prices, the Commission applied interim measures, and thus, in practice, overrode the opposition of Germany. Finally, the Single European Act introduced a qualified majority voting within the Council as a principle. This has been reinforced by the TEU.

The Merger Treaty

The idea of rationalising the institutional structure of the Communities was first introduced by the Convention of 25 March 1957 on Certain Institutions Common to the European Communities. The Convention provided for the establishment of a single Assembly (EP), a single Court of Justice and a single Economic and Social Committee for all three Communities. Further rationalisation took place in April 1965 when the Treaty establishing a Single Council and a Single Commission of the European Communities known as the Merger Treaty was signed. The Treaty came into force on 13 July 1967. Under the Merger

---

[58] *IXth General Report on the Activities of the EEC*, 1965–1966, p3; see J Lambert, 'The Constitutional Crises, 1965–66' (1966) 4 Journal of Common Market Studies 226.

[59] [1988] ECR 855; see also Teasdale, 'The Life and Death of the Luxembourg Compromise' (1993) 31 Journal of Common Market Studies 567.

Treaty the three Communities share the same institutions, although they remain legally independent and the competencies of the institutions are subject to the respective Treaties.

The Hague Summit

An important development in the consolidation process, and more precisely in the shaping of future co-operation among Member States, took place at the proposal of George Pompidou, the successor of Charles de Gaulle. A meeting was convened in The Hague in December 1969, and Pompidou, more flexible in his approach toward the development of the Community but as opposed to the construction of supra-national Europe as de Gaulle,[60] invited all Heads of State or Government of the Member States to a meeting. The main decisions taken by The Hague Summit concerned:

1. enlargement of the Communities (admission of the UK, Denmark, Norway and Ireland);
2. establishment of European Political Co-operation;
3. adoption of measures leading to the economic and monetary union among Member States;
4. introduction of regular meetings of foreign ministers of the Member States;
5. reform of CAP financing;
6. establishment of technical co-operation, introduction of development aid and the social policy on the Community agenda; and finally
7. creation of a European University.

In the immediate period after The Hague Summit the oil crisis at the international level and the budgetary crisis within the Community asphyxiated its growth for almost two decades. Nevertheless, since The Hague Summit the EC's ambitious agenda has been further developed.

Establishment of European Political Co-operation (EPC)

The Hague Summit decided to examine the best ways of achieving progress in the establishment of a political union. In October 1970, the Davignon Report named after its author, the political director of the Belgian Foreign Ministry, was adopted by foreign ministers of the Member States as a basic strategy in this area. It was further approved by the Copenhagen Summit on 23 July 1973.[61] It proposed the harmonisation of foreign policy outside the Community framework and consisted of regular exchanges of information between foreign ministers aimed at facilitating the harmonisation of their respective views and, when possible, leading to a common position. It therefore recommended the traditional inter-governmental co-operation in political matters without any supporting common structures. Some changes to the European Political Co-operation were introduced in a subsequent report which was adopted by foreign ministers meeting in London on 13 October 1981.[62] The above-mentioned reports and the Solemn Declaration on European

---

[60] H Simonian, *The Privileged Partnership: Franco-German Relations in the European Community, 1968–1984*, Oxford: OUP, 1985, p35.

[61] *Seventh General Report on the Activities of the European Communities*, Brussels, Luxembourg, 1973, p502 et seq.

[62] EC Bull Suppl 3/81, p14 et seq.

Union agreed at the Stuttgart Summit in 1983 constituted the foundation of the EPC.[63] It was incorporated in Title III of the Single European Act.[64]

Economic and Monetary Union (EMU)

The establishment of the Werner Committee was a concrete response to the Hague Summit of 1969 in this area. The Werner Report outlined three stages in the economic and monetary union, although only the first stage was comprehensively drafted. Its main objective was to create full monetary union by 1980. The first stage of the EMU is better known as 'the snake in the tunnel'. The Werner Plan was modified as a result of crises within the International Monetary Fund.[65] These modifications put it in line with the Smithsonian Agreement of December 1971. In its final version it consisted of the reduction of exchange rate fluctuation among currencies of the Member States to a band of 2.25 per cent of their central parities – it was the 'snake' which was allowed to move within the wider band of 4.5 per cent maximum against the US dollar, that was 'the tunnel'. The 'snake in the tunnel' was launched on 24 April 1972. The currencies of nine countries (six full Members) participated in the EMU. Three other States were about to join, that is the UK, Ireland and Denmark, but the devaluation of sterling in June 1972 forced the UK and Ireland to leave the EMU within eight weeks. Denmark left in June 1972 but returned in October. When the International Monetary Fund (IMF) collapsed in October 1972 and speculation against the US dollar caused its second devaluation, the EMU fell in disarray. Indeed, the tunnel disappeared but the 'snake' survived. The participating Member States were leaving and joining the EMU at their convenience (Italy left in February 1973, France in January 1974 and then again in March 1976, etc). However, the 'snake' remained but had changed its nature. It became a mainly 'German snake', that is, it was essentially composed of the deutschmark and currencies of small countries closely linked with Germany (eg The Netherlands).

The failure of the EMU can be explained by the conjunction of internal and external factors. The external factor was the collapse of the IMF. As to the internal factors, it was the weak commitment of the Member States to the EMU which was treated as an additional option in national policies and not as a priority (eg France joined in 1972, left in 1974, joined again in 1975, left again in 1976).

The EMU was replaced by the European Monetary System (EMS) adopted at the Bremen and Brussels Summits in 1978. It came into force on 13 March 1979. The EMS was created by Roy Jenkins in 1977[66] and strongly supported by Helmut Schmidt, the Chancellor of Germany. The main elements of the EMS are the European Currency Unit (ECU) and the Exchange Rate Mechanism (ERM). The ECU constitutes the Community's alternative

---

[63] EC Bull 6–1983, pp18–29.

[64] Article 30 SEA and arts 1 and 3 SEA Title I.

[65] The Bretton Woods system established in 1944 provided for the exchange market intervention. The US dollar was tied to gold at $US 35 per ounce and the US government promised to buy and sell at that price. All other Member States of the IMF accepted to specify a par value for their currencies in terms of the $US. As a result, their currencies were tied together at stable exchange rate. On 15 August 1971 President Richard Nixon announced the end of the US commitment to buy and sell at $US35 per ounce: G Milton, *Quest for World Monetary Order*, New York: John Wiley, 1980.

[66] R Jenkins, 'European Monetary Union' (1978) 127 Lloyds Bank Review 1–14.

currency. It is a unit of currency against which the values of national currencies are measured. The ECU is a composite currency, a 'weighted basket' of currencies of all Member States. The percentage of each national currency is determined by the size of the country, the relative size of its GNP and the share it commands of the Community's total trade. The ECU, being a composite currency, has become very popular in international credit deals for both businesses and individuals as it reduces monetary risks inherent to any international transactions. Member States were forced to accepted the ECU as a part of their foreign exchange reserves. The ECU has many functions: it is used in financial settlement between different States; the EC issues its bonds in ECUs; and, most importantly, the ECU is at the heart of the ERM as it is used for the credit and intervention mechanism of the ERM.

Under the ERM the currency of each Member State has a value against the ECU, as well as a cross-rate against all of the other EMS currencies – the bilateral central rate. Member States agreed to fix their exchange rate against each other within a band of 4.5 per cent but not allowing the value of their currencies to rise or fall by more than within 2.25 per cent around the central rate (except for Italy which was allowed a 6 per cent range). The ERM currencies float against all other world currencies. The rates of exchange are not irrevocably fixed and thus may be changed by a decision of Member States, although Italy unilaterally devalued the lira in July 1985. In order to ensure the proper functioning of the ERM some intervention and assistance mechanisms are provided:

1. The intervention of central banks. When the currency of one Member State reaches the upper or lower limit of the permitted band against the currency of another Member State, the central banks of both countries have to co-operate in order to maintain both currencies within their bilateral limits, that is sell or buy the currency of another State.

2. The reserve pooling system. The Basle/Nyborg Agreement of September 1987 opened up access to short-term finance for central banks of the ERM States in need. Medium term finance can be provided through the Council. The European Monetary Co-operation Fund[67] provides long term financial assistance. Its objective is to promote:

   '(a) the proper functioning of the progressive narrowing of the margin of fluctuation of the Community currencies against each other;
   (b) interventions in Community currencies on the exchange markets, and settlements between central banks leading to a concerted policy on reserves'.[68]

3. Subsidised loans for ERM members through the European Investment Bank.

The UK joined the EMS in October 1990 but left in September 1992.

The EMS ensures exchange-rate stability, discourages speculation, controls inflation and reinforces the co-operation among its members in monetary matters. The EMS was very successful until 1992 when it faced a serous problem created by the German government that decided for political reasons (against the advice of the Bundesbank) to unify the currencies of West and East Germany at a 1:1 ratio for much of the money supply, and 2:1 for the rest, although the actual exchange ratio should have been 4:1. It resulted in inflation in Germany, followed by the Bundesbank tightening money supply. At that time the UK was

---

[67] OJ L89 14.7.73 p2.
[68] Ibid.

entering a recession. The response of the Bank of England was to reflate the British economy which, against the policy of the Bundesbank, forced the UK to leave the EMS. Italy left a few days later. The EMS had to adopt to a new challenge. As a result, the permitted fluctuation bands have been widened from 2.24 per cent to 15 per cent (in fact 30 per cent, 15 per cent on each side of central rate). It meant that floating exchange rates were re-introduced within Europe. The difficulties did not, however, discourage the Member States from signing the TEU.

Establishment of technical co-operation, the introduction of development aid and the social policy on the Community agenda

Technical co-operation

In the area of technical co-operation, the Colonna Report of 1970 was a response to The Hague Summit of 1969. Mostly ignored by Member States, this report nevertheless inspired the Commission to create a common industrial policy, especially in the new 'high technology industries'. The Commission has been very successful in this area. From the first programmes – the European Space Agency, Airbus Industries and Euronet-DIANE (Direct Information Access Network for Europe) – it has mobilised and brought together many researchers, industrialists and academics. The major achievements in this area are the creation of such programmes as ESPRIT (the European Strategic Programme for Research and Development and Information Technology), BRITE (the Basic Research in Industrial Technologies for Europe), RACE (Research into Advanced Communications in Europe), etc.[69]

Development aid

The introduction of development aid has two aspects: aid for developing countries which will be examined elsewhere in the book,[70] and aid to the poorest regions of the Community in order to reduce disparities in economic conditions both within its borders and in each Member State. The main body in charge of promoting economic activities and improving living conditions in the less prosperous regions of the Community is the European Regional Development Fund (ERDF) created as a temporary body in 1975 at the initiative of the UK in order to compensate for her small share of agriculture subsidies. The ERDF has become a permanent feature of the Community. The development of regional policy, especially after subsequent enlargements allowing poor countries, like Greece and Ireland, to join the Community, has become an important matter for the Community. From 1975 to 1986, a time of a major reform of the ERDF, it distributed nearly ECU 18 billion to the poorest regions in the Community, 91 per cent of which was allocated to five countries: the UK, France, Greece, Ireland and Italy[71] in the form of non-repayable grants. After 1986, new 'quota ranges' have been introduced for each Member State, followed by some structural changes in the allocation of the ERDF funds, that is, 30 per cent to 50 per cent of its

---

[69] For details see: S A Budd and A Jones, *The European Community, a Guide to the Maze*, London: Kogan Page, 4th ed, 1992, pp87–109.

[70] Chapter 5.

[71] E Wistrich, *The United States of Europe*, London, New York: Routledge, 1996, p66.

spending are grants for infrastructure projects, and more emphasis is put on regional and sectorial programmes and projects. The ERDF applies to two categories of programmes: purely Community, long-term programmes aimed at areas with social and economic difficulties, and national programmes of interest to the Community which, in general, are jointly financed by a Member State applying for a grant and the Community.

Social policy

The social policy of the Community was in a state of infancy until the adoption of the Single European Act (new arts 118a and 118b EEC). The ECSC Treaty contains some social provisions designed to alleviate the effect of the reconstruction of steel and coal industries for workers employed in these sectors. The preamble to the EEC Treaty set out as main long-term objectives 'the constant improvement of the living and working conditions' of peoples of the Member States, and underlines the Community commitment to the economic and social progress of the Member States by common action to eliminate the barriers which divide Europe. In practice, social policy lacked direction and it had been mainly developed by the creative approach of the ECJ based on art 7 EEC (non-discrimination based on nationality), art 119 EC (equal pay for men and women), art 48 EEC (free movement of workers), art 51 EEC (social security), etc, or some occasional intervention of the Community such as the First Social Action Programme of 1974. The Social Fund established by the EEC Treaty has played an important role from its inception. Its main task, at that time, was to compensate for the difficulties that some social groups might experience resulting from structural changes due to the operation of the common market. During the 1960s, a period of economic boom and low employment, the Social Fund was mainly involved in the retraining of workers affected by structural changes, but after the problems of 1973 (see below), its priority was to combat unemployment. In 1986, 16 million workers in the Community, that is 16 per cent of its work force, were out of work. In these circumstances the Single European Act acknowledged the need for reformulating the social policy of the Community and set out a new task for the Social Fund.

The Community from 1970 to 1985 – years of stagnation

From 1970 to 1985 the Community was in a state of stagnation. The so-called 'Eurosclerosis' can be explained by the difficult international situation, but more importantly by lack of commitment from the Member States to further integration. Instead of developing an effective strategy for dealing with common problems created by the oil embargo in 1973, each Member State decided to act on its own. As a result, the UK and France signed bilateral agreements with Iran and Saudi Arabia for oil supplies, while The Netherlands was left in the cold with its supplies completely cut off by OPEC. National interests and national policies prevailed over Community objectives. The crisis within the Community was also enhanced by three major issues: the budgetary matters; the UK contribution to the Community budget; and the reform of the CAP. However, during that period some positive developments took place, such as the reform of the Community budget, the creation of 'own resources' of the Community aimed at replacing the system of national contributions and, finally, in June 1979, for the first time the European MPs were directly elected by people of the Member States.

Major developments

The European Parliament The Parliamentary Assembly by its own resolution of 30 March 1962 changed the name to 'the Parliament'[72] in order to emphasise the role it wanted to play within the Community. In the struggle to become a 'real Parliament' with legislative powers and directly elected members by universal suffrage in all Member States, the EP won two major victories in the 1970s. First, the budgetary reform of the Community allocated important new powers to the EP. Based on two Treaties signed on 22 April 1970[73] and 22 July 1975[74] known as the Budgetary Treaties, the EP acts in conjunction with the Council in the budgetary procedures. Their respective competencies are determined by the distinction between 'compulsory expenditure' that automatically arises from, or forming the inevitable consequence of, the Treaty obligations to third parties (eg mainly expenditure on the Common Agricultural Policy), and 'non-compulsory expenditure' regarding expenditure in respect to the institutions (eg structural funds, research, etc). The EP was granted the right to block non-compulsory expenditure. The 1975 Budgetary Treaty has also created a new Community institution: the Court of Auditors in charge of the finances of the Community.

The second victory of the EP concerns the introduction of direct elections to the EP. In this respect, the Council Decision and Act of 20 September 1976 on Direct Elections[75] states in art 1 that the Members of the Parliament should be elected by direct universal suffrage. The first election took place in June 1979.[76]

Budgetary matters The Budgetary Treaties were completed by the introduction of the Communities 'own resources'. Article 201 EC provides for the establishment of 'own resources' of the Community, thus replacing the system of national contributions to the Community budget. In 1970 the Member States agreed on the new system,[77] although it was only implemented in 1980. At this stage the 'own resources' consisted of revenue from the common external tariff (custom duties, agricultural levies) and up to 1 per cent of VAT levied on the common assessment base.[78]

Recognition of the European Council Informal meetings of the Heads of State or Government of the Member States initiated by The Hague Conference in 1969 within the framework of the Common Political Co-operation were recognised as a Community institution by the Paris Summit in December 1974.[79] The European Council was to meet regularly three times a year. The number of meetings was reduced to two in 1985.

---

[72] OJ 1962 p1045.

[73] OJ L2 2.1.71 p1.

[74] OJ L359 31.12.77 p1.

[75] Council Decision 76/787 (OJ L278 8.10.76 p1) and the Act concerning the election of the representatives of the Assembly by direct universal suffrage (OJ L278 8.10.76 p5).

[76] For details see Chapter 6.

[77] Council Decision 70/243 on the Replacement of Financial Contributions from the Member States by the Communities' Own Resources OJ L94 28.4.70 p19).

[78] A common assessment base is a percentage of the total value of good and services on which VAT is levied. It means that if a Member State's VAT rate is 20 per cent, 1 per cent is allocated to the Community.

[79] EC Bull 12–1974, p7ff.

Major problems

The three major problems that had arisen during the years of stagnation were inter-related. On one hand, the UK contribution to the Community budget was the main reason for UK dissatisfaction with the Community; on the other hand, two-thirds of the Community budget was spent on financing the Common Agricultural Policy. These difficulties were compounded by the intra-Community struggle between the Council and the European Parliament. The crisis reached a climax in December 1979 when the EP rejected the budget in order to express its dissatisfaction regarding its limited participation in the budgetary procedure, and in 1983 it blocked the UK rebate in an attempt to force budgetary reforms. These problems were solved later when the process of European integration was set on course. As to the UK contribution to the Community budget the Fontainebleau Summit in June 1984 solved the dispute by introducing a 'correction' to the UK net contribution based on the rules for the calculation of the 'own resources' of the Community.[80] The revision of the Common Agricultural Policy was even more complex. The Delors 1 package provided a solution for the financing of the CAP which was approved by a special summit in Brussels in February 1988. The budgetary disagreement between the EP and the Council was settled by the Inter-institutional Agreement between the Commission, the Council and the EP in 1988.[81] The Delors 1 package has eliminated to a great extent the possible disagreements between the Community institutions in budgetary matters as it: introduced a five-year (1988–92) 'financial perspective', that is, a draft budget for each year; put a ceiling for expenditure from 1.15 per cent of Community GNP in 1988 to 1.2 per cent in 1992; introduced a new 'own resource' to the Community budget consisting of a percentage of each Member State's share of the Community's GNP; and finally reduced substantially the Community's spending on the CAP – a maximum of 74 per cent of the growth rate of the Community's GNP – thus allocating more money to structural funds.

Relaunch of European integration

The early 1980s witnessed the new attitude of the Member States towards the Community. The unexpected enthusiasm, optimism and commitment to European integration, and a political will on the part of Member States to further the development of the Community, are difficult to explain. Indeed, the change in mood was surprising, but essential to the survival of the idea of European unity. Among the factors that certainly contributed to the 'Europhobia' was: the improvement of international economic situation; the commitment of a new French President, F Mitterrand, to the development of the Community, strongly supported by the German Chancellor Helmut Kohl; and the appointment of Jacques Delors, the new President of the Commission in 1985, who decided to accelerate the process of integration by submitting concrete projects. An additional stimulus was the realisation by the Member States that only a common action could improve the competitiveness of national economies and increase their share in world exports, especially vis-à-vis the United

---

[80] Decision 85/257 (OJ L128 14.5.85 p15), which was replaced by Decision 88/376 (OJ L185 15.7.88 p24). Now in force in Decision 94/278 (OJ L293 12.11.94 p9). The advantage of the system of periodical revision is that the decision in this area requires a unanimous vote by the Council.

[81] It was replaced by the Inter-institutional Agreement of 29 October 1993 (OJ C331 7.12.93 p1), which covers the period from 1993–1999.

States, Japan and the newly industrialised countries. A greater convergence in all fields within the framework of the Community was the answer to the growing inter-dependence of international trade. Furthermore, national solutions to international problems proved unrewarding, and the economic turmoil of 1973 when Member States resorted to protective measures at a national level was the best example in this respect. As a result, some of the earlier proposals at reforming the Community were re-examined.

In December 1974 the Commission was asked to prepare a report on European Union which was submitted in 1976 by the Belgian Prime Minister, Leo Tindemans.[82] The Tindemans Report set up a bold agenda for economic, monetary and political integration headed by a supra-national body to supervise its functioning which would be accountable to directly elected bi-cameral parliament. The Report was considered as very controversial and was never seriously examined. Its only practical result was an invitation to the Council and the Commission to prepare annual reports on progress towards the creation of the European Union. More realistic reforms were proposed in 'The Three Wise Men' report prepared at the request of the European Council of 1978 and submitted to it in October 1979.[83] This report emphasised the role of the European Council as a true contributor to the improvement of the decision-making procedure within the Community, examined the reasons for failures of the Community institutions to perform their task efficiently which 'lie rather in political circumstances and attitudes that sometimes produced conflicting conceptions of the right way forward, and sometimes produced no clear conceptions at all',[84] and called for solidarity among the Member States. However, it did not produce concrete results.

Another important initiative in this area was the report submitted by Altiero Spinelli, a strong supporter of the reforms of the Community leading to closer integration. He founded the so-called 'Crocodile Club' named after a restaurant in Strasbourg, a meeting place of the reformers. Their proposal for institutional reforms was endorsed by the European Parliament. As a result the EP set up an Institutional Committee, with Spinelli as a co-ordinating *rapporteur*, responsible for preparing a comprehensive draft regarding the creation of a European Union. The Spinelli Draft Treaty on European Union was adopted with enthusiasm by the EP on 14 February 1984 (out of 311 MPs, 273 were in favour, 31 against and 43 abstained).[85] The Draft Treaty was strongly supported by President Mitterrand, and, indeed, at Fontainebleau in June 1984 under his initiative an *ad hoc* committee made up of representatives of the Member States under the chairmanship of James Dooge, leader of Irish Senate, was set up in order to examined the Draft. At the same time, the Fontainebleau Summit created the Addonnino Committee and entrusted it with the preparation of proposals concerning the free movement of persons within the Community with a view to the establishment of a Citizen's Europe.[86] The final report of the Dooge Committee was presented at the Brussels Summit in March 1985[87] and adopted by the majority of its members. The report recommended the introduction of the co-decision

---

[82] EC Bull Suppls 5/75 and 9/75.

[83] A N Duff, 'The Report of the Three Wise Men' (1981) 21 Journal of Common Market Studies 237 et seq.

[84] Ibid, p19.

[85] OJ C77 19.3.84 p27.

[86] *XVIII General Report on the Activities of the European Communities*, 1984, point 5.

[87] EC Bull Suppl 3/85, point 3.5.1. et seq.

procedure designated to give more powers to the EP, the recognition of the European Council as a Community institution and the preparation of a new treaty on the European Union.

On 1 January 1985 Jacques Delors was appointed the new President of the Commission. Lord Cockfield, the Commissioner in charge of the internal Community market, volunteered to prepare the complete Internal Market Programme. His initiative was not only endorsed by Delors but he extended the initial proposal to cover all industries, including steel and coal.[88] The Cockfield White Paper was very detailed. It identified the remaining barriers to trade within the Community and set up a timetable for their elimination at the end of 1992. The White Paper and comments on the Dooge Committee Report from Member States were submitted to the Milan Summit in June 1985, which welcomed the White Paper and instructed the Council to initiate a precise programme based on it. However, the main achievement of this summit was the decision of the Heads of State or Government to convene an Inter-governmental Conference (IGC) despite opposition from the UK, Denmark and Greece.

The conference met in Luxembourg and Brussels during the autumn of 1985. The three dissenting Member States decided to participate in the Inter-governmental Conference (IGC). The outcome of the IGC was the Single European Act.

The Single European Act

The SEA was signed on 17 and 28 February 1986 and came into effect on 1 July 1987. Its ratification encountered some difficulties in four Member States: Italy considered that the SEA was not bold enough; Greece dragged its ratification waiting for Denmark's decision on whether to ratify or not; for Denmark it was necessary to hold a national referendum; and in Ireland, the Irish government was forced by the ruling of its Supreme Court[89] to hold a referendum as the Court held that the SEA provisions on security were in conflict with the Irish constitution.

The SEA was not very ambitious which was the main reason for its acceptance by the Member States, but had much potential for expansion.

The main features of the SEA are:

1. The completion of the internal market by 31 December 1992. This objective is contained in Article 7a EC. The creation of a single market involved the elimination of physical barriers to trade, such as frontier documentation processes, as well as physical barriers to the free movement of people within the Community, such as passport control, immigration procedures, baggage searches, etc. It also involved the removal of technical barriers in relation to all four freedoms – for goods it meant the harmonisation of national technical standards and governmental procurement policies; for people it consisted of the facilitation of the mobility of labour, both workers and self-employed, as well as the creation of a common market for services. The free movement of capital, the harmonisation of company and intellectual property law, and the removal of fiscal

---

[88] Lord Cockfield, *The European Union, Creating the Single Market*, London: Wiley Chancery Law, 1994, pp28–59.
[89] *Crotty* v *Taoiseach* [1987] 2 CMLR 666 (Irish SC).

barriers by the equalisation of VAT and excise duties were priority objectives. They were successfully completed on time.[90]

Nearly 300 measures were enacted in order to create an European Economic Area without frontiers.

2. The key to the completion of a single market was the introduction of qualified majority voting within the Council which covered two-third of the 300 measures necessary to create a common market. Nevertheless under art 100a EC, regarding the approximation of national legislation aimed at completing the internal market, unanimity was required in the following areas: taxation, freedom of movement for persons, and measures concerning the rights and interests of employed persons.

3. The extension of legislative powers of the European Parliament. A new co-operation procedure enhancing the participation of the EP in the decision-making procedure in ten areas was introduced (art 189c EC). Furthermore a second procedure, the 'assent procedure', has given the EP a new and important role. The approval of the EP (by an absolute majority) is required for the admission of new members to the Community, and in the case of association agreements with third countries. The decision-making procedures will be discussed elsewhere in the book.[91]

4. The formalisation of the European Council as a Community institution.

5. The creation of the Court of First Instance in order to ease the workload of the ECJ.

Many amendments introduced by the SEA have been further developed by the Treaty of Maastricht. Consequently, they will be discussed in the next chapter. Among them the following are of great importance:

1. The formalisation by the SEA of the mechanism for the European Political Co-operation.

2. The extension of the Community competences to new areas. In some areas the Community was already active, such as environment, research and regional policy, protection of consumer and social cohesion.

The impact of the SEA on the European integration is twofold: it has successfully created a single market, and psychologically it has encouraged the Member States to pursue common objectives within the framework of the Community. It paved the way to the Treaty of Maastricht.

From the Single European Act to the Treaty on European Union

The Commission commented on the SEA that 'if the programme succeeded, it would fundamentally alter the face of Europe',[92] especially as it contained a hidden agenda, that is the creation of economic and monetary union, a necessary complement to the single

---

[90] The Commission in order to convince the Member States of the benefit flowing out of the establishment of a common market asked P Cecchini to prepare a report: P Cecchini, *The European Challenge 1992, the Benefits of a Single Market*, Aldershot: Wildwood, 1988. According to the Report the overall cost of non-tariff barriers was approximately ECU 200 billion and the benefit ranged between 4 and 7 per cent of Community GDP.

[91] See Chapter 6.

[92] EC Bull 6–1985, p18.

market. This approach confirms the 'spillover' theory according to which integration in one area of activity leads to integration in others. However, in order to achieve the objectives laid down in the SEA it was necessary to deal first with persisting internal conflicts. In this respect, the adoption of the Delors 1 package, which introduced the budgetary discipline, ended the 'British rebate' saga and reformed the CAP, permitting the Commission to put forward new initiatives. The Commission under the Presidency of Jacques Delors was committed to further integration with a view to introducing EMU. Its motto was 'one market, one money'.

The Hanover Summit of June 1988 reappointed Jacques Delors as President of the Commission. It also reaffirmed his vision of the Community by declaring that 'in adopting the Single Act, the Member States of the Community confirmed the objective of progressive realisation of economic and monetary union'.[93] The Hanover Summit, most importantly, set up a Committee, chaired by Jacques Delors, to examine the measures necessary for the establishment of EMU. The task of this Committee was to prepare concrete stages leading towards monetary union for the Madrid Summit in June 1989. Jacques Delors, in his annual speech on 17 January 1989 to the EP, assessed progress in the completion of a single market and set the agenda for the newly appointed Commission, that is, to devolve more power to the EP and to create EMU by successive stages. His vision of the Community was clear: it was a 'frontier free economic and social area on the way to becoming a political union',[94] although at this stage political union was not his priority. The Madrid Summit in June 1989 examined the Delors Report[95] without taking particular notice of the changing situation in Europe.[96]

The dismantling of the barbed wire border between Hungary and Austria on 2 May 1989 was the first tear in the 'iron curtain' and started the sequence of events which led to the creation of the political union. Indeed, the 'German question' became the main preoccupation of Member States. The old political division between West and East was abolished, the Soviet Union was in a coma, the old order was shattered. Under the pressure of events and uncertainty, the Federal Republic of Germany (FRG) accelerated the reunification process. Helmut Kohl in his ten-point programme on German reunification, submitted to Bundestag on 28 November 1989, underlined that German unity was entirely a German question, but nevertheless in six points emphasised the FRG's commitment to the Community, the necessity to embed inter-German relations in an all-European process, as well as further strengthening the Community, especially in the light of the historical changes occurring in Europe.[97] The official policy of Germany on reunification echoed the famous call of Thomas Mann in 1953 'not a German Europe but for a European Germany'.

---

[93] EC Bull 6–1988, point 1.1.14.

[94] EC Bull Suppl 1/89, p18.

[95] J Delors, *Report on Economic and Monetary Union in the EC,* Luxembourg: Office for Official Publications of the European Communities, 1989.

[96] Only a very brief discussion on the changes in the Soviet bloc: EC Bull 6–1989, Presidency Conclusion, point 1.1.16.

[97] E Kirchner, 'Genscher and What Lies Behind Genscherism' (1990) 13 West European Politics 159–177.

The hegemony of Germany within the Community haunted all European leaders.[98] Jacques Delors considered that German reunification was a matter the Germans had to deal with. In his annual speech on 17 January 1990 to the EP he presented his programme for the Commission's forthcoming year and emphasised that East Germany was a special case, that reunification of Germany, although being left to the German nation, nonetheless must be achieved 'through free self-determination, peacefully and democratically, in accordance with the principles of the Helsinki Final Act, in the context of an East-West dialogue and with an eye to European integration'.[99] Indeed, at that time the Brandenburg Gate in Berlin was opened and the first democratic elections announced in the former German Democratic Republic (GDR). It was clear that, at this stage, nothing could really stop the inevitable reunion of the German nation. The President of France, François Mitterrand, began to put pressure on other Member States to create a political union to counterbalance the implications of German reunification by closely linking the largest Member State with the Community in political matters.[100] The extraordinary summit held in Dublin on 28 April 1990 formally welcomed East German integration into the Community, and in reply Helmut Kohl agreed on the political union alongside EMU. The Dublin Summit asked foreign ministers to prepare proposals regarding co-operation in political matters among Members States for the Dublin Summit in June 1990, and these were to constitute the basis of a second Inter-governmental Conference.[101]

The second summit in Dublin on 25–26 June 1990 decided to convene two Inter-governmental Conferences on 14 December 1990: one on EMU and the other on political union. The two IGCs were intended to be parallel, with ratification of both instruments taking place within the same time frame. In the course of negotiations two approaches emerged: one favoured a 'Three Pillars' structure, the so-called Temple, consisting of a main agreement based on the EC Treaty and two separate arrangements outside the main framework covering judicial co-operation and a common foreign and security policy (CFSP). The second proposal was more ambitious and suggested the 'tree' model, a single 'trunk' having several branches and treating integration in all three areas as a common foundation (the tree), with special arrangements in particular fields (the branches). The second proposal was strongly federalist and as such judged too controversial by the foreign ministers to be submitted for consideration at Maastricht. The deliberations of the Inter-governmental Conference were based on the first proposal with modifications introduced by a second Netherlands proposal presented on 8 November 1989, which provided for unanimous voting within CFSP while submitting its implementation to qualified majority

---

[98] British Prime Minister Margaret Thatcher strongly opposed reunification of Germany and tried to convince President Mitterrand that indeed, within the EC, Germany's hegemony would assert itself and that France and the UK should act together like in the past to prevent, or at least slow, the process of reunification. Mitterrand agreed with her but considered that the reunification was inevitable, and instead of preventing it that is was better to strengthen the EC through further political integration. (Thatcher wanted to widen the EC to include central European countries and thus counterbalance the excessive influence of reunited Germany.): M Thatcher, *The Downing Street Years*, New York: Harper Collins, 1993, pp688–726.

[99] EC Bull Suppl 1/90, p6.

[100] United Germany with its 77 million people, that is 25 per cent of the entire population of the Community would account for 27 per cent of its GDP.

[101] R Corbett, '*The Intergovernmental Conference on Political Union*' (1992) 30 Journal of Common Market Studies 274.

vote. The Inter-governmental Conferences began on 15 December 1990. The Maastricht Summit held on 9 and 10 December 1991 approved the text of the TEU. The final version was signed on 7 February 1992 at Maastricht. It was agreed that the process of ratification should be completed at the end of 1992, and its entry into force was to coincide with the completion of a single market. In practice, the process of ratification was fraught with difficulties, it became even more troublesome than the ratification of the SEA.[102]

Ratification of the TEU

The first impediment to the ratification of the TEU was its rejection by the Danish Parliament. It failed to obtain the required five-sixths majority in the Danish Folketing on 13 May 1992. As a result, the Danish government had to organise a national referendum on 2 June 1992. By the small margin of 46,000 votes the people of Denmark rejected the TEU. The negative referendum plunged the Community in a state of uncertainty. The UK decided to delay ratification until settlement of the Danish problem. The European Summit of 26 and 27 June 1992 declared that it would observe the timetable for the ratification of the TEU notwithstanding the Danish 'No'. However, its entry into force on 1 January 1993 was, at this stage, unrealistic.

The reasons for the Danish rejection were analysed and presented in the memorandum 'Denmark in Europe'[103] prepared by the Danish government. The Danish objections were numerous, ranging from the lack of openness and transparency in Community decision-making, the extension of the EU competences in common defence policy and co-operation in justice and home affairs, EU citizenship and the third stage of EMU, to the rejection of the TEU's federalist approach which was perceived as undermining the national independence and sovereignty of Denmark. As a result, the government of Denmark requested 'special arrangements' in order to accommodate its people and ensure acceptance of the TEU in a second referendum on 18 May 1993. Under the Presidency of the UK the European Summit held in Edinburgh on 11 and 12 December 1992 examined the Danish memorandum. Its deliberations are contained in the Part B of the Edinburgh Conclusions on 'Denmark and the Treaty on European Union'.[104] Before examining the 'concessions' made for Denmark it is necessary to stress that the text of the TEU itself was not amended by the Edinburgh Summit in order to accommodate the Danes. The text submitted to the Danish people for the second referendum was identical to that already rejected on 2 June 1992. The Edinburgh Summit explained, clarified and interpreted those TEU provisions considered unacceptable by the Danish electorate. The Danish 'opt-outs' concerned:

1. Citizenship of the European Union. Denmark in its unilateral declaration in Annex III states that citizenship of the EU does not mean that a national of another Member State is entitled to obtain Danish citizenship, nor may he claim any rights, privileges, etc, which derive from Danish citizenship. This point has been clarified by the Declaration on Nationality of a Member State annexed to the Treaty on European Union. The

---

[102] See F Laursen and S Vanhoonacker (eds), *The Ratification of the Maastricht Treaty: Issues, Debates and Future Implications*, Dordrecht/Boston/London: M Nijhoff Publishers, 1994.
[103] *Europe*, 5 November 1992.
[104] OJ C348 31.12.92 p1.

combined effect of the Declaration and art 8(1) EC, as amended by the TEU, confirmed the Danish understanding of the concept of citizenship of the EU, that the question of nationality is within the exclusive prerogatives of a Member State and any dispute in this area is decided by reference to the national law of the Member State concerned. As a result, Denmark is bound by arts 8–8e EC but clarification was necessary in order to reassure the Danish electorate that the question of nationality remains within the exclusive realm of Danish law.

2. Participation in the third stage of EMU. In this respect, the 12th Protocol annexed to the TEU does permit a Member State not to participate in the third stage of EMU. The Edinburgh Summit confirmed, or activated, the option that already existed under this protocol and, taking into account the Danish notification concerning its non-participation in the third stage of EMU, granted an exemption in this respect. However, the exemption neither applies to the second stage of EMU nor to Danish participation in the European Monetary System.

3. Participation in common foreign and security policy which might involve a common defence policy. Denmark objected to compulsory membership of the Western European Union. This question will be examined elsewhere in the book (see Chapter 3), but it seems that art J4(4) TEU, which states that 'the policy of the Union ... shall not prejudice the specific character of the security and defence policy of certain Member States', in conjunction with the 13th Declaration on Western European Union annexed to the TEU which invites Members States of the EU but not of the WEU to become observers or to join this organisation 'if they so wish', is far from imposing a legal obligation to accede to the WEU. The Edinburgh Summit clarified the matter by stating that nothing in the TEU committed Denmark to the WEU.

4. The application of more favourable national provisions in the fields of social policy, protection of consumers, environment and the distribution of income. The Declaration of the European Council regarding these matters states that the TEU does not prevent any Member State from maintaining or introducing more stringent protection measures in these areas provided that are in conformity with the EC Treaty. Many provisions of the EC Treaty – arts 118a(3), 129a(3) and 130t – together with art 2(5) of the Agreement on Social Policy between the Member States of the European Community, expressly permit stricter national policies in these areas. Finally, the Declaration specifies that the distribution of income and maintenance or improvement of social welfare benefits remains within the competence of Member States, and that nothing in the TEU prevents them from pursuing national policies in this respect.

In the second referendum held on 18 May 1993 56.8 per cent of the Danes voted in favour of the TEU.[105]

It is submitted that the Danish opposition to the TEU was more based on an insufficient understanding of the TEU by the Danish electorate rather than its actual content.

---

[105] D Howarth, 'The Compromise on Denmark and the Treaty on European Union: a Legal and Practical Analysis', 31 CMLR 765–805.

An interesting legal question arises in relation to the Edinburgh Summit. Annex 1[106] to Part B of the Conclusions contains a 'Decision of the Heads of State or Government, meeting within the European Council, concerning problems raised by Denmark on the Treaty on European Union'. The decision is divided into five sections: sections A–D refer to the 'derogations' from the TEU granted to Denmark, and section E contains final provisions. The decision provides that Denmark may at any time inform the other Member States that it will set aside all or part of the decision. It also specifies that it will enter into force at the same time as the TEU. The interesting point is that the decision is the first legally binding decision of the Heads of State or Government meeting within the European Council. Therefore, it is not a decision of the European Council but a decision of the Heads of State or Government of the Member States adopted within the framework of the European Council and as such it is really an international agreement concluded among them. The practical and legal implications are interesting: first it confirms that the Head of States or Government have their own agenda in European integration; second, that they feel competent to provide 'legal interpretations' of the TEU; and, third, this approach deepens the problem of democratic accountability as it deprives national parliaments of their say in important matters and thus their 'constitutional law [is] completely glossed over by the governing elite'.[107] It also undermines the role of the ECJ since any dispute in relation to the Danish decision is, as an international agreement, within the jurisdiction of the International Court of Justice at the Hague not the ECJ. Finally, it destroys the unitary character of the EU by creating a 'Europe à la carte' (Europe of 'bits and pieces').

The negative Danish referendum had implications in other Member States. The following day François Mitterrand announced a referendum in France, although he initially had no intention of submitting the TEU to a popular vote. Indeed, the Constitutional Council (le Conseil Constitutionnel), seised by the President of the French Republic, ruled that the ratification of the TEU necessitated the revision of the French Constitution[108] which was carried out according to the 'Congres' procedure without involving a referendum. The constitutional law of 25 June 1992 enacted the necessary amendments to the French Constitution and so permitted the parliament to apply the usual procedure in order to ratify the TEU. However, Mitterrand took the gamble and decided to organise a referendum. The French vote reflected more the unpopularity of the government than the genuine position of the French people on the TEU. The vote was close, with a 30 per cent abstention, 51 per cent voted in favour.

---

[106] Only Annex 1 of Part B of the Conclusions is published (OJ C348 31.12.92 p1). Part B is devoted to the 'Denmark question'. It comprises three annexes: Annex 1 concerns the 'Decision of the Heads of State or Government, meeting within the European Council, concerning certain problems raised by Denmark on the Treaty on European Union'; Annex 2 contains two Declarations of the European Council, one on social policy, consumer protection, the environment and the distribution of income, and the other on defence; Annex 3 consists of two unilateral declarations of Denmark, the first on the citizenship of the EU, the second on co-operation in the fields of justice and home affairs. Both declarations are attached to the Danish Act of ratification of the TEU and are addressed to all Member States which have to take cognisance of their existence.

[107] D Curtin and R van Ooik, 'Denmark and the Edinburgh Summit: Maastricht without Tears', in *Legal Issues of the Maastricht Treaty*, D O'Keefe, and P M Twomey (eds), London: Wiley Chancery Law, 1994, p365. On this subject see pp353–358.

[108] Decision 92–308 DC of 9 April 1992.

In Ireland, the outcome of the referendum was an overwhelming 'Yes' vote – 69 per cent – although once again the issue of abortion emerged to complicate the referendum campaign. The referendum allowed the Irish parliament to amend the constitution and the TEU was adopted by the parliament with large majority.

In Germany, the ratification was challenged before its Constitutional Court.[109] In its decision of 12 October 1993, the Court dismissed the constitutional complaints against the ratification of the TEU and held that Germany's participation in the EU and the subsequent transfer of powers that it involved could be reconciled with constitutional standards of democratic participation.[110]

In the UK, despite major concessions obtained during the negotiations, such as the rejection of the social dimension of the TEU resulting in a special Protocol on Social Policy annexed to the Treaty and the right to opt-out of the third stage of EMU, the process of ratification was slowed down by growing opposition within the governing Conservative Party. Eventually, the European Communities (Amendment) Bill 1993 was passed by a large majority in the House of Commons (292 votes to 112). However, final ratification was delayed by a judicial review of its terms in *R* v *Secretary of State for Foreign and Commonwealth Affairs, ex parte Rees-Mogg*.[111]

The TEU was ratified by the UK and all Member States on 7 February 1992. TEU Titles II, III, IV and its Protocols by s1(1)(a) European Communities (Amendment) Act 1993 were deemed to be treaties under ss1(2) and 2(1)(b) European Communities Act 1972 and thus had legal effect in the UK. By s1(2) European Communities (Amendment) Act 1993 the TEU was approved for the purposes of s6(c) European Parliamentary Elections Act 1978, which provided that no further increase in the European Parliament's powers could be ratified by the UK unless by Act of Parliament. Mr Rees-Mogg by judicial review sought a declaration that the UK could not ratify the TEU contending:

1. As the TEU Protocol on Social Policy extended the European Parliament's powers the government were in breach of s6 European Parliamentary Elections Act 1978 as by para 3 of the Protocol it formed part of the EC Treaty not the TEU. Thus any approval in s1 European Communities (Amendment) Act 1993 did not cover this Protocol.
2. By ratification the government altered the content of Community law under the EC Treaty without an Act of Parliament, since by virtue of s2(1) European Communities Act 1972 the EC Treaty was deemed to be given legal effect in the UK. Thus statutory approval was required under s6 European Parliamentary Elections Act 1978.
3. TEU Title V establishes a common foreign and security policy which is a transfer of the royal prerogative to Community institutions without statutory authority.

The Court held:

1. Ratification of the Protocol on Social Policy would not increase the powers of the European Parliament since protocols were ancillary to the TEU. Ratification of the TEU automatically ratified the protocols. The TEU referred to in s1(2) European

---

[109] M Herdegen, 'Maastricht and the German Constitutional Court: Constitutional Restraints for an "Ever Closer Union"' (1994) 31 CMLR 235–249.

[110] *Bundesverfassungsgericht*, Judgment of 12 October 1993, 2BvR and 2BvR 2159/92.

[111] [1994] 1 All ER 457 (QBD).

Communities (Amendment) Act 1993 meant the whole Treaty, including protocols, since the purpose of that section was to ensure that the TEU could be ratified without any breach of s6 European Parliamentary Elections Act 1978.

2. The government were not altering domestic law under the EC Treaty without statutory approval contrary to s6 European Parliamentary Elections Act 1978, since if Parliament had wished to fetter the Crown's treaty-making power it would have done so expressly. There were insufficient grounds to find that it had been fettered even by implication. Further, the Protocol would not alter domestic law since it was not a treaty for purposes of s2(1) European Communities Act 1972 as it was specifically excluded by s1(1) of that Act. The Protocol did not become one of the treaties covered merely by being annexed to the EC Treaty.

3. Title V was an exercise, not of abandonment or transfer, of the Crown's prerogative powers in relation to foreign affairs.

4. Application failed.

The TEU was ratified in the UK on 2 August 1993.

In Portugal and Spain, the ratification of the TEU necessitated amendments to their constitutions which went smoothly.

Finally in Belgium, Greece, Italy, Luxembourg and The Netherlands the TEU was ratified according to their parliamentary procedures. The parliamentary majorities in favour of the TEU were overwhelming.

3 The Treaty on European Union and Beyond

3.1   Pillar 1: the European Community

3.2   Pillar 2: Common Foreign and Security Policy

3.3   Pillar 3: Co-operation in Justice and Home Affairs

3.4   Draft Treaty of Amsterdam

The Treaty on European Union (TEU) was signed on 7 February 1992 and entered into force on 1 November 1993, almost a year later than stated in art R(2) TEU. Indeed, in its ratification the Member States experienced great difficulties; for some the TEU was not ambitious enough, others resisted its federalist approach as being contrary to their national interests.

This chapter will examine the main features of the Treaty on European Union, in itself no easy task. As McAllister said:

'Maastricht is like Janus. It faces both ways: towards inter-governmentalism, and towards some kind of "federal vocation". It is as ambiguous as the oracle of Delphi; as the Community itself. It reflects the extent to which the States are, and are not, able to agree.'[1]

The Treaty itself is a lengthy document – consisting of seven Titles, 17 legally binding Protocols and 33 Declarations which have only an interpretive function – and is considered badly drafted. *The Economist* reported, half jokingly, that the negative referendum in Denmark, and a very narrow majority vote in a French referendum, regarding the ratification of the TEU could be explained by the fact that these governments gave their people the original version to read, as opposed to Ireland, where the Irish government published a booklet summarising the Maastricht Treaty in plain language and consequently won a two-thirds vote in favour.[2] The only justification for producing such a confusing legal document is that the TEU is a transitory treaty. It establishes a procedure for its own revision.[3] It provided that an inter-governmental conference (IGC) should be convened in 1996 to make necessary modifications to the TEU. The IGC opened in Turin on 29 March 1996 and its work culminated in the Draft Treaty adopted by the Amsterdam Summit of 17–19 June 1997.[4]

The TEU is based on the so-called 'Temple' structure which consists of three pillars, each representing different competences of the European Union. Pillar 1 embraces all existing

---

[1] R McAlister, *From EC to EU, an Historical and Political Survey*, London: Routledge, 1997, p225.

[2] Quoted by P Demaret, 'The Treaty Framework', in *Legal Issues of the Maastricht Treaty*, D O'Keeffe and P M Twomey (eds), London: Wiley Chancery Law, 1994, p3.

[3] Article N TEU.

[4] The pluses and minuses of the Draft Treaty of Amsterdam are examined at the end of this Chapter.

policies under the previous Treaties and introduces fundamental amendments to the Communities (Title II – EC, Title III – ECSC, Title IV – Euratom), Pillar 2 concerns inter-governmental co-operation on a common foreign and security policy (Title V), and Pillar 3 covers inter-governmental co-operation in the fields of justice and home affairs (Title VI). The roof of the Temple consists of Common Provisions which lay down the objectives of the TEU (Title I). The Temple is based (its 'plinth') on the Final Provisions (Title VII). The three Pillars are linked by the Council of the European Union, a decision-making body common to all Pillars, and to some extent by the Commission, although it has no implementing powers regarding Pillars 2 and 3 but is associated with the work of the Council in these areas. Since these two Pillars are based on inter-governmentalism, they create obligations only amongst the Member States and as such are not incorporated into UK law and therefore cannot be enforced in British courts. The EU is like a ghost, its spirit is omnipresent but it has no material existence. The EU has neither legal personality, nor its own institutions, nor its own budget. It acts through the Communities in regard to the Pillar 1 and Member States in the areas within the scope of the Pillars 2 and 3.

The objectives of the EU are set out in the common provisions and the preamble to the TEU. The main goal of the EU is to 'establish the foundations of an ever closer union among the people of Europe'. To attain this objective, concrete actions of the EU consist of:

1. the promotion of balanced and sustainable economic progress through the establishment of an area without internal frontiers, the reinforcement of internal cohesion, the establishment of a single currency within the framework of economic and monetary union;
2. the promotion of an international identity for the EU through implementation of a common foreign and security policy (CFSP) which might lead to a common defence policy;
3. the establishment of citizenship of the EU;
4. the development of closer co-operation in the fields of justice and home affairs (JHA);
5. the improvement in the effectiveness of the EU institutions mostly by extending the legislative powers of the EP;
6. the extension of EU competences to new policies while reinforcing the existing ones;
7. the reaffirmation of its commitment to the protection of human rights;
8. the introduction of the principle of subsidiarity; and
9. the introduction of the concept of variable geometry which permits differential integration, that is, while all Member States pursue common activities, in certain projects only some of them will participate. The best examples are provided by the economic and monetary union, the Schengen Agreements, and some aspects of CFSP and JHA.[5]

---

[5] For excellent studies see J A Usher, 'Variable Geometry or Concentric Circles: Patterns for the European Union' (1997) 46 ICLQ 243.

3.1 Pillar 1: the European Community

The European Economic Community, as the most important of the three Communities, has been renamed. The TEU substitutes the term 'European Community' for 'European Economic Community' in order to underline the fundamental changes in its objectives as it now deals with more than just economic issues. The most important changes introduced at Maastricht to the EC Treaty are:

1. recognition of the principle of subsidiarity which operates to restrict the Community's involvement in national matters;
2. establishment of European citizenship which creates new rights for the nationals of the Member States;
3. redefinition of the objectives of the Community in areas such as health, education, training, industrial policy, telecommunication and energy networks, research and development, consumer protection, trans-European networks, and culture;
4. extension of EC competences in environmental protection and development aid for poor countries;
5. deepening the Commission's accountability to the European Parliament while extending EP participation in decision-making procedures;
6. establishment of the European Economic and Monetary Union depending on the extent to which Member States' economies converge in terms of inflation, interest rates and other criteria laid down in the EC Treaty; and
7. extension of the ECJ powers in relation to Member States who refuse to comply with its judgments.

Each amendment to the EC Treaty is worth a separate examination.

Principle of subsidiarity

The principle of subsidiarity has not been invented by the TEU. It has a long history, it derives from the Catholic doctrine of Thomas Aquinas and has been mainly used by the Church – by Pope Pius XI in his Encyclical letter *Quadragesimo Anno* (1931) and later by Pope John XXII in his *Pacem in Terris* (1963) – to enhance the role of an individual in society in the context of a corporate State (especially a Communist State). According to Pius XI:

> 'It is an injustice, a grave evil and disturbance of right order for a larger and higher association to arrogate to itself functions which can be performed efficiently by smaller and lower societies'.[6]

In the context of social organisation the principle of subsidiarity means that decisions affecting individuals should always be taken at the lowest practical level, as closely as possible to the individuals concerned, and that their initiatives should not be impeded by any authorities in those areas where individuals are the most competent to decide for themselves.

---

[6] Cited by J Steiner, 'Subsidiarity under the Maastricht Treaty', in *Legal Issues of the Treaty of Maastricht*, supra note 2, p50.

The principal of subsidiarity has its constitutional and political dimension in federations. It allocates powers between federal and state authorities in order to strike a balance between the needs of the federation and the protection of interests of members of the State, and thus decides which function should be performed at the federal level, which should be shared by federal and state levels, and which are within exclusive competence of the latter.

The principle of subsidiarity is entrenched in the German Constitution; some authors consider that it was the German model of subsidiarity which was adopted by the EU.[7] In the context of the German federation, subsidiarity sets up a presumption in favour of the lower authorities (Länder) in decision-making procedures.[8] The allocation of power is clearly regulated by the German Constitution, that is, art 73GG enumerates exclusive competences of federal authorities such as foreign policy, citizenship, customs matters, etc, while art 74GG provides a list of 27 areas of concurrent power in which federal and Länder authorities share competencies. However, once federal authorities legislate in a specific area of shared competences, they 'occupy the field' and thus the Länder is prevented from making any further regulations and its existing rules in this area are inoperative. The transfer of powers from a lower political unit to the centre is effected only if the former cannot discharge certain powers adequately and effectively, otherwise central authorities cannot interfere. The main function of subsidiarity under the German Constitution is to give adequate weight to the interests of Länder. It also protects individuals' freedom, which in the context of the German experience under the Nazi regime constitutes an additional safeguard in that decisions are taken as close as possible to the individuals concerned.

Subsidiarity under the Treaty of Maastricht

The allocation of power between the Community and the Member States is one of the most controversial aspects of European integration. If the distinction between confederation and a federation is based on the degree of sovereignty that the participating units enjoy then the EU is neither a federation nor a confederation. It is true that the EC operates in many areas as a federation but it has institutions which are typical of a confederation. It is submitted that the EU is a *sui generis* organisation. For that reason, the principle of subsidiarity can play many roles in the context of European integration. In order to determine its precise meaning and the functions that it is supposed to fulfil, it is necessary to examine the provisions of the TEU which make reference to subsidiarity.

The principle of subsidiarity, although in a state of gestation, was mentioned in art 5 ECSC. Also, it was implicit in art 235 EC concerning the extension of competences of the Community. The Single European Act introduced it explicitly in relation to the protection of environment – art 130r(4) EEC states that the Community shall intervene in environmental matters '... to the extent to which the objectives referred to in paragraph 1 cannot be attained better ... at the level of the individual Member States'.

In the Treaty of Maastricht the principle of subsidiarity in first mentioned in its preamble and in arts A and B. Article A TEU states that decisions should be taken as closely

---

[7] Scharpf, 'The Joint-decision Trap: Lessons from German Federalism and European Integration' (1988) 66 Public Administration 239–278.
[8] Article 30GG (German Constitution).

as possible to the citizen of the EU. This is solely a political statement, as under art L TEU the ECJ has no jurisdiction in matters outside Pillar 1, arts L to S and art K3(2)(c). As a result, the Preamble and art A have no legal effect. Article B plays a similar function, and states that the objectives of the EU should be achieved in conformity with the principle of subsidiarity as defined in art 3b EC.

Article 3b applies to the EC Treaty only, is very complex and defines three legal concepts: the concept of conferred powers ('The Community shall act within the limits of the powers conferred upon it by this Treaty and of objectives assigned to it therein'); the principle of proportionality ('Any action by the Community shall not go beyond what is necessary to achieve the objectives by the Community'); and the principle of subsidiarity. Subsidiarity is defined in the following terms

> 'In areas which do not fall within its exclusive competence, the Community shall take action, in accordance with the principle of subsidiarity, only if and in so far as the objectives of the proposed action cannot be sufficiently achieved by the Member States and can therefore, by reason of the scale or effects of the proposed action, be better achieved by the Community.'

Subsidiarity and the allocation of competences between the Community and the Member States

Unlike the German Constitution, the allocation of power between the Community and the Member States is neither clearly regulated nor is there any mechanism for the allocation of competences within the Community. For that reason, the Commission decided that it has the responsibility to determine which competences are exclusive to the Community and which can be shared between the Community and the Member States.[9] According to the Commission the Community has exclusive powers in all essential areas covered by the original EC Treaty.[10] This is seen as being extended to new policy areas established under the SEA and TEU. As a result, the exclusive competences of the EC cover 'at least, those aspects of health, safety environmental and consumer protection policies which are connected with the internal market'.[11]

Indeed, the exclusive competence of the Community in these areas is a logical consequence of the theory of 'occupied fields', also known as the concept of pre-emption. It means that once the Community has legislated in a particular area, the field is occupied and a Member State is precluded from introducing any legislation. The rule has no exception. As a result, a Member State cannot justify its action even though it may improve the existing EC measure. The most spectacular example of this was provided in Case 60/86 *Commission v United Kingdom*.[12] In this case Directive 76/756/EEC, which harmonised technical requirements regarding motor vehicles, did not mention the 'dim dip' devices which were, for safety reasons, considered as necessary in all motor vehicles sold on the territory of the UK. The ECJ decided that the directive provided an exhaustive list of devices and the reason

---

[9] EC Bull 10–1992, p1.16.
[10] Such as removal of obstacles to the free movements of goods, persons, services and capital, the Common Commercial Policy, competition policy, the CAP, the conservation of fishery resources and the common organisation of the fishery markets, the Common Transport Policy.
[11] A G Toth, 'A Legal Analysis of Subsidiarity', in *Legal Issues of the Maastricht Treaty*, supra note 2, p41.
[12] [1988] ECR 3921.

UK. The ECJ decided that the directive provided an exhaustive list of devices and the reason for the UK regulation was irrelevant.

The delegation of certain powers by Member States to EC institutions under the provisions of the EC Treaty ensures that in order to attain the Treaty's objectives action is taken at Community level. It results in the creation of uniform rules throughout the Community. By the transfer of powers to the institutions the Member States have surrendered their power to act unilaterally in these areas. Consequently, action taken by the Community in a particular field is fully justified. The concept of pre-emption is easy to grasp but its actual application is more complex because in many instances it is difficult to determine to what extent the action of the Community pre-empts national competences (provided the Member States are allowed to share competences in that area).[13] Indeed, if the matter is within the exclusive competences of the Community, Member States have no concurrent power, even though the Community has failed to exercise its competences.[14]

The exclusive competence of the Community in the areas in which it has taken action can be explained without reference to the concept of pre-emption. The principle of supremacy of EC law over national law provides sufficient justification for precluding any unilateral legislation by a Member State in an area already regulated by the Community. The principle provides that any national legislation in conflict with EC law must be set aside.

However, the exclusive competence of the Community by pre-emption should be distinguished from that which has been inferred from the EC Treaty by the ECJ. So far, there are only two areas in which the exclusive competence of the Community has been firmly established by the ECJ. In its Opinion 1/75 (OECD/Local Cost Standard),[15] as confirmed later in Case 41/76 *Donckerwolcke*,[16] and more recently in the Court Opinion 1/94 on Various Agreements Relating to the Establishment of the World Trade Organisation,[17] it was held that the common commercial policy is within the exclusive competence of the Community. The second area of exclusive competence of the Community is conservation of the biological resources of the sea.[18]

Implementation of the principle of subsidiarity

The Edinburgh Summit in December 1992 examined the reports of the Commission and the Council on the procedural and practical steps needed to implement subsidiarity, which were prepared at the request of the Lisbon Summit of June 1992.[19] The Edinburgh Summit also took into considerations a draft Inter-Institutional Agreement on the application of art 3b EC presented by the European Parliament[20] and a report from the President of the

---

[13] For details see S Weatherill, 'Beyond Pre-emption? Shared Competence and Constitutional Change in the European Community', in *Legal Issues of the Maastricht Treaty*, supra note 2, pp13–33.

[14] Case 804/79 *Commission* v *UK* [1981] ECR 1045 concerning the adoption by the UK of conservation measures, albeit the Community has exclusive competences under the Common Fisheries Policy; see Chapter 4, section 4.1.

[15] [1975] ECR 1355.

[16] [1976] ECR 1921.

[17] [1994] ECR I–5267; also in Case C–83/94 *Criminal Proceedings against Peter Leifer and Others* [1995] ECR I–3231.

[18] Case 804/79 *Commission* v *UK* [1979] ECR 2923.

[19] EC Bull 6–1992, p8.

[20] EC Bull 12–1992, p9.

Commission regarding the Commission's review of existing and proposed legislation in the light of the principle of subsidiarity,[21] and established guidelines regarding practical and procedural implications deriving from the principle of subsidiarity for EC institutions. The guidelines which were later completed by the 1993 Inter-Institutional Agreement on Procedures for Implementing the Principle of Subsidiarity[22] created certain obligations for the EC institutions.

The European Commission. The Commission has to submit an annual report to the European Council and the European Parliament on the application of art 3b EC. Since the Edinburgh Summit the Commission has submitted three annual reports on the application of the principle of subsidiarity. The first two reports – to the Brussels Summit in December 1993 and to the Essen Summit in December 1994 – both contained concrete proposals regarding withdrawal, revision and modification of a number of Community legislative measures in the light of the principle of subsidiarity. In its last report 'Mieux Légiférer' (Better legislation), submitted to the Madrid Summit in December 1995, the Commission confirmed the reduction of proposed legislative measures for 1996 – only 19 proposals, as compared to 61 in 1990.[23]

The Commission emphasised that the application of the principle of subsidiarity to new legislative measures requires:

1. generalisation of wide consultation before the Commission puts forward a proposal for a legislative measure;
2. in secondary legislation, the Commission has to give preference to directives rather than regulations and, especially, framework directives should prevail over detailed directives as they allow Member States to select the most appropriate methods of implementing EC law. Similarly, non-binding measures – such as recommendations, opinions and non-compulsory codes of conduct – should be used when appropriate, rather than binding measures. This approach was applied by the Commission prior to the TEU in the framework for the completion of a single market. Co-operation between Member States should be encouraged and thus the Commission is required to support, complete or supervise such joint action;
3. voluntary withdrawal by the Commission of 60 proposals, such as those concerning directives (the packaging of foodstuffs, allocation of radio frequencies) and harmonisation measures in such matters as vehicle number plates, the regulation of gambling, structure and equipment for fun-fairs and theme parks, etc;[24]
4. the Commission has to take the principle of subsidiarity into account in proposing any new legislation. In its preamble it has to justify a Community action in the light of subsidiarity which becomes part of the measure's legal basis. As a result it is the function of the Commission to show that it is more appropriate to act at the Community level.

---

[21] Ibid, p16.
[22] EC Bull 10–93, point 2.2.2.
[23] EC Bull 11–95, point 1.9.2.
[24] Overall Approach to the Application by the Council of the Subsidiarity Principle and art 3B of the Treaty on European Union, Conclusions of the European Council, Edinburgh, December 1992, Annex 2 to Part A.

This is very important as it regulates the burden of proof and sets the direction for future developments of the Community.

In relation to the existing legislative acts, the Commission underlined that they are currently subject to consolidation and codification. Furthermore, they are revised in the light of the principle of subsidiarity in such areas as technical standards, mutual recognition of qualifications, animal welfare, etc. In competition policy, the Commission decided that national authorities, and especially national courts, should play a more important role in the application of arts 85 and 86 EC.[25]

The Council of the European Union The Council must examine each proposal submitted by the Commission, as well as its own amendments to such proposals, in the light of subsidiarity. However, the Council must not dissociate from its deliberations on the merits the application of the principle of subsidiarity. Both aspects must be examined at the same time.

The European Parliament The application of subsidiarity implies the co-operation of the EP, especially since the EP has important legislative competences in many areas under the co-operation procedure (art 189b EC) and the new co-decision procedure (art 189c EC). The Inter-Institutional Agreement on Procedures for Implementing the Principle of Subsidiarity provides that the EP must take into account the principle of subsidiarity and justify any amendment which substantially changes a proposal submitted by the Commission in the light of art 3b EC.

The European Court of Justice The principle of subsidiarity is not only a socio-political concept but also a fundamental principle of EC law. No special procedure has been established to bring an issue of subsidiarity before the ECJ, although this solution was supported by the EP.[26] As a result, the principle of subsidiarity can arise in two types of action: against EC institutions or under art 177 EC. As to judicial review of acts of EC institutions (art 173), the applicant can challenge the act itself by claiming that it was adopted in violation of the requirements laid down in art 3b EC. Article 177 enables national courts and tribunals to refer questions of Community law that require to be decided in a case pending before them to the ECJ for a preliminary ruling. For the first time[27] the issue of subsidiarity arose in Case C–84/94 *United Kingdom* v *Council (Re Working Time Directive)*.[28]

Here, the UK brought an action for annulment of Council Directive 93/104 concerning certain aspects of the organisation of working time or in alternative of its art 4, the first and second sentences of art 5, art 6(2) and art 7. The UK challenged the legal base of the Directive. The UK argued that the Directive should have been adopted under art 100 EC or

---

[25] Notice on co-operation between national courts and the Commission in applying arts 85 and 86 EC Treaty (OJ C39 13.2.95 p6).

[26] A G Toth, 'Is Subsidiarity Justiciable?' (1994) 19 ELR 268 especially 273.

[27] The CFI was in two cases seised with the question of subsidiarity but left them unanswered: Case T–5/93 *Tremblay* [1995] ECR II–185; Case T–29/92 *SPO* [1995] ECR II–289.

[28] [1996] ECR I–5758.

art 235 EC which require unanimity within the Council instead of art 118a(2) which imposes only qualified majority voting within the Council. Second, the UK claimed that the Directive was in breach of the principles of proportionality and subsidiarity since the Council failed to demonstrate that the objective of the Directive could better be achieved at Community level than at national level. Finally, the UK claimed that the Council had infringed essential procedural requirements by not providing sufficient reasons for the adoption of Directive 93/104 in the preamble.

The ECJ held that art 118a(1) was an appropriate legal base for the Directive since it refers to 'working environment' and 'health and safety' which should be interpreted broadly for two reasons. First, the words 'especially in the working environment' favour a broad interpretation of the Council powers under art 118a and, second, it is supported by the constitution of the World Health Organisation which describes health as a state of complete physical, mental and social well-being and not the absence of illness or infirmity. This definition is recognised by all Member States as they are Members of WHO. Thus, the organisation of working hours must be included in the meaning of 'working environment' since it is capable of affecting the health and safety of a particular worker. Only the second sentence of art 5 of the Directive was annulled. It referred to Sunday as a weekly rest period. The ECJ held that in the context of the diversity of cultural, ethnic and religious factors in Member States it should be left to each Member State to decide which day of the week is the most appropriate for a weekly rest day.

The question of subsidiarity and proportionality is the most interesting part of the judgment. The ECJ confirmed that the principle of subsidiarity can be relied upon by the applicant, although in this case it was invoked to support the main claim and not as an autonomous ground for annulment. Thus, all disputes as to whether subsidiarity as such can be invoked before the ECJ seemed settled. The ECJ made a clear distinction between the principle of proportionality and the principle of subsidiarity. It held that the argument of the UK that the Council could not adopt measures as general and mandatory as those forming the subject- matter of the Directive must be examined in the light of the principle of proportionality, while the argument that the objective of the Directive would be better served at Community level than at national level concerned the principle of subsidiarity. Also, Advocate-General Leger emphasised that the principle of subsidiarity answers the question at which level, Community or national, the adoption of a legislative measure is more appropriate, while the principle of proportionality governs the intensity of the Community action. In the other words, the ECJ on the ground of subsidiarity would examine whether a measure adopted by a Member State would achieve the desired Community objective. Under the principle of proportionality the ECJ examines whether less onerous, less restrictive measures adopted by the Community would achieve the aims pursued. In respect of subsidiarity the ECJ demonstrated the necessity of an action at the Community level since the objective of raising the level of health and safety through harmonisation 'presupposes Community-wide action'. As to proportionality, in order to verify whether the measure complies with the principle of proportionality it is necessary to ascertain 'whether the means which it employs are suitable for the purpose of achieving the desired objective and whether they do not go beyond what is necessary to achieve it'. In this respect, the ECJ held that the measures adopted by the Directive were necessary and appropriate as they contributed directly to achieving the objective of raising the health and safety protection of workers and did not exceed what is necessary to achieve such an objective. The third plea of infringement of essential procedural requirements was also dismissed. The ECJ stated that the preamble clearly explained the objectives of the Directive and a specific reference to scientific material justifying its adoption was not necessary.

In this context it is interesting to mention that the Edinburgh Summit in its conclusion declared that art 3b has no direct effect.[29] Also, the Council of the European Union in its answer to a written question asked by Victor Arbeloa regarding the direct effect of art 3b EC emphasised that 'it would appear difficult to attribute to this provision the direct effect that the EC has acknowledged, though a quite specific and constant jurisprudence, in respect of certain other provisions of this Treaty' because on the one hand the application of subsidiarity by the EC institutions calls for an essentially political appraisal, and on the other hand it leaves the institutions a wide margin of discretion.[30] It is submitted that the conclusions of the Edinburgh Summit are irrelevant in that if a question of validity of an act of EC institution arises before a national court, and the latter refers it to the ECJ under art 177, the Court will decide whether the act is valid and therefore the question of direct effect is not pertinent. The drawback of this solution is that individual applicants under arts 3 and 5 EC will have to bring an action before national courts instead of Community courts. It will leave privileged and semi-privileged applicants without remedy. In this respect it seems that the way to alleviate lack of direct effect of art 3b EC in relation to all applicants, whether privileged or not, is to challenge the act in question on two grounds: subsidiarity and proportionality, as the latter is directly effective.

Assessment of the principle of subsidiarity

The concept of subsidiarity is, indeed, an elusive concept. It is submitted that its best definition is the following: 'It is a principle for allocating power upwards as well as downwards, but it incorporates a presumption in favour of allocation downwards in case of doubt'.[31] It is not tantamount to decentralisation and it admits degrees of exercise of powers.

This entails that the decision should always be taken at the lowest practical level thus leaving the Community to concentrate on the essential and vital objectives. The principle of subsidiarity maintains the integrity of the Community while allowing the participation of national authorities in decision-making procedures, provided they can exercise their functions satisfactorily. Subsidiarity maintains the balance of power between the Community and the Members States and, by imposing the burden of proof upon the Community institutions, it affects the allocation of power not only today but, most importantly, in the future. The principle of subsidiarity has been introduced in order to increase efficiency, accountability and transparency in the decision-making procedures of the EC.

However, the practical implications deriving from the principle of subsidiarity will have to be further clarified by ECJ case law, in itself no easy task taking into account its highly

---

[29] Presidency Conclusions, Annex 1 to Part A, under 1(4) fifth indent.
[30] OJ C102 11.4.94 p3.
[31] A CEPR Annual Report, 1993: 'Making Sense of Subsidiarity: How Much Centralisation for Europe' (1993) 4 Monitoring European Integration 4.

political aspects. So far, it has many different interpretations. For Member States hostile to a federal structure of the EU, such as the UK, the principle of subsidiarity constitutes a guarantee of national sovereignty as it precludes the Community from undue interference in their affairs. For the Commission it is a necessary component of a federal State. Jacques Delors has underlined that subsidiarity is the essence of federalism since 'the federal approach is to define clearly who does what'.[32]

Citizenship of the European Union

The concept of European citizenship highlights a new dimension of European integration and especially underlines that the Community has extended its competences beyond economic and social domains.[33] Indeed, it seems unrealistic to build a political union without granting special rights and imposing some obligations upon its citizens. Article B TEU provides that the objective of the Union is to 'strengthen the protection of the rights and interests of the nationals of its Member States through the introduction of a citizenship of the Union'. In order to give substance to these rights, and thus to go beyond a mere declaration, the provisions on citizenship are contained in arts 8–8e EC which form a new Part II of the EC Treaty. Article 8(2) EC states that: 'Citizens of the Union shall enjoy the rights conferred by this Treaty and shall be subject to the duties imposed thereby', albeit no specific duties are mentioned in the Treaty. It seems that apart from an implied civic duty to vote there are no duties imposed on EU citizens.

Union citizenship as it stands now is more a symbol of European identity, as is the European flag adopted in 1986 (the 12 stars will remain no matter how many new States join the EU as they represent as a 'symbol of perfection'), the European anthem adopted in 1972 (the prelude to the 'Ode of Joy' from Beethoven's Ninth Symphony), and European Day (9 May to commemorate the Schuman Declaration). Its main objective is to bring European integration closer to ordinary people rather than to confer important rights and benefits to them. Indeed, citizenship of the Union has three main limitations.

First, it is based on nationality of a Member State. Article 8(1) EC states that: 'Every person holding the nationality of a Member State shall be a citizen of the Union.' In the light of the Declaration on Nationality of a Member State attached to the TEU which provides that:

> '... wherever in the Treaty establishing the European Community reference is made to nationals of the Member State, the question whether an individual possesses the nationality of a Member State shall be settled solely by reference to the national law of the Member State concerned'

and that a Member State may make declarations as to the determination of their nationals, it is clear that nationality is within the exclusive prerogative of a Member State. This was confirmed by the ECJ in Case C–369/90 *Michelletti*[34] where the Court held that the determination of conditions governing the acquisition and loss of nationality were,

---

[32] (1992) Le Figaro 8 June p1.
[33] For the historical background see D O'Keeffe, 'Union Citizenship', supra note 2, pp87–89.
[34] [1992] ECR I–4239.

according to international law, matters which fell within the competence of each Member State, whose decision must be respected by the other Member States. As a result, a Member State has to accept as an EC national anyone who has nationality of another Member State regardless of the conditions of acquisition of that nationality. Furthermore, the EU cannot interfere in nationality laws of the Member States as they are outside the scope of the TEU.

The requirement of nationality of a Member State as a prerequisite of EU citizenship means that nationals of third countries legally residing in a Member State, refugees and stateless persons have not acquired any rights under art 8 EC. In practice about 8–9 million people residing legally in the EU are excluded from benefiting from EU citizenship, although they contribute to prosperity of the EU and in the Member States are treated on equal footing with nationals.

Second, human rights are not part of EU citizenship. In this respect, the Rome Summit of December 1990 decided to dissociate the protection of human rights from the concept of citizenship, despite opposition from the Commission and the European Parliament.[35] The Commission has twice raised the issue of Community accession to the European Convention on Human Rights (ECHR). Its 1979 Memorandum on the Accession of European Communities to the Convention for the Protection of Human Rights and Fundamental Freedoms[36] was left unanswered by the Council until April 1986, when the latter decided to leave it for further consideration. The Commission presented another communication on 19 November 1990.[37] The Council decided three years later to ask the ECJ for an opinion which was given on 28 March 1996.[38] In its opinion the Court held that the Community has no competence to accede to the European Convention on Human Rights.[39] Therefore, this question must be settled by the Member States since only they are entitled to amend the TEU and decide unanimously to accede to ECHR. It is submitted that this is unlikely to happen. At Maastricht, the EC accession to the European Convention on Human Rights was blocked by countries with dualist legal orders: the UK, Ireland and Denmark.

The third limitation concerns the material scope of application of arts 8–8e EC. Only seven rights are enumerated, some of which are of a little practical importance to EC nationals for two reasons: some rights have already been granted to EC nationals residing in another Member State and thus the TEU only confirms the existing situations; and others need to be further developed in order to grant real benefits to EU citizens. The rights confirmed by the TEU are as follows: the right of free movement and residence within the territory of the Member States; the right to vote and stand for municipal elections in the State of residence, under the same conditions as nationals of that State, as well as passive and active voting rights for elections to the European Parliament; the right to diplomatic and consular protection in a third State in which the Member State of the national is not represented; the right of petition to the EP and application to the Ombudsman. These rights

---

[35] Union Citizenship. Contributions by the Commission to the Intergovernmental Conference, EC Bull Suppl 2/91; EP–Bindi Report on Union Citizenship, PE Doc A3–0139/91, 23 May 1991.

[36] EC Bull Suppl 2/79.

[37] Doc SEC(90) 2087.

[38] Opinion 2/94 Accession by the Community to the European Convention for the Protection of Human Rights and Fundamental Freedoms, 28 March 1996, not yet reported.

[39] For detailed analyses, see G Gaja, 'Case Law, Court of Justice, Opinion 2/94' (1996) 33 CMLR 973–989.

may be added to, or strengthened by, the Council and a mechanism for their review is provided in this respect.

Right of free movement and residence within the territory of the Member States

Article 8a(1) EC recognises the right of free movement and provides for freedom of residence within the territory of the Member States. However, it specifies that those rights are conditional upon limitations and conditions laid down in the Treaty and by measures adopted to give them effect. Under art 8a(2) the Council shall adopt measures facilitating the exercise of those rights. Such measures must be proposed by the Commission and require the unanimous vote of the Council and the assent of the European Parliament.

In practice, art 8a(2) is of real importance for EC nationals who are not economically active since the right of free movement and residence of persons economically active has already been recognised under the EC Treaty.[40] Workers, self-employed persons, providers of services and their families, as defined in secondary legislation, are entitled to move freely and to reside in other Member States unless their presence is contrary to the public policy, public security or public health of the host State. Therefore, the right of the economically inactive to move freely and to reside in another Member State is within the ambit of art 8a(2). On 28 June 1990 the Council adopted three directives: Directives 90/364–366 granting the right of free movement to three categories of persons – employees and the self-employed, who have ceased their occupational activity, and the right of residence for students.[41] The important limitation is that these persons must not become a burden on the social security system of the State of residence. As a result they must have health insurance and adequate means of support. Their right expires if they default on any of the conditions of their residence as prescribed by the Directives,[42] or they may be precluded on the grounds of public policy, public security and public health. The definition of family members is more restrictive than that regarding economically active persons. Article 8a was invoked in *R v Home Secretary, ex parte Vitale and Do Amaral*.[43] In this case the applicants, both EC nationals, challenged a deportation order. They had been receiving income support for a number of months and, according to the Department of Employment, were not actively seeking employment. Both applicants disagreed with the Department of Employment and argued that, regardless of the allegations made by the Department, as EU citizens they were allowed to reside in the UK. The Divisional Court rejected their argument and held that neither the right to free movement, nor the right to reside freely, were free-standing or absolute and that taking into account limitations imposed in arts 8a(2) and 8e, art 8a did not provide every citizen of the Union with an open-ended right to reside freely within every Member State.[44]

---

[40] B Wilkinson, 'Towards European Citizenship? Nationality, Discrimination and Free Movement of Workers in the European Union' (1995) 3 European Public Law 417–529. He examines the right of free movement for workers in the light of art 8 EC.

[41] OJ L180 13.7.90 p28.

[42] Article 3 of Directive 90/364 (OJ L180 13.7.90 p26); art 3 of Directive 90/365 (O L180 13.7.90 p28); and art 4 of Directive 90/366 (OJ L180 13.7.90 p30).

[43] (1995) The Times 18 April; [1995] NLJ 5 May.

[44] The ECJ will soon decide under art 177 EC in *R v Secretary of State for the Home Office, ex parte Adams* [1995] All ER (EC) 177 as to the scope of art 8a EC, ibid.

It seems that no further legislation will be adopted under art 8a. Economically active EU citizens are already protected by the EC Treaty and retired persons and students are covered by Directives 90/364–366.

Participation in municipal elections and in elections to the European Parliament

Article 8b covers both active (right to stand as a candidate) and passive (right to vote) rights at municipal elections for a national residing in a Member State of which he is not a national under the same conditions as nationals of that State,[45] and participation in elections to the European Parliament.[46] Both provisions necessitated further implementing measures which have already been adopted by the Council.

Participation in municipal elections Participation in municipal elections for EC nationals residing in a Member State of which they are not nationals is important as it contributes to their integration in the host State. It is also in line with the Council of Europe Convention of 5 February 1992 on the Participation of Foreigners in Public Life at Local Level, provided they fulfil the requirements of residence. The situation in Member States before the TEU was disparate. Some like Ireland, Denmark and The Netherlands granted generous access to all foreign residents to participate in local elections; in the UK, Irish and Commonwealth citizens were given local voting rights; in Spain these rights were based on reciprocity; and in France, Germany and Luxembourg only nationals had electoral rights at the municipal level.

The Council adopted Directive 94/80[47] on 19 December 1994 which confers on citizens of the Union the right to vote and stand as candidates in local elections in their Member State of residence under the same conditions as nationals of that State. The deadline for adoption was also met.[48] The deadline for its implementation expired on 1 January 1996. The Directive allows multiple voting – for example, a French national residing in England and Belgium is entitled to exercise his voting rights in both countries. Furthermore, the Directive gives no definition of residence. It only provides that the owners of holiday homes are not considered as residents in the Member State where their holiday homes are situated, unless they are allowed to participate in municipal elections on the basis of reciprocity.[49] To illustrate reciprocity: an Englishman who owns a holiday home in Spain will be allowed to vote and stand at municipal elections in Spain only if a Spanish national who owns a holiday home in, for example, Southampton has the same rights in England.

Some derogations are permitted in order to accommodate Member States with a very high percentage of resident nationals from other Member States. If more than 20 per cent of foreign residents are nationals of the EU, without being nationals of that State, the exercise of their electoral rights may be subject to the requirement of a certain period of residency in that State. This derogation concerns mostly Luxembourg where 26.3 per cent of the population are foreign residents and 92.7 per cent of them are EC nationals.[50]

---

[45] Article 8b(1).
[46] Article 8b(2).
[47] OJ L368 31.12.94 p38.
[48] Article 8b(1) stated that this measure should be adopted before 31 December 1994.
[49] Article 4(2) of Directive 94/80.
[50] Commission Report on Voting Rights in Local Elections for Community Nationals: EC Bull Suppl 2/86.

The adoption of Directive 94/80 posed three problems. First, in some Member States granting local election rights to EC residents was contrary to their constitution; second, there were difficulties in defining the local government unit; and, third, determining the offices which nationals of other Member States may hold gave rise to controversies.

As to the first problem, at the time of ratification of the TEU the necessary amendments to constitutions of the following Member States were introduced: France,[51] Germany, Spain and Portugal.

The second question was partially solved by Directive 94/80 which in art 2(1) provides a definition of the basic local government unit, and partially by Member States which in the Annex to the Directive listed the administrative entities for which they permit the EU citizens residing in their country to exercise electoral rights. Article 2(1) defines the basic local governmental unit as 'certain bodies elected by direct universal suffrage and ... empowered to administer, at the basic level of political and administrative organisation, certain local affairs on their own responsibility'. However, the reference to national law in determination of those bodies resulted in wide diversity in the levels of government accessible to EC citizens. In the UK, Ireland and Denmark, resident EU nationals are entitled to passive and active voting rights to all levels of government below national government, while in France, Belgium and The Netherlands they are limited to the lowest level.[52] The list of administrative entities provided by the UK encompasses: 'counties in England, counties, county boroughs and communities in Wales, regions and islands in Scotland, districts in England, Scotland and Northern Ireland, London boroughs, parishes in England, the City of London in relation to ward elections for common councilmen'.[53]

Finally, the question of access to certain offices elected by direct universal suffrage, such as the post of mayor or alderman (a member of the local executive), is regulated in art 5(3) of Directive 94/80 which states that 'the office of elected head, deputy or member of the governing college of the executive of a basic local government unit if elected to hold office for the duration of his mandate' may be reserved to nationals of a Member State. This solution is contrary to European integration but in line with arts 48(4) and 55 EC which exclude nationals of Member States resident in another Member State from access to the public service and from activities which involve the exercise of official authority. As a result Directive 94/80 strengthens the limitations already existing under the EC Treaty instead of abolishing any difference in treatment between nationals and non-nationals of the EU. In general Directive 94/80 is very modest. It confers passive and active voting rights in municipal elections which are of little importance in the political life of any Member State. The grant of electoral rights in national parliamentary elections, in direct presidential elections or in referenda would give real meaning to citizenship of the EU.

Participation in elections to the European Parliament Article 8b(2) EC confers on citizens of the EU the right to vote and stand in elections to the European Parliament in their Member State of residence, under the same conditions as nationals of that State. The Council wanted to adopt a measure in this respect before the elections to the EP which were

---

[51] P Oliver, 'The French Constitution and the Treaty of Maastricht' (1994) ICLQ 1.
[52] For details see P Oliver, 'Electoral Rights under Article 8b of the Treaty of Rome' (1996) 33 CMLR 473–498.
[53] Annex to Directive 94/80.

to be held in June 1994. As a result, Directive 93/109[54] was adopted on 6 December 1993 and successfully implemented in all 12 Member States before the elections to the EP.[55] The main feature of Directive 93/109 is its minimal interference in national electoral laws of the Member States.

Diplomatic and consular protection

Article 8c states that an EC national is entitled to the diplomatic and consular protection of any Member State, in the territory of a third country in which the Member State of which he is a national is not represented, under the same conditions as nationals of that State. This is a new right for EC nationals, albeit in international practice, for when a State has no representation in the territory of another State it often conducts diplomatic relations, including protection of its nationals, indirectly with the assistance of other States which have permanent diplomatic offices there. Many countries cannot afford embassies, even in the most strategic places from a point of view of international politics.[56] Also, diplomatic relations between two countries can be suspended or terminated which often requires third countries to act on their behalf.[57] The innovation introduced in art 8c is that now any EC national in a third country where his Member State is not represented may ask for assistance from any Member State, and the latter is obliged to offer him diplomatic and consular protection on the same conditions as to its own nationals. However, it is uncertain whether a Member State can actually endorse a claim on behalf of an EC national, although this is more an academic question than a real problem for an EC national since as an EC national he possesses nationality of one Member State which under international law can act on his behalf.

The scope of art 8c is limited by the procedure provided for further enactment measures in this area. It is based on inter-governmental co-operation. Article 8c states that Member States 'shall establish the necessary rules among themselves and start the international negotiations required to secure this protection' before 31 December 1993. As a result, the extent of diplomatic and consular protection must be viewed in the light of art J6 TEU which requires diplomatic and consular missions of the Member States, and the Commission delegation in third countries, to co-operate by exchanging information and carrying out joint missions in order to uphold the common position and measures adopted by the Council within the framework of the Common Foreign and Security Policy. Co-operation under art J6 contributes to further develop rights granted to EC nationals under art 8c.[58]

In the context of diplomatic protection it is interesting to mention Case T–572/93 *Odigitria*[59] in which the Court of First Instance seems to recognise that the Community has

---

[54] OJ L329 30.12.93 p34.

[55] The deadline for its implementation was very tight, 1 February 1994.

[56] For example, Gambia closed its embassy in Washington in 1985 for financial reasons.

[57] For example, when Fidel Castro came to power, the US cut off all diplomatic relations with Cuba. The Swiss and Czechoslovakian embassies in Havana acted on behalf of the US and Cuban governments for many years.

[58] See Decision 95/553 of the Representatives of the Governments of the Member States meeting within the Council of 19 December 1995 regarding protection for the citizens of the European Union by diplomatic and consular representations (OJ L314 28.12.95 p73).

[59] [1995] ECR II–2025.

a duty to offer diplomatic protection to EC citizens and EC firms. In this case the applicant brought and action under art 215(2) against the Commission for failure to take appropriate measures for the protection of his rights and interests before the authorities of a third State. The application was rejected on the ground that the applicant did not submit the evidence of the failure to act by the Commission. The ECJ rejected the appeal from the decision of the CFI on the basis that the applicant did not submit new elements.[60] Both decisions suggest that the Commission is under obligation to provide diplomatic protection to EC citizens. Unfortunately, the ECJ did not explain whether it rejected the appeal because under art 51 of its Rules of Procedure no new legal arguments were invoked by the applicant, or whether it agreed with the decision of the CFI. It is submitted that the obligation of the Community to provide diplomatic protection to EC citizens is doubtful. First, the one and only provision of the Treaty which refers to the exercise of the diplomatic protection is art 8c. It expressly imposes this duty on Member States and not on the Community. Second, this area is within the competence of the Council and implicitly within the scope of inter-governmental co-operation of the Member States.

Right of petition and applications to the Ombudsman

Article 8d EC states that a citizen of the Union may petition the European Parliament and apply to the Ombudsman according to the procedure provided in art 138d EC. The right to petition the EP already existed under arts 156–158 of the Rules of Procedure of the European Parliament.[61] The innovation is that not only citizens of the EU are entitled to exercise their right of petition but also any natural or legal person residing or having its registered office in a Member State. There are certain limitations under art 138d EC. First, the matter must come within the fields of activity of the Community and excludes from EP supervision matters covered by Pillars 2 and 3, as well as all other issues subject to inter-governmental co-operation; and second, the matter must affect the petitioner directly.[62] In order to ensure the right of petition under the two remaining Treaties, new provisions identical to art 138d were added.[63]

The right to apply to the Ombudsman is now defined in arts 138e EC, 20d ECSC and 107d Euratom. Article 138e EC provides that 'The European Parliament shall appoint an Ombudsman empowered to received complaints'. This article was completed by Council Decision 94/262 of 9 March 1994[64] which laid down the regulations and general conditions governing the performance of the Ombudsman's duties.

The Ombudsman is nominated by the European Parliament after its elections and holds office for the duration of its term and may be reappointed. The procedure for his appointment is provided in art 159 of the Rules of Procedure of the European Parliament. According to art 2(2) of Decision 94/262 the Ombudsman must be a citizen of the EU, chosen from persons whose independence is beyond doubt, and who possesses the

---

[60] Case C–293/95P *Odigitria* [1996] ECR I–6129, *Europe*, January 1997, no 6, comm FL.

[61] In 1977 the EP adopted a resolution demanding that the right of petitions be attributed to EC nationals.

[62] On the subject see E Marias, 'The Right to Petition the European Parliament after Maastricht' (1994) 19 ELR 169–185.

[63] Articles 20c ECSC and 107c Euratom.

[64] OJ L113 4.5.94 p15.

qualification required for appointment to the highest judicial offices in his country, or has experience and recognised competences necessary for exercise of the functions of Ombudsman. He may be removed from office by the ECJ, at the request of the European Parliament, if he no longer satisfies the conditions required for the performance of his duties, or meets the obligations resulting from his office, or is guilty of serious misconduct. He may not hold any office of an administrative or political nature, nor engage in any occupation or profession paid or unpaid during his term of office. His role it to act independently, in the general interests of the Community and thus he must neither seek nor take instructions from any body. The Ombudsman provides a guarantee of independence and impartiality.

He is empowered to receive complaints from citizens of the EU as well as any natural and legal person residing or having its registered office in a Member State. The Ombudsman competences *ratione materiae* are limited to maladministration in the activities of EC institutions or bodies, with the exception of the ECJ and the Court of First Instance acting in their judicial role. Such limitation is very disappointing since complaints regarding maladministration by national bodies in pursuance, or in violation, of EC law are the most important and vital to ordinary people. The remedies for maladministration by Community institutions are already provided by Community Treaties; it should be noted that they are more adequate and more efficient than those resulting from the successful intervention of the Ombudsman. The Ombudsman may make investigations on his own initiative, as well as from complaints coming from individuals or submitted to him through members of the European Parliament, except where the alleged facts are or have been subject of legal proceedings of the Community courts. If the Ombudsman decides that the complaint is well founded, he refers the matter to the institution concerned which has three months to express its views. After the expiry of that period if the institution in question has not taken appropriate measures to resolve the matter, the Ombudsman has to draft a report, which may include recommendations, and then forwards it to the EP and the institution concerned. He may then only inform the complainant of this process, however; no legal remedy is provided. In this context, the existence of the Ombudsman seems superficial,[65] and this is emphasised by his subordination to the ECJ in that he cannot investigate complaints against maladministration in the activities of the ECJ or the Court of First Instance.

In practice, up to the end of October 1996, the first European Ombudsman elected by the EP in 1995, Mr Jacob Soderman, had received 984 complaints; 11 were resolved in the same month and up to 60 per cent were considered inadmissible.[66]

Assessment of Union citizenship
The introduction of the Union citizenship responds to the concern of the EU to emphasise that the EU is of direct relevance to the individual citizen. It is of great practical importance to EC nationals who directly live and work in another Member State. In this respect, it is interesting to mention that there are 420,000 UK citizens living in other Member States,

---

[65] As the competences of the Committee on Petitions and the Ombudsman overlap, the EP stated that they should complement each other rather than compete: PE 200.788/fin, p23.

[66] (1996) The European December (EP News) p3. For legal analyses of the complaints see S Tierney, 'European Citizenship in Practice? The First Report of the European Ombudsman' (1996) 2 European Public Law 517 et seq.

and nearly a quarter live in Germany. Also, UK citizens are the largest EU minority group in six of the 15 Member States: Denmark, Greece, Spain, Ireland, Portugal and Sweden. They are second largest group in Italy and The Netherlands. Furthermore, in the UK there are 768,000 non-national EU residents, 1.3 per cent of the entire population. About 140,000 EU students study in another EU country and their favourite destinations are Germany, the UK and France.[67]

The most important aspect of Union citizenship is its dynamic character, one which is evolving to follow the progress achieved by the EU. In this respect art 8e provides that:

'... the Council, acting unanimously on a proposal from the Commission and after consulting the European Parliament, may adopt provisions to strengthen or to add to the rights laid down in this Part, which it shall recommend to the Member States for adoption in accordance with their respective constitutional requirements'.

As a result, the Council can only increase the list of rights granted to the EU citizens but not reduce them. Also art 8e make no reference to the imposition of new duties.[68]

Economic and monetary union (EMU)

The most controversial issue of European integration is certainly the creation of the economic and monetary union. The new Title VI of the EC Treaty contains provisions concerning the economic and monetary policy of the Union. It is completed by a number of protocols (3, 4, 5, 10 and 11) which introduced detailed provisions including special arrangements, the so-called opt outs for the UK and Denmark regarding their participation in the third stage of EMU.

Economic union

Economic union entails the close co-ordination of economic policies of the Member States which constitutes the foundation of monetary union. It reflects the so-called 'coronation' or 'economic' theory according to which monetary union is the final result, the 'coronation' of the process of economic convergence. This theory is strongly supported by the German government and especially the Bundesbank.[69] Surprisingly, the TEU devotes only a few, broadly formulated provisions to the creation of economic union. The TEU provides for two concrete actions in this respect: the adoption of a common policy of price stability which will be developed once the EU achieves a full monetary union; and the introduction of fiscal discipline by controlling national budget deficits.

In regard to the first objective, it will be the responsibility of the European Central Bank (ECB) to stabilise the internal price level despite changes in the external exchange rate of the Euro,[70] in order to avoid destabilisation of the overall price structure which would result

---

[67] (1996) The European December (EP News) p2.
[68] On the reform of EU citizenship see J H H Weiler, 'The European Union Belongs to Its Citizens: Three Immodest Proposals' (1997) 22 ELR 150–156.
[69] D R R Dunnett, 'Economic and Monetary Union', in *Legal Issues of the Maastricht Treaty*, supra note 2, p136.
[70] As agreed by the Madrid Summit in 1995.

in the inability of the Euro to function as a stable store of value.[71] The control of excessive budget deficits is the second objective of economic union. Under art 104c(1) the Member States are required to avoid excessive governmental deficits and maintain budgetary discipline. The TEU introduces a surveillance procedure which empowers the Commission to monitor the budgetary situation and governmental debts in Member States. The Commission has to submit reports within the framework of the surveillance procedure on economic co-ordination and convergence of the economic performance of Member States. The Council, acting by qualified majority on the basis of a report prepared by the Commission, may issue a recommendation to a Member State which conducts its economic policy in a manner incompatible with the broad economic guidelines set by the Council. The latter may also make its recommendation public if necessary.[72] Furthermore, the Council has to carry out an overall assessment on the co-ordination of economic policies and convergence of the economic performance of the Member States, and submit an annual report on the results of multilateral surveillance to the EP.

The creation of an economic union is completed by further obligations imposed on Member States: art 103(1) EC requires that they should consider their economic policies as a matter of common concern and thus must co-ordinate them within the Council; and art 109m(1) provides that they must treat their exchange rate polices as a matter of common concern.

Monetary union

Unlike the TEU provisions on economic union, those concerning the creation of monetary union are well developed and detailed. In Title VI, arts 102a–109m EC laid down the institutional and policy requirements necessary to create monetary union and formally sanctioned the three-stage programme towards EMU.

Stage 1 (from 1 July 1990 to 31 December 1993) This stage is broadly outlined in art 102a EC. The main objective of the first stage of EMU was: the completion of the Single European Market; the abolition of the existing restrictions to the free movement of capital; the participation of all Member States in the Exchange Rate Mechanism (ERM); the reduction of exchange-rate fluctuations; and the establishment of a closer co-ordination of economic and monetary policies.

Stage 2 (from 1 January 1994) Its main objectives are: to further develop convergency of national economies of the Member States; to gradually ensure independency for the national central banks; and to establish the European Monetary Institute (EMI).[73]

The first objective is to be attained by introducing the supervision system described in art 104c aimed at eliminating excessive government deficits.

---

[71] It means that without the price stability policy the prices change whenever the exchange rate of the Euro changes, that is, if the Euro depreciated all prices would rise, etc. For details see E Tower and T Willet, *The Theory of Optimum Currency Areas and Exchange Rate Flexibility, Special Papers in International Economics, No 11,* New York: Princeton University Press, 1976.

[72] Article 103(4) EC.

[73] M Moore and T O'Connell, *Monetary Policy in Stage Two of EMU,* Centre for Economic Policy Research Discussion Paper 616, 1992.

With regard to the independence of national banks from governments, all Member States have already introduced necessary legislation in this respect and, as a result, most central banks are now fully independent.

The European Monetary Institute (EMI) was officially inaugurated on 1 January 1994. It has its seat in Frankfurt and employs about 200 staff. Its Council is made up of an independent president, who is also a president of the EMI, and the governors of the national central banks. EMI has its own resources consisting of contributions from the central banks. The European Monetary Institute is a temporary body, a forerunner of the European Central Bank. EMI is in charge of preparing the third stage of monetary union, strengthening co-operation between national central banks, supervising proper functioning of the European Monetary System (EMS), encouraging the use of the Euro and furthering co-operation among Member States in monetary matters. The European Monetary Institute will also prepare a draft agreement on financial and technical arrangements between the European Central Bank and central banks of Member States that will not participate in the third stage, mostly because they did not meet the convergence criteria on time or received a derogation as to their participation in the third stage. The first group of Member States will join the third stage once they meet the convergence criteria, the second group of Member States comprises Denmark and the UK. Denmark notified its non-participation in the third stage at the Edinburgh Summit, which granted a derogation in this respect, while the UK is allowed under Protocol 11, annexed to the TEU, to decide whether or not to participate at the beginning of the third stage provided she meets the convergence criteria. Another task of EMI consists of preparing Euro banknotes. In this respect, on 13 December 1996 in Dublin the President of EMI presented the winning designs for Euro money created by Robert Kalina.[74] Another important task of EMI is to prepare reports for the Council on progress achieved by Member States in relation to convergence criteria on the basis of which, and together with a report from the Commission, the Council submits its recommendations to the European Council. The latter, taking into account Council recommendations and the opinion of the EP, will decide which Member States will be allowed to participate in the next stage of EMU and acting by qualified majority determine its commencement. The first EMI President, Alexander Lamfalussy, set a precedent in presenting the Institute's annual report to the European Parliament in June 1995.

This stage of EMU is crucial for the Member States' participation in the third stage. They must meet the following convergence criteria:

1. Low inflation, which must not exceed that of the three best performing Member States by more than 1.5 per cent.
2. The currency must remain within the normal fluctuation margins of the ERM for at least two years and without being devalued, by unilateral action of a Member State, against the currency of any other Member State. Currently, the margins of fluctuations are very wide – 15 per cent. The objective of this criterion is to maintain stable exchange rate for at least two years.

---

[74] The Euro banknotes got a mixed review. They were praised by the Belgian *Le Soir* ('the European currency at last has a face') and much criticised by the UK (*The Sun*: 'We hate funny money', the *Daily Telegraph*: 'garish Dutch style sweet wrappers'), and in Finland (*Helsinginsanomat*: 'They look a bit like old Tsarist notes and will probably wind up being worth about as much'): (1996) The European 19–25 December p17.

3. Government debts must not exceed 60 per cent of GDP and annual government borrowing (budget deficit) must be less than 3 per cent of GDP.
4. Long-term interest rates must not exceed the average rate of the three lowest rates by more than 2 per cent.

These criteria are very stringent and few Member States are currently able to meet them. In order to further EMU, and to clarify the uncertainties surrounding the single currency, the Dublin Summit of 13 December 1996 adopted 'The Stability and Growth Pact' which focuses on the Member State's budget deficit. It was agreed that the Council of Finance Ministers can impose financial sanctions on a government if its budget deficit exceeds 3 per cent of GDP. The financial sanctions are imposed by qualified majority vote excluding the culprit Member State. The government will be required to pay a fine of up to 0.5 per cent of GDP in a form of an interest-free deposit equivalent to 0.2 per cent of GDP, plus 0.1 per cent for every percentage point above the 3 per cent deficit ratio, up to the maximum deposit of 0.5 per cent of GDP. However, the deposit will only be required if the government concerned fails to take remedial action within four months. If the government's deficit results from exceptional circumstances beyond its control, such as natural disasters or severe recession – the decline of 2 per cent of GDP over a single year, or in the case of a 'grey area' when GDP declines between 0.75 per cent and 2 per cent – no sanctions will be imposed. The deposit will be lost if the excessive deficit persists after more than two years.

The stability and growth pact on budget discipline was discussed and formally endorsed by the Amsterdam Summit in June 1997. The candidates for the third stage of EMU were given nine months to prepare to switch to the single currency, and selection will take place in spring 1998 on the grounds of their 1997 performance. It will be a final date for the UK to decide whether or not to participate in the launching of a single currency. In summer 1998 the European System of Central Banks must be established. The EMU timetable was confirmed by the Amsterdam Summit of June 1997. If it is kept the third stage will commence on 1 January 1999.

Stage 3 (from 1 January 1999) [75] In the third stage the monetary union will become reality. Special bodies will be created in order to conduct economic and monetary policy: the European System of Central Banks (ESCB) which under art 105(1) EC will be responsible for maintaining price stability; and an independent European Central Bank (ECB) in charge of the formulation and implementation of the monetary policy of the EU. Under art 105(2) EC the Governing Council of the ECB, which will be made up of the members of the Executive Board and the governors of the national central banks participating in the third stage,[76] will formulate the monetary policy, that is, will establish intermediate objectives of the monetary policy, will determine interest rates and the supply of reserves in the ESCB, and will set up necessary guidelines for their implementation; while the Executive Board of

---

[75] C Monticelli and J Vinals, *European Monetary Policy in Stage Three, What Are the Issues?*, Centre for Economic Policy Research, Occasional Paper 12, 1993.
[76] See I Harden, 'The European Central Bank and the Role of National Central Banks in Economic and Monetary Union', in K Gretschmann (ed), *Economic and Monetary Union: Implications for National Policy-Makers*, Dordrecht: Kluwer, 1993, p149 et seq.

the ECB, comprising the President, the Vice-President and four other members, will implement monetary policy, including giving necessary instructions to national central banks. The ECB will be an independent body, although it will not enjoy the status of a Community institution. Its status is set out in a separate Protocol which can only be amended in relation to its substantive prerogatives by amendments of the EC Treaty under art N TEU.[77] It will have legal personality[78] unlike the ESCB. Only persons from Member States without derogations under art 109k(1) EC may be members of the Governing Council and the Executive Board of the ECB. In order to integrate the Member States with derogations from the third stage another body will be set up, the General Council (GC), made up of the President and Vice-President of the ECB and all governors of the national central banks, including governors from Member States with derogations. Their participation in the General Council will ensure that they are fully informed and involved in the work of the ESCB. The GC will be set up under art 45 of the Protocol, albeit without prejudice to art 106(3) EC which provides that the ESCB is to be governed by the decision-making bodies of the ECB, that is, the Governing Council and the Executive Board. The General Council will replace the EMI in relation to those tasks which, by the reason of derogations, still have to be performed in the third stage of EMU. Furthermore, it will be a consultative body providing legal advice in the preparations for abrogations of the derogations, and on the scope and implementation of EC law on the prudential supervision of credit undertakings and the stability of the financial system at the request the Council, the Commission and competent authorities of the Member States.

On 1 January 1999 the currencies of participating Member States will be replaced by the Euro, which will also become the unit of account of the European Central Bank and of the central banks of the participating Member States. The Euro is divided into 100 cents. Although the TEU requires that the Euro became a single currency from 1 January 1999, in practice there will not be sufficient notes and coins to be in circulation at that date.[79] Probably after 2002 a single currency will replace national currencies.[80] From 1 January 1999 to the year 2002/2003 national currencies will continue to be used in the Member States as means of payment. Dual pricing of products will gradually appear with conversion tables displayed wherever necessary. The official exchange rate of national currencies against the Euro will have to be fixed by EU legislation, and financial institutions and banks will start to conduct transactions in Euros. In 2002/2003 the Euro will take over as the national currency, although national notes and coins will be exchanged in banks for a considerable period. From that point financial transactions, wages, salaries, bank accounts, etc, will be in the Euro.

It is interesting to mention that a newly designed symbol for the Euro is closely

---

[77] J V Louis, 'The Project of the European Central Bank', in J Stuyck, (ed), *Financial and Monetary Integration in the European Economic Community: Legal, Institutional and Economic Aspects*, Deventer and Boston: Kluwer Academic, 1993, p13 et seq.

[78] Article 107 EC.

[79] At present there is about 12 billion banknotes in use, 8 billion notes in store and 6.5 billion new notes printed each year in all 15 Member States.

[80] On policy recommendations for the transition to EMU, S Collignon, *Europe's Monetary Future, a Study Prepared at the Request of the European Parliament*, London: Pinter Publishers, 1994, especially pp205–229.

modelled on the Greek letter *epsilon*. The Commission considers that it 'points back to the cradle of European civilisation and is the first letter of Europe'.[81]

Assessment of EMU

The creation of EMU requires significant convergence of national economies of Member States which involves their close co-operation in these matters at the Community level. In practice a considerable amount of national economic sovereignty will be transfer to EU institutions. Member States participating in EMU will no longer be able to control their economic policy, especially to set interest rates or devalue their currency. This is the main disadvantage of EMU. However, this argument must be considered in the light of the growing interdependence and internationalisation of economies. Do countries actually have any real economic sovereignty left to exercise? On the one hand interest rates depend on market forces, and on the other hand devaluation of a national currency is only a temporary measure which backlashes in creating inflationary consequences, which in turn leads to pressure for higher wages, thus undermining competitiveness of national products.

It is submitted that the creation of EMU will result in a number of advantages:

1. It will be a powerful symbol of European integration.
2. The Euro will become one of the dominant world currencies and be in competition with the US dollar and the Japanese yen. It will highlight the importance of Frankfurt and London (if the UK joins EMU) as world financial centres. Also, it might result in the Euro enjoying the *seigniorage* position, that is, the ability to finance balance of trade deficits by having other countries keep the Euro as part of their reserves.
3. It will result in considerable savings in transactions costs as the cost of exchanging one currency for others will be eliminated. The Euro will become the major transaction or invoicing currency. According to the Financial Market Group of the London School of Economics, by 2002 a global invoicing share for the Euro will be about 28 per cent, with growing potential in trade with central and eastern European countries. For tourists there will be no extra cost for converting one currency into another while travelling in the EMU territory.
4. It will increase the attractiveness of the EU to foreign investors and increase the share of the EMU-participating countries in world export from 17 to 25 per cent. In this respect Andrew Crockett, general manager of the Bank for International Settlements in Basle, said: 'Monetary union in Europe holds the promise of profound change in international finance. The economies sharing the Euro could face the world as the largest single currency area and the largest single trading bloc.'[82]
5. It will result in the same inflation rate throughout the EMU territory which will probably be very low taking into account the independence of the ESCB. Anti-inflationary discipline will be imposed upon Member States like France, Spain, or Italy, well known for their high inflation rates.
6. Management of the EU will be simplified as all payments will be made in the same currency.

---

[81] (1997) The European 24–30 July p23.
[82] K Engelen, 'Why US is Beginning to Worry about the Euro' (1997) The European 9–15 January p18.

3.2 Pillar 2: Common Foreign and Security Policy (CFSP)

The realistic objective of the common foreign policy for the EU is more to agree on a common position in international politics, that is, to speak with one voice, rather than achieve a unified foreign policy conducted by supra-national bodies, with the EU raised to the status of a superpower.

The EC is often described as an economic giant but a political dwarf. Its economic weight in the international arena has not been counterbalanced by a similar political role, except in trade which is considered as a politically neutral activity. The dichotomy can be explained by historical reasons. From its inception the Community was a 'civilian power', that is, an organisation implicitly rejecting power politics and concentrating on economic aspects of European integration.[83] In reality, it lacked military capacity to conduct a defence policy, and this aspect of European affairs had been developed mainly within the framework of the North Atlantic Treaty Organisation (NATO). However, the collapse of Communism, the reunification of Germany and the American policy of burden-shedding in military matters have changed perspectives on Europe's future foreign and defence policy.

The Common Foreign and Security Policy covers two distinct, although closely related, areas. Co-operation in foreign matters was initiated at The Hague Summit in 1969 and resulted in the establishment of European Political Co-operation (EPC), albeit outside the Treaty. It became recognised and incorporated into the structure of the Community in Title III of the Single European Act, but was not subject to judicial review of the ECJ. Title III SEA declared that Member States would endeavour jointly to formulate and implement a European foreign policy. The improvements to EPC brought about by the SEA are:

1. the distinction between foreign ministers' meeting within the EPC and the Council was abolished;
2. an EPC Secretariat was set up in Brussels;
3. a mechanism was provided to convene emergency meetings of the Political Committee or Community foreign ministers within 48 hours upon the request of at least three Member States;
4. the Commission and the EP became associated with EPC; and
5. the Commission and the Presidency were responsible for ensuring consistency between the external policies of the Community and policies agreed within the framework of the EPC.

The EPC resulted in adoption of common positions on many issues such as the Middle East, eastern Europe and South Africa but, in practice, its vague declarations after events had taken place and little direct action undermined its importance. Jacques Delors strongly advocated a new approach in the development of a common foreign policy. He distinguished between a single and a common policy which is akin to the distinction between a regulation and a directive, and decided that the second option was more realistic. It means that only broad guidelines are established, as in the case of EC directives. This flexible approach in implementation of a common foreign policy will allow Member States to take into

---

[83] P Tsakaloyannis, 'From Civilian Power to Military Integration', in J Lodge (ed), *The EC and the Challenge of the Future,* London: *Pinter,* 1989, p243.

consideration their national traditions and interests. Furthermore, the necessity of adopting a new approach was highlighted when Member States were faced with the Gulf crisis and the deteriorating situation in the former Yugoslavia.

In the Gulf crisis, no agreement was reached among Member States on the use of force against Iraq; the position of Members States varied from immediate and unconditional support for the US military action (the UK Prime Minister, M Thatcher, was at that time in Colorado with President Bush and promised UK support), to the Irish policy of non-intervention based on neutrality.

In relation to the crisis in the former Yugoslavia, the Rome Summit in October 1990 firmly declared its support for unity and territorial integrity of Yugoslavia.[84] However, sympathy for the breakaway Yugoslav republics in some Member States led to a challenge of the Summit declaration. Germany put pressure on other Member States to recognise immediately Croatia and Slovenia. At the meeting of foreign ministers on 16 December 1991 it was decided that the Community should have a uniform policy on the recognition of new States. A special Commission was set up under the chairmanship of Judge Robert Badinter to assess criteria for recognition of new States by the Community.[85] Germany announced that, regardless of the Badinter Report, it would delay recognition of Croatia and Slovenia only until 15 January 1992. As a result, Germany forced the Community's hand, despite the fact that the criteria for recognition laid down in the Badinter Report were not being satisfied in either case. Croatia was recognised without safeguards being obtained for a large Serbian minority living there. As a result, Serbia accused the Community of hypocrisy and its credibility as a neutral force was lost. On 6 April 1992 the Community recognised Bosnia, a gesture which to some extent triggered the Serbian 'cleansing' policy, and resulted in widespread atrocities unknown in Europe since World War II.

Finally, the Lisbon Summit of 1992 refused to recognise Macedonia, with firm opposition mounted by Greece. The summit even ignored its own criteria for recognition which, in the case of Macedonia, were fulfilled, thus destabilising one of a few peaceful regions in the Balkans and increasing the risk of internationalisation of a conflict outside the territory of former Yugoslavia. The Community management, or rather mismanagement, of the crises in former Yugoslavia exacerbated rather than alleviated the situation. As Dinan stated: 'Far from reflecting well on the Community, the Yugoslav war emphasised deep foreign policy differences between Member States and showed the limits of EC international action. The Community's involvement also sapped popular support for European integration and contributed to the Maastricht Treaty ratification crises.'[86]

Indeed, each international crisis revealed divergencies in opinion between Member States and the impossibility of presenting a common front to the outside world. This has also contributed to the incorporation of the Common Foreign and Security Policy (CFSP) into the Treaty of Maastricht.[87]

---

[84] EC Bull 10–1990, Presidency Conclusions, point 1.8.
[85] EPC Press Release, P129/91, 16 December 1991.
[86] D Dinan, *Ever Closer Union?*, London: Anne Rienner Publishers, 1994, pp489–490.
[87] The circumstances leading to the incorporation of Common Foreign and Security Policy (CFSP) into the Treaty of Maastricht were examined in Chapter 2.

Main objectives of CFSP and the mechanisms for pursuing them

Article J of the TEU describes the principles of the CFSP. Under art J1(2) the CFSP has the following objectives:

1. to safeguard the common values, fundamental interests and independence of the Union;
2. to strengthen the security of the Union and its Member States in all ways;
3. to preserve peace and strengthen international security, in accordance with the principles of the United Nations Charter as well as the principles of the Helsinki Final Act and the objectives of the Paris Charter;
4. to promote international co-operation; and
5. to develop and consolidate democracy and the rule of law, and respect for human rights and fundamental freedoms.

The objectives of the CFSP are to be pursued through two forms of co-operation: the first consists of adoption of a common position and is defined in art J2; the second concerns a joint action which is described in art J3. There is no definition of either. However, practice shows that a common position is similar to a declaration and thus sets out general guidelines on important international questions. The decision whether to define a common position is taken by unanimity and must be upheld by Member States in international organisations and international conferences.[88]

The necessity for adopting a joint action is assessed by the Council on recommendations from the European Council. The Council decides by unanimity whether to adopt a joint action and, if so, sets out its scope, general and specific objectives and, if necessary, its duration, means, conditions and procedures for implementation. However, implementation measures are decided by a qualified majority. A Member State's binding commitment to implement a joint action in the conduct of its national foreign policy may be set aside under one of derogations introduced in the TEU: art J3(6) allows a Member State in case of urgency to conduct national policy provided it takes into account the general objectives of the joint action and informs the Council immediately afterwards; art J3(7) provides that a special solution may be adopted for Member States that have major difficulties in implementing a joint action, although this special arrangement should neither undermine the objectives of the action nor impair its effectiveness; and, finally, art J3(3) states that the Council can always revise a joint action by taking into consideration the changing circumstances affecting its subject matter. So far some joint actions have been adopted but its number is steadily rising. Among them are: humanitarian aid for Bosnia; support for the transition to democracy in South Africa and the peace process in the Middle East; administration of Mostar, a Bosnian town, for two years, at the request of the Bosnian Federation (May 1994); the dispatch of a team of observers to Russian parliamentary elections; control on the export of dual-use goods; participation in the Korean Peninsula Energy Development Organisation; the nomination of a special envoy for the African Great Lakes Region; and, the most important, a 'Stability Pact' in Europe.

---

[88] For the Permanent Members of the UN Security Council see art J5(4).

Institutions of the CFSP

The main decision-making body within the CFSP is the Council made up of foreign ministers of the Member States which acts as the General Affairs Council. It defines a common position and decides on foreign and security policy matters subject to a joint action. It meets monthly but can meet anytime, if necessary. Decisions are taken by unanimity, apart from procedural questions or in cases when, by mutual consent, a decision is taken by qualified majority. The CFSP Council is assisted as any council by COREPER (Committee of Permanent Representatives), which is often overridden by the Political Committee reporting directly to the CFSP Council and consisting of the political directors of the foreign ministries of the Member States. The Corresponding Group, made up of other foreign ministry officials, is in charge of preparing work not dealt with by the Political Committee as well as liaison functions. Also various working groups made up of officials from foreign ministries, situated in the capitals of the Member States, are entrusted with specific subjects (horizontal – UN, or vertical – Asia, eastern Europe, etc). The EPC Secretariat has been incorporated into the Council's General Secretariat.

Role of Community institutions under the CFSP

The TEU has abolished the distinction between the Council acting in the EPC and EC areas. The Council has become a common institution to all three Pillars. The main advantage is that the Council must ensure consistency between action under the CFSP and under the other Pillars. In this respect art J8 emphasises that the Council must ensure 'the unity, consistency and effectiveness of action by the Union'. It has also acquired an executive role under the CFSP which under EPC was assigned solely to the Member States.

The Commission is fully associated with the CFSP. It shares the right of initiative with Member States but it is not involved in the implementation of the CFSP. In this context it is interesting to mention the European Community Humanitarian Office (ECHO) as it is the area of foreign policy where the Commission has a direct role. The ECHO was set up in 1992 with the objective of funding and co-ordinating emergency humanitarian aid in both natural and man-made disaster situations. In 1996, ECHO donated ECU 660 million to more than 60 developing countries. The Commission has signed a framework agreement with more than 170 working partners of ECHO, national and international organisations active in this area, in order to co-ordinate its humanitarian assistance and financial support.

The role of the European Parliament has not changed, it is still a consultative body. The Presidency of the Council is required to inform and consult with the EP on the 'main aspects and basic choices' of CFSP and to take into account its opinions. The EP is entitled to ask the Council questions and to make recommendations. It also holds an annual debate on progress in implementing the CFSP. As a result, democratic control by the Union of the CFSP is still weak as it consists mainly of consultations with the EP.

Commitments of Member States under the CFSP

The EU has strengthened the commitment of Member States to a common foreign policy. It reinforces the obligations of the Member States to conform to the common positions.

Article J1(4) stresses that 'Member States shall support CFSP and shall refrain from action impairing its effectiveness.' Further, it has introduced the concept of a joint action and provided procedures for selecting and implementing such actions.

The main commitment of the Member States within the CFSP is to implement the common position and any joint action of the EU. Member States have obligations vis-à-vis each other in consulting and exchanging information, especially when only some of them are members of international organisations or attend international conferences where decisions that potentially affect all of them may be taken.

On the other hand, Member States have obligations vis-à-vis the Union. In this respect, the Members States must support the CFSP 'actively and unreservedly in a spirit of loyalty and mutual solidarity'.[89] Once again, where the State is a member of an international organisation where decisions that potentially affect the Union may be taken, that Member State must defend the interests of the EU.[90] In the case of the Permanent Members of the UN Security Council this must be achieved without compromising their responsibilities deriving from the UN Charter. Secondly, diplomatic and consular missions of Member States and Commission delegations in third countries and international organisations must co-operate, especially to exchange information, carry out joint assessments and contribute to the implementation of art 8c EC, that is, ensure diplomatic and consular protection of EU citizens in countries where their governments are not represented. The Commission has a mission in more than 100 countries and in many international organisations.

Management of the CFSP

The Presidency of the Council is to represent the EU on CFSP matters in international organisations and international conferences. Article J5 defines its functions which consist of implementation of common measures and representation of the EU worldwide. A system of 'troika' is maintained, that is the current Presidency, the preceding and the succeeding Presidencies, accompanied by representative of the Commission, act together in order to ensure the continuity and consistency of the CFSP. In case of emergency the Presidency on its own motion, or at the request of the Commission or a Member State, must convene an extraordinary meeting within 48 hours or a even a shorter period of time.[91]

Common defence policy

With regard to a common defence policy, the Gulf crisis enhanced the attractiveness of the Western European Union (WEU) comprising at that time nine countries: UK, France, Germany, Belgium, The Netherlands, Luxembourg, Italy, Spain and Portugal. Unlike NATO, the WEU can operate outside Europe and the USA is not a Member State. France is the most enthusiastic supporter of WEU and when holding the Presidency of WEU invited all EC countries to attend a meeting on 21 August 1990 to examine the possibility of a military

---

[89] Article J2(1).
[90] Article J5(4).
[91] Article J8(4).

intervention in the Gulf,[92] and especially to assess the role of WEU in the context of military action outside the remit of NATO. This meeting was parallel to a meeting of foreign ministers of the Community.

On 18 September 1990 Italy, which held the Presidency of the Council, submitted a proposal aimed at merging the Community and WEU.[93] The proposal was too controversial to be seriously considered by Member States, but the Rome Summit on October 1990 agreed in principle on the development of a common security policy without specifying its content and procedures of co-operation. The future role of WEU was not decided but the Summit took the position that WEU should not undermine NATO. In June 1992, at the meeting in Bonn, the foreign ministers and defence ministers of WEU countries adopted the 'Peterberg Declaration' which set out the objectives for WEU's future development, mainly conflict prevention and peace-keeping action under the auspices of the Organisation for Security and Co-operation in Europe[94] and the UN Security Council.

At Maastricht the Member States agreed to include 'the eventual framing of a common defence policy, which might in time lead to a common defence' into the scope of the TEU.[95] The crucial question regarding the relationship between NATO and WEU was solved. The WEU was recognised as a means to strengthen the European pillar of the Atlantic Alliance. In this respect art J4(4) and (5) underline the fact that the EU defence policy is without prejudice to the obligations arising out of security arrangements whether bilateral (the Eurocorps) or multilateral (NATO) to which Member States are party, provided they are compatible with the objectives of the Treaty. The WEU has become a defence component of the EU and is entrusted with elaboration and implementation of actions and decisions of the EU which have defence implications.[96]

Also at Maastricht WEU countries made a declaration stating that they welcomed the development of the European security and defence identity. They emphasised that they were determined, taking into account the role of WEU as the defence component of the European Union and as the means to strengthen the European pillar of the Atlantic Alliance, to put the relationship between WEU and the other European States on a new basis for the sake of security and stability in Europe.[97] Also, WEU granted full membership to Greece at Maastricht and invited EC members to join or to become observers if they wished to. As a result, Ireland, Denmark, Sweden, Finland and Austria have the status of observer which entitles them to participate in the WEU Council and working group meetings, and even take part in deliberations if requested. Apart from observers, some European countries become 'associate partners': Norway, Iceland, Turkey and nine central and eastern European countries. Their status allows them to fully participate in WEU Council meetings, to associate themselves with the decisions of WEU and to participate in WEU military operations.

---

[92] During the Gulf War WEU was in charge of the co-ordination of naval units of Member States (Operation Cleansweep).

[93] D Dinan, *Ever Closer Union?*, supra note 86, p471.

[94] The Organisation for Security and Co-operation in Europe (OSCE) was formerly known as the Conference on Security and Co-operation in Europe (CSCE). Its name and status were changed by the Budapest Review Conference and Summit of 10 October–6 December 1994.

[95] Article J4(1).

[96] Article J4(2).

[97] N Foster, *EC Legislation*, 5th ed, London: Blackstones, 1994, pp132–135.

The future of WEU is still under discussion. Some decision must be taken as the WEU Treaty expires in 1998. The main problem concerns the relationship between NATO and WEU. It seems unlikely that WEU will replace NATO, most probably it would run parallel with it and at the same time it would allow countries with close connections to former colonies, such as the UK and France, to continue to exercise their responsibilities as before. It will probably permit the EC countries to participate in all existing bilateral and multilateral military arrangements, provided they are compatible with the objectives of the EU. Neutral countries like Ireland, Sweden, Austria and Finland strongly object to a military dimension of the EU. Under the Irish Presidency a draft text was submitted at the December 1996 Dublin Summit limiting the role of WEU to peace-keeping tasks on behalf of the EU. The forthcoming enlargement of NATO, to include countries like Poland, Hungary the Czech Republic and possibly in the near future Romania and even Ukraine, changes the image of NATO beyond recognition. Therefore, WEU may provide an alternative to present NATO members dissatisfied with their NATO obligations (each signatory has to defend other signatories) within the enlarged membership (for example, France may object to defending Bulgaria or Romania). Finally, the EU countries have about two million soldiers under arms. France and Spain decided to abandon conscription, and other States have embarked upon a reduction in armed forces which will result in huge savings (about £15 billion for the UK alone). The development of WEU may also be attractive to other countries, taking into account that, apart from the resurgent nationalism in Russia, there is no serious threat to Europe's security.[98] Smaller, common, armed forces within WEU will provide necessary safeguards to Europe's security, while allowing individual EU Member States to reduce their military expenditure.

In the context of the European defence policy, it is necessary to mention Eurocorps which may become a foundation for the future European army at the disposal of WEU. Eurocorps was born out of a Franco-German initiative and became operational in 1994. It comprises one French, one German division and contingents from Belgium, Spain and Luxembourg, a total of approximately 35,000 solders. Eurocorps is under NATO command when operations are taking place within the territorial ambit of NATO, but is expected to act independently outside NATO territory, or when the latter declines to act.

Assessment of the CFSP

The CFSP is based on inter-governmental co-operation. As a result it is not subject to judicial review by the ECJ, and the involvement of the Commission and the European Parliament is very limited. Progress in the development of the CFSP has been hindered by the requirement of unanimity within the Council on proposed measures, although the decision of the foreign ministers in March 1997 to impose sanctions on Burma in response to its abuse of human rights, especially in relation to child labour, could be considered as a

---

[98] On 28 May 1997 the Founding Act on Mutual Relations, Co-operation and Security was signed between Russia and NATO. The Act emphasises that Russia and NATO are no longer adversaries as they have overcome the vestiges of earlier confrontation and competition. The Act re-affirms 'the determination of Russia and NATO to give concrete substance to their shared commitment to build a stable, peaceful and undivided Europe, whole and free, to the benefit of all its people': (1997) The European 29 May–4 June p2.

real breakthrough. In this context it is necessary to mention a very successful initiative of CFSP. Under its auspices a conference attended by 40 countries on 'Stability in Europe' was organised in May 1994 in Paris which focused on ethnic disputes and maintaining peace and stability in eastern Europe. It resulted in the establishment of the 'Stability Pact' in Europe in March 1995 under the supervision of the Organisation for Security and Co-operation in Europe.

3.3 Pillar 3: Co-operation in Justice and Home Affairs

Title VI of the TEU containing arts K–K9 is devoted to co-operation in Justice and Home Affairs (JHA) among the Member States. The framework of co-operation is based on a inter-governmental decision-making procedure with marginal contributions from Community institutions. Pillar 3 of the TEU consists of determination of nine areas listed in art K1 which are considered as 'matters of common interest' to the Member States in their effort to achieve the objective of the Union – mainly the free movement of persons – but without prejudice to the powers of the EC. These nine areas are:

1. asylum policy (art K1(1));
2. rules governing the crossing by persons of the external borders of the Member States and the exercise of controls thereon (art K1(2));
3. immigration policy and policy regarding nationals of third countries which establishes the conditions of entry, movement and residence on the territory of Member States, as well as combatting their illegal immigration, residence and work (art K1(3));
4. combating drug addiction in so far as this is not covered by points 7–9 below (art K1(4));
5. combating fraud on an international scale as far as this is not covered by points 7–9 below (art K1(5));
6. judicial co-operation in civil matters (art K1(6));
7. judicial co-operation in criminal matters (art K1(7));
8. customs co-operation (art K1(8));
9. police co-operation for the purposes of preventing and combating terrorism, unlawful drug trafficking and other serious forms of international crime, including if necessary certain aspects of customs co-operation, by way of the organisation of a Union-wide system of exchanging information within a European Police Office (Europol) (art K1(9)).

The procedural aspect of co-operation in these areas is described in art K3, and a distinction is made between items mentioned in art K1(1)–(6) and K1(7)–(9). The Commission has right of initiative only in relation to issues covered by art K1(1)–(6). Furthermore, under art K9, the so-called 'passerelle' provision, the Council acting unanimously on a proposal from the Commission or a Member State may allow the transfer of competence from Pillar 3 to Pillar 1 (EC Treaty) in relation to the areas referred to under art K1(1)–(6). As a result, matters covered in art K1(7)–(9) which are considered as vital and essential for internal security and the exercise of national sovereignty by the Member States are subject to double exclusions. This is unjustified taking into account that some of them directly affect proper functioning of a single market, such as customs co-operation and police co-operation in preventing and combatting terrorism, drug trafficking, money-laundering, etc. Such exclusions undermine the dynamic character of Pillar 3, that is its prospect of becoming a part of the EC Treaty. If the Council decides to transform a 'matter of common interest' into a Community matter two conditions must be satisfied: at the Community level, the Council must adopt that decision unanimously; and, at the national level, the Council's decision must be ratified in accordance with constitutional law of Member States. It means in practice, that under art K9 the EC Treaty can be amended without following the procedure laid out in art N TEU.

Organisational structure of JHA

Procedurally, the Council translates the objectives of co-operation in the fields of justice and home affairs (JHA) into action by adopting joint positions, promoting joint co-operation, and adopting joint action subject to the principle of subsidiarity and conventions without prejudice to art 220 EC. It should be noted that the Council acting in JHA cannot use the well established forms of secondary legislation: regulations, directives and decisions. The legal status and the difference between joint positions and joint action are still unclear, although art K5 provides that Member States 'shall defend the common positions' within international organisations and international conferences. It seems that common positions are similar to declarations and thus are not binding. As to joint action opinions diverge,[99] although it is certain that measures implementing such joint action must have legal effect. Only a few joint actions have been adopted so far, for instance on the Europol Drugs Unit,[100] on group travel by school children,[101] etc, although there is a steady increase in their number.[102]

Comparison between Pillars 2 and 3 of the TEU demonstrates that under JHA Member States' obligations are less stringent. They have neither the duty to defend joint action in the international fora, that is within international organisations or at international conferences, nor are they bound by common positions in the conduct of their national policy.

Unlike the Presidency under Pillar 2, in JHA the implementation of common measures, the representation of the Union interests in these fields within international organisations and at international conferences, as well as the implementation of material consistency, are not incumbent on the Presidency. In this respect, it seems that inconsistency between the action of the Union and action by the Member State in JHA will prove the most problematic. Indeed, art A TEU, which states that the task of the EU must be organised in such a manner as to ensure consistency and solidarity in relations between the Member States and between their peoples, ensures organisational consistency in the Union, that is, it contains a general requirement that the allocation of competencies between Union institutions should be based

---

[99] For Muller-Graff, 'The Legal Bases of the Third Pillar and Its Position in the Framework of the Union Treaty', 31 CMLR 493–510, joint actions have no legal effect, but D O'Keeffe states that 'I Submit that they do have legal effects and are legally binding, insofar as they are part of the implementation of the TEU' in 'Recasting the Third Pillar' (1995) 32 CMLR 914.

[100] Adopted on 10 March 1995 by virtue of art K3 TEU (OJ L62 20.3.95 p1).

[101] Council Decision on a joint action concerning travel facilities for school pupils from third countries resident in a Member State adopted on 30 November–1 December 1994 on the ground of art K3(2)(b) (OJ L327 19.12.94 p1).

[102] For example, in 1996 ten joint actions were adopted as compared to three in 1995.

requirement that the allocation of competencies between Union institutions should be based on rational grounds. Article C TEU provides for material consistency. It states:

> 'The Union shall be served by a single institutional framework … The Union shall in particular ensure consistency of its external activities as a whole in the context of its external relations, security, economic and development policies. The Council and the Commission shall be responsible for ensuring such consistency.'

Article C deals with situations where there is an overlap between various provisions of the TEU. Actions or measures taken under different provisions, but concerning the same policy, must not clash but should complement each other in order to render the policy in question more efficient. Article C ensures consistency between different pillars of the TEU. The consistency between action by the Union and action by the Member States within the framework of the CFSP is governed by art J8(3). Pillar 3 neither contains a similar provision nor mentions the system of Troika which ensures consistency within the JHA Council.

The main instruments of co-operation in JHA are conventions which are legally binding. Under art K3(2)(c) the Council is in charge of preparing and recommending them to the Member States for adoption. Their implementation is conferred upon the Council, unless otherwise provided by such conventions. In the adoption of implementing measures the Council is required to act by a majority of two-thirds of the Contracting States to a particular convention. Also, if international conventions attribute jurisdiction to the ECJ, the latter can interpret them and give rulings on any dispute concerning their application.

A very important new body has been set up under Pillar 3 – the Co-ordinating Committee (the so-called K4 Committee) which is defined in that article.[103] The K4 Committee is made up of senior officials from Member States. It main tasks are to co-ordinate the activities falling under JHA, to submit opinions to the Council on its own initiative or at the request of the Council, and to prepare meetings of the Council in all areas covered by art K1 (without prejudice to art 151 EC), as well as matters within the scope of art 100c EC (visa policy).

Role of Community institutions in JHA

The involvement of the Commission and the EP in the procedure under JHA is minimal as they both lack any binding force in the enforcement of JHA. The Commission, the Member States and the K4 Committee have the right to initiate measures under JHA, but the Commission is limited to areas referred to in art K1(1)–(6). Notwithstanding art K4(2) that

---

[103] It does not replace the Committee of Permanent Representatives (COREPER), which prepares work for any council including the JHA Council. The K4 Committee co-ordinates the work of steering groups, and as such is a vital intermediary between the Council and the Steering Groups which are divided into three categories: Immigration and Asylum, Security and Judicial Co-operation. The group on Immigration and Asylum is subdivided into: Migration, Asylum, Visas, External Frontiers, Forged Documents and Clearing Houses on Immigration and Asylum and Customs groups; on Security the vertical groups are: Police and Customs Co-operation, Terrorism, Police Co-operation (operational and technical), Drugs and Serious Organised Crime, Ad hoc Group Europol; and on Judicial Co-operation there are: Extradition, Internal Organised Crime, Penal Law/Communitarian Law, Withdrawal of Driving Licence, Trial Documents, Application of 1968 Brussels Convention groups. Horizontal Information Group comprises, for example, the European Information System.

the Commission should be fully associated with the work regarding Pillar 3, no concrete procedure is provided in this respect, apart its participation in the K4 Committee. The European Parliament must be informed by the Presidency and the Commission of discussions in the areas covered by Title VI. The EP should be consulted by the Presidency on important aspects of activities in areas covered by Title VI and its opinion taken into consideration. The most important practical competence of the EP in relation to Title VI is that it must hold an annual debate on the progress made in the implementation of the areas covered by Pillar 3, and may also ask questions and make recommendations to the Council in this respect. This may become a means to pressurise the Council and the K4 Committee. Finally, the EP involvement may increase if the expenditure in relation to Title VI, which so far has been charged to the Member States, is charged to the EC budget.

The activities under Title VI can be divided into three main categories: immigration and asylum, security and judicial co-operation.

Immigration and asylum

Immigration and asylum, although separate issues are, nevertheless, interrelated. The EU Member States become countries of immigration for people who are using the application for asylum as a gate for immigration. Until the TEU these issues were mostly left to the Member States. For a few reasons the EC decided not to deal with immigration and asylum: this has already been done by the Schengen group, and the ad hoc Group on Immigration. Some governments, the UK in particular, considered that these matters were within its exclusive competences and refused to surrender its sovereign rights in border checks, even for travellers from the EC, not trusting continental immigration authorities to keep illegal immigrants outside the UK.

However, action at Community level became necessary with the creation of a single market. Internal borders had to be removed in order to ensure the free movement of workers in conformity with art 48a EC. Co-operation on immigration and asylum under the umbrella of the EC started when the Council established a 'Group of Co-ordinators' which was instructed to prepare proposals for measures to be implemented by 1 January 1993. It resulted in the submission of the so-called 'Palma Document' which was adopted at the Madrid Summit in June 1989. The essential measures proposed by the Palma Document concerned: the introduction of accelerated procedures and common criteria for 'manifestly unfounded' asylum applications; a procedure for preventing asylum-seekers from applying for asylum in more than one Member State; determination of a Member State responsible for removing immigrants and asylum seekers from the EC; the establishment of a financing system for expulsion; a common list of countries whose nationals require an entry visa to the EC; a regularly updated and a common list of inadmissible persons and wanted persons; the introduction of common measures for checks on external borders, accompanied by exchange of information between police and customs, etc. The Commission approved the Palma Document, and in October 1991 issued its own communication on Immigration and Asylum to the Council and the European Parliament in which it recognised the link between both matters.[104]

---

[104] SEC(91)1857.

Co-operation between Member States has been mostly based on *ad hoc* arrangements. Indeed, the removal of internal borders, a necessary condition of the completion of a single market, created a need for closer co-operation among the Member States on immigration and asylum. They considered it necessary to keep a strict control on the admission of non-EC nationals. In October 1986, on a proposal by the UK to curb illegal immigration and especially to 'end abuses of the asylum process', an *ad hoc* Group on Immigration was created, made up of interior ministers of all Member States. The ad hoc Group on Immigration drafted many important proposals in this area: in April 1987 on sanctions on airlines bringing in undocumented asylum seekers and those with false documents which was implemented in the UK in the Carriers Liability Act in 1987;[105] in 1990 a draft convention to prevent asylum seekers to make more than one application in the EC which was transformed into the Dublin Convention; in 1990 a draft convention on harmonisation of controls at external borders; in 1991 a proposal for fingerprinting asylum seekers; and in 1992 a draft resolution on criteria and procedures on 'manifestly unfounded' asylum applications, as well as proposals on harmonisation of policies on expulsion, on the admission of non-EC nationals for employment, etc. The work of the *ad hoc* group was presented at the meetings of immigration ministers within the framework of the European Political Co-operation (EPC). Many initiatives of the *ad hoc* Group on Immigration were approved by the Council of Ministers' meetings within the EPC, such as the creation at the end of 1991 of the Centre for information, discussion and exchange on asylum (CIREA) containing information on countries of origin of asylum seekers to assist in deciding which are 'safe' and in which the risks of persecution for political reasons are serious. Although CIREA was strongly criticised by non-governmental organisations (NGOs), at the end of November 1992 another Centre for information, discussion and exchange on the crossing of borders and immigration (CIREFI) was set up to supervise the common immigration policy, and especially to store information on unlawful immigration methods, forged documents, rejected asylum applications, etc.

At the meeting in London in November 1992 the ministers approved the Resolution on Manifestly Unfounded Applications for Asylum. They expressed the wish to incorporate the principles of the Resolution into a legally binding instrument and many States have already introduce national legislation based upon it.[106] The Resolution sets out criteria and the procedure for handling manifestly unfounded applications for asylum. It also introduces an accelerated procedure for processing asylum claims within one month. Another important resolution on a harmonised approach to questions concerning host third countries approved by the 1992 meeting is contained in the Dublin Convention. If an asylum seeker on the way from a country where he was persecuted went through a host third country, that is a country which is considered safe or where he could apply for asylum, his application in the EC would be deemed unlawful and he would be returned to the host country. The most important proposals of the *ad hoc* Group on Immigration are the Dublin Convention and the draft convention on the external borders.

Dublin Convention
The Convention Determining the State Responsible for Examining Applications for Asylum

---

[105] Under its provisions carriers' liability doubled to £2,000 per passenger.
[106] In the UK the Asylum and Immigration Appeals Act 1993.

Lodged in One of the Member States of the European Communities was signed on 15 June 1990 in Dublin. The Amsterdam Summit of June 1997 welcomed the completion of the ratification procedures of this Convention which allowed its entry into force on 1 September 1997. The main objective of the Convention is to prevent an asylum seeker from making multiple applications and from selecting the country of asylum. As a result, if his application is refused in one country, the application is considered as refused by all other Member States. It also acknowledged the first 'safe' country principle. The Convention determines the Member State which should deal with an asylum application, that is, the one which granted him a visa or allowed him illegal entry into the Community, unless he has a close family – only husband or wife or parents or children – with refugee status in an EC country. In that case the State of residence of his close family will deal with his application. The receiving State notifies the responsible State of the presence of an asylum seeker and sends the asylum seeker to that State. Under the Dublin Convention the entire Union is treated as one country for the purposes of an asylum application.

Draft Convention on the Crossing of External Frontiers

The Draft Convention on the Crossing of External Frontiers was expected to have been signed in 1991. It contains common rules for the crossing of external borders by third countries' nationals; introduces stringent conditions for entry of non-EC nationals; and establishes a joint computerised list of inadmissible third country nationals via the European Information System (EIS). The Convention was drafted in such a way as to allow its ratification by the UK. It does not mention internal borders. Nevertheless, the UK refuses to accede to the Convention because of her dispute with Spain over Gibraltar. On 10 December 1993 the Commission submitted amendments to the draft Convention under art K3(2) which avoids the issue of the territorial application of the Convention to Gibraltar and confers an interpretative role to the ECJ.[107] It is considered that the new version will be approved by the UK.

Schengen II

The agreement between France and Germany in July 1984 in Saarbrucken on the elimination of frontier controls between the two countries, which was intended as a way of strengthening Franco-German relations, gave birth to the Schengen system. The Benelux countries had already abolished border checks for their nationals. They decided to join the Franco-German project. It resulted in the adoption of the Schengen Convention on the gradual abolition of checks at the common borders (Schengen I), signed between the Benelux countries and France and Germany on 14 June 1985. The Schengen agreement provided that border controls should be abolished on 1 January 1990 between their territories. In order to achieve this objective, working groups were established to draw up necessary measures on the relaxation of border controls, such as the introduction of mixed checks at the borders, visual checks on EC nationals (green sticker at the front window of cars), and co-ordination of measures strengthening external borders control to keep out undesirables by harmonising visa controls, asylum and deportation policies. Also issues relevant to internal security – such as harmonisation of firearms and ammunition laws,

---

[107] COM(93)684.

police co-operation in combating illegal trade in drugs and serious international crimes – were addressed. Their work culminated in the adoption of the Schengen Implementing Convention on 19 June 1990 (Schengen II) between the same five contracting States. This Convention entered into force on 1 September 1993 and became operative from 26 March 1995 between the five original members and Spain and Portugal, which had ratified both instruments in the meantime. The following countries have also acceded to the Schengen system – Italy, Greece, Austria, Denmark, Sweden and Finland – although the Schengen system is not yet implemented in most of these countries. The UK and Ireland are outside the Schengen system; the UK considers that the Schengen II will not achieve tight external frontiers, and the UK objections prevent Ireland from acceding to the Convention since it will modify special arrangements between both countries on border controls. The Amsterdam Summit of June 1997 decided to incorporate the Schengen system into the revised TEU. From a legal point of view art K7 TEU permits its incorporation into the JHA. This provision states that:

'The provisions of this Title shall not prevent the establishment or development of closer co-operation between two or more Member States in so far as such co-operation does not conflict with, or impede, that provided for in this Title.'

The Protocol integrating the Schengen II into the framework of the Union and the Protocol on Denmark (which allows Denmark to accede to the Schengen system by preserving the Nordic Union Passport) will enter into force when the Treaty of Amsterdam becomes operative. The Protocol leaves open the opportunity for the UK and Ireland to join at a later date which is unlikely to happen.[108]

Schengen II consists of eight Titles: Title I (Definitions), Title II (The Abolition of Checks at Internal Borders and Movement of Persons), Title III (Policy and Security), Title IV (The Schengen Information System (SIS)), Title V (Transport and Movement of Goods), Title VI (Protection of Personal Data), Title VII (The Establishment of an Executive Committee), Title VIII (Final Provisions).

In the relationship between the Schengen group and the EC, the Commission has always had status of observer at the Schengen meetings. The Schengen system is subordinate to EC law through the compatibility requirement established in art 134 of Schengen II, which states that Schengen provisions shall only apply if they are compatible with EC law. For that reason it was quite easy to incorporate the Schengen system into the TEU. Also, the areas covered by the Schengen II which overlap with measures adopted by the EU or other conventions ratified by all Member States are rendered inoperative and are replaced by the latter. In this respect, the Protocol of 26 April 1994 adopted in Bonn provides that the Schengen II provisions on asylum are replaced by the Dublin Convention from its entry into force.

Consequently, Schengen II constitutes the main arrangement concerning the common treatment of non-EC nationals and a system of common control at external borders. The main features of the Schengen II is that it relaxes internal control at the borders but increases checks at the external borders. Furthermore, if a non-EC national is considered to be unlawfully in one Schengen country, he is deemed to be illegally in all and will be expelled from the Schengen territory. Also, it introduces tight controls on non-EC nationals

---

[108] See the comments of the Amsterdam Summit at the end of this Chapter.

entering the Schengen territory, aimed at eliminating illegal immigration, and strengthens the co-operation between police and immigration authorities. Finally, it sets up a computerised exchange of information known as the Schengen Information System (SIS), located in Strasbourg, which contains information on policing, crime and immigration, including arrest warrants, missing persons, stolen documents and goods, etc. At its heart is the SIRENE system (Supplementary Information Request at the National Entries), an emergency communications system and the central contact point for each Schengen country. Requests for information through the EIS are verified and legally validated.

Schengen II is completed by agreements on readmission concluded with countries neighbouring to the Schengen territory such as Poland, Hungary, the Czech Republic, the North African countries, etc. Under the agreements these countries are obliged to take back those who illegally cross from that country into Schengen territory, overstay or in any other manner break the conditions of entry to Schengen countries, whether their nationals or not. The readmission agreements create a buffer zone outside the Schengen countries. As a result, it offloads a large part of the Schengen countries' responsibility towards refugees and other undesirables to countries which have neither the financial resources nor sufficient experience to deal with these problems. To prevent entry of illegal immigrants or refugees these countries have negotiated similar readmission agreements with their neighbours (for example Poland with Ukraine, etc).

Assessment of JHA on immigration and asylum

The main benefit of having immigration and asylum matters included in the TEU is that all previous informal inter-governmental arrangements are now co-ordinated by the JHA Council. Some of them such as the Dublin Convention are part of JHA, others like Schengen II will be incorporated into it.

Before the TEU inter-governmental co-operation in these matters was criticised for lack of transparency as it deprived the European Parliament and national parliaments of any control over immigration and asylum policy. The old system was outside the EC structure, deliberations of interior ministers were confidential and their agreements secret. In this respect the TEU constitutes an improvement but democratic input is still lacking since Title VI is still based on inter-governmentalism and the involvement of EC institutions is still insufficient. The question of accountability is also important as the EP is more liberal than the Commission or the Council, and by keeping those matters outside the EC structure, the EP cannot scrutinise Member States' policy in these areas.

The separation of competence in visa policy between art 100c EC and art K1(1)–(6) produces surprising results. In this respect in October 1995 the Council on the grounds of art 100c EC issued Regulation 2317/95[109] which enumerates 101 countries whose nationals must be in possession of a visa when entering the territory of the Union. However, the conditions for issue and other aspects of visa policy are within the scope of Title VI. As a result, the arrangements under Schengen II, or national policy on visas in the UK and Ireland, are still valid.

Concrete actions of the JHA Council are based on old arrangements, for example the Dublin Convention is modelled on Schengen II which has been strongly criticised, *inter*

---

[109] OJ L234 3.10.95, p1.

alia, for creating the 'fortress Europe', that is, immigrants and asylum seekers unable to enter nearly all EC and EFTA countries.[110] Even if they cross the external frontiers, almost all EU countries have introduced new stringent laws on asylum, accelerated procedure for 'manifestly unfounded' applications without appeal, and instituted detention for those that could not prove their identity, or prisons and detention centres for all asylum seekers accompanied by mandatory fingerprinting, etc. In addition, measures such as carriers' liability for bringing a person without proper documents into the territory of a Member State, or the examination of asylum request at the border, mean that border guards and stewardesses decide whether a person is entitled to obtain refugee status. Furthermore, the readmission agreements have created the buffer zone outside the EC which in practice means that other countries guard the frontiers of the Union to prevent the entry of undesirables. It confirms the policy of Member States and the Union of shedding the burden in immigration and asylum matters to others – to less developed friendly neighbours in the case of readmission agreements,[111] or to other Contracting Parties to the Geneva Convention of 1951[112] – despite art K2 TEU which provides important safeguards in relation to measures adopted under JHA. They must be dealt with in compliance with the European Convention for the Protection of Human Rights and Fundamental Freedoms and the Convention relating to the Status of Refugees of 28 July 1951, as well as national protective measures granted by Member States to persons persecuted on political grounds.

Finally, while Member States seek to eliminate racial violence they are using the same violence to justify more immigration controls and anti-refugee measures. In this respect, in 1994 the Commission issued a Communication on Immigration and Asylum Policy which set out the approach that should be taken in order to tackle immigration problems. First, the Union must help to eradicate the causes for immigration. The economic conditions many of the immigrants have to live under at home are so appalling that they will try anything to cross the external borders of the Union. They are forced into the asylum admission procedure since there are no other possibilities for them to improve their living standards. Second, the Commission proposes to control immigration by formulating basic principles on admission, conditions of stay and other aspects of immigration policy. Finally, it highlights the necessity of combating racism and xenophobia, and in July 1996 the JHA Council adopted a joint action concerning measures to fight against racism and xenophobia.[113] Each Member State has a duty to ensure effective judicial co-operation to punish racism and xenophobia.[114] The EU proclaimed 1997 the European Year against

---

[110] D O'Keeffe, 'The Schengen Convention: a Suitable Model for European Integration?' (1992) 11 YEL 185–219.

[111] These countries have obtained in return visa-free travel and work opportunities for their nationals and other benefits such as trade concessions, investment, etc.

[112] H U Jessurun d'Oliveira, 'Expanding External and Shrinking Internal Borders: Europe's Defence Mechanism in the Areas of Free Movement, Immigration and Asylum', in *Legal Issues of the Maastricht Treaty*, supra note 2, pp273–274.

[113] OJ L185 24.7.96 p5.

[114] It is worth mentioning that a political party such as Le Front National in France legally exists and has seats in the parliament (only one in the last parliamentary elections in 1997, but it is one to many). The leader of Front National, Jean Marie Le Pen, publicly calls for an end of the 'Islamification of France', claims that gas chambers were an insignificant detail and that all immigrants who entered France after 1974 should be sent home. He also favours the introduction of racial segregation at schools. The following Member States have racist electoral parties: Sweden, France, Belgium, Germany and Italy.

racism and xenophobia. The Amsterdam Summit of June 1997 welcomed the agreement on the establishment of the European Monitoring Centre on Racism and Xenophobia which will be based in Vienna.

Internal security

The first initiative in this area went back to 1976 when the Trevi group (an acronym for Terrorism, Radicalism, Extremism, and Political Violence) of interior ministers was established to co-operate on issues of terrorism. This group expanded in mid-1980 to cover the following areas: Trevi 1 (terrorism), Trevi 2 (police training, public order, forensic science, fingerprint data bases, football hooliganism), and Trevi 3 (organised crime and drug traffic, law enforcement on environmental offences, art theft). There are also some *ad hoc* groups, for instance on International Organised Crime set up in 1992, and on Yugoslavia (1993). The Trevi working groups prepare recommendations on topics they examine which serve as the basis for Trevi senior officials reports, which in turn are submitted to Trevi ministers meetings held twice a year prior to the summit meetings of the European Council.

There are many examples of co-operation in internal security matters among Member States before the TEU:[115]

1. On drugs: CELAD (Comité Europénne de Lutte Anti-Drogues) created in 1989 in order to co-ordinate cross-border inquiries and exchange of information. It works with the Pompidou Group which was set up in 1972 under the auspices of the Council of Europe to combat drug abuse and unlawful traffic in drugs, and it comprises almost all European States. CELAD also co-operates with the Dublin Group, which is an international forum as it comprises all EU Members, except Finland, plus the Commission, Australia, Canada, Japan, Norway and the USA, for discussion and co-ordination of police assistance against drug producing and transit countries.
2. On money-laundering of drug profits: GAFI (Groupe d'Action Financière Internationale).
3. On terrorism: PWGOT (the Police Working Group on Terrorism) which was set up in 1979. It is made up of the special branches of all Member States. There is also the Vienna Group which was established in 1978 to combat terrorism and comprises Germany, Italy, Austria, Switzerland and France.
4. On fraud: UCLAF (Unité de Co-ordination de la Lutte Anti-Fraude), which was established in 1988 and acts under the umbrella of the Commission. It comprises officials from the Commission's directorates and representatives from the Member States. It has its own computerised information system, the IRENE (IRregularities, ENquiries, Evaluation). It is considered that each year the EC loses over 10 per cent of its budget due to various kinds of fraud.[116] The EU Convention on the Protection of the European Communities' Financial Interests and its second Protocol are expected to be operational by mid-1998.[117]

---

[115] For a review see R Clutterbuck, *Terrorism, Drugs and Crime in Europe after 1992*, London: Routledge, 1990.

[116] According to the Report on Fraud issued by the Commission in 1996 losses caused by fraud were estimated at ECU 1.3 billion ($1.4 billion): (1997) The European 8–14 May p2. In general for comparative treatment of fraud see J van der Hulst (ed), *EC Fraud*, Deventer: Kluwer, 1993; for fraud in the EC see L de Moor, 'The Legal Protection of the Financial Interests of the European Community', ibid, pp11–17.

[117] OJ C316 27.11.95 p48.

Under Title VI the work of Trevi groups and other organisations, is co-ordinated by the JHA Council. Among the new initiatives, the most interesting is the creation of Europol (European Police Office), a European criminal investigation body. According to art K1(9) Europol is one of the matters of common interest, and the aim is to strengthen police co-operation in 'preventing and combating terrorism, unlawful drug trafficking and others serious forms of international crime, including if necessary certain aspects of customs co-operation'. The functions of Europol have been further specified in the Declaration on Police Co-operation annexed to the TEU. The Convention on the Establishment of Europol has not yet come into force,[118] but the first project the European Drugs Unit (EDU) became operational on 1 January 1994 and has its seat in The Hague. Under the Ministerial Agreement on the Establishment of the Europol Drug Unit signed in Copenhagen on 2 June 1993, the EDU's main objective is to co-ordinate and examine intelligence on drugs trafficking and associated money laundering.[119]

The work of EDU is taken into consideration by the European Monitoring Centre for Drugs and Addiction (EMCDDA) which was set up in February 1993. It collects, examines and compares the existing data in this area and co-operates with European and international bodies. It has its own computer network the European Information Network on Drugs and Drug Addiction (REITOX).

Judicial co-operation

Very often judicial co-operation is treated as a less important component of Title VI, although its contribution to the domain of justice should not be undermined. It is indeed a necessary complement of police co-operation.

Judicial co-operation is carried out by two working groups: on criminal and civil law. They draft conventions and agreements in those areas, submit amendments concerning existing conventions, for example the Brussels Convention on Jurisdiction and the Enforcement of Foreign Judgments in Civil and Commercial Matters, the Convention on Extradition, etc. Also they recommend adoption of international conventions prepared by the Council of Europe, The Hague Conference on Private International Law, the Rome Institute, etc, to Member States.

The importance of judicial co-operation was acknowledged by the JHA Council when it adopted a common action on 22 April 1996 concerning the exchange of liaison magistrates which aimed to improve judicial co-operation among the Member States of the Union.[120]

---

[118] OJ C316 27.11.95 p2.

[119] M den Boer, 'Police Co-operation in the TEU: Tiger in a Trojan Horse' (1995) 32 CMLR pp569–72.

[120] Joint Action of 22 April 1996 concerning a framework for the exchange of liaison magistrates to improve judicial co-operation between Member States (OJ L105 27.4.96 p1). Closer co-operation in judicial matters has been re-inforced by two joint actions: Joint Action of 28 October 1996 on a programme of incentives and exchanges for legal practitioners (Grotius) (OJ L287 8.11.96 p3), and Joint Action of 28 October 1996 introducing a programme of training exchanges and co-operation in the field of identity documents (Sherlock) (OJ L287 8.11.97 p7).

3.4 Draft Treaty of Amsterdam

At 3 am on 18 June 1997 the draft Treaty intended to revise the TEU was signed by Heads of State or Government in Amsterdam. Its final version was to be submitted for approval to the European summit in October 1997. The Commission President, Jacques Santer, resumed the Amsterdam Summit in the following words: 'We set our sights high but had to make do with something less ambitious',[121] although the European Council congratulated itself for successfully concluding the Inter-governmental Conference and achieving a consensus on the project of a new treaty on the basis of Document CONF 4001/97. Indeed, the biggest disappointment of the Amsterdam Summit was the abandonment of further integration of the EU into a federal structure which is clearly demonstrated by the disagreement on the institutional reform. Such important issues as the size of the Commission, the redistribution of voting weights at the Council, etc, were left unsettled. In this respect art 2 of the Protocol on the Institutions with the Prospect of Enlargement of the EU annexed to the Draft Treaty provides: 'At least one year before the membership of the European Union exceeds twenty, a conference of the governments of Member States shall be convened in order to carry out a comprehensive review of the provisions of the Treaties on the composition and functioning of the Institutions.' The small Member States, which usually strongly support supra-nationality, were neither prepared to renounce to their right to national representation in the Commission nor to agree on the reform on voting within the Council which would diminish their importance but make the Council more representative of the interests of people of the EU as opposed to the Member States. Furthermore, Germany, one of the main driving forces of unification at Maastricht, strongly opposed any expansion of the EU competences at the expense of national and regional governments. Helmut Kohl blocked the extension of the majority voting in the Council in industrial policy, social policy, transfer of pensions, social security rights, recognition of professional diplomas, and many other areas. He also opposed the majority voting in asylum, visa and immigration policies. As a result, for at least five years, that is until the review is due, unanimity will be required in decisions concerning those areas. The reversal of the priorities of Germany which now focuses on EMU, instead of the political union as a main instrument of the integration of Germany into the EU, led to the confirmation by the Amsterdam Summit of the Stability Pact and the adoption of the future European Monetary System (EMS II) for the final stage of monetary union and the texts establishing the legal status of the single currency. In order to avoid the French veto on those issues, a resolution on growth and employment to complement the stability pact was adopted by the Amsterdam Summit, although the basic disagreement between France and Germany over macro-economic policy is far from being settled.

The UK, Finland, Sweden and Ireland blocked the merger of the Western European Union with the EU. As a result, NATO remains the main defence force of Europe. The Amsterdam Summit agreed to incorporate the Schengen system into the EU but the UK and Ireland opted out from common border control. The implementation of a common foreign policy is subject to unanimity. A Member State may block any decision in this area on the

---

[121] (1997) The Guardian 19 June p16.

113

ground of the Luxembourg-style agreement, that is that if its vital interests are affected. Other important issues such as the reform of the Common Agricultural Policy, the structural funds and the EU budget were left unresolved until the enlargement negotiations. Furthermore, the Amsterdam Summit accepted a multi-speed Europe. Thus, under the enhanced co-operation flexibility, some Member States will be able to move forward in a number of areas without waiting for other Member States, provided that the Council agrees by a qualified majority. Finally, the decision concerning future enlargement was postponed. The Amsterdam Summit declared that in the December meeting in Luxembourg it would take necessary decisions on the overall enlargement process based on the Commission opinions issued by mid-July, its communication 'Agenda 2000' and the comments of the Council (General Affairs) on both documents.

On the brighter side, the main points of the new draft Treaty of Amsterdam are:

1. The confirmation of the Stability Pact and the timetable for EMU.
2. The suspension of rights of a Member State which violates basic freedoms. The principles of liberty, democracy, respect for human rights and fundamental freedoms and the rule of law on which the EU is founded have been recognised as conditions for admission of a new Member, and thus resulted in the amendment of art O TEU and, more importantly, their violation by a Member State is punishable under a new art FA. This provision states that Council meeting in the composition of the Heads of State or Government and acting by unanimity on the proposal by one-third of the Member States or by the Commission and after obtaining the assent from the EP may determine the existence of a violation of those fundamental freedoms, and then acting by a qualified majority may decide to suspend certain rights of the defaulting Member State, including the suspension of its voting rights in the Council.
3. The creation of the zone of freedom, security and justice for EC citizens within five years of the Treaty's ratification, which encompasses the establishment of the freedom of movement throughout the EU and thus the abolition of the border controls between Member States. This is a sign of a supreme trust of one Member State in other Member States, especially taking into account that some Member States such as Italy or Greece have long and open coasts, and others such as Austria have a small number of external border guards. This is to be completed by the incorporation of the Schengen system into the EC Treaty.[122] The new arrangements bring the areas of visa policy, the terms of issuing residence permits to immigrants, asylum procedures and rules governing judicial co-operation in civil matters, such as divorce laws, within the realm of the Community rules with a role to play for the EP, the Commission and the ECJ, which will have jurisdiction over those matters. However, for the next five years decisions in those areas will be adopted by unanimity in the Council. At the end of that period a majority vote may be introduced. However, the UK and Ireland will retain border controls at ports and airports. The UK justified its opt-out on the basis of its special situation as an island nation, as well as the importance of passport controls which is the main tool in the fight against organised crime and drug smuggling. Furthermore, the acceptance of open borders by the UK would necessitate the introduction of identity cards which is a very

---

[122] See Chapter 5.

controversial issue in the UK. Also, the question of immigration and asylum seekers will remain within the national competences of both countries, although it seems that despite tight border controls there are an estimated one million illegal immigrants in the UK.[123] Similarly, it is considered that estimated £2.4 billion of criminal money is laundered through the City of London.[124] However, co-operation between the police forces and other national bodies in charge of criminal matters is still subject to Pillar 3, and as such based on inter-governmental arrangements and takes two forms: through Europol or directly between the policies of the Member States. The Amsterdam Summit decided to confer an operational role to Europol, the intelligence-gathering agency and the EU's embryonic police force. Its priority is to co-ordinate Member States' actions against international money laundering, and to combat drug smuggling as well as the illegal import of nuclear materials, stolen vehicles, illegal immigration networks, trafficking of human beings and the sexual exploitation of children.

Furthermore, the scope of the principle of non-discrimination was extended to cover discrimination based on 'sex, racial or ethnic origin, religion or belief, disability, age or sexual orientation'.[125] This was completed by a Declaration to the Final Act regarding persons with a disability, which emphasises that their situation should be taken into account in drafting proposals under art 100a. The prohibition of discrimination between men and women was strengthened by amendments to arts 2 and 3 EC requiring the Community to promote equality between men and women. Also, the Amsterdam Summit issued a Declaration on the Abolition of the Death Penalty which has been abolished in most of the Member States and has not been applied in any of them.

4. The inclusion of a chapter on employment. France threatened to veto the Stability Pact if its project on a Europe-wide job-creation scheme was rejected. As a result, a new approach towards policy co-ordination, in respect of growth and employment as part of the preparation for EMU, was adopted by the Amsterdam Summit. First, the European Investment Bank[126] will finance socially useful employment projects and, second, anti-unemployment strategy will be co-ordinated at the Community level in order to ensure that Member States' combined policies do not result in a recession for the whole area. Maximising opportunities for growth could reduce unemployment in the EU by between five and seven per cent. This policy is based on the US model, that is the use of monetary expansion and very low interest rates to launch the economy, which resulted in sustainable non-inflationary growth for the last six years and reduced unemployment to 4.8 per cent, while in Europe more than 10.8 per cent of workforce are out of jobs, that is 18.2 million people. The employment policy has been added to the objectives of the

---

[123] (1997) The European June (EP News) p3.

[124] Ibid.

[125] A new art 6a in the EC Treaty.

[126] The European Investment Bank is ready to spend up to ECU one billion by the year 2000 to implement the Amsterdam Summit Resolution on Growth and Employment. On 13 September 1997 the President of the EIB presented an interim report in this respect to the informal Council meeting of EU Economy and Finance Ministers at Mondorf-les-Bains. A comprehensive report on the EIB's three-year Amsterdam special programme will be presented during the Special Job summit on 21 November 1997 in Luxembourg: *European Report*, no 2251, 17 September 1997, p2.

Treaty.[127] In the Resolution of the European Council on Growth and Employment it was stressed that employment is at the top of the political agenda of the EU. The new title on Employment involves the Community institutions in the task of fighting unemployment in the EU and co-ordinating national employment policies of the Member States. A new advisory body, the Employment Committee, will be created by the Council after consulting the EP to promote co-ordination between Member States on employment and labour market policies. Social protection of workers has been strengthened and special emphasis is put on combating 'social exclusion', and those living on the margins of society. The UK decided to join the Social Protocol. As a result it has been incorporated into the Treaty provisions on social policy, education, training and youth.

5. The extension of powers of the EP. The clear winner at the Amsterdam Summit is the EP. The co-decision procedure has been extended to 15 existing Treaty provisions (such as free movement and right of establishment, social security for migrant workers, transport policy, and including the implementation of decisions concerning the Social and Regional Funds and vocational training, trans-European networks, research, environment and development aid) and eight new Treaty areas (such as employment policy, equal opportunities, public health, measures aimed at combating fraud, transparency, customs co-operation, statistics and the establishment of the new body on data protection). However, in some areas, for example in asylum and immigration matters which were transferred to Pillar 1, the requirement of unanimity in the Council limits the application of the co-decision procedure. The attempt by the EP to include the freedom of movement and social security of immigrant workers were defeated. The co-decision procedure itself has been simplified. The assent procedure has been extended to only one area, that is concerning sanctions imposed on a Member State in breach of fundamental principles under art FA. It was also agreed that the EP should not exceed 700 members. In addition, the EP is to prepare a proposal concerning a uniform electoral procedure to the EP based on proportional representation, but taking into account principles common to all Member States which must be submitted to them. In this respect the EP may resubmit its 1993 draft since the UK agreed to proportional representation for the 1999 elections to the EP.

The draft Treaty encompasses national parliaments in the legislative decision-making procedures in the EU in order to give then an opportunity to express their views on matters which may be of particular interest to them. It requires the Commission to promptly forward all proposals to national parliaments. Proposals cannot be placed before the Council for six weeks after it is made available to national parliaments subject to exceptions based on urgency.

6. In the area of foreign and security policy there are no major changes. As before it is based on inter-governmental co-operation. The decisions are taken by unanimity; however, in the case of a decision adopted by a majority voting, a Member State may declare it contrary to its national interests and thus block its adoption. The President of the Council will represent the Union and will be assisted by a Secretary-General.

7. The establishment of a general principle of 'openness' on the basis of which EU citizens will be entitled to have access to documents from the Council, the Commission and the

---

[127] Amendments to art B TEU and arts 2 and 3 EC.

EP. However, a Member State can ask that some documents may not be consulted without its consent.

8. Among miscellaneous matters, Belgium was particularly pleased by a declaration on sports teams which emphasises the social importance of sport 'in particular its role in forging identity and bringing people together'. France and Spain were very satisfied by the amendment of art 227(2) EC which now expressly acknowledges special needs of outermost regions such as the French overseas departments, Madeira, the Canary Islands and the Azores. Austria and the UK praised new clauses on animal welfare inserted into the Treaty.

It is interesting to note that Mr Blair, the UK Prime Minister, made a constructive contribution at the Amsterdam Summit which was noticed by representatives of other Member States.[128] He himself declared before the British House of Commons that:

> 'We have proved to the people of Britain that we can get a better deal by being constructive, and we have proved to Europe that Britain can be a leading player, setting a new agenda that faces the real challenges of the new century'.[129]

---

[128] (1997) The Guardian 19 June p16.
[129] Ibid, p10.

4 External Competences of the European Community[1]

4.1 Competences of the Community

4.2 Competences of the Community in international relations

Competences of the Communities[1] will be examined from two perspectives: international (or external) in this chapter, since the Communities are subjects of public international law and possess international legal personality; and national (or internal) in Chapter 5, that is from the point of view of the important competences attributed to the Communities by Member States resulting in the shrinkage of their individual spheres of competence or by limitations imposed on their sovereignty.

The term 'competence' means that the Communities are empowered to take legislative measures and participate in some international activities. It has a different meaning in relation to the European Communities and the European Union.[2]

In relation to the European Communities this term refers to the allocation of competences to entities which have legal personality. Articles 6 ECSC, 210 EC and 184 Euratom expressly state that the Communities enjoy distinct legal personality. However, apart from art 6(2) ECSC, which expressly refers to international legal personality by stating that 'in international relations, the Community shall enjoy the legal capacity it requires to perform its functions and attain its objectives', it was uncertain whether the remaining Communities were also endowed with international personality or solely enjoyed legal personality in each Member State. The uncertainty resulted from the combined effect of arts 210 and 211 EC. Article 210 EC states that the Community shall have legal personality, while art 211 EC adds that in each Member State the EC:

'... shall enjoy the most extensive legal capacity accorded to legal persons under their laws; it may, in particular, acquire or dispose of movable and immovable property and may be a party to legal proceedings'.[3]

This point was clarified in Case 6/64 *Costa* v *ENEL*[4] in which the ECJ extended international legal personality to the EC. The ECJ emphasised that under art 210 EC it is 'a Community of

---

[1] The competences of ECSC and the Euratom are not examined in this chapter since ECSC is limited to coal and steel while Euratom deals with nuclear energy. The subject-matter of both Communities determine their competences.

[2] Under public international law the term 'power' or 'jurisdiction' is used to describe what the term 'competence' means under EC law. These terms are interchangeable. However, in relation to external competence of the EC the term 'jurisdiction' is used to emphasise the special status of the Community in international relations.

[3] In relation to this capacity the Communities are represented in Member States by the Commission on the ground of the Protocol on the Privileges and Immunities of the European Communities annexed to the Merger Treaty of 1965 (OJ L152 13.7.67 p1). For a recent case on the Protocol see Case C–88/92 *Van Rosendaal* v *Staatssecretaris van Financien* [1993] ECR I–3315.

[4] [1964] ECR 585.

unlimited duration, having its own institutions, its own personality, its own legal capacity, and capacity of representation on the international plane'.[5] In Opinion 1/78[6] the ECJ interpreted art 184 Euratom is a similar way.[7] However, international personality is conferred only to the Communities not to their institutions.[8]

The Merger Treaty of 8 April 1965 envisaged the fusion of all Communities and thus the creation of a single legal personality for all Communities. Nevertheless, it was decided, at that time, to postpone their merger for an indefinite period. As a result, the three Communities established by, and made up of, the Member States possess competences similar to these enjoyed by sovereign States under public international law. The ECJ has jurisdiction to ensure that the Communities act within the limits of their competences and can take sanctions against any *ultra vires* act of the Communities, or against any transgression by the Member States into competences allocated to the Communities.

In the context of the European Union the terms 'competences' means that certain areas are open to common actions of the Member States which must be adopted within a specific institutional framework but without any intervention from the ECJ since the latter has no jurisdiction in matters falling under inter-governmental co-operation among Member States. The Union has no international personality and no treaty-making power. However, the recommendation of the 1996 IGC has been taken into consideration by the Member States. The final report of the Reflection Group for the 1996 IGC highlights the advantages and disadvantages of conferment of international personality to the Union in the following terms:

> 'A majority of members point to the advantage of international legal personality for the Union so that it can conclude international agreements on the subject-matter of Titles V and VI concerning the CFSP and the external dimension of justice and home affairs. For them, the fact that the Union does not legally exist is a source of confusion outside and diminishes its external role. Other consider that the creation of international legal personality for the Union could risk confusion with the legal prerogatives of Member States.'[9]

At the Amsterdam Conference, 16–18 June 1997, the Member States decided that the advantages outweighed the disadvantages. As a result, the draft Treaty of Amsterdam invests the European Union with international personality.

4.1 Competences of the Community

The allocation of competences between the EC and the Member States, whether in international or internal relations, is based on three principles which are defined in art 3b EC, that is the principle of limited powers, the principle of subsidiarity and the principle of proportionality.

---

[5] Ibid.
[6] Opinion 1/78 (Natural Rubber) [1979] ECR 2871.
[7] [1978] ECR 2151.
[8] Case C–327/91 *France v Commission* [1994] ECR I–3641.
[9] RG2, p40.

General principles concerning the allocation of competences

The Treaty of Maastricht for the first time expressly acknowledged all three principles, albeit the ECJ already recognised the principle of limited powers and often made reference to the principle of proportionality to the extent of transforming them into general principles of EC law.

Principle of limited powers

The principle of limited powers is inherent to any legal person. It permits achievement of the objectives assigned to the legal person which constitute its *raison d'être*. Particularly, it applies in the context of international organisations or federal States. The principle of limited powers is defined in art 3b EC in the following terms:

> 'The Community shall act within the limits of the powers conferred upon it by this Treaty and of the objectives assigned to it therein.'

It is also implicit in art 4(1) EC, which requires that EC institutions, in carrying out their task, must act within the limits of powers granted to them by the Treaty.

The principle of limited powers serves as both a justification for a Community action and as its legal basis. It is enforced in the last resort by the ECJ under art 173, which permits annulment of any measure adopted by the Community institutions for lack of competence or infringement of essential procedural requirements. In practice the allocation of powers between the Community and the Member States is neither clearly regulated nor is there any mechanism for the allocation of competences within the Community. As a result, the principle of limited powers is undermined since there are no rigid limits to, or prohibitions against, any extension of Community competences.

Indeed, the case law of the ECJ confirms that it is not necessary to revise the Treaty to expand EC external and internal powers, which is the usual procedure in respect of any international organisation. To the contrary, often amendments to the Treaty recognise a *de facto* expansion of Community competence which had already occurred due to judicial or legislative practice. For instance, EC competence concerning the protection of the environment was recognised by the ECJ in Case 240/83 *ADBHU* [10] which held that environment protection constitutes one of the Community's essential objectives despite the lack of any provision in this respect in the EC Treaty. Subsequently, by virtue of the SEA, protection of environment was added to the Community competence.[11] The ECJ's attitude is not surprising taking into account the following: the EC Treaty refers to the objectives to be attained by the Community but not to its competences; the ECJ applies the teleological method of interpretation of EC law and also favours dynamic expansion of the EC competence. In this respect, it is sufficient to compare the judgment of the ECJ in Case 26/62 *Van Gend en Loos* [12] which stated that by joining the Community the Member States

---

[10] [1985] ECR 531.
[11] Another example is provided in the area of consumer protection, Case C–362/88 *GB-INNO* v *CCL* [1990] ECR I–667. The TEU included consumer protection by virtue of art 129a EC among the activities of the Community, although in practice under the SEA, mainly art 100a(3) EC, many measures were introduced in this area.
[12] [1963] ECR 1.

attributed to the EC institutions their powers 'albeit in limited fields' with the Opinion 1/91[13] which makes reference to 'ever wider fields' of the Community competence.

Principle of proportionality
Article 3b provides that:

> 'Any action by the Community shall not go beyond what is necessary to achieve the objectives of this Treaty.'

The principle of proportionality was recognised by the ECJ in Case 8/55 *Fédération Charbonnière de Belgique v High Authority*[14] and has since become a general principle of Community law. It imposes a limitation upon the exercise of a Community competence because it requires that any action of an EC institution should not go beyond what is necessary to achieve the declared, lawful objective.[15] Second, the measure must be adequate and appropriate vis-à-vis the legitimate objective. Finally, when an EC institution has a choice between a number of appropriate measures it should choose the one which is the least burdensome and the least restrictive, and the disadvantage caused must not be disproportionate to the aims pursued.[16]

Principle of subsidiarity
This has already been examined in Chapter 3. Article 3b EC has an important role to play, although its exact scope of application is still uncertain. It was inserted into the Treaty of Maastricht to counterbalance the Community's tendency to excessively expand its external and internal competences without revising the Treaties.

Acquisition of new competences by the Community without revising the Treaty

In general, the acquisition of a new competence by the Communities requires the revision of the Treaties. Nevertheless, in practice the Communities have extended their powers without revising the Treaties in the following circumstances: on the basis of a general authorisation to legislate (arts 235 EC, 203 Euratom and 95(1) ECSC); and under the doctrine of implied powers.

The general authorisation to legislate: art 235 EC
Article 235 EC provides that if action by the Community is necessary in order to achieve one of the objectives of a common market, but the Treaty has not assigned appropriate competences to the EC in this respect, the Council is empowered to take that necessary measure acting unanimously on a proposal from the Commission and after consulting the European Parliament. As a result, art 235 EC provides the EC with a residual legislative power which has been used extensively to take measures in important areas not covered, at

---

[13] Opinion 1/91 (First EEA Opinion) [1991] ECR 6079.
[14] [1954–56] ECR 245 at 299.
[15] Case 154/78 *Valsabbia* [1980] ECR 907.
[16] Case 265/87 *Schrader* [1989] ECR 2227; Case C–331/88 *Fedesa* [1990] ECR I–4023.

that time, by the EC Treaty, such as environmental protection, regional aid, research and technology.

The acquisition of new competences under art 235 EC has been restricted for three reasons. First, amendments to the founding Treaties have extended EC powers in a number of areas: under the SEA the Community acquired new powers in environmental policy, social and economic cohesion, research and development; and under the Treaty of Maastricht in industrial policy, the trans-European networks, public health, education and cultural policy, consumer protection, energy, civil protection, tourism and economic and monetary union.[17] Second, the principle of subsidiarity, with its presumption in favour of competence at national or regional level, imposes important limitations in this area. Finally, although art 235 has been widely interpreted by the ECJ, there are limits to the objectives of the EC regarding the operation of the common market.[18]

In the past, the Council leant, probably too frequently, upon art 235 EC for two reasons. First, the Paris Summit in October 1972 decided that in order to establish an economic and monetary union, as well as promote the social dimension of the Community, all provisions of the EC Treaty, including art 235, should be widely used. As a result, in the 1970s the Council referred to art 235 EC extensively and systematically. On 15 March 1992, 677 measures both internal and external were adopted on the basis of this provision, and 407 are still operational.[19] It has been used in order to establish new Community bodies such as the European Monetary Co-operation Fund,[20] the Regional Development Fund,[21] and to develop new policies such as protection of consumers, the protection of environment, research outside the programmes covered by Euratom, and energy outside of coal and atomic energy which were within the scope of ECSC and Euratom Treaties. Furthermore, art 235 EC can also provide a legal basis for an external measure and, indeed, has been invoked on many occasions by the EC. For example, to justify its participation in international environmental conventions prior to the SEA,[22] to set up the European Bank for Reconstruction and Development,[23] or to allow the EC to become a contracting party to the World Trade Organisation.[24]

Second, the Council may adopt a measure on the ground of art 235 EC acting unanimously. This requirement constitutes an additional protection for the Member States as it ensures that no measure contrary to interests of any of them is likely to be adopted.

---

[17] Indeed, the extension of competences under the SEA and TEU, as well as the supervision exercised by the Commission over the choice of a legal basis for a Community measure, made by Council deterred the latter from referring to art 235 EC when there is a more appropriate provision in the Treaty for the adoption of a measure in question. Also, recently the ECJ has given restrictive interpretation to art 235 EC: Opinion 1/94 [1994] ECR I–5267; Opinion 2/92 [1995] ECR I– 521; Opinion 2/94 of 28 March 1996, not yet reported.

[18] The 1996 ICG decided not to change art 235: Progress Report on IGC (1996), Presidency Conclusions, European Council in Florence, 21–22 June 1966, Doc. SN 300/96, Annexes, p16. Consequently, it remains exactly the same under the draft Treaty of Amsterdam.

[19] Question no 1130/92 (OJ C285 3.11.92 p1).

[20] Regulation 907/73 (OJ L89 5.4.73 p2).

[21] Regulation 724/75 (OJ L73 21.3.75 p1).

[22] For example, Decision 81/462 concerning the adoption of the Convention on the Conservation of Migratory Species of Wild Animals.

[23] Decision 90/674.

[24] Opinion 1/94 (WTO) [1994] ECR I–5267.

The Commission has challenged before the ECJ the legal basis of certain measures adopted by the Council under art 235 EC. As a result, the ECJ decided in Case 45/86 *Commission v Council*[25] that a measure can only be adopted under art 235 if there is no other appropriate provision in the Treaty which would provide a legal basis for Community action. Article 235 EC was considered as a possible legal basis for the accession of the EC to the European Convention of Human Rights, but the ECJ stated in Opinion 2/94 that this provision is an integral part of the EC institutional system and cannot serve as justification for widening the scope of the EC powers beyond the general framework set up by the Treaty provisions in general and those provisions which refer to the EC's task and activities in particular. It held that:

> '... Article 235, cannot be used as a basis for the adoption of provisions whose effect would, in substance be to amend the Treaty without following the procedure which it provides for that purpose'.[26]

Thus, art 235 EC has been restored to its initial role, that is a measure can be based on this provision only if no other appropriate legal ground can be found in the Treaty.

Implied powers

Certain provisions of EC Treaty determine explicitly the powers of the Community. Articles 3 and 3b EC, together with Title V and VI TEU, enumerate the objectives of the Community which are in fact the EC competences. In these areas the Community is empowered to take all necessary measures to achieve these objectives. In external relations competence of the Community is expressly stated in a number of articles, for example: art 18 EC on the reduction of custom duties; art 109 EC concerning the exchange-rate system for the ECU in relation to non-Community currencies; art 130m EC on co-operation in research, technical development and demonstration; art 130r(4) EC on the protection of environment; art 130y EC on development co-operation; art 238 EC on association agreements, etc.

Powers which do not result directly and expressly from a provision or a number of provisions of the Treaty, but from global and general objectives laid down by the Treaty as interpreted by the ECJ, are known as implied powers. The doctrine of implied powers was recognised by the International Court of Justice in its Advisory Opinion on Reparation for Injuries Suffered in the Service of the United Nations,[27] and endorsed by the ECJ in Case 8/55 *Fédéchar*.[28] The ECJ has mainly applied it in relation to the external competences of the EC, although it also has an internal dimension. In the internal sphere it relates to the powers of EC institutions vis-à-vis Member States. The ECJ held in joined Cases 281, 283–285 and 287/85 *Germany v Commission*[29] that when the Commission is under an

---

[25] [1987] ECR 1493; Case 165/87 *Commission v Council* [1988] ECR 5545, Cases C–51 and 94/89 *UK, France and Germany v Council* [1991] ECR I–2757; Case C–295/90 *EP (supported by the Commission) v Council (supported by the UK and The Netherlands) (Re Student Directive)* [1992] ECR I–4913. On this subject see G Close, 'Harmonisation of Laws: Use or Abuse of the Powers under the EEC Treaty' (1978) 3 ELR 461–81.

[26] Opinion 2/94 (ECHR) of 28 March 1996, para 30 (not yet reported).

[27] [1949] ICJ 174.

[28] [1956] ECR 291.

[29] [1987] ECR 3203.

obligation to carry out a specific task assigned to it by the Treaty, the latter confers on the Commission the necessary powers to carry out that task.

In external relations the general principles on implied powers have been established in Case 22/70 *Commission v Council (ERTA)*.[30] The judgment of the ECJ in this case is also of considerable importance because on the one hand, for the first time the Commission brought an action against the Council and, on the other hand, the so-called ERTA principles have been recently confirmed in Opinion 1/94 (WTO),[31] and thus the ECJ rejected its own interpretation of external implied powers[32] and returned to the doctrine of parallelism.

ERTA, a European agreement on the working practices of international road transport crews, was signed in Geneva on 19 January 1962. Amongst the signatories were five of the original Member States. The agreement did not come into force as it lacked sufficient ratification and negotiations resumed in 1967. Similar work at a Community level resulted in Regulation 543/69 of 25 March 1969. On 20 March 1970 the Council discussed the attitude to be taken in the ERTA negotiations. Member States conducted and concluded the ERTA negotiations on the basis of the 20 March 1970 meeting. The Commission lodged an application for annulment of the proceedings of the Council 20 March 1970 on the grounds that the issue of Regulation 543/69 transferred the competence for a common transport policy to the Community and that the Council had infringed arts 75 and 228 EC Treaty.

The ECJ held that the ERTA agreement had been in the process of negotiation since 1962, a considerable time before the issue of Regulation 543/69. Despite the Commission's claim that the Council had infringed art 75, the Commission had in fact made no attempt to make any submission to the Council under art 75(c), nor did the Commission make any application to the Council in pursuance of its right to carry out these negotiations under art 228(1). In the light of the above the submission was rejected.

In this case the Court not only settled a dispute between the Commission and the Council but also adopted a radical approach towards the expansion of Community competences by establishing important general principles in this area, first, on the attribution of powers to the EC, and, second, on their exclusive nature. With regard to attributed powers the ECJ stated that in order to determine in a particular case the Community competence to enter into international agreements 'regard must be had to the whole scheme of the Treaty no less than its substantive provisions'. As a result, the EC powers 'arise not only from an express conferment by the Treaty – as is the case with arts 113 and 114 EC for tariff and trade agreements and with art 238 EC for association agreements – but may equally flow from other provisions of the Treaty and from measures adopted, within the framework of those provisions, by the Community institutions'.[33] The ECJ endorsed the doctrine of parallelism under which the external competence is not limited to express provisions of the Treaty but may also derive from other provisions of the Treaty and from internal measures adopted within the framework of those provisions.

On the exclusive nature of Community powers the ECJ stated that where the Community has adopted Community rules within the framework of a common policy, the

---

[30] [1971] ECR 263.
[31] [1994] ECR I–5267.
[32] In Cases 3, 4 and 6/76 *Kramer* [1976] ECR 1279 and Opinion 1/76 (Rhine Navigation) [1977] ECR 741.
[33] Ibid, note 30, para 16.

Member States are not allowed, individually or collectively, to enter into agreements with third States in the areas affected by those rules. 'As and when such common rules come into being, the Community alone is a position to assume and carry out contractual obligations towards third countries affecting the whole sphere of application of the Community legal system.'[34]

Under art 228 EC the ECJ further clarified its position on both points.

Doctrine of parallelism The doctrine of parallelism means that the internal competence of the Community should be matched by the external competence – *in interno in foro externo* – that is, if the EC has express powers in internal matters it should also be entitled to extend them to external relations in those areas. Implied powers may be based on the provisions of the Treaty or upon measures adopted by Community institutions within the framework of those provisions. In Opinion 2/91(ILO)[35] the ECJ held that implied external powers may flow even from measures adopted under art 235 EC. The most controversial question in relation to implied external powers of the Community is whether the latter is empowered to exercise external powers in the absence of any internal measures. In the *ERTA* case the ECJ held that the Community cannot use an implied external competence in the absence of internal measures. The limitation thus imposed was slowly lifted in the subsequent cases. In Opinion 1/75 (OECD Local Cost Standard)[36] the ECJ held that the common commercial policy consisted of interaction between external and internal measures and refused to give priority to either. In Opinion 1/76 (Rhine Navigation Case)[37] the Court decided that when EC law had created powers for the institutions of the Community within its internal system in order to attain a specific objective, the EC had authority to enter into the international commitments necessary for the attainment of that objective, even in the absence of any internal measure. The ECJ held that:

> 'Although the internal Community measures are only adopted when the international agreement is concluded and made enforceable, as is envisaged in the present case by the proposal for a Regulation to be submitted to the Council and the Commission, the power to bind the Community vis-à-vis third countries nevertheless flows by implication from the provision of the Treaty creating the internal power and in so far as participation of the Community in the international agreement is, as here, necessary for the attainment of one of the objectives of the Community.'[38]

In joined Cases 3, 4 and 6/76 *Kramer*[39] the ECJ has reconfirmed the existence of the implicit competence of the Community corresponding to its internal competence and susceptible to be extended *ratione materiae* if an analogous competence is conferred to a State under public international law. This wide interpretation of the Community implied external competences was first limited in Opinion 2/91 (ILO Convention) in which the ECJ held they arise only 'whenever Community law created for the institutions of the

---

[34] Ibid, note 30, para 18.
[35] [1993] ECR I–1061.
[36] [1975] ECR 1355; [1976] 1 CMLR 85.
[37] [1977] ECR 741.
[38] Ibid, para 4.
[39] [1976] ECR 1279, paras 44–45.

Community powers within its internal system for the purpose of obtaining a specific objective'.[40] As a result, the participation of the EC in external relations based on the doctrine of implied powers is conditional upon the necessity to achieve a 'specific objective' of the EC which cannot be attained without the participation of third States. In Opinion 1/94 (WTO)[41] the ECJ abandoned altogether its generous interpretation of external implied powers and re-affirmed its judgment in *ERTA*. Thus, the Community is prevented from exercising its implied external powers in the absence of internal measures.[42]

Exclusive competence The distinction between exclusive competences of the Community and competences which the EC shares with Member States has important practical implications. If the competence is exclusive, Member States are prevented from acting unilaterally or collectively in this area, once the Community has itself acted. This principle also applies to implicit external competences as the ECJ pointed out in the *ERTA* judgment. The EC, in internal or external relations, replaces the Member States.

In Opinion 1/75 (OECD Local Cost Standard)[43] the Court stated that the Community has exclusive competence in the area of commercial policy and, as a result, Member States must refrain from concurrent actions. In this opinion export credit agreements within the Organisation for Economic Co-operation and Development, an organisation closely connected with export trade, raised the question whether the Member States had concurrent competences within the framework of common commercial policy. The ECJ was clear, the common commercial policy which resulted from art 113 EC was within the exclusive competence of the Community and necessary to ensure proper functioning of the common market. As such any concurrent action on the part of the Member States in this area would risk undermining the efficient defence of Community's global interests, distort the institutional framework of the EC and call into question the mutual trust within the Community, since Member States would pursue commercial policy based on their national interests. An exclusive competence over the conservation of fisheries has also been confirmed.[44]

The latest statement of the ECJ in this area was delivered in Opinion 1/94 (WTO).[45] The Commission asked the ECJ a number of questions in relation to the WTO:

1. Whether the EC has exclusive competence to conclude the Multilateral Agreements on Trade in Goods, in so far as those Agreements covered products under the ECSC and Euratom Treaties.
2. Whether the EC has exclusive competence under art 113 EC, or alternatively under other provisions of EC Treaty, to conclude the General Agreement on Trade in Services (GATS) and the Agreement on Trade-related Aspects of Intellectual Property Rights (TRIPs) within the framework of the GATT agreements which culminated in the Uruguay Round.

---

[40] [1993] ECR I–1061, para 7.
[41] [1994] ECR I–5267.
[42] It was confirmed in Opinion 2/92 (OECD National Treatment Instrument) [1995] ECR I–521.
[43] [1975] ECR 1355; [1976] 1 CMLR 85.
[44] Case 804/79 *Commission v UK* [1981] ECR 1045.
[45] [1994] ECR I–5267.

The GATS and TRIPs agreements are modelled on GATT rules; GATS applies to trade in all services apart from services supplied in the exercise of governmental authority and regulates four forms of services, that is, cross-border supply of services, consumption abroad, commercial presence and movement of persons. As a result, it covers not only supply of services but also establishment of the supply of services. The TRIPs agreement encompasses all intellectual property rights.

On 15 November 1994 the ECJ delivered advisory Opinion 1/94 (WTO)[46] and held that the EC has exclusive competence under art 113 EC to conclude Multilateral Agreements on Trade in Goods, including the Agreement on Agriculture and goods subject to the Euratom and ECSC Treaties. In relation to the first point, that is, the Multilateral Agreements on Trade in Goods, the situation required clarification since the Tokyo Round Agreement on Technical Barriers to Trade was concluded jointly by the EC and the Member States, and the ECJ confirmed the exclusive competence of the EC in this area. On trade in ECSC and Euratom products with third countries the ECJ restated its previous position, that it is covered under art 113 and as such within the exclusive competence of the EC apart from agreements relating specifically to ECSC products.

However, many areas were excluded by the ECJ from the scope of art 113 EC: international transport, all services but the cross-frontier supplies of services, the TRIPs agreement apart from its provisions regarding the prohibition of the release into free circulation of counterfeit goods already governed by Regulation 3842/86. As a result, competence to conclude GATS and TRIPs is shared between the EC and the Member States.

There is one passage in Opinion 1/94 which especially elucidates this matter. It provides that:

> '... the Community's exclusive external competence does not automatically flow from its power to lay down rules at internal level. As the Court pointed out in the *ERTA* judgment (paragraphs 17 and 18), the Member States, whether acting individually or collectively, only lose their right to assume obligations with non-Member countries as and when common rules which could be affected by those obligations come into being. Only in so far as common rules have been established at internal level does the external competence of the Community become exclusive.'[47]

Opinion 1/94 has limited the competences of the EC as it excluded many areas from the scope of art 113 EC.

The situation is different if the Community has not exercised its powers in the area in which it has exclusive competence. In Cases 3, 4–6/76 *Kramer* (see above) the ECJ confirmed that the Community has exclusive competence in the protection of fishing grounds and conservation of the biological resources of the sea once the transitional period provided for in art 102 of the Act of Accession of the UK expires, that is from 1 January 1979. It meant that until that date, the Community and the Member States had concurrent competence in this area and thus the latter were empowered to adopt national measures in the absence of Community measures, provided they observed procedural and substantial

---

[46] For commentary on Opinion 1/94 see J H J Bourgeois, 'The EC in the WTO and Advisory Opinion 1/94: AN Echternach Procession' (1995) 32 CMLR, 763–787.

[47] [1994] ECR I–5267, para 77.

provisions of Community law in this respect.[48] If the Community persists in its failure to act, the Member States have a duty to act but the adopted conservation measures must respond to the collective interest of the Community.[49] With the expiry of the transitional period, and provided the Community fails to act national measures continue to apply and may even be modified in order to respond to the changing biological and technical requirements. However, the Member States are regarded as not exercising national competence but acting in a framework of the exclusive competence of the Community. As a result, they are the depository of a common interest of the Community and as such they must not only consult but also obtain the approval of the Community in respect of the adopted measures.[50]

With respect to concurrent competence, the Member States are allowed to act within the limitations imposed by the Treaty provisions as long as the EC is inactive. Those limitations mean that a Member State cannot adopt measures contrary to the Community's position, for example the principle of non-discrimination on the ground of nationality,[51] and more importantly it must pay a special regard to art 5 EC, that is take all appropriate measures to ensure fulfilment of its obligations arising out of the Treaty or resulting from action taken by Community institutions, and abstain from any measure which could jeopardise the attainment of the Treaty objectives. The obligation of co-operation between the Community and the Member States has been emphasised by the ECJ in Opinion 1/94 in which the Court held that:

> '... where it is apparent that the subject-matter of an agreement or convention falls in part within the competence of the Community and in part within that of the Member States, it is essential to ensure close co-operation between the Member States and the Community institutions, both in the process of negotiation and conclusion and in the fulfilment of the commitments entered into. That obligation to co-operate flows from the requirement of unity in the international representation of the Community'.[52]

Once the Community takes action in a particular area, the field is occupied and under the principle of supremacy of Community law the Member States are prevented from taking any action, even if it improves any EC measure in this area. Community action transforms concurrent competence in the field which it occupies into exclusive competence.

Mixed agreements

An agreement is considered as mixed when the Community and one or more of the Member States are contracting parties to it. The basic feature of a mixed agreement is that neither party can conclude an agreement without the other as only together are the Community and the Member States able to fulfil all their obligations deriving from it. Mixed agreements are necessary if the Member States and the Community share competence in a particular field or if, for whatever reason, the participation of the Member States is required. They may

---

[48] Case 141/78 *France* v *UK* [1979] ECR 2923.
[49] Case 32/79 *Commission* v *UK* [1980] ECR 2403.
[50] Case 804/79 *Commission* v *UK* [1981] ECR 1045.
[51] Case 61/77 *Commission* v *Ireland* [1978] ECR 417.
[52] [1994] ECR I–5267, para 108; also see Ruling 1/78 (Nuclear Material Case) [1978] ECR 2151 and Opinion 2/91 (ILO) [1993] ECR I–1061.

be bilateral like the Lomé Conventions, which create obligations between the ACP (African, Caribbean and Pacific) countries on one side and the EC and the Member States on the other side, or multilateral such as the UN Convention on the Law of the Sea 1982 which imposes obligations upon all contracting parties. Only art 102 ECSC expressly provides for mixed agreements, but the ECJ has extended this possibility to EC and Euratom.[53]

The Treaty of Maastricht has expressly recognised mixed agreements in many areas such as protection of environment (art 130r(4) EC), development co-operation (art 130y EC), etc.[54] There is a growing tendency for the Member States to include the EC in any international agreements by inserting provisions which require the participation of the Community and which result in a mixed agreement. Whether this attitude undermines the credibility of the EC or, to the contrary, enhances its international position is a matter of controversy. It is submitted that the opinion of Weiler, who emphasised the positive influence of mixed agreements on European integration as they bring together the EC and the Member States, eliminate tension and 'by constituting a growing network whereby Community and Member States gain in international strength simultaneously and become among themselves even further inextricably linked',[55] should be preferred.

Mixed agreements can also be concluded for other reasons, such as reinforcing the Community influence within an international organisation by securing voting rights for the Member States or ensuring that the Member States rather than the Community financially contribute to the achievement of the objectives of an agreement. In the first case, the best example is provided by the Community membership in the World Trade Organisation which has replaced the General Agreement on Tariffs and Trade (GATT). The WTO came into existence on 1 January 1995. If the EC, but not the Member States, is a sole contracting party to the WTO then it would have only one vote as any other contracting party. However, if the EC and all Member States are the members of the WTO, its bargaining power and international standing greatly increases as together they would have 16 votes. Whether this is a wise strategy is doubtful in the context of the WTO. Nowadays, trade negotiations are conducted between the three competing blocs: the EC, NAFTA (the North American Free Trade Agreement formed by the United States together with Canada and Mexico) and ASEAN (the Association of South East Asian Nations, led by Japan). The interdependence and the globalisation of the economy require that all three blocks act within the international framework, and thus it seems unrealistic that any important decision would be adopted by the WTO with the opposition of one of the major world commercial powers.

As to the conclusion of mixed agreements for financial reasons in Opinion 1/78 (Natural Rubber)[56] the ECJ stated that the an agreement setting up a buffer stock in relation to trade in natural rubber financed by the contracting parties was not within the EC exclusive competence since it established a 'financial instrument'. Therefore, participation of the

---

[53] Ruling 1/78 (Nuclear Material Case) [1978] ECR 2151; Opinion 1/78 (Natural Rubber) [1979] ECR 2871; Opinion 2/91 (ILO) [1993] ECR I–1061; Opinion 1/94 (WTO) [1994] ECR I–5267; Case 316/91 *Parliament v Council* [1994] ECR I–625, especially the opinion of the A-G Jacobs.

[54] These provisions state that the EC and the Member States 'shall act within their respective spheres of competence'.

[55] J Weiler, 'The External Relations of Non-Unitary Actors: Mixity and the Federal Principle', in D O'Keeffe and H G Schermars (eds), *Mixed Agreements*, Dordrecht: Nijhoff, 1983, p85.

[56] [1979] ECR 2871.

Member States was necessary since the agreement imposed not only important financial obligations upon them but also because that financial commitment constituted the essence of the agreement. Indeed, the nature of agreement, rather than the manner of financing it requires, is crucial. When the Member States invoked the financial argument in relation to the agreement on the WTO, the ECJ specified that in the case of an international organisation which has no financial policy instrument, but only an operating budget, the fact that its expenditure would be charged directly to the contracting parties cannot in itself justify the participation of the Member States in the conclusion of the WTO agreement.[57]

However, mixed agreements create many difficulties at the internal and external levels, mainly because the allocation of competence between the Community and the Member States is still unclear and is especially confusing for third countries. They often require specific declarations on the respective competences of the EC and the Member States regarding negotiation, conclusion and implementation of international agreements.[58]

4.2 Competences of the Community in international relations

International personality refers to the capacity to be a bearer of rights and duties under public international law. The typical subjects of international law are sovereign States. International personality may be unlimited as it is in the case of independent States or limited which applies to dependent States or international organisations. The International Court of Justice has recognised the diversity of international personality by stating that: 'the subjects of law in any legal system are not necessarily identical in their nature or in the extent of their rights'.[59] The Communities as international organisations enjoy limited international personality. The extent of their competences has been determined by the Member States in the original Treaties as amended over the years and clarified by case law of the ECJ. The Communities have been granted the capacity to enter into relations and to conclude treaties with third States and other organisations. Further, the Communities and especially the most active and important among them, the EC, are the only international organisations that possess and exercise an independent power to make binding decisions which affect Member States, corporate bodies situated inside and outside the territory of the Community, for example in competition matters, and EC nationals. Whenever the jurisdiction of a sovereign State is limited, or excluded, by rules of international law, or by voluntary attribution of a State competence to an international entity, it does not disappear. It accrues to other entities which became the actual beneficiaries of such rules. As a result, the Communities to a certain extent exercise powers similar to sovereign States: they have power to regulate the activities of people and to control the use of property within the territory of the Union. This function in relation to a sovereign State is described as jurisdiction. For that reason it seems justified to use the term 'jurisdiction' in order to describe the Communities' competences which usually are enjoyed only by sovereign States.

---

[57] Opinion 1/94 (WTO) [1994] ECR I–5267, para 21.
[58] C D Ehlermann, 'Mixed Agreements, a List of Problems', in D O'Keeffe and H G Schermars (eds), *Mixed Agreements*, supra note 55.
[59] Advisory Opinion in *Reparation for Injury Suffered in the Service of the United Nations* [1949] ICJ 174.

The classification of forms of State jurisdiction can be based on various criteria. For our purposes the selected criteria are:

1. the object of jurisdiction which distinguishes between personal and territorial jurisdiction;
2. the character of the exercise of a State's jurisdiction which results in the forms of ordinary jurisdiction and extraordinary jurisdiction; and
3. the limitations imposed upon the exercise of sovereignty which leads to a distinction between unlimited and limited, the latter concerns the exercise of jurisdiction in the nexus of a plurality of sovereign States.

These classifications can be transposed to the Communities in order to emphasise the special status of the Communities in international relations. Nevertheless, the Communities are supra-national organisations and for that reason the term 'competence' will be used again in relation to their external powers *ratione materiae*. The Community, as an international organisation, suffers some limitations in the exercise of its external competences in the nexus of a plurality of sovereign States and other international organisations.

Territorial and personal jurisdiction of the Community

The most important of the typologies of jurisdiction under public international law is the classification based on territorial and personal jurisdiction. Territorial jurisdiction concerns the authority of a sovereign State over a geographically defined portion of the surface of the earth, and the space above and below it which a State claims as its territory, including all persons and things therein. Personal jurisdiction refers to the jurisdiction assumed by a sovereign over individuals based on allegiance they owe to that sovereign wherever they happen to be, or in the protection of his nationals abroad against breaches of international law by the State of their sojourn or residence.

Territorial jurisdiction

The Communities have no jurisdiction over the territory of the Union in the sense of public international law; they cannot cede or acquire any part or the whole of their territory. The territory of the Union is made up of the territories of the Member States. Any territorial change affecting a Member State affects the territory of the Union. The best example in this respect is provided by the reunification of Germany, and another is provided by Greenland whose secession from the Community was negotiated between Member States. However, the Community may interfere in the delimitation of the spatial scope of application of Community law and thus modify territorial[60] and personal[61] jurisdiction of a Member State. Furthermore, even the ECJ refers to the 'territory of the Community'[62] in the sense of the spatial scope of application of Community law which is not fixed but varies depending on

---

[60] For example, Case 61/77 *Commission v Ireland* [1978] ECR 448 at 509.
[61] Cases 3, 4 and 6/76 *Kramer* [1976] ECR 1279; Case C–286/90 *Poulsen* [1992] ECR I–6019; Case C–280/89 *Commission (supported by Spain) v Ireland* [1992] ECR–6185.
[62] Case 36/74 *Walrave* [1974] ECR 1405.

the subject-matter of Community rules. The recognition of the doctrine of variable geometry emphasises the differentiation in the application of Community law. In addition, the geographical scope of application of each Treaty is not identical.

The ECSC Treaty states in art 79 that it applies to 'European territories of the Member States'; art 198 of Euratom includes within its scope of application non-European territories over which Member States exercise their jurisdiction. Article 227 EC provides that the Treaty applies to all Member States, enumerates the French overseas departments and specific areas of EC law which shall apply to them as soon as the Treaty enters into force, and recognises special arrangements for association set out in Part Four of the Treaty which apply to the overseas countries and territories listed in Annex IV of the Treaty. Finally, art 227(4) EC extends the geographical scope of application of the Treaty to the European territories for whose external relations the Member States are responsible, but expressly excludes the following: the Faroe Islands and the sovereign base areas of the UK in Cyprus. Also, art 227(5)(c) EC specifies that the EC Treaty applies to the Channel Islands and the Isle of Man 'only to the extent necessary to ensure the implementation of the arrangements for those islands set out in the Treaty concerning the accession of new Member States to the European Economic Community and to the European Atomic Energy Community signed on 22 January 1972'.

Since the territorial jurisdiction of the Community is conditional upon the jurisdiction of its Member States, the territorial scope of application of EC law includes air, space and both internal and territorial waters of the Member States.

Personal jurisdiction of the Community

There is no EC nationality, nevertheless nationals of the Member States are afforded important rights under the Treaties which resulted in the establishment of the concept of EC nationals. In addition, the Treaty of Maastricht created citizenship of the Union which is not tantamount to nationality in the sense of international law but it adds important, supplementary rights to EC nationals. Nationality of the Member States and national citizenship are unaffected by Union citizenship. It is a complementary citizenship as it is based on the possession of the nationality of one of the Member States. European citizenship confers new rights on EC nationals such as the right of free movement and residence on economically inactive persons; the right of all EC nationals to vote and stand at municipal elections in their Member State of residence, under the same conditions as nationals of that State; the passive and active voting rights for elections to the European Parliament; the right to diplomatic and consular protection in a third State in which their State of nationality is not represented from the diplomatic and consular authorities of any Member State, on the same conditions as the nationals of that State; and the rights of petition to the EP and application to the Ombudsman.[63]

The concept of the EC national is peculiar. In other Member States EC nationals enjoy a special status, that is between that of nationals and foreigners but on the grounds of the principle of non-discrimination enshrined in art 6 EC they are the most privileged foreigners. The originality of EC law and its impact on EC nationals is highlighted by the fact that some of its provisions are directly applicable and directly effective. Directly

---

[63]See Chapter 3.

applicable provisions of EC law are automatically part of national law. Apart from the founding Treaties, as amended, legal measures enumerated in art 189 EC, such as regulations and decisions, are directly applicable. In this respect, EC regulations are analogous to statute law. EC regulations create uniform rules throughout the Community, their implementation into national law or any further action in the Member State is not only unnecessary but even contrary to EC law[64] since they must be enforced as they stand. Under art 172 EC regulations adopted by the Council, or jointly with the European Parliament, may give the ECJ unlimited jurisdiction with regard to the penalties provided for in such regulations, including pecuniary sanction imposed on individuals.

Decisions issued by the Council or the Commission may be addressed to Member States, individuals or corporate bodies. They may impose pecuniary sanctions. Under art 192 EC decisions of the Council or the Commission which impose a pecuniary obligation on persons other than States must be enforced according to the rules of civil procedure in force in the State in the territory of which the enforcement is carried out.

Directly effective Community law allows individuals to rely on its provisions in proceedings before national courts. Furthermore, other binding acts than those contained in art 189 EC[65] are capable of creating enforceable rights such as resolutions,[66] administrative memoranda,[67] or international agreements with third countries.[68] Also, since the judgment of the ECJ in Cases C–6 and 9/90 *Francovich and Others* v *Italian Republic*,[69] a Member State may be liable, in certain circumstances, in damages for its own breach of Community law. It is a powerful remedy for those individuals who seek redress for a loss directly caused by a Member State breach of Community law.

Individuals may have direct access to ECJ in certain circumstances: under art 173 EC to challenge acts adopted by Community institutions; under art 175 EC to force the latter to act when the Treaty imposes upon them a positive obligation to act; or under art 215(2) EC to sue Community institutions for damage caused by their unlawful conduct. As a result, EC institutions have important administrative, economic and legal powers which may affect individuals directly. This kind of power is normally reserved to a sovereign State.

As to other objects of international law capable of having a nationality, such as ships and aircraft, the rules are similar to those applicable to individuals – there is no EC nationality. It is for each Member State to lay down conditions and national rules of registration on which it grants ships or aircraft the right to operate under its flag. This was confirmed by the ECJ in Case 223/86 *Pesca Valentia*.[70] However, rules of Community law and, especially in this case, the principle of non-discrimination must apply to registration of objects from other Member States.[71]

---

[64] Case 40/69 *Hauptzollamt Hamburg* v *Bollmann* [1970] ECR 69; Case 93/71 *Leonesio* v *Ministry of Agriculture and Forestry* [1972] ECR 287.
[65] Regulations, directives and decisions.
[66] Case 22/70 *Commission* v *Council (ERTA)* [1971] ECR 263.
[67] Case 366/88 *France* v *Commission* [1990] ECR I–3571.
[68] Case 181/73 *Haegemann* v *Belgian State* [1974] ECR 449; Case 104/81 *Hauptzollamt Mainz* v *Kupferberg* [1982] ECR 3641; Case C–192/89 *Sevince* v *Staatssecretaris van Justitie* [1990] ECR I–3461; Case C–432/92 *R* v *Minister for Agriculture, Fisheries and Food, ex parte Anastasiou (Pissouri) Ltd* [1994] ECR I–3087.
[69] [1991] ECR I–5403.
[70] [1988] ECR 83.
[71] Case C–246/89 *Commission* v *UK* [1991] ECR 4585.

Ordinary and extraordinary jurisdiction of the Community

Ordinary jurisdiction of a State (or the Communities) is exercised over persons within its territory. In certain circumstances a State may regulate or interfere with the conduct of individuals outside its boundaries without violating international law. The extraordinary jurisdiction was developed to respond to the internationalisation of criminal activities at the end of nineteenth century. The improvements in travel, transport and communication highlighted the problem of the enforcement of criminal law. In 1935, the Harvard Law School conducted an extensive study in this area which culminated in an unofficial Draft Convention on Jurisdiction with Respect to Crime which set up five permissible bases on which a State can legitimately act beyond its borders.[72] In the case of the Community, the principle of territoriality is the most important. Under public international law the principle of territoriality allows a State to exercise its jurisdiction when certain unlawful activities take place partially within and partially outside its borders. Its subjective form allows the exercise of the territorial jurisdiction when the conduct commences within a State and is completed abroad, while its objective form applies when a conduct commences outside a State and is completed within it. The latter is also known as the 'effects doctrine' and was developed in the context of international criminal law. However, it has also found its application in anti-trust cases, especially in the US anti-trust laws and the EC competition rules.

The Community extra-territorial jurisdiction is based on the effects doctrine and exercised in the area of competition law. It means that in certain circumstances the exercise of the jurisdiction by the EC is justified when the effect of some anti-competitive conduct of foreign undertakings is realised or felt within the territory of the Union. The best example of the extraterritorial application of EC competition rules is provided by the *Wood Pulp* case[73] in which a number of undertakings all located outside the territory of the Community were engaged in a concerted practice which affected the selling price of woodpulp to purchasers established in the Community. The ECJ held that their activities were within the scope of application of EC competition rules because implementation of their agreement was effected within the Community. Implementation was defined as trading directly into the Community or using sales offices or agents to trade in the Community. Their concerted practice had intended a direct and substantial effect on trade within the Community through a reduction in competition in terms of price in sales of woodpulp to the Community undertakings. As a result, the concerted practice restricted competition within in the EEC. The Commission in the *Wood Pulp* case emphasised that:

---

[72] The research in international law of the Harvard Law School: 'Jurisdiction with Respect to Crime' (1935) 29 American Journal of International Law (Special Supp). There are the following: territorial principle, nationality principle, passive personality principle, protective principle and universality principle. In international practice States follow these principles, although it is still a matter of controversy whether they are part of international customary law and to what extent they are recognised under public international law. According to M Dixon: 'It is implicit in the identification of permissible heads of jurisdiction that any State which exercise a jurisdiction not justified by these criteria may be acting outside its power [ultra vires]', *Textbook on International Law*, London: Blackstone, 3rd ed, 1996, p128

[73] Cases 89, 104, 114, 116–117, 125–129/85 *A Ahlstrom OY and Others v Commission* [1988] ECR 5193; (1988) 4 CMLR 901.

'Article 85 of the EC Treaty applies to restrictive practices which may affect trade between Member States even if the undertakings and associations which are parties to the restrictive practices are established or have their headquarters outside the Community, and even if the restrictive practices in question also affects markets outside the EEC.'[74]

In Case 84/76 *Hoffman-La Roche*[75] the ECJ held that a Swiss multinational with subsidiaries in the Community was in breach of art 86 as it abused its dominant position by inserting so-called 'fidelity rebates' into its purchase agreements, which granted substantial discounts to customers buying all or most of their vitamins requirements from La Roche. The ECJ has confirmed the extra-territorial application of EC competition rules in many cases.[76]

The extra-territorial application of EC competition law creates many problems. The investigation of alleged breaches of EC competition rules outside the territory of the Union pose a difficult task for the Commission and often necessitates co-operation of competent authorities of a third State. Even more challenging is the actual enforcement of decisions of the Commission and judgments of the ECJ in competition cases outside the territory of the Union, as a third State where the undertaking is located has no obligation to co-operate or assist the Commission.

Limited international personality of the Communities

The Communities are the subject of international law since they possess international personality. Only independent States have unlimited international personality. The Communities are still classified as international organisations and as such their international personality is limited to the extent granted by the Member States. In general, the Communities, and especially the EC, enjoy a large measure of international personality.

An international organisation must satisfy three conditions to have legal capacity under international law: it must be a permanent association of States created to attain certain objectives and having administrative organs; it must exercise some power that is distinct from the sovereign power of its Member States; and, finally, its competences must be exercisable on an international level and not confined exclusively to the national systems of its Member States. The Communities satisfy these requirements and as such are vested with an international personality distinct from their Member States. As a result, the Communities have the capacity to conclude treaties with third States and international organisations (*ius tractatus*), to engage in diplomacy (*ius missionis*) and to sue an individual State for injuries to it,[77] or to be sued.

The most important aspect of conducting international relations for the Communities is their recognition by third States and international organisations. In this respect subjects of international law are entitled to use their discretion. Recognition means acknowledgment of the existence of a new subject of international law and the legal effect it entails.

In the absence of such recognition, acts of a new entity in international law would not be

---

[74] Ibid.
[75] [1979] ECR 461.
[76] P Torremans, 'Extraterritorial Application of EC and US Competition Law' (1996) 21 ELR 280–294.
[77] Supra note 59.

opposable by those who refuse to recognise it. The Communities were not recognised by the Soviet Union and the central and eastern European countries of the former Soviet block associated within the Council for Mutual Economic Co-operation (COMECON). The COMECON refused to deal with the Communities, even in those areas in which the EC had exclusive competence. This situation should have resulted, logically, in the severance of all relations with them. The Member States favoured a more 'political solution', that is individual Member States were allowed to conclude co-operation agreements with east European countries under the supervision of the Community.[78] This problem disappeared with the establishment of official relations between the EC and the COMECON. They were formalised in the Joint Declaration of 21 June 1988 of the EC and the Council for Mutual Economic Co-operation which implicitly recognised the Community.[79]

External competences of the EC ratione materiae

The EC Treaty contains specific provisions determining areas in which the EC has capacity to conclude certain types of international agreements with a third State, a group of States or international organisations. This competence has been expanded by the SEA and the Treaty of Maastricht. Under the TEU the EC may conclude international agreements in the following areas:

1. reduction of customs duties (art 18 EC);
2. exchange-rate system for the ECU/Euro in relation to non-Community currencies (art 109 EC);
3. the common commercial policy including tariff rates, tariff and trade agreements, liberalisation of international trade, export policy and protective measures such as dumping or subsidies (art 113 EC);
4. co-operation in research, technical development and demonstration (art 130m EC);
5. protection of environment (art 130r(4) EC);
6. development co-operation (art 130y EC); and
7. association agreements (art 238 EC).

Also in other areas such as education, vocational training and youth,[80] culture,[81] public health[82] the EC has certain specific powers.

It is interesting to examine in more details the most important areas of external competence of the EC.

Common commercial policy

One of the most important areas is the common commercial policy in which the EC has exclusive external competences. Even before the end of the transition period, that is before 1 January 1970, based on art 111 EC the Community was authorised to negotiate and enter

---

[78] Council Decision of 22 July 1974 (OJ L208 30.7.74 p3). Decision 74/393/EEC.).
[79] The Council issued a decision in this respect on 24 June 1988 (OJ L157 24.6.88 p34. Decision 88/345/EEC.
[80] Articles 126(3) and 127(3) EC.
[81] Article 128(3) EC.
[82] Article 129(3) EC.

into agreements on tariffs with third countries. As a result, the Community participated in tariff negotiations conducted under the auspices of GATT aimed at substantial reductions in tariff levels among the contracting parties, first in the Dillon round from 1960 to 1962 and then in the Kennedy round from 1964 to 1967. After 1970 the competences of the EC were expanded on the basis of art 113 EC to cover quantitative restrictions to trade, export policy, and protective measures such as dumping and subsidies, etc. At that time the EC agreed on a common external tariff among the six original Member States, and became responsible for conducting a common commercial policy at the international level. Under art 113 EC the Community has concluded many bilateral commercial and economic co-operation agreements, for example with Canada, India, Israel, etc, sectoral agreements, on such products as sugar, wine, cheese, manioc, etc, both non-preferential and preferential. Under the auspices of UNCTAD (the United Nations Commission on Trade and Development based in Vienna), the EC concluded various multilateral trade agreements on international commodities such as natural rubber, coffee, cacao, tin, jute, etc. In respect to new forms of international trade agreements, such as international agreements on commodities, and other instruments aiming at stabilising the price or the quantity of certain products at the international or regional level, the ECJ in Opinion 1/78 (Natural Rubber)[83] confirmed that they are within the scope of application of art 113 EC since its interpretation should be made in the light of changes in the international economy and its structure. The ECJ declared that competences under the commercial policy should be understood in a broad sense and that the list of measures under art 113 EC:

> '... is conceived as a non-exhaustive enumeration which must not, as such, close the door to the application in a Community context of any other process intended to regulate external trade'.[84]

The EC in the framework of the Tokyo round contributed to a substantial reduction in tariff levels on industrial products. Indeed, they became so low that they no longer constituted a barrier to trade. However, the elimination of tariffs resulted in the increase of non-tariff barriers to trade. In the next round of GATT, the Uruguay Round, the EC negotiated on behalf of all Member States, although they were contracting parties to GATT not the EC. The Uruguay Round was completed in December 1993 and the individual Member States, not the EU, signed the GATT agreements in Marrakesh in April 1994. This was later ratified by the Council, the EP and the Member States according to their national procedures.

Associations agreements under art 238 EC

Under art 238 EC the Community is empowered to conclude association agreements involving reciprocal rights and obligations, common action and special procedures with a third State, a group of States or international organisations. The ECJ held in Case 12/86 *Demirel*[85] that art 238 EC is not limited to commercial activities and includes any area covered by the EC Treaty. The agreements concluded on the basis of art 238 EC can be

---

[83] [1979] ECR 2871.
[84] Ibid, para 45.
[85] [1987] ECR 3719.

divided into four categories: association agreements with States-candidates for accession to the EU; the Lomé Conventions; the agreement creating the European Economic Area (EEA); and other agreements.

States-candidates for accession to the EU This category encompasses association agreements with States-candidates for accession to the Community, such as the Europe Agreements with some central and eastern European Countries. So far ten agreements have been concluded with the following countries: Poland, Hungary, the Czech Republic, Slovakia, Bulgaria, Romania, Latvia, Lithuania, Estonia, and Slovenia. The Europe Agreements create a very close relationship between these countries and the EU in all areas.[86] An Association Council supervises the proper functioning of the Agreements, any dispute arising under the Agreements which cannot be resolved by the Association Council can be referred to international arbitration. Also under Protocols to the Europe Agreements the associated countries have access to various EC programmes.[87] An interesting feature of the Europe Agreements is the establishment of a regular political dialogue between the EU and the associate countries with a view of achieving a convergence of position on important international questions.

Association agreements have been concluded with Turkey, Cyprus and Malta, and prior to their accession to the Communities with Greece, Portugal and Spain.

Lomé Conventions The Lomé Conventions are agreements between the EU and 70 former colonies of the Member Sates in Africa, the Caribbean and the Pacific (ACP).[88] The special relationship between some Member States and their former colonies has been recognised by the Treaty of Rome[89] and its annexes. Initially, the agreements were confined to French-African colonies, hence the first and second Yaoundé Conventions of 1963 and 1969. With the accession of the new Members to the Communities, especially the UK, and on the insistence of The Netherlands and Germany, a new approach towards developing countries was adopted. Instead of the French-oriented relationship based on donor-recipient concept, the Community has set up an original partnership with these countries offering not only generous access to a common market for ACP products, but most importantly setting up a development-assistance framework. This consists of a system of generalised preferences in trade, substantial financial assistance, including project aid, and the export stabilisation earnings of ACP countries through two mechanisms: the Commodity Export Earnings Stabilisation Scheme (STABEX of Lomé I); and the Mineral Accident Insurance System (SYSMIN of Lomé II) which guarantees ACP export prices regardless of fluctuations in world

---

[86] Together with the pre-accession strategy adopted in 1993 the Europe Agreements constitute actual schemes preparing the associated countries for membership of the EU. The Commission's White Paper on the Preparation of the Association Countries for Integration, COM(95)163.

[87] EU Bull 3–1995, point 1.4.68.

[88] M Addo, 'A Critical Analysis of the Perennial International Economic Law Problems of the EEC-ACP Relationship' (1990) 33 GYIL 37–60.

[89] Articles 131–136 EC.

commodity and minerals prices.[90] The first Lomé Convention was signed in 1975 and provided for its renewal every five years. The last Lomé Convention, number IV, introduces important innovations. It is concluded for ten years from 1990 to 2000.[91] It maintains the old provisions on trade, modifies the STABEX by adding new commodities such as cacao derivatives, essential oil products and squid, lowering the threshold for its application and increasing available funds under the STABEX by 66 per cent compared to Lomé III which amounts to ECU 1.4 billion.[92] Under the financial protocol of Lomé IV ACP countries will receive ECU 12 billion for development aid and ECU 1.15 billion for structural adjustment support. The Lomé IV Convention also contains a political agenda, such as strengthening democracy and respect for the rule of law and human rights in these countries.[93] It also encompass environmental protection, regional economic integration and emphasises self-reliant and self-sustained development.

European Economic Area (EEA) The most important and the most sophisticated agreement concluded under art 228 which has created a *sui generis* form of integration was concluded between the EC and EFTA. It resulted in the establishment of the European Economic Area.

EFTA was the biggest commercial partner of the EC, but following the accession of Austria, Finland and Sweden to the EU on 1 January 1995, which resulted in their desertion from EFTA, has become almost an obscure, insignificant and redundant organisation. The main reason for the accession of Austria, Finland and Sweden to the EU was the disintegration of the Soviet bloc which removed any security threat and undermined the concern to preserve their neutrality.

The Treaty establishing the European Economic Area (EEA) was signed on 2 May 1992 in Oporto between the 12 Member States of the European Economic Communities (EEC, ECSC, but not the Euratom) and the seven Members of the European Free Trade Association: Austria, Finland, Iceland, Liechtenstein, Norway, Sweden and Switzerland. Its main objective was the creation of the biggest trade area in the world which would account for 46 per cent of the world trade. It was beneficial for both parties: for EFTA countries it secured access to a single market which was essential for their economic survival; for the EC it ensured the expansion of its economy and constituted a counterbalance for the influence of NAFTA and Japan in international markets. The original Treaty provided for the free

---

[90] Many ACP countries export just one commodity. Therefore, when the price for that commodity diminishes as a result of price fluctuations in the world markets that country's economy is adversely affected. The STABEX applies to exports to the EC and other ACP markets. It provides funds to cover shortfalls of export earnings due to external factors. The poorest countries are not require to reimburse them, while other ACP countries have to pay back at very favourable terms.

[91] The Lomé Convention IV was revised in 1995. Its modified version was signed in Mauritius in November 1995: EU Bull 11–1995, point 1.4.102.

[92] C Cosgrove and P-H Laurent, 'The Unique Relationship: the European Community and the ACP', in John Redmond (ed), *The External Relations of the European Community: the International Response to 1992*, New York: St Martin, 1992, pp351–352.

[93] The Council adopted in November 1991 a resolution on Human Rights, Democracy and Development. It provides for incorporation of human rights and democracy clauses in the preambles and the text of international agreements concluded with third countries. They provide legal justification for suspension of an agreement when a contracting party is in breach of the fundamental human rights. See Case C–268/94 *Portugal v Council* [1996] ECR I–6177.

movement of goods, except for sensitive products such as steel, coal, and energy. Agriculture and fisheries were also left outside its scope. It further encompassed the free movement of persons, capital, services, rules on consumer protection, the protection of the environment (apart from the agreement with Austria on truck emissions),[94] social policy, statistics, company law and competition law. It also provided for closer co-operation in such areas as research and development, the environment, education, small and medium-sized enterprises (SMEs) and tourism. EC law, consisting of more than 1,600 EC measures, the *acquis communautaire*, applies to the EEA as well as new EC legislation adopted with consultation with the EFTA countries but without their actual participation in the decision-making procedure of the EU after the entry into effect of the EEA.

Under the EEA Treaty, EFTA countries agreed to contribute ECU 1.5 billion in low-interest loans and ECU 500 million in grants into a cohesion fund to equalise economic conditions within the EEA, and to provide assistance in environmental and educational projects in less-developed EC countries such as Spain, Portugal, Greece and Ireland.

To supervise the functioning of the EEA, and especially to solve any dispute between EFTA and the EC, the original Treaty envisaged the establishment of a common and independent mixed tribunal. The ratification of the original EEA Treaty was hindered by a number of obstacles. First, the ECJ challenged the creation of a mixed EFTA/EC tribunal on the grounds that five judges from the ECJ would also be judges at the mixed tribunal. Therefore, the question arose whether the delegated judges should be allowed to hear similar cases on EC law already decided by the mixed tribunal. As a result of the negative opinions of the ECJ[95] the idea of a mixed tribunal was abandoned in favour of arbitration. The EFTA countries committed themselves to the application of EC law in areas under the agreement.[96] Furthermore, in order to ensure uniformity in the application of EC law, the EFTA Court and the ECJ established a system for the exchange of information which allows for the intervention of the EEA Joint Committee, made up of representatives of the contracting parties and a main decision-making body, if necessary.

Second, the Swiss rejected the EEA in a referendum held in December 1992. The non-participation of Switzerland in the EEA necessitated amendments of the original agreement. The Commission presented a modified text of the EEA Treaty on 9 March 1993 which was embodied in a Protocol annexed to the Treaty and signed on 17 March 1993. It offered Switzerland the opportunity to accede to EEA at a later date, it provided that 60 per cent of the Swiss contribution to the cohesion plan was to be made by the remaining EFTA countries, and made special arrangements for Liechtenstein which is linked with Switzerland by a customs union. The EEA Treaty as amended entered into force on 1 January 1995.

Under the EEA six institutions were set up: the EEA Council, EEA Joint Committee, EEA Joint Parliamentary Committee, EEA Consultative Committee, EEA Surveillance Authority and the EFTA Court. The main difference in the functioning of the EEA bodies and the EU is

---

[94] Which was to be reduced by 60 per cent over 12 years.

[95] Opinion 1/91 (First EEA Opinion) [1991] ECR I–6079; Opinion 1/92 (Second EEA Opinion) [1992] ECR I–2821; and also case C–188/91 *Deutche Shell AG* v *Hauptzollamt Hamburg-Harburg* [1993] ECR I–363.

[96] M Cremona, 'The "Dynamic and Homogenous" EEA: Byzantine Structures and Variable Geometry' (1994) 19 ELR 508–526.

that the decision-making procedures are based upon consensus between the EU and its Member States and the EFTA countries. Furthermore, the EEA institutions are classical inter-governmental bodies since they have no legislative power. Presently, there are only three EFTA countries within the EEA: Iceland, Liechtenstein and Norway.

Other agreements Another category of agreements concluded under art 228 EC offer varying degrees of economic co-operation between the Community and third countries – ranging from the lowest form of economic integration, represented by partnership, to the most elaborate such as free trade and customs union agreements. The EU has concluded partnership and co-operation agreements with Russia, Ukraine, Belarus, Moldovia, Kazakhstan, Kyrgyzstan, Uzbekistan, etc. The Community has also concluded some agreements creating a customs union, *inter alia*, with Andorra in 1990 and Turkey in December 1995.

Another type of association agreement was signed with Mediterranean countries: Tunisia in April 1995, Israel in September 1995 and Morocco in November 1995. They strengthen the commitment of these countries to the protection of human rights and democracy, provide for a political dialogue, and the establishment of a free trade area within twelve years, as well as approximation of laws. The Mediterranean association agreements will be extended to other countries such as Lebanon, Jordan, Egypt, etc.

Protection of the environment: art 130r(4) EC

The protection of the environment has become a major issue for the Community at internal and international levels. The environmental protection policy has developed gradually and reflects the growing concern and awareness of the people and governments of the Member States. This issue transcends national borders and as such requires international action and close co-operation between all countries. In the Treaty of Rome no reference is made to environmental policy. The question appeared on the EC agenda for the first time in 1971 when the Commission prepared a detailed report on the environment for the European Council. It resulted in the adoption of an EC environmental policy and the establishment of an Environmental Protection Service by the Paris Summit in 1972.[97] Within the framework of the newly established environmental policy the Commission has played a leading role. So far it has prepared five Environmental Action Programmes (EAPs) which set up the major objectives of the Community policy. The internal aspects of environmental policy will be discussed elsewhere in the book (see Chapter 5). However, it is important to note that before the SEA all measures in this area were taken on the basis of arts 100 and 235 EEC. The explicit legal base for the Community legislation on environmental matters, which at the same time constitutes the confirmation of EEC *de facto* competences, was provided by the new arts 130r–130t EEC inserted into the SEA. The Treaty of Maastricht has expanded and highlighted the Community commitment to the protection of environment. Its external aspect is regulated in art 130r(4) EC which states:

> 'Within their respective spheres of competence, the Community and the Member States shall co-operate with third countries and with the competent international organisations.

---

[97] J Hassan, 'Environmental Policy', in F McDonald and S Dearden (eds), *European Economic Integration*, London: Longman, 1992, p122.

The arrangements for Community co-operation may be subject of agreements between the Community and the third parties concerned, which shall be negotiated and concluded in accordance with art 228.

The previous subparagraph shall be without prejudice to Member States' competence to negotiate in international bodies and to conclude international agreements.'

The provision clearly provides for concurrent competences of the EU and the Member States in the conduct of external environmental policy.

The Community has been deeply involved in shaping global environmental policy. One of the first initiatives of the Community at the international level was the ratification of the 1973 Washington Convention on Trade in Endangered Species (CITES). It was implemented in Regulation 3626/82.[98] The Community, together with the Member States, became a party to the 1987 Montreal Protocol on the protection of the ozone layer which was implemented in Decision 88/540.[99] The Community has set up a system of quotas and licensing for imports of ozone-depleting substances among parties to the Protocol, and established a total ban on imports of these substances and products containing them for non-contracting States in Regulation 594/91.[100] Also, the EC has ratified 1989 Basle Convention on the Control of Trans-Boundary Movement of Hazardous Wastes and Their Disposal in Decision 93/38,[101] which applies between the Community and third States but not between Member States since this constitutes an internal aspect of the common market. The Community attended the 1992 Earth Summit in Rio de Janeiro which resulted in the adoption of three major texts: The Rio Declaration on the Environment and Development which highlights general principles relating to the impact of economic development on the environment; Agenda 21 which contains a comprehensive programme regarding virtually every aspect of environment and development and a non-binding statement of forest principles.[102] In addition, there were two conventions prepared before the Earth Summit in 1992, but agreed at Rio, that is, the UN Framework Convention on Climate Change[103] and the Convention on Biodiversity, both ratified by the EC.[104] The financial and political implications of the commitments made at the 1992 UN Conference on the Environment and Development at Rio de Janeiro enhance the EU's role in these matters at the international level. However,

---

[98] OJ L384 31.12.82 p7. Other measures adopted by the Community relating to trade in species in danger of extinction are, for example: Regulation 348/81/EEC imposing a ban on importation of certain whale products for commercial purposes (OJ L39 12.2.81 p1); Regulation 2496/89/EEC prohibiting the importation of raw and worked ivory from African elephant (OJ L240 17.8.89 p5), etc.

[99] Decision 88/540 on the Vienna Convention for the protection of the ozone layer and the Montreal Protocol on substances that deplete the ozone layer (OJ L297 31.10.88 pp10 and 21). The EU extended its commitment resulting from the Montreal Protocols which require to reduce by 50 per cent the production of chlorofluorocarbons by the end of 1999 by announcing that the Community would cut the production of these chemicals by 85 per cent as soon as possible and ban all production by the year 2000: see D Vogel, 'Environmental Protection and the Creation of a Single European Market', Paper submitted at the 1992 Annual Meeting of the American Political Science Association, Chicago, 3–6 September 1992, p11.

[100] OJ L67 14.3.91 p1.

[101] OJ L39 16.2.93 p3.

[102] See Council Regulation 3062/95 on operations to promote tropical forests (OJ L327 30.12.95 p9).

[103] OJ L33 7.2.94 p13.

[104] Decision 94/69 concerning the UN Framework Convention on Climate Change (OJ L33 7.2.94 p13); and Decision 93/626 on the Convention of Biodiversity (OJ L309 13.12.93 p3).

the United Nations Earth Summit Review Conference which was held in New York in June 1997 declared that progress on many important environmental issues was slow. Only three OECD countries were likely to reach their commitments under the Climate Change Convention for the year 2000, and the growing black market in the substances banned under the Montreal Protocol undermined efforts made by contracting States. In this respect, a new initiative of the World Bank which will allocate up to £20 million to phase out production of ozone-depleting chemicals in seven factories in Russia within 18 months will help to restrict the damage to the ozone layer.[105] The preservation of forests is another controversial issue. The President of the World Bank announced at the Review Conference that together with the World Wide Fund for Nature they would sponsor a plan to conserve 10 per cent of the forests cover in every country. Although the concrete results of international actions relating to the protection of environment are disappointing, the EU has kept its international commitments and puts more a more emphasis on environmental issues in its dealings with third countries.

The tangible results are, for example, the introduction of environmental protection into the Lomé IV Convention, which provides for environmental assessment of certain development projects,[106] exchange of information on the safety of pesticides and other chemical substances,[107] technical co-operation aiming at combatting desertification,[108] and imposes a ban on exports of hazardous waste to the ACP countries. Also protection of the environment is emphasised in the Europe Agreements and in the partnership and co-operation agreements with former Republics of the Soviet Union and Russia itself. The environmental renovation and protection constitutes essential elements of the EU aid programmes for the central and eastern European countries.

The EU participates in the work of many international organisations such as the OECD, the UN Environmental Programme and the UN Economic Commission for Europe in environmental matters.

Development co-operation: art 130y EC

The Treaty of Maastricht formally recognises the EU competence in development policy in arts 130u–130y EC. It was previously exercised on the grounds of arts 113, 229–231, 235 and 238 EEC. The most ambitious initiative in this respect is certainly the Lomé Convention. In the future, art 130y EC will provide legal basis for a new arrangements with ACP countries. The objectives of the development policy are laid out in art 130u EC. Under this article the development policy of the EU should complement national policy of the Member States. The development policy of the EU according to art 130u EC should foster:

'–the sustainable economic and social development of the developing countries, and more particularly the most disadvantaged among them;
– the smooth and gradual integration of the developing countries into the world economy;
– the campaign against poverty in the developing countries'.

---

[105] (1997) The Guardian 26 June p21. Half of the world's production of CFCs takes place in Russia.
[106] Article 37.
[107] Article 40.
[108] Articles 54–57.

The external competence of the EU in development co-operation is regulated in art 130y which allows the Community to conclude agreements with third parties and to participate in international organisations. The EU shares competence with the Member States.

Community development policy is very ambitious. Outside Lomé it consists of lowering or exempting from customs duties most of the industrial and other processed exports from developing countries under the Generalised System of Preferences.[109] It should, however, be kept in mind that developing countries' industrial products are generally not competitive in the EC markets, and the impact of custom duties on international trade in industrial goods has been virtually eliminated under the GATT agreements. As a result countries like China, Brazil, Taiwan, Singapore, etc, are the main beneficiaries of the Generalised System of Preferences.

Under the auspices of the EU development projects are being conducted in more than 100 developing countries. A new project, HORIZON 2000, has been set up to increase aid for public health, AIDS prevention, food distribution and to combat poverty. Through the European Community Investment Partners scheme the EU encourage private businesses to invest in developing countries by entering joint ventures and other forms of co-operation. The aid and assistance from the EU to the central and eastern European countries under the Phare and TACIS programmes (see Chapter 2, section 2.2) constitute the largest and most generous international contributions made towards their development. Under a new regulation for TACIS adopted in June 1996, covering the period 1996–99, ECU 2.224 billion is allocated to this programme. Development policy is also conducted on contractual basis, and the EU has concluded many trade and aid agreements with developing countries. In this respect some regions are treated more favourably than others. From 1992 to 1996 the EU allocated ECU 4.4 billion for the Mediterranean region and 2.7 billion for Latin America and Asia.[110]

As already noted, an important new aspect of EU development policy is the emphasis on the protection of human rights, the rule of law and democratic institutions by the developing countries.

Finally, the EU is one of the major donors of humanitarian aid. The European Community Humanitarian Office (ECHO) is in charge of managing all EU emergency humanitarian aid.

Procedure for conclusion of international agreements

A new art 228 EC defines the general procedural requirements that the EC has to satisfy in order to conclude international agreements, although its application is excluded in relation to CFSP, JHA, monetary agreements on the currency rate under art 109 EC, etc.

Under art 228 the Commission submits recommendations in the form of a 'communication' to the Council which may or may not authorise the opening of negotiations. If the Council approves, the negotiations are conducted by the Commission in consultation with a special committee which may be appointed by the Council on a

---

[109] A new scheme for 1995–98 is contained in the Council Regulation 3281/94 (OJ L348/1 1994).

[110] For more on development policy see E Grilli, *The European Community and the Developing Countries*, Cambridge University Press, 1994.

consultative rather than a directive basis to assist the Commission. The special committees are working groups of the Council. The Commission must conduct negotiations within the framework of any Council's directives that may be issued. As a general principle, the Council concludes international agreements by qualified majority vote on the basis of the proposal submitted by the Commission and after consultation with the EP. There are many exceptions to the general procedure.[111] In the case of association agreements, and in relation to certain internal measures, the Council must act unanimously when it authorises the opening of negotiations and concludes the final agreements.[112] If an agreement amends the Treaty, a special procedure for amendments contained in art N TEU must first be adopted.[113]

An important aspect regarding international agreements which involves the contribution of the ECJ in their conclusion is envisaged in art 228(2) EC. The Council, Commission or a Member State may request an opinion from the ECJ on the compatibility of a new agreement with the EC Treaty.[114] Since 1990 the ECJ has been asked more frequently to deliver its opinions on internal and external implications deriving from the envisaged conclusion of international agreements. The procedure under art 228(2) EC has been examined by the ECJ in the Opinion 2/94 (ECHR). The Court held that it is:

> 'A special procedure of collaboration between the Court of Justice on the one hand and the other Community institutions on the other whereby, at a stage prior to the conclusion of an agreement which is capable of giving rise to a dispute concerning the legality of a Community act which concludes, implements or applies it, the Court is called upon to ensure, in accordance with art 164 of the Treaty, that in the interpretation and application of the Treaty the law is observed.'[115]

An interesting feature of the procedure is that all the Advocates-General deliver an opinion to the ECJ under art 228(2), but these are neither published nor referred to by the ECJ in its opinion. Furthermore, the ECJ has shown willingness to accept the request for an opinion and so far has dismissed only one such request. In Opinion 3/94 (Bananas Agreement)[116] the ECJ decided that the request was submitted too late since the Framework Agreement on Bananas had already been concluded. As a result, Germany, which asked for an opinion, could only bring an action for annulment under art 173 EC of the Council's decision approving the conclusion of the agreement.

Participation of the Communities in international organisations

Membership of international organisations is in principle limited to sovereign States. In the case of the Communities this limitation creates serious problems, taking into account their competences in many areas which sometimes lead to the substitution of the Member States by the Communities in international relations. Furthermore, the admission of the EC together with the Member States to an international organisation is hardly acceptable to

---

[111] See Chapter 6.
[112] Article 228(2) EC.
[113] Article 228(5) EC; also Opinion 2/94 (ECHR) [1996] ECR (not yet reported).
[114] K P E Lasok, *The European Court of Justice*, London: Butterworths, 1994, pp588–92.
[115] [1996] ECR (not yet reported).
[116] [1995] ECR I–4577.

other States, which are members of the organisation. Nevertheless, the participation of the EC in international organisations has been gradually accepted by the international community, although it is still rather exceptional. The decision of the UN Food and Agriculture Organisation (FAO) concerning the admission of the EC constitutes an important step towards the recognition of a special status of the EC. Also, the entry into force of the third stage of EMU would certainly require the admission of the EC to the International Monetary Fund and the World Bank.

There is no express provision in the Treaty allowing the EC to join international organisations. The ECJ in Opinion 1/76[117] recognised that the Treaty has conferred on the Community, inter alia, the competence to participate in the establishment and to become a member of international organisations. Nevertheless, international organisations decide whether or not to accept the EC. For that reason EC participation or membership in many international organisations has been difficult to obtain. In many organisations the EC has only a status of observer, and has held this position since 1974 in the United Nations[118] and in its bodies such as the General Assembly, the Economic and Social Council, which encompasses its Regional and Functional Commission including the Commission on Human Rights and the Commission on Sustainable Development,[118] and most of the UN specialised Agencies such as the International Labour Organisation, the World Health Organisation, UN Commission on Environment and Development (UNCED), UN Educational, Scientific and Cultural Organisation (UNESCO), etc. Also the EC has a formal status of observer in the International Monetary Fund, the World Bank, the International Atomic Energy Agency (IAEA) and certain regional organisations such as the Conference on Security and Co-operation in Europe (CSCE). The EC has also established close links with some international organisations on a contractual basis, without enjoying a status of an observer, for example in relation to the Council of Europe, the OECD, etc.

If the EC does not participate in some international organisations, the Member States that are members of that organisation are obliged under art 5 EC to co-operate with the Community,[120] and especially to defend Community interests as well as common positions adopted within the CFSP.

So far the EC enjoys membership of three international organisations: the UN Food and Agriculture Organisation (FAO), the European Bank for Reconstruction and Development (EBRD), and the World Trade Organisation (WTO).[121] Furthermore, the EC is a member of more than 60 international organisations created for a specific purpose of monitoring the implementation of a treaty dealing with a specific subject-matter, such as the protection of environment, fisheries, and commodity agreements concluded under the auspices of UNCTAD. These agreements vary as to the extent of supervision or assistance required for their implementation, for example agreements concluded outside the existing international

---

[117] Opinion 1/76 [1977] ECR 741, 756.
[118] Resolution 3208(XXIV) of the General Assembly.
[119] EC Bull 6–1992.
[120] In Opinion 2/94 (ECHR) [1996] (not yet reported), the ECJ enhanced the obligation of co-operation between the Community and the Member States based on art 5 EC.
[121] The condition of membership in the three organisations vary considerably: see J Sack, 'The European Community's Membership of International Organisations' (1995) 32 CMLR 1227–56.

organisations providing for the establishment of a complex structure such as the International Seabed Authority under the UN Convention on the Law of the Sea.

Ius missionis

Diplomatic relations are based on mutual consent of the sending and the receiving State. There is no right under public international law to diplomatic relations.[122] As a result, no State can compel another State to establish diplomatic relations. If, however, two States decide to enter into diplomatic relations with each other, they exchange representatives who usually work in the respective capitals of each State. The Vienna Convention on Diplomatic Relations 1961, which entered into force on 24 April 1964, codifies customary law in this area and governs all matters concerning diplomatic relations between sovereign States. The EC participated in the UN Conference on Diplomatic Intercourse and Immunities of 1961 which adopted the 1961 Vienna Convention. However, as an international organisation, the Community is not a contracting party to it. Another international convention relevant to the conduct of diplomatic relations by the Community is the Vienna Convention on the Representation of States in their Relations with International Organisations 1975 which is very similar to the 1961 Vienna Convention but has not yet come into force. As a result, the right to conduct diplomatic relations by the Communities is based on a practice acquiesced to by third States.

Indeed, an increasing number of States have found it advantageous to be represented at the headquarters of the European Communities by permanent delegations with diplomatic status. In 1952 the Foreign Office of the United Kingdom, followed by the United States and Sweden and, in 1954, by Japan, sent permanent delegations to the High Authority of the ECSC. In 1958 the United States accredited to the European Economic Community a permanent delegation headed by an envoy of ambassadorial rank.[123]

The right to conduct diplomatic relations by the Communities is recognised in art 17 of the Protocol on the Privileges and Immunities of the European Communities annexed to the Merger Treaty of 1965. It provides that the Member States in whose territory the Communities have their seat shall grant to diplomatic missions of third States accredited to the Communities all customary diplomatic privileges and immunities. In June 1996, 168 States and territories had their representation in Brussels.[124] Nineteen international organisations have set up their 'bureaux de liaison' in Brussels.[125] Presently, the procedure of accreditation is governed by the Luxembourg Accords.[126] The decision to establish diplomatic relations is taken by the Council unanimously. The Council decides not only whether to enter into diplomatic relations, but also must consent to the particular diplomat. The letters of credence are submitted separately to the President of the Council and the

---

[122] Article 2 of the Vienna Convention on Diplomatic Relations 1961.

[123] The first ambassador accredited to the EEC, *First General Report EEC*, point 168.

[124] *Corps Diplomatique accredite aupres des Communautes europeennes et representations aupres de la Commission, Commission*, Brussels, June 1966.

[125] I Macload, I Hendry and S Hyett, *The External Relations of the European Communities: a Manual of Law and Practice*, Oxford: OUP, p220, n85.

[126] *Ninth General Report, EEC*: EC Bull 3–1966, pp31–33. The Luxembourg Accords amended the previous procedure according to which the Commission enjoyed a leading role in the procedure of accreditation.

President of the Commission, usually the same day and without any official ceremony. The diplomat is then fully accredited and permitted to engage in diplomatic relations on behalf of his country.

Also, the Member States have established 'permanent representations' to the Communities which enjoy diplomatic status. A permanent representative is integrated into the Community system since he is a member of the COREPER.

Diplomatic relations between sovereign States entails that each State is represented in the territory of another and the rights and privileges of the diplomatic agents are granted on the basis of reciprocity. The representation of the Communities in third States is less developed because the Communities are not sovereign States and thus a third State has a discretion whether to grant diplomatic status to the representatives of the Communities. As a result, representation differs from country to country, and in practice certain rivalries between the Commission and the Council has led to peculiar arrangements. The Commission has its 'delegations' in third States, a group of States and international organisations. The delegations are created by the Commission which also appoints particular delegates, and this is based on the Commission's power to set up its own departments.[127] The first mission of the three Communities was established in London in 1968, the second in Washington in 1972 and the third in Japan in 1974. Today, the Commission has 104 delegations, two representations and ten offices in third States or territories. The existence of Commission delegations has been recognised by art J6 TEU. The Commission has also established a number of missions to international organisations such as ILO, UNESCO, United Nations Economic Commission for Europe, UNCTAD, International Atomic Energy Agency (IAEA), OECD, etc.

The Council is represented in third States by diplomatic agents of the Member State which holds the Presidency of the Council.

Assessment of international relations of the Communities and the European Union

The conduct of external relations by the Communities, and especially by the EC, highlights their peculiar status under public international law. Indeed, the EC can be considered as a mutant; it is not yet a federal State and does certainly differ from traditional international organisations. The ratification of the Treaty of Amsterdam, which endows the European Union with international legal personality, will certainly enhance its political weight in international relations. The Community almost from its inception has been recognised as a world economic power. Today, the Union is reaching a next, logical step in its development – it has become an important player in international politics. Within the framework of the Common Foreign and Security Policy, which is a concept of enormous potential, the EU will be able to take advantage of its new status in international law and thus strengthen the image of Europe as a single entity in all international relations.

The European Community's external relations are well developed, and it can be said that it has a major presence in the world. The relations between the United States and the

---

[127] Case C–327/91 *France* v *Commission* [1994] ECR I–3641, para 28, (opinion of Advocate-General Tesauro).

Community has always been of utmost importance. The US has encouraged European integration since 1945. Twice a year the President of the US and the Presidency of the European Union hold a summit-meeting. The last one in The Hague on 28 May 1997 set up a new transatlantic agenda and a joint EU-US action plan. Together with the EU, the US promotes stability and development of a democratic and united Europe. The celebration of the fiftieth anniversary of the Marshall Plan, which coincided with the EU-US summit, provided an opportunity for the US President to call for a new economic approach of the EU towards eastern Europe and Russia. He emphasised that the EU should revitalise their economies and infrastructures, just as the Marshall Plan did.[128] The response of the Community is very promising. The Commission's President, Jacques Santer, proposed a new ECU 75 billion Marshall Plan to improve economic conditions in eastern European countries and to prepare them for membership of the EU between the years 2000 and 2006. This new strategy for an enlarged EU within the framework of 'Agenda 2000' is perfectly feasible provided the existing regional assistance for the poorest areas of the EU is substantially reduced.[129] Furthermore, as Europe is unable to provide for its own defence, the US commitment to Europe is vital. The NATO-Russia Founding Act signed in Paris on 27 May 1997, which establishes a new partnership between the former Cold War adversaries, is a landmark document in this respect. The Amsterdam Summit in June 1997 welcomed its signing as 'a fundamental contribution to the development of a new European security architecture in which Russia finds its due place'. Russian-EU relations are based on the partnership and co-operation agreement signed in June 1994.[130] Its importance for both parties is significant as Russia is the largest trade partner of the EU. The communication submitted by the Commission on 'The EU and Russia – the Future Relationship'[131] was adopted in November 1995 by the Council and contains the general outlines of the EU policy towards Russia.[132] The EU provides assistance, humanitarian aid and incorporates Russia in many co-operation programmes in various fields, as well as in its TACIS scheme.

Another important area of the EU's external relations is its Mediterraenian policy. It is based on the Global Mediterranean Policy providing for preferential trade relations adopted at the 1972 Paris Summit. However, the preferential treatment excluded sensitive industries, agriculture, fisheries, etc, and no agreement was reached on migrant workers. With the accession of Greece, Spain and Portugal further development of Mediterraenian policy was blocked since these countries became main suppliers of commodities, peculiar for this region, which were in demand in the EC. In order to revive the Community policy, the Commission prepared a draft plan outlining proposed strategy toward Mediterranean non-EU Member States called 'Vers une Politique Mediterranienne Renovée: Proposition pour la Période 1992–96'. However, this general guideline was not ambitious enough. The Corfu Summit in June 1994 instructed the Commission to prepare a new strategy for the Mediterraenian basin which proposed the creation of the largest free trade in the world

---

[128] D Kunz, 'Bill's Marshall Plan: You Foot the Bill' (1997) The Times 29 May, p20. These countries desperately need help. In Russia, according to Kunz: 'Life expectancy has dropped by seven years since 1991. Deaths exceed births. Diphtheria, polio and tuberculosis are spreading as health services collapse.'

[129] (1997) The European July (EP News, European Parliament) p1.

[130] Council Decision 95/414 (OJ L247 13.10.95 p2) implemented by Decision 95/415 (OJ L247 13.10.95 p30).

[131] COM(95)73.

[132] EU Bull 11–1995, point 2.2.1.

including the EU, North African and Middle East countries. Approved by the Essen Summit, the Euro-Mediterranean Agreement was signed in October 1995 and further elaborated in the 'Barcelona Declaration' which was the outcome of the Euro-Mediterranean Conference held on 27–28 November 1995 between the EU and 12 Mediterranean non-Member States.[133] The objectives agreed at Barcelona were reaffirmed at the Second Euro-Mediterranean Conference held at Valletta (Malta) on 15 and 16 April 1997. The Amsterdam Summit reviewed the EU Mediterranean policy. It welcomed the extension of a network of Euro-Mediterranean agreements, especially in the context of the signing of a Interim Association Agreement with the Palestine Liberation Organisation for the benefit of the Palestinian Authority of the West Bank and the Gaza strip, and recommended the conclusion as quickly as possible of similar agreements with Egypt, Lebanon, Jordan and Algeria.

The relations with Central and South American countries were boosted by a co-operation agreement signed between the EU and MERCOSUR, that is a common market comprising Argentina, Brazil, Paraguay and Uruguay in December 1995. In addition, since 1985 there are annual meetings between the EU and countries of Central America and, since 1991, with the Rio Group of Latin American countries. These meetings have led to the conclusion of a number of free trade agreements and partnership agreements between the EU and Central and Southern American countries.[134]

The Amsterdam Summit of June 1997 adopted many resolutions regarding future EU policies towards third countries which illustrate the complexity and extent of its external relations. Among them are resolutions concerning the Congo, Albania, Hong Kong and Macau, Latin America, Africa, former Yugoslavia, South Africa, etc.

---

[133] COM(95)72 final, Barcelona Declaration and Work Programme: EU Bull 11–1995, point 2.3.1; F S Hakura, 'The Euro-Mediterranean Policy: the Implications of the Barcelona Declaration' (1997) 34 CMLR 337.

[134] Commission Communication on a closer relationship with Latin America (1996–2000), COM(95)495.

5 Internal Competences of the European Community

5.1 Creation of the internal market

5.2 Common policies

5.3 Legislative competences in other sectors

5.4 Competences similar to those exercised by any international organisation

Internal competences of the Communities are based on the founding Treaties, as amended. Each Community has been assigned different objectives, although the establishment of a common market in certain products such as coal and steel under the ECSC Treaty, atomic energy under the Euratom Treaty or a single market in which goods, labour, services and capital are in a free circulation under the EC Treaty constitutes their common goal. The Treaty of Maastricht has neither modified the competence of ECSC nor Euratom, although it has amended and extended the competences of the EC and added new areas of co-operation in Common Foreign and Security Policy (CFSP) and Justice and Home Affairs (JHA) for the Union.

The competences of the European Communities are characterised by a triple heterogeneity. First, the diversity of the areas in which the Communities are empowered to act. Their competences are defined in the form of the task conferred upon them (art 2 ECSC and EC, art 1 Euratom), and the activities which they have to carry out in order to fulfil their tasks (art 3 ECSC and EC and art 2 Euratom).

In this context, it is interesting to examine the activities of the EC which are at the same time EC competences *ratione materiae*. Article 3 EC states that in order to accomplish the task set out in art 2 EC, the activities of the Community shall include:

'(a) the elimination, as between Member States, of customs duties and quantitative restrictions on the import and export of goods, and all other measures having equivalent effect;
(b) a common commercial policy;
(c) an internal market characterised by the abolition, as between Member States, of obstacles to the free movement of goods, persons, services and capital;
(d) measures concerning the entry and movement of persons in the internal market as provided for in art 100c;
(e) a common policy in the sphere of agriculture and fisheries;
(f) a common policy in the sphere of transport;
(g) a system ensuring that competition in the internal market is not distorted;
(h) the approximation of the laws of Member States to the extent required for the functioning of the common market;
(i) a policy in the social sphere comprising a European Social Fund;
(j) the strengthening of economic and social cohesion;

153

(k) a policy in the sphere of the environment;

(l)   the strengthening of the competitiveness of Community industry;

(m) the promotion of research and technological development;

(n) encouragement for the establishment and development of trans-European networks;

(o) a contribution to the attainment of a high level of health protection;

(p) a contribution to education and training of quality and to the flowering of the cultures of the Member States;

(q) a policy in the sphere of development co-operation;

(r)   the association of overseas countries and territories in order to increase trade and promote jointly economic and social development;

(s) a contribution to the strengthening of consumer protection;

(t)   measures in the spheres of energy, civil protection and tourism'.

Article 3a EC adds to those activities the adoption of an economic policy and the establishment of EMU.

Second, the terminology employed in art 3 EC suggests that competences of the EC vary according to the importance of a particular area for the purposes of European integration. Indeed, in order to determine whether a particular field is within the exclusive competence of the EC or the Community shares its powers with the Member States, the typology can be useful, for instance a common policy is certainly within the exclusive competence of the EC, but other areas of potential competence whether exclusive or concurrent can only be determined by reference to the principle of subsidiarity.

Finally, the legal measures that the Community is empowered to adopt in pursuance of the objectives stated in art 3 EC depend upon the competence the EC enjoys in relation to a particular area and its specificity. The choice between regulations, directives, decisions, recommendations and opinions must be based upon the principles of subsidiarity and proportionality, which should lead to a wider application of non-binding instruments such as recommendations and opinions.

In relation to internal competences of the EC it is necessary to underline that the extensive use of art 235 EC as well as the development by the ECJ of the doctrine of implied powers[1] have considerably extended the Community's internal powers.[2] As a result, the EC internal competences are impressive. It is impossible to examine all of them in detail. Nevertheless, certain areas are of such importance that a brief summary of the activities of the EC seems necessary. Among them, the creation of the internal market merits particular attention, as it constitutes the most interesting and important achievement of the EC.

5.1 Creation of the internal market

The creation of a common market where goods, people, services and capital move freely was one of the main objectives of the EEC Treaty. The SEA gave a new impetus to the

---

[1] For example, in Case 36/74 *Walrave* [1974] ECR 1405 the ECJ held that the EC has competence in the area of sport; in Case 293/83 *Gravier* [1985] ECR 593, the ECJ stated that professional training and access to it were covered by art 127 EC.

[2] See Chapter 4.

achievement of this objective. The SEA replaced the term 'common market' by 'an internal market' which is defined in art 7a EC as:

> 'an area without internal frontiers in which the free movement of goods, persons, services and capital in ensured in accordance with the provisions of the Treaty'.

Based on the White Paper prepared by Lord Cockfield, more than 300 measures were introduced to converge the national markets of all Member States into a single economic area without internal frontiers. Officially on 31 December 1992 an internal market was completed.

Whilst the Community has competence to take all appropriate measures with the aim of establishing the internal market, those competences are difficult to determine *a priori*. During the period leading to the completion of the common market the Community harmonised the laws in the Member States which directly affected its establishment and proper functioning. In this respect arts 100 and 100a EC were most frequently used. Under art 100 EC the Council may issue directives for the approximation of national laws, regulations, and administrative procedure, acting unanimously upon a proposal from the Commission and after consulting the EP.[3] Article 100a EC grants the Council similar powers in the context of the internal market, but imposes a very important limitation upon a Member State as it allows the Council to act by qualified majority[4] and thus makes it possible to bypass the opposition of one or more Member States to the proposed measure.

The free movement of goods is the foundation of the Single European Market (SEM). It involves the elimination of all obstacles to trade such as custom duties and charges having an equivalent effect,[5] and quantitative restrictions and all measures having an equivalent effect,[6] although art 36 EC provides for exceptions to arts 30–34. It also prohibits discriminatory internal taxation upon goods of other Member States.[7] The removal of barriers to the free movement of goods within the framework of the SEM encompasses such areas as State aid and subsidies[8] *per se* in breach of art 30 EC but still considered as necessary elements of national economic policy.[9] Public procurement of both goods and services, as Member States often favour national contractors in major public contracts for the supply of goods, work and services to public authorities and utilities, is included in the SEM. The EC has adopted a number of measures to combat domestic bias in this area.[10] The

---

[3] Article 100 EC.

[4] However, certain areas are excluded: fiscal provisions, provision relating to the free movement of persons and the rights and interests of employed persons (art 100a(2) EC).

[5] Articles 12–29 EC.

[6] Articles 30–37 EC.

[7] Article 95 EC.

[8] Articles 92–94 EC.

[9] Case 103/84 *Commission* v *Italy* [1986] ECR 1759; Case 249/81 *Commission* v *Ireland* [1982] ECR 4005 where the ECJ held that a state-sponsored campaign to 'Buy-Irish' was in breach of art 30 EC, notwithstanding a claim of the Irish government in its support under art 92 EC.

[10] Directive 90/531/EEC on the Procurement Procedures of Entities Operating in the Water, Transport, Energy and Telecommunication Sectors (OJ L297 29.10.90 p1) as amended by Directive 93/38/EEC (OJ L199 9.8.93 p84); Directive 93/36/EEC Co-ordinating Procedures for the Award of Public Supply Contracts (OJ L199 9.8.93 p1); Directive 93/37/EEC Concerning the Co-ordination of Procedures for the Award of Public Works Contracts (OJ L199 9.8.93 p54); in relation to public service contracts Directive 92/50/EEC Concerning the Co-ordination of Procedures for the Award of Public Service Contracts (OJ L209 24.7.92 p1); the so-called Remedies Directives 89/665/EEC (OJ L395 30.12.89 p33) and 92/13/EEC (OJ L76 1.6.94 p3) which require establishment of a national body controlling public procurement and empowered to adopt interim measures, suspend the award procedure of its implementation and nullify the decision and to award damages to persons who suffered as a result of it.

SEM in the context of art 30 EC also regulates intellectual property rights which are considered an exception to the free movement of goods, but nevertheless are limited to the 'specific subject matter' of the property rights.[11] The most difficult obstacles to the free movement of goods are technical barriers. The Community tries to tackle this problem by means of exchanging information on national measures allowed under art 36 EC within a procedure established under Decision 95/3052[12] and Directive 83/189.[13] They require the Member States to notify their draft technical regulations to the Commission and other Member States, thus providing the Commission with an opportunity to verify their conformity with EC law and, if necessary, to exercise its right to impose a standstill. The procedure is currently under review.

The free movement of people and services allows EC nationals to work as employees or to be self-employed anywhere in the EU, and to be treated without discrimination based on nationality in the host State. The national treatment of such people is vital to the exercise of the free movement of workers, the right of establishment and the provision of services. There are still some obstacles, especially in relation to the recognition of professional qualifications which must be recognised by a host Member State even though they are not identical to those required for their own nationals. Recognition is granted only if the professional capacity is sufficient to guarantee the proper exercise of such activities.[14] The Commission in its Work Programme 1997 emphasised its continual commitment to harmonisation of this area and proposed legislation for European articles of apprenticeship, that is, educational qualifications obtained in one Member State would be accepted in another Member State for the purpose of obtaining apprenticeship and training contracts.[15]

The self-employed enjoy similar rights as workers under the freedom of establishment and the freedom to provide services. The right of establishment means that any EC national is entitled to set himself up in whichever Member State he wishes and to conduct business under the conditions laid down for the nationals of that State. The rights of establishment and provision of services are also granted to companies and firms situated in the territory of the EU. The free movement of services is mainly hindered by the fact that the service sector is difficult to deregulate.

The free movement of capital has been successfully accomplished. Directive 88/361[16] eliminated all restrictions on capital and ensured access of EC nationals and businesses to the financial systems and products of other Member States.

The European Union is the biggest internal market in the world, 40 per cent larger than the US market. In general, Member States have successfully implemented almost all legislation necessary to the proper functioning of the internal market, with Denmark in the lead (95.9 per cent of all Single European Market legislation has been transposed into

---

[11] Case 119/75 *Terrapin* v *Terranova* [1976] ECR 1039; the ECJ made a distinction between the existence and the exercise of intellectual property rights. The existence is guaranteed under EC law but certain forms of exercise are restricted as contrary to art 30 EC.

[12] OJ L321 30.12.95 p1.

[13] OJ L109 26.04.83 p1.

[14] Case C–76/90 *Sager* [1991] ECR I–4221.

[15] The European Commission's 1997 Work Programme, Special Report, *European Law Monitor*, February 1997, ppi–iv.

[16] OJ L178 8.7.88 p3.

Danish national law) and Greece trailing with 77.9 per cent.[17] In 1993 the Commission produced a White Paper on Growth, Competitiveness and Employment which summarises the achievements of the internal market: 70 million documents were eliminated by abolishing the internal borders; it expanded investment by one-third between 1985 and 1990; mergers and acquisitions within the EU trebled between 1986 and 1992 and doubled outside of the EC; transportation costs were reduced to 3 per cent; and nine million jobs were created between 1986 and 1990.

Nevertheless there are still some areas which remain outstanding and require further action. In its Work Programme for 1997 the Commission underlined the fact that a number of measures in relation to the SEM which have been prepared by the Commission require adoption by the Council – such as the statute which would enable a European company to operate freely throughout the EC under a single legal regime, the legal protection of biotechnical inventions and a single market in gas.[18]

5.2 Common policies

There are four common policies: Common Commercial Policy (CCP), Common Agricultural Policy (CAP), Common Fisheries Policy (CFP) and Common Transport Policy (CTP). The Member States still have important powers, but the basic assumption behind common policies is that the Community enjoys exclusive powers. The Common Commercial Policy having already been covered, we shall first examine the most important and the most controversial of these policies.

Common Agricultural Policy (CAP)

The Common Agricultural Policy (CAP) was established by the Treaty of Rome in arts 38–47 and came into force in 1964. A common agricultural policy which would ensure market stability for agricultural products, protection against outside exports, technical progress, reasonable prices for consumers and ensure the availability of food supplies making the Community self-sufficient was a very attractive idea to the original Member States. Hunger and food shortages during World War II and its immediate aftermath prompted the Member States to ensure that Europe would never again be hungry.

The main objectives of the CAP are set out in art 39 EC.[19] The ECJ held in Case 5/73 *Balkan v Hauptzollamt Berlin-Packhof*[20] that any one of the objectives stated in art 39 EC may be given temporary priority to satisfy the requirements of the economic factors and

---

[17] In May 1996 it was reported that in all Member States 93 per cent of legislation was transposed into domestic legislation, L Tsoukalis, *The New European Economy Revisited*, Oxford: OUP, 1997, p74.

[18] See note 15, piv.

[19] Article 39(1) EC provides that the EC should have the following objectives in the CAP: '(a) to increase agricultural productivity by promoting technical progress and by ensuring the rational development of agricultural production and the optimum utilisation of the factors of production, in particular labour; (b) thus to ensure a fair standard of living for the agricultural community, in particular by increasing the individual earnings of persons engaged in agriculture; (c) to stabilise markets; (d) to assure the availability of supplies; (e) to ensure that supplies reach consumers at reasonable prices'.

[20] [1973] ECR 1091.

conditions in the context in which the decision is made within the framework of the CAP. The objectives of the CAP could only be achieved in a controlled market. The basic principles governing the CAP were set out by the Council in 1960. They comprise the free movement of agricultural products within the Community, the establishment of a common customs tariff for imported products while promoting Community agricultural exports, and the joint responsibility of the Member States in financing the CAP regardless of whether or not the benefits received are equivalent to their financial contributions. Various instruments necessary to the proper functioning of the CAP were introduced: the price support system, direct subsidies to farmers, import barriers, the agrimonetary system, etc.

The price support system involves the fixing of target and intervention prices for agricultural products by the Agricultural Council in the spring of each year. A target price is the price which should be obtained under normal market conditions. However, if a farmer cannot obtain the target price the support system offers him the opportunity to sell his products to an intervention agency in each Member State that has to buy at the pre-set intervention price. National agencies intervene in two situations: when the price for certain agricultural products falls below a certain level by acquiring them at the intervention price; and, conversely, supplying a particular commodity to the market when its price rises above the maximum level as a result of its shortage. Almost 70 per cent of agricultural products benefit from the price support system.

For some products Community assistance consists of financial support only for storage,[21] or is offered to the buyer organisations or importers under the so-called threshold prices when the import price is lower than the EU price. The price support system distorts the normal interaction of market forces and results in the creation of false prices. This is reinforced by art 42 EC which provides that the competition rules apply to the production and trade in agricultural commodities 'only to the extent determined by the Council within the framework of art 43(2) and (3)'.[22] In particular, the Council is empowered to grant aid to enterprises handicapped by structural or natural conditions or, if it is necessary, within the framework of economic development programmes. Another consequence of the price support system is overproduction as the false price encourages farmers to increase production, which results in 'butter mountains', 'beef mountains', 'wine lakes', 'milk lakes', and so on. In order to ease the problem certain measures have been introduced, such as the maximum guaranteed quantity, the milk quota, the co-responsibility levies, subsidies for imports and donation of food to poor countries or countries with dramatic shortages of food.

Among other intervention mechanisms – such as direct subsidies for certain products based on the area under cultivation (by hectare) or quantity produced, import barriers, export subsidies, etc – the most controversial used to be the agrimonetary system. It was an adjustment mechanism allowing compensation for the difference in the exchange rates of national currencies and the ECU. All CAP prices are expressed in the ECU but farmers receive payments in their national currency, calculated at the 'green rate' which does not follow the currency market exchange rate. The difference between the green rate and the

---

[21] For example, pigmeat.
[22] Normally, a legislative measure adopted by the Council cannot override the provisions of the Treaty: Cases 80 and 81/77 *Ramel* v *Receveur des Douanes* [1978] ECR 927.

market rate was covered until December 1992 by a system of monetary compensation amounts (MCAs). It meant in practice that when a national currency was devalued, compensatory amounts were levied on agricultural exports and granted on agricultural imports. Conversely, in the case of a revaluation of a national currency the compensatory amounts were paid on exports and levied on imports. This system was particularly appreciated by countries with a strong currency and it took years to abolish. A new arrangement was agreed by the Agricultural Council in June 1995 which has introduced a dual green currency system: exchange rates are fixed for strong currency countries and based on the ECU for weak currency countries.

The main problem with the CAP is that it was too successful. It created high productivity and regular food supplies. On the one hand, the Community has become not only self-sufficient in many agricultural products, but also the second largest exporter of agricultural products and first in many commodities such as wine, sugar beet, etc. On the other hand, the CAP system is costly to operate: the major part of the EC budget is spent on agriculture which has lost its previous importance in the economy of the Member States. This protectionist system results in high prices to consumers since the interference of the Community distorts market mechanisms and artificially fixes prices much higher than world prices for agricultural products. The CAP is unfair as it affords a special protection to only one group of people, farmers, and even among them the producers of some specific products and large agricultural businesses are more protected than others – 20 per cent of farmers receive more than 80 per cent of the CAP spending. Finally, the CAP constitutes the main source of disagreement among the Member States and the Community and the EC and third countries.

Many different reforms of the CAP were submitted over the years but until 1992 were *ad hoc* and limited in scope. In 1992 the then Agricultural Commissioner, Ray MacSharry, recommended a radical reform of the CAP.[23] The main features of the MacSharry reforms were: reduction in price support for cereals of 35 per cent, 10 per cent for milk, 15 per cent for butter over three years, 5 per cent for skimmed milk and 15 per cent for beef; withdrawal of approximately 15 per cent of land out of production and promoting its use for other environment-friendly purposes such as afforestation, conservation reserves or tourism, while compensating farmers for the loss of income; early retirement for farmers and mandatory retirement for farmers without a pension over 55 (over four million farmers were over 65 years old and two in three farms was less than five hectares)[24]; subsidies for farms in less-favoured regions and mountains; emphasis on product quality; eco-friendly production; and, finally, support for small and medium-sized farms.[25]

MacSharry's proposals were opposed by farmers, agricultural organisations and the agricultural ministers of the Member States. In his own country, Ireland, MacSharry, was compared by the chairman of the Irish Farmers' Association to Oliver Cromwell, who in the

---

[23] Before the EP he pleaded for the reform by depicting the existing situation in the following terms: 'we have 20 million tonnes of cereals in intervention ... almost 1 million tonnes of dairy produce in intervention ... there are 750,000 tonnes of beef in intervention and rising at the rate of 15,000 to 20,000 per week': OJ C–407 11.7.92 p282.

[24] COM(91)258/3 final:36).

[25] J Gibbons, 'The Common Agricultural Policy', in F McDonald and S Dearden (eds), *European Economic Integration*, London: Longman, 1992, p139 et seq.

seventeenth century destroyed Irish towns and murdered their inhabitants.[26] After much criticism from almost everybody, and long debates, the MacSharry Plan was adopted by the Agricultural Council in May 1992, albeit in a modified version. The proposed price reductions were smaller than originally suggested, but other measures were accepted. As a result, under the reformed CAP the emphasis changed from the price support system to direct income support granted to large producers willing to set aside 15 per cent of their land, and pensions for retired farmers. The environment-friendly measures and the ecological dimension of the EC agriculture are now important elements of the CAP.

The reform of the CAP made possible further liberalisation of trade in agricultural products under the auspices of GATT. One of the most contentious questions examined by the Uruguay round was agriculture. The United States and the 'Cairns group', that is, 14 agricultural exporting countries, including Australia and New Zealand, bitterly attacked the CAP albeit it seems that it was unfair to focus their attention on the Community alone. According to Tsoukalis, agricultural support levels were 35 per cent of output in the US, 46 per cent in Canada, 75 per cent in Japan, and 49 per cent in the EU.[27] The situation was exacerbated by the threat of the US to impose punitive tariffs on many EC agricultural products. The Commission and the US finally reached a compromise in November 1992 known as the Blair House Accord. Its main points are: reduction of subsidised farm exports to 21 per cent in volume over six years and in value to 36 per cent with internal support cut by 20 per cent; limitation of oilseeds production in terms of land (5.128 million hectares with 10 per cent of oilseeds land set aside permanently with compensation for farmers) and volume (to one million tons for industrial production); conversion of protective measures, such as export levies, into customs tariffs (the so-called tariffication); minimum access to national markets for imports which should not exceed 3 per cent (and 6 per cent in six years); and the prevention of unilateral action against each other in trade by accepting a six-year 'peace clause on outstanding disputes'.[28]

The Blair House Accord was bitterly opposed by France, the second biggest exporter of agricultural products. Although France has only one million full-time farmers, who constitute 5 per cent of its working population, and agriculture accounts for a mere 4 per cent of French GDP, farm lobbies are very powerful. The Blair House Accord was considered by France as contrary to the CAP as reformed by MacSharry. However, French attempts at renegotiation of the Blair House Accord were unsuccessful, although France has obtained all the guarantees asked for from both the US and the EU. They made mutual concessions in order to secure French acceptance of the Uruguay Round Accords.[29]

One of the first steps in the implementation of the Uruguay Round agreements was

---

[26] (1991) Irish Times 10 July p1.

[27] L Tsoukalis, *The New European Economy*, Oxford: Oxford University Press, 1991, p260.

[28] (1993) Financial Times 20 September p3.

[29] The US has agreed to exempt 25 million tons of cereal in storage in the EU from the Blair House Accord, to compare the EU's export subsidies not to average annual volume exported between 1986–1990 but in 1992 which allows the EU (but mainly France) to export an additional 8 millions tons of cereals, and to extend the peace clause from six to eight years. In counterpart the EU has widened access to its market of some agricultural products of the US such as pork, grains, dairy products, processed turkey, nuts, etc, and abolished tariffs on sensitive industrial products such as steel, wood, paper, semiconductor equipment but reduced it on semiconductors themselves to 3 per cent, etc: (1993) Financial Times 6 December p3.

Council Regulation 3290/94[30] (in force since 1 January 1995) which introduced 'tariffication'. In order to ensure transparency import levies have been replaced by customs duties which are easier to detect and compare than any non-tariff barriers to trade. Many other necessary measures have been adopted by the Council in order to comply with the EU obligations deriving from the accords. The overall effect of the Uruguay Round agreements is not as dramatic as it may look, but they confirm and amplify the EU long-term objectives, that is, creation of a much smaller and efficient agricultural sector.

Agriculture is still a very sensitive area. Many Member States benefit considerably from the CAP and the next enlargement of the EU will necessitate another reform. Indeed, the current agricultural policy would be unsustainable when the Union accepts countries like Poland and Hungary which have a substantial agricultural base. Even now, the support of CAP costs the EU about ECU 35 billion per annum, half of the total EU budget. The Argicultural Council of the EU will submit a detailed report on the CAP reform in the light of the next enlargement in January 1998.

Common Fisheries Policy (CFP)

The CFP was established in 1970, but not fully implemented until 1983, and is based on the same provisions of the EC Treaty as the CAP, that is arts 38–43 EC. The basic principles are similar to the CAP, that is: the establishment of a common organisation over the fishing market; its protection from outside imports by imposing a common external tariff; access to EU fishing waters to all Union fisherman;[31] allocation of quotas to each Member State,[32] accompanied by technical conservation measures that regulate the fishing gear, impose limitations on the minimum size of fish caught and prohibit fishing for certain periods of the year in specific areas; introduction of market intervention instruments, such as a system of guide prices for more than 100 fish species; and subsidies for catches withdrawn from the market based on a decreasing scale, etc.[33]

The financial involvement of the Community in subsidising the CFP is very low – 1 per cent of the EC spending. The entire EU fishing industry employs about 300,000 fisherman and 1.5 million people in associated industries.

The problems which the Community faces in relation to the CFP are universal: too many boats chasing too few fish. The EU fleet operates at 40 per cent above capacity while the fish stocks are dwindling, and scientific evidence shows that many species are endangered, for example cod, hake, North Sea plaice, herring and downs herring, Baltic salmon, etc. Overfishing and modern fishing practices, which permit the taking of adolescent and young adult fish before they have spawned, and the quota system itself which leads to the discard of a high quantity of fish, have resulted in a dramatic fall in fish stocks. Paradoxically, quotas

---

[30] OJ L349 31.12.94 p105.

[31] EU fishing waters consists of the waters around Member States to 200 nautical miles offshore, ie the EEZ, and exclude the 12 mile Territorial Seas, but also include overseas waters where the EC has negotiated rights, ie North West Atlantic Fisheries – Canadian turbot, etc.

[32] A vessel registered in a Member State can fish anywhere in EU fishing waters provided that Member State has not exceeded quota.

[33] Based on Council Regulation 3759/92 (OJ L388 32.12.92 p1), as amended by Regulation 3318/94 (OJ L350 31.12.94 p15).

were introduced to protect fish stocks but they force fisherman to discard fish caught in excess of the quota amount, all undersize fish of the quota species and all fish other than the quota species. These fish are usually dead by the time that they are returned to the sea.[34] In order to avoid an ecological disaster it is necessary to reduce catches and to introduce stringent conservation measures. The most difficult problem is to convince fisherman of the validity of scientific evidence. Fisheries disputes between international fleets for the remaining stocks are common, but the complete collapse of stocks would spell disaster for all of them.[35]

In Case 804/79 *Commission* v *United Kingdom*[36] the ECJ held that the conservation and management of the fisheries resources is within the exclusive competence of the Community. As a result, the Community has introduced a number of measures in this area which are presently contained in Council Regulation 3760/92[37] and will apply until 2002. Its practical enforcement is monitored by the EC fisheries inspectors.

Common Transport Policy (CTP)

Articles 74–84 of the Treaty of Rome established a legal framework for a CTP. The principles of the CTP were further developed in the Schaus Memorandum of 1961 which proposed three types of measures necessary to pursue the CTP: abolishing discrimination both between the different modes of transport and between Member States; liberalising the cross-border supply of services for carriers; and harmonising various aspects of transport, such as standardising the weight and dimension of road vehicles, taxation of vehicles, etc.[38] The TEU in Title XII arts 129b–129d establishes trans-European networks in the fields of transport, telecommunication and energy infrastructures which aim at connecting national networks into an integrated EU networks. The Council and the EP have already adopted a decision which lays down guidelines for measures necessary to ensure the inter-operability of networks and provides a list of projects of common interest.[39]

In practice, progress towards the CTP was both slow and piecemeal for a number of reasons, the main being that Member States jealously protected their competences in transport matters in view of its importance to their domestic economy. This was exacerbated by providers of different modes of transport who wanted to protect their competitive and financial advantages in national markets.

The breakthrough came with the judgment of the ECJ in Case 13/83 *European Parliament* v *Council*[40] in which the EP successfully challenged the inaction of the Council in relation to the introduction of the CTP, and its failure to act on 16 Commission proposals relating to transport. The Court held that the Council of Transport Ministers was required

---

[34] It is estimated that up to 50 per cent of cod and haddock caught are discarded: (1997) The European 17–23 April.

[35] In this respect, the collapse of cod stocks in Newfoundland in early 1990 resulted in 40,000 jobs loss in the area: (1997) The European 17–23 April p3.

[36] [1981] ECR 1045; see also Cases 3, 4 and 6/76 *Kramer* [1976] ECR 1279.

[37] OJ L389 31.12.92 p1; also Regulation 894/97 (OJ L132 23.5.97 p1) laying down certain technical measures for the conservation of fishery resources.

[38] See J Whitelegg, *Transport Policy in the EEC*, London: Routledge, 1988.

[39] Decision 96/1254 (OJ L161 19.6.96 p147).

[40] [1985] ECR 1513.

under arts 3(e) and 74 EC to adopt measures to liberalise transport services within a reasonable time whether in a single decision or a series of decisions. At that time the Transport Council acted unanimously and on its own initiative. As a result of the Court judgment, and with the advent of the common market, the Council was prompted to act, but the measures it adopted were still piecemeal and limited to areas as disparate as tachographs, licences for inland waterway vessels, noise emission from subsonic aircraft, etc. During that period, transport matters arose more frequently in the context of competition policy, which were initially excluded from its scope of application[41] but later governed by specific regulations of the Council.

The deregulation of transport at an international level and the establishment of an internal market necessitated a new approach towards the CTP. Under the SEA and the TEU in certain areas of transport the Council is empowered to act by qualified majority. Furthermore, transport safety and evaluation of the CTP must now be viewed in the light of art 2 EC, that is, it must reflect the general objectives of the EU such as 'the harmonious and balanced development of economic activities', sustainable and non-inflationary development of economic activities respecting the environment, convergence of economic performance, high employment and social protection, etc.

As a result, the Commission prepared a report on *The Future Development of the Common Transport Policy* in 1992 which highlighted three main objectives of the CFP: the elimination of existing obstacles within the internal market in order to create a safe, efficient, integrated and modern transport system; the incorporation of the protection of the environment within the CTP; and, finally, the integration of all transport networks into a single trans-European network.[42] In 1995 the Commission submitted the Second Action Programme 1995–2000 which outlines necessary legislative measures required to achieve those objectives. Since then an impressive number of measures has been introduced to complete a single market in all sectors of transport, including: road freight and road passenger transport, rail and inland waterway transport, maritime and air transport. The development of an infrastructure in all forms of transport based on the existing facilities and future needs which necessitates important investment is one of the main preoccupations of the Community.[43]

The Commission in its 1997 Work Programme identifies a number of specific measures which must be adopted in this area, such as training of safety advisors for the transport of dangerous goods by road, rail and inland waterways, regulation of the composition of ships' crew, harmonisation in the use of long-distance transfer of computerised information in road transport, issuing of air carrier certificates, and the adoption of its draft directive on the registration of persons sailing on board passenger ships.[44] They will complete the creation of the single market in transport in 1997.[45]

---

[41] Council Regulation 17/62 (OJ Sp Ed 1959–62 p87).

[42] COM(92)494.

[43] The Council Regulation 3359/90/EEC on an Action Programme in the Field of Transport Infrastructure with a view to the Completion of an Integrated Transport Market in 1992, Council of the European Communities, Brussels, 1990.

[44] OJ C31 31.1.97 p5.

[45] Special Report, 'The European Commission's 1997 Work Programme', *European Law Monitor*, February 1997.

5.3 Legislative competences in other sectors

The original Treaty of Rome conferred competences to the Community in a limited number of areas. Apart from the fields already mentioned, the Treaty provides for competence in social competition and association policies. Under art 235 EC the Community has added new areas such as regional, environmental, research and development and energy policies, all of them confirmed and recognised under the SEA, apart from energy policy. The Treaty of Maastricht has considerably extended the areas of EC competence, but in all new areas the Community has only complementary powers, that is, the Member States are basically responsible for development of new policies. This is highlighted by the legal terminology used in arts 3 and 3b EC in relation to those areas. The Community contributes to, promotes, etc, action in a particular domain.

The diversity of the competences of the EC makes their classification difficult. Nevertheless, in some of them the EC has legislative powers – competition policy, social policy, environmental policy, protection of consumers, free movement of persons within the EU – in others it intervenes only to co-ordinate, recommend and provide financial support from the EC budget.

Competition policy

The competition policy is vital for the proper functioning of the common market. From their inception the ECSC and EEC Treaties established frameworks for competition between undertakings. The ECSC Treaty provides for a wider role of the Commission in the enforcement of competition policy than the EEC Treaty.[46]

The EEC Treaty required the Community to establish 'a system ensuring that competition in the internal market is not distorted'.[47] The main objective of the EC competition policy is the integration of the Member States into the single market, although the social and economic development of the Community also plays an important role. Indeed, some anti-competitive arrangements of undertakings which are *prima facie* in breach of art 85(1) EC may be exempt from the general prohibition set out in this provision if they contribute 'to improving the production or distribution of goods or to promoting technical or economic progress, while allowing consumers a fair share of the resulting benefit', but they may not impose on the undertakings concerned restrictions which are not indispensable or which eliminate competition in respect of a substantial part of the products in question.[48]

In order to cover all forms of anti-competitive behaviour by any commercially active entity dealing in goods, services or carrying out any other commercial activity, the EC

---

[46] The Commission has similar powers under arts 65 ECSC and 85 EC, but art 66(7) ECSC, concerning abuse of a dominant position by an undertaking, empowers the Commission to determine prices and conditions of sale or draw up production and delivery programmes where the undertaking is or acquires a dominant position within the common market in breach of EC law. Also, under art 66(1) and (2) ECSC the High Authority/Commission has important powers regarding mergers between undertakings, while the EC Treaty has no similar provision.

[47] Article 3f EEC, now art 3g EC.

[48] Article 85(3) EC.

Treaty contains many provisions relating to its competition policy. The most important are: arts 85 and 86 which regulate the conduct of undertakings within the common market; art 90 which concerns State monopolies; and arts 92–94 EC on State aid. These provisions are further developed by secondary legislation, the most important being Regulation 4064/89 on the control of concentration between undertakings (Merger Control Regulation),[49] and Regulation 17/62[50] on enforcement powers and procedures of the Commission in relation to the application of arts 85 and 86 EC.

Before examining the main features of competition policy it is necessary to emphasise that Community policy in this area has a federal dimension. National competition rules have not been harmonised by the EC. To the contrary, they are left unchanged. The EC is solely concerned with the Community dimension of competition issues.

Article 85 deals with anti-competitive conduct between undertakings; it prohibits arrangements between them which have as their object or effect the prevention, restriction or distortion of competition within the common market. Such arrangements are in breach of art 85(1) EC if they have direct or indirect, actual or potential effect on the pattern of trade between Member States.[51] However, if this effect is insignificant, under the *de minimis* rule[52] the anti-competitive agreements are excluded from the scope of application of art 85(1) EC. The Commission issued in 1968 a Notice on Agreements of Minor Importance[53] which provides guidelines as to the application of the *de minimis* rule. Its art 7 states that an agreement is of minor importance if the goods and services, subject of the agreement, together with the participating undertakings' other goods and services which are considered by users as equivalent in terms of their characteristics, price and use, do not represent more than 5 per cent of the total market for such goods and services in the area affected by the agreement, and when the aggregate turnover of the participating undertakings amounts to no more than ECU 200 million. However, it is only a Notice and as such it is not legally binding. In practice the ECJ, in deciding whether an agreement is of minor importance, takes into consideration the structure of the market for a particular product, rather than relying on a purely quantitative approach.[54] Article 85(1) provides a non-exhaustive list of arrangements between undertakings which are incompatible with the common market and as such are prohibited. It encompasses: fixing purchase or selling prices or any other trading conditions; limiting or controlling production, marketing technical development or investment; sharing markets or sources of supply; discriminating between parties in equivalent transactions; and subjecting transactions to unconnected supplementary obligations. As already mentioned, under certain circumstances the undertakings may be exempted from the prohibition even though they have entered into anti-competitive agreements in breach of art 85(1). Also, art 85 applies to both horizontal (between competitors in the same market) and vertical (between undertakings at a different level of an economic process, eg manufacturers and distributors) agreements.[55]

---

[49] OJ L257 21.9.90 p13.
[50] OJ O13 21.2.62 p204 (SE SERI (59–62) p87).
[51] Case 56/65 *Société Technique Minière* v *Maschinenbau Ulm GmbH* [1966] ECR 235.
[52] This principle was introduced by the ECJ in Case 5/69 *Volk* v *Etablissements Vervaecke* [1969] ECR 295.
[53] The version in force was adopted in 1986: OJ C231 12.9.86 p2.
[54] Case 30/78 *Distillers Co Ltd* v *Commission* [1980] ECR 2229.
[55] Joined Cases 56 and 58/64 *Consten and Grundig* v *Commission* [1966] ECR 299.

Article 86 concerns the conduct of an undertaking within the market structure. It prohibits any abuse of a dominant position by one or more undertakings, but does not prohibit being in the dominant position itself, unlike the United States' anti-trust law where the Sherman Act prohibits such dominance. The notion of a dominant position and its abuse have been defined by the ECJ. In Case 27/76 *United Brands* v *Commission*[56] the ECJ held that the dominant position is 'a position of economic strength enjoyed by an undertaking which enables it to prevent competition being maintained on the relevant market by affording it the power to behave to an appreciable extent independently of its competitors, its customers and ultimately of the consumers'.[57] The dominance is assessed not in abstract but in relation to a relevant product market[58] geographically delimited.[59] Abuse has been defined in Case 85/76 *Hoffman-La Roche* v *Commission*[60] as an objective concept; it relates to the behaviour of an undertaking in a dominant position which influences the structure of a market resulting in its weakening and which 'through recourse to methods different from those which condition normal competition in products or services on the basis of the transactions of commercial operators, has the effect of hindering the maintenance of the degree of competition still existing in the market or the growth of that competition'.[61]

The abuses are divided into two categories: exploitative and anti-competitive. The first, exploitative abuse, occurs when an undertaking imposes unfair conditions on consumers, while the second, anti-competitive abuse, takes place when a dominant undertaking through its conduct prevents or weakens the position of other undertakings in the context of the relevant product market. Finally, the abuse of a dominant position must have an effect on trade between Member States, and the meaning of the effect is similar under arts 85 and 86 EC.

In competition matters important enforcement powers have been delegated to the Commission by the Council under Regulation 17/62[62] and other specific regulations in the area of transport. The Commission's decisions are subject to an appeal to the Court of First Instance and, only on a point of law, from that jurisdiction to the ECJ. In order to enforce EC competition law the Commission has investigative and punitive powers. The investigative powers permit the Commission to request information from the Member States about any undertakings including the undertaking under investigation, to carry out on-the-spot investigations, to impose interim measures during the investigation and require the discontinuance of prohibited conduct. As to punitive powers the Commission may impose substantial fines upon undertakings in breach of arts 85 or 86 EC amounting to the maximum of ECU one million or 10 per cent of turnover calculated on the basis of group

---

[56] [1978] ECR 207.

[57] Ibid, para 38.

[58] Case 6/72 *Europemballage and Continental Can Co* v *Commission* [1973] ECR 215. The ECJ referred to characteristics of the product in terms of their interchangeability in consumption or use. Thus, a product with close substitutes is considered as a relevant product market.

[59] In Case 27/76 *United Brands Co* v *Commission* [1978] ECR 207 the ECJ held that the relevant geographical market is the one in which objective conditions of competition are the same for all traders.

[60] [1979] ECR 461.

[61] Ibid, para 91.

[62] Supra note 50.

turnover in the relevant market sector, and not just in the Member State where the offence occurred, whichever is greater.

In addition, the Commission alone has powers to grant exemption from the prohibition contained in art 85(1) EC on an individual basis if an agreement is notified to it or collectively under regulations issued by the Council or the Commission providing for block exemptions. Block exemptions are adopted in relation to general categories of agreements such as exclusive distribution agreements, exclusive purchase agreements, etc. A particular regulation serves as a model for an agreement between undertakings concerned. Block exemptions contain a list of permitted clauses (white list), prohibited clauses (black list) and those which must be notified to the Commission, but if not opposed by the latter within six months of notification are deemed to be exempt (grey list). Their objective is to avoid individual assessment of applications for exemption which imposes a heavy administrative burden on the Commission and considerably delays the conclusion of an agreement between undertakings under art 85(1) EC. Under art 86 there is no exemption from liability but an undertaking may ask the Commission for negative clearance by virtue of art 2 of Regulation 17/62. In this respect, a decision of the Commission assures the undertaking concerned that its envisaged action in not contrary to art 86 EC.

Since September 1990 the Commission has enforcement powers in relation to mergers with a Community dimension. Under Regulation 4064/89[63] mergers with a Community dimension, that is where the undertakings concerned have an aggregate worldwide turnover of more than ECU 5,000 million and the aggregate Community turnover of each of at least two of the undertakings is more than ECU 250 million, must be notified to the Commission within one week of the conclusion of the agreement or the announcement of a public bid or the acquisition of a 'controlling interest', whichever is the earliest. The Commission must issue a decision within one month, and up to six weeks if informed by the Member States that the proposed merger threatens to create or strengthen the compartmentalisation of a common market. If the Commission decides to investigate, the investigation must commence within one month or six weeks of notification and must be completed within four months by a final decision. The Commission may prohibit the merger, order its divestiture if already completed, impose fines up to 10 per cent of turnover on parties involved in prohibited merger, and/or require the parties to amend the proposed merger agreement.

Social policy

Social policy was not of major importance to the six original Member States. They focused on economic integration which resulted in a low-key approach to social issues. Two aspects of social policy are mentioned by the original Treaty of Rome: the establishment of the European Social Fund and powers of the Community to promote social progress, although in the latter the EEC was limited to recommending certain measures to the Member States without any possibility of forcing them to adopt these measures. Only in two areas did the Treaty confer legislative powers on the EEC: the protection of health and safety at work through directives, and in the social security matters of 'migrant workers' through

---

[63] OJ L257 21.9.90 p13.

regulations. Also under art 119 EEC the Community is empowered to take binding measures to ensure equal pay for equal work performed by men and women.

The European Social Fund (ESF) based on arts 3 and 123–128 EEC was set up in 1960. At the beginning it focused on the retraining and resettlement of unemployed workers and maintaining existing workplaces in the context of changes in economic conditions due to the creation of the Communities. However, its objectives and the operational design have changed many times. The last reform took place in 1994. Now, its main objectives are to promote employment opportunities and labour mobility within the EC and to facilitate these objectives by offering vocational training and retraining.[64] Under Council Regulations 2081/93,[65] 2082/93[66] and 2084/93[67] the European Social Fund, within a framework of the Community programme of economic and social development which set up five main objectives in this area, is in charge of Objective Three, that is, action for combating long-term unemployment (over 12 months), together with adopting measures facilitating the occupational integration of young people (under 25) and those threatened with exclusion from the labour market. Between 1994 and 1999 9 per cent of the ESF will be spent on measures providing employment opportunities for disadvantaged groups. Under Objective Five the ESF has to facilitate the worker's adaptation to industrial changes and to changes in production systems. It is also involved in Objectives One and Two covering regional and rural assistance. The fund is administered by the Commission but the Council establishes guidelines for ESF. The Fund provides financial support for various projects in Member States sponsored mostly by public and private sectors on all levels – national, regional and local – aimed at reducing unemployment in certain areas suffering from a decline in industry, underdevelopment or among certain groups such as the young unemployed, the long-term unemployed, women re-entering the work market, the disabled, etc. Its budget, although considerably increased, is relatively small. For 1995 it was ECU 6.5 billion – a sum which has been outstripped by demand.

Under the umbrella of ESF a European Employment Services agency was established to serve not just as an employment agency but also a forum for discussion on employment.

The social dimension of the Community and, consequently, the allocation of important powers to the Community in this area was initiated by the Paris Summit of 1972 which asked the Commission to prepare proposals on social policy. It resulted in the creation of a Social Action Programme in 1973 which was adopted by the Council in January 1974.[68] It has three main objectives: to ensure full and better employment in the Community; to improve living conditions; and to promote industrial democracy, that is participation of management and labour in the economic and social policy-making of the EC and participation of workers in the decision-making processes of their companies. However, the implementation of these measures was hindered by economic recession. As a result, it was in the 1980s, under the French concept of the Social Area, that these measures were finally adopted. Indeed, the electoral victory of François Mitterrand in France and the appointment

---

[64] Articles 123 et seq, Title XIV EC and Protocol 15.
[65] OJ L193 31.7.93 p5.
[66] OJ L193 31.7. 93 p20.
[67] OJ L193 31.7. 93 p39.
[68] OJ C13 21.1.74 p1.

of Jacques Delors as the President of the Commission gave a new impetus to the development of social policy. The SEA confirmed in its preamble the necessity to 'improve the [Community's] economic and social situation by extending policies and pursuing new objectives'. It introduced a new Title on economic and social cohesion and under art 118a EEC provided for qualified majority voting in the health and safety of workers which resulted in adoption of many measures.

In 1985 at Val Duchesse, a Belgian chateau, Jacques Delors initiated dialogue between 'social partners', that is business leaders and trade unions. The outcome of the Val Duchesse social dialogue was the reinforcement of employment policies of the Community. Furthermore, Delors considered that the successful completion of the internal market necessitated adoption of measures in social policy. The social dimension of the Single European Market (SEM) had been endorsed by the Hanover summit in 1988. The Presidency conclusions emphasised that the SEM should benefit all people by improving working conditions, living standards, protection of health and safety, access to vocational training and further development of the Val Duchesse social dialogue.[69] As a result the Commission presented a working paper on the social dimension of the single market in September 1988.[70] Based on this paper, and backed by the French government, Delors proposed to draft the Community charter of basic social rights. The first draft of the Social Charter was ready in May 1989. The final version of Community Charter of the Fundamental Social Rights of Workers was presented by the Commission in October 1989 and adopted by the Strasbourg summit in December 1989 by all Member States except the UK. The Charter was strongly criticised by the government of the UK and, although many amendments were introduced, it was considered unacceptable[71] as it was viewed as an attempt to introduce socialism by the back door.

The Community Charter of the Fundamental Rights of Workers is a non-binding document which lays down 12 categories of social rights: the right to work in the chosen country by a worker; the right to choose an occupation and to be fairly paid; the right to improve working and living conditions; the right to social protection under the same conditions as nationals of a host State; the right to freedom of association and collective bargaining; the right of workers to information, consultation and participation; the right to vocational training; the right to equal treatment between men and women; the right to health and safety at work; social protection for children and adolescents; the right to a minimum income for the elderly; and the right to professional integration for disabled persons.

The Social Charter, although a declaratory and hortatory document, is of great importance. Not only has it set the Community agenda in social matters, but it has also empowered the Commission to take appropriate measures in order to implement the rights enumerated in the Social Charter and to prepare annual reports on its application in the Member States. As a result, the Commission prepared a Social Action Programme which contained 47 measures of which only 17 were new.[72]

The Treaty of Maastricht has further developed Community social policy, although the opposition of the UK prevented the Social Charter from being incorporated into the Treaty

---

[69] EC Bull 6–1988, point 1.1.1.
[70] EC Bull 9–1988, point 1.1.–6.
[71] EC Bull 12–1989, Presidency Conclusions, point 1.1.10.
[72] COM(89)568 final, November 29, 1989.

itself. The remaining Member States adopted a Protocol on Social Policy and confirmed their commitment to an EC-wide social policy.[73]

The Social Protocol contains only seven articles. Article 1 defines the objectives of the Protocol and art 2 concerns the Council voting procedures, that is it provides for qualified majority voting in the following areas – health and safety at work, working conditions, information and consultation of workers, equal opportunities between men and women and integration of people excluded from the labour market – and for unanimity in matters related to social security, such as social protection, protection of redundant workers, representation, collective defence of workers and employers, employment conditions for non-EC nationals, and finance for employment generation. Article 3 requires that the Commission engages in consultation with management and labour in order to prepare proposals under the Protocol, art 4 encourages the pursuit of a dialogue between management and labour which may result in agreements even at EU level, art 5 states that in order to achieve the objectives enumerated in art 1 of the Protocol, the Commission should encourage the Member States to co-operate and to co-ordinate their national social policies, art 6 emphasises the obligation of Member States to abolish sex discrimination between men and women, and, finally, art 7 calls on the Commission to submit annual reports on the implementation of measures adopted in view of the achievement of the art 1 objectives.

The decision of the UK to reject the social dimension of the EC as presented in the Social Charter and the Social Protocol led to the adoption of the Agreement on Social Policy among the 11 other Member States. The UK is a contracting party to the Social Protocol as it constitutes an integral part of the Treaty under art 239 EC, but is excluded from its application on the grounds of the Agreement on Social Policy to which the UK is not a party. However, the accession to the Social Protocol by the new government of the UK has resolved complicated issues of its legal status. The Labour government signed an agreement at the Amsterdam Conference on 17 June 1997 ending Britain's opt-out and allowing the incorporation of the Social Protocol into the revised Treaty.[74] Until the entry into force of the Treaty of Amsterdam the UK will have no right to vote on legislation adopted under the Social Protocol but will take part in deliberations. Already the UK has given its first approval for a directive which assists victims of sexual discrimination to prove their case. It requires an employer to prove that there has been no discrimination once the applicant demonstrates that there is a case to answer.[75]

Environmental policy

As already mentioned, the environmental policy was established outside the Treaty framework at the Paris Summit shortly after the UN Stockholm Conference on Environment in 1972. The summit asked the Commission to prepare the Environmental Action Programmes (EAPs). So far the Commission has submitted five action programmes for approval by the Council. The programmes are indicative rather than legally binding, but

---

[73] B Springer, *The Social Dimension of 1992*, Westport: Praeger, 1992, pp39–42.
[74] See Chapter 3.
[75] Ch Bremner, 'Britain Approves its First Law under the Social Chapter' (1997) The Times 28 June.

many of their proposals are later transposed into Community law. The first EAP (1973–1977)[76] laid down general principles of EC environmental policy which are still in effect, for example: the 'polluter pays' principle – that the polluter should pay for the damage he caused to the environment – which was given legally binding effect in art 130r(2) EC; the importance of preventive measures; and the impact of Community's socio-economic development on the environment. The second EAP (1977–1981) and the third EAP (1982–1986) consolidated and further developed general principles of the first EAP. The fourth EAP (1987–1992) put more emphasis on preventive measures, set up common standards for environmental protection and tried to intertwine environmental protection with other EC policies.[77] In order to stimulate and assist in the implementation of the action programmes the European Environmental Agency, a successor to the 'Corine' programme (1985–1990), was established in 1990. It is entrusted with the collection and publication of data on environmental issues and the preparation of reports on the state of environment in the Community every three years. The European Environmental Agency, which started its activities in the spring of 1994, has its seat in Copenhagen. The EP wanted the Agency to have enforcement powers but this was opposed by the Council.

The fifth action programme 'Towards Sustainability: a European Community Programme of Policy and Action in Relation to the Environmental and Sustainable Development (1993–2000)'[78] reinforces the prevention principles and introduces a new approach towards the protection of environment by replacing the traditional 'top-down' by a 'bottom-up' policy, that is, it involves broader categories of actors and a broader range of policy instruments such as incentives to promote environment-friendly products, and emphasis on education and information. The fifth EAP sets up general long-term objectives in five sectors: industry, energy, transport, agriculture and tourism. Also, the fifth EAP requires that any Commission proposal is assessed in the light of its effect on the environment. Public access to information on environmental issues held by public bodies has been facilitated by Directive 90/313 on Access to Information on the Environment[79] (in force since 31 December 1992) which provides that any person is entitled to obtain information from these bodies at a reasonable charge. It also establishes an appeal procedure in the case of refusal or failure to respond.

The legal bases of environmental policy are now contained in Title XVI, arts 130r–130t EC, which should be assessed in the light of art 2 EC which states that the task of the Community is to promote 'sustainable and non-inflationary growth respecting the environment'. Article 130r(1) EC establishes the Community objectives in its environmental policy, adding to those stated in the SEA – preservation, protection and improvement of the quality of the environment, protection of human health and the prudent and rational utilisation of natural resources – and including a new one relating to the international dimension of the EC environmental policy. The action of the EC is subject to the principle of subsidiarity which determines whether these objectives could be better achieved at the

---

[76] OJ C112 20.12.72 p1.
[77] Hassan, 'Environmental Policy', in F McDonald and S Dearden (eds), *European Economic Integration*, London: Longman, 1992, p124.
[78] OJ C138 17.5.93 p1.
[79] OJ L158 23.6.90 p56.

Community level or the national level. The principles of the Community policy in this area are set out in art 130r(2) EC. They should apply in the context of regional diversity. Among the principles enumerated in art 130r(2) EC the most important is the precautionary principle which puts emphasis on the prevention of environmental damage rather than remedying its effects, and which permits the EC to take preventive measures against environmental damage before it occurs. The ECJ has confirmed its application in Case C–2/90 *Commission v Belgium (Walloonian Waste)*[80] when it held that wastes should be disposed as close as possible to their place of origin in order to reduce the possibility of any damage to environment taking place. Even though there is insufficient scientific proof that the harm will occur, the precautionary principle permits anticipatory measures on the grounds that many environmental processes are irreversible. Article 130r(2) EC also states that environmental damage should as a priority be rectified at source and that the 'polluter pays' principle applies in this area. Finally, the principle of integration provides that the requirements regarding the protection of environment must be incorporated into the definition and implementation of other EC policies.

Under art 130t(2) EC Member States are allowed to adopt more stringent measures providing they are in conformity with the EC Treaty and are notified to the Commission. Also, the TEU introduces an important innovation as to voting in the Council on environmental issues. Article 130s EC restricts the unanimity to three main areas: fiscal measures, town and county planning and measures significantly affecting the Member States' choices between different energy sources, and extends qualified majority voting to other environmental matters.

The linkage between environmental and economic issues is obvious. It has been acknowledged by the ECJ in Case 91/79 *Commission v Italy*[81] in the context of the EC competition policy. The Court held that different standards concerning the protection of environment in the Member States may put additional burdens on some undertakings and thus place them at a competitive disadvantage vis-à-vis undertakings from other Member States, which would result in the distortion of competition within the Community.

The economic dimension of environmental problems, and the use of economic instruments in order to achieve environmental objectives, are important considerations of environmental policy. In this respect, some economic theories link economic growth with the accelerating rates of depletion of natural resources and increasing levels of waste disposal. Sustainable economic growth is stifled because of the limited stock of natural resources and the capacity of the environment to assimilate growing accumulation of waste. Other theories emphasise that this effect may be reduced or even eliminated where markets work efficiently. It seems that the second approach has gained considerable support. The current EAP has as its long-term objective sustainable economic growth. The Commission has emphasised that the relationship between environment and development:

> '[it] entails preserving the overall balance and value of the natural capital stock, redefinition of short, medium and long-term cost/benefit evaluation criteria and instruments to reflect the real socio-economic effects and values of consumption and conservation, and the equitable

---

[80] [1992] ECR I–4431.
[81] [1980] ECR 1099.

real socio-economic effects and values of consumption and conservation, and the equitable distribution and use of resources between nations and regions over the world'.[82]

The current environmental issues such as acidification and air pollution, depletion of natural resources, biodiversity, climate change, etc, are only symptoms – the main problem is the management of resources which can be solved, *inter alia*, by the greater use of market-based instruments to direct producers and consumers alike towards responsible use of natural resources. In particular, in five sectors – industry, energy, transport, agriculture and tourism – which are the main source of current environmental problems, the incorporation of environmental considerations into their future development and operation is required.

The Community applies both economic and regulatory instruments as tools of environmental policy. Economic instruments consist of financial incentives and disincentives to encourage eco-friendly behaviour of both consumers and producers, such as charges and taxes, grants and subsidies, etc. The EC has been very successful in introducing many measures relating to waste management, land use, water and air pollution. Three stages can be distinguished in the developments of EC environmental policy, reflecting chronologically the EC priorities in this area.[83]

First stage in the development of environmental policy
In the early 1970s the main emphasis was on corrective measures designed to clean up and to control problems in specific sectors – mainly air and water pollution and the reduction, processing and recycling of waste – which were strengthened later by more stringent requirements. The following measures have been adopted:

Water pollution In the 1970s primary legislative measures aimed at reducing and preventing water pollution were issued in Directive 76/464 on pollution caused by certain dangerous substances discharged into the aquatic environment of the Communities,[84] which divided dangerous substances into two categories: those totally banned such as carcinogens, mercury, cadmium, etc; and other less harmful products for which discharges should be limited. This framework directive was completed by a number of measures setting quality standards for water intended for human consumption in Directive 80/778[85] for the quality of

---

[82] Commission of the European Communities, *Towards Sustainability: a European Community Programme of Policy Action in Relation to the Environment and Sustainable Development*, vol 2, COM 23, Brussels, CEC, p18.

[83] For details see Kiss and Shelton, *Manual of European Environmental Law*, Cambridge: Cambridge University Press, 1994.

[84] OJ L129 18.5.76 p23, as amended by Directive 91/692 Concerning Standardising and Rationalising Reports on the Implementation of Certain Directives Relating to the Environment (OJ L377 31.12.91 p48). Many directives have been adopted on its basis such as Council Directive 86/280 on limit values and quality objectives for discharges of certain dangerous substances included in List I of the Annex to Directive 76/464 as amended by: Directive 86/280 (OJ L158 25.6.88 p35) and Directive 90/415 amending Annex II to Directive 86/280 (OJ L219 14.8.90 p49); Directive 83/513 on limit values and quality objectives for cadmium discharges (OJ L291 24.10.83 p1); Directive 82/176 on limit values and quality objectives for mercury discharges by the chlor-alkali electrolysis industry (OJ L81 27.3.82 p29); Directive 84/156 on limit values and quality objectives for mercury discharges by sectors other than the chlor-alkali electrolysis industry (OJ L74 17.3.84 p49); Directive 84/491 on limit values and quality objectives for discharges of hexachlorocyclohexane (OJ L274 17.10.84 p11), etc.

[85] OJ L229 30.8.80 p11, amended by Directive 81/858 (OJ L319 7.11.81 p19).

bathing water (beaches) in Directive 76/160,[86] on fresh waters needing protection or improvement in order to support fish life in Directive 78/659,[87] on the quality required of shellfish waters in Directive 79/923,[88] and on the quality required of surface water intended for the abstraction of drinking water in the Member States in Directive 75/440.[89] These measures have been completed by Directive 80/68[90] on discharges of dangerous substances to groundwater and a Council Decision on sea pollution.[91]

Air pollution The establishment of quality standards which set maximum limits for discharges of pollutants into the air have been regulated by a number of EC directives such as Directive 80/779 on pollution by sulphur dioxide and suspended particulates,[92] Directive 82/884 on limits for lead in the air,[93] Directive 85/203 on pollution by nitrogen dioxide,[94] etc. Also, the emission of pollutants by industrial plants, incinerators, etc, is regulated by EC directives.[95] The discharge into air of other substances such as carbon monoxide and ozone are not restricted by the EC legislation but is controlled by Member States.

For motor vehicle emissions the Community has steadily introduced stricter standards which resulted in reducing pollutants by 80–90 per cent since 1980, and culminated in Directive 89/458[96] which requires all new cars marketed in the EC after 1 January 1993 to be equipped with catalytic converters. The adoption of Directive 91/441[97] (as amended in 1993) imposes even stricter limits for emissions for gasoline-fuelled motor vehicles as it requires that all new petrol engine cars must be fitted with a three-way catalytic converter. It seems that any further reduction of motor vehicle emission can only be achieved by alternative measures such as replacement of the existing carbon fuels by more environmentally friendly mixes, reduction in the use of cars, better control and inspection of existing cars, etc.

The protection of the ozone layer is a world-wide problem that has given rise to the adoption of a number of measures aiming at reducing the use of chlorofluorocarbons (CFCs).[98] The EC has participated in the preparation of international agreements in this area and has ratified the 1985 Vienna Convention for the Protection of the Ozone Layer, the 1987

---

[86] OJ L31 5.2.76 p1, amended many times.

[87] OJ L222 14.8.78 p1.

[88] OJ L281 10.11.79 p47, amended by Directive 91/692 OJ L377 31.12.91 p48.

[89] OJ L194 25.7.75 p26.

[90] OJ L20 26.1.80 p43.

[91] OJ L188 13.12.80 p11.

[92] OJ L229 30.8.80 p30, amended by Directive 89/427 (OJ L201 14.7.89 p53).

[93] OJ L378 31.12.82 p15.

[94] OJ L87 27.3.85 p1, amended by Directive 85/580 (OJ L372 31.12.85 p36).

[95] For example Directive 84/360 on the combatting of air pollution from industrial plants (OJ L188 16.7.84 p20), Directive 88/609 on the limitation of emissions of certain pollutants into the air from large combustion plants (OJ L366 7.12.88 p1), Directive 89/369 on the prevention of air pollution from new municipal waste-incineration plants (OJ L163 14.6.89 p32) and Directive 89/429 on the reduction of air pollution from existing municipal waste-incineration plants (OJ L203 15.7.89 p50).

[96] OJ L226 3.8.89 p1.

[97] OJ L242 30.8.91 p1, amended by Directive 93/59 on the approximation of the laws of Member States relating to measures to be taken against air pollution by emissions from motor vehicles (OJ L186 28.7.93 p2), amended by the Commission Directive 97/20 (OJ L125 16.5.97 p21), completed by Directive 94/22 relating to measures to be taken against air pollution by emissions from motor vehicles (OJ L100 19.4.94 p42).

[98] Regulation 3093/94 on substances that deplete the ozone layer (OJ L333 22.12.94 p1).

Montreal Protocol, and subsequent protocols in 1991 and 1992. The emission of carbon dioxide which contributes to the climate change by causing global warming (the greenhouse effect) and can only be tackled at the international level[99] is also an EU concern.

Noise abatement has been the subject of many EC directives. They focus on the methods of measuring noise levels and set standards for its maximum levels.[100]

Waste management In the EU more than two billion tons of waste are produced each year, including 100 million tons of municipal waste and 21 million tons of toxic waste. Since 1974 the Community has tried to tackle the problem of reducing and recycling of waste. The first Directive 75/442,[101] as amended by Framework Directive 91/156,[102] defines waste as any substances disposed of by the holder, and requires the Member States to establish a permit system for waste handling and general guidelines for the collection, disposal, recycling and processing of waste. Some measures have been enacted for specific wastes, such as polychlorinated biphenyls (PCBs), polychlorinated terphenyls (PCTs), asbestos, batteries and accumulators, liquid containers, etc, and those not covered by the framework directives such as toxic and hazardous wastes,[103] and their transport across national borders[104] which allows the EC to adhere to the Basel Convention on the Regulation and Disposal of Cross-border Movements of Dangerous Waste.[105] In December 1994 the Council adopted a Directive on packing and packaging waste which will result in the recovery and recycling of between 50 per cent and 65 per cent of such waste and 30 per cent energy saving due to their incineration within ten years.[106]

Chemicals Directive 67/548 on Classification, Packaging and Labelling of Dangerous Substances[107] and Directive 76/769/EEC[108] on the use and marketing of them, as amended and adapted many times over the years in order to reflect advances in science, constitute the main EC legislation in this area. They are complemented by Regulation 1734/88[109] which sets up a common notification system for the export/import of dangerous chemicals. In

---

[99] See Chapter 4.

[100] For example, Directive 70/157 relating to the possible sound level and the exhaust system of motor vehicles (OJ L042 23.2.70 p16 (SE SERI 70(1) p111)), amended many times, and its last version is contained in Directive 92/97 (OJ L371 19.12.92 p1); Directive 79/113 relating to the determination of the noise emission of construction plant and equipment (OJ L33 08.2.79 p15), also amended many times; Directive 80/51 on the limitation of noise emissions from subsonic aircraft (OJ L18 24.1.80 p26), also amended many times.

[101] OJ L194 25.7.75 p39.

[102] OJ L78 26.3.91 p32.

[103] Directive 78/319 (OJ L84 31.3.78 p43) which was replaced by Directive 91/689 (OJ L377 31.12.91 p20) and amended by Directive 94/31 (OJ L168 2.7.94 p28).

[104] Regulation 259/93 on the supervision and control of shipments of waste within, into and out of the European Community (OJ L30 6.2.93 p1).

[105] The version in force is contained in Regulation 120/97 (OJ L22 24.1.97 p14).

[106] EP and Council Directive 94/62 on packing and packaging waste (OJ L365 31.12.94 p10) complemented by Commission Decision of 28 January 1997 establishing the identification system for packaging materials (OJ L52 22.2.97 p28), and Commission Decision of 3 February 1997 establishing the formats relating to the database system (OJ L52 22.2.97 p22).

[107] OJ L196 16.8.67 p1, amended many times.

[108] OJ L262 27.9.76 p201 has been amended 14 times, the last amendment is contained in OJ L116 6.5.97 p31.

[109] OJ L155 22.6.88 p2.

order to prevent and limit damage to humans and the environment caused by industrial accidents, and following the Seveso disaster in Italy which involved contamination of a large area by dioxins, highly carcinogenic substances, the Community adopted Directive 82/501 (the so-called Seveso Directive)[110] which imposes on manufacturers using dangerous materials a duty to notify local authorities of their use including storage, handling, quantities used, etc, and requires that manufacturers and local authorities prepare emergency measures in case of such disasters.

Second stage in the development of environmental policy

In the second stage of development of the Community environmental policy the emphasis was put on the protection of specific uses of land, which included protection of natural habitats and the promotion of large-scale environmental programmes. The first Directive 79/409 on the Conservation of Wild Birds[111] requires the Member States to maintain populations of wild birds and to preserve, maintain and re-establish habitats for birds covered by the Directive. It also regulates their hunting, trapping, killing, possession and transport, while Directive 92/43 on the Conservation of Natural Habitats and of Wild Flora and Fauna[112] sets up a general scheme for the protection of natural habitats and the species inhabiting them. Its objective is to create a 'European ecological network' called 'Natura 2000', comprising the existing areas designated to protect natural habitats as well as new conservation sites, and it provides a list of protected species.[113]

Further examples of the extent of environmental protection are: Regulation 563/91 on Action by the Community for the Protection of the Environment in the Mediterranean Regions;[114] Regulation 3908/91 on Community Action to Protect the Coastal Zones and Coastal Waters in the Irish Sea, North Sea, English Channel, Baltic Sea, and North East Atlantic Ocean;[115] and Regulation 170/83 on the Community System for the Conservation and Management of Fishery Resources.[116] These large-scale environmental programmes are complemented by Directive 85/337/EEC on the Assessment of the Effects of Certain Public and Private Projects on the Environment[117] which provides procedures for carrying out an environmental impact assessment of public and private projects that the Member States must apply for certain types of installation such as oil refineries, nuclear power stations, steel mills, dangerous waste plants, etc, and may also be applied for assessment of twelve other types of activities in such areas as mining, metal processing, food processing, etc. Only after conducting the environmental impact assessment under the procedure prescribed by the Directive may the Member States decide whether or not the submitted project should be approved.

---

[110] OJ L230 5.8.82 p1. It has been replaced by Directive 96/82 'Seveso II' (OJ L10 14.1.97 p13).
[111] OJ L103 25.4.79 p1.
[112] OJ L206 22.7.92 p7.
[113] Commission Decision of 18 December 1996 concerning a site information format for proposed Natura 2000 sites (OJ L107 24.4.97 p1).
[114] OJ L63 9.3.91 p1.
[115] OJ L370 31.12.91 p12.
[116] OJ L24 27.1.83 p1.
[117] OJ L175 5.7.85 p40, amended by Directive 97/11 (OJ L73 14.3.97 p5).

Third stage in the development of environmental policy

The third stage of the EC environmental policy focuses on preventive, voluntary and integrated measures. In this respect, the collection, assessment and dissemination of information on the state of environment by the European Environmental Agency assists the Community in the formulation and enforcement of EC environmental laws. Also, public access to information on the environment under Directive 90/313[118] ensures more efficient enforcement of EC environmental law as it allows the environmental groups and members of public to act on the basis of information obtained from industry and enforcement agencies. The voluntary participation of industry and businesses in the EC environmental policy has been introduced by Regulation 880/92 on a Community Eco-Labelling Scheme[119] which allows national bodies to award 'eco-labels' to environmentally friendly products based on uniform Community criteria. As a result, the Regulation sensitises both producers and consumers towards environmental issues. More than 160 products now carry the EU's eco-label.[120] Regulation 1836/93 on the establishment of an Eco-Management and Auditing Scheme[121] is also based on voluntary participation by manufacturing companies, producers of electricity, gas, hot water, and enterprises involved in waste management and on experimental basis a Member State may allow other businesses to participate. Each participant, using the rules laid down by the Regulations, prepares an environmental policy programme for all its activities on a given site which is rigorously verified, and this validated environmental statement is made public. At this stage participating companies may apply for registration by national authorities and their participation is rewarded by allowing companies so registered to use a logo on reports, headed papers, corporate brochures, etc, which shows to the public that they take part in the scheme, although their participation cannot be publicised in the advertisement of their products. Registration is subject to periodic review and a triennial audit.

In relation to integrated measures, the best example is provided by Directive 96/61 on Integrated Pollution Prevention and Control[122] which requires the Member States to set up regulatory systems under which a single permit covering all types of emissions (air, water and soil) is granted to undertakings. The regulatory authorities assess on the grounds of environmental criteria as well as from the point of view of the 'best available technology', that is comparing emission levels to those which would be obtained using the best technology, and the overall impact of a given operation on the environment. It is interesting to note that the Commission itself in order to become more 'green' decided to use eco-friendly office materials, to encourage its staff to use public transport and to prevent energy waste in its buildings.[123]

---

[118] OJ L158 23.6.90 p56.
[119] OJ L99 11.4.92 p1.
[120] It is a small flower logo.
[121] OJ L168 10.7.93 p1.
[122] OJ L257 10.10.96 p26, which came into force on 30 October 1996.
[123] (1997) The European 31 July – 6 August p13.

Consumer protection

The development of consumer protection at the Community level was slow, although a consumer protection unit had been established in 1968 within the Directorate-General for Competition. For the first time in 1975 the Council adopted a programme for consumer protection and information which recognised five fundamental rights of consumers: protection of consumers' health and safety; protection of consumers' economic interests; the right to information and education; the right to redress; and the right to consumer representation and participation.[124] The second programme added two new objectives to the first programme, that is the incorporation of consumer protection in all Community policies and the promotion of dialogue between representatives of consumers, producers and distributors.[125] The third consumer programme was submitted to the Council in 1985[126] and suggested a radical change in the Community attitude towards the protection of consumers. On one hand, the judgment of the ECJ in Case 120/78 *Rewe-Zentral AG* v *Bundesmonopolverwaltung fur Branntwein*[127] had established two important principles: it permitted a Member States to introduced restrictions to the free movement of goods *prima facie* contrary to art 30 EC, but justifiable on the grounds of the protection of consumers, the so-called 'rule of reason'; and, second, it held that goods lawfully manufactured and marketed in one Member State were entitled to free circulation throughout the territory of the Community. Both principles required the harmonisation of consumer protection laws at a Community level but the unanimity requirement for the adoption of such measures was slowing down progress in this area. On the other hand, the creation of a single internal market necessitated more stringent measures as the opportunity for abuse of consumers would greatly increase. It was hoped that the SEA would reflect these considerations and, indeed, it has integrated consumer protection into the framework of the Treaty. In this respect art 100a(3) EC provides for a high degree of protection for consumers in legislation necessary to the creation of an internal market and imposes qualified majority voting in the Council. All these considerations led the Community to abandon its piecemeal approach and to decide that only essential requirements formulated in general terms regarding the protection of consumers would be specifically adopted at the Community level, and that details would be left to the standardisation bodies. As a result, under the fourth programme (1988–1992),[128] an independent Consumer Policy Service was established by the Commission and entrusted with the promotion of consumer interests. The Treaty of Maastricht has further developed the protection of consumers, and it has become one of the policies of the Union[129] as reflected in art 129a EC which constitutes a specific provision on consumer policy. It provides that the Community

'shall contribute to a high level of consumer protection through:
(a) measures adopted pursuant to art 100a in the context of the completion of the internal market;

---

[124] Annex to Council Resolution of 14 April 1975 (OJ C92 25.4.75 p1).
[125] OJ C133 3.6.81 p1.
[126] 'A New Impetus for Consumer Protection Policy' COM(83)314 final.
[127] [1979] ECR 649.
[128] COM(92)23 Final.
[129] Article 3(s) EC.

(b) specific action which supports and supplements the policy pursued by the Member States to protect the health, safety and economic interests of consumers and provide adequate information to consumers.'

However, under art 129a(2) Member States are allowed to introduced more stringent measures than those taken by the Community, provided they are compatible with the Treaty and notified to the Commission. As a result, the Community only contributes to consumer protection and thus supplements national measures – as such it plays a complementary, but very important, role in this area.[130]

5.4 Competences similar to those exercised by any international organisation

In many areas the competences of the EC can be compared to those which traditional international organisations enjoy under public international law. The requirement of unanimity in the enactment of Community measures in these areas enhances the limitations imposed upon its powers. This category of EC competences encompasses the following areas: contributions in health protection; education; professional training; culture; promotion of research and technical development; encouragement of the establishment and development of trans-European networks; strengthening of economic and social cohesion; the competitiveness of Community industry; and promoting measures in the spheres of energy, civil protection and tourism.

Contributions in health protection

The Treaty of Maastricht has introduced the possibility for the Union to contribute to health protection in the Member States. The EC action is based on art 129 EC which provides that:

'The Community shall contribute towards ensuring a high level of human health protection by encouraging co-operation between the Member States and, if necessary, lending support to their action. Community action shall be directed towards the prevention of diseases ... by promoting research into their causes and their transmission, as well as health information and education.'

As a result, it mainly concerns the prevention of diseases and especially infectious diseases. The EC has no competence to legislate in the area of health protection, that is, to harmonise laws in this areas by imposing its own measures. It can only adopt actions of encouragement and issue recommendations, as well as promoting co-ordination of health protection policies of the Member States.

The health ministers of the Member States have adopted resolutions on many aspects of health policy, including action programmes on cancer, Aids, tobacco, alcohol abuse and the introduction of the European health card.[131] Furthermore, on the grounds of art 129 EC the Commission has submitted a public health programme[132] which constitutes the EC strategy

---

[130] See the Commission Communication on the priorities in consumer policy for 1996–1998 (COM(95)519 Final).
[131] COM(93)559, para39.
[132] COM(93)559.

in this area. It enhances co-operation and co-ordination of national policies, such as the exchange of information, assessment of preventive policies, research, and training. The external aspect of the health policy is included as the Commission's health programme covers co-operation with third countries and international organisations active in this field.

EC competences under art 129 EC must be distinguished from those concerning the protection of health and safety at work in the context of the single market, which allow the Community to adopt various measures under arts 100a EC and 118a EC. The latter served as a legal basis for almost 20 directives, the most important being the Framework Directive 89/391[133] which imposes on employers the burden of assessing risks to health and safety of workers in all stages of production and providing them with information and training regarding health and safety at work as well as supervising their health. Under the Framework Directive 89/391, especially art 16, a number of complementary directives has been introduced covering a wide range of issues concerning health and safety of the workforce, from the use of machinery[134] to the protection of pregnant workers and workers who have recently given birth or are breastfeeding.[135] All measures under art 118a EC aim at 'encouraging improvements, especially in the working environment, as regards the health and safety of workers'. In the Case C–84/94 *UK* v *Council*,[136] in which the UK challenged the use of art 118a EC as a legal basis of Directive 93/104 on working times,[137] the ECJ reaffirmed the internal competence of the EC in social matters conferred by art 118a EC and stated that 'the working environment' encompasses measures regarding the organisation of working time.

As to art 100a EC it has been widely used, *inter alia*, as a legal basis of Directive 92/59 on Product Safety.[138] In 1994 the Commission set up the European Agency for Health and Safety[139] in Bilbao, Spain and entrusted it with the mission of assisting the Commission and conducting research on the health and safety of the EU workforce.

Education

In this area similar limitations as in health protection are imposed upon the Community competences. Any harmonisation of the national laws and regulations by the Community is expressly prohibited in art 126(4) EC.

A new art 126(1) EC expressly recognises the Community action in the field of education. It states that:

> 'The Community shall contribute to the development of quality education, by encouraging co-operation between Member State and, if necessary, by supporting and supplementing their action.'

As a result, recommendations and incentives are the main media for EC thrusts.

---

[133] OJ L183 29.6.89 p1.
[134] Council Directive 89/655 (OJ L393 30.12.89 p13).
[135] Council Directive 92/85 (OJ L348 28.11.92 p1).
[136] [1996] ECR I–5758.
[137] OJ L307 13.12.93 p18.
[138] OJ L228 11.8.92 p24.
[139] Council Regulation 2062/94 (OJ L216 20.8.94 p1).

EC action in this area began in 1971 on the initiative of ministers of education and culminated with the adoption of the first Community action programme in the field of education. No major changes have since been introduced to the Community's education policy.[140] Article 126 confirms EC priorities in the field of education. It states (under art 126(2)) that the Community action shall consist of:

1. developing the European dimension in education, particularly through the teaching and dissemination of the languages of the Member States;
2. encouraging mobility of students and teachers, *inter alia*, by encouraging the academic recognition of diplomas and periods of study;
3. promoting co-operation between educational establishments;
4. developing exchanges of information and experience on issues common to the education systems of the Member States;
5. encouraging the development of youth exchanges and of exchanges of socio-educational instructors; and
6. encouraging the development of distance education.

These priorities of the Community have been translated into practice through the establishment of numerous educational programmes such as: the SOCRATES programme[141] which replaces the previous programme ERASMUS (European Community Action Scheme for Mobility of University Students); TEMPUS, its equivalent for the former Communist countries (but it is not applicable to the CIS and parts of former Yugoslavia); COMETT (Community Programme for Education and Training for Technologies); PETRA (Action Programme for the Vocational Training of Young People and Their Preparation for Adult and Working Life); LINGUA, which promotes quantitative and qualitative improvements in competence in a foreign language, etc. The mobility of students is encouraged by the establishment of the European Credit Transfer System which translates local grades into the European grades and thus facilitates recognition and validation of courses taken abroad and supported by mobility grants. The ECJ has contributed to the development of educational policy of the EC: in Case 242/87 *Commission* v *Council (Erasmus Case)*[142] it confirmed that the funding of non-mandatory activities from the EC budget was permitted under EC law, even if they involved a research element.[143]

Professional training

The question of professional training arose in the context of the single market. The diversity of educational policies and vocational training in terms of structure, qualifications and resources allocated to them in the Member States became an apparent obstacle to the free movement of workers, the right of establishment and the provision of services. On the basis of art 127 EC which empowered the Council to adopt measures regarding a common

---

[140] Resolution of the Council and the Ministers of Education meeting within the Council of 9 February 1976 comprising an action programme in the field of education (OJ C38 19.2.76 p1).
[141] Council Decision 95/819/EC (OJ L87 20.4.95 p10).
[142] [1989] ECR 1425.
[143] Joined Cases C–51 and 94/89 *UK* v *Council* [1991] ECR I–2757.

vocational training policy, aimed at the harmonisation of both the national economies and the common market, the ECJ has defined and developed the EC position on vocational training. In Case 152/82 *Forcheri*[144] the ECJ held that although vocational training was not within the competences of the Community, art 127 EC conferred legislative competences on the Community in this area. In Case 293/83 *Gravier v City of Liege*[145] the ECJ provided a definition of vocational training which was 'any form of education which prepares for a qualification for a particular profession, trade or employment or which provides the necessary skills for such profession, trade or employment in vocational training whatever the age and level of the pupil or student'.[146] This broad interpretation of vocational training was further extended in Case 263/86 *Belgium v Humbel*[147] in which courses of general education were considered as vocational provided they were part of an overall programme of vocational education. Based on this definition almost all courses offered by professional bodies, universities, etc, satisfy the criteria of vocational training. However, the main issues for the ECJ were the fees paid for vocational training and the availability of scholarship and grants in a host Member State. The first question was resolved by the ECJ on the grounds of art 6 EC which prohibits discrimination based on nationality. As a result, other EC nationals in a host Member State were entitled to equal access to vocational courses in terms of payment of fees and admission criteria as nationals of that State. The second question was answered by the ECJ in Case 197/86 *Brown v Secretary of State for Scotland*[148] and in Case 39/86 *Lair v University of Hanover*.[149] The Court held that grants did not fall within the scope of the Treaty as they were a matter of the educational policy of each Member State. Nevertheless, if the applicant was considered as a worker under EC law or a child of a worker then he was entitled to the financial assistance of a host Member State in the form of scholarship and grants.

The Treaty of Maastricht has recognised the importance of vocational training in art 127 EC. However, the competences of the Community are, once again, restricted in a similar manner as those regarding educational policy. The EC can only supplement the action of the Member States through the adoption of non-binding measures, excluding any harmonisation of the laws and regulations of the Member States. Article 127(2) EC laid down the priorities in development of vocational training which are the following: adaption to industrial changes; vocational integration and reintegration into the labour market; access to training; mobility of instructors and trainees; co-operation between educational and training establishments and firms; and exchanges of information and experience.

Culture

For the first time, the Treaty of Maastricht included culture within the competences of the EC, albeit in a limited manner. A new Title IX, devoted to culture, emphasises in art 128(1) that the EC shall contribute to:

---

[144] [1983] ECR 2323.
[145] [1985] ECR 593.
[146] Ibid, at 606.
[147] [1988] ECR 5365.
[148] [1988] ECR 3205
[149] [1988] ECR 3161.

'the flowering of the cultures of the Member States, while respecting their national and regional diversity and at the same time bringing the common cultural heritage to the fore'.

Nevertheless, culture is still within the exclusive competence of the Member States as art 128(5) EC expressly denies the EU any power to harmonise national laws and regulations in this area. As a result, the Council by a unanimous vote may solely adopt non-binding incentive measures. Therefore, as before, the cultural matters are subject to Council resolutions and the EC-sponsored programmes which support and complement actions adopted by the Member States. Nevertheless, the EC has regulated some cultural activities of the Member States in the context of the common market. In this respect, art 36 EC permits Member States to derogate from their obligation to ensure the free movement of goods[150] on the grounds of the protection of national treasures possessing artistic, historic or archaeological value. There is no case law on this aspect of art 36 EC. However, in Case 7/68 *Commission* v *Italy*[151] which was decided under art 12 EC and concerned a tax on the export of artefacts, where Italy argued that they were not goods and as such were outside the scope of the Treaty, the ECJ held otherwise. It stated that paintings possess an economic value, were capable of forming the subject of commercial transactions and thus satisfied the criteria of being considered as goods under the Treaty. The ECJ added that any restrictions to the free movement of goods on the grounds of protection of national treasures could only be justified under art 36 EC. The ECJ has strictly interpreted derogations under art 36 EC, and if a Member State invoked this derogation[152] 'it would be incumbent on a Member State to demonstrate why the item in question possesses such importance that it goes beyond mere high artistic quality and impinges on the cultural or historical heritage of the nation'.[153] Also, among derogations to the free movement of goods judicially created by the ECJ, the protection of cultural values is considered as a justification for trade restrictions between the Member States. In *Torfaen Borough Council* v *B & Q plc*, the ECJ held that English legislation prohibiting large shops from opening on Sunday might be justified in the context of 'national or regional socio-cultural characteristics'.[154] In *Cinétheque* v *Fédération Nationale de Cinemas Françaises*[155] the ECJ, without expressly recognising that the protection of cultural values may justify restrictions to the free movement of goods, decided in favour of France, that is that the prohibition of marketing of video versions of films within 12 months of first showing was not in breach of art 30 EC.[156]

The Commission in its Communication to the Council enhanced the impact of the common market on the unlawful exportation of national treasures.[157] As a result the Council adopted measures on trade of works art such as Regulation 3911/92/EEC on the Control of the Export of Cultural Goods[158] and Directive 93/7/EEC on the Return of Cultural Objects

---

[150] It concerns derogation from arts 30–36 EC.

[151] [1968] ECR 423.

[152] Case 120/78 *Rewe-Zentrale* v *Bundesmonopolverwaltung fur Branntwein (Cassis de Dijon Case)* [1979] ECR 649.

[153] S Weatherill and P Beaumont, *EC Law*, Penguin: London, 1995, p476

[154] Case 145/88 [1989] ECR 765, para 14.

[155] Cases 60 and 61/84 [1985] ECR 2605.

[156] In these cases Advocate-General Slynn suggested that the protection of artistic activities constituted a mandatory requirement under the *Cassis de Dijon* rule of reason.

[157] COM(89)594.

[158] OJ L395 31.12.92 p1.

Unlawfully Removed from the Territory of a Member State.[159] The protection of cultural values has been examined by the ECJ in the context of competition law, although this consideration has been so far disregarded by the Court in favour of strict application of EC competition law.[160]

Promotion of research and technical development

The Treaty of Maastricht introduced a new Title XV on Research and Technological Development, although the Community competences in this area had already been recognised in art 130f EC. The Community action in Research and Technological Development is based on a multiannual framework programme which is implemented through specific programmes developed within each activity. The Council adopts unanimously such multiannual programmes according to the procedure laid down in art 189b EC and specific programmes in accordance with the procedure contained in art 189c EC. The current Fourth Framework Programme (1994–98)[161] highlights the following areas of activity: a research programme which includes information and communications technologies, industrial technologies, environment, life science and technologies, energy, transport and targeted socio-economic research; co-operation with non-EC countries and international organisations; dissemination and exploitation of conducted research and training and mobility. The main purpose of these programmes is to encourage co-operation among undertakings, research centres and universities in their research and technical development activities of high quality.[162] In practice, the Community financially contributes to research and technical development projects, although it may also set up joint undertakings or other structures necessary for the efficient execution of the programmes.[163] In that case the Council must act unanimously on a proposal from the Commission and after consulting the EP and the Economic and Social Committee. Under the TEU the role of the Commission has been enhanced; under art 130h EC covering the co-ordination of research between the Member States and the Community any initiative in this area is given to the Commission.

Another important new feature is contained in art 130p EC which requires the Commission to present an annual report to the EP on research and development (R & D) activities and the dissemination of results from the previous year, as well as a work programme for the current year.

The budget allocated to the Fourth Framework Programme on R & D for 1994–1998 amounts to ECU 12.3 billion. From a modest beginning initiated with the creation of the Joint Research Centre in 1959 under the Euratom Treaty, R & D has become one the priorities of the Community which is reflected in the funds allocated to this area and in the number of programmes set up by the EU.

---

[159] OJ L74 1993.
[160] Cases 43 and 63/82 *VBVB* v *VBBB* [1984] ECR 19 and Case T–66/89 *Publishers' Association* v *Commission* [1992] ECR II–1995.
[161] EC Bull 4–1993, point 1.26.
[162] Article 130f(2) EC.
[163] Article 130n EC.

Among such programmes Eureka, founded by Margaret Thatcher and François Mitterrand ten years ago to support trans-national co-operation on research projects, is one of the most successful. There are currently 700 projects running under the scheme and the Commission celebrated its tenth anniversary by offering an additional ECU 2.7 billion available in grants for 150 new projects.[164]

Development of trans-European networks

Differences in standards and technical specifications of the Member States in transport, telecommunication and energy systems constitute an important hindrance to the proper functioning of the common market. A good example is provided by national rail systems which are highly developed around capitals (Paris, London, Brussels) but often neglect both peripheral regions and Community needs. Another example is the different voltages of electrical systems in the Member States, varying from 25 KV ac in France and the UK to 1.5 KV dc in the Netherlands. The necessity for integration of national infrastructures in these areas into one coherent system at the Community level has been acknowledged by Title XII of the TEU. Article 129b EC provides that in order to derive full benefit from a common market the Community shall contribute to the establishment of trans-European networks in transport, telecommunications and energy infrastructures. To promote interconnection and inter-operability of national networks, and to ensure full access to such networks by the peripheral regions, the Community is empowered: to establish guidelines identifying projects of common interest which relate to objectives and priorities in the sphere of trans-European networks; to implement measures necessary to ensure the inter-operability of the networks, especially in relation to technical harmonisation; and to identify and support projects of common interest financed by the Member States through feasibility studies, loan guarantees, subsidies or in transport infrastructure to finance directly specific projects through the Cohesion Fund.[165] Guidelines and projects of common interest are adopted by the Council under the procedure set up in art 189b EC, and in addition they must be approved by the Member States concerned. Other measures under Title XII should be adopted by the Council in accordance with the procedure referred to in art 189c EC. In Case C–127/94 *European Parliament v Council*[166] the EP challenged the legal basis of Council Decision 94/445[167] on the inter-administration transfer by automatic and electronic transmission of data relating to the trading of goods between Member States which was adopted under art 100a. It argued that it should have been taken under art 129c(1) EC. The ECJ has made two important statements which strengthened the autonomy of trans-European networks: first, it held that the legislative measures taken in this area did not need to be envisaged in the guidelines referred to in art 129c(1) EC prior to their enactment; and, second, that the appropriate legal basis for Decision 94/445 was art 129c(1) EC, a more specific provision than art 100a EC.

The development of coherent European systems up to year 2000 will cost the

---

[164] P Matthews, 'Eureka Comes of Age with New Initiatives' (1997) The European 23–29 January p26.
[165] Article 129c(1) EC.
[166] [1996] ECR I–1689.
[167] OJ L183 19.7.94 p42.

Community approximately ECU 250 billion for transport and energy and ECU 150 billion for telecommunications.[168]

Economic and social cohesion

The level of economic development and the capacity of the national economy of Member States to compete within the internal market differ from one State to another. In order to reduce economic disparities and lessen the impact of the economic reconstruction due to the creation of an internal market on the least prosperous Member States in terms of their competitiveness, and to assist less-developed or declining industrial regions, the EC has developed its economic and social cohesion policy. The strengthening of economic and social cohesion was introduced into the EC Treaty by arts 130a and 130b EC. It was also confirmed as an important objective of the internal market by the Lisbon Summit[169] and further developed by Title XIV of the Treaty of Maastricht. The main objective of economic and social cohesion policy is defined in art 130a EC which states that:

'the Community shall aim at reducing disparities between the levels of development of the various regions and the backwardness of the least-favoured regions, including rural areas'.

In order to achieve these objectives the Community co-ordinates national economic policy of Member States, implements the EC common policies and measures relating to the internal market in a manner which takes into account the objectives set out in art 130a EC, and thus contributes to their achievements and provides financial support through structural funds: the European Regional Development Fund, the European Social Fund, and the Guidance Section of the European Agricultural Guidance and Guarantee Fund which constitutes one-third of the total EC budget. Also, loans and loan guarantees and other financial instruments provided by the Community and the European Investment Bank can be used to financially assist some of the poorest countries and regions in the EU. Title XIV, art 130d EC provides for the creation of a new Cohesion Fund to finance projects in transport infrastructures in two areas: in the context of trans-European networks for projects which are identified as being of 'common interest';[170] and in relation to environmental projects which contribute to achievement of the objectives enumerated in art 130r(1) EC. The Cohesion Fund was set up by Council Regulation 1164/94[171] under the assent procedure. It is designated to offer funding for the above-mentioned projects to Member States with a per capita GDP less than 90 per cent of the Community average. For the period 1993–99 countries eligible for assistance from the Cohesion Fund are Greece, Spain, Portugal and Ireland and the planned expenditure amounts to ECU 15.15 billion at 1992 prices, approximately ECU 240 per capita.[172] The Cohesion Fund, as all other structural funds, is intended to complement public structural expenditure of the Member States, not to replace it. This consideration is very important since Member States often abuse EC

---

[168] COM(93)700, pp82–95.

[169] EC Bull 6–1992, p11.

[170] Under Article 129c EC.

[171] OJ L130 25.5.94 p1.

[172] Regulation 1164/94 ibid, art 4 and Annexe 1.

to replace it. This consideration is very important since Member States often abuse EC structural funds[173] through lack of discipline and transparency in their administration.[174]

Additional measures necessary to attain cohesion may be taken by the Council acting unanimously on a proposal from the Commission and after consultation with the EP, the Economic and Social Committee and the Committee of the Regions.

Industrial policy

To improve the position of EC industry in the world markets and make it more competitive vis-à-vis the United States and Japan the industrial policy was added to the list of activities of the Community in art 3(l) and further developed in Title XIII[175] on Industry at Maastricht. Prior to the Treaty of Maastricht industrial policy was indirectly developed by the Community through the exercise of its powers in a number of areas such as internal market measures, competition, research and development, etc.

Under art 130(1) EC Member States and the Community are required to establish conditions necessary for competitiveness through the promotion of technical innovation, training, rapid structural adjustment, co-operation between undertakings and the development of undertakings, especially those of small and medium-size. The industrial policy encompasses the adoption of positive measures such as: harmonisation of technical standards; development of infrastructures; various programmes aimed at promoting or assisting declining industries; industries in trouble or strategic sectors of industries and facilitative measures which concern the proper functioning of the markets, such as elimination of remaining barriers to trade and ensuring fair conditions of competition within the common market.

Under art 130 EC the Community is entitled to develop a global strategy for all industries. Thus, factors such as the EC social policy, protection of environment, protection of consumers, etc, which contribute to competitiveness of a particular sector of industry, are duly taken into consideration as well as the importance of the development and application of new technology, especially in three areas: information technology, communication and biotechnology.

Under art 130(2) EC the Council acting unanimously may decide on specific measures in support of action taken by the Member States to achieve objectives of industrial policy set out in art 130(1) EC. However, these measures may not distort competition within the EC. The Commission shall initiate measures regarding industrial policy and co-ordination of action among Member States in this area.

The Amsterdam Summit of 16–17 June 1997 emphasised that competitiveness of industry is a key to prosperity in the EC as it provides the foundation for growth, creating jobs and raising living standards. It approved the conclusion of the Industrial Council of 24 April 1997 on the organisation of work concerning the competitiveness of European industry and especially its initiative of organising annual debate within the Industrial

---

[173] Regulation 2082/93, art 9, emphasises that the Member States must at least maintain public expenditure at its previous level.
[174] COM(93)67, p21 et seq.
[175] It contains only one Article, art 130 EC.

Council on the basis of programme prepared by the Commission which is to be assisted in its work by a new Competitiveness Advisory Group.[176]

Measures in the spheres of energy, civil protection and tourism

The three areas are mentioned together in art 3t EC which provides that the Community should take measures in those spheres. They are new activities of the Community introduced by the TEU. Tourism was for the first time included within the Community competences when the Council designated 1990 as a 'European Tourism Year'.[177] Unfortunately, the Community action in tourism has proved so far inefficient for two reasons. First, Directorate-General 23 in charge of tourism and enterprise has a very small budget (ECU 3 million) for studying and measuring the industry's performance, and the damaging audit presented by its Commissioner on the widespread misuse of the EU's funding for tourism policy, mainly in the form of payments for consultancies and reports, further undermined EU credibility in this area.[178] Second, the problem of defining tourism resulted in its scattering over all departments. It seems that in every Commission department there are at least 50 programmes more or less connected with tourism. However, the situation is going to change as the EU intends to allocate ECU 6 billion (£9 billion) to develop and promote tourism.[179] The Commission is expected to present a comprehensive report on this subject, as well as the EU's spending priorities for the available ECU 6 billion tourism support. Indeed, a new approach is necessary when one takes into account that nine million people in the EU work in this sector and that it generates 5.5 per cent of the EU's gross domestic product. Furthermore, tourism is expected to become one of the biggest industries in the twenty-first century.

---

[176] Its first meeting took place at the beginning of August 1997.
[177] Twenty-third General Report, point 302.
[178] (1997) The European 24–30 July p23.
[179] P Matthews, 'Brussels to spend £9 billion on tourism' (1997) The European 29 May–4 June p24.

6 The Institutions of the European Communities and the European Union and their Participation in the Decision-making Procedures

The institutional structure of the Communities and the European Union is based on original concepts, new to public international law. The ECSC, the EEC and the Euratom were each at their inception endowed with an autonomous institutional framework. In reality, a set of single institutions serving all three Communities has been established in two stages. First, the Convention on Certain Institutions Common to the European Communities was signed on 25 March 1957, at the same time as the Treaties of Rome, which merged Assemblies (European Parliaments), the Court of Justice and the Economic and Social Committees of the three founding Treaties. Second, the Merger Treaty signed on 8 April 1965 which entered into force on 13 July 1967 replaced the High Authority and the Commission of the ECSC – which until then were independent institutions – with a Single Council and a Single Commission, common to all three Communities. Thus, instead of 12 institutions a quadric structure, with some variations, was put in place which ensures that each institution carries out simultaneously all tasks conferred to it under the three founding Treaties. The Treaty of Maastricht recognised the unitary framework for the Communities, while adding the Court of Auditors, first established in 1975, as a fifth common institution. Article 4 EC and art 3 Euratom enumerate five bodies which are entitled to use the name Community institutions. Article 4 EC states that:

'The tasks entrusted to the Community shall be carried out by the following Institutions:
– a European Parliament,
– a Council,

- a Commission,
- a Court of Justice,
- a Court of Auditors.'

The first four mentioned institutions constitute the basic structure of the institutional system of the Communities, although the Treaties provide for the establishment of a number of additional bodies, for example under art 4(2) EC the Economic and Social Committee and the Committee of the Regions to assist the Council and the Commission, while art 4a EC provides for the establishment of institutions necessary to carry out particular tasks of the Economic and Monetary Union – a European System of Central Banks and a European Central Bank. Furthermore, the Treaty of Maastricht in art 4b EC adds the European Investment Bank,[1] and by virtue of art 168a EC the Court of First Instance (CFI) is 'attached' to the ECJ.

The basic institutional structure is completed by two further categories of body: the European Council and a number of bodies which are within the scope of the Treaties and which assist the Council and the Commission in the accomplishment of their tasks. These are agencies, offices and centres such as the European Environmental Agency, the European Training Foundation, the European Agency for the Evaluation of Medicinal Products, the Office for Veterinary and Plant Health Inspection and Control, the European Monitoring Centre for Drugs and Drug Addiction, Europol, etc,

Each of the five institutions has a specific role to play in the functioning of the Community. The Council represents the interests of the Member States; the Commission, the interests of the Community; the European Parliament (EP), the interests of the people of the Member States; the Court of Justice (ECJ) ensures that in the functioning of the institutional system law is observed; and the Court of Auditors is charged with supervising financial aspects of the Community. However, the division of functions between the five institutions does not reflect the Montesquieu system of the 'separation of powers' under which the Parliament is responsible for the performance of the legislative functions, the government for executive functions and the courts for judicial functions. In the Community system the homologue of legislative powers is the Council, which also has executive and governmental functions, and the Commission is the 'guardian of the Treaty' and as such supervises and, if necessary, enforces Community law. It also initiates and implements Community legislation. The European Parliament, from being solely an advisory body, has evolved into a directly elected body and now participates, to some extent, in the law-making procedures of the Community. The ECJ and the CFI ensure the observance of law in the implementation of the Treaty by the Community institutions and the Member States. Furthermore, the ECJ under art 177 EC assists national courts in their difficult task of interpretation of Community law and thus ensures homogeneity and uniformity in its application in all Member States. The legal protection of individuals, in the context of the limited nature of parliamentary supervision of the institutional system of the Community, also constitutes an important consideration in the work of the ECJ.

Until the Treaty of Maastricht the main features of the evolution of the institutional system of the Communities were:

---

[1] The European Investment Bank is an international organisation established by art 198d EC. Its Statute is annexed to the Treaty.

1. The spontaneous creation of a new inter-governmental body, the European Council, which was first recognised as a Community institution by the SEA. The European Council is a political body which defines the general political objectives of the Community and the Union, although it neither adopts legislative acts nor participates in the formal decision-making procedures.
2. The gradual acquisition by the European Parliament of legislative powers, firstly in budgetary matters and then under the SEA in the assent procedure.
3. The establishment of co-operation in political matters outside the framework of the Treaty.

The Treaty of Maastricht has modified the Community institutional system by strengthening the legislative powers of the EP and establishing new institutions entrusted with the adoption and the implementation of monetary policies of the Union. The Treaty of Maastricht has created the European Union which, under art C, 'shall by served by a single institutional framework'. It means that certain Community institutions have different roles to play, depending whether they act as a Community institution or as a body of the European Union. The roles that the Council, the Commission, and the ECJ play within Pillars 2 and 3 of the Treaty on European Union are fundamentally different from the exercise of their powers under the Treaty of Paris or the Treaties of Rome as amended. Indeed, the institutional structure of the Union which exists alongside that of the Community mainly uses the Community institutions for the achievement the Union's objectives. It results in a complex relationship between the Communities and the Union. Furthermore, the democratic accountability of Union institutions is even weaker than under the Treaties of Rome.

The balance of power among the institutions has changed since the creation of the Communities. As H Wallace wrote:

> 'The institutional powers and relationships have varied across policy sectors and over time in complex and inconsistent ways. These reflect the interplay of ideas, interests and policy substance. A succession of different policy modes with different institutional configurations has marked the history of European integration.'[2]

It is important to mention that there are certain common rules applicable to all institutions. First, they concern the seat of the institutions. Under art 216 EC, art 77 ECSC and art 189 Euratom the seat of the Community institutions should be determined by common accord of the Member States. In practice, the determination of the permanent seats of the Community institutions has always been subject to fierce competition among the Member States. The Decision of 8 April 1965[3] provided for a temporary solution by which the seats of the institutions were assigned to three different places: Luxembourg, Brussels and Strasbourg. This compromise gave rise to many political, financial and legal difficulties, especially in respect to where the sessions of the EP were to be held.[4] In this

---

[2] H Wallace and W Wallace (eds), *Policy-Making in the European Union*, Oxford: OUP, 1996, p37.
[3] OJ 152 13.7.67 p18.
[4] Case 230/81 *Luxembourg* v *EP* [1983] ECR 255; Case 108/83 *Luxembourg* v *EP* [1984] ECR 1945; Cases 358/85 and 51/86 *France* v *EP* [1988] ECR 4821; Cases C–213/88 and C–39/89 *Luxembourg* v *EP* [1991] ECR I–5643.

context, an agreement was reached at the Edinburgh Summit on 12 December 1992,[5] which was further completed by the European Council Decision adopted at the Brussels meeting on 29–30 October 1993.[6] As a result, the Council, the Commission and the Economic and Social Committee have their seats in Brussels, although the Council, under this agreement, holds its meetings in Luxembourg in April, June and October, and certain departments of the Commission, namely the administrative services of ECSC and Euratom, as well as its Statistical Office and the Office for Official Publications, are located in Luxembourg. The ECJ, the CFI, the Court of Auditors and the European Investment Bank have their seats in Luxembourg. The European Parliament is required to hold 12 periods of monthly plenary sessions in Strasbourg and any additional sessions in Brussels. Its secretariat is still located in Luxembourg. The Member States are very sensitive to any changes regarding the seats of the Community institutions. The action for annulment brought by France against the EP's calendar for 1996 provides a good illustration of this point. In Case C–345/95 *France v EP*, France argued that the EP calendar for 1996 was invalid as it provided for only 11 sessions in Strasbourg, instead of 12 sessions.[7]

The seats of the European Monetary Institute and the European Central Bank are located in Frankfurt. The Brussels European Council in its Decision of 29 October 1993 expressed a preference for the allocation of seats for various bodies and agencies in the Member States who did not host any Community institutions. As a result, the European Environmental Agency is located in Copenhagen, the European Agency for Evaluation of Medical Products in London, the Agency for Health and Safety at Work in Bilbao, Europol and the Europol Drugs Unit in The Hague, the Office for Harmonisation in the Internal Market (Trade Marks, Designs and Models) in Alicante, the Office for Veterinary and Plant Health Inspection and Control in Dublin, the European Monitoring Centre for Drugs and Drug Addiction in Lisbon. Also, the new policy of the European Union to establish different agencies and bodies in different Member States led the Council to move the European Centre for the Development of Vocational Training from Brussels to Thessaloniki.

Second, the rules governing the languages of the institutions are also determined by the Council, acting unanimously, without prejudice to the provisions contained in the Rules of Procedure of the ECJ.[8] This question was resolved in Regulation 1 of 1958 in which the Council decided that national languages of the Member State are official languages of the Community and are all equal in rank and status. This principle applies to the ECSC and Euratom Treaties as well as to the Treaty of Maastricht. Since 1 January 1995 there are 11 official languages of the European Union: Danish, Dutch, English, Finnish, French, German, Greek, Italian, Portuguese, Spanish and Swedish. Also, all language versions of the Treaties and of Community measures are equally authentic. The Treaty of Paris was drafted in French and only the French version is considered as being authentic. The Treaties of Rome were drawn up in Dutch, French, German and Italian, all

---

[5] The Decision of 12 December 1992 (OJ C341 23.12.92 p1).
[6] OJ C323 30.11.93 p1.
[7] OJ C351 30.12.95 p7.
[8] See the proceedings before the ECJ. The language is chosen by the applicant subject to exception laid down in arts 29–31 of its Rules of Procedure.

four texts being equally authentic.[9] However, upon the accession of new Member States it was specified that versions in English, Irish, Danish, Greek, Spanish, Finnish, Portuguese and Swedish are also authentic. If there are any discrepancies between different language versions they should be resolved without giving priority to any particular language.[10]

The 11 official languages of the Community mean that all official meetings are conducted in all official languages which are translated from one to another. Also, all official documents are in 11 languages, although French and English are imposed as working languages. Furthermore, all individual acts, that is addressed to the Member States or individuals under jurisdiction of a Member State, are written in the language of that State, while Community acts of a general scope of application, for example regulations, are written in nine official languages but published in the Official Journal in all 11 official languages. The use of multiple languages in the everyday running of the Community is very costly, but is necessary to ensure equality between the Member States and transparency vis-à-vis the citizens of the European Union. In addition, national authorities and courts which often have to apply the Community acts directly to their nationals must have the relevant text in their own national language. The principles of legal certainty and the protection of individual rights strengthen this requirement. Furthermore, conferring official status on 11 languages permits EC nationals to submit their complaints to a particular institution in their own language.

Third, there is a common status applicable to all staff of the Community and the European Union. The Protocol on the Privileges and Immunities of the European Communities, annexed to the Merger Treaty of 1965 and in force since 13 July 1967, provides that the officials and other servants of the Communities should be: treated as officials of international organisations; immune from legal proceedings in respect of acts performed in their official capacity; exempt from national taxes on salaries, wages and emoluments paid by the Community; subject to the social security benefits established by the Communities, etc. In addition, the status of the officials and other servants of the Communities was completed by Council Regulation of 29 February 1968[11] as amended many times.

In this chapter the role of the four main institutions and the European Council will be examined in the context of the complex relationship between the Communities and the European Union. The powers that each institution exercises will be assessed in the light of art 4(1) EC which states that: 'Each institution shall act within the limits of the powers conferred upon it by this Treaty.' Finally, the participation of Community institutions in the decision-making procedure will complete this Chapter.

6.1 The European Council

The European Council plays a very important role in the institutional system of the Communities and the Union, although *sensu stricto* it is neither an institution nor a

---

[9] Article 248 EC.
[10] Case 29/69 *Stauder* [1969] ECR 419; Case 80/76 *Kerry Milk* [1977] ECR 425. In practice, common points of the different version should be sought.
[11] OJ L56 4.3.68 p1.

Community body. It is common to both the European Communities and the European Union. The informal summit meetings of Heads of State or Government of the Member States that have been held since 1961,[12] and which were officially agreed in Paris in December 1974 to be held on a regular basis, were brought within the framework of the Community by art 2 of SEA and further recognised by art D of the TEU which provides that:

'The European Council shall provide the Union with the necessary impetus for its development and shall define the general political guidelines thereof.

The European Council shall bring together the Heads of State or of Government of the Member States and the President the Commission. They shall be assisted by the Ministers for Foreign Affairs of the Member States and by a Member of the Commission. The European Council shall meet at least twice a year, under the chairmanship of the Head of the State or Government of the Member State which holds the Presidency the Council

The European Council shall submit to the European Parliament a report after each of its meetings and a yearly written report on the progress achieved by the Union.'

The formula 'Heads of State or Government' is used to take into account the special constitutional position of the President of the French Republic.

Main tasks

The importance of the European Council stems from the political role it plays in shaping the future of the Communities and the European Union. It exercises four main functions in the context of the Community: it serves as a platform for the exchange of informal views and for unofficial discussions among the leaders of the Member States; it may examine any matter within the competence of the Community, as well as any subject of a common interest; it may decide to give the necessary impetus for the development of the Community; and, finally, it settles sensitive matters and disputes which the Community institutions are unable to resolve, especially those forwarded by the Council of the European Union (for example, the question of the determination of the UK contribution to the Community budget was settled by the Fontainebleau Summit). The political decisions adopted by the European Council are not legal acts in the sense of the EC Treaty and as such not reviewable under art 173 EC. Furthermore, their implementation is usually left to the Council. In its exercise of the supreme political power the European Council can be compared to holding a kind of presidential authority of the Community.

The European Council's role within the framework of the European Union is to define the general principles and guidelines. It also extends to 'ensure the consistency and the continuity of the activities carried out in order to attain its [Union] objectives'[13] between the three Pillars as well as their internal coherence. The European Council acts under two Pillars, that is in relation to the Common Foreign and Security Policy (CFSP) and in the area of Justice and Home Affairs (JHA), as an inter-governmental body according to rules and procedures provided in Titles V and VI of the TEU.[14] Under both Pillars the European Council adopts common positions or joint actions by unanimity.[15] However, when adopting

---

[12] From 1961 to 1974 seven unofficial summit meetings took place.
[13] Article C TEU.
[14] For details see Chapter 4.
[15] Articles J8 and K4 TEU.

a joint action or a common position at any stage during their development, it may also define those matters on which decisions will be taken by a qualified majority.[16] In the area of CFSP the European Council is assisted by the Political Committee, which consists of political directors from the 15 ministers of foreign affairs.[17] In JHA the Co-ordinating Committee, made up of senior officials, contributes to the preparation of the European Council's agenda.[18]

The European Council is not a Community institution, even when referred to expressly under the EC Treaty, for example in art 103(2) EC. Article D TEU has clarified its position in this respect. It eliminates any possibility that the European Council can be considered as a peculiar form of the Council of the European Union. As a result, the European Council has an important impact on the functioning of other Community institutions. The Council of the European Union is no longer the supreme decision-making body. Furthermore, the intervention of the European Council in disputes which the Council of the European Union is not able to resolve risks dissuading the latter from making all necessary efforts to achieve their settlement within the Community framework. Also, the Commission is deprived of the political initiatives and thus its contribution to the future shape of the Community is very limited, although the Commission is often involved in bringing forward new policy initiatives. If they are supported by the European Council they may lead to major developments, as for example the adoption of the Social Charter at the Strasbourg Summit in 1989. Finally, the non-accountability of the European Council vis-à-vis the people of the Member States is emphasised by the lack of control by the EP over its activities. Consequently, the scope of dialogue between the EP and the European Council suffers further limitations.

Functioning

The European Council meets twice a year – usually its meetings coincide with the end of a Council of the European Union Presidency. Extraordinary meetings may also take place, as was the case at the end of in October 1993 before the entry into force of the Treaty of Maastricht. Meetings are attended by the Heads of State or Government of the Member States accompanied by their foreign ministers. The Commission, represented by its President and Vice-President, participates in all deliberations, even the most restricted. All deliberations are confidential. The Declarations of the European Council are adopted at the end of each meeting on all matters on which the summit reached a consensus.

The preparation of the European Council meetings is undertaken by specialised Councils of the European Union. However, the ministers of foreign affairs of the Member States, helped by the Committee of Permanent Representatives (COREPER), supervise the preparations. Usually, a meeting of foreign ministers is organised before the European Council meeting. Nevertheless, certain matters which are within the exclusive competences of the Member States, although formally prepared by the Community, that is the appropriate Council and COREPER, are outside its powers. In addition, the European

---

[16] Articles J3 and K3 TEU.
[17] Article J8(5) TEU.
[18] Article K4(1) TEU.

Council may set up its own working group made up of national officials and experts to prepare the meeting and to report directly to the European Council. For example, the preparation of the second scheme concerning the creation of the European Monetary System during 1978 took place outside the Community institutional structure. As a result, the Community institutions did not contribute to its elaboration and their role was limited to its implementation.

6.2 The Council of the European Union

The Council of Ministers is referred to in the Treaties as the Council. Following the entry into force of the Treaty on European Union the Council of Ministers adopted Decision 93/591 on 8 November 1993,[19] in which it decided to rename itself the Council of the European Union. It is the principal political and legislative institution of the European Communities and the European Union. The Council of the European Union represents the national interests of each Member State and as a purely inter-governmental body has risked degenerating into a diplomatic conference which sometimes it has not been possible to avoid.

Composition

By virtue of art 146 EC:

'The Council shall consists of a representative of each Member State at ministerial level, authorised to commit the Government of that Member State.'

This formula introduced by the TEU allows Member States with a federal structure to be represented when the Council is examining matters within the exclusive competence of regional governments, for example a minister of a land in Germany or a region in Belgium, instead of a minister in the federal government. In such a case, the regional minister is authorised to act on behalf of the Member State and thus commits the federal government both legally and politically. However, the TEU excluded the Council meeting at the level of the Heads of Government unless this possibility is expressly provided by the Treaty.[20]

The Council has no fixed composition and its membership varies according to the matters under discussion, but has always the same number of members as the number of Member States. Each minister is accompanied by a civil servant as part of a negotiating team. The Commission is also represented, although its influence depends upon the subject-matter under discussion and the competences of the Commission in the area discussed. There are currently about 20 formations of the Council of the EU. Among the specialised Councils are: the General Affairs Council, comprising foreign ministers of the Member States which co-ordinates the activities of other Councils, examines external affairs and matters of general Community concern; Ecofin, which is attended by finance ministers; and the Internal Market Council which is made up of ministers in charge of a particular aspect

---

[19] OJ L281 16.11.93 p18.
[20] For example arts 109j and 109k EC.

of the internal market. There are also specialised Council meetings in other subject areas such as agriculture, transport, budget, energy, education, culture, etc.

The nature of the Council meetings poses certain problems as they are, simultaneously Council meetings and meetings of the representatives of the Member States. As a Community institution, the Council must follow the rules and procedures prescribed by the Treaties, but as a diplomatic conference the rules of public international law apply. For that reason, it is sometimes difficult to determine the legal nature of the acts adopted by the Council.[21]

Presidency

Council meetings are chaired by the Member State holding the Council Presidency, which rotates every six months according to the order established by art 146 EC. Under Council Decision 95/2[22] – which laid down the holders of the Presidency for eight-and-half years from the accession of Austria, Finland and Sweden – from July 1997 Luxembourg holds the Presidency followed by: (from January 1998) the United Kingdom, (from July 1998) Portugal, (from January 1999) Germany, and (from July 1999) Finland.

The Member State which holds the Presidency of the Council presides also, during that period, over other bodies, for example, the European Council, COREPER, committees and organs of political co-operation, etc. In addition, at the meetings of the Council of the European Union, that Member State is represented in two capacities – as a Member State and as a President of the Council.

In practice, the role of the President is very important since the Member State holding it is responsible for setting the priorities for the Council during its six months in office. Thus, the Presidency determines the agenda and the calendar of the Council. It also submits at the end of Presidency a detailed report of its achievements to the European Parliament which is discussed by the latter. The Member States have become more and more ambitious in determining the objectives they want to attain during the Presidency.[23] Each tries to make a lasting contribution to the development of the Communities and the Union. In addition, they may put on the agenda issues of vital national importance which are not considered essential in the context of the Community. Outside its political functions, the Presidency also has administrative tasks to fulfil such as: convening the Council meetings on its own initiative or at the request of one the Member State or of the Commission; determining the agenda, to chair the deliberations of the Council; assisting Member States to reach a compromise; and deciding the time to vote. In the context of the European Union, in the area of CFSP the Presidency represents the Union in international organisations and international conferences and is responsible for the implementation of joint actions and common positions adopted by the Member States.[24] In order to ensure continuity in the work of the Council the troika system has been developed which associates the previous and

---

[21] See Chapter 7; also Case 22/70 *Commission* v *Council* [1971] ECR 263.

[22] OJ L1 1.1.95 p22.

[23] For example, The Netherlands decided to finalise the Inter-governmental Conference during its Presidency (from January 1997 to the end of June 1977). This objective was successfully achieved when the draft Treaty of Amsterdam was signed on 17 June 1997.

[24] Article J5(1) and (2) TEU.

the next Member States to hold the Presidency with its current holder. Also, the General Secretariat of the Council of the European Union contributes to the continuity of Community policies.

COREPER

The Council is not a permanent body. Each meeting has to be prepared by civil servants convened in a number of committees, the most important being the Committee of Permanent Representatives (COREPER).[25] This body was initially established on an informal basis to ensure the continuity of the Council's work. It was formally recognised by art 4 of the Merger Treaty and is now defined in arts 151 EC and 121 Euratom. COREPER is made up of permanent representatives of the Member States to the European Union. Indeed, each Member State has a permanent delegation in Brussels similar to an embassy, which comprises national civil servants with ambassadorial rank. Article 151(1) EC set out the tasks of COREPER. It states that:

'A committee consisting of the Permanent Representatives of the Member States shall be responsible for preparing the work for the Council and for carrying out the tasks assigned to it by the Council.'

The main objective of COREPER is to prepare proposals which are negotiated prior to the Council meeting and thus to avoid unnecessary discussion at ministerial level. The timetable of the Council meetings is prepared in advance. Regular meetings are usually convened once a month, whilst extraordinary sessions can take place any time, but the agenda must be forwarded by the President to the Member States at least ten days in advance. The Council agenda is divided into two parts: so called 'A' items and 'B' items. The former are those on which an agreement was reached during the preparatory meeting of COREPER, while the latter are referred to the Council for debate since no satisfactory solution was found for their settlement.

There are two COREPERs: COREPER I made up of deputy permanent representatives which concentrates on more technical issues; and COREPER II, comprising the permanent representatives themselves, which focuses on more general and political matters. The Council forwards a matter to be discussed to COREPER which may create specialist or *ad hoc* committees, working groups, etc, in order to examine it. The matter is then referred back to COREPER for further study. The Commission and often the European Parliament are also involved as they discuss and negotiate the submitted proposal. If there is a unanimous agreement on the proposal it is put in Part A of the Council agenda. Unless the Council opposes the proposal and sends it back to COREPER, it will be adopted by the Council. If there is no agreement in COREPER, the matter is put in Part B of the Council agenda for resolution.

---

[25] Its name is the French acronym for this Committee of Permanent Representatives. Apart from COREPER three permanent specialised committees assist the Council of the EU: the Agricultural Committee; the Monetary Committee, which will be replaced by the Economic and Financial Committee in the third stage of EMU; and the K4 Committee in matters relating to Pillar 3.

Sessions

The Council sessions are very frequent and often very long.[26] The deliberations are in camera: only the members of the Commission have access and the right to speak. However, in order to ensure transparency the Edinburgh Summit of 11–12 December 1992 introduced the possibility of public debates.[27] The Council responded by amending its Rules of Procedure. As a result, certain sessions are open to the public and may be broadcast.[28] Also, the results of voting are now made public unless the Council by simple majority decides otherwise. Finally, the Council adopted a Code of Conduct in this respect on 2 October 1995 concerning access to its working sessions and any statement that result from them.[29]

Voting

The vote in the Council is personal, although under the Council Rules of Procedure a Member of the Council may arrange to be represented at a meeting which he is not able to attend. Usually, he is replaced by the permanent representative or the deputy permanent representative of that Member State. However, his replacement has no right to vote. For that reason, another member of the Council under art 150 EC usually acts on behalf of the absentee member and thus the non-ministerial representative votes in accordance with the instruction forwarded by his government under 'cover' of one of the ministers present. A present member of the Council cannot act on behalf of more that one other Member.

The Treaties provided for three modes of voting: by simple majority, by qualified majority or by unanimity. The choice of mode is not left to the Council but depends upon the legal basis of the act in question. Under art 148(1) EC in the absence of any specific provision the Council acts by a simple majority of its members. Paradoxically, simple majority voting – which was foreseen as a norm – is exceptional[30] as the Treaties often require qualified majority or unanimity votes. It is worth mentioning that the decision to revise the Treaties which led to the adoption of the SEA was taken by simple majority against the opposition of three Member States, although they later accepted it.

Unanimous voting, which was assigned the privileged place in the original Treaties has lost its importance due to the amendments introduced by the SEA and the TEU. It is still applied to constitutional or paraconstitutional matters,[31] certain aspects of harmonisation of national law in the context of the internal market,[32] and the adoption of measures concerning the common policies.[33] By contrast, in the Common Foreign and Security Policy and Co-operation in the Fields of Justice and Home Affairs unanimity is the predominant mode of voting. It is also interesting to note that under art 148(3) EC abstentions by a

---

[26] For example, in 1986 the Council held 79 sessions for a total of 107 days of meetings.
[27] The first broadcast took place on 1 February 1993.
[28] Council Decision 93/662/EC of 6 December 1993 (OJ L304 10.12.93 p1); also, the EP demanded to make the deliberations of the Council public, Report Hansch, Doc EP A3–189/92 and Report Giovanni, Doc EP A3–190/92.
[29] EU Bull 10–1995, point 1.9.1.
[30] Articles 152, 153 and 213 EC. Also, the Council modifies its Rules of Procedure by simple majority.
[31] Articles 8a, 8b, 8e, 138, 201, 228, 235 EC.
[32] Articles 51, 57(2), 99, 100a(2), 100c EC.
[33] Articles 73c(2), 103a, 104c(14), 105(6), 109(1) and (4), 109f(4) and (5), 128(5), 130(3), 130b, 130e, 130i, 130o, 130s(1) EC.

member present or represented at the Council do not prevent the adoption of measures which required unanimity. Also, unanimity constitutes the only means for the Council to reject a proposal originating from the Commission under the procedure of art 189a and in certain cases the position adopted by the EP under arts 189b and 189c procedures.

Qualified majority voting (QMV) has gradually become the most frequently used within the Council. It is based on a 'weight' given to each Member State, which is designed to ensure their equality in the decision-making process. The system of weighted votes reflects the size of a Member State, its demographic, economic and political 'weight' within the Community. It has two objectives: first, to ensure that small Member States are not able themselves to block a measure; and, second, that small Member States have sufficient representation to avoid being systematically outvoted by the larger Member States. Under art 148(2) EC, when the Council is required to vote by a qualified majority, the votes are weighted as follows:

Germany, France, Italy and the United Kingdom – 10 votes each;
Spain – 8 votes;
Belgium, Greece, The Netherlands and Portugal – 5 votes each;
Austria and Sweden – 4 votes each;
Denmark, Ireland and Finland – 3 votes each;
Luxembourg – 2 votes, making a total of 87 votes.

A qualified majority requires 62 of the total of 87 votes. If the measure is based on a Commission proposal it requires any 62 votes; in other cases, that is if a proposal is submitted by the Council, the 62 votes must by cast by at least ten Member States. The latter has been introduced to ensure the protection of interests of smaller Member States which are normally taken into consideration by the Commission in its proposal.[34]

A qualified majority vote was foreseen as the norm at the end of the transition period. The opposition of France to its introduction in a wide range of policies from 1966 led to a major crisis which was resolved by the Luxembourg Accord in January 1966.[35] The question of qualified majority voting reappeared at the end of admission negotiations with Austria, Finland, Norway and Sweden. Subsequent to the pressure exercised by the United Kingdom and Spain to maintain the number of votes required to block a proposal at 23 votes,[36] the foreign ministers of the Member States reached a compromise at an informal meeting held on 27–29 March 1994 which is known as the Ioannina Compromise. Under Council Decision of 29 March 1994[37] if members of the Council representing a total of between 23 and 35 votes indicate their intention to oppose the adoption of a measure taken by QMV, the Council will do all in its power to reach, within a reasonable time, a satisfactory solution which will lead to its adoption by 65 votes. During that period the President of the Council with the assistance of the Commission and members of the Council will take all necessary initiatives to facilitate the broadest possible consensus within the Council. The Ioannina

---

[34] For example, art 8(1) EC.

[35] On the Luxembourg Accord and its implications see Chapter 3.

[36] The majority of the Member States wanted a proportional increase in the number of the votes necessary to block a proposal, from 23 to 26, which fixed the blocking minority at 30 per cent. The UK considered that this increase would give smaller Member States an unfair advantage.

[37] OJ C105 13.4.94 p1, as amended (OJ C1 1.1.95 p1).

Compromise means that if there is a sufficient number of votes to constitute a blocking minority under the pre-accession rules, but not under the new rules, then the President of the Council will interfere in order to obtain a number of votes which could not block the proposal under the old voting rules. This system is of very little practical importance since under old and new rules only a group of Member States can block a measure and it has not yet been relied upon. It was hoped that the Inter-governmental Conference would reform the voting system within the Council. However, this decision was delayed by the Amsterdam Conference of 1997 until the number of the Member States reaches at least 20.

Competences

In the context of the European Communities the Council is the ultimate legislative body, although under the ECSC Treaty it exercises a very unusual role. The Council is mainly a consultative body and as such in certain cases it is only consulted by the High Authority, in others it gives its assent in respect of legislative measures adopted by the High Authority.[38] Also, under art 50 ECSC the Council may authorise the High Authority to debit Member States and fix a levy exceeding 1 per cent, and in the absence of an initiative from the High Authority the Council may force the latter to establish a system of quotas in respect of the production[39] or maximum and minimum prices.[40] Under the EC Treaty in certain decision-making procedures the Council shares its legislative powers with the European Parliament.[41]

The Council has some 'governmental' functions which it may exercise directly by implementing its own measures or it may confer powers on the Commission for the implementation of those measures. Also, in external relations the Council acts in a similar way as a government. It authorises the opening of negotiations, confers on the Commission the power to negotiate international agreements on behalf of the Community, and decides whether or not to conclude them. For some agreements, for example in respect of admission of a new Member, the assent of the EP is required. In international organisations and international conferences the President of the Council represents the Communities. In budgetary matters the Council drafts the proposed budget and participates it its adoption together with the EP. Under art 152 EC the Council may ask the Commission to undertake any studies that the Council considers desirable for the attainment of the common objectives, and to submit to it any appropriate proposals. Furthermore, the Council fixes the remuneration of the Commissioners, Judges, Advocates-General and Registrar of the ECJ,[42] appoints the members of the Court of Auditors,[43] amends the Statute of the ECJ and approves its Rules of Procedure,[44] and may increase the number of Commissioners, Judges, or Advocates-General.[45]

Under arts 145 EC, 26 ECSC and 115 Euratom the Council must ensure co-ordination of

---

[38] Articles 14 and 28 ECSC.
[39] Article 58 ECSC.
[40] Article 61 ECSC.
[41] See section 6.4 of this Chapter.
[42] Article 6 of the Merger Treaty.
[43] Article 206 EC; also the Economic and Social Committee under art 194 EC.
[44] Article 188 EC.
[45] Commissioners (art 10 of the Merger Treaty), Judges (art 165 EC), Advocates-General (art 166 EC).

the general policies of the Member States. The task is mainly carried out by means of deliberations, consultations, recommendations and studies, although some binding acts may also be adopted by the Council.[46]

In the context of the European Union, that is in the Common Foreign and Security Policy and Co-operation in the Fields of Justice and Home Affairs, the Council is the ultimate decision-making body. It adopts common positions under arts J2(2) and K3(2) TEU, defines joint actions under arts J3(1) and K3(2) TEU, as well as representing the EU in the person of its President under art J5.

6.3 The European Commission

Like the Council of Ministers, the Commission has renamed itself following the entry into force of the Treaty of Maastricht. Instead of the Commission of the European Communities a new name, the European Commission, should be used. The Commission represents the interests of the Communities. As a 'revolutionary' body within the institutional system of the Community, it is also the most controversial institution. It exercises many functions, the most important being the guardian of the Treaty and the initiator of Community measures.

Composition

Since the last enlargement, the Commission is made up of 20 members, at least one and not more than two from each Member State. By convention larger Member States, that is Germany, France, Italy, Spain and the United Kingdom have two members. The Commissioners must be chosen on the basis of their general competence. Article 157(1) EC specifies that only nationals of the Member States may be appointed Commissioners. In the general interest of the Community their independence must be beyond doubt. In this respect they take a solemn oath before the ECJ. Their independence requires that, as art 157(2) provides, they:

> 'shall neither seek nor take instructions from any government or from any other body … Each Member State undertakes to respect this principle and not to seek to influence the Members of the Commission in the performance of their tasks'.

Also, in order to reinforce their independence during their term of office, they are prohibited from engaging in any other occupation, whether gainful or not, and from any action incompatible with their duties as Commissioners, which excludes the possibility that they may be members of a national Parliament or the European Parliament. However, academic activities, research and teaching are compatible with the status of Commissioner.[47]

By virtue of the founding Treaties, the Commissioners are designated by the common accord of the Member States, although in practice each Member State submits its candidates subject to the veto from other Member States. The Treaty of Maastricht has modified the

---

[46] For example, on the basis of arts 103, 116 EC.
[47] For more on incompatibility see Question E–2752/94 by F Herman (OJ C88 10.4.95 p39).

procedure of designation in order to strengthen the position of the President of the Commission,[48] to ameliorate the cohesion of the Commission and, especially, to ensure effective control by the EP over the nomination of Commissioners. New art 158(2) EC provides that the Member States must nominate the President of the Commission by common accord, after consulting the EP, and that:

> '... The governments of the Member States shall, in consultation with the nominee for President, nominate the other persons whom they intend to appoint as Members of the Commission. ...
>
> The President and the other Members of the Commission thus nominated shall be subject as a body to a vote of approval by the European Parliament. After approval by the European Parliament, the President and the other members of the Commission shall be appointed by common accord of the governments of the Member States.'

For the first time, this procedure was applied to the appointment of the current Commission (its term of office is from 1995 to 2000). The European Parliament was strongly criticised for interviewing each candidate, since under art 158(2) EC its vote of approval should concern the entire Commission and not a particular Commissioner.

Under art 161 EC the Commission may appoint one or two Vice-Presidents from among its members. Currently there are two Vice-Presidents: Sir Leon Brittan from the United Kingdom and Manuel Marin from Spain.

Term of office

The term of office for Commissioners has been extended to five years by the TEU in order to synchronise it with that of the EP. The mandate is renewable. Any vacancy, whether by normal replacement, death, resignation or compulsory retirement, is filled for the remainder of the member's term of office by a new member appointed by common accord of the Member States. However, the Commission may decide by unanimity not to fill such vacancy. The procedure concerning the appointment of the President applies also in the case of his replacement due to the circumstances stated above.[49]

If the Commissioner no longer fulfils the conditions required for the performance of his duties, or if he has been guilty of serious misconduct, the ECJ may, on application by the Council or the Commission, compulsorily retire him. So far this possibility, contained in art 160 EC, has been applied only once in a case of complete incapacity (he was paralysed). Also in the event of any breach of obligations imposed upon Commissioners, which includes their duty to behave with integrity and discretion even after they have ceased to hold office, sanctions may be imposed by the ECJ, depriving him or her of pension rights or other benefits. Furthermore, the European Parliament also may exercise some disciplinary power, but only over the entire Commission – by submitting a motion of censure under art 144 EC.[50]

---

[48] Jacques Santer has been President of the Commission since 26 January 1995. Among his famous predecessors are: Jacques Delors (France) from 1981 to 1985; François Xavier Ortoli (France) from 1973 to 1977; Sicco Manshott (The Netherlands) from 1972 to 1973; and Walter Hallstein (Germany) from 1958 to 1967. Two presidents, in particular, exercised great influence on the development of the Communities: Hallstein and Delors.

[49] Article 158(2) EC.

[50] See in the Chapter, section 6.4: the competences of the EP.

Functioning

The Commission is a collegiate body. It means that each member of the Commission is not empowered to take any decision on his own and that once he makes a decision, issues a declaration, etc, he expresses the position of the entire Commission. This principle requires that each measure must be formally approved by the college; its violation may render that measure invalid.[51] However, for practical reasons this principle has been attenuated.[52] Apart from the exceptions provided in arts 10 and 11 of the Commission's Rules of Procedure, the collegiate principle requires that the Commission seeks a broad consensus among its members, although it may also submit the matter to a formal vote.[53] The President of the Commission is only *primus inter pares* – there is no casting vote.

Despite the collegiate principle, the Commission divides its tasks among its members, with each Commissioner being allocated one or more policy area(s) and the Directorate(s)-General in charge of those areas. Currently, there are 25 Directorates-General and each deals with a policy area or administrative tasks.

Each Commissioner has personal advisors, his so-called *Cabinet*, which acts as a liaison between the Commissioner and his Directorate(s)-General. The chief of his *Cabinet* is usually the same nationality as the Commissioner and deputises for him as necessary. He also meets weekly with the other *Cabinet* chiefs in order to prepare the agenda for the Commission.

The Director-General is in charge of a particular Directorate-General. The Directorates-General are located in Luxembourg, while the Commission is based in Brussels. The Commission usually meets on the Wednesday of each week in Brussels or during the Parliamentary sessions in Strasbourg.

The Commission employs approximately 16,000 officials, and about 12 per cent of its administrative staff are involved in translation.

Competences

The competences of the European Commission are different under the Treaty of Paris and the Treaties of Rome. Under the ECSC the High Authority (Commission) enjoys wide direct powers while under the EC and Euratom Treaties its role is more limited. The competences of the European Commission are described in art 155 EC which provides that:

> 'In order to ensure the proper functioning and development of the common market, the Commission shall:
> – ensure that the provisions of this Treaty and the measures taken by the Institutions pursuant thereto are applied;
> – formulate recommendations or deliver opinions on matters dealt with in this Treaty, if it expressly so provides or if the Commission considers it necessary;
> – have its own power of decision and participate in the shaping of measures taken by the Council and by the European Parliament in the manner provided for in this Treaty;

---

[51] In Case C–137/92P *Commission* v *BASF* [1994] ECR I–2555 the ECJ confirmed the decision of the CFI (Cases T–79 , 84–86, 91–92, 94, 96 and 98/89 *BASF* [1992] ECR II–315) which considered it as violation of substantive requirements rendering the act in question unlawful.

[52] Case 5/85 *AKZO* [1986] ECR 2614; Cases 43 and 63/82 *Hoechst* [1989] ECR 2930.

[53] Under art 163 EC a simple majority of its members is required.

– exercise the powers conferred on it by the Council for the implementation of the rules laid down by the latter.'

In addition, the Commission has important managerial and administrative functions and plays a modest role under Pillars 2 and 3 of the TEU.

The European Commission as the 'Guardian of the Treaty'

The most important function of the Commission is to ensure that the provisions of the Treaty and the acts of the institutions are applied by the Member States, the individuals and even other EC institutions. In order to fulfil this task the Commission has at its disposal important powers.

First, the Commission is empowered to obtain any necessary information from Member States, individuals and undertakings. The Member States have a duty to forward information required by the Commission, to notify measures and projections of measures they intend to adopt, and to send explanations concerning any question of law or fact which the Commission considers important. This obligation derives variously from specific provisions of the Treaty,[54] from measures adopted by the EC institutions,[55] or from art 5 EC which requires the Member State to co-operate with the Commission in order to facilitate the achievement of the Community's tasks. Also, the Commission may ask individuals and undertakings to forward information,[56] and under its investigative powers to verify them. Indeed, the request for information is often the first step in the Commission's investigation of an alleged infringement of Community law by an undertaking in competition matters.[57]

Second, the Commission may take preventive actions. Usually, as mentioned in art 155 EC, the Commission formulates recommendations and delivers opinions intended to ensure effective application of EC law in the future or to determine the objectives for the Member States in areas within the exclusive national competences. In this respect an interesting example is provided by Recommendation 91/131 of 27 November 1991 to which is annexed the code of practice aiming at combating sexual harassment at the work place.[58]

Third, the Commission is empowered to enforce Community law. The obligation to observe Community law binds individuals, and the Commission may impose pecuniary and/or administrative sanctions upon them by virtue of specific provisions of the ECSC Treaty, in matters concerning the control of security under the Euratom Treaty, and in competition issues under the EC Treaty. Also the Commission may bring an action before the ECJ against a Member State in breach of Community law under arts 88 ECSC, 169 EC and 141 Euratom.[59] Furthermore, if any Community institution violates Community law the Commission may bring an action under arts 173 or 175 EC; this is mostly applied in respect of the Council.[60]

---

[54] For example, arts 72, 73, 93, 100a(4), 102 EC, etc.
[55] Especially, the final provisions of EC directives which impose upon the Member States the obligation to notify the Commission of the adoption of implementing measures.
[56] For example, arts 47 and 86 ESCS, and art 213 EC.
[57] See Regulation 17/62 , especially its art 14; Regulation 4064/89 on the Merger Control, arts 11 and 12.
[58] Commission recommendations on the protection of the dignity of women and men at work (OJ L49 24.2.92 p1).
[59] See Chapter 9.
[60] See Chapter 10.

Fourth, the Commission may authorise, in certain circumstances, derogations to the provisions of the Treaties. The expiry of the transition period made most derogations redundant, although under the Acts of Accession, measures adopted by Community institutions and international agreements still permit them in exceptional circumstances and on a temporary basis under the supervision of the Commission. Also under arts 223 and 224 EC or art 100a(4) EC the Commission is empowered to authorise measures incompatible with the common market if the Member State is seeking derogation from the application of the Treaty on the grounds of serious economic difficulties, internal disturbances, serious international tension, or if its essential interest of national security is in jeopardy.[61] In the context of the Economic and Monetary Union the Commission will monitor budgetary discipline in Member States in order to avoid excessive governmental deficits,[62] as well as supervising their balance of payments.[63]

The European Commission as the initiator of legislative measures

The general interest of the Community requires that the Commission's main objective is to foster European integration. Consequently, its right to initiate legislative measures in order to further develop the Community is well justified. In Cases 88–90/75 *SADAM*[64] the ECJ emphasised that the Commission is entrusted with a general mission of initiative. Therefore, the Commission may proceed, not only by drafting proposals for legislative measures, but also by adopting non-binding measures such as communications, action programmes, reports, white papers, etc, which define general objectives and the means necessary to their attainment which often result in formal proposals and, ultimately, in binding acts. In respect of proposals for legislative measures many provisions of the Treaties of Rome provide that only the Commission may initiate them. The special position of the Commission is recognised in art 189a EC which provides that:

> '(1) Where, in pursuance of this Treaty, the Council acts on a proposal from the Commission, unanimity shall be required for an act constituting an amendment to that proposal …
> (2) As long as the Council has not acted, the Commission may alter its proposal at any time during the procedures leading to the adoption of a Community act.'

It means that the Council may only amend the Commission proposal acting unanimously, although for its adoption without an amendment often a simple majority or QMV is sufficient. Furthermore, if there is any disagreement among the Member States, and unanimity can not be achieved, the Commission, which is the only institution entitled to change the proposal in question, acts as a broker between various governments and may negotiate a compromise by modifying the original proposal or even withdrawing it. This solution emphasises that the priority conferred upon proposals drafted by the Commission, which express the interest of the Community as a whole, may only be rejected if all Member States agree. Thus, the interest of the Community should prevail over national interests.

Although about 95 per cent of all legislative measures are initiated by the Commission, its exclusivity in this respect has been limited. First, the Council and the European

---

[61] See Chapter 9.
[62] Article 104c EC.
[63] Articles 109h and 109i EC.
[64] [1976] ECR 323.

Parliament may request the Commission to submit proposals on matters on which they consider that a Community act is necessary for the purpose of implementing the Treaty.[65] Second, under the TEU other institutions are empowered to submit proposals. In matters relating to the Economic and Monetary Union, the European Central Bank (ECB) shares the initiative with the Commission.[66] The Council and the Member States enjoy an autonomous right to initiate legislative measures.[67] In this area in a number of situations the initiative of the Commission is exercised by means of recommendations instead of proposals.[68] Also, the principle recognised under art 189a(1) EC, that a proposal emanating from the Commission may only be amended by the Council acting unanimously, is called into question by the decision-making procedure contained in art 189b EC. Indeed, if the Conciliation Committee reaches an agreement between the Council and the EP on a joint text, the text of the original proposal of the Commission is adopted in the modified version.[69]

Executive powers of the European Commission

Article 155 EC provides that the Commission shall 'have its own power of decision and participate in the shaping of measures taken by the Council and by the European Parliament in the manner provided for in this Treaty'.

Unlike the wide direct powers conferred upon the High Authority (Commission) by the ECSC, under the Treaty of Rome the Commission is empowered to enact normative measures of a general scope of application only in a limited areas such as the establishment of the customs union on the basis of the timetable determined by the Treaty,[70] or in the framework of common policies, the CAP being the best example. However, the Commission is more involved in issuing individual legislative measures addressed to Member States, undertakings and individuals. Under the EC Treaty it is mainly involved in competition matters. Furthermore, the administration of Community policies necessitates the adoption of numerous binding measures. The Commission also implements the Community budget and administrates four special funds: the European Social Fund; the European Development Fund; the European Agricultural Guidance and Guarantee Fund; and the European Regional Development Fund.

By virtue of art 155 EC the Commission exercises the powers conferred on it by the Council for the implementation of measures adopted by the latter. As a result, the Commission has delegated implementation powers which in practice means that while the Council adopts a framework act (usually a regulation), for example in relation to the CAP, the Commission is in charge of its details, for example it must fix the quotas, determine the price, etc, through regulations or decisions. The Commission must act within the limits of the authority delegated by the Council, although the ECJ has given a broad interpretation to such delegated implementation powers as it recognises the wide discretion of the

---

[65] The Council under art 152 EC and the EP under art 138b(2) EC. However, the Commission is not obliged to respond favourably to their requests: Case C–331/88 *Fedesa* [1990] ECR I–4057.

[66] Articles 106(5) and 109 EC.

[67] Article 109d EC.

[68] Articles 103(1) and (4), 104(6) and (13), 109(1), (2) and (3), 109j(2), 109k(1) EC.

[69] See end of this Chapter.

[70] Articles 12–37 EC.

Commission in this respect, including the possibility of imposing sanctions and of authorising derogations.[71]

Comitology The drawback to the delegated implementing powers conferred on the Commission is that a system of procedural mechanisms has been established by the Member States in order to supervise the way the Commission exercises those powers. The 'comitology' system was established as a necessary element in the introduction of the CAP in 1962. At that time it was thought to be politically unacceptable that the Commission alone implemented delegated legislation and a supervision committee was set up comprising national civil servants and presided over by a non-voting Commission representatives. With time, the system flourished and was extended to many areas. This pathological growth of 'comitology' was recognised by the Single European Act.[72] However, the necessity to rationalise the system prompted the Council to establish principles and rules governing comitology. Council Decision 87/373[73] lays down the procedures for the exercise of the delegated implementation powers. It provides for three types of committees: the regulatory committee, which must approve the proposal prior to its implementation by a qualified majority; the management committee, whose approval is not required but should it disapprove by a qualified majority then the Council must substitute its own measure for that of the Commission; and, lastly, the advisory committee, which must be consulted on the draft measure although its opinion is not binding. As a result, the Commission acts either alone or by one of three committee procedures.[74]

Since the SEA the principle is that the Commission implements measures adopted by the Council and the latter may exercise such powers itself only in 'specific cases' and in such event 'must state in details the grounds for such a Decision'.[75]

The hostility of the EP towards 'comitology' was resolved by the *modus vivendi* concluded between the EP, the Council and the Commission on 20 December 1994, which aims at ensuring the EP's influence on measures adopted under the co-decision procedure (art 189b EC).[76]

International functions

The European Commission has delegations which enjoy diplomatic status in more than 100 countries. The Commission also liaises with international organisations such as specialised bodies of the United Nations, the World Trade Organisation,[77] the Council of Europe,[78] the Organisation for Economic Co-operation and Development,[79] etc. The Commission, under art 228 EC, is entrusted with negotiating international agreements between the Community

---

[71] Case 41/69 *ACF Chemiefarma* [1970] ECR 661; Case 57/72 *Westzuker* [1973] ECR 321; Case 230/78 *Eridania* [1979] ECR 2749; Case C–296 and 307/93 *France and Ireland* v *Commission* [1996] ECR I–795.

[72] Article 145 EC.

[73] OJ L197 18.7.87 p33.

[74] See K Bradley, 'Comitology and the Law: Through a Glass, Darkly' (1992) 29 CMLR 693.

[75] Case 16/88 *Commission* v *Council* [1989] ECR 3457.

[76] OJ C293 8.11.95 p1.

[77] Article 229 EC.

[78] Article 230 EC.

[79] Article 231 EC.

and third countries. Its powers are strictly defined by the Council which may issue directives and appoint a special committee to assist the Commission and to ensure that the latter acts within the framework of its directives. The necessity for the Commission to conduct negotiations within the limits determined by the Council was emphasised in Case C–327/91 *France v Commission*,[80] in which the ECJ annulled an agreement on competition matters between the Commission and the United States when the former exceeded those limits. Under the new art 228(4) EC the Council may, by way of derogation, authorise the Commission to conclude international agreements adopted according to a simplified procedure introduced by the Treaty of Maastricht.[81]

6.4 The European Parliament

The European Parliament, previously known as the Assembly of the European Communities, renamed itself in 1962 in order to emphasise the role it should play in the Communities' policy-making process. This role is still limited although it has been dramatically increased by each revision of the original Treaties. The Single European Act recognised the new name, which was further confirmed by the TEU. In comparison to other Community institutions, the European Parliament has undergone the most dramatic changes since its inception in terms of attributed competences and the way it is constituted. Indeed, since 1979 it is the only directly elected body in the Communities and, as such, its claim to be a real parliament like any national legislature in a democracy is, to a certain extent, justified. Nevertheless, the EP it still a body which exercises its influence more through powers of persuasion than through votes. And unlike national parliaments it is still not a real, sovereign parliament as it has no power to initiate legislation or to impose taxes.

Composition

In accordance with Council Decision 76/787 and the annexed Act on direct elections of 20 September 1976[82] adopted by the Council on the ground of art 138(3) EC, the members of the European Parliament are elected in direct universal suffrage. The Treaty of Maastricht amended the EC Treaty so that art 8b(2) specifies that every citizen of the EU residing in a Member State of which he is not a national is entitled to vote and stand as a candidate in elections to the EP in the Member State in which he resides, under the same conditions as nationals of that State.[83] Contrary to art 138 EC a uniform electoral procedure has not yet been agreed. The first elections were held in 1979 and now take place every five years. In the last election, in June 1994, 567 MEPs were elected by the people of the European Union. Subsequent to the accession of Austria, Finland and Sweden on 1 January 1995, the number of MEPs was increased by 59 Members. The total number of MEPs is now 626. The number of parliamentary seats is determined on the basis of the size of population in each Member

---

[80] [1994] ECR I–3641.
[81] International aspect of the competences of the Commission are examined in detail in Chapter 4.
[82] OJ L278 8.10.76 p1.
[83] For details see Chapter 3.

State, but this is not a strict mathematical formula in the light of the wide difference between large and small Member States. For example, Luxembourg only has a population of 350,000, while the UK has 60 million inhabitants.[84] As a result, a compromise was reached which takes into consideration the size of the population in a Member State, while ensuring that the smallest Member States are adequately represented in the EP and that its overall size does not produce an over-large, unwieldy body.

The Member States' allocation of MEPs is as follows: Austria (21), Belgium (25), Denmark (16), France (87), Finland (16), Germany (99), Greece (25), Italy (87), Ireland (15), Luxembourg (6), The Netherlands (31), Portugal (25), Spain (64), Sweden (22) and the UK (87).

Any citizen of a Member State may stand as a candidate to the EP. However, certain offices are incompatible with membership of the EP, such as membership of national governments of a Member State, of the European Commission, the ECJ or employment by a Community institution. The dual mandate, that is being an MEP at the same time as being a member of a national parliament, is now permitted.

Members of the EP enjoy certain privileges and immunities, such as: freedom of movement when they travel to or from the place of meeting of the EP; immunity from any form of inquiry, detention or legal proceedings in respect of opinions expressed or votes cast in the performance of their duties; during the session of the EP they are accorded the same immunities as members of their national parliaments in the territory of their own State; and immunity from any measures of detention and from legal proceedings in the territory of any other Member State.[85] However, the immunity can be waived if an MEP commits a criminal offence. In this respect, it is interesting to note that the EP has modified its Rules of Procedure following the problem raised by the personal bankruptcy of Bernard Tapie during his mandate in order to regulate this kind of situation in the future. In the absence of a uniform electoral procedure at the Community level the question is governed in each Member State by its national electoral laws.[86] According to French electoral procedure, when a bankruptcy judgment is rendered against the debtor, that person cannot be elected to Parliament or continue to exercise his mandate as a Member of Parliament. The Decree of the French Conseil d'Etat of 28 October 1996, based on the judgment of the Tribunal de Commerce de Paris delivered on 14 December 1994 which declared Mr Tapie personally bankrupt, terminated his mandate as an MEP. Mr Tapie appealed against the decree on the grounds that it was incompatible with the Act on direct elections to the EP annexed to Council Decision 76/787. The French Conseil d'Etat rejected his appeal and held that French electoral law and the Act in question were compatible since the electoral procedure applicable to MEPs is governed by national electoral law unless covered by the Act. The latter is silent as to personal bankruptcy and, in addition, does not impose any restriction on the Member States in respect of measures which may be taken in this area.[87] Unfortunately,

---

[84] As a result, the number of people represented by a seat varies widely: eg, France has one seat for more than 670,000 people, while Luxembourg has one seat for approximately 61,000 inhabitants.

[85] See arts 8–10 of the Protocol on the Privileges and Immunities of the European Communities annexed to the Merger Treaty of 1965.

[86] On the consequences of the absence of uniform electoral procedure see: Case 294/83 *Les Verts* [1986] ECR 1339; Case C–41/92 *The Liberal Democrats* [1993] ECR I– 3153.

[87] Conseil d'Etat, 9 January 1997, *Tapie,* Req No 183363, *Europe,* April 1997, note 100, comm D Simon.

the Conseil d'Etat did not consider necessary to consult the ECJ on this matter under art 177 EC.

The remuneration of MEPs is paid by the Member State of their nationality. They receive the same salary as MPs in their own countries. As a result, there are wide differences in their salaries, especially in relation to the Portuguese (the lowest paid),[88] British and Italian MEPs which the EP tries to rectify by granting them generous allowances and expenses. The reimbursement of fees relating to the exercise of a mandate is within the exclusive competence of the EP.

Unlike national parliaments, the EP is not divided into the government and the opposition. MEPs sit in multinational political groupings and not in national groups. Under the Rules of Procedure of the EP a political group is recognised by the EP if it comprises a minimum of 29 members from one Member State, 23 if they are from two Member States, 18 if they are from three Member States and 14 if they are from four or more Member States.

In 1997 there were eight political groups: Party of European Socialists (214); European People's Party (Christian Democrats) (181); Union for Europe (57); European Liberal, Democratic and Reformist Group (43); European United Left/Nordic Green Left Group (33); Greens (28); European Radical Alliance (20); Independent Europe of the Nations Group (18); and Independents (non-affiliated) (32).

The Treaty of Maastricht emphasised the importance of political parties at European level as an important factor for integration since they 'contribute to forming a European awareness and to expressing the political will of the citizens of the Union'.[89] There are important incentives to form political groups, such as allocation of an office and staff, appointment to parliamentary committees, allocation of speaking time, various rights of initiative and disbursement of funding which is made on a political group basis.

Functioning

From its inception, the EP has considered itself as a parliament. The Assembly of the ECSC adopted rules of procedure similar to any parliament. This was recognised by the Treaties of Rome and enhanced by the universal suffrage to the EP. Under art 142 EC the EP adopts its own Rules of Procedure.[90] However, the power of the EP is limited by the obligation to respect the allocation of competences between the Community institutions as determined by the Treaties.[91] Also, the EP cannot unilaterally decide on the location of its seat. As a result, the MEPs travel between three working places: Luxembourg, Brussels and Strasbourg.[92]

The EP elects its President for two-and-half years. The President chairs the debates, exercises an administrative and disciplinary function similar to those of a leader of any national parliament and, together with the President of the Commission and the President

---

[88] The best paid are the French and German MEPs.
[89] Article 138a EC.
[90] OJ L49 19.2.97 p1.
[91] This was emphasised by the ECJ in Case 294/83 *Les Verts* [1986] ECR 1339.
[92] Supra note 2.

of the Council of the European Union, represents the European Union. Fourteen vice-presidents and five quaestors[93] are elected by the EP and with the President they form the Bureau of Parliament which is responsible for the organisation and administration of the EP. Until 1993 the Bureau and the chairman of the political groups formed the Enlarged Bureau which set the detailed agenda for the parliamentary sessions. Since then it has been replaced by the Conference of Presidents,[94] comprising the chairmen of the political groups, the president of the EP and the presidents of the EP Committees. The non-attached MEPs delegate two of their number to attend meetings of the Conference but they have no right to vote. In addition to the tasks carried out by the Enlarged Bureau, it organises meetings and relations with other Community institutions, bodies and organisations, and the national parliaments of Member States. The Conference is responsible for the composition and competence of committees, committees of enquiry, joint parliamentary committees, standing delegations and *ad hoc* delegations. It also submits proposals to the Bureau concerning administrative and budgetary matters relating to the policial groups. The Secretary-General and Secretariat assists the EP in administrative and organisational matters.

The EP may establish permanent, temporary, specialised and general commissions. They examine in detail particular topics, and prepare opinions at the request of the Council and resolutions concerning new initiatives of the EP. There are 20 permanent (standing) commissions, each dealing with a specific aspect of Community activities. They are of particular importance as they ensure the continuity in the work of the EP. They prepare reports for debates in the EP and liaise with the Commission and the Council in the interim between parliamentary sessions. They can meet at any time at the request of their chairman or the President of the EP. The members of commissions are elected on the basis of proposals submitted by political groups. Political and geographical factors, as well as equitable representations of the parliamentary political groups within a commission, determine its composition. In principle, each MEP is a sitting member of one commission and an advisory member-suppliant of another. Article 138c EC, as amended by the TEU, permits the EP to set up a temporary Committee of Inquiry to investigate alleged contravention and maladministration in the implementation of Community law.[95]

Sessions

Article 139 EC provides that:

> 'The European Parliament shall hold an annual session. It shall meet, without requiring to be convened, on the second Tuesday in March.
>
> The European Parliament may meet in extraordinary session at the request of a majority of its members or at the request of the Council or of the Commission'.

In practice, the annual session is never closed; there are monthly plenary sessions, including the budget session, when the MEPs meet for one week except in August. Between each

---

[93] They are in charge of administrative and financial matters directly concerning the MEPs.
[94] The Decision of the EP of 15 September 1993 (OJ C268 4.10.93).
[95] See Chapter 3.

annual session two weeks are set aside for meetings of the parliamentary commissions and a third week for meetings of the political groups. The sessions are open to the general public.

In principle, the EP acts by an absolute majority of votes cast, although in many matters the positive vote by a majority of its members is required.

Competences

Under the original Treaties the EP was only a supervisory and advisory body. Gradually in its 'fight for power' which was enhanced by direct election, the EP has achieved, apart from sharing budgetary power, an actual role in the decision-making procedures of the Community and in the conduct of external relations. There are four main functions which the EP exercises at present: political control, budgetary powers, participation in decision-making procedures and in the external relations of the Communities and the Union.

Political control

Political control exercised by the EP over the Commission was first provided in the ECSC Treaty. However, its form has changed over the years as the Commission, under the TEU, has become directly accountable to the EP. Furthermore, the political control of the EP now extends over other institutions such as the Council, the bodies in charge of the political co-operation and the European Council.

General and permanent political control is exercised by the EP over the Commission and the Council by means of various techniques. The EP has power to ask questions: written, oral without debates, oral with debates, question-times, etc. Written questions and answers to them are published in the Official Journal. Oral questions without a debate, which must be first approved by the Bureau, may be put to the Council and the Commission during the plenary session. Oral questions with a debate may only be put by a parliamentary commission, a political group or at least 29 MEPs. Sometimes they lead to a resolution being adopted by the EP. Question-time, which is modelled on the British parliamentary tradition, was introduced in 1973: in each plenary session a period of time is specially set aside for questions regarding current affairs. The questions are brief and precise and so are the answers. After each answer any MEP may ask an additional question and, if necessary, at the request of 29 MEPs question-time may lead to a debate. The possibility of asking questions ensures a follow-up to the legislative and administrative activities of the Commission and the Council, and imposes an obligation to justify them before the EP. Also, the EP is entitled to ask questions concerning the development of political co-operation by the foreign ministers of the Member States.

Another general method of political control involves the ability of the EP to examine annual and periodical reports, programmes of action, etc, submitted by various bodies. By virtue of art 143 EC the Commission must submit an annual report on activities of the Communities, to which the Commission on its own initiative decided to annex its annual work programme. In February each year both are discussed by the EP and resumed under a resolution on the general policy of the Communities. Also, every six months the Presidency of the Council submits its report, and the foreign minister of the Member State which holds the Presidency presents the report after each session of the European Council, a symbolic

213

gesture which was subsequent to a request of the EP in 1981. Margaret Thatcher was the first to establish a formal link between the European Council and the EP.[96] Since 1973 the President of the Council of Foreign Ministers issues an annual declaration addressed to the EP on progress achieved in the matters relating to political co-operation.

Another means of political control by the EP consists of the establishment of a temporary Committee of Inquiry at the request of a quarter of its members which investigates alleged contravention or maladministration in the implementation of the Community law. This body ceases to exists on the submission of its report.[97] Furthermore, by virtue of art 8d EC every citizen of the EU has the right to petition the EP and may apply to the Ombudsman appointed by the EP.[98]

In relation to the Commission, under the TEU the EP has the right to approve the nomination of the President of the Commission and its members.[99] The extensive interviews of the candidates conducted by the EP in relation to the nomination of the current Members of Commission demonstrate that the power is far from being theoretical. In addition, under art 144 EC the EP may table a motion of censure and thus force the entire Commission to resign, but not its President or a particular Commissioner. In order to avoid abuse art 144 EC laid down stringent requirements as to the motion of censure: it must be tabled by at least one-tenth of the MEPs; a time of reflection of at least three days after the motion has been tabled is required; a two-thirds majority of the votes cast, representing a majority of the MEPs, is necessary to carry the motion of censure; and the vote must be open. Before direct elections to the EP began, four such motions were tabled, two subjected to the vote of the EP and none were successful. Since then, one motion of censure has been tabled and voted but failed.[100] Indeed, a motion of censure is an exceptional measure which could lead to a serious crisis in the EU without achieving the desired objective, unless the objective was to remove the whole Commission. The Commission is not a decision-making body and represents the interest of the Communities. Often the actual culprit is the Council and, rather than fighting it, the EP must seek co-operation with the Commission to secure the interests of the Communities. Also, the final result of the motion of censure, provided it is successfully carried out, is doubtful. The Commissioners are nominated by the Member States. Nothing would prevent the Member States from nominating the same persons, although it is difficult to envisage how the Commission would operate without the approval of the EP. Nevertheless, art 144 EC provides a powerful weapon for the EP in the complex political interaction between the three institutions: the EP, the Council and the Commission.

Budgetary powers

Before the Budgetary Treaties of 1970 and 1975 the EP was only consulted on the Communities budget. Since then it has acquired important powers over the budget, not only of the Communities but also of the European Union. Indeed, under arts 199–209 EC, as

---

[96] Report Antoniozzi, EP Doc, session 1–737/81.
[97] See Chapter 3.
[98] Ibid.
[99] Article 158(2) and (3) EC.
[100] In 1990 by Jean-Marie Le Pen, 16 in favour, 243 against and 5 abstention, Bradley, 'Legal Developments in the European Parliament' (1991) 10 YEL 367 at 381.

amended by the TEU, the budget comprises: 'All items of revenue and expenditure of the Community including those relating to the European Social Fund' as well as 'administrative expenditure occasioned for the institutions by the provisions of the Treaty on European Union relating to the Common Foreign and Security Policy and to co-operation in the fields of Justice and Home Affairs'.[101]

The Commission prepares a preliminary draft based on estimates of expenditure submitted by each institution which is placed before the Council no later than 1 October for the following financial year (from 1 January to 31 December). The Council is entitled to make amendments and, acting on qualified majority, approves a draft budget which is forwarded to the EP for its first reading, no later than 5 October. The EP has 45 days to accept, reject or amend the budget. No action amounts to the acceptance of the submitted draft budget. The power of the EP to amend the budget depends on the classification of the expenditure. Compulsory expenditure (CE) which relates to those items resulting from Treaty obligations or secondary legislation, mainly the financing of the Common Agricultural Policy, etc, cannot be amended by the EP. The EP may, acting by the simple majority of MEPs present, adopt proposals for their modification. Non-Compulsory Expenditure (NCE) covers other items such as social and regional policy, research and aid, etc. The EP acting by the majority of all MEPs may amend NCE. In both cases the budget is sent back to the Council which must within 15 days modify the budget in line with the amendments or reject them by QMV, otherwise the amendments are deemed to be accepted. The modifications proposed by the EP are dealt with according to their content. If the modifications increase CE they are deemed to be rejected, unless the Council accepts them within 15 days acting by QMV. In the event of reduction of CE the Council has 15 days to reject, otherwise it is deemed to be accepted. However, in respect of CE the Council may, instead of rejecting the modifications, fix different amounts that those submitted in the first draft. If the Council disagrees with the amendments and modification, which usually is the case, the budget is forwarded to the EP for a second reading. At this stage the EP cannot change CE but in relation to NCE it has 15 days to reject or amend the changes made by the Council to its original amendments acting by a majority of its Members by three-fifths of the votes cast. After 15 days the budget is automatically adopted or the EP, using the same voting majority, may reject the Council's amendments. The last word of the EP on NCE should be assessed in the light of constant increase of NCE in the Community budget, from 3.5 per cent in 1970 to 23 per cent in 1980 and 42 per cent in 1992. However, NCE cannot be increased without limits. Article 203(9) EC provides that 'the actual rate of increase in the draft budget established by the Council is over half the maximum rate, the European Parliament may, exercising its right of amendment, further increase the total amount of that expenditure to a limit not exceeding half the maximum rate'.

The most important prerogative of the EP in budgetary matters is that it may reject the budget as a whole acting by a majority of its members and two-thirds of the votes cast. If the budget is rejected a new draft must be prepared. The inconvenience it creates for the institutions is significant, as the previous year's budget continues to operate on a one-twelfth basis for each month. It means that the institutions cannot exceed the previous year's limits, although now art 204 EC permits an increase in expenditure on the approval of

---

[101] Article 199 EC.

the Council and the EP. The EP rejected the 1980 and 1985 budgets.[102] As a result, inter-institutional agreements on budgetary discipline and improvement of the budgetary procedure were concluded in 1988[103] and in 1993.[104] Furthermore, in a Joint Declaration of 30 June 1982 the EP, the Commission and the Council agreed on a common classification of compulsory expenditure.[105]

Legislative powers

Unlike national parliaments the EP has neither the right to initiate legislative measures nor to adopt them by acting on its own accord. Since the introduction of direct elections to the EP the EP has sought to impose on the Commission the duty to be unofficially consulted in respect of its proposals prior to their presentation to the Council. Under pressure the Commission agreed to inform the EP of the content and financial implications of its proposals under consideration. The Treaty of Maastricht grants power to the EP, acting by a majority of its members, to request that the Commission submits appropriate proposals on matters on which the EP considers that a Community act is required for the purpose of implementing the Treaty.[106]

In relation to the participation of the EP in the decision-making procedures of the Community,[107] each revision of the original Treaty has increased the EP powers in the adoption of legislative measures. At the beginning, the participation of the EP in the decision-making was limited to the obligation imposed on the Council to ask the EP for its opinion in only limited areas specified by the Treaty. The SEA has introduced the co-operation procedure[108] and the assent procedure.[109] The TEU has strengthened the legislative role of the EP by adding the procedure under art 189b, generally known as the co-decision procedure, under which the EP may, in specific situations, block the adoption of a measure by the Council.

Role of the European Parliament in external relations of the Communities and the Union

Until the Treaty of Maastricht the EP played a limited role in the conduct of external relations of the Community. Under art 238 EEC and 206 Euratom the EP was consulted in relation to association agreements prior to their conclusion but after they were signed. The EP fight for more involvement in external aspects of the Communities was quite successful. Under the 'Luns/Westerterp'[110] procedure the EP is notified of any envisaged agreements – not only association agreements but also commercial and economic agreements between the Communities and third countries – and is able to discuss them before the opening of

---

[102] See Chapter 2.

[103] OJ L185 15.7.88 p33.

[104] OJ C331 7.12.93 p1. For details see Zangl, 'The Interinstitutional Agreement of Budgetary Discipline and Improvement of the Budgetary Procedure' (1989) 26 CMLR 675.

[105] OJ C194 28.7.82 p1.

[106] Article 138b EC.

[107] The decision-making procedure will be discussed in section 6.9 of this Chapter.

[108] Article 149 EC as amended by art 7 SEA.

[109] Articles 237 and 238 EC as modified by arts 8 and 9 SEA.

[110] The surnames of the Presidents of the Council who accepted the participation of the EP in external matters on behalf of the Council.

negotiations. During negotiations the appropriate parliamentary commission is informed of their progress by the Commission. After the agreement is signed, but before its conclusion, the EP is formally consulted and informed of its content and essential features. The amendment of art 238 EC by the Treaty of Maastricht has given the EP a real veto in relation to association agreements. The procedure used for this purpose, the assent procedure, requires that the EP by an absolute majority of its members approves that agreement. Under art 228(3) EC, apart from association agreements, the assent of the EP is required in relation to 'agreements establishing a specific institutional framework by organising co-operation procedures, agreements having important budgetary implications for the Community and agreements entailing amendment of an act adopted under the procedure referred to in art 189b'.

In addition, for the conclusion of almost all international agreements, apart from those referred to in art 113 EC, the EP must be consulted prior to their conclusion.

6.5 The Court of Justice of the European Communities (ECJ)

The ECJ is located in Luxembourg. It has been created separately under each founding Treaty: ECSC, EEC and Euratom, although since the 1957 Convention on Certain Institutions Common to the European Communities it has been recognised as a common institution for all three Communities. The Protocol on the Statute of the ECJ annexed to each founding Treaty which regulates its organisation and competences is still a formally distinct legal instrument. For that reason the TEU provides that Title III of each Protocol, which concerns the procedure before the ECJ, may be modified by the Council acting unanimously at the request of the ECJ and after the consultation with the Commission and the EP. However, there are the same Rules of Procedure[111] for the three Communities. They are adopted by the ECJ but require the unanimous approval of the Council. The ECJ's main task is to ensure that in the interpretation and application of the Treaties the law is observed.

Composition

The ECJ consists of 15 judges and nine Advocates-General, both nominated by the Member States by a common accord. The number of judges and Advocates-General may be increased by the Council acting unanimously at the request of the ECJ, especially in order to ease the Court's workload or to accommodate a Member State which considers that it is under-represented in the ECJ. Article 167 EC provides that the judges and the Advocates-General are chosen from persons 'whose independence is beyond doubt and who possess the qualifications required for appointment to the highest judicial offices in their respective countries or who are jurisconsults of recognised competence'. The inclusion of jurisconsults

---

[111] The last modification of the Rules of Procedure has taken into consideration the accession of Austria, Finland and Sweden to the Communities, but especially was designated to make the work of both courts more efficient, Modifications of the Rules of Procedure of the ECJ of 11 March 1997 and the Rules of Procedure of the CFI of 12 March 1997 (OJ L103 19.4.97 p1).

allows academics, solicitors, civil service lawyers and jurists, that is lawyers without professional qualification, to be appointed even though in their own country they would not be eligible for the highest judicial offices. There is one judge from each Member State although no provision of the Treaties provides for a national balance. In practice, it facilitates the work of the ECJ to have a judge who is an expert in national law of a Member State and in addition speaks the language of that State. The originality of the composition of the ECJ is emphasised by the presence of Advocates-General, who are also members of the Court. By virtue of art 166 EC the function of the Advocates-General is the following:

> 'It shall be the duty of the Advocate-General, acting with complete impartiality and independence, to make, in open court, reasoned submissions on cases brought before the Court of Justice, in order to assist the Court in the performance of the task assigned to it in art 164.'

Thus, their function is similar to that of the *commissaire du gouvernement* in the French *Conseil d'Etat* (the highest administrative court). Especially at the beginning the post was justified by the importance of an action for annulment in the ECSC Treaty.[112] The Advocate-General is required to be neutral as between the applicant and the defendant. He represents the interests of justice. He reviews factual and legal aspects of the case and must reach a conclusion which constitutes his recommendation of how the ECJ should decide the case. The conclusion is very detailed and often suggests original and new legal approaches to the disputed matter, but is not binding on the ECJ. Even if rejected by the ECJ in a particular case, the opinion of a Advocate-General may be later reconsidered in a similar case since it often indicates the direction in which the Community should evolve. Furthermore, the opinion is very useful to understanding the case as the ECJ's judgment is usually very short.

The posts of Advocates-General are allocated according to a non-written agreement among the Member States, that is, one from each of the largest Member States – Germany, France, Italy, Spain and the UK – with the remaining four posts[113] held on a rotating basis.

Term of office

Judges and Advocates-General are appointed for six years, renewable without any limitation. Usually, they hold the office for two terms. In order to ensure continuity in the work of the ECJ there is a partial replacement of the judges and Advocates-General every three years.

The judges and Advocates-General have privileges and immunities similar to other officials of the Communities and additionally are immune from legal proceedings in respect of acts performed in their official capacity, including words spoken or written, but this may be waived by the ECJ. In criminal proceedings in any of the Member States against a judge or an Advocate-General, provided the immunity is waived, he should be tried only by the court competent to judge the members of the highest national judiciary. Before taking up his post at the ECJ each judge or Advocate-General must take a solemn oath that he will perform his duties impartially and conscientiously and preserve the secrecy of the

---

[112] For details see A Barov, *Le Commissaire du Gouvernement Devant le Conseil d'Etat et L'Avocat Général Près de la Court de Justice des Communautés Européennes*, Revue International de Droit Compare, 1974, p809; in English, N Brown, *The Court of Justice of the European Communities*, 3rd ed, 1989, p53.

[113] Under art 166 EC there should be eight Advocates-General but nine have been appointed until 6 October 2000.

deliberations of the Court. The independence of judges and Advocates-General requires that they cannot hold during their term of office any political or administrative post or engage in any occupation incompatible with their mandate unless an exceptional exemption is granted by the ECJ. They must behave with integrity and discretion both during and after their term of office.

A judge or an Advocate-General may resign but should hold his office until his successor is appointed. Usual disciplinary measures apply to both judges and Advocates-General. However, the unanimous opinion of the judges and Advocates-General is required in order to decide that the person concerned no longer fulfils the requisite conditions or meets the obligations arising from his office and thus should be disciplined, dismissed or deprived of his right to pension or other benefits.

Organisation

The ECJ remains permanently in session although hearings do not usually take place during the judicial vacations. Their duration is determined by the ECJ in the light of the needs of the Court's business. In case of urgency, the President may convene the ECJ during vacations.

The President of the ECJ is elected by judges from among their own number by an absolute majority vote in a secret ballot for a period of three years, which is renewable. He directs the judicial business and administration of the Court, chairs hearings and deliberations and exercises its competences in relation to applications for interim measures. He supervises the services of the ECJ.

The Registrar is appointed for six years by the ECJ after consultation with the Advocates-General. He is in charge of the day-to-day administration of the ECJ, financial management and accounts. In particular he assists the ECJ in the act of procedure, that is the acceptance, transmission and custody of documents, and is present in person or by a substitute at all hearings of the ECJ in chambers and all meetings of the ECJ apart from the disciplinary proceedings and matters outside its competence. He is also in charge of archives and of the publication of the decisions rendered by the ECJ. Officials and other employees attached to the ECJ are accountable to him under the authority of the President of the ECJ.

Each judge and Advocate-General is assisted by three *référendaires*, who usually have the same nationality as their senior and form his *Cabinet*. They are lawyers, usually with a Doctorate in Law. They prepare pre-trial studies on the legal aspects of the case at issue and assist in the drafting of judgments and opinions.

In principle, the ECJ sits in plenary session. However, in order to facilitate and accelerate proceedings, art 165 EC allows the Court to form chambers consisting of three or five judges in two events, either to undertake certain preparatory inquiries or to adjudicate a particular category of cases. Since 1995 there are four chambers, each comprising three or five judges, and two chambers of seven judges each. The frequent use of chambers was approved by the Council in its Decision of 26 November 1974,[114] following a request by the ECJ in order to cope with its increasing workload. As a result, the ECJ may forward to its chambers all preliminary questions and all other cases when the applicant is an individual

---

[114] OJ L318 28.11.74 p22.

or an undertaking if it considers that the importance or the complexity of the matter does not require that the ECJ sit in plenary session, and provided there is no opposition from either a Member State or a Community institution.[115] In any event, a chamber may decide to send back the case to the ECJ if necessary. The TEU has recognised the tendency of the ECJ to work in chambers. By virtue of art 165 EC:

> 'The Court of Justice shall sit in plenary session when a Member State or a Community institution that is a party to the proceedings so requests.'

In all other cases the ECJ decides whether or not to sit in plenary session.

Functioning

The quorum for a plenary session is nine judges, for chambers of three or five judges it is three, and for chambers of seven judges it is five. In addition, art 15 of the Protocol on the Statute of the ECJ provides that the decisions of the ECJ will only be valid when an uneven number of judges sit in deliberations. The President has no casting vote.

A party to the proceedings cannot apply for a change in composition of the ECJ or its chamber on the basis that there is a judge who has the nationality of that party or that there is no judge from the Member State of that party. In order to ensure that there is no conflict of interest, a judge or Advocate-General is not permitted to take part in a case in which he has previously participated as agent or adviser or has acted for one of the parties or in any other capacity. Also, the President of the ECJ may decide for some special reason that a judge or Advocate-General should not take part in the disposal of a particular case.

Procedure

The procedure before the ECJ has been inspired by that of the French *Conseil d'Etat*. There are two stages to the proceedings before the ECJ: written and oral. The written stage begins when the application from the plaintiff is received by the Registrar. The application should contain the names and permanent addresses of the parties, the subject-matter of the dispute, legal arguments invoked by the applicant and the form of the order sought by him. It must be lodged within the time-limit prescribed for such action by the Treaty. Once it is filed with the Registrar, the President of the ECJ appoints from among the judges a judge-rapporteur who prepares a preliminary report on the case. The defendant is notified and has one month to submit a written defence. Then each party may submit a further written pleading, the applicant to reply to the defendant's submission and the defendant to lodge a rejoinder (reply to the applicant's reply to his application). As a result, there are usually two written pleadings from each party. After the written part is closed the judge-rapporteur submits his report to the ECJ which may recommend certain procedural steps, such as the ordering of a preparatory inquiry, witnesses to be examined, experts' reports, inspection of a place, etc. The oral procedure, which is fixed at the closing of the written stage, commences with the reading of the preliminary report of the judge-rapporteur. This is forwarded to the parties before the opening of the oral stage, and comprises the summary of the case, the legal

---

[115] But not if the case is a staff dispute between the Community and its officials or servants.

arguments invoked by the parties, and the factual situation based on the evidence presented during the written stage and preparatory enquiry. The next step is the hearing of the parties through their representatives: the Court may also examine experts and witnesses.[116] At the conclusion of the oral stage the representatives of the parties make closing speeches to the Court, first the plaintiff and then the defendant. At the end, the Advocate-General delivers his opinion. Usually, at that stage, the oral proceedings are closed, although it is still possible in certain circumstances to reopen the oral procedure, and the ECJ proceeds to deliberate on the case. The deliberations are, and remain, confidential. Neither the Advocate-General nor translators, nor legal secretaries are present. During the deliberations the judges will try to reach consensus on the matter. If not, the decision is reached by a majority vote. There are no dissenting or separate opinions, it is a single collegiate judgment. It must state the reasons on which it is based and must be signed by all judges who took part in the deliberations. It is delivered in open court and binding from that date.

There are a number of specific issues in respect of the procedure before the ECJ which require some comment: the parties to the proceedings, the language, the cost of the proceedings and the intervention of a third party.

Parties to the proceedings

The parties must be represented even in actions for annulment under art 173 EC. The Community institutions and the Member States must be represented by an agent appointed for each case, usually a member of the legal services of the institution concerned and by a member of the legal services of the foreign ministry of a Member State. Individuals and undertakings must be represented by a lawyer authorised to practise before a court of a Member State. However, the latter cannot represent himself. In Cases C–174 and 175/96P *Orlando Lopes*[117] the ECJ rejected an application submitted by a Portuguese lawyer who refused to be represented by another lawyer on the ground that no one is permitted to represent himself. University teachers and nationals of a Member State whose law accords them the right of audience (Germany) may represent parties to the proceedings before the ECJ. The representations of the parties enjoy rights and immunities necessary to the independent exercise of their duties.

Language

The ECJ is multilingual. Any official language may be chosen but there is an important limitation. Only one language may be used as the procedural language in a particular case. It is the language of the defendant in the case of an individual or an undertaking or a Member State. If a Community institution is a party to the proceedings, the applicant may choose the language of the procedure. All procedure is conducted in that language: written pleadings, examination of witnesses, etc. The last modification of the Rules of Procedure has introduced some changes in respect of the choice of the procedural language.[118] Any

---

[116] Article 29 of the Protocol on the Statute of the ECJ.

[117] [1996] ECR I–6401. It seems that the applicant was not only stubborn as his appeal from the decision of the CFI was submitted twice and consequently refused on the same ground but he was also disbarred from the Portuguese Bar.

[118] The Modification of the Rules of Procedure of the ECJ of 11 March 1997 and of the CFI of 12 March 1997 (OJ L103 19.4.97 p1).

derogation from the rules applicable to the choice of the procedural language is decided by the President of the ECJ or the CFI and not by the courts themselves unless the other party to the proceedings opposes such derogation.[119] In case of the preliminary ruling the procedural language is that of the court or a tribunal which referred the question to the ECJ. Under new rules in art 177 proceedings, a party to national proceedings may request a change of language in oral pleadings before the ECJ. The President of the ECJ may authorise it if a request lodged by that party is well justified and provided the views of the other party and the Advocate-General are duly taken into account.

The working language of the ECJ is French and, *inter alia*, the deliberations are conducted in that language.

Costs

The ECJ does not charge parties for its services, although in exceptional circumstances the parties may pay the fees, for example for translation of certain documents. The ECJ, however, determines which party should pay the cost of the proceedings. Usually it is the losing party, although the ECJ may decide otherwise. The Rules of Procedure of the ECJ adopted the German and Italian system in respect of the fees paid to a lawyer of the winning party. Thus, the losing party pays the fees of the experts, witnesses, his own lawyer and the lawyer of the other party. Usually, the ECJ does not fix the costs of the proceedings and leaves this question to the parties, although in the case of a disagreement the party concerned may apply to the ECJ which will settle the matter by an order.

Intervention of a third party

The ECJ permits the intervention of a third party in proceedings which have already commenced. Member States and Community institutions may intervene without establishing an interest in the result of the case. Such an interest is required in respect of any other person, that is individuals and undertakings. The latter cannot intervene in cases between Member States, between Community institutions and between Member States and Community institutions. Individuals and undertakings may obtain the necessary information concerning the case from the Official Journal. Indeed, the Registrar must publish a notice in the latter which specifies the date on which the application was lodged, gives the names and the addresses of the parties, indicates the subject matter of the dispute, the form of the order sought by the parties and contains a brief statement of the pleas in law on which the application is based. The application to intervene must be limited to supporting the form of order sought by one of the parties and must be lodged within one month from the publication of the notice in the OJ. The last modification of the Rules of Procedure shortened the time-limit from three months to the present one month.[120]

Revision and interpretation of judgments

There is no appeal from the judgments rendered by the ECJ. The only possibility is the revision of a particular judgment, although its conditions are very stringent. An application

---

[119] Ibid, RP of the ECJ art 29(2) and RP of the CFI art 35(2).
[120] RP of the ECJ, art 123.

for revision of a judgment will only be admissible by the ECJ 'on discovery of a fact which is of such a nature as to be a decisive factor, and which, when the judgment was given, was unknown to the Court and to the party claiming the revision'.[121] Furthermore, the application must be lodged within ten years from the date of the judgment and within three months of the discovery of that fact.[122]

A party to the proceedings before the ECJ or a Community institution, provided it demonstrates an interest in the decision, may ask the ECJ for the interpretation of a judgment if its meaning or scope gives rise to uncertainty.[123] In Case 5/55 *Assider v High Authority*[124] the ECJ emphasised that: 'the only parts of a judgment which can be interpreted are those which express the judgment of the Court in the dispute which has been submitted for its final decision and those parts of the reasoning upon which this decision is based and which are, therefore, essential to it ... the Court does not have to interpret those passages which are incidental and which complete or explain the basic reasoning'. Thus, only the operative part of the judgment, the *ratio decidendi*, may be interpreted by the ECJ. The request for interpretation may concern the effect of the judgment but not its application or legal implications arising from it.[125]

Jurisdiction of the ECJ

By virtue of art 164 EC:

'The Court of Justice shall ensure that in the interpretation and application of this Treaty the law is observed.'

The ECJ exercises its powers under the conditions and for the purposes provided for in the Treaties as amended.

Since its inception to 31 December 1996 some 9,468 cases have been brought before the ECJ. Of the 420 cases in 1996, the three most important areas were: the free movement of workers and social security (70); environmental policy (59); and agriculture (57). The ECJ delivered 297 judgments and, again, the three most important areas were: the free movement of workers and social security (41); the free movement of goods and environmental matters (36); and agriculture (34). Between 1954 and 1994 the United Kingdom was an applicant in 24 cases and a defendant in 36 cases.[126]

There are three categories of proceedings which can be brought before the ECJ: contentious, non-contentious and consultative.

---

[121] Article 41 of the Protocol on the Statute of the ECJ.

[122] Case 1/60 *Belgium* [1962] ECR 331.

[123] Article 40 of the Protocol on the Statute of the ECJ; see also Case 41/73 *Société Anonyme Générale Sucrière* [1977] ECR 445.

[124] [1954–56] ECR 125.

[125] Case 9/81 *Court of Auditors v Williams* [1983] ECR 2859.

[126] Among the Member States France was an applicant in 48 cases, Spain in 38 cases, while Denmark only in 5 cases and Portugal in 6 cases. Italy was a defendant in 298 cases, Belgium in 159 cases, France in 131 cases, while Portugal in 11 cases and Denmark in 20 cases: D Leonard, Guide *to the European Union*, 5th ed, London: The Economist, 1997, pp70–71.

Contentious proceedings

In contentious proceedings the ECJ is seised by the parties to a dispute which the ECJ decides in the first and last resort, that is the ECJ decides on the merits and delivers a final judgment. This category of disputes in the most common and comprises:[127]

1. actions for annulment of an act having legal effect adopted by a Community institution (arts 173 EC and 33 ECSC);
2. actions for failure to act brought against a Community institution which has a positive obligation to act imposed by the Treaties (arts 175 EC and 35 ECSC);
3. pleas of illegality (art 184 EC);
4. actions brought by any natural or legal person to make good damage caused by the Community institution, or by its servants, in the performance of their duties – non-contractual liability of the Community (arts 178 and 215(2) EC);
5. action against sanctions imposed by the Community institutions (art 172 EC);
6. appeals from the Court of First Instance including staff disputes (art 179 EC);
7. actions against a Member State for failure to fulfil a Treaty obligation (arts 169 and 170 EC, art 88 ECSC);
8. action against a Member State for failure to fulfil its obligation under the Statute of the European Investment Bank and the European Central Bank (art 180 EC);
9. action based on the arbitration clauses contained in a contract by or on behalf of the Community (art 181 EC);
10. actions brought by one Member State against another in the context of a dispute which relates to the subject matter of the Treaty on the basis of a special agreement between the parties (art 182 EC);
11. the application for interim measures (art 186 EC); and
12. actions brought in relation to disputes arising from the Agreement on the setting up of the European Economic Area.

Non-contentious proceedings

At the request of a national court, the ECJ rules on questions of Community law which have arisen in the national forum. The judgment on the principal issue is given by a national court, and the ECJ answers only the referred question. These include:

1. preliminary rulings concerning the validity of an act adopted by a Community institution (art 41 ECSC);
2. preliminary rulings concerning the interpretation of EC law and of acts of the Community institutions and the validity of such acts (art 177 EC and 150 Euratom); and
3. preliminary rulings concerning the interpretation of certain Conventions concluded among the Member States but outside the Community framework, such as the Brussels and Lugano Conventions on Recognition and the Enforcement of Judgments in Civil and Commercial Matters, the Rome Convention on the Law Applicable to Contractual Obligations, etc.

---

[127] It is examined in detail in Chapters 8 and 10.

Consultative jurisdiction

Despite its name, the consultative jurisdiction of the ECJ results in binding decisions, although it is not necessary for a dispute to exist on the matter brought to the attention of the ECJ even though in practice it is often the case. The consultative jurisdiction is provided for all three Communities: arts 95(3) and (4) ECSC, 103 and 104 Euratom, and 228(6) EC. In the case of the EC it arises in the context of international agreements between the Community and a third country or countries or international organisations. The Council, the Commission or a Member State may ask the ECJ for its opinion as to whether the envisaged agreement is compatible with the provisions of the Treaty. If the ECJ considers that the agreement in question is contrary to EC law the only possibility for that agreement to enter into force, apart from its renegotiation, is to revise the Treaty in accordance with art N TEU. The consultative jurisdiction of the ECJ has become quite popular in the recent years.

6.6 The Court of First Instance (CFI)

The CFI is attached to the ECJ. It was created to ease the workload of the ECJ and to enable the latter to concentrate on its fundamental tasks without affecting the effectiveness and the quality of the Community judicial system. It was established by Council Decision 88/591 of 24 October 1988.[128]

It is made up of 15 judges nominated by the common accord of the Member States, one from each Member State, although there is no nationality requirement for their appointment. Judges are appointed for a renewable term of six years and a partial replacement is taken place every three years. The same requirements for nomination, enjoyment of privileges and immunities, and disciplinary measures are applied as those regarding judges of the ECJ. However, it is not necessary for judges of the CFI to possess the qualifications required for appointment to the highest judicial offices in their respective countries but only for the exercise of judicial offices. No Advocates-General are appointed to assist the CFI, but in some cases the judges are called upon to perform the task of an Advocate-General. The CFI sits in chambers of three judges in cases concerning Community staff and five judges in all other cases, but if an important and complex legal matter is under consideration the CFI may sit in plenary session. The CFI has its own Registrar, appointed by its judges, who is in charge of the judicial and practical organisation of the Court. The procedure before the CFI is the same as before the ECJ.

The transfer of jurisdiction to the CFI is based on art 168a EC. It provides that the Council acting unanimously at the request of the ECJ and after consulting the EP and the Commission, determines the classes of action or proceedings within the jurisdiction of the CFI. As a result, the CFI has jurisdiction in the following matters:

1. disputes between the Communities and its staff (arts 179 EC and 152 ECSC);
2. under Council Decision of 8 June 1993[129] all actions under arts 173, 175 and 178 brought by any natural or legal person against a Community institution under all three Treaties;

---

[128] OJ L319 25.11.88 p1.
[129] OJ L144 16.6.93 p21.

3. disputes concerning the application of the competition rules to undertakings; and
4. actions against the Commission by virtue of arts 33 and 35 ECSC brought by undertakings and associations of undertakings concerning the application of arts 50 and 57–66 ECSC (levies, production, prices, restrictive agreements, decisions or practices and concentrations).

The transfer of jurisdiction may be extended to other areas with an exception established in art 168a(1) EC which clearly states that only the ECJ has jurisdiction to hear and determine questions referred for a preliminary ruling under art 177 EC.

6.7 The Court of Auditors

The Court of Auditors was established in 1975, constituted in 1977 and recognised as a Community institution by the Treaty of Maastricht. It has no judicial functions, thus it is not really a court but an independent auditing body, the Community's financial watchdog.

The Court of Auditors is composed of 15 members, one from each Member State, although there is no specific requirement as to their nationality. Each member must either have belonged to a national external audit body or be 'especially qualified' to carry out the audit. Their independence must be beyond doubt. They are nominated by Member States and appointed by the Council acting unanimously after consulting the EP for a six-year renewable term. The usual limitations aimed at ensuring the independence of the members of the Court of Auditors as well as privileges, immunities, disciplinary measures, etc, apply to them. The main task of the Court of Auditors is to ensure that the financial affairs of the Community are properly managed and, especially, that all revenue has been received and all expenditure incurred in a lawful and regular manner. At the end of a fiscal year the Court of Auditors produces annual accounts which, together with the replies of the institutions, are published in the Official Journal. Furthermore, at the request of the institutions the Court of Auditors may prepare special reports and opinions. It may also on its own initiative draft reports on the financial implications of certain programmes or measures envisaged by the Community. In order to fulfil its tasks the court has extensive investigative powers.

6.8 Other Community bodies

The Treaty of Maastricht has established a number of new bodies such as the Ombudsman,[130] two consultative bodies – the Economic and Social Committee and the Committee of the Regions – and provided for the creation of new institutions within the framework of EMU: the European Central Bank, the European Monetary Institute, and the European System of Central Banks.[131]

---

[130] See Chapter 3.
[131] See Chapter 3.

The Economic and Social Committee[132]

The Economic and Social Committee was created by the Treaty of Rome. At present arts 193–198 EC and its Rules of Procedure[133] apply to the Economic and Social Committee. Currently it comprises 222 representatives of various categories of economic and social activity, in particular farmers, producers, workers, dealers, craftsman, professionals, as well as representatives of the general public from all Member States – 24 from each of the largest Member States, 12 or less from others. They are appointed by the Council for a four-year renewable term. The Economic and Social Committee is divided into three groups: 'employers' comprising the representatives of employers' organisations and chambers of commerce; 'workers' comprising trade union representatives; and 'various interests' which includes representatives of small businesses, farmers, the professions, craftsmen, environmental and consumer groups, etc. The members of each group are spread over nine working sections, each in charge of a specific policy area. The Committee is an advisory body entrusted with the task of expressing the opinions of these groups in respect of legislative measures prepared by the Council and the Commission, although its opinions are non-binding. The consultation of the Economic and Social Committee is compulsory for the Commission when the latter prepares proposals in a number of areas such as the CAP, the right of establishment, the mobility of labour, transport, approximation of laws, social policy, the European Social Fund and vocational training. In other areas consultation is optional. Furthermore, the Committee may issue opinions on its own initiative. So far the Committee has played a very constructive role within the Community as its represents the citizens of the EU and their interests and thus constitutes a step towards a people's union.

The Committee of the Regions[134]

The Committee of the Regions was set up by the TEU[135] and consists of 222 representatives of regional and local bodies of the Member States. Their terms of appointment, office, privileges, etc, and organisational structure are identical to those on the Economic and Social Committee. It was created to allow the regions and local authorities to influence and participate in the Community's legislative process. The Commission must consult the Committee of the Regions in a limited number of areas, fewer than in the case of the Economic and Social Committee, and these include public health, culture and education. In other areas the Commission and the Council may consult the Committee. If the Economic and Social Committee is consulted pursuant to art 198 EC (compulsory consultation), the Committee of the Regions must be informed by the Commission or the Council of the request for an opinion and may, if specific regional interests are involved, issue an opinion on the matter. It may also give an opinion on its own,[136] but – as in the case of the Economic and Social Committee – its opinions are not binding. Also, if the Council or the Commission

---

[132] Articles 193–198 EC.
[133] OJ L82 30.3.96 p1.
[134] Articles 198a–198c EC.
[135] Articles 198a–198c EC.
[136] See Hessel and Mortelmans, 'Decentralized Government and Community Law: Conflicting Institutional Developments' (1995) 30 CMLR 905.

fixes a time-limit for the submission of the opinion from the Committee of the Regions or the Economic and Social Committee this may not be less than one month from the notification of the request. The absence of an opinion will not prevent the Council or the Commission from further action.

Other bodies

Among other Community bodies worthy of mention are the specialised advisory committees created on the ground of art 153 EC, such as the Committee of Transport under art 83 EC, the Monetary Committee under art 109c EC, special committees set up on the grounds of arts 113 and 228 EC, the Committee on the European Social Fund under art 124 EC, and the Scientific and Technical Committee under art 134 Euratom. In addition, there are a number of bodies created for the administration of the Community affairs. Subsequent to the agreement reached in 1993[137] on the location of their seats a number of bodies were established such as the European Environmental Agency, the European Training Foundation, Office for Veterinary and Plant Health Inspection, etc.[138] In addition, the Community operates a number of funding programmes which benefit both Member States and countries outside the EU, the most important being its structural funds: the European Social Fund, the European Agricultural Guidance and Guarantee Fund, and the European Regional Development Fund. Concerning programmes designated for businesses located outside the EU, two are especially important: PHARE (Aid and Assistance for the Reconstruction of the Economy in Central and Eastern Europe) and TACIS (Technical Assistance to the CIS and Georgia).

6.9 The legislative decision-making procedures

The legislative process of the Community is very complex for two reasons: first, the revisions of the decision-making procedures in order to give more powers to the EP have led to compromises of extreme complexity; and, second, the tension between inter-governmentalism and supranationality in the context of a democratic deficit which the EP, the only democratically elected body in the Community, claims to be able and entitled to legitimately overcome, is reflected in those procedures. The Draft Treaty of Amsterdam failed to simplify the legislative process in the Community, although its reform is necessary in the light of envisaged enlargements of the EU.

The legislative process involves the co-operation of different institutions even though their contribution varies to a great extent. In principle, the legislative process is commenced by the Commission which initiates legislation, although the Council under art 152 EC, and the EP under art 138b(2) EC, are entitled to ask the Commission to prepare any proposals considered desirable for the attainment of the objectives of the Treaty. Also, in rare cases, the Council may adopt legislation without a previous proposal from the Commission, acting by a QMV cast by at least ten Member States in favour.[139]

---

[137] Decision of the Representatives of the Governments of the Member States on the Location of Seats of Certain Bodies and Departments (OJ C323 30.11.93 p1).
[138] These are mentioned in the introduction to this Chapter.
[139] Article 148(2) EC.

The adoption of a proposal by the Commission starts when an appropriate Directorate-General formulates a broad outline of an envisaged measure. The draft proposal is then submitted to the widest possible consultation with all interested parties, including governmental authorities, professional bodies, experts, consumer groups, etc, and the Commission's own legal service. This requirement of consultation has been strengthened by the principle of subsidiarity. The external and internal opinions often lead to redrafting or even abandonment of proposals. Provided this stage has been successfully completed and resulted in a firm proposal the latter is then forwarded to all Directorates-General for assessment and amendments. Once again, in the light of comments provided by Directorates-General, the proposal may be changed accordingly. In this version it is then submitted to the College of Commissioners which decides by a simple majority vote whether or not the Commission should proceed. In the affirmative, the proposal is submitted to the Council, translated into all official languages of the Community and published in the Official Journal.

Upon receipt of the proposal the Council sends it to the COREPER for further study. In practice, the Commission also forwards the proposal to the EP. Indeed, the EP has gradually extended its consultation prerogatives to areas in which their consultation is not mandatory or otherwise required by the Treaty. This new 'acquisition' of powers by the EP in respect of the legislative process in the Community was consolidated by the Code of Conduct adopted jointly by the Commission and the EP on 9 March 1995.[140]

The inter-institutional triangle – the Commission, the Council and the EP – in the decision-making process constitutes one element common to all types of procedure, although the degree of the actual involvement of the EP as well as the Council's vote (whether by unanimity, QMV or a simple majority), varies depending on the area of policy concerned.

There are four main decision-making procedures in the Community provided for in the Treaty: the consultation procedure; the co-operation procedure; the co-decision procedure; and the assent procedure. In addition, a conciliation procedure was established by a Joint Declaration of the EP, the Commission and the Council on 4 March 1975.[141]

Consultation procedure

The consultation procedure was the only one involving the EP under the original Treaty. It requires the Council to obtain the opinion of the European Parliament. This procedure starts with the submission of a formal proposal by the Commission to the Council. The latter must – it is a mandatory requirement – ask the EP for its opinion on the proposal. The Council is not obliged to follow the opinion delivered by the EP but it must receive it. In Cases 138 and 139/79 *Roquette*[142] the Council had adopted Regulation 1293/79 on the basis of art 43(2) which required the consultation of the EP but without receiving the opinion from the latter. The Council argued that it requested the opinion but the EP did not reply and thus by its own conduct, and knowing the urgency of the matter, the EP made it

---

[140] Its text in French in *Revue Trimestriel de Droit Européen*, 1995, p338.
[141] OJ C89 22.3.75 p1.
[142] [1980] ECR 3333.

impossible for the Council to comply with the consultation requirement. The ECJ held that when the Treaty provides for the consultation of the EP, this requirement must be strictly complied with since 'due consultation of the Parliament in the cases provided for by the Treaty ... constitutes an essential formality disregard of which means that the measure concerned is void'. The arguments of the Council would have been accepted if they had exhausted all existing procedural possibilities provided by Community law[143] to force the EP to deliver its opinion, which was not the case in *Roquette*. Indeed, the EP has a duty to loyally co-operate with other Community institutions and especially to deliver its opinion within a reasonable time in order to allow the Council to adopt a measure within a required time frame.[144] If the Council or the Commission amends its initial proposal substantially the EP must be consulted a second time, unless the modification embodies the amendments suggested by the EP.[145]

Under the 1995 Code of Conduct the Commission agreed to give the EP reasons why its amendments were not taken into account, to withdraw proposals which were rejected by the EP or, if the Commission decided to proceed with the proposal despite its rejection by the EP, to provide justification for its position. The Council also agreed, under the procedure known as 'Scheel', to justify its rejection of EP amendments.

The consultation procedure has thus evolved, especially in the light of the 1995 Code of Conduct, in two key ways: first, it allows the EP to play an active role in the decision-making procedures; and, second, it emphasises the democratic character of the Community by taking into account the will of the people of the EU through the intermediary of their representatives, the EP.

The consultation procedure must be applied, for example, if a measure is to be adopted on the basis of the following provisions of the EC Treaty: art 14 on custom duties; art 43(2) on the CAP; art 54(1) on the abolition of existing restrictions on freedom of establishment; art 63 on the abolition of existing restrictions on freedom to provide services; and art 100 on the approximation of laws. The SEA extended the consultation procedure to the following areas: art 84 on certain aspects of transport policy; art 99 on the harmonisation of indirect taxes, etc. Under the TEU the following areas were added: art 8b on voting rights for nationals of other Member States in municipal and European elections; art 8e on recommendations to Member States to increase the rights granted to EU citizens; art 94 on State aids; art 100c on the determination of third countries whose nationals must be in possession of a visa when crossing the external borders of the EU; art 109(1) on formal agreements on the exchange rate for the ECU vis-à-vis non-Member States; art 109j(2)–(4) and 109k(2) on the fulfilment of necessary requirements by a Member State for the adoption of a single currency, etc.

The TEU replaced the consultation procedure by a procedure more favourable to the EU in some areas: art 130i(1) regarding multiannual framework programmes on research and technical development to which the procedure of art 189b now applies; art 75(1) regarding

---

[143] For example the Council may request emergency procedures which are envisaged in the EP Rules of Procedure or an extraordinary session of the EP provided for in art 139 EC.

[144] Case C–65/93 *EP v Council* [1995] ECR I–643, *Europe*, August/September 1995, no 281, comm FG and DS.

[145] Case 41/69 *Chemiefarma v Commission* [1970] ECR 661; Case 1253/79 *Battaglia* [1982] ECR 297; Case C–65/90 *EP v Council* [1992] ECR I–4593; Cases C–13 to 16/92 *Driessen v Zonen* [1993] ECR I–4751; Case C–65/93 *EP v Council* [1995] ECR I–643; Case C–21/94 *EP v Council* [1995] ECR I–1827.

common transport policy; art 125 concerning implementing decisions relating to the European Social Fund; and art 130s(1) concerning environmental measures, to them the co-operation procedure provided for in art 189c applies.

Co-operation procedure

The co-operation procedure was introduced by the Single European Act. It strengthens the legislative role of the EP without substantially modifying the powers of the Council. Indeed, under this procedure the last word belongs to the Council which still enjoys exclusive legislative competences as it may override the EP and adopt the disputed measure. This procedure preserves the Commission's exclusive right of initiating the legislative measures. The co-operation procedure involves two readings. The first reading takes place when the EP gives its opinion on the measure. This part is identical to the consultation procedure. However, once the Council receives the opinion of the EP it seeks to achieve a 'common position' acting by QMV or by unanimity if the common position modifies the original proposal submitted by the Commission. The text of the common position is then forwarded to the EP (the second reading) which has three months to endorse, reject or amend it. If there is no reply from the EP within the three months, or if the EP endorses the common position, the measure will be adopted by the Council as it stands. The rejection of the common position by the EP by an absolute majority does not preclude the measure from being adopted, but imposes the requirement of a unanimous vote of the Council if it still wishes to enact it. Amendments to the common position approved by absolute majority of the EP require intervention by the Commission. The latter has one month to decide whether: to modify its original proposal by incorporating all or some of the amendments; to reject the amendments while providing an explanation for doing so; or to withdraw its proposal, in which case the Council will be prevented from adopting the measure. If the Commission decides to send the proposal to the Council, the latter must vote by a qualified majority if the Commission has endorsed the EP's amendments and unanimously if the Commission has rejected them or if the Council decides to modify the proposal by incorporating the amendments suggested by the EP. However, if the Commission has substantially modified its original proposal otherwise than suggested by the EP, the latter must be reconsulted. If the Council does not take any action, the proposal is deemed to be definitely rejected.

Under the SEA the co-operation procedure was applied, inter alia, in the following areas: prohibiting discrimination based on nationality (art 7); free movement of workers (art 49); freedom of establishment (arts 54(2), 56(2) and 57, except its para 2 second line); harmonisation of national laws for the purposes of the internal market (art 100a but not its para 2); harmonisation and improvement of the conditions in the working environment, especially health and safety of workers (art 118a); implementation of decisions relating to the European Regional Development Fund (art 130e), etc.

The TEU moved the co-operation procedure from arts 149(2) EEC to 189c EC and extended its scope of application to new areas such as common transport policy (arts 75(1) and 84 EC), economic and monetary policies (arts 103(5), 104a(2), 104b(2) and 105a(2) EC), social policy (arts 118a(2) and 125 EC), vocational training (art 127 EC), trans-European networks (art 129d EC), economic and social cohesion (art 130e EC), research (art 130o(1) EC), environment (art 130s EC), co-operation and development (art 130w(1) EC and art 2(2) of the Agreement on Social Policy annexed to the Protocol on Social Policy but not applicable to the UK), etc.

Co-decision procedure: art 189b EC

The co-decision procedure is referred as the procedure of art 189b EC. It is known as a co-decision procedure, although the EP and the Council do not enjoy the same powers even though for the first time legislation cannot be adopted against the will of the EP acting by absolute majority and within a specific time-limit. The co-decision procedure was introduced by the TEU in 15 areas. It is a very complex and time-consuming legislative procedure.

Article 189b EC provides that:

'(1) Where reference is made in this Treaty to this article for the adoption of an act, the following procedure shall apply.

(2) The Commission shall submit a proposal to the European Parliament and the Council.

The Council, acting by a qualified majority after obtaining the opinion of the European Parliament, shall adopt a common position. The common position shall be communicated to the European Parliament. The Council shall inform the European Parliament fully of the reasons which led it to adopt its common position. The Commission shall inform the European Parliament fully of its position.

If within three months of such communication, the European Parliament:

(a) approves the common position, the Council shall definitively adopt the act in question in accordance with that common position;

(b) has not taken a decision, the Council shall adopt the act in question in accordance with its common position;

(c) indicates, by an absolute majority of its component members, that it intends to reject the common position, it shall immediately inform the Council. The Council may convene a meeting of the Conciliation Committee referred to in paragraph 4 to explain further its position. The European Parliament shall thereafter either confirm, by an absolute majority of its component members, its rejection of the common position, in which event the proposed act shall be deemed not to have been adopted, or propose amendments in accordance with subparagraph (d) of this paragraph;

(d) proposes amendments to the common position by an absolute majority of its component members, the amended text shall be forwarded to the Council and to the Commission, which shall deliver an opinion on those amendments.

(3) If, within three months of the matter being referred to it, the Council, acting by a qualified majority, approves all the amendments of the European Parliament, it shall amend its common position accordingly and adopt the act in question; however, the Council shall act unanimously on the amendments on which the Commission has delivered a negative opinion. If the Council does not approve the act in question, the President of the Council, in agreement with the President of the European Parliament, shall forthwith convene a meeting of the Conciliation Committee.

(4) The Conciliation Committee, which shall be composed of the members of the Council or their representatives and an equal number of representatives of the European Parliament, shall have the task of reaching agreement on a joint text, by a qualified majority of the

members of the Council or their representatives and by a majority of the representatives of the European Parliament. The Commission shall take part in the Conciliation Committee's proceedings and shall take all the necessary initiatives with a view to reconciling the positions of the European Parliament and the Council.

(5) If, within six weeks of its being convened, the Conciliation Committee approves a joint text, the European Parliament, acting by an absolute majority of the votes cast, and the Council, acting by a qualified majority, shall have a period of six weeks from that approval in which to adopt the act in question in accordance with the joint text. If one of the two institutions fails to approve the proposed act, it shall be deemed not to have been adopted.

(6) Where the Conciliation Committee does not approve a joint text, the proposed act shall be deemed not to have been adopted unless the Council, acting by a qualified majority within six weeks of expiry of the period granted to the Conciliation Committee, confirms the common position to which it agreed before the conciliation procedure was initiated, possibly with amendments proposed by the European Parliament. In this case, the act in question shall be finally adopted unless the European Parliament, within six weeks of the date of confirmation by the Council, rejects the text by an absolute majority of its component members, in which case the proposed act shall be deemed not to have been adopted.'

This procedure differs from the co-operation procedure in two aspects: first, it provides for the establishment of the Conciliation Committee in order to reach an agreement on a joint text; and, second, if no joint text can be agreed the EP may override the Council confirmation of its original position with or without the amendments suggested by the EP.

The co-decision procedure is applied mainly to all internal market legislation, including: the free movement of workers and the right of establishment; general action programmes relating to environment, research and development; and also education, culture, trans-European networks, and protection of consumers.

The application of the co-decision procedure in practice was favourably assessed by the Commission. In its report submitted to the Council and required under art 189b(8) EC the Commission recommended future widening of its scope by the Treaty of Amsterdam on the grounds that 49 texts were adopted according to the co-decision procedure, and out of 20 cases when the establishment of the Conciliation Committee was necessary in 19 a joint text was agreed. In one case the Council confirmed its common position and incorporated some of the amendments suggested by the EP, but it was nevertheless rejected by the EP. In one case a joint text was agreed but was not confirmed by the EP. On average the co-decision procedure takes from 18 to 24 months. The Commission provided a long list of areas in which co-decision should be introduced, *inter alia*, non-discrimination (art 6(2) EC), citizenship of the EU (arts 8a(2) and 8b(1) EC), certain aspects of the internal marker (arts 51, 55, 57(2), 59, 73c and 100 EC), social policy (arts 118a(2) and 125 EC), environment (art 130r EC), vocational training (art 127(4) EC), and different aspects of common policies.[146]

The draft Treaty of Amsterdam has, indeed, extended the co-decision procedure to most of the proposed areas and made some modifications. For example, if the Conciliation Committee approves a joint text both institutions have six weeks to adopt the measure; if either fails to do so the measure is deemed not to have been adopted. Similarly, if the Conciliation Committee does not approve a joint text the proposed measure is deemed not

---

[146] Agence Europe, Europe Doc no 1994, 11 July 1996. The annexes to the report indicating the possible areas of application of the co-decision procedure were reproduced in *Europe*, August/September 1996, no 229.

to have been adopted and thus the part of the procedure concerning the confirmation of the Council of its original common position and the possibility for the EP to override it is deleted.

Assent procedure

The assent procedure was introduced by the SEA in respect of two aspects of the external relations of the Community: the admission of a new member under art 237 EEC and in the conclusion of association agreements provided for in art 238 EEC. The assent procedure is in fact a pure co-decision procedure in which the Council acts on a proposal of the Commission after obtaining the assent from the EP. The Council is usually required to act by unanimity but QMV is sufficient in the conclusion of international agreements. The EP acts by a majority of the votes cast except for a decision upon an application for membership of the EU where an absolute majority is required.

The TEU has extended the scope of the assent procedure to the following areas: art 8a(2) EC on measures facilitating the exercise of rights of free movement and residence for citizens of the EU; art 105(6) EC conferring upon the European Central Bank specific tasks concerning policies relating to the prudential supervision of credit institutions, and other financial institutions with the exception of insurance undertakings in the third stage of economic and monetary union; art 106(5) EC concerning the amendments of certain articles of the Statute of the European System of Central Banks; art 130d(1) EC defining the task, objectives and functioning of the structural funds, and art 138(3) EC concerning proposals on a uniform procedure for elections to the EP.

Conciliation procedure

The conciliation procedure was set up by a Joint Declaration of the EP, the Commission and the Council in 1975 subsequent to the Paris Summit in December 1974. It constitutes a logical extension of the powers the EP acquired in budgetary matters. The Joint Declaration provides that a conciliation procedure applies if three conditions are satisfied:

1. a proposed legislative measure must be of a general application;
2. it must have 'appreciable financial implications'; and
3. it must relate to non-compulsory expenditure.

In the case of disagreement between the position of the Commission, the Council and the European Parliament in respect of such a measure, a conciliation procedure may be opened. A Conciliation Committee is set up comprising an equal number of representatives of the EP and the Council. The Committee seeks within a time-limit of three months to reach an agreement. The Commission also takes part in the Conciliation Committee's proceedings and must take all the necessary initiatives with a view to reconciling the positions of the European Parliament and the Council. If the conciliation is successful the EP delivers a new opinion and the Council proceeds to the adoption of the measure in question. If the conciliation fails, the Council may, notwithstanding, adopt that measure. As a result, the conciliation procedure only suspends the adoption of a proposal since the last word belongs to the Council. It allows the EP to negotiate directly with the Council and thus may improve relations between them. In practice, the conciliation procedure has been a failure and has rarely led to a successful outcome. At one stage, the EP wanted to extend the scope of this procedure,[147] but its growing participation in other procedures, and especially in the co-operation and co-decision procedures, put an end to this initiative.

The conciliation procedure applies to the adoption of legislative measures in very limited areas, such as in respect to art 201 EC concerning the Community's own resources, art 209 EC concerning financial regulation, etc.

---

[147] See project of the second Declaration concerning the conciliation procedure: EC Bull 3–1982.

7 Sources of Community Law

There is no classification of sources of Community law in the Treaties. In its absence, the classification must be based on other factors, such as indications provided by the Treaties, practice established by the Community institutions and the Member States, and judgments rendered by the ECJ. The classification of sources of Community law can be founded on various criteria. Thus, it is possible to distinguish between written and unwritten sources, internal and external sources, primary and secondary sources, sources established by the Treaty of Paris and those provided for by the Treaty of Rome, sources mentioned by the Treaties and those which have been introduced by practice, *senso stricto* sources of EC law which comprise primary and secondary sources, and sources in a broad sense containing all rules applicable to the Community legal order written and unwritten, external and internal.

In order to simplify the classification of sources of Community law, the following typology is suggested: fundamental or primary sources of EC law which are contained in the founding Treaties as amended over the years; secondary sources of EC law which are unilateral acts adopted by the EC institutions on the basis of Treaties; external sources which derive from international treaties concluded between the Communities and third countries; complementary sources of EC law which encompass international conventions, decisions, accords, declarations, resolutions, etc, adopted by the Member States outside the framework of the Treaties, but which nevertheless apply only between them; and, finally, sources resulting from the interpretation of Community law by the ECJ, such as general principles of Community law, and the decisions of the ECJ.

7.1 Primary sources of Community Law

The primary sources of Community law comprise the three founding Treaties, together with the Protocols annexed to them, as amended over the years and the Acts of Accession of new Member States to the existing Communities.

The three founding Treaties

These are:

1. The Treaty of Paris of 18 April 1951 established the European Coal and Steel Community (ECSC) which entered into force on 25 July 1952, was for a 50-year term, and will expire on 23 July 2002.
2. The Treaty of Rome of 25 March 1957 established the European Economic Community (EEC) which entered into effect on 1 January 1958 and was concluded for an unlimited period.
3. The Treaty of Rome of 25 March 1957 established the European Atomic Energy Community (Euratom) which entered into force on 1 January 1958 and, like the EEC Treaty, was concluded for an unlimited period.

The primary sources are at the top of the hierarchy of sources of EC law, their supremacy implies that all other sources of Community law are subordinate to them. The superiority of the primary sources over other sources is strengthened by the prohibition of any revision of the Treaties either by an act or practice of the Community institutions or the Member States outside the procedures set out in the Treaties themselves. In Case 43/75 *Defrenne*[1] the ECJ rejected the possibility of revision of the Treaties based on art 39 of the 1969 Vienna Convention on the Law of Treaties which provides that a revision of a particular treaty may result from a common accord of all contracting parties. The Court held that a modification of the Treaty can only take place, without prejudice to other specific provisions contained in the Treaty, on the grounds of art 236 EEC. Thus, since 1957 it has been well established that the Member States are not permitted to act by a common agreement to revise the Treaties outside the existing procedures and, especially, by excluding the Community institutions from participating in these procedures,[2] although in the early days of the Communities two exceptions to this principle occurred, which are examined below in this section (see below in this section **Common consent of the Member States**). Not only the formal requirements prohibit the revision of the founding Treaties outside the procedures envisaged in the Treaties, but also there are some limitations *ratione materiae*. In this respect, the ECJ held that some provisions of the EC Treaty, such as art 164 which defines the tasks of the ECJ, are not revisable.[3] As a result, some provisions of the founding Treaties are intangible and constitute a '*noyau dur*' of the constitutional identity of the Communities. The Common Provisions of the Treaty of Maastricht, and provisions relating to the constitutive elements of Communities, can be considered as immutable.[4]

The primary sources also prevail over international treaties concluded between the Communities and third countries. In order to avoid any conflict between them art 228 EC provides for a consultative role by the ECJ in the conclusion of international agreements. In

---

[1] [1976] ECR 455.

[2] Agreements with third countries which would alter the provisions of the Treaties are included: Opinion 1/91 [1991] ECR I–6079 and Opinion 1/92 [1992] ECR I–2821, both relating to the agreement on the establishment of the European Economic Area.

[3] Ibid.

[4] R Brieber, 'Les Limites Materielles à la Revision des Traités Institutant les Communautés Européennes?' [1993] RMC 343.

addition, a decision of the Council relating to the conclusion of an international agreement with a third country which is in breach of the provisions of the founding Treaties is susceptible to annulment by the ECJ.[5]

The relationship between international agreements entered into by the Member States and the primary sources of EC law is more complex. It depends whether a Member State concluded the agreement in question prior or subsequent to its accession to the Communities. In both cases, the principle of public international law, which provides that subsequent international agreements should not affect earlier agreements, applies. As a result, international agreements concluded by Member States after their accession to the Communities will be disregarded if incompatible with Community law. Conversely, international agreements concluded before the accession of a Member State to the Communities prevail over EC law. Article 234 EC confirms this position by stating that:

> 'The rights and obligations arising from agreements concluded before the entry into force of this Treaty between one or more Member States on the one hand, and one or more third countries on the other, shall not be affected by the provisions of this Treaty.
>
> To the extent that such agreements are not compatible with this Treaty, the Member State or States concerned shall take all appropriate steps to eliminate the incompatibility established. Member States shall, where necessary, assist each other to this end and shall, where appropriate, adopt a common attitude.'

As a result, in case of incompatibility between previous international commitments of a Member State with the obligations arising out of its membership of the Community, the Member State concerned should take all necessary measures to eliminate this incompatibility and under art 234(2) other Member States have to offer their assistance in this respect. However, a Member State is not allowed to invoke previous international agreements in order to escape its obligations imposed by the Treaties. In this respect, in Case 10/61 *Commission* v *Italy*[6] the ECJ held that Italy could not invoke GATT provisions on customs duties in relation to inter-Community exchanges.[7] Nevertheless, art 234 EC imposes an important limitation on a Member State's obligations arising out of an international agreement concluded prior to its accession: the Community cannot be bound by such an agreement vis-à-vis third countries.[8] In practice, the principle contained in art 234 EC poses difficult problems for national judges in the case of a conflict between international agreements and Community law. This problem is best illustrated by the contradictions between the Conventions of the International Labour Organisations and the EC Directive relating to the night work of woman.[9] Finally, all international agreements between the Member States concluded before their accession to the Communities are subject to special provisions of the Treaty.[10]

---

[5] Case C–327/91 *France* v *Commission* [1991] ECR I–3641.

[6] [1962] ECR 22.

[7] Also, in Case C–144/89 *Commission* v *United Kingdom* [1991] ECR I–3533, the ECJ held that the provisions on Common Fisheries Policy could not be replaced by conventional rules emanating from an international convention entered into by the UK prior to the accession to the Communities.

[8] Case 812/79 *Burgoa* [1980] ECR 2787.

[9] Case C–345/89 *Stoeckel* [1991] ECR I–4047; Case C–158/91 *Lévy* [1993] ECR I–4287; Case C–13/93 *ONEM* v *Minne* [1994] ECR I–371.

[10] For example, art 233 EC concerning the customs union between Belgium and Luxembourg as well as the Benelux Union.

The primary sources of EC law, the founding Treaties and their amendments, are considered as the constitutional Treaties. The idea that the founding Treaties establishing the three Communities are different from classical international treaties has been recognised by the ECJ in Case 26/62 *Van Gend en Loos*,[11] the first case decided by the Court in which it held that 'this Treaty is more than an agreement which merely creates mutual obligations between the Contracting States', and that 'the Community constitutes a new legal order of international law' which creates rights and obligations not only for the Member States but, more importantly, for their nationals which 'become part of their legal heritage'. The constitutional nature of the founding Treaties, as well as the legal implications deriving from their peculiar status under public international law, has been progressively developed by the ECJ. In Case 294/83 *Parti Ecologiste Les Verts v Council*[12] the ECJ considered the EC Treaty as the 'basic constitutional Charter' of the Community and in Opinion 1/91 (First EEA Opinion)[13] refused to interpret international accords in the same manner as the EC Treaty taking into account their peculiar nature.

The three founding Treaties are independent vis-à-vis each other. The Merger Treaty had envisaged their fusion but it was decided, at that time, to postpone their merger for an indefinite period. The relationship between all three founding Treaties is governed by art 231 EC which provides that, in conformity with public international law, the EC Treaty as a general Treaty shall neither modify the ECSC Treaty nor derogate to the provisions of the Euratom Treaty, both being specific Treaties. As a result, the provisions of ECSC Treaty do not apply to the EC Treaty as the ECJ decided in Case 17/62 *Confédération Nationale des Producteurs de Fruits et Légumes*,[14] in which it rejected the application by analogy of more liberal provisions of the ECSC Treaty regarding the conditions of admission of applications challenging the validity of Community acts under art 173 EC. Also, in Cases 27–29/58 *Hauts Fourneaux de Givors*[15] the ECJ held that each time the ECSC Treaty regulates a specific subject-matter exhaustively, the application of the EC Treaty is excluded. However, if there is a gap in the specific Treaties, that is in ECSC and Euratom Treaties, the EC Treaty as a general Treaty and secondary legislation adopted on the basis of the EC Treaty will fill that gap without the necessity of adopting any specific measures or any declarations on its interpretation being required. In Case 328/85 *Deutsche Babcock*[16] the ECJ held the EC Treaty applied to products covered by the ECSC Treaty when the latter contained a gap on a specific point. This approach was confirmed in Opinion 1/94.[17]

The autonomy of each founding Treaty has been undermined by the ECJ; in order to achieve greater uniformity of EC law the ECJ has interpreted the provisions contained in one founding Treaty in the light of analogous provisions of the other Treaties. The obvious similarity between them has allowed the ECJ to clarify, by analogy, an obscure provision of one Treaty on the basis of clear and precise meaning of a similar provision of the other

---

[11] [1963] ECR 1.
[12] [1986] ECR 1339.
[13] [1991] ECR 6079.
[14] [1962] ECR 901.
[15] [1960] ECR 527.
[16] [1987] ECR 5119.
[17] [1994] ECR I–5267.

Treaty. In this respect, in Case 13/60 *Comptoirs de Vente de la Ruhr*,[18] the ECJ held that the exact meaning of art 65 ECSC can be inferred from art 85 EEC as the latter can serve as 'indirect support' in the interpretation of art 65 ECSC while in Case 15/57 *Meroni*[19] it has extended the scope of application of art 156 ECSC concerning the plea of illegality by virtue of an analogous ambit of application of art 184 EEC. There are two possible justifications that can be invoked to explain this tendency of the ECJ. First, the EC Treaty can be considered as a fundamental Treaty since it establishes general principles relating to the creation of a common market in all products and services, while Euratom and the ECSC Treaties cover only limited markets. As a result, reference to the EC Treaty as a general and fundamental Treaty is fully justified. Second, the future incorporation of the provisions of the ECSC Treaty, that is once it expires in 2002, into the EC Treaty emphasises the fundamental nature of the latter.[20]

Protocols, Declarations and Conventions annexed to the Treaties

Protocols and Conventions annexed to the founding Treaties, or to the treaties amending the founding Treaties, have the same legal effect as the Treaties themselves in accordance with art 2(2) of the Vienna Convention of 23 May 1969 on the Law of the Treaties. Also art 239 EC provides that:

> 'The Protocols annexed to this Treaty by common accord of the Member States shall form an integral part thereof.'

This has been confirmed by the ECJ many times.[21] In Case 260/86 *Commission v Belgium*[22] the ECJ held that the violation of provisions contained in the Protocol on the Privileges and Immunities by Belgium constituted a breach of its obligations deriving from the Treaties. More and more often the Member States use the Protocols (the Treaty of Maastricht has 17 Protocols attached). Although the terms of Protocols could be incorporated into the founding Treaties, their existence avoids too lengthy texts of the revised Treaties.

The Declarations annexed to the Treaties are not legally binding and most express an intention or a wish of the Member States on a particular point, although there are some unilateral declarations emanating from a particular Member State which wishes to clarify its position vis-à-vis other Member States in relation to a particular question. However, the specific nature of Community law prevents unilateral Declarations acquiring any legal effect, and other Member States merely take cognisance of Declarations. The theory of acquiescence, which applies in public international law and under which unilateral

---

[18] [1960] ECR 165.
[19] [1958] ECR 185.
[20] Nevertheless, the case law of the ECJ on this point is confusing, even for the judges of the Court of the First Instance. In Case C–220/91 *Stahlwerke Peine Salzgitter* [1993] ECR I–2393, the ECJ rejected the judgment of the Court of First Instance (Case T–120/89 [1991] ECR II–279) in which the latter emphasised that the existence of a 'unique legal order', as well as the necessity of strengthening coherence within that system, required that the conditions which give rise to the Community's liability were the same under the ECSC and EEC Treaties, and held that although there were some similarities on this point between the ECSC and the EEC Treaty, these conditions must be construed on the basis of the ECSC Treaty alone.
[21] Case 149/85 *Wybot* [1986] ECR 2403; Case 314/85 *Foto-Frost* [1987] ECR 4199.
[22] [1988] ECR 966.

declarations are legally binding on other contracting States provided they accept them, is rejected under Community law. The ECJ is empowered to resolve any dispute between Member States and provides clarifications on a particular point of law. Declarations are, nevertheless, of some importance. The ECJ makes reference to Declarations in the interpretation of EC law since they often express the intention of Member States or a particular Member State.

Acts of Accession

Acts of Accession are legally binding. They are similar, from the point of view of the legal effect they produce, to the founding Treaties.

Modifications and amendments of the founding Treaties

Modifications and amendments of the founding Treaties can take various forms: within the framework of the founding Treaties by the adoption of new Treaties; or outside the procedure of revision in three situations – when there is a consensus of all Member States, when particular provisions of the founding Treaties permit Member States to avoid the necessity to revise the founding Treaty and, finally, when the particular nature of a 'decision' adopted by the Council necessitates its ratification by all Member States.

Revision of the founding Treaties according to the procedure provided by the Treaties themselves: art N TEU

The most straightforward manner consists of the adoption of new treaties under the procedures provided by the founding Treaties themselves. In this respect, art N TEU contains a uniform procedure of revision for all three founding Treaties and replaces arts 96 ECSC, art 236 EEC and art 204 Euratom. Under this provision, a proposal for revision is submitted either by the governments of the Member States or by the Commission to the Council, which after consulting the EP and, depending upon the subject-matter of the proposal, the Commission and the Council of the European Central Bank decides whether or not to accept the proposal by a simple majority of votes. If accepted, the Council convenes a diplomatic conference of all representatives of the Member States who negotiate and prepare a draft treaty which will enter into effect once ratified by all Member States according to their constitutional laws.

Among the most important treaties which have revised the founding Treaties are: the Merger Treaty 1965;[23] the Single European Act signed at Luxembourg and The Hague on 17 and 28 February 1986 which became operational on 1 July 1987;[24] and the Treaty on European Union signed at Maastricht on 7 February 1992 and entered into force on 1 November 1993. Only some provisions of the TEU are considered as primary sources of EC law, that is those which modified the founding Treaties: Title II which amended the European Community Treaty, Titles I, III and IV, Final Provisions (arts L–S) and Protocols annexed to the TEU.

---

[23] OJ 152 13.7.67 p1.
[24] OJ L169 1987 p1.

Revision of the founding Treaties outside art N TEU
There are certain mechanisms permitting the revision of the founding Treaties outside art N TEU.

Common consent of the Member States Under public international law, only the consent of all contracting parties to a particular treaty is required for its revision. Within the Community this approach has been used twice: the Convention of 27 October 1957 concerning the legal implications of the return of the Sarre to the Federal Republic of Germany and the Convention of 25 March 1958 relating to Certain Institutions Common to the Communities. This manner of revising the founding Treaties should be considered as obsolete for two reasons: first, since 1958 it has never been applied and, second, the Community institutions have expressly recognised the revision procedure provided for by the founding Treaties as appropriate and confirmed their attachment to it: the ECJ in Case 43/75 *Defrenne;*[25] the Council in its written answer to question no 398/77;[26] and the European Parliament in its Resolution of 8 May 1969 and in the Burger Report.[27]

Simplified procedures provided for in the founding Treaties The simplified procedures involve only the Community institutions. Under art 95(2) and (3) ECSC it requires obligatory consultation with the ECJ and its negative opinion blocks any proposed revision. This procedure has been used three times. In two cases the ECJ issued a negative opinion and thus opposed the proposed measures from being adopted. Under both Treaties of Rome the Council acts unanimously on a proposal from the Commission and after consulting the EP.[28] Under arts 168a and 188(2) EC the proposal must be submitted by the ECJ and a consultation with the Commission and the EP is required. The simplified procedure provided for in art 106(5) EC requires the Council to act by qualified majority on the recommendation from the ECB and after obtain the assent of the EP.

'Decisions' of the Council The Council may revise the founding Treaties on the basis of certain provisions, mainly art 201 EC relating to the 'own resources' of the Community, art 138 EC concerning the conditions regarding elections to the EP, art 8e EC which permits the Council to complement the list of rights of the EU citizens by an unanimous decision based on a proposal from the Commission, and art K9 TEU which provides that certain actions under the JHA may be submitted to the procedure laid down in art 100c EC (visas). These decisions require ratification by all Member States according to national constitutional procedure. The Treaty of Maastricht added a new requirement to art 138 EC, that is, an 'avis conforme' of the EP and specified procedure under each provision (arts 8e and K9). The most important decisions modifying the founding Treaties adopted under these procedures are: Council Decision and Act of 20 September 1976 on Direct Elections to the European Parliament; Budgetary Treaties of 1970 and 1975; decisions under art 8e EC concerning Union citizenship; and decisions based on art 100c.

---

[25] [1976] ECR 455.
[26] OJ C270 10.11.77 p18.
[27] EP Doc Session no 215/1968/69.
[28] For example, arts 76, 85, 90 Euratom and under arts 14(7), 33(8), 38(3), 84(2), 104c(14), 106(5), 126, 165, 166 EC.

Doctrine of implied powers Based on arts 95(1) ECSC, 235 EC and 203 Euratom the Council may extend Community competences in internal and external matters. This question has already been examined in Chapter 4.

7.2 Secondary sources of Community Law

Secondary sources of EC law are, in terms of quantity,[29] the most important source of Community law but in the hierarchy of sources they are classified after the primary sources and general principles of EC law. Under the founding Treaties, Member States have attributed important legislative powers to the Community institutions which enable them to further develop the provisions of the Treaties and thus give full effect to Community law and policies. The founding Treaties carefully avoid any mention of 'law-making powers' or 'legislation' in relation to Community institutions. However, the ECJ has not hesitated to expressly refer to 'legislative powers of the Community' in Case 106/77 *Simmenthal*[30] or a 'legal system of the Treaty' in Case 25/70 *Köster*,[31] at least in relation to the EEC Treaty.

Secondary sources of EC law are enumerated in arts 189 EC, 161 Euratom and 14 ECSC. Articles 189 EC and 161 Euratom are identical. Both provide that:

> 'In order to carry out their task and in accordance with the provisions of this Treaty, the European Parliament acting jointly with the Council, the Council and the Commission shall make regulations and issue directives, take decisions, make recommendations or deliver opinions.'

Article 14 ECSC enumerates similar sources of Community law but uses a different terminology. General decisions mentioned by this provision are equivalent to regulations under art 189 EC and art 161 Euratom, ECSC recommendations are same as EC/Euratom directives, and ECSC individual decisions to EC/Euratom decisions.

The secondary sources of EC law are unilateral acts adopted, until the entry into force of the TEU, solely by the Council and the Commission, but now they may also be adopted jointly by the Council and the European Parliament under art 189b EC, as well as the European Central Bank from the beginning of the third stage of EMU under arts 4a and 108a EC. Unilateral acts of the Community institutions are enacted on the basis of the Treaties, which explains the reason why they are considered as secondary or derived legislation. Only regulations, directives and decisions are legally binding acts. Article 189(5) expressly states that recommendations and opinions have no binding force and thus they are neither legal acts nor considered as sources of Community law.

The ECJ has confirmed many times that the classification of a particular act, that is whether it should be considered as regulation, directive or decision, depends upon the

---

[29] In this respect, it is interesting to note that at the end of 1992 in France 22,445 regulations were in force, 1,675 directives, 1,198 accords and protocols: *Le Rapport du Conseil d'Etat Français*, Documentation Françaises, pp19 et seq.
[30] [1978] ECR 629.
[31] [1970] ECR 1161.

content not its nomenclature and has often reclassified them.[32] The choice of a particular form – regulation, directive or decision – for a specific act is determined by reference to a provision of the founding Treaties which constitutes its legal basis. In Case 20/59 *Italy* v *High Authority*[33] the ECJ held that if the form is expressly provided in a provision of the Treaty, the competent authority has no choice but to enact it accordingly. For example, arts 13, 33, 54, 63 and 100 EC expressly state that only directives are appropriate to adopt measures under these provisions, as a result regulations are ruled out. The question of whether a less restrictive measure can be adopted, for example instead of issuing a regulation the Council adopts a directive, even though a particular provision provides for the first mentioned, is answered affirmatively in art 14 ECSC. This solution, however, cannot be transposed to EC and Euratom Treaties, although the principle of subsidiarity and art 155 EC may justify the use of non-binding measures, such as recommendations and opinions, but not the substitution of one binding measure by another. However, if there is no indication on this point, or a particular provision leaves the choice open as, for example, in arts 49 and 87 EC which provide for regulations or directives, or refers only to 'measures' in general as in art 100a EC, the EC institution invested with power to adopt the necessary measures must decide which one is the most appropriate to achieve the objective prescribed by the provision in question.[34] This choice is nevertheless subject to the control of the ECJ.

Also, some formal requirements must be satisfied for a measure to be legally binding. Article 190 EC provides that measures must 'state the reasons on which they are based and shall refer to any proposals or opinions which were required to be obtained pursuant to this Treaty'. The objective of this requirement has been explained in Case 24/62 *Germany* v *Commission (Brennwein)*[35] by the ECJ as permitting the parties concerned by that measure to defend their rights, to the ECJ to exercise its supervisory functions and to all Member States and to all EC nationals to ascertain the circumstances in which the EC institutions apply the provisions of the Treaty. The absence, or insufficient 'motivation', of a measure must be raised *ex officio* by courts[36] and may result in its annulment by the ECJ. The motivation must indicate the legal basis of the act and the detailed reasons for its enactment.[37] It must be clear and unequivocal,[38] taking into account its context and other rules applicable to that subject-matter, and especially precise if the adoption of that measure is subject to the assessment of an economic situation by an EC institution.[39] Less detailed motivation is accepted if the applicant has contributed or participated in the procedure leading to the adoption of a measure,[40] or if it derives from a constant practice of EC

---

[32] Case 16–17/62 *Confédération Nationale des Producteurs de Fruits et Légumes* [1962] ECR 901; Case 25/62 *Plaumann* [1963] ECR 197.
[33] [1960] ECR 665.
[34] Cases 8–11/66 *Cimenteries CBR* [1967] ECR 93.
[35] [1963] ECR 63.
[36] Case T–471/93 *Tiercé Ladbroke SA* [1995] ECR II–2537, Judgment of 18 September 1995.
[37] For example, Case C–27/90 *SITPA Oniflhor* [1991] ECR I–133; Case C–69/89 *Nakajima* [1991] ECR I–2069; Case C–352/92 *Greece* v *Council* [1994] ECR I–3507.
[38] Case 1/69 *Italy* v *Commission* [1969] ECR 277.
[39] Case 24/62 *Germany* v *Commission* [1963] ECR 63.
[40] Case 13/72 *The Netherlands* v *Commission* [1973] ECR 27; Case 1252/79 *Lucchini* [1980] ECR 3753.
[41] Case 73/74 *Groupement des Papiers Peints de Belgique* [1975] ECR 1491; Case 102/87 *France* v *Commission* [1988] ECR 4067.

institutions,[41] but any change in the those practices requires more detailed explanations as to its legal basis and the objectives which the measure aims to achieve. Another formal requirement concerns the publication of a measure. In Case 98/78 *Racke*[42] the ECJ held that the fundamental principle of the Community legal order requires that an act emanating from public authorities cannot produce legal effect unless it come to the knowledge of its addressees. Thus, notification or publication depending upon the form of a measure constitutes a necessary condition of its entry into force but does not affect its legality.[43] Article 191 EC requires that only regulations, EC measures adopted under the co-decision procedure of art 189b EC and directives addressed to all Member States must be published, but in fact EC directives are usually also published in the Official Journal of the European Communities (OJ). The Official Journal of European Communities constitutes an important source of information on many aspects of the Community activities, including EC legislation. It is published on most weekdays simultaneously in all official languages of the Community, each version has the same pagination. Under the 'L' series legislation, treaties, the budget and all binding acts are published; the 'C' series comprises miscellaneous information and notices, such as draft legislation prepared by the Commission, common positions adopted by the Council and minutes of the plenary sessions of the European Parliament; and the 'S' series is devoted to the specialised use of firms competing for public contracts. An annex to the OJ contains the debates of the European Parliament.

In this context it is interesting to mention Case T-115/94 *Opel Austria Gmbh*[44] in which the CFI held that the Council by expressly antedating the publication of the regulation at issue in the OJ was in breach of the principle of legal certainty.

Under art 191 EC other measures must be notified to their addressees – that is directives which are not adopted by the Council and the EP within the framework of the co-decision procedure (art 189b EC), which are not addressed to Member States, as well as decisions which are not adopted jointly by the Council and the EP under the co-decision procedure (art 189b EC) – to natural or legal persons by registered/recorded delivery or often by diplomatic channels, that is ambassadors accredited to the EU instititions if undertakings are situated outside the territory of the EU. Member States are notified through their permanent representatives in Brussels.

The date of an entry into force of a particular measure may be specified in the measure itself, if notified on the day of its notification, if published and in the absence of any specification art 191 EC provides that a measure is deemed to become operative 20 days after its publication. The ECJ held in Case 98/78 *Racke*[45] that the day of publication means not the day on which the OJ is available in the territory of each Member State, but the day when it is available at the seat of the Office of Official Publications of the Communities at Luxembourg which coincides, except with proof to the contrary, with the day the OJ containing the text of an act in question is published. In relation to acts which require publication, usually a specific date is fixed since the immediate entry into force of a specific measure without any transitory period risks undermining the principles of legal security

---

[42] [1979] ECR 69.
[43] Case 185/73 *Hauptzollamt Bielefield* [1974] ECR 607.
[44] [1997] ECR II–39.
[45] [1979] ECR 69.

and legitimate expectation.[46] In Case 17/67 *Max Neumann*[47] the ECJ held that immediate entry into force of an act, that is on the day of its publication in the OJ, may be resorted to only in the case of extreme necessity resulting from the obligation to avoid a legal void or to prevent speculation and, in addition, the institutions concerned must have serious reasons to believe that the delay between the date of the publication of an act and its entry into force would cause prejudice to the Community.

The ECJ has added certain essential requirements in relation to secondary legislation. The ECJ rejected the retroactive application of secondary legislation apart from exceptional cases, provided that the legitimate expectations of the persons concerned by that measure are respected[48] and that the measure does not apply to penal matters.[49] Also, the ECJ confirmed the right to withdraw or to abrogate a measure: when individual rights have been created it is permitted only when the withdrawal is made within a reasonable time which is determined by the ECJ (approximately six months), solely for reason of illegality,[50] provided public and private interests are duly taken into account,[51] and when a measure does not afford rights to individuals it may be done within a reasonable time (two to three years).[52]

Regulations

EC/Euratom Treaty regulations, or their equivalent under the ECSC Treaty (general decisions), constitute *par excellence* the expression of legislative powers of the Community institutions. Regulations ensure uniformity of solutions throughout the Community. They apply *erga omnes* and simultaneously in all Member States. Article 189 EC defines regulations in the following terms:

> 'A regulation shall have general application. It shall be binding in its entirety and directly applicable in all Member States.'

Thus, a regulation is comparable to statutory law in England. First, it has general applications, and the ECJ in Case 101/76 *Koninklijke Scholten-Honig NV v Council and Commission*[53] has explained this feature of a regulation by stating that it applies 'to objectively determined situations and produces legal effects with regard to persons described into a generalised and abstract manner'. Regulations are expressed in general, abstract terms. The ECJ has emphasised in many cases that the mere fact that is possible to determine the number, or even identity, of the persons concerned by a particular measure does not call into question its nature as a regulation, provided that the class of those potentially within its scope of application is not closed at the time of its adoption.[54]

---

[46] Case 74/74 *CNTA* [1975] ECR 533.

[47] [1967] ECR 571.

[48] Case 98/78 *Racke* [1979] ECR 69; Case 14/81 *Alpha Steel* [1982] ECR 749. See also F Lamoureux, 'The Retroactivity of Community Acts in the Case Law of the Court of Justice' (1983) 20 CMLR 269–283.

[49] Case 63/83 *Kirk* [1984] ECR 2689; Case C–331/88 *Fedesa* [1990] ECR I–4023.

[50] Cases T–79, 84–86, 91–92, 94, 96, 98, 102 and 104/89 *BASF* [1992] ECR II–315.

[51] Cases 42 and 49/59 *SNUPAT* [1961] ECR 101; Case 11/63 *Lemmerz-Werke* [1965] ECR 835; Case 15/85 *Consorzio Cooperative d'Abruzzo* [1987] ECR 1005.

[52] Case 14/61 *Hoogovens* [1962] ECR 485.

[53] [1977] ECR 797.

[54] Case 231/82 *Spijker Kwasten BV v Commission* [1983] ECR 2559.

Second, a regulation is binding in its entirety which means that its incomplete[55] or selective[56] application is prohibited under Community law. Also, its modification, adjunction[57] or introduction of any national legislation likely to affect its content or scope of application is contrary to EC law.[58] These well established principles acquire a special importance in the case of an incomplete regulation. EC regulations are incomplete in the sense that they require Member States to adopt necessary measures to ensure their full application. Sometimes this requirement is expressly stated in a regulation itself, as for example the obligation to adopt penal measures in order to ensure efficient application of a regulation as was held by the ECJ in Case C–52/95 *Commission v France*[59] or Case 128/78 *Commission v United Kingdom (Re Tachographs)*,[60] in which a duty to create new criminal offences was imposed on the UK in order to implement some of its provisions. Sometimes this obligation is based on art 5 EC which provides that Member States shall take all necessary measures to fulfil their obligations deriving from the Treaty. Whichever applies, national measures are subordinate to the provisions contained in regulations and must neither alter them nor hinder their uniform application throughout the Community.[61]

Finally, regulations are directly applicable in all Member States. It means that they become part of national law of the Member States at the date of their entry into force. Their implementation into national law is not only unnecessary but, more importantly, prohibited by Community law.[62]

The direct effect of EC regulations will be examined in Chapter 8.

Directives

EC/Euratom directives or their equivalent under the ECSC Treaty (recommendations) are defined in art 189 in the following terms:

> 'A directive shall be binding as to the result to be achieved, upon each Member State to which it is addressed, but shall leave to the national authorities the choice of form and methods.'

The main difference between EC/Euratom directives and ECSC recommendations is that the former are addressed solely to the Member States, while the latter may be addressed to Member States and undertakings. Apart from this, in Case C–221/88 *Busseni*,[63] the ECJ held that rules applicable to EC directives apply also to ECSC recommendations.[64]

Directives are used to harmonise national legislation, regulations and administrative provisions. Unlike regulations they require co-operation between the Community and the Member States, they respect the autonomy of national institutional and procedural systems

---

[55] Case 39/72 *Commission v Italy* [1973] ECR 101.
[56] Case 18/72 *Granaria* [1972] ECR 1172.
[57] Case 3/70 *Norddeutsches Vieh-und Fleischkontor* [1971] ECR 49.
[58] Case 40/69 *Bollmann* [1970] ECR 69.
[59] [1995] ECR I–4443.
[60] [1979] ECR 419.
[61] Case C–290/91 *Peter* [1993] ECR I–2981.
[62] Case 39/72 *Commission v Italy* [1973] ECR 101
[63] [1990] ECR I–495.
[64] [1991] CMLR 415, note G Bebr.

while imposing upon the Member States the obligation of achieving a necessary result and thus an identical legal solution for a particular question in all Member States. That is why a directive is described as being able to 'intrigue, derange, devise, all this is due to its peculiarity'.[65] There are three main features of EC directives.

First, unlike regulations, directives have no general application. Indeed, EC/Euratom directives are binding only on their addressees, that is a particular Member State or some Member States, or all of them. Nevertheless, under certain circumstances, namely when a directive is addressed to all Member States, for example they are the favoured legislative act of the internal market programme under arts 99, 100, 100a EC,[66] the required result must be obtained throughout the Community within a determined time-limit, and they have general scope of application. In that situation, in Case 70/83 *Kloppenburg*[67] the ECJ qualified them as acts having general application. Second, art 5 EC imposes upon an addressee Member State an obligation to achieve the objective of a directive but leaves the choice of measures, procedures, methods, etc, required to achieve that result at its discretion. However, in order to achieve the prescribed result EC directives in many cases must be precise, sometimes extremely precise. For that reason EC directives have become very detailed and often leave little or no choice to their addressees. As a result, in many cases, EC directives must be implemented into national law as they stand. In this respect in Case 38/77 *Enka*[68] the ECJ held that it results from art 189(3) EC that a discretion left to the Member States as to the choice of forms and methods is subject to the result that the Council or the Commission wishes to obtain. Thus, if necessary, an addressee Member State may be left without any margin of appreciation as to the manner of its implementation.[69] In particular, EC directives aimed at creating the common market are very detailed. The drawback of this approach is that the drafting process is very long. A new approach based on the principle of subsidiarity recommends the use of framework directives which leaves a large margin of discretion to Member States as to the choice of forms and methods of their implementation, but results in an increase in litigation as to whether or not they have been correctly introduced into national law.[70]

Indeed, the essential objective of directives is to achieve the prescribed result. It means that the national law of the Member State must be in conformity with the prescribed results once the time-limit for the implementation of a directive elapses. For that reason, sometimes no changes are necessary at the national level if under national law the prescribed result has already been achieved. Nevertheless, in majority of cases, an addressee Member State has to implement national measures in order to bring a directive into effect. In many cases the ECJ held that it is not necessary to copy the text of a directive into a national text, although it seems the best way to avoid any disputes in this respect, provided

---

[65] R Kovar, *Observations sur l'intensité normative des directives*, Mélange P Pescatore, p359. 'La directive intrigue, derange, devise, sa singularité en est la cause.'

[66] Article 100 EC prescribes the exclusive use of directives. Articles 99 and 100a EC provide for other measures but, in practice, only directives have been adopted on the basis of these provisions.

[67] [1984] ECR 1075.

[68] [1977] ECR 2203.

[69] This position has been confirmed in other cases: Case 102/79 *Commission* v *Belgium* [1980] ECR 1473; Case C–150/88 *Provide* [1989] ECR 3891; Case C–29/90 *Commission* v *Greece* [1992] ECR 1971.

[70] See QE, no E–3106/93 (OJ C102 11.4.94 p27).

that national measures are sufficiently clear and precise as to ensure its application.[71] Partial or selective implementation of a directive is contrary to EC law as well as its implementation being limited to a certain territory of a Member State. In this respect, in Case C–157/89 *Commission* v *Italy*[72] the ECJ held that a Member State cannot invoke the autonomy of some of its regions in order to derogate to some from its provisions.

Also, the choice of methods and forms of their implementation has been delimited by the ECJ. The Court held that they must ensure legal certainty and transparency.[73] As a result, a simple administrative practice is not sufficient, as the ECJ stated in Case 102/79 *Commission* v *Belgium*,[74] since it is easily modified by national administration and lacks adequate publicity, or an internal circular, which once again cannot ensure legal certainty.[75]

In the United Kingdom EC directives are usually implemented by statutory instruments under the European Communities Act 1972 and sometimes by an Act of Parliament.

Third, it is clear from the wording of art 189(3) EC that an addressee Member State is responsible for their implementation into national law. For that reason usually directives grant a specific time-limit to a Member State within which they must be brought into effect in the territory of that Member State. It is very important to note that directives enter into force at the date specified by them or in its absence 20 days after their publication, but produce their legal effect after the expiry of a fixed time-limit which varies depending upon the subject-matter of a directive. In most cases the time-limit is restricted to two years. Before the expiry of the purported time-limit no obligations arise from a directive for individuals as the ECJ held in Case 80/86 *Kolpinghuis*.[76] However, once the time-limit elapses the situation changes dramatically.[77] In Case 270/81 *Felicitas*[78] the ECJ held that the general principle is that in all cases when a directive is correctly implemented into national law it produces legal effects vis-à-vis individuals through the implementing measures adopted by the Member State concerned. Thus, it becomes a part of national law. An individual is entitled to invoke a directive and base his claim upon it if that directive has been incompletely or incorrectly implementated by a Member State. However, non-implementation of a directive within a prescribed time-limit produces the following results: a directive becomes directly applicable as it was held by the ECJ in Case 148/78 *Ratti*,[79] and if its provisions are directly effective an individual may start proceedings before a national court based on an unimplemented directive; the Commission can bring an action under art 169 EC against a Member State concerned for breach of EC law;[80] and, finally, provided certain conditions are satisfied, an individual may sue a defaulting Member State for damages.[81]

---

[71] Case 252/85 *Commission* v *France* [1988] ECR 2243; Case C–360/87 *Commission* v *Italy* [1991] ECR I–791; Case C–190/90 *Commission* v *The Netherlands* [1992] ECR I–3265.

[72] [1991] ECR I–57; also Case C–33/90 *Commission* v *Italy* [1991] ECR I–5987.

[73] Case C–131/88 *Commission* v *Germany* [1991] ECR I–825; Case C–58/89 *Commission* v *Germany* [1991] ECR I–5019.

[74] [1980] ECR 1473; Case C–360/88 *Commission* v *Germany* [1991] ECR I–2567.

[75] Case C–58/89 *Commission* v *Germany* [1991] ECR I–5019.

[76] [1987] ECR 3969.

[77] On direct applicability and direct effect of EC directives see Chapter 8.

[78] [1982] ECR 2771.

[79] [1979] ECR 1629.

[80] See Chapter 9.

[81] Case C–6/90 *Francovich* [1991] ECR I–5359; Case C–91/92 *Faccini Dori* [1994] ECR I–3325.

In this context, it is interesting to note that all directives in their final provisions impose upon addressee Member States an obligation to provide a list of measures which have been taken in order to implement them. This facilitates the task of the Commission as well as it provides information on the state of national law in this area. When a Member State fails to notify the Commission, or provides an incomplete notification even though it has taken all necessary measures, it is still in breach of its obligations deriving from the Treaty, that is art 5 EC, and the Commission is empowered to bring an action before the ECJ[82] on the grounds of art 169 EC.

Decisions

EC/Euratom decisions and ECSC individual decisions have no general application. They may be addressed to a particular Member States or any legal or natural person. The definition of a decision is provided in art 189 which states that:

'A decision shall be binding in its entirety upon those to whom it is addressed.'

and explained in Case 54/65 *Compagnie des Forges de Châtillon Commentry & Neuves-Maisons* v *High Authority*[83] as:

'A measure emanating from the competent authority, intended to produce legal effects and constituting the culmination of procedure within that authority, whereby the latter gives its final ruling in a form which its nature can be identified.'

Usually, decisions are similar to administrative acts issued by national authorities and are as such legal instruments permitting Community institutions to force their addressees to comply with the provisions of the Treaty. In most cases, decisions are issued by the Commission or the Council within their competences relating to competition policy. Decisions are binding in their entirety, which means that they may prescribe not only a particular result to be achieved but also forms and methods necessary to achieve this objective. As a result, a decision may be very detailed. Decisions are directly effective vis-à-vis their addressees, but in certain cases, that is if a person (natural or legal) proves that they are directly and individually concerned by it, that person may bring annulment proceedings under art 173 EC as well as claim damages under art 215(2).[84]

Non-binding acts: recommendations and opinions

Article 189 EC expressly provides that recommendations and opinions have no binding force. Although they are not sources of EC law, their importance should not be underestimated. Recommendations issued by the Council or the Commission invite a Member State to adopt a specific line of conduct. Recommendations and opinions are adopted in areas in which the Community has no legislative powers or when a transitional period is necessary in order to achieve a certain stage in which the EC institutions would be empowered to exercise their competences. In the latter case, recommendations and opinions

---

[82] See Chapter 9.
[83] [1966] ECR 265.
[84] See Chapter 10.

are aimed at preparing the next stage of development in a particular area, for example this is the case of art 37 EC relating to State monopolies. In Case C–322/88 *Grimaldi*[85] the ECJ held that recommendations are not devoid of all legal effect. National judges are obliged to take them into consideration in the interpretation of national law when they provide some clarifications and explanation. Recommendations are also used as an aid to interpretation if they have as an objective to complete provisions of EC law.

7.3 Other Community acts not expressly mentioned in art 189 EC

In Case 59/75 *Manghera*[86] the ECJ held that art 189 EC does not provide an exhaustive list of acts of EC institutions producing legal effect; other acts not mentioned in that provision are also lawful provided they are not contrary to the provisions of the Treaty. Indeed, outside art 189 EC there are other sources of EC law which are not secondary legislation *stricto sensu* but nevertheless constitute an important source of EC law.[87] In this category two kinds of acts can be distinguished:

1. Acts which are recognised by the founding Treaty such as: internal regulations which regulate the composition, functioning and procedures of each EC institution; directives, recommendations and opinions which one EC institution addresses to another; and decisions issued by EC institutions which are known under a German name as 'Beschlusse' – such decisions should not be confused with decisions under art 189 EC which in the German version of the Treaty are called 'Entscheidunsen'.
2. Acts outside the framework of the EC Treaty such as resolutions, deliberations, conclusions, communications, common declarations of two or more EC institutions, etc, adopted by various EC institutions. The European Parliament has expressed its concern as to the increasing number of new acts adopted by EC institutions outside the EC Treaty,[88] but in Case 59/75 *Manghera*[89] the ECJ held that EC institutions were empowered to issue those acts provided that their provisions are in conformity with the EC Treaty.

7.4 External sources which derive from international commitments of the Communities

International competences of the Communities, as well as the main international conventions concluded between the Communities and third countries, have already been examined in Chapter 4.

By virtue of art 228(7) EC international agreements entered into by the Community and

---

[85] [1989] ECR 4407.
[86] [1976] ECR 91.
[87] See European Parliament, Report Kirk, Doc 148/78 of 30.5.78.
[88] See Report Burger, EP Doc, session no 215/68–69 of 12.03.69.
[89] [1976] ECR 91.

third countries or international organisations are binding upon the Community institutions and the Member States. This provision has been inserted to underline that the principle of public international law according to which only contracting parties to an international agreement are bound of its provisions does not apply in the context of the Community. In addition, the principle of supremacy of Community law strengthens the peculiar position of the Member States vis-à-vis international agreements concluded between the Community and third parties. In Case 181/73 *Haegeman*[90] the ECJ held that the provisions of international agreements, from their entry into force, form an integral part of the Community legal order. This is also extended to mixed agreements.[91] It means that international agreements acquire *ipso facto*, that is solely because they are international agreements and from the date of their entry into effect, force of law in the Community legal order. No express incorporation into Community law is required. Indeed, the decision of the ECJ in *Haegeman* has resolved doubts as to whether an international agreement needs to be implemented into EC law by an internal act of the Council. This uncertainty was highlighted by the fact that in practice the Council has always concluded an international agreement by adopting a decision or a regulation to which in its annex the text of the agreement was added. Thus, it is clear that international agreements become an integral part of Community law, independently of any internal act adopted by the Council in this respect and without any need for their implementation into EC law. As the Advocate-General Rozes stated in Case 270/89 *Polydor*,[92] an internal act by which the Council expresses the willingness of the Community to be bound by a international agreement does neither modify its nature nor its legal effects, but has only 'instrumental' character.

As to the conditions of an entry into force of an international agreement, the EC Treaty is silent. In practice, a decision or a regulation reproducing in its annex the text of an agreement and relating to its conclusion adopted by the Council is published in the Official Journal. In Case 98/78 *Racke*[93] the ECJ held that an international agreement cannot produce legal effects before its publication. As to their entry into force, usually international agreements in their final provisions specify that date. For that reason, a decision or a regulation relating to the conclusion of an international agreement contains a provision stating that the date of its entry into force will be published in the OJ.

If an international agreement to which the Community is a contracting party provides for the establishment of a body empowered to supervise or monitor its proper functioning or its uniform application in all contracting States, then any decisions adopted by such a body also form an integral part of the Community. This was confirmed by the ECJ in many cases.[94] The same solution applies to 'recommendations' of such bodies because of its 'direct link' with an international agreement.[95]

In the hierarchy of sources of EC law, international agreements concluded between the Communities and third countries or international organisations are situated below primary

---

[90] [1974] ECR 449.
[91] Case 12/86 *Demirel* [1987] ECR 3719.
[92] [1982] ECR 239.
[93] [1979] ECR 69.
[94] Case 87/75 *Bresciani* [1976] ECR 129; Case C–192/89 *Sevince* [1990] ECR I–3461; Case C–69/89 *Nakajima* [1991] ECR I–2069.
[95] Case C–188/91 *Deutsche Shell* [1993] ECR I–363; [1993] CMLR 1043–1050, note by F Castillo de la Torre.

sources and general principles of EC law but above the secondary sources. Its secondary position vis-à-vis primary sources is justified on the grounds of art 228(7) EC which provides that:

> 'Agreements concluded under the conditions set out in this article shall be binding on the institutions of the Community and on Member States.'

In Case 40/72 *Schroeder*[96] the ECJ held that international agreements, and all unilateral acts of the EC institutions adopted in relation to their conclusion within the meaning of art 228(7) EC, prevail over secondary sources of EC law. As a result, all unilateral measures such as regulations, directives and decisions must be interpreted in conformity with international agreements and any conflicting secondary legislation may be annulled by the ECJ by virtue of art 173 EC,[97] or any breach of an international agreements by EC institutions may give rise to their liability for damages under art 215(2) EC.[98]

Direct effect of international agreements will be discussed in Chapter 8.

7.5 Complementary sources of Community law

Complementary sources of EC law result from agreements among Member States in the areas which are within national competences. Those agreements are classical international treaties in the sense they create legal obligations between the contracting parties, although they are not independent vis-à-vis the Community legal order. Indeed, they are considered complementary sources since the subject-matters of these agreements are within the scope of the Treaty or constitute the extension of the objectives defined in the EC Treaty. The relationship between these agreements and EC law is peculiar depending upon the form they take. In this respect a distinction should be made between: international conventions concluded by the Member States on the basis of EC Treaty; various decisions and agreements concluded by the representatives of governments of the Member States within the Council; and, finally, declarations, resolutions and common positions adopted by a common accord of the Member States.

Conventions concluded between the Member States

The EC Treaty itself provides for the conclusion of international agreements between Member States in order to avoid difficulties which may arise due to the intensification of exchanges and the increased mobility of natural and legal persons within the common market. In this respect art 220 EC enumerates four areas belonging to private international law which are recommended for harmonisation: the protection of persons and their individual rights in the context of art 6 EC; the elimination of double taxation, mutual recognition of companies or firms within the meaning of art 58(2) EC; the retention of legal personality in the event of transfer of their seats from one Member State to another and

---

[96] [1973] ECR 125.
[97] Case C–188/88 *NMB* [1992] ECR I–1689.
[98] Case 181/73 *Haegeman* [1974] ECR 449.

merger between companies and firms registered in different Member States; and the recognition and enforcement of judgments and arbitral awards throughout the Community. By virtue of art 220 EC the following conventions have been concluded between the Member States:

1. The 1968 Brussels Convention on Recognition and the Enforcement of Judgments in Civil and Commercial Matters which entered into force on 1 February 1973 among the six original Member States. Since then, it has been modified many times over the years. Indeed, each enlargement of the Communities has necessitated its amendment and provided an opportunity for modifications. Today, there are five versions of the Brussels Convention. In order to achieve uniformity in its application, a Protocol of 3 June 1971 gives the ECJ jurisdiction to interpret the Convention.[99]

2. The 1968 Convention on Mutual Recognition of Companies and Legal Persons, together with a Protocol on its interpretation which has not yet entered into force.[100]

3. The Transfer Pricing Arbitration Convention adopted on 23 July 1990 which entered into force on 1 January 1995.

4. The Convention relating to the procedure of Insolvency of 23 November 1995.

5. The 1980 Rome Convention on the Law Applicable to Contractual Obligations which entered into force on 1 April 1991.

6. The Convention relating to bankruptcy which is in a stage of advanced negotiations.

The characteristic features of these conventions which distinguishes them from other international agreements are: first, they are concluded for an undefined period of time; second, only the Member States may become contracting parties to those Conventions and with each enlargement new Member States must ratify them as an 'acquis communautaire'; third, their entry into force is conditional upon their ratification by all Member States; fourth, in order to ensure uniformity in their application the ECJ has jurisdiction to interpret them; and, finally, the Council and the Commission are involved in their preparation. In this last respect they initiate work relating to a particular convention; the Commission assists the representatives of the Member States in the drafting of its text; the Council and the Commission formally express their views on the draft convention which are published as their opinions in the OJ; a convention is signed during the session of the Council by the plenipotentiaries of the Member States; and the instruments of ratification are deposited with the General Secretariat of the Council.

However, the participation of the Council and the Commission in the preparation of conventions under art 220 EC is also common to other conventions concluded among the Member States outside the provisions of the Treaty but which are nevertheless considered as necessary in order to facilitate the application of Community law. In this respect, the following conventions have been concluded:

1. The 1967 Naples Convention on the Mutual Assistance between Customs Administrations.

2. The Community Patent Convention 1975 and the Community Agreement on the Community Patent 1989.

---

[99] Its codified version is contained in OJ C189 28.7.90 p1.
[100] EC Bull Suppl 2/69.

The Treaty of Maastricht set out a new basis for international conventions among the Member States which have been previously concluded outside the framework of the EC Treaty but which were important, useful and relevant to the achievement of the objectives of the Treaty. In the area of Justice and Home Affairs art K3(2)(c) TEU provides for conclusion of international conventions among the Member States. It states that:

'Without prejudice to art 220 of the Treaty establishing the European Community, [the Council may] draw up conventions which it shall recommend to the Member States for adoption in accordance with their respective constitutional requirements.'

On the basis of this provision a number of conventions has already been concluded among the Member States: the Convention of 10 March 1995 concerning the Simplified Extradition Procedure,[101] the Europol Convention and the Convention of 26 July 1995 concerning the Protection of Financial Interests of the European Communities.[102]

Decisions and agreements concluded by the representatives of the governments of the Member States meeting within the Council

These kinds of decisions and agreements are concluded by the representatives of the governments of the Member States meeting within the Council, so that it acts not as a Community institution but as a diplomatic conference. The Treaty itself provides for them in certain circumstances, for example under art 158 EC for nomination of members of the Commission, or appointments of judges of the ECJ under art 167 EC, or by virtue of art 216 EC for determination of the seat of EC institutions. From early days, the representatives of the governments of the Member States decided to take opportunity of these meetings to adopt measures necessary to the proper functioning of the Community even outside the framework of the Treaty. These measures, although necessary, cannot be taken by the EC institutions since the latter can only act within the limit of their competences (art 4 EC).

There are three areas in which this type of decision or agreement have been adopted by representatives of the governments of the Member States meeting within the Council:

1. In matters which the Treaty itself reserves for the Member States. For example, under arts 15 and 24 EEC concerning the acceleration of elimination of customs duties and the establishment of a common custom tariffs, a number of decisions relating to the acceleration were adopted: on 12 May 1960[103] and on 15 May 1962.[104]
2. In matters outside the Treaty. For example, a Decision of 18 December 1978 concerning the suppression of certain postal taxes on presentation to the customs.[105]
3. In matters partially within the scope of the Treaty. For example, a Decision of 20 September 1976 concerning Economic Co-operation within the Mixte Committee EEC/Canada.[106]

---

[101] OJ C78 30.3.95 p1.
[102] OJ C316 27.11.95 p1.
[103] OJ L215 12.9.60 p1.
[104] OJ L284 28.5.62 p1.
[105] OJ L6 10.1.79 p26 Decision 79/8 EEC.
[106] OJ L260 24.9.76 p36 Decision 76/755/ECSC, EEC, Euratom.

The decisions and agreements of the representatives of the governments of the Member States are usually adopted on the proposal submitted by the Commission and after consulting the EP. They are published in the OJ and often their implementation is left to the EC institutions. Another feature of this type of act is that they are adopted by unanimity and signed by all representatives of the governments of the Member States, unlike acts of the Council which are signed only by the President of the Council.

From a legal point of view these decisions and agreements are considered as international treaties concluded in a simplified form. As a result, Member States are bound by these decisions and agreements and they constitute a complementary source of Community law.

Declarations, resolutions and common positions adopted by a common accord of the Member States

These are basically political statements of the Member States. They have no legal effect and are non-binding. In most cases they are adopted jointly by the Council and the Member States and contain guidelines as to the future policy of the Community in an area of shared competences. There are many examples of these kinds of non-binding acts such as the Resolution of the Council and the Representatives of the Government of the Member States Concerning the Progressive Creation of the Economic and Monetary Union,[107] the Declaration concerning the Action Programme in the Field of Environment,[108] the Resolution of the Council and the Ministers of Education Concerning the Action Programme in the Field of Education,[109] etc.

Complementary sources in the hierarchy of sources of Community law

The complementary sources of Community law are in the position of inferiority vis-à-vis primary sources and general principles of EC law. They originate outside the framework of the Treaty. As a result of the combined effect of arts 236 and 5 EC complementary sources of EC law cannot derogate from the provisions of the Treaty. The relationship between complementary sources and secondary sources is more complex. In the areas in which the Community has exclusive competences the complementary sources are excluded and the Member States, unless they are expressly authorised, have no powers to adopt legislative acts, otherwise they will be in breach of EC law. In the areas of concurrent competences, and especially on the grounds of art 235 EC, the secondary sources prevail over complementary sources. This solution has a double justification. First, it results from art 5 EC which requires that Member States facilitate the accomplishment of the tasks conferred upon the EC institutions and imposes a duty upon the Member States to abstain from adopting any act likely to jeopardise the objectives of the Treaty. Second, art 20 of the Rome Convention on the Law Applicable to Contractual Obligations expressly states that:

---

[107] OJ C28 27.3.71 p1.
[108] OJ C112 20.12.73 p1.
[109] OJ C38 19.2.76 p1.

'This Convention shall not affect the application of provisions which, in relation to particular matters, lay down choice of law rules relating to contractual obligations and which are or will be contained in acts of the institutions of the European Communities or in national laws harmonised in implementation of such acts.'

In the area of exclusive competences of the Member States, the Community institutions may solely adopt secondary legislation when authorised by the complementary. Thus, they prevail over secondary legislation.

The complementary sources occupy a special place in the legal system of the Community. They cannot derogate to the provisions of the Treaty. Article 5 EC ensures that any violation of the Treaty by complementary law may give rise to proceedings under arts 169 and 170 EC. Nevertheless, proceedings under arts 173[110] or 177 EC are excluded in relation to complementary law,[111] although the ECJ may have jurisdiction to interpret some complementary law on the basis of specific provisions contained in a particular convention, such as art 73 of the Convention on the Community Patent, or a special protocol, such as the 1971 Protocol concerning the interpretation of the 1968 Brussels Convention on Jurisdiction and the Enforcement of Judgments in Civil and Commercial Matters.

7.6 General principles of Community law and the case law of the ECJ

The last category of sources of EC law results from the activities of the ECJ (including the Court of First Instance). The special position of the ECJ as a law-maker requires some explanation.

Case law of the Community courts

First, the ECJ as a Community institution enjoys a special status. Until the establishment of the Court of First Instance, the ECJ was the one and only judicial institution in the Community. Its authority is similar to those of national supreme courts such as the House of Lords in the United Kingdom or the Cour de Cassation in France. There in no control over, and no appeal against, its decisions. The creation of the Court of First Instance has not changed the position of the ECJ. The latter constitutes an appellate court on points of law from the decisions of the Court of First Instance.

Second, under art 164 EC the ECJ must 'ensure that in the interpretation and application of this Treaty the law is observed'. Thus, its mission is not only to apply the law expressly laid down by the Treaty but, more importantly, to promote its continuous development, to supplement its provisions as well as to fill gaps in the Treaty. Bingham J in *Customs and Excise Commissioners* v *Samex SpA* has described this as the '... creative process of supplying flesh to a spare and loosely constructed skeleton'.[112]

Third, the ECJ, in order to carry out its tasks, relies on a variety of methods of

---

[110] However, an action against measures adopted on the basis of complementary law is permitted: Case C–316/91 *Parliament* v *Council* [1994] ECR I–625.

[111] Case C–248/91 *Parliament* v *Council* [1993] ECR I–3685.

[112] [1983] 3 CMLR 194; [1983] 1 All ER 1042 (Commercial Court).

interpretation and a number of interpretive devices. The interpretation of Community law is based on art 31 of the 1969 Vienna Convention on the Law of the Treaties, which provides that the interpretation should be based on the ordinary meaning of the terms of a treaty, in the context of, and in the light of, its object. The ECJ has given priority to the interpretation 'in the general context' (systematic method) 'and in the light of its object and goal' (teleological method) over the literal interpretation of the Treaty.[113] In Case 283/81 *CILFIT*[114] the ECJ emphasised the particular difficulties in the interpretation and application of EC law. The Community legislation is drafted in several languages and each version is authentic. Thus, the comparison of different versions is sometimes necessary. Furthermore, the Community law uses terminology and refers to legal concepts which are peculiar to it. It is autonomous and community meaning of legal concepts differ from those known under national laws of the Member States. Finally, the ECJ held in *CILFIT* that:

> 'every provision of the Community law must be placed in its context and interpreted in the light of the provision of Community law as a whole, regard being had to the objectives thereof and to its state of evolution at the date on which the provision in question is to be applied'.

Nevertheless, the ECJ relies on other methods of interpretation depending upon the case and the degree to which the provision to be interpreted is ambiguous, obscure, etc. Indeed, this is the most characteristic feature of the ECJ; the wide eclectism of the methods used to interpret EC law, combined with the willingness to draw from each of them the maximum of effectiveness. The originality and autonomy of Community law vis-à-vis international law and national laws of the Member States, the need to maintain the coherence of the Community system and to ensure its unity and homogeneity require and, at the same time, allow the ECJ to become a law-maker. Whether this 'judicial legislation' should be criticised, or to the contrary considered as an asset, is a different matter.[115] In reality, the ECJ has considerably contributed to European integration and to the creation of dynamic and evaluative Community law.

General principles of Community law

In the 'judicial legislation' a special place is given to the general principles. They are unwritten rules of law which a judge has to apply, but not to create, although the preliminary stage to their application is necessary creative. The reference to the general principles has two objectives: to avoid the denial of justice and to strengthen the coherence of the Community law.

There is no reference to general principles in the ECSC Treaty. However, in Case 7/56, 7/57 *Algera*[116] the ECJ confirmed the existence of general principles applicable to the Community legal order on the basis that these principles are recognised by all legal systems of the Member States. The EC Treaty in art 215(2) has expressly referred to 'general principles common to the laws of the Member States' according to which the non-contractual liability of the Community is to be determined. However, the ECJ has not

---

[113] Case 6/60 *Humblet* [1960] ECR 1125.
[114] [1982] ECR 3415.
[115] See R Lecourt, *L'Europe des juges*, Bruxelles: Bruylant, 1976.
[116] [1957] ECR 39.

limited the reference to the general principles to this area. To the contrary, it has applied them to all aspects of Community law.

In formulating general principles the ECJ draws inspiration from many sources:

1. public international law and its general principles inherent to all legal systems;
2. national laws of the Member States by identifying the general principles common to the laws of the Member States,
3. Community law by inferring the general principles from the nature of the Communities; and
4. fundamental human rights.

General principles inherent to all legal systems

The creation of a new international legal order by the Community did not preclude the ECJ from making reference to the general principles of public international law. The ECJ recognised and incorporated into Community law such universal principles as the compatibility of the successive conventional obligations[117] or the right of a national to enter and remain in the territory of his own country,[118] although some of them have been rejected as contrary to this new legal order. For example, the principle of reciprocity especially under its form of the *exceptio non adimpleti contractus* was considered by the ECJ as incompatible with the Community legal order.[119] The most important principle of public international law recognised by the ECJ is the principle of legal certainty which is in itself vague. In the context of the Community legislation it means that the latter must be certain, its legal implications foreseeable especially in its application to financial matters.[120] At a national level, it means that national legislation implementing Community law must be worded in such a way as to be clearly understandable to those concerned as to their rights and obligations.[121] The ECJ has given a concrete scope of application and a more specific application to the principle of legal certainty in order to escape its tautological nature and to clarify its content. As a result, under the principle of legal certainty, the following rules has been established by the ECJ:

1. the principle of non-retroactivity of administrative acts;[122]
2. the principle of good faith which requires that Community institutions in administrative and contractual matters act in conformity with that principle;[123]
3. the principle of *patere legem*;[124]
4. the principle of vested or acquired rights;[125] and
5. the principle of legitimate expectations which means that 'those who act in good faith on the basis of law as it is or seems to be should not be frustrated in their expectations'.[126]

---

[117] Case 10/61 *Commission v Italy* [1962] ECR 3.
[118] Case 41/74 *Van Duyn* [1974] ECR 1337.
[119] Cases 90 and 91/63 *Commission v Luxembourg and Belgium* [1964] ECR 1217.
[120] Case 325/85 *Ireland v Commission* [1987] ECR 5041.
[121] Case 257/86 *Commission v Italy* [1988] ECR 3249.
[122] Case 234/83 *Gesamthochschule Duisburg* [1985] ECR 333.
[123] Case 43/59 *Van Lackmuller* [1960] ECR 933.
[124] Case 38/70 *Deutsche Tradex* [1971] ECR 154; Case 68/86 *United Kingdom v Council* [1988] ECR 855.
[125] Case 100/78 *Rossi* [1979] ECR 831; Case 159/82 *Verli Wallace* [1983] ECR 2711.
[126] Wyatt and Dashwood, *European Community Law*, section on The General Principles of Community Law, Chapter 4.

It has given rise to many cases in the context of commercial activities of individuals and undertakings,[127] and has been invoked in the famous milk quota cases: first, under art 173 EC to annul the Council regulations limiting the milk quotas by milk producers who under the previous Community legislation did not deliver any milk during the year which the Council chose as a base of the calculation of the new quota;[128] and, second, under art 215(2) for damages suffered by them as a result of an unlawful action of the EC institutions.[129]

Another category of general principles taken from public international law concerns the procedural rights necessary to safeguard the protection of substantive rights, such as the right to defence and, especially, to a fair hearing in administrative proceedings[130] and before courts,[131] including those concerned in the preliminary enquiry of the Commission in competition cases.[132] In addition, certain principles relating to the proper and sound administration of justice,[133] such as the refusal to recognise the possibility of an extraordinary appeal without any written text,[134] or the continuity of the composition of an administrative body in a procedure susceptible to entail pecuniary sanctions,[135] are also inspired by general principles of law.

General principles common to the laws of the Member States

It is not necessary that a general principle is recognised by legal systems of all Member States. It is sufficient if a given principle is common to a certain number of national legal systems, although 'non-negligible divergences' constitute an obstacle to its recognition.[136] Advocate-General Slynn in Case 155/79 *AM and S v Commission* explains the manner in which the ECJ discovers unwritten principles of EC law by citing H Kutscher, a former judge at the ECJ. Kutscher explained that:

> '... when the Court interprets or supplements Community law on a comparative law basis it is not obliged to take the minimum which the national solutions have in common, or their arithmetic mean or the solution produced by a majority of the legal systems as the basis of its decision. The Court has to weigh up and evaluate the particular problem and search for the "best" and "most appropriate" solution. The best possible solution is the one which meets the specific objectives and basic principles of the Community ... in the most satisfactory way'.[137]

Therefore, the discovery of general principles common to the Member States is based on a comparative study of national laws of the Member States, but avoids any mechanical or mathematical approach leading to the lowest common denominator. To the contrary, the spirit of national laws, their evolution and general features are taken into consideration by

---

[127] See Sharpston, 'Legitimate Expectations and Economic Reality' (1990) 15 ELR 103.
[128] Case 120/86 *Mulder* [1988] ECR 2321; Case 170/86 *Von Deetzen* [1988] ECR 2355.
[129] Joined Cases C–104/89 and C–37/90 *Mulder v Council and Commission* [1992] ECR I–3061.
[130] Case 7/69 *Commission v Italy* [1970] ECR 117; Case 17/74 *Transocean Marine Paint* [1974] ECR 1063; Case 85/76 *Hoffman-La Roche* [1978] ECR 461; Case 53/85 *AKZO* [1986] ECR 1985.
[131] Case 42/59 *SNUPAT* [1961] ECR 101.
[132] Case 374/87 *Orkem* [1989] ECR 3283.
[133] Case 63/72 *Werhahn Hansamuhle* [1973] ECR 1229.
[134] Case 12/68 *X* [1969] ECR 116.
[135] Case 41/69 *ACF Chemiefarma* [1970] ECR 661.
[136] Case 46/87 *Hoechst* [1989] ECR I–3283.
[137] [1982] ECR 1575 at 1649.

the ECJ. The general tendency, or sometimes lack of it, may also inspire the judges. For example, the principle of proportionality was known only to German law but has become a general principle of Community law since it responds to the needs of the Community legal order. In the process of discovery of general principles, the ECJ is entitled to choose the most appropriate from the point of view of the objectives of the Community law. It has, for example, recognised a principle which is rejected by all Member States but one, as was the case of the concept of exercise of public functions by an agent which has a broad meaning in five Member States but the ECJ favoured its narrow meaning which is recognised only in one Member State,[138] or rejected a principle common to national laws of all Member States but incompatible with the requirements of Community law.[139] Once the ECJ incorporates a national principle into Community law, it becomes an independent, autonomous principle which may have different meaning from the one known to national laws. Among the principles common to the national laws of the Member States the ECJ has discovered the following:

1. the principle of equality before economic regulation;[140]
2. the principle of the hierarchy of legal measures which allows distinguishing between legislative acts and measures necessary to their implementation;[141]
3. the principle of unjust enrichment;[142]
4. the principles concerning tortious liability of the EC institutions;[143]
5. the principle of confidentiality of written communications between lawyer and client;[144]
6. the principle of access to the legal process;[145] and
7. the principle of the protection of business secrets by an undertaking.[146]

General principles inferred from the nature of the Communities

The ECJ has inferred from the specific nature of the Communities, and from the context of the Treaties and their objectives, a certain number of principles. Some of them concern institutional law of the Communities, other are inherent to the creation of a common market. The first category of general principles reflect the political and economic structure of the Community. These principles are:

1. The principle of solidarity which is based on mutual trust among the Member States.[147] Solidarity is required in internal and external relations of the Member States. The Treaty of Maastricht has further developed the principle of solidarity and recognised it as a binding objective of the Treaty. Under the TEU it has two aspects: within the Community it applies to all Member States, and in the context of the European Union it extends to

---

[138] Case 9/69 *Sayag* [1969] ECR 3219.
[139] Case 26/67 *Dausin* [1968] ECR 464.
[140] Case 8/57 *Hauts Fourneaux et Acieries Belges* [1958] ECR 225.
[141] Case 25/70 *Köster* [1970] ECR 1161.
[142] Case 26/67 *Danvin* [1968] ECR 463.
[143] Case 83/76 *Bayerische HNL* [1978] ECR 1209.
[144] Case 155/79 *AM and S v Commission* [1982] ECR 1575.
[145] Case 222/84 *Johnston v Chief Constable of the Royal Ulster Constabulary* [1986] ECR 1651.
[146] Case 53/85 *AKZO* [1985] ECR 1985; Case 36/92 *SEP* [1994] ECR 1911.
[147] Case 39/72 *Commission v Italy* [1973] ECR 101.

the people of the Member States. In practice it means that all Member States should contribute to the harmonious development of the Union, and thus the principle of solidarity strengthens the economic and social cohesion within the EU.

2. The principle of loyal co-operation between EC institutions and Member States, and Member States themselves based on art 5 EC.

3. The principles of subsidiarity and equality between Member States which have already been examined in Chapter 3.

4. The principle of limited powers which is implicit in art 4(1) EC and according to which EC institutions must act within the limits of the powers conferred upon them by the Treaty.

5. The principle of occupied fields and attributed powers which concerns the division of competences between the Community and the Member States, also discussed earlier.

As to the second category, these principles strengthen the objectives of the Community and the neo-liberal philosophy of the Common market. These include the principle of equality which prohibits all forms of discrimination, direct and indirect based: on nationality[148] as recognised by art 6 EC; on gender[149] which is embodied in art 119 EC; and on producers and consumers within the framework of the common agricultural market under art 40(3) EC. It also applies to similar situations unless the differentiation is objectively justified,[150] and vice versa the same treatment of different situations.[151] The principle of proportionality which has already been discussed is also included in this second category.[152]

Some principles are well rooted in Community law, other are more dubious. In this respect the ECJ in Case C–352/92 *Greece* v *Council*[153] followed Advocate-General Jacobs' opinion and rejected the principle of Community preference which was acknowledged as a general principle of EC law in previous decisions.[154] This rejection demonstrates that the list of general principles is not exhaustive or definitive.

Also related to the proper functioning of the common market are the principles of the free movements of goods, people, services and capital, the principle of the homogeneity of the Common market, the principles relating to the competition, etc.

The most important principles which derive from the objectives of the Treaty, and have been developed by the ECJ in order to promote effective enforcement of EC law within the national legal systems of the Member States, are the principles of direct effect, direct applicability, supremacy of EC law, *effet utile*, and the principle of the liability of Member States in damages for breaches of Community law vis-à-vis individuals. These questions will be examined in Chapter 8.

Fundamental human rights

From their inception the Communities focused on economic objectives. This consideration, and the existence of the European Convention on Human Rights, explain the reason why

---

[148] Case 155/80 *Oebel* [1981] ECR 1993.
[149] Case 149/77 *Defrenne* [1978] ECR 1365.
[150] Joined Cases 124/76 and 20/77 *Moulins Point-a-Mousson* [1977] ECR 1795.
[151] Case 106/83 *Sermide* [1984] ECR 4209.
[152] See also De Burca, 'The Principle of Proportionality and Its Application in EC Law' (1993) 13 YEL 105.
[153] [1994] ECR I–3411.
[154] Case 5/67 *Beus* [1968] ECR 125, especially 147.

the question of human rights has been relatively neglected. Nevertheless, the ECJ was confronted with fundamental human rights issues quite early on. The question of the fundamental rights which arose before the ECJ concerned the alleged contradictions between obligations imposed by the High Authority of the ECSC and the rights which were granted to undertakings under their national constitutional law. On the one hand, the rights and freedoms contained in national constitutions were superior to any other sources of law and their observance was imposed on any public authority of the Member States in dealings with the public. Thus, it was impossible to permit national constitutional laws to prevail over Community law without compromising its uniform application throughout the Community. On the other hand, the founding Treaties neither contained any reference to fundamental human rights nor imposed on Community institutions any requirement to observe these rights. It was the task of the ECJ to find a solution to this legal impasse. For the first time, in Case 1/59 *Stork v High Authority*,[155] the ECJ when determining the relationship between the fundamental human rights and Community law refused to allow the examination of Community law in terms of its compliance with fundamental human rights and freedoms contained in national constitutions, as this approach would challenge the supremacy of Community law. The criticism expressed by Member States, and especially the German Constitutional Court, led the ECJ to alter its position in an *obiter* statement in Case 29/69 *Stauder v City of Ulm*,[156] in which it held that fundamental human rights constituted general principles of Community law and as such were protected by the ECJ. This position was further elaborated in Case 11/70 *Internationale Handelsgesellschaft* when the Court emphasised that:

> 'The protection of such rights, whilst inspired by the constitutional traditions common to the Member States, must be ensured within the framework of the structure and objectives of the Community.'[157]

Very soon this solution was considered as insufficient. In order to increase the protection of fundamental human rights, the ECJ decided to make reference to international conventions in this area, especially to the European Convention on Human Rights and Fundamental Freedoms signed in Rome on 4 November 1950 to which all Member States were contracting parties. In Case 4/73 *Nold KG v Commission* the ECJ held that '... international treaties for the protection of human rights on which the Member States have collaborated or of which they are signatories, can supply guidelines which should be followed within the framework of Community law'.[158]

Nevertheless, the ECJ in *Nold* highlightened that these rights are not absolute and '... far from constituting unfettered prerogatives, [they] must be viewed in the light of the social function'. Thus it is legitimate that 'these rights should, if necessary, be subject to certain limits justified by the overall objectives pursued by the Community, on condition that the substance of these rights is left untouched'.

Since then the ECJ has recognised, *inter alia*, the following rights:

---

[155] [1959] ECR 17; also Case 40/59 *Comptoirs de vente de la Ruhr* [1960] ECR 890.
[156] [1969] ECR 419.
[157] [1970] ECR 1125.
[158] [1974] ECR 491.

1. the right to equal treatment including non-discrimination based on gender;[159]
2. the right to exercise economic and professional activities, although it may be legitimately restricted in the light of the social function of the protected activity;[160]
3. the right to private and family life, domicile and correspondence as enounced in art 8 of the ECHR, but it does not exclude the interference of public authorities under the conditions defined by law and necessary to ensure public security and economic welfare of a country, or actions exercising the enforcement powers of the Commission in competition matters;[161]
4. the right to property,[162] but commercial interests in which the risks factor is inherent to its substance are not protected;[163]
5. the right to medical secrecy;[164]
6. the right to association;[165]
7. the right to free speech;[166]
8. the right to religious freedom;[167]
9. the principle of non-retroactivity of penal measures;[168] and
10. the principle *'nulla poena sine lege'*.[169]

The procedural rights – such as the right to defence, access to the court, fair hearing, etc – protected under the ECHR have also been recognised by the ECJ. In addition, in Case 5/88 *Wachauf* [170] the ECJ held that the protection of fundamental human rights is not only imposed on EC institutions, especially while they adopt binding measures, but also on the Member States in their application of such measures. Thus, national authorities in applying EC law must ensure 'as far as possible' that human rights are protected.

The importance of fundamental human rights prompted the Council, the Commission and the European Parliament to sign a Joined Declaration on 5 April 1977 which expressed their attachment to the protection of human rights. Although the declaration is solely a political statement it has initiated a new approach, that is the need for the Community to incorporate the European Convention on Human Rights into Community law. As already discussed, this initiative was blocked by the Member States at the Maastricht Conference and, finally, in Opinion 2/94[171] the ECJ held that the EC has no competence to accede to the ECHR without a Treaty amendment. However, the TEU contains two provisions relating to human rights. Article F(2) which provides that:

---

[159] Case 149/77 *Defrenne* [1978] ECR 1365.
[160] Case 4/73 *Nold* [1974] ECR 491; Case 44/79 *Hauer* [1979] ECR 3727; Case 234/85 *Keller* [1986] ECR 2897; Cases C–90 and 91/90 *Neu EA* [1991] ECR I–3617.
[161] Case 136/79 *National Panasonic* [1980] ECR 2033; Case C–404/92 *PX v Commission* [1994] ECR I–4737; Case C–76/93P *Piera Scaramuzza v Commission* [1994] ECR I–5173.
[162] Case 44/79 *Hauer* [1979] ECR 3727.
[163] Case 154/78 *Valsabbia* [1980] ECR 907.
[164] Case C–62/90 *Commission v Germany* [1992] ECR I–2575.
[165] Case 175/73 *Union Syndicale* [1974] ECR 917.
[166] Case C–200/89 *Elliniki* [1991] ECR I–2925; Case C–23/93 *TV 10 SA* [1994] ECR I–4795.
[167] Case 130/75 *Prais* [1976] ECR 1589.
[168] Case 63/83 *Kent Kirk* [1984] ECR 2689.
[169] Case C–328/89 *Berner Allemeine* [1991] ECR I–3431.
[170] [1989] ECR 2609.
[171] 28 March 1996, not yet reported.

'The Union shall respect fundamental rights, as guaranteed by the European Convention on Human Rights and Fundamental Freedoms signed in Rome on 4 November 1950 and as they result from the constitutional traditions of the Member States, as general principles of Community law.'

Although art F(2) envisages fundamental human rights in Community context, that is as general principles of Community law, the Community judges have explicitly referred to this provision in a number of cases.[172] Also, art K2 TEU provides that matters of common interest in co-operation in the fields of Justice and Home Affairs shall be dealt with in accordance with the requirements of the ECHR and the 1951 Refugee Convention.

The Draft Amsterdam Treaty further develops the protection of human rights.[173]

Assessment of general principles of Community law

In the hierarchy of sources, general principles are as important as founding Treaties, especially fundamental principles which are expressly acknowledged by art F(2) TEU. The protection of fundamental human rights is imposed on Community institutions and Member States. Other general principles are theoretically less important, although in practice the ECJ only recognises those principles which are compatible with the founding Treaties and fundamental human rights.

In the hierarchy of Community sources the general principles of Community law are superior to secondary legislation but nevertheless inferior to the primary sources, that is the three founding Treaties, together with the Protocols annexed to them as amended over the years and the Acts of Accession of new Member States to the existing Communities.

---

[172] Article F(2) is not enforceable before the ECJ. For that reason, Community judges can only make reference to this provision, see Case T–13/94 *Century Oil Hellas* [1994] ECR II–431; Case C–415/93 *Bosman* [1995] ECR I–4921; [1996] Europe (February), no 61, comm FG and DS.

[173] See Chapter 3.

8 Fundamental Principles of Community Law: Direct Applicability, Direct Effect, Supremacy of Community Law

8.1   Direct applicability of Community law

8.2   Direct effect of Community law

8.3   Supremacy of Community law

Community law is neither foreign nor external to the legal systems of the Member States. To the contrary, it forms an integral part of national laws. Its peculiar position is due to the manner it which it penetrates the national legal order of the Member States. The three legal concepts developed by the ECJ, – that is, direct applicability, direct effect and supremacy of Community law – strengthen its autonomy and determine the degree of its integration into national laws of the Member States.

The definition of direct applicability of Community law was given in Case 106/77 *Amministrazione delle Finanze* v *Simmenthal*[1] by the ECJ in the following terms:

> 'Direct applicability ... means that rules of Community law must be fully and uniformly applied in all Member States from the date of their entry into force and for so long as they continue in force'

and further explained in Case 28/67 *Firma Molkerei*[2] in which the ECJ held that direct applicability ensures that the provisions of Community law penetrate into national legal order of the Member States without the need for their incorporation. Furthermore, direct applicability depends on the sources of Community law, for some of them it is automatic and general in scope, for others it is conditional and limited.

The concept of direct effect is the most complex and difficult part of Community law. In Case 26/62 *Van Gend en Loos*[3] the ECJ has divorced Community law from recognised principles of public international law relating to the law of the treaties and held that 'Community law ... not only imposes obligations on individuals but it also intended to confer upon them rights' which national courts must protect.'

These provisions are not only entirely independent from national law but in most cases an individual can rely on them precisely where national rules precludes enforcement of Community law. The ECJ has established the general criteria of direct effect which requires that a provision, in order to produce direct effect, must be clear and precise, unconditional

---

[1] [1978] ECR 629.
[2] [1968] ECR 211.
[3] [1963] ECR 1.

and must penetrate into the internal legal order of the Member States without any national or Community measures designed to transpose it into domestic law.

The supremacy of Community law means that primacy must be accorded to Community law over national laws of the Member States. This fundamental principle was established by the ECJ in Case 6/64 *Costa* v *ENEL*[4] in which the ECJ held:

'... the law stemming from the Treaty, an independent source of law, could not, because of its special and original nature, be overridden by domestic provisions, however framed, without being deprived of its character as Community law and without the legal basis of the Community itself being called into question'.

This chapter focuses on these fundamental concepts and examines the complex relationship between Community law and national law of the Member States.

8.1 Direct applicability of Community law

Direct applicability is a question well known to public international law. It concerns the manner of introduction of international law into municipal law. Public international law does not regulate the conditions in which provisions of international treaties become incorporated into municipal laws in order to be applied by national courts. It is left to each country to decide on the relationship between international and municipal law. In this respect, there are two theories: dualist and monist. Under the dualist theory international law and municipal law are independent and separate systems. As a result, an international treaty duly ratified produces legal effect only at the international level, that is, it is only binding on the contracting States. In order to be applied by national courts it is necessary to incorporate an international treaty into the State's legal system to enable it to take effect at the national level. The reception of international law by municipal law constitutes the most important feature of the dualist doctrine. However, once an international provision is transformed into a national provision by means of implementing measures or its transposition, it is applied by national courts as any other municipal provision not as an international one.

In the monist system the unity between international and municipal law means that international law automatically becomes law within a contracting State. It is directly applicable. There is no need for reception of an international treaty as it becomes an integral part of national law of a contracting State once the procedure for it ratification is completed. An international provision is applied by municipal courts as such and not as a provision of domestic law.

Community law, due to its specificity, gives preference to the monist theory. In this respect, art 189 EC provides that regulations are directly applicable in all Member States. More importantly, the preference for the monist theory derives from the nature of the Community. Only a monist system is compatible with the idea of European integration. In

---

[4] [1964] ECR 585.

Case 6/64 *Costa* v *ENEL*[5] the ECJ emphasised its peculiar nature by stating that the Member States have created:

> 'a Community of unlimited duration, having its own institutions, its own personality, its own legal capacity and capacity of representation on the international plane and, more particularly, real powers stemming from a limitation of sovereignty or a transfer of powers from the States to the Community, the Member States have limited their sovereign rights, albeit within limited fields, and have thus created a body of law which binds their nationals and themselves'.

This confirmation is even more evident in the following passage extracted from the same decision in which the ECJ held that:

> 'By contrast with ordinary international treaties, the Treaty has created its own legal system which, on the entry into force of the Treaty, became an integral part of the legal systems of the Member States and which their courts are bound to apply.'

As a result, Community law cannot tolerate national divergencies as to their relations vis-à-vis international law since the dualist system jeopardises the attainment of the objectives of the Treaty and is contrary to the spirit of the Community objectives and Community law. Member States may preserve the dualist system in relation to international law but it is excluded in relations between Community law and national law. As a result, Community law becomes an integral part of national law without any need for its formal incorporation, and national judges are bound to apply it. Furthermore, it occupies a special place in domestic legal systems of the Members States as it is applied as Community law and not as municipal law.

Direct applicability of the founding Treaties

The original signatories of the three founding Treaties have ratified them according to national constitutional procedures. In monists countries such as France, on the basis of art 26 of the French Constitution of 1946, the Treaties were incorporated into municipal law on the basis of their ratification authorised by La Loi of 2 August 1957 and a *Décret de publication* of 28 January 1958.[6] In dualist countries such as Belgium, Germany and Italy it was necessary for national parliaments to intervene in order to supply the national legal basis for the Treaties and thus recognise their binding effect in municipal law, first by authorising their government to ratify them and then to incorporate them into domestic law in a legislative measure similar to the British Act of Parliament. To neutralise the effects of the dualist approach, in Case 9/65 *San Michele*[7] the ECJ refused to acknowledge the conditions of their incorporation into municipal laws of the Member States and held that they are binding and should be applied by national judges not as internal law but as Community law.

For Member States which joined the Communities the principle of direct applicability of the Treaties was obvious and case law of the ECJ clarified this point beyond any doubt. Since membership is conditional upon of the acceptance of the 'acquis communautaire', the Acts

---

[5] [1964] ECR 585.
[6] JORF of 22.2. 58.
[7] [1965] ECR 1967; [1965] ECR 35 Ord.

of Accession expressly recognised direct applicability, direct effect and supremacy of Community law. In the United Kingdom s2(1) of the European Communities Act 1972 recognises direct applicability of Community law. It provides that:

'All such rights, powers, liabilities, obligations and restrictions from time to time created or arising by or under the Treaties ... as in accordance with the Treaties *are without further enactment to be given legal effect* or used in the United Kingdom shall be recognised and available in law, and enforced, allowed and followed accordingly; and the expression "enforceable Community right" and similar expressions shall be read as referring to one to which this subsection applies.'

Section 2(2) of the Act further confirms that Community law forms an integral part of the law of the United Kingdom.

Although Community law is incorporated into the law of the United Kingdom by means of implementing legislation, more specifically by the European Communities Act 1972, it does not emanate from the British Parliament and cannot be applied by British courts as municipal law. Upon their ratification, the Treaties automatically became law in the United Kingdom. Implementing legislation was not necessary but the UK as a dualist country decided that upon accession, from a purely national perspective, it was necessary to make Community law applicable within the national legal system by means of an Act of Parliament. In Ireland the Treaties were implemented by an act of Parliament very similar to the 1972 British European Communities Act. Article 2 of the Irish act provides expressly that from 1 January 1973 the Treaties, as well as measures adopted by EC institutions, shall be binding and form an integral part of Irish law. In Denmark art 3 of the law of 11 October 1972 relating to the Accession of Denmark to the European Communities introduces the Treaties directly into national law without any implementing measures, although Denmark is also a dualist country.

Regulations

The direct applicability of regulations is expressly recognised in art 189 EC. Their direct applicability is recognised by s2(1) of the European Communities Act 1972 in the United Kingdom. Not only are any implementing measures unnecessary, they are prohibited by Community law. In Case 34/73 *Variola*[8] the ECJ was asked whether the provisions of a regulation can be introduced into Italian law by internal measures reproducing the contents of that regulation in such a way as not to affect its substance. The ECJ held that:

'By virtue of the obligations arising from the Treaty and assumed on ratification, Member States are under a duty not to obstruct the direct applicability inherent in regulations and other rules of Community law.'

As a result, implementing measures or transposition of regulations into national law is considered as a hindrance to their direct applicability and as such prohibited under Community law. The Constitutional Court of Italy recognised the arguments of the ECJ in the *Frontini* case[9] where it held that it 'derived from the logic of the Community system that

---

[8] [1973] ECR 981.
[9] Judgment of 27 December 1973, Frontini Foro it. 1974, I, 314.

EC regulations should not, as directly applicable legislative acts, be subject to national reproducing or implementing measures susceptible to modify, impose conditions as to their entry into force, substitute, derogate or abrogate them, even partially'.[10] In monist countries direct applicability of EC regulations is self evident. In France, in *Syndicat des Hautes Graves de Bordeaux Case*[11] the French Conseil d'Etat (highest administrative court) in its Decision of 22 December 1978 held that EC regulations by virtue of art 189 EC become, from their publication, an integral part of national law of the Member States. The French Constitutional Council also confirmed this solution.[12]

Directives and decisions

Directives are addressed to the Member States under the Treaties of Rome and to undertakings under the ECSC Treaty. Article 189 EC provides that Member States are under an obligation to achieve the objectives set up in EC directives but forms, procedure and methods necessary to attain these objectives are left to the discretion of the addressee Member States. Whether EC directives are directly applicable is a matter of controversy. For English scholars EC directives are not directly applicable since they require implementing measures.[13] For others, especially from monist Member States, States have only powers to implement directives, which is quite different from the reception of international treaties into the municipal system.[14] They made a distinction between the competence *d'execution* and the competence of *reception*. Member States exercise the former in relation to EC directives but not the latter. Those authors refuse to accept that until the transposition of EC directives into municipal law they do not exist from a legal point of view. In this respect, Judge P Pescatore said that a directive cannot be considered as 'a judicial non-entity from an internal viewpoint'.[15]

It is submitted that the conditions for implementation of EC directives are different from those required for incorporation of international law into domestic law. In addition, the peculiar nature of Community law within the Member States calls into question the non-direct applicability of EC directives. Indeed, it stems from art 5 EC as well as from s2(1) of the British European Communities Act 1972 quoted above.

EC directives as legal acts of the Community should be directly applicable. From the date of their publication until their implementation or the expiry of the time-limit for their implementation, they exist. Thus, they cannot be ignored since Community law is not international law *sensu stricto*. Indeed, as the ECJ highlighted in Case 26/62 *Van Gend en*

---

[10] In its French version: 'Il est conforme à la logique du système communautaire que les règlements de la CEE [...] ne doivent pas, en tant que source immédiate de droits et d'obligations [...] faire l'objet de mesures étatiques à caractère reproductif ou exécutif, susceptibles d'en modifier ou d'en conditionner de manière quelconque l'entrée en vigueur, et moins encore de s'y substituer, d'y déroger ou de les abroger, même partiellement': [1974] RTDE 148.

[11] [1979] RTDE, R.526, 717, concl. Genevois.

[12] Decisions of 30 December 1977 [1979] RTDE 142, note G Isaac and J Molinier.

[13] See for example J Tillotson, *European Community Law*, 2nd ed, London: Cavendish, 1996, p69.

[14] For example R Kovar, 'La contribution de la Cour de justice à l'édification de l'ordre juridique communautaire', in *Collected Courses of the Academy of European Law*, IV–I, especially p57.

[15] 'A non-être juridique du point de vue interne' in *L'effet des directives communautaires, Essay de démythification*, Paris: Dalloz, 1980, p171.

Loos, 'the Community constitutes a new legal order of international law'[16] which was later, in Case 6/64 *Costa* v *ENEL*,[17] considered as *sui generis* when the ECJ held that 'the Treaty has created its own legal system'. As a result, the law of the Treaties does not apply to this new system. The implementation of EC directives cannot be assimilated to the reception of an ordinary international treaty by a dualist Member States. First, because Community law is different, it is autonomous; and, second, because the Community rejects the dualist theory in so far as Community law in concerned. For all these reasons, EC directives are directly applicable, they do form an integral part of domestic law of the Member States from the time of their publication in the Official Journal, although they do not produce legal effects. In this respect, the French Conseil d'Etat in the *Cohn-Bendit* case,[18] in which it refused to recognise the supremacy of EC law, held that national judges have an obligation to verify the compatibility of national measures which implement EC directives with the provisions of those directives, before the expiry of the time-limit for their implementation. This recognises that EC directives are part of domestic law and thus have legal existence even before their transposition into domestic law or the expiry of the time-limit provided for their implementation. This reasoning also applies to decisions[19] addressed to the Member States and international agreements concluded between the Community and third countries.

8.2 Direct effect of Community law

Under public international law, some provisions of international treaties may confer rights on individuals or impose some obligations upon them. This approach has been developed as a result of the recognition of fundamental human rights, since individuals were not considered as subjects of public international law. This possibility was recognised for the first time by the Permanent Court of International Justice (PCIJ) in the *Case Concerning Competences of the Courts of Danzig*[20] in which it was held that an exception to the principle of individuals not being subject of public international law arises if the intention of contracting parties was to adopt a treaty which creates rights and obligations for them which may be enforced before national courts. The PCIJ emphasised that this intention must be express and not inferred from the treaty, since this kind of international treaty constituted an exception to a general principle. These treaties are qualified under public international law as 'self-executing'. They become automatically part of the national law of contracting parties and are directly applicable by their national courts.

However, this exception has become a principle under Community law. In Case 26/62 *Van Gend en Loos*[21] the ECJ delivered one of the most important decisions from a point of view of development of Community law: it held Community law directly effective and thus

---

[16] [1963] ECR 1.

[17] [1964] ECR 585.

[18] [1979] CDE 265.

[19] Decisions addressed to natural and legal persons are usually adopted in the area of competition and thus are of quasi-judicial nature. Indeed, they may be compared to judgments issued by national courts. They are binding upon their addressees.

[20] Advisory Opinion of 3 February 1928, Series B, no 15, esp 17.

[21] [1963] ECR 1.

creating rights and obligations for EC nationals enforceable before national courts. The Court rejected the solution of public international law and, without any justification based on the provisions of the Treaty, since there is neither an express provision in the Treaty nor a clear intention of the Member States in this respect, decided that Community law is directly effective.

In 1960 Van Gend imported unreaformaldehyde, a chemical product, into The Netherlands from Germany. In December 1959 The Netherlands had enacted legislation which modified the Benelux tariff system and which brought into effect the Brussels Convention on Nomenclature unifying the classification of goods for customs purposes. Under the new nomenclature Van Gend's product was reclassified. It resulted in an increase in the duty payable on unreaformaldehyde to 8 per cent on an *ad valorem* basis as compared to 3 per cent payable previously under Dutch law. On the 14 January 1958 the EC Treaty came into force. Its art 12 provides that:

> 'Member States shall refrain from introducing between themselves any new customs duties on imports or exports or any charges having equivalent effect, and from increasing those which they already apply in their trade with each other.'

Van Gend challenged the increase as contrary to art 12 EC. When his claim was rejected by the customs inspector he appealed to the Dutch Tariecommissie (Customs Court) in Amsterdam. Under art 177 EC the Customs Court submitted two questions to the ECJ: first, whether art 12 EC could create rights for individuals as claimed by Van Gend and, second, provided the answer to the first question was affirmative, whether the modification in customs duties was prohibited by art 12.

The governments of Belgium, West Germany and The Netherlands submitted additional memoranda to the ECJ claiming that art 12 EC created obligations for Member States and not rights for individuals. As a result, if a breach of EC law occurred the proceedings should solely be based on arts 169 and 170 EC.

The ECJ based its decision on a teleological interpretation of art 12 EEC and held that: 'Article 12 of the Treaty establishing the European Economic Community produces direct effect and created rights which national court must protect.' The Court invoked a number of arguments in support of its decision. It stated that direct effect confirms the peculiar nature of Community law. First, the objectives of the Treaty imply that the Treaty itself is 'more than an agreement which created mutual obligations between the contracting States'. Indeed, the Community 'constitutes a new legal order of international law ... the subjects of which comprise not only Member States but also their nationals'. Second, it stems from the Treaty's preamble which refers not only to the Member States but also to its people and Community institutions that Community law affects both the Member States and their citizens. It also requires the co-operation of the latter in the functioning of the Community through its institutions such as EP and the Economic and Social Council. Furthermore, the Court invoked an argument drawn from art 177 EC that the Member States 'have acknowledged that Community law has an authority which can be invoked by their nationals before those courts and tribunals'. From all these arguments the ECJ inferred that Community law 'independently of the legislation of Member States ... not only imposes obligations on individuals but is also intended to confer upon them rights which become part of their legal heritage'. The rejection of public international law is clear-cut when the

ECJ states that: 'Those rights arise not only where they are expressly granted by the Treaty, but also by reason of obligations which the Treaty imposes in a clearly defined way upon individuals as well as upon the Member States and upon the institutions of the Community.' Therefore, the fact that the addressees of a provision of the EC Treaty are the Member States 'does not imply that their nationals cannot benefit from this obligation'. To the contrary, the Treaty confers rights upon EC nationals not only when its provisions expressly provide so but also when they impose clearly defined obligations upon the Member States. In addition, direct effect of Community law ensures its effectiveness since: 'The vigilance of individuals concerned to protect their rights amounts to an effective supervision in addition to the supervision entrusted by arts 169 and 170 to the diligence of the Commission and of the Member Sates.'

Criteria of direct effect

It was also left to the ECJ to determine the conditions under which a provision of Community law becomes directly effective. The criteria that emerged from the decisions of the ECJ rendered mostly under art 177 EC are simple. A provision of Community law in order to produce direct effect must be: sufficiently clear and precise;[22] unconditional;[23] and self-executing, that is, must not require implementation by the Member States or EC institutions.[24]

However, the ECJ has substantially modified these requirements. First, it held that lack of clarity or precision did not hinder a provision from producing direct effect if that provision may be clarified or defined in more precise terms by means of interpretation by the Community or national judge.[25] Second, a condition attached to the provision which suspends its application does not nullify its direct effect but merely delays it until the realisation of the conditions or the expiry of the time-limit.[26] A provision is still considered as unconditional, although it requires the adoption of some implementing measures on the part of a Member State or an EC institution, if neither a Member State nor an EC institution has a discretion to adopt those measures. In this respect, under art 95(3) EC Member States are required to eliminate or to 'correct' provisions of national fiscal laws which discriminate imports from other Member States. In Case 57/65 *Alfons Lütticke* v *Hauptzollamt Saarlouis*[27] the ECJ held that the Member States in order to implement art 95(3) EC had no discretionary powers and thus decided this provision was directly effective. In Case 8/81 *Ursula Becker* v *Finanzamt Munster-Innenstadt*[28] the ECJ held that if implementation measures concerned solely procedural matters, a provision in question is still considered as unconditional and as such may be enforced before national courts.

---

[22] Case 148/78 *Ministere Public* v *Ratti* [1979] ECR 1629; Case 8/81 *Ursula Becker* [1982] ECR 53. The formula 'clear and precise' was examined in Case C–236/92 *Comitato di Coordinamento per la Difesa della Cava* v *Regione Lombardia* [1994] ECR I–483.

[23] Case 203/75 *Casati* [1981] ECR 2595; also *Ursula Becker*, ibid.

[24] Case 43/75 *Defrenne* [1976] ECR 455.

[25] Case 26/67 *Fink Frucht* [1968] ECR 327; Case 43/75 *Defrenne*, ibid; Case C–262/88 *Barber* [1990] ECR I–1889.

[26] Case 2/74 *Reyners* [1974] ECR 631; Case 59/75 *Manghera* [1976] ECR 101.

[27] [1966] ECR 205.

[28] [1982] ECR 53.

It is submitted that the criteria of direct effect are not set in concrete but depend upon the context in which Community law is applied by a national court. If a national judge has to apply Community law in the absence or in place of national law then a provision of Community law must, from all points of view, be unconditional, clear and sufficiently precise to take the place of national law. However, if a national judge has to verify whether national law is compatible with a provision of Community law, even though in its implementation national authorities have a discretion as to the form and method of implementation, the provision produces direct effect if the 'limits of appreciation' which it contains are unconditional, clear and sufficiently precise.[29] Finally, if a national judge has to interpret national law in the light of Community law, or determine the liability of national authorities stemming from its violation of Community law, the criteria of direct effect are further attenuated.

Vertical and horizontal direct effect

Vertical direct effect means that an individual may enforce Community law before national courts against the State, while horizontal direct effect means that he may rely on Community law in proceedings before a national court against another individual, that is any natural or legal person. In practice, this distinction is very important since it considerably limits the scope and the effectiveness of Community law in the case of a provision which may only produce vertical direct effect.

Direct effect of the Treaties

The ECJ in *Van Gend en Loos* (see above) held that direct effect of the Treaties' provisions is not automatic since they must be clear and precise, but it established that art 12 EC is vertically directly effective. The question whether other provisions of EC Treaty can produce vertical direct effect was confirmed by the ECJ in Case 57/65 *Alfons Lütticke v Hauptzollampt Saarlouis*.[30]

Lütticke imported whole milk powder from Luxembourg on which German customs levied duty and a turnover tax. Lütticke claimed that the imported product should be exempt from turnover tax as domestic natural milk and wholemilk powder were exempt under the Turnover Tax Law. The Finangericht des Saarlands referred the ECJ under art 177 to ascertain whether art 95 EC, which prohibits the imposition of such taxes, has direct effect and so thus confers rights upon individuals which a national court must protect. The ECJ held that art 95 EC does produce such individual rights which must be enforced by national courts.

Therefore, all doubts as to vertical direct effect of the founding Treaties were dissipated. The question of horizontal direct effect of EC Treaty provisions was decided by the ECJ in Case 43/75 *Defrenne v SABENA*.[31] Here, Miss Defrenne was employed as an air hostess by a Belgian airline company, SABENA. She claimed for losses she sustained in terms of pay she received as compared with male cabin stewards doing the same work. The Court de Travail referred to the ECJ under art 177 to ascertain whether she could rely on art 119 EC which

---

[29] Case 51/76 *Nederlandse Ondernemingen* [1977] ECR 113.
[30] [1966] ECR 205.
[31] [1976] ECR 455.

275

prohibits all discrimination between men and women workers and thus requires that they receive equal pay for performing the same task in the same establishment or service. However, art 119 EC requires further implementation measures.

The ECJ held that in her case it was not difficult to apply art 119 EC as the fact clearly showed that she was discriminated against. It stated that:

> '... the prohibition on discrimination between men and women applies not only to the action of public authorities, but also extends to all agreements which are intended to regulate paid labour collectively, as *contracts between individuals*'.

However, in cases of discrimination which could not be easily identified implementation measures adopted by the Community or the Member States may be necessary. Therefore, this case has established that some provisions of the Treaty may produce horizontal direct effect.

The case law of the ECJ has gradually elucidated which provisions of the Treaty have direct vertical and horizontal effect.

The Treaties' provisions which produce both vertical and horizontal direct effect In this respect, the Treaties' provisions relating to competition policy are particularly apt to produce vertical and horizontal direct effect and thus can be invoked by one undertaking against another undertaking before national courts.[32] These are: arts 85 and 86 EC, 65–66 ECSC, and 78, 81 and 83 Euratom concerning security control. Second, the provisions concerning the free movement of workers and self-employed, that is arts 48, 52, 59, 60 EC, as well as the art 7 EEC (now art 6 EC), which prohibits discrimination based on nationality, are both vertically and horizontally directly effective.[33] In this respect Case 36/74 *Walrave and Koch* v *Association Union Cycliste Internationale*[34] is particularly interesting.

The plaintiffs were prohibited by their sports association from competing in professional events on the grounds of their nationality. The ECJ held that discrimination as prohibited under art 6 EC applies not only to the action of local authorities but extends likewise to rules emanating from private bodies which aim at collectively regulating gainful employment as an employee under art 48 EC or as a self-employed person under arts 52–59. Sport is also an economic activity.

As already examined, art 119 EC produces vertical and horizontal direct effect. Also, art 30 EC, which provides for the free movement of workers, can be relied upon by an individual against another individual in proceedings before national courts as stated in Case 58/80 *Dansk Supermarked*.[35]

The Treaty provisions which have only direct vertical effect These provisions create rights and obligations for individuals which can only be enforced against the Member States. The first group of provisions concerns those which impose upon the Member States a prohibition. For example:

---

[32] Case 127/73 *BRT* v *Sabam* [1974] ECR 51; Case 13/61 *Bosch* [1962] ECR 97.
[33] For vertical direct effect see Case 14/68 *Walt Wilhelm* [1969] ECR 1.
[34] [1974] ECR 1420.
[35] [1981] ECR 181. For vertical direct effect see Case 74/76 *Iannelli* [1977] ECR 557.

1. art 12 EC which prohibits imposition of new customs duties and charges having equivalent effect;[36]
2. arts 31 and 32(1) EC which prohibits quantitative restrictions;[37]
3. art 37(2) EC which prohibits the introduction of new discriminatory measures relating to State monopoly of commercial nature;[38]
4. art 53 EC which prohibits the introduction of new restrictions relating to the freedom of establishment;[39]
5. art 73b(1) EC which prohibits restrictions on the free movement of capital between the Member States and between the Member States and third counties;[40]
6. art 90(2) EC which prohibits the development of trade which would be contrary to the interests of the Community;[41]
7. art 93(3) EC which prohibits granting by a Member State new aid without notifying the Commission;[42]
8. art 95(1) and (2) EC which prohibits discriminatory taxation of imports.[43]

The second category concerns provisions of the Treaty which impose on a Member State an obligation to adopt necessary measures in specific areas. For example:

1. art 13(2) EC concerning the elimination of customs duties on imports;
2. art 16 EC concerning the elimination of customs duties on exports;[44]
3. art 37(1) EC concerning State monopoly;[45]
4. art 95(3) EC concerning the elimination of discriminatory taxation on imports.[46]

Provisions of the Treaty having no direct effect[47] These are:

1. art 2 EC which enumerated objectives of the Treaty;[48]
2. art 5 EC which requires that Member States must take all necessary measures to fulfil their obligations arising out of the Treaty;[49]
3. arts 32(2) and 33(1), (2) EC relating to the elimination of quantitative restrictions;[50]
4. arts 92 and 93(1), (2) EC which prohibit State aid;[51]

---

[36] Case 26/62 *Van Gend en Loos* [1963] ECR 1.
[37] Case 13/68 *Salgoil* [1968] ECR 661.
[38] Case 6/64 *Costa* [1964] ECR 585; Case 91/78 *Hansen* [1979] ECR 935.
[39] Case 6/64 *Costa*, ibid.
[40] Cases C–163, 165 and 250/94 *Sanz de Lera* [1995] ECR I–4821.
[41] Case 57/65 *Lütticke* [1966] ECR 205.
[42] Case 120/73 *Lorenz* [1973] ECR 1471; Case C–354/90 *Fédération Nationale du Commerce Exterieur des Produits Alimentaires (Fenacomex)* [1991] ECR I–5505.
[43] Case 57/65 *Lütticke* [1966] ECR 205; Case 27/68 *Fink-Frucht* [1968] ECR 341.
[44] Case 18/71 *Eunomia* [1971] ECR 811.
[45] Case 59/75 *Manghera* [1976] ECR 91.
[46] Case 57/65 *Lütticke* [1966] ECR 205.
[47] On this subject see R Kovar, *Note sur les criteres du droit communautaires non directement applicable*, Mélange Dehousse, Nathan, Paris, Labor, Bruxelles, volume II, 1979, p227.
[48] Case C–339/89 *Alsthom Atlantique* [1991] ECR I–107.
[49] Case 9/73 *Schlüter* [1973] ECR 1161.
[50] Case 13/68 *Salgoil* [1968] ECR 661.
[51] Case 74/76 *Iannelli* [1977] ECR 557; Case 78/76 *Steinicke and Weinlig* [1977] ECR 595.

5. art 97 EC;[52]
6. art 102 EC relating to the obligatory consultation of the Commission by the Council on some legislative measures;[53]
7. art 107 EC;[54]
8. art 117 and 118 EC relation to social policy.[55]

To this list certain provisions of the Treaty of European Union must be added: namely its Title I (Common Provisions contained in Articles A–F which are expressly excluded from jurisdiction of the ECJ by virtue of Article L), as well as the provisions of Pillars 2 and 3 of the TEU.

Regulations

Regulations are the only Community acts which are directly applicable and may produce both vertical and horizontal direct effect. The vertical direct effect of EC regulations was recognised in Case 93/71 *Leonesio v Italian Ministry of Agriculture*.[56] In this case, under the EC regulation relating to a scheme to reduce dairy herds and over-production of dairy products, payments to farmers who slaughtered their dairy cows should have been made within two months. The Italian government delayed implementation of the scheme until the introduction of necessary budgetary provisions as part of the cost was paid by national authorities. Leonesio slaughtered her dairy cows and did not receive payment within the two-month period. Leonesio brought an action before a national court against the Italian Ministry of Agriculture for payments.

Under art 177 proceedings the ECJ held that:

> 'Regulations were of direct effect, creating a right in the applicant Leonesio to a payment which could not be conditional or altered by national authorities, and which was immediately enforceable in the national courts.'

Case 43/71 *Politi SAS v Ministry of Finance of the Italian Republic*[57] is the leading case concerning horizontal direct effect. Here the Politi organisation imported meat, and under Italian Law, no 330 of 15 June 1950, they were required to pay a duty at 0.5 per cent of the consignment value and a statistical levy which was imposed under art 42 of the Decree of the Italian President, no 1339 of 21 December 1961 and no 723 of 26 June 1965. Politi considered the statistical levy should not have been imposed and sought judicial review before the court of the President of the Tribunale di Torino on the grounds that under art 14(1) EC and EC Regulation 20/62 of 4 April 1962 'charging of any customs duty or charge having equivalent effect' on imports from Member States was incompatible with the intra-Community levy system. Further, art 18(1) provided that all levies equivalent to customs duties or charges having equivalent effect on imports from third countries should be abolished. The Italian court sought advice from the ECJ under art 177 to determine whether

---

[52] Case 28/67 *Firma Molkerei Zentrale* [1968] ECR 143.
[53] Case 6/64 *Costa v ENEL* [1964] ECR 585.
[54] Case 9/73 *Schlüter* [1973] ECR 1161.
[55] Case 126/86 *Gimenez Zaera* [1987] ECR 3697; Cases C–72 and 73/91 *Firma Sloman Neptun* [1993] ECR I–887.
[56] [1972] ECR 287.
[57] [1973] ECR II–1039.

Regulation 20/62, which was by then replaced by Regulation 121/67, conferred individual rights which the national courts must protect.

The ECJ held that charges having equivalent effect to customs duties are prohibited under art 9 EC. As a result Regulation 20/62 was unlawful and individuals were permitted to challenge it before national courts.

Directives – the recognition of vertical direct effect of EC directives by the ECJ

There are three main arguments invoked against direct effect of EC directives. First, art 189 EC provides that only EC regulations are directly applicable. *A contrario*, EC directives are neither directly applicable nor directly effective. Second, EC directives have no general application. They are addressed only to the Member States and leave to them the form, methods and procedures necessary to attain the objectives pursued by an EC directive. Therefore, EC directives cannot create rights for individuals since the latter are not addressees of EC directives and individual rights can only by conferred by national measures implementing EC directives. Finally, the difference between EC regulations and EC directives disappear if the latter produce direct effect. This equality between them from a legal point of view would be incompatible with the EC Treaty when its provisions expressly provide that only EC directives are appropriate to harmonise specific areas of Community law.

The ECJ answered those arguments by emphasising the necessity to confer direct effect to EC directives. First, the binding force of EC directives is incompatible with the refusal to confer them direct effect. Individuals should invoke them in appropriate circumstances. Second, the principle of *effet utile*, which has been applied by the ECJ in order to promote effective enforcement of Community law within the legal systems of the Member States,[58] requires the recognition of the direct effect of EC directives which entails their application by national courts. The third argument is inferred from art 177 EC which provides a procedure for national courts to consult the ECJ on interpretation and validity of EC law, without any distinction among various legislative acts adopted by EC institutions. The ECJ considered that art 177 EC implies that EC directives can also be invoked by individuals in proceedings before national courts. As a result, EC directives should be directly effective.

The ECJ first invoked the possibility that EC directives may produce direct effect in Case 9/70 *Franz Grad* v *Finanzampt Traustein*.[59] In this case the question concerned direct effect of a Council decision, and the ECJ stated that other measures mentioned in art 189 EC may produce direct effect, *inter alia*, EC directives. In Case 33/70 *SACE*[60] the ECJ was asked to give its ruling on the combined effect of directly effective provisions of EC Treaty and EC directives implementing them. The first decision of the ECJ in which direct the effect of an EC directive was expressly recognised was Case 41/74 *Van Duyn*.[61]

Miss Van Duyn, a Dutch national, arrived at Gatwick Airport on 9 May 1973. She intended to work as a secretary at the British headquarters of the Church of Scientology of

---

[58] See R Ward, 'National Sanctions in EC law: a Moving Boundary in the Division of Competence' [1995] 1 ELR p205.

[59] [1970] ECR 825.

[60] [1970] ECR 1213.

[61] [1974] ECR 1337.

California. British immigration authorities refused her leave to enter on the grounds of public policy. Although it was not unlawful to work for the Church of Scientology, the government of the United Kingdom warned foreigners that the effect of the Church's activities were harmful to the mental health of those involved. Miss Van Duyn challenged the decision of immigration authorities on two grounds: the basis of art 48 EC which grants workers the rights to free movement between Member States, subject to its para 3 which imposes limitations on grounds of public policy, public security or public health; and on the basis of art 3(1) of Directive 64/221 which further implements art 48(3) EC and which provides that measures taken by Member States regarding public policy must be 'based exclusively on the personal conduct of the individual concerned'. She claimed that art 3(1) of Directive 64/221 was directly effective and that her refusal to enter the UK was not based on her conduct but on the general policy of the British government towards the Church of Scientology.

For the first time an English court referred to the ECJ under art 177 EC. The High Court asked whether both art 48 EC and the Directive were directly effective. The ECJ held that they both produced direct effect. In particular, the ECJ held that 'given the nature, general scheme and wording [of art 3(1) of Directive 64/221] its effectiveness would be greater if individuals were entitled to invoke it in national courts'. Therefore, based of the principle of *effet utile* the ECJ decided that art 3(1) of Directive 64/221 was directly effective.

The case law of the ECJ regarding EC directives has further elucidated the concept of direct effect. Three main tendencies have appeared. The general principle is that EC directives should be correctly implemented into national law which means that individuals could rely on their provisions before national courts through the national implementing measures.[62] As a result, there should be no need to verify whether a provision of an EC directive satisfies the three criteria for direct effect, that is, it must be clear and precise, unconditional and self-executing. In this way, an individual may secure rights conferred by EC directives in the manner envisaged by art 189 EC. Therefore, the question of direct effect does not arise since the correct transposition of provisions of an EC directive means that they are part of national law. The question whether an EC directive has been correctly implemented into national law concerns in reality the conformity of national law with EC law and not the question of direct effect.[63] Thus, any provision of an EC directive transposed into national law may be invoked in any dispute (including a dispute between individuals) in order to verify whether national authorities have implemented it in accordance with requirements specified in the directive.[64] Furthermore, implementing measures may be called into question in the process of interpretation of national law in conformity with Community law. In this respect in Case 14/83 *Von Colson and Kamann* the ECJ held that national courts in applying national law, and especially its provisions implementing EC directives, have a duty to interpret national law in the light of the text and objectives of that directive in order to achieve the results envisaged in art 189(3) EC.[65]

In order to curtail non-implementation of EC directives by the Member States within a

---

[62] Case 270/81 *Felicitas* [1982] ECR 2771.
[63] Case 51/76 *Nederlandse Ondernemongen* [1977] ECR 113.
[64] Ibid at 127.
[65] [1984] ECR 1891; also Case 31/87 *Bentjes* [1988] ECR 4635.

specific time-limit, usually laid down in the measures themselves, the ECJ held in Case 148/78 *Publico Ministero* v *Ratti*[66] that provided the provisions of an EC directive are sufficiently precise and unconditional its non-implementation in the prescribed period results in their direct effect.

Ratti was selling solvents and varnishes. He fixed labels to certain dangerous substances in conformity with Directive 73/173 and Directive 77/128 but contrary to Italian legislation of 1963. He was prosecuted by Italian authorities for breach of Italian legislation. Directive 73/173 was not implemented in Italy, although the time-limit prescribed for its implementation elapsed on 8 December 1974. Also Directive 77/128 was not transposed into Italian law but the time-limit for its implementation had not yet expired. The Milan Court asked the ECJ under art 177 EC which set of rules should be applied, national law or Directives 73/173 and 77/128.

The ECJ held that if the provisions of an EC directive are sufficiently precise and unconditional, although not implemented within the prescribed period, an individual may rely upon them. However, if the time-limit for implementation into national law had not been reached at the relevant time, the obligation was not directly effective.

A logical corollary to *Ratti* is that a Member State which failed to transpose an EC directive within the prescribed time-limit cannot rely on an unimplemented directive in proceedings against individuals.[67]

Direct effect of an EC Directive becomes an issue only if the implementation measures adopted by a Member State are incompatible with its provisions,[68] or insufficient,[69] or as in *Ratti* when a Member State failed to implement a directive within the prescribed time-limit.

Finally, EC directives can only produce vertical direct effect. This solution has been confirmed many times by the ECJ despite contrary opinions of Advocates-General.[70] It has been expressly confirmed in Case C–91/92 *Faccini Dori* in the following terms:

> 'The effect of extending that case law [horizontal direct effect] to the sphere of relations between individuals would be to recognise a power in the Community to enact obligations for individuals with immediate effect, whereas it has competence to do so only where it is empowered to adopt regulations.'[71]

Indirect horizontal direct effect of EC directives

To refuse horizontal direct effect to EC directives means that if conditions for direct effect are satisfied by provisions of an EC directive, an individual cannot rely on them in proceedings brought against another individual. As a result, a individual cannot defend his rights because the other party involved is an individual.[72] This is obviously an unjust and unfair solution since, for example, if an individual is employed in public sector he may bring proceedings against his employer based on the direct effect of EC directive, but if he works

[66] [1979] ECR 1629.
[67] Case 80/86 *Kolpinghuis Nijmegen* [1987] ECR 3969.
[68] Case 38/77 *Enka* [1977] ECR 2203; Case 103/88 *Fratelli Constanzo* [1989] ECR 1839.
[69] Case 36/75 *Rutili* [1975] ECR 1219.
[70] Conclusions of Van Gerven in Case C–271/91 *Marshall* [1993] ECR I–4367 at 4381; Jacobs in Case C–316/93 *Vaneetveld* [1994] ECR I–763 at 765; Lenz in Case C– 91/92 *Faccini Dori* [1994] ECR I–3325.
[71] Ibid, para 24, confirmed in Case C–472/93 *Luigi Spano and Fiat Geotech* [1995] ECR I–4321.
[72] On this question see V Prechal, 'Remedies after *Marshall*' [1990] CMLR 451.

in the private sector he has no remedy against an employer in breach of an EC directive. In order to overcome the practical implications deriving from its refusal to confer horizontal direct effect on EC directives, the ECJ has developed two approaches: it has extended the meaning of a State or a body emanating from the State and has imposed a duty on national courts to interpret national law in conformity with Community law. The main reason why the ECJ opted for such complex legal devices, especially in the light of difficulties which raise the rejection of horizontal direct effect in practice,[73] is that many Member States have resisted the recognition of vertical direct effect of EC directives.[74] But, more importantly, the imposition of horizontal direct effect on EC directives by the ECJ risks causing more harm than good to European integration. Indeed, the ECJ is much criticised for its revolutionary approach toward the application and interpretation of Community law. Its use of the concept of *effet utile* provides a good example. In public international law the concept of *effet utile* is applied by an international judge when he is confronted with two possible interpretations of a legal provision, one which confers to it some meaning and other which devoids it of any significance. He gives priority to the former. The ECJ not only sets aside the interpretation which destitutes a provision of its *effet utile*, but more importantly rejects any interpretation which results in limitations or weakening of *effet utile* of that provision. In Case 9/70 *Franz Grad* the ECJ held that:

> 'it would be incompatible with the binding effect attributed to decisions by art 189 to exclude in principle the possibility that persons affected might invoke the obligation imposed by a decision'.[75]

Furthermore, the ECJ in interpreting Community law, takes into consideration the evolving nature of the Community and thus interprets Community law in the light of new needs which did not exist at the time of ratification of the founding Treaties. The development of the Common Commercial Policy provides the best illustration in this respect.[76] Also the ECJ has inferred from Community law concepts such as supremacy of Community law, direct applicability, direct effect, the existence of external competences based on parallel internal competence and 'acquis communautaire'. The Court is a guardian of unity and the very existence of the Communities. On the one hand, the ECJ, if possible, introduces concepts which are necessary for the survival of the Community as a special species of international law but, on the other hand, it is sometimes more diplomatic in its approach towards Member States. Instead of antagonising them the ECJ achieves its objectives by more subtle means. The indirect horizontal affect of EC directives is the best example in this respect.

However, before examining this question, one explanation seems necessary. It concerns the French Conseil d'Etat. Many English authors wrongly state that the French highest administrative jurisdiction has changed its attitude towards vertical direct effect of EC

---

[73] Case C–221/88 *Busseni* [1990] ECR I–495.

[74] See Traversa, 'La Jurisprudence Italienne concernant le Droit Européen' [1988] RMC 341; or in France where the Conseil d'Etat in the *Cohn-Bendit* decision of 22 December 1978 refused to recognise vertical direct effect to EC directives and still maintains its position; see D Simon, 'Le Conseil d'Etat, la Directive, la Loi, le Droit: ad augusta per angusta?' [1992] Europe (April) Chron 1.

[75] [1970] ECR 825.

[76] See Chapter 4.

directives.[77] This is not the case,[78] the French Conseil d'Etat has attenuated its position in the sense that:

1. an individual may invoke the provisions of EC directives in order to challenge national implementing measures;[79]
2. an individual may challenge national provisions contrary to EC directives including those national provisions which were enacted before the implementation of EC directives;[80]
3. an individual may invoke provisions of an EC directive, regardless of whether they are directly applicable or not, as a point of reference in interpretation of national law and especially national implementing measures;[81]
4. an individual may on the basis of EC directives seek compensation against administrative bodies which acted in breach of EC law;[82]
5. if an EC directive has been transposed into national law, an individual may invoke its provisions to demonstrate that national implementing measures are incompatible with that directive and thus challenge an administrative individual act based on the national implementing measures.[83]

However, an individual is not entitled to rely on directly effective provisions of an EC directive before administrative courts in France in order to challenge an individual decision based on that directive itself.[84]

Extension of the concept of a State On the basis of vertical direct effect of EC directives an individual has directly enforceable rights on which he may rely in an action against a Member State in proceedings before the national courts. The obvious question is what bodies are considered as belonging to the State. In general, the answer is rather simple. The dichotomy of public/private body is known in all Member States. Nevertheless, the ECJ in order to maximise the effect of EC directives has introduced an autonomous meaning of public body. First in Case 152/84 *Marshall* v *Southampton and South-West Hampshire Area Health Authority (Teaching) (No 1).*[85]

Miss Marshall, an employee of the AHA, was forced to retired at the age of 60 while for her male colleagues the retirement age was 65. She was dismissed at 62 at that ground. Miss Marshall who wished to remain in employment argued that the British Sex Discrimination

---

[77] For example J Tillotson, *European Community Law*, 2nd ed, London: Cavendish, 1996, p163.

[78] The principle was established in *Cohn-Bendit* [1979] Dalloz-Sirey 155; *Sovincast*, Judgment of 28 November 1980; *Association Fédérale régionale pour la protection de la nature*, Judgment of 16 February 1994 [1994] Europe (November) 6.

[79] *Confédération nationale des sociétés de protection des aimaux en France* [1984] AJDA 695, concl Jeanneney (in this case the provisions of EC directive were incorporated into national law via a act of general application which was annulled by the Conseil d'Etat as not conforming with the Directive).

[80] *Alitalia* [1990] AJDA 387.

[81] *Ministeur du budget* v *Cercle militaire de la caserne France* [1990] AJDA 328.

[82] *SA Rothmans International France et SA Philip Morris France, Soc Arizona Tobacco et SA Philip Morris France* [1992] AJDA 210, concl M Laroque.

[83] *Giuseppe Palazzi* [1991] AJDA 827.

[84] *Cohn-Bendit* [1979] CDE 265, obs G Isaac.

[85] [1986] ECR 723.

Act 1975, which excluded from its scope of application provision in relation to death and retirement, was contrary to Council Directive 76/207 on Equal Treatment. The UK adopted this Directive but had not amended the 1975 Act considering that discrimination in retirement ages was allowed. The Court of Appeal asked the ECJ under art 177 EC whether the dismissal of Miss Marshall was unlawful and whether she was entitled to rely upon Directive 76/207 in national courts.

The ECJ answered in the affirmative to both questions. It held that the AHA was a public body regardless of the capacity in which it was acting, that is a public authority or employer. It added that:

> 'The argument submitted by the United Kingdom that the possibility of relying on provisions of the directive against the respondent qua organ of the State would give rise to an arbitrary an unfair distinction between the rights of State employees and those of private employees does not justify any other conclusion. Such a distinction may easily be avoided if the Member State concerned has correctly implemented the directive into national law.'

Subsequently, the ECJ has elucidated the concept of a State and given to it a wide interpretation.[86] In Case C–188/89 *Foster and Others v British Gas plc*[87] the ECJ has provided a definition of a body which is an emanation of a State. It is a body

> 'whatever its legal form, which has been made responsible pursuant to a measure adopted by a public authority, for providing a public service under the control of that authority and had for that purpose special powers beyond those which resulted from the normal rules applicable in relations between individuals'.

It results from that definition that three criteria should be satisfied in order to consider an organisation as an emanation of the State. First, it must be made responsible for providing a public service; second, it must provide that service under the control of the State; and, third, it must have special powers to provide that service beyond those normally applicable in relations between individuals. This test has been applied by national courts, including, British courts, to determine whether an organisation can be considered an emanation of the State. In *Doughty v Rolls Royce*,[88] the Court of Appeal decided that although Rolls Royce was 100 per cent own by the State as the latter was its sole shareholder, and thus any services it provided was under control of the State, it did not fulfil the remaining criteria established in *Foster*. As a result, Doughty in a very similar situation to Miss Marshall could not invoke Directive 76/207 and was barred from commencing proceedings against Rolls Royce.

Interpretation of national law in conformity with Community law by national courts
National judges are required to interpret national law in conformity with Community law. This principle constitutes a logical consequence of the supremacy of EC law and applies in relation to all Community law[89] irrespective of whether or not a provision of Community law

---

[86] Case 222/84 *Jonhston v Chief Constable of the Royal Ulster Constabulary* [1986] ECR 1651. The latter was considered as an emanation of a State.
[87] [1990] ECR I–33/3.
[88] [1992] 1 CMLR 1045.
[89] In relation to a provision of the Treaty see Case 157/86 *Murphy* [1988] ECR 686.

is directly effective. National law, whether posterior or subsequent, must be conform to Community law. Furthermore, in Case 14/83 *Von Colsen and Kamann*[90] the ECJ emphasised that national judges are obliged to interpret national law in the light of the text and objectives of Community law and in this particular case it was an EC directive. This solution is based on two premises. First on arts 5 EC, 86 ECSC and 172 Euratom which impose upon the Member States a duty of loyal and active co-operation. Article 5 EC provides that the Member States must take all appropriate measures, whether general or particular, to fulfil their obligations arising out of the Treaty and resulting from measures adopted by EC institutions. They must facilitate accomplishment of the tasks of EC institutions. It means that the Member States must adopt implementing measures vis-à-vis the Treaties and acts of EC institutions. Second, in Case 30/70 *Scheer*[91] the ECJ held that under art 5 EC the Member States have a duty to do whatever possible to ensure *effet utile* of the provisions of Community law. According to the ECJ, art 5 EC applies to all national bodies, including national courts, which have a duty to ensure that national law conforms with Community law and thus the requirement of the principle of *effet utile* is satisfied, that is, rights vested on individuals by Community law are protected by national courts. This device is especially useful to ensure indirect horizontal effect to EC directives as the combined effect of art 189 EC, art 5 EC and the principle of *effet utile* secures adequate enforcement of any obligations imposed on individuals.

The possibility to require from national courts that they interpret national law in conformity with Community law was for the first time mentioned in Case 111/75 *Mazzalai*,[92] when the ECJ approved the conclusion of Advocate-General Darmon who emphasised the usefulness of EC directives as means of interpretation of national law. However, it was in two decisions of the ECJ rendered the same day, Case 14/83 *Von Colson and Kamann* (see above) and Case 79/83 *Harz*,[93] that provided a new solution to the problem of lessening the vertical/horizontal public/private dichotomy regarding EC directives.

Both Von Colson and Harz were females discriminated against on grounds of gender when applying for job. Von Colson was in public service as she applied for the post of prison social worker, and Harz was in the private sector when she applied to join a training programme with a commercial company. Under German law implementing Council Directive 76/207 they were entitled to receive only nominal damages that is, reimbursement of their travel expenses. They claimed that such implementation was contrary to art 6 of Directive 76/207 which provides that: 'Member States shall introduce into their national legal systems such measures as are necessary to enable all persons who consider themselves wronged by failure to apply to them the principle of equal treatment ... to pursue their claims by judicial process after possible recourse to other competent authorities'. Both applicants argued that they should be offered the post or receive substantial damages. The German labour court referred under art 177 to ECJ the following question: whether art 6 of Directive 76/207 was directly effective and whether under that Directive Member States were required to provide for particular sanctions or other legal consequences in cases of discrimination on grounds of sex against a person seeking employment.

---

[90] [1984] ECR 1891.
[91] [1970] ECR 1197.
[92] [1976] ECR 657, para 10.
[93] [1984] ECR 1921.

The ECJ avoided the question of direct effect of art 6 of Directive 76/207 and instead concentrated on the interpretation of national law in conformity with EC law. It held that national law must be interpreted in such a way as to achieve the result required by the Directive regardless of whether the defendant was the State or private party. It stated that sanctions for discrimination were left to national law and that, on the one hand, the employer is not obliged to offer a contract of employment to an applicant being discriminated against on the ground of gender but, on the other hand, decided that *effet utile* requires that

'if a Member State chooses to penalise breaches of ... prohibition by the award of compensation, then in order to ensure that it is effective and that it has a deterrent effect, that compensation must in any event be adequate in relation to the damage sustained and must therefore amount to more than purely nominal compensation such as, for example, the reimbursement only of the expenses incurred in connection with the application. It is for the national court to interpret and apply the legislation adopted for the implementation of the Directive in conformity with the requirements of Community law, in so far as it is given discretion to do so under national law.'

The German labour court found that it had power to award damages to both plaintiffs not exceeding six months gross salary.

In both cases the interpretation of national law in conformity with the Directive resulted in providing an efficient remedy to the applicants tantamount to conferring to art 6 of Directive 76/207 horizontal direct effect. The question arose whether the interpretation in conformity with Community law was restricted to national law implementing EC measures or extended to all law. The answer was provided by the ECJ in Case C–106/89 *Marleasing*.[94]

Under the Spanish Civil Code a company could be nullified on the grounds of 'lack of cause'. Marleasing claimed that the defendant company was established in order to defraud its creditors, that the founders' contract was a sham and, since the contract of association was void for 'lack of cause', he as one of the lenders could recover his debt personally from those behind the scheme. The defendants argued that under art 11 of the EC first Company Directive 68/151, which provided an exhaustive list of the grounds on which the nullity of a company may be declared, lack of cause was not mentioned. Directive 68/151 was not implemented in Spain although the prescribed time-limit for its implementation had elapsed. The Spanish court asked the ECJ under art 177 proceedings whether art 11 of Directive 68/151 was directly effective and whether it prevented a declaration of nullity on the grounds other than enumerated in that provision.

The ECJ confirmed that EC directives could not produce horizontal direct effect, thus the defendants could not rely on art 11 in proceedings against another individual. Also art 11 of Directive 68/151 exhaustively listed the grounds of nullity and did not include the grounds on which Marleasing relied. Nevertheless, the ECJ held that based on its judgment in *Von Colsen* a Spanish court was obliged 'so far as was possible' to interpret national law, whether it pre-dated or post-dated the Directive in the light of its its terms. It meant that a Spanish court had to interpret Spanish law in such a way as to disregard provisions of the Spanish Civil Code which pre-dated Directive 68/151.

Marleasing is a very controversial case. On the one hand, it states that the obligation to

---

[94] [1990] ECR I–4135.

interpret national law in conformity with EC law is demanded only 'as far as possible', and on the other hand it does not require a national judge to interpret a national provision in the light of the Directive. It simply strikes down a conflicting national provision which was never intended to implement this Directive.[95] The ECJ has, to a certain extent, elucidated the meaning of *Marleasing* in Case C–334/92 *Wagner Miret v Fondo de Garantia Salarial.*[96]

Wagner Miret was employed as a senior manager in a Spanish company that became insolvent. Under Directive 80/897 Member States were required to set up a fund compensating employees in the case of insolvency of their employer. Spain established such a fund but it did not apply to senior management staff. The ECJ held that Directive 80/897 was not precise enough to produce direct effect and that Spanish law clearly limited access to the fund. Spanish law could not be interpreted in such a way as to include senior management staff within a group of people to be compensated from that fund. As a result, the duty to interpret national law in conformity with Community law is not absolute so as to interpret national law *contra legem* but only 'so far as possible'. However, Wagner Miret was not left without remedy as he could bring proceedings against Spain for incorrect implementation of Directive 80/987 which caused him damage (the so-called *Francovich* remedy which will be discussed below in section 8.3).

It seems that the ECJ has limited the scope of *Marleasing*. National courts are under a duty to take into consideration all national law, whether adopted before or after the directive, concerning the matter in question in order to determine whether national legislation can be interpreted in the light of the wording and the purpose of the directive. The interpretation *contra legem* is required 'as far as possible'. The question arises as to the meaning of the formula 'as far as possible', that is the limit of national courts' obligation regarding the interpretation of national law in the light of the wording and the purpose of the directive in order to achieve the results prescribed in art 189 EC.

In this respect the ECJ established that the uniform interpretation of Community law must be qualified in criminal proceedings, where the effect of interpreting national legislation in the light of the directive would be to impose criminal liability in circumstances where such liability would not arise under the national legislation taken alone. In Case 80/86 *Kolpinguis Nijmegen*[97] the ECJ held that the obligation for a national judge to make reference to the terms of the directive, when he interprets relevant provisions of national law, is limited by general principle of Community law and especially by the principle of legal certainty and non-retroactivity.[98] This was further explained in Joined Cases C–74 and 129/95 *Criminal Proceedings against X* [99] in which an Italian judge within the preliminary ruling proceedings under art 177 EC asked the ECJ to interpret some provisions of Directive 90/270 on the minimum safety and health requirements for working with display screens. The Italian court did not exclude that the interpretation provided by the ECJ would have determined or aggravated liability of individuals in breach of that Directive, although Italian law which implemented its provisions did not provide for any penal sanctions. The ECJ held that:

---

[95] See also Case C–472/93 *Luigi Spano and Fiat SpA* and Case C–449/93 *Rockfon* [1995] ECR I–4291.

[96] [1993] ECR I–6911.

[97] [1987] ECR 3969.

[98] Ibid, paras 13 and 14.

[99] [1996] ECR I–6609.

'the obligation on the national court to refer to the content of the Directive when interpreting the relevant rules of its national law is not unlimited, particularly where such interpretation would have the effect, on the basis of the Directive and independently of legislation adopted for its interpretation, of determining or aggravating the liability in criminal law of persons who act in contravention of its provisions'.[100]

The ECJ explained that the principle of legality in relation to crime and punishment and especially the principle of legal certainty, its corollary, which precludes bringing criminal proceedings in respect of conduct not clearly defined as culpable by law. In support of its decision the ECJ referred to the general principles of law which result from the common constitutional tradition of the Member States and art 7 of European Convention of Human Rights.

The 'as far as possible' caveat, which attenuates the requirement of the principle of uniform interpretation, will certainly allow national courts to avoid *contra legem* interpretation of national law, but the circumstances in which this possibility may be invoked will have to be determined by the ECJ.

The Marleasing *principle in the United Kingdom* In *Webb* v *EMO Air Cargo (No 2)*,[101] the first British case after *Marleasing*, the House of Lords asked the ECJ under art 177 EC for some clarifications on the question of interpretation of national law in conformity with the ECJ and, especially, on its application to pre-dating national legislation.

Ms Webb was offered a temporary job to replace her colleague on the maternity leave. Before the commencement of her employment she discovered that she was pregnant and as a result dismissed. She argued that her dismissal was unlawful under Directive 76/207 which prohibits discrimination based on sex. The House of Lords called to interpret the Sex Discrimination Act 1975 which implemented Directive 76/207 asked the ECJ under art 177 EC proceedings whether Ms Webb's dismissal was contrary to Directive 76/207.

The ECJ held that Ms Webb's dismissal was in breach of Directive 76/207. As a result the House of Lords had to interpret the Sex Discrimination Act 1975 as required by Directive 76/207. To achieve this objective the House of Lords interpreted s5(3) of the Act, which provides that, in order to determine discrimination, a comparison between the treatment of women and men must be based on similar 'relevant circumstances', as meaning that 'relevant circumstances' meant in the case of Ms Webb's unavailability for work due to pregnancy and not as previously stated by the House of Lords as simply her unavailability to work. The House of Lords held that a male employee could not be dismissed on those grounds and thus Ms Webb's dismissal was discriminatory.

The House of Lords in *Webb* has clearly accepted the decision of the ECJ in *Marleasing*, that is, that national legislation pre-dating Community law must be interpreted in conformity with the latter.

Decisions

A decision adopted under art 198 EC addressed to a legal or natural person is directly effective both vertically and horizontally. It creates rights and obligations vis-à-vis its

---

[100] Ibid, para 24.
[101] [1995] 4 All ER 577.

addressee. A decision is directly effective and may be enforced by a Member State under art 192 EC. Also, a decision may confer rights on a third party which may be invoked in proceedings before a national court. For example, a decision adopted by the Commission vis-à-vis an undertaking in breach of competition law may be relied on by another undertaking, a victim of anti-competitive practice of the former.

The direct effect of a decision addressed to the Member States was a matter of controversy. Similar arguments as in the case of EC directives were advanced. The main difference between EC decisions and EC directives is that usually no implementation measures are required as the obligations imposed by EC decisions concern only a Member State, although it is not always the case. The ECJ has recognised that the combined effect of a Treaty provision, a directive and a decision may create rights for individuals enforceable before national courts as in Case 9/70 *Franz Grad v Finanzampt Traunstein*.[102]

Council Decision 65/271 of 13 May 1965 placed the German government under an obligation to introduce the common VAT system to road haulage and abolish specific taxes in existence and not to introduce new ones thereafter. A harmonising directive laid down the deadline for the implementation of the Decision. In addition, art 12 EC prohibits introduction of any new customs duties or charges having equivalent effect. In those circumstances, the German government levied a tax on the carriage of goods, in this case a consignment of preserved fruit from Hamburg to Austria. The plaintiffs, a haulage contractor, challenged the transport tax as contrary to Decision 65/271. The court, Finanzgericht Munchen, made reference under art 177 to the ECJ to determine whether the Decision produce direct effect.

The ECJ held that the Decision did have direct effect and thus conferred individual rights which must be protected in the national courts. The ECJ emphasised that '... it would be incompatible with the binding effect attributed to decisions by art 189 to exclude in principle the possibility that persons affected might invoke the obligation imposed by a decision'. The ECJ decided that the obligation in question was sufficiently clear and unconditional to produce direct effect.

The ECJ based its reasoning exclusively on *effet utile*. This approach has been confirmed in relation to a decision alone in Case C–156/91 *Hansa Fleisch*.[103] Also decisions adopted by a body created by an international treaty concluded between the Community and third countries may produce direct effect.[104] There are not many cases on direct effect of decisions.

Decisions can only produce vertical direct effect. The justification for the rejection of horizontal direct effect is the same as for EC directives although there is no case law in this respect.

International agreements concluded between the Community and third countries

The ECJ has the same approach towards international agreements concluded between the Community and third countries as monist countries. Thus, an individual may invoke

---

[102] [1970] ECR 825.

[103] [1992] ECR I–5567.

[104] For example, a decision adopted by the Association Council EEC–Turkey: Case C–192/89 *Sevince* [1990] ECR I–3461. See also Case C–237/91 *Kazim Kus* [1992] ECR I–6781; Case C–171/95 *Recep Tetik* [1997] ECR I–329.

provisions of an international agreement in proceedings before national courts provided they confer rights upon individuals and satisfy the criteria for direct effect, that is they are clear and precise, unconditional and self-executing. This principle was established in Cases 21–24/72 *International Fruit Company NV and Others v Produktschap voor Groenten en Fruit*.[105]

Here, the plaintiffs challenged import licensing regulations and quota-setting imposed upon importers as being contrary to art XI GATT. Under art 177 the ECJ was asked whether measures adopted by Community institutions are valid under international law in that Regulations 459/70, 565/70 and 686/70 are contrary to art XI GATT. The ECJ held that the provision of international law must be capable of conferring rights on individuals before they can be invoked. Article XI did not create rights for individuals. As a result, EC regulations cannot be affected by art XI GATT.

In Case 87/75 *Bresciani*[106] the ECJ has allowed individuals to rely on provisions of international agreements concluded between the Community and third countries. In Case 104/81 *Kaupferberg*[107] the ECJ held that neither the nature nor the economy of an international agreement can prevent an individual from relying on its provisions in proceedings before national courts. The best summary of the case law of ECJ in this respect is given in the conclusion of Advocate-General M Darmon in Case 12/86 *Demirel*.[108] He emphasised that a provision of an agreement concluded between the Community and third countries may be considered as producing direct effect when, in relations to its terms, object and nature, it contains a clear and precise obligation which is not subordinated in its implementation to the intervention of any subsequent act. It means that a provision of an international agreement, which may be drafted in identical terms as a provision of EC Treaty, which was recognised as capable of producing direct effect may not be regarded as directly effective since the object and nature of that agreement constitutes a *sine qua non* of direct applicability. The ECJ recognised direct effect of provisions in free trade,[109] co-operation[110] and association[111] agreements.

Finally, the form in which an international agreement was introduced into Community law, that is by a decision or a regulation adopted by the Council, is not taken into consideration by the ECJ in determining whether or not its provisions produce direct effect.

8.3 Supremacy of Community law

There is no mention of supremacy of Community law in the founding Treaties. The absence of any express provision is not, however, a gap in Community law but a result of diplomacy and caution. Indeed, an express provision would have confirmed the federal nature of the

---

[105] [1972] ECR 1219.
[106] [1976] ECR 129.
[107] [1982] ECR 3641.
[108] [1987] ECR 3719.
[109] Case 104/81 *Kaupferberg* [1982] ECR 3641.
[110] Case C–103/94 *Zoulika Krid* [1995] ECR I–719.
[111] Case 87/75 *Bresciani* [1976] ECR 136 (Yaoundé Convention); Case 17/81 *Pabst* [1982] ECR 1331 (association agreement between the EEC and Greece).

Community and thus prevented some Member States from acceding to the Communities. For that reason less controversial formulas were used such as art 189 EC, which recognised binding effect to measures adopted by EC institutions, or art 5 EC, which required that Member States abstain from taking measures which could jeopardise the attainment of objectives of the Treaty.

In practice, however, this question arose before national courts which referred to the ECJ for clarification under the procedure laid down in art 177 EC. Thus, it was the task of the ECJ to firmly establish the principal of supremacy of Community law as the *sine qua non* of the existence of the Community itself, and its peculiar nature in international legal order. In Case 6/64 *Costa* v *ENEL*[112] the ECJ recognised the primacy of Community law over national law of the Member States.

Costa was a shareholder of one of private undertakings nationalised by the Italian Government on 6 September 1962. Assets of private undertakings were transferred to ENEL. Costa, who was also a lawyer, refused to pay an electricity bill for £1 sent by ENEL and was sued by the latter. He argued, *inter alia*, that the nationalisation legislation was contrary to various provisions of EC Treaty. The Milanese Giudice Conciliatore referred this question the ECJ under art 177 EC. The Italian government claimed that the referral was 'absolutely inadmissible' since a national court which is obliged to apply national law cannot avail itself of art 177 EC. In the meantime the Italian Constitutional Council decided on 7 March 1964 in favour of national legislation.

The ECJ posed one of the most important principles of Community law: the supremacy of EC Law. The ECJ based its reasoning on three arguments:

1. Direct applicability and direct effect of Community law would be meaningless if a Member State were permitted by subsequent legislation to unilaterally nullify its effects by means of a legislative measure which could prevail over Community law. The Court held that:

   'The Treaty has created its own legal system which on the entry into force of the Treaty, became an integral part of the legal systems of the Member States and which their courts are bound to apply ... The integration into the laws of each Member States of provisions, which derive from the Community and more generally the terms and the spirit of the Treaty, make it impossible for the State, as a corollary, to accord precedence to a unilateral and subsequent measure over a legal system accepted by them on a basis of reciprocity.'

   Furthermore the ECJ stated that:

   'The precedence of Community law is confirmed by art 189, whereby a regulation "shall be binding" and "directly applicable in all Member States". This provision, which is subject to no reservation, would be quite meaningless if a State unilaterally nullifies its effects by means of a legislative measure which could prevail over Community law.'

2. By transferring certain competences to the Community institutions the Member States have limited their sovereignty. The ECJ held that:

---

[112] [1964] ECR 585.

'By creating the Community of unlimited duration ... and more particularly real powers stemming from a limitation of sovereignty or a transfer of powers from the States to the Community, the Member States have limited their sovereign rights, albeit within limited fields, and have thus created a body of law which binds both their nationals and themselves.'

3. Uniformity of application of Community law which ensures homogeneity of the Community legal order. In this respect the ECJ held that:

'The executive force of Community law cannot vary from one State to another in deference to subsequent domestic laws, without jeopardising the attainment of the objectives of the Treaty set out in art 5(2) and giving rise to the discrimination prohibited by art 7.'

The ECJ has summarised its reasoning in the following terms:

'... the law stemming from the Treaty, an independent source of law, could not, because of its special and original nature, be overridden by domestic legal provisions, however framed, without being deprived of its character as Community law and without the legal basis of the Community itself being called into question'.

This statement constitutes the essence of supremacy of Community law. The position of the ECJ has not changed since its decision in *Costa*. If anything, the ECJ has become more radical in confirming obvious implications of supremacy of Community law vis-à-vis the Member States. Indeed, whatever the reaction of the Member States and no matter how long it takes to gain full recognition of this principle by the Member States, for the Community supremacy is a necessary requirement of its existence. In order to achieve the objectives of the founding Treaties, to uniformly apply EC law throughout the Community,[113] to ensure the proper functioning of the internal market, and to become a fully integrated structure, the supremacy of Community law must be respected by the Member States. Otherwise, the Community will cease to exist.[114]

Supremacy of Community law is based on the fact that contrary to ordinary international treaties the founding Treaties have created their own legal system. It primacy results from the peculiar nature of the Community and not from concessions made by constitutional laws of the Member States. For that reason, primacy of Community law does not depend on which theory each Member State applies in order to determine the relationship between national and international law and which, in addition, varies from one Member State to another.

The supremacy of Community law is unconditional and absolute – all Community law prevails over all national law. It means that all sources of Community law, the provisions of the Treaties, and secondary legislation – regulations,[115] directives,[116] decisions,[117] general principles of Community law,[118] international agreements concluded between the

---

[113] In Cases C–143/88 and 92/89 *Zuckerfabrik Suderdithmarschen* the ECJ held that uniformity of application of EC law constitutes a fundamental requirement of the Community legal order: [1991] ECR I–415 at para 26.

[114] As the ECJ explained in Case 14/68 *Walt Wilhelm* [1969] ECR 15.

[115] Case 43/71 *Politi* [1971] ECR II–1039; Case 84/71 *Marimex* [1972] ECR 89.

[116] Case 158/80 *Rewe* [1981] ECR 1805; Case 8/81 *Becker* [1982] ECR 53.

[117] Case 130/78 *Salumificio de Cornuda* [1979] ECR 867.

[118] Case 5/88 *Wachauf* [1989] ECR 2609.

Community and third countries[119] – irrespective whether or not they are directly effective, prevail over all national law. Also Community law is superior to all provisions of national law: legislation, administrative, jurisdictional and constitutional. In relation to constitutional laws of the Member States in Case 9/65 *San Michele*[120] the ECJ confirmed that a provision of national constitutional law cannot be invoked in order to nullify the application of Community law since it was contrary to the Community public order.

In Case 11/70 *International Handelsgesellschaft*[121] the ECJ held that Community law prevails over national constitutional law, including fundamental human rights enshrined in the constitution of a Member State. In this case EC regulations set up a system of export licences guaranteed by a deposit for certain agricultural products and required that during the validity of a licence products were exported or otherwise a forfeited deposit would be lost. The plaintiffs lost a deposit of DM 17,000 and argued that the system introduced by EC regulations, which was run by the West Germany National Cereals Intervention Agency, was in breach of the fundamental human rights provisions contained in the German Constitution and especially the principle of proportionality as it imposed obligations, that is the forfeited deposit, which were not necessary to achieve the objectives pursued by EC regulations, that is the regulation of the cereals market. The Frankfurt Administrative Court referred to the ECJ under art 177 EC to determine the validity of one of the two regulations in question.

The ECJ confirmed the supremacy of Community law over national constitutional law in the following terms:

'... the law stemming from the Treaty, an independent source of law, cannot because of its very nature be overridden by rules of national law, however framed, without being deprived of its character as Community law and without the legal basis of the Community itself being called in question. Therefore, the validity of a Community measure or its effect within a Member State cannot be affected by allegations that it runs counter to either fundamental rights as formulated by the constitution of that State or the principles of a national constitutional structure'.

Nevertheless, the ECJ held that fundamental human rights, taking into account their importance, cannot be disregarded by the Community. The protection of fundamental human rights forms an integral part of the general principles of EC law and the protection of such rights must be ensured within the framework of the structure and objectives of the EC. In this case, the ECJ declared the regulation in question as valid and the system of deposit as appropriate methods of attaining the objectives of arts 40(3) EC and 43 EC concerning the common organisation of the agricultural markets.

The conflict between national law enacted prior to the entry into force of the Treaties is resolved in favour of Community law. All pre-dating national law is deemed to be abrogated or at least devoid of its legal effect inasmuch as it is contrary to Community law. This has been confirmed in the case examined above. Similarly, in a conflict between Community law and national law post-dating the entry into force of the Treaties the former prevails. One of the most important cases in this respect is Case 106/77 *Amministrazione delle Finanze* v

---

[119] Case 38/75 *Nederlandse Spoowegen* [1975] ECR 1439; Cases 267–269/81 *SPI and SAMI* [1983] ECR 801.
[120] [1965] ECR 35. The decision was rendered in relation to ECSC.
[121] [1970] ECR 1125.

Simmenthal[122] in which the ECJ defined the task of national judges faced with conflicting provisions of national law and Community law.

Simmenthal imported a consignment of beef from France to Italy. He was asked to pay for veterinary and public health inspections carried out at the frontier. He paid but sued for reimbursement of the money in the Italian court, arguing that the fees were contrary to Community law. After reference to the ECJ, which held that the inspections were contrary to art 30 EC as being measures having equivalent effect to quantitative restrictions and consequently charges were unlawful under art 12 EC being charges equivalent to customs duties, the Italian court ordered the Italian ministry to repay the fees. The ministry refused to pay, claiming that the national statute of 1970 under which Simmenthal was liable to pay fees still prevented any reimbursement and could only be set aside by an Italian constitutional court. The question was referred once again to the ECJ under art 177 EC.

The ECJ confirmed that in the event of incompatibility of a subsequent legislative measure of the Member State with Community law every national judge must apply Community law in its entirety and must set aside any provision of national law, prior or subsequent, in conflict with Community law. The ECJ held that:

> 'any provision of a national legal system and any legislative, administrative, or judicial practice which might impair the effectiveness of Community law by withholding from the national court having jurisdiction to apply such law the power to do everything necessary at the moment of its application to set aside national legislative provisions which might prevent Community rules from having full force and effect are incompatible with those requirements which are the very essence of the Community law'.

As a result, national courts should not request or await the prior setting aside of an incompatible national provision by legislation or other constitutional means but of its own motion, if necessary, refuse the application of conflicting national law and instead apply Community law.

The obligation to give full effectiveness to Community law, and thus to protect rights which the latter confers upon individuals, empowers a national judge to suspend, as an interim measure, the application of a national law which he suspects is in conflict with Community law,[123] although it might be contrary to national law to do so.

As a result, based on the supremacy of Community law, national judges are able to resolve any difficulties with they may encounter while facing a conflict between national law and Community law. Similarly, administrative authorities are required to set aside any national provision incompatible with Community law.[124] In relation to sanctions, especially of a penal nature, ordered by virtue of national law incompatible with Community law, those sanctions are considered as devoid of legal basis.[125]

---

[122] [1978] ECR 381.
[123] Case C–213/89 *R* v *Secretary of State for Transport, ex parte Factortame (No 2)* [1990] ECR I–2433; see the principle of supremacy in the United Kingdom.
[124] Case 103/88 *Fratelli Costanzo* [1989] ECR 1861.
[125] Case 88/77 *Schonenberg* [1978] ECR 473; Case 269/80 *Regina and Robert Tymen* [1981] ECR 3079.

Practical implications of supremacy of Community law

EC institutions are not empowered to apply the principle of supremacy in the Member States. They cannot invalidate a national measure incompatible with Community law. Only under art 169 EC, which will be examined in Chapter 9, may the Commission commence proceedings against a Member State in breach of EC law. For that reason national authorities, and especially national courts, are required to ensure effectiveness of Community law, to protect rights conferred by the latter upon individuals, and to supervise the proper application of the principle of supremacy. The ECJ has gradually developed and imposed upon national courts substantive and procedural rules applicable to Community issues which on the one hand limit the autonomy of national law but on the other hand are necessary to the proper functioning of the Community. From the principal of supremacy of Community law and the case law of the ECJ national judges have inferred important practical consequences.

Interpretation of national law in conformity with Community law

This consequence deriving from the principle of supremacy of Community law has been examined in relation to indirect horizontal effect of EC directives. Indeed, the supremacy of Community law requires that if there is any doubt as to the meaning of a provision of national law, this provision should be interpreted in the light of Community law. This principle is very useful, especially in relation to national implementing measures. Often national law is not in conflict with Community law but has a gap which using an interpretation based on Community law may be filled by a national court. The interpretation of national law in conformity with EC law is, however, limited in scope, that is, in the event of patent incompatibility of national law with Community law, no interpretation is possible.

Tortious liability of a Member State in breach of Community law

The principle that a Member State should be liable in damages to individuals who have suffered loss as a result of its infringement of Community law is today one of the cornerstones of Community law. Its origin can be found in Case 69/75 *Russo v Aima*[126] in which the ECJ held that a Member State should compensate for damage caused by its own breach of Community law but refer to national law to lay down the necessary conditions applicable to tortious liability.

There are many justifications for the introduction of this principle into Community law. The less obvious and not mentioned in Joined Cases C–6 and 9/90 *Francovich v Italian State* and *Bonifaci v Italian State*,[127] which established Member States' liability in tort, is that many Member States in the late 1980s delayed the implementation of EC directives which were mainly used to complete the internal market. There was no effective remedy since, as previously examined, penalties against defaulting Member States were introduced in the amended art 171 EC by the TEU. The best way to ensure implementation of an EC directive was to allow individuals to enforce their rights before national courts, that is to permit them to sue a defaulting Member State for loss that they have suffered, especially in cases where

---

[126] [1976] ECR 45.
[127] [1991] ECR I–5357.

the EC directives were not directly effective or when individuals had no remedy based on indirect horizontal effect. This was the case in *Francovich*.

As a result of the bankruptcy of his employer Francovich lost 6 million lira. He sued his former employer but could not enforce the judgment against him (the latter was insolvent). He decided to commence proceedings against the Italian State for sums due under Council Directive 80/987, which was not implemented in Italy, although the prescribed time-limit had already elapsed, or for compensation in lieu. Directive 80/987 on protection of employees in the event of the insolvency of their employers, required that the Member State set up a scheme under which employees of insolvent companies would receive at least some of their outstanding wages.[128] In Case 22/87 *Commission v Italy*[129] the ECJ under art 169 EC had held Italy in breach of EC law for non-implementation of Directive 80/987. The Italian court made reference to the ECJ under art 177 to determine whether the provision of the Directive in relation to payment of wages was directly effective and whether the Italian State was liable for damages arising from its failure to implement the Directive. The ECJ held that the provision in question was not sufficiently clear to be directly effective but made a following statement in relation to the second question: 'It is a general principle inherent in the scheme of the Treaty [that] a Member State is liable to make good damage to individuals caused by a breach of Community law for which it is responsible.' The ECJ justified the new principle on the basis of supremacy of Community law, *effet utile*, and art 5 EC which requires Member States to take all appropriate measures to ensure the fulfilment of their obligations arising out of the Treaty.

In *Francovich* the ECJ, in upholding a claim against the Italian Government for non-implementation of a directive, held that a Member State may be liable for losses that could be directly attributed to its failure to implement a directive provided that the date for such implementation has expired; that the provisions of that directive are unconditional and sufficiently precise as to confer rights upon individuals; and the action is brought against the State. This judgment firmly accepts that a plaintiff may rely upon the vertical effect of a directives and rejects reliance upon its horizontal effect to the dismay of some who consider that 'the distinction between public and private [law] is unjustified'.[130]

In this case the ECJ has established three conditions necessary to give rise to liability in the case of total failure of a Member State to implement a directive:

1. the result required by the directive must include the conferring of rights for the benefit of individuals;
2. the content of those rights must be clearly identifiable by reference to the directive; and
3. there must be a causal link between the breach of the State's obligation and the damage suffered by the individual.

Under Community law it has been established that any provision is unconditional where neither a Member State nor a Community institution is required to take any measures in its

---

[128] Council Directive 80/987 was implemented in the United Kingdom in the Employment Protection (Consolidation) Act 1978 as amended. It set up the Redundancy Fund which provides payments for employees of insolvent companies.

[129] [1989] ECR 143.

[130] Lord Slynn of Hadley, 'A Judgement on the European Court' (1993) 30 International Corporate Law 32.

implementation or effects.[131] To be sufficiently precise in the above context requires that the terms relied upon by the plaintiff define with sufficient clarity as to enable a national court to decide the identity of the persons entitled to the benefit from that right and to ascertain whether the plaintiff is such a beneficiary, the extent and content of that right and the identity of the legal body charged with providing that right.[132]

There is academic opinion that the principle of strict liability applies especially in regard to cases of persistent non-implementation of EC directives by a Member State.[133] This opinion is firmly rejected by the ECJ which has re-confirmed *Francovich*[134] and held that liability would depend on the nature of the breach in question.[135] This may be demonstrated by considering the following joined cases:

1. Case C–46/93 *Brasserie du Pêcheur v Germany*

   Brasserie, a French brewer, was forced to cease exports to Germany as its beer did not comply with the purity standards imposed by the Biersteuergesets.[136] In Case 178/84 *Commission v Germany*[137] the ECJ had already ruled that such a ban was incompatible with art 30 EC. Germany's omission in not repealing such domestic legislation was, therefore, a sufficiently serious breach.

2. Case C–48/93 *R v Secretary of State for Transport, ex parte Factortame*

   The United Kingdom government enacted the Merchant Shipping Act 1988 which made the registration of fishing vessels dependent upon conditions as to the nationality, residence and domicile of their owners. Factortame, being a Spanish owned company was deprived of its right to fish. In Case C–221/89 *Factortame (No 3)*[138] the ECJ held such regulations as being contrary to EC law. This was confirmed in Case C–246/89 *Commission v United Kingdom.*[139] The United Kingdom's action was clearly such a sufficiently serious breach.

However, it became apparent to Member States that some considerable disparity existed between the burden of proof required to substantiate a breach of duty by a Community institutions in actions under art 215 EC and that applicable against a Member State as developed by case law. Further, there was a huge disparity between an award of damages for non-implementation and the applicable sanctions against Community institutions under art 215 EC. As a result the ECJ modified their position on the ground that:

> 'the conditions under which the State may incur liability for damage caused to individuals cannot, in the absence of particular justification, differ from those governing the liability of the Community in like circumstances. The protection of the rights of individuals derive from Community law cannot vary on whether a national authority or a Community institute is

---

[131] Case 28/67 *Molkerei-Zentrale Westfalen/Lippe GmbH v Hauptzollamt Paderborn* [1968] ECR 143.

[132] Case C–6/90 *Francovich*, ibid.

[133] J Convery, 'State Liability in the United Kingdom after *Brasserie du Pêcheur*' (1997) 34 CMLR 603–634

[134] Case 6/90 *Francovich*, ibid, para 38.

[135] Joined Cases C–46 and C–48/93 *Brasserie du Pêcheur v Germany*; *R v Secretary of State for Transport, ex parte Factortame* [1996] ECR I–1029.

[136] Law on Beer Duty, BGBl.I p144.

[137] [1987] ECR 1227.

[138] [1991] ECR I–3905.

[139] [1991] ECR I–4585.

Community law cannot vary on whether a national authority or a Community institute is responsible for the damage'.[140]

and confirmed the criteria laid down in *Francovich*. In the same case the ECJ further stated that 'reparation for loss or damage cannot be made conditional upon fault (whether intentional or negligent) going beyond that of a sufficiently serious breach of Community law'.[141]

The obvious question as to what is to be considered as a sufficiently serious breach was referred by the High Court to the ECJ for a preliminary ruling under art 177 EC; it was held that 'where a Member State was not called upon to make any legislative choices and possessed only considerably reduced, or even no discretion, the mere infringement of Community law may be sufficient to establish a sufficiently serious breach'.[142] This approach was confirmed in Case 392/93 *R v HM Treasury, ex parte British Telecom plc*[143] which concerned the failure to properly implement art 8(1) of Directive 90/531. In this case the ECJ found that the Member State concerned had a wide discretion of power in the field in which it was acting; that the wording of the provisions of the original Directive was imprecise and as a result was capable of being interpreted in the manner implemented; that implementation had been carried out after taking legal advice as to the Directive's meaning; and that there was no ECJ case law on the subject nor any objection from the Commission as to the interpretation applied. In the light of the above there was not a sufficiently serious breach of Community law. Conversely in the Case C–5/94 *R v Ministry of Agriculture, Fisheries and Food, ex parte Hedley Lomas*[144] a case which concerned the United Kingdom authorities' refusal to grant an export licence in breach of a directive, the ECJ stated that 'where the Member State was not called upon to make any legislative choices and possessed only considerably reduced, or even no discretion, the mere infringement of Community law may be sufficient to establish a sufficiently serious breach'. The apparent disparity between the original criteria laid down in *Francovich* and those adopted above have been explained by the ECJ as being 'in substance ... the same since the condition that there should be a sufficiently serious breach, although not expressed in *Francovich*, was never the less evident from the circumstances of the case'.[145]

It is submitted that the actual test for liability may be expressed as follows:

1. a State becomes liable if it has enacted (as per *Factortame*) or retained (as per *Brasserie*) practices contrary to Community law; and
2. where the State has a wide discretion in the exercise of legislative power in the manner of implementation of the directive then it must have 'manifestly and gravely' disregarded the limits on its discretion (*British Telecom*); or
3. where the State has little or no legislative choice as to implementation then only a mere infringement is necessary (*Hedley Lomas*).

---

[140] Case C–46/93 *Brasserie du Pêcheur v Germany*, ibid, para 51.
[141] Ibid, para 80.
[142] Case C–5/94 *R v Minister of Agriculture, Fisheries and Food, ex parte Hedley Lomas (Ireland) Ltd* [1996] ECR I–2553.
[143] [1996] ECR I–1631.
[144] [1996] ECR I–2553.
[145] Case C–178/94 *Dillenkofer v Germany* [1996] 3 CMLR 469

It also results from the case law of the ECJ that the conditions of a State's liability apply to all breaches of Community law, whether legislative, executive or administrative. Second, a State is liable regardless of the organ of State whose act or omission infringed Community law. Also, it is irrelevant whether the provision in question is directly effective or not. Whichever is breached, a Member State may be liable. The ECJ emphasised that direct effect constitutes a minimum guarantee and thus *Francovich* liability is a necessary corollary of the *effet utile* of Community law.

The ECJ has placed the onus upon national courts to uphold such rights under national rules for public tortious liability,[146] by imposing upon them the duty to 'verify whether or not the conditions governing state liability for a breach of Community law are fulfilled'.[147] National courts are charged with ensuring that the protection of Community law rights is given equal status and may not be less favourable than the protection afforded to similar rights arising under domestic law.[148] National courts may not impose any procedure that makes it more difficult, or even impossible, for an individual to rely upon those rights.[149] As has been amply demonstrated in the United Kingdom this may involve setting aside or modifying domestic legislation.[150]

The principle of supremacy of Community law in the Member States

Two of the original Member States (Italy and Germany) had difficulties in accepting the principle of supremacy of Community law as such, and most of them to recognise it in the light of their constitutions. This principle was not expressly mentioned in the founding Treaties but the necessity to ensure uniform application of EC law in all Member States, as well as the requirements of the evolving Community, resulted in its slow recognition although for reasons other than those stated by the ECJ in *Costa*. It seems that only the two original Member States, that is Belgium and Luxembourg, accepted the reasoning of the ECJ and recognised the supremacy of Community law based on a peculiar nature of the Community legal order.[151]

Italy

Italy, after the decision of the ECJ in *Costa v ENEL,* which called in question a previous judgment rendered by the Italian Constitutional Court in the same case (the latter decided that subsequent legislation may be contrary to Community law) abandoned its position in the *Frontini* case (see section 8.1 above). Nevertheless, the Constitutional Court held that every Italian judge faced with a question of incompatibility of subsequent Italian legislation

---

[146] Case 45/76 *Comet BV* v *Produktschap voor Siergewassen* [1976] ECR 2043, para 43.

[147] Case 392/93 *R* v *HM Treasury, ex parte British Telecom plc* [1996] ECR I–1631.

[148] Case 158/80 *Rewe-Handelsgesellschaft Nord mbH* v *Hauptzollamt Keil* [1981] ECR 1805.

[149] Case 811/79 *Amministrzione della Stato* v *Arieta SpA* [1980] ECR 2545.

[150] Case 213/89 *R* v *Secretary of State for Transport, ex parte Factortame (No 2)* [1991] ECR I–2433.

[151] The Cour de Cassation of Belgium in the decision of 27 May 1971, *SA Fromagerie Franco-Suisse Le Ski* [1971] CDE 561, note Pescatore; V K Lenaerts , 'The Application of Community Law in Belgium' [1986] CMLR 253; and the Supreme Court of Justice of Luxembourg in its decision rendered on 14 July 1954 although Luxembourg is a dualist country: M Thill, 'La primaute et l'effet direct du droit communautaire dans la jurisdrudence luxembourgeoise' [1990] RFDA 978.

with Community law was not empowered to suspend or disregard national law but to refer that question to the Constitutional Court. The Decision of the ECJ in *Simmenthal* was finally approved by the Constitutional court on 8 June 1984 in the *Granital* case and since then has been confirmed many times.[152] However, the Italian Constitutional Court refuses to accept the supremacy of Community law vis-à-vis fundamental rights enshrined in the Italian Constitution.[153]

France

Even France, a monist country, was reluctant to recognise the principle of supremacy of Community law in relation to subsequent national legislation. The reason was based on judicial practice, the so-called 'Matter' doctrine,[154] which prohibited national courts from disregarding a national provision which was in conflict with a provision of an international treaty if the incompatibility was patent and impossible to resolve by means of interpretation. However, this theory was rejected by the Cour de Cassation (highest judicial court in France) in its decision rendered on 24 May 1973 in *Société des Cafes Jacques Vabre*.[155] The Conseil d'Etat (highest administrative court in France) recognised the supremacy of the Community Treaty over subsequent national legislation in its decision rendered on 20 October 1989 in *Nicolo*.[156] The French Constitutional Court has a different position than constitutional courts in Italy or Germany. It has limited jurisdiction *ratione materiae*; it is empowered to control the constitutionality of legislation before its entry into force and also international treaties before they enter into effect. On the other hand, neither national courts nor individuals may appeal to the Constitutional Court but only certain expressly determinated entities. In this context, it seems that in general the French Constitutional Court has been in favour of the supremacy of Community law.

The French Constitution itself, in art 55, provides that international treaties prevail over national law. The French Cour de Cassation in Vabre justified the supremacy of Community law on art 55 of the French Constitution.

Germany

The recognition of the supremacy of Community law over fundamental human rights as embodied in the German Constitution was the main challenge for the German Constitutional Tribunal. In its decision of 29 May 1974 (So lange I) the Constitutional Tribunal held that as long as the Community had no codified list of fundamental human rights, those rights as enshrined in the German Constitution would override Community law. However, in the decision of 22 October 1986 (So lange II)[157] the Tribunal considered that the case law of the ECJ demonstrated that Community law ensured efficient protection

---

[152] L Daniele, 'Après l'arrêt *Granital*: droit communautaire et droit national dans la jurisprudence récente de la Cour constitutionnelle italienne' [1992] CDE 3.

[153] On the decisions of constitutional courts in the Member States see *Les constitutions à l'epreuve de l'Europe*, Paris: La Documentation française, 1993.

[154] Matter was Advocate-General at the French Cour de Cassation.

[155] [1975] Dalloz-Sirey 497, concl Touffait.

[156] [1989] ECR 190, concl Frydman; D Somon, 'Le juge administrative et le juge européen', in *Le juge administrative à l'aube du XXIe siècle*, Grenoble: PUG, 1995, p369.

[157] M Hilf, 'So lange II: wie lange noch Solange?' [1987] EuGRZ 1.

of fundamental human rights equal to the protection offered by the German Constitution. As a result, the Tribunal would declared as inadmissible any application relating to incompatibility of Community law with German law.

The United Kingdom

In principle, there should be no difficulties with the recognition of supremacy of Community law in the United Kingdom since when a State accedes to the Communities it must accept the 'acquis communautaire'. At the time of accession of the United Kingdom, the principle of supremacy was already well rooted in Community law. Furthermore, s2(4) of the European Communities Act 1972 provides that 'any enactment passed or to be passed … shall be construed and have effect subject to the foregoing provisions of this section'. As a result, all legislative acts enacted subsequent to the European Communities Act 1972 are subject to Community law, and thus any conflict between Community law and national subsequent legislation should be resolved in favour of the former on the grounds of supremacy of EC law. For many years, however, the judiciary tried to reconcile the irreconcilable: the principal of supremacy of EC law with Dicey's model of parliamentary sovereignty according to which there are no limits to the legislative power of the Parliament subject to the exception that Parliament cannot limit its own powers for the future. It means that no legislation enacted by Parliament is irreversible. The breakthrough came in Case C–221/89 *R* v *Secretary of State for Transport, ex parte Factortame (No 3)*[158] in which the Merchant Shipping Act 1988 made the registration of fishing vessels dependent upon conditions as to the nationality, residence and domicile of their owners. Factortame's vessels, being Spanish owned, were refused registration in the UK. Their Lordships accepted the decision of the ECJ gracefully. Lord Bridge said:

> 'If the supremacy within the European Community of Community law over national law of Member States was not always inherent in the EEC Treaty it was certainly well-established in the jurisprudence of the European Court of Justice long before the United Kingdom joined the Community. Thus, whatever limitation of its sovereignty Parliament accepted when it enacted the European Communities Act 1972 it was entirely voluntary. Under the terms of the Act of 1972 it has always been clear that it was the duty of a United Kingdom court, when delivering final judgment, to override any rule of national law found to be in conflict with any directly enforceable rule of Community law'.

---

[158] [1991] ECR I–3905.

9 Actions against Member States

9.1 Action under art 169 EC

9.2 Action against a Member State by another Member State under art 170 EC

9.3 Effect of a ruling confirming a failure of a Member State to fulfil its obligations under the Treaty

9.4 Simplified procedures

This Chapter, together with Chapter 10, is concerned with the enforcement of Community law. The European Union is based on law and has as its ultimate objective the creation of the 'Union of Law'. The 'Union of Law', an expression first employed by the President of the Commission, Walter Hallstein, has since been referred to in many decisions of the ECJ.[1] The preamble to the Treaty of Maastricht emphasises this feature of the Union. It confirms the Member States' attachment to 'the principle of liberty, democracy and respect for human rights and fundamental freedoms and the rule of law'.

Consequently, Member States, Community institutions, undertakings and citizens of the Union have to observe Community law. The control of legality of acts of Community institutions and the enforcement of Community law vis-à-vis Member States ensures that the creation of the Union of Law is not an empty word.

An action for failure to fulfil an obligation arising from the Treaty which may be brought against a defaulting Member State enhances the originality of the Community legal order. The fact that the Community can enforce compliance with its rules through effective sanctions against a Member State in breach of its obligation confers a unique status to the Community law. Its peculiarity is further emphasised by the Commission's powers to initiate proceedings against a defaulting Member State in its role as the 'guardian of the Treaties' within the meaning of art 155 EC. Thus, contrary to rules of public international law, an EC institution, and not the other Member States,[2] is responsible for ensuring that the Member States comply with Community law. Furthermore, the ECJ has exclusive, mandatory and unreserved jurisdiction in all types of actions for failure to fulfil an obligation by a Member State. The system of sanctions which may be imposed upon a defaulting Member State refusing to comply with the judgment rendered by the ECJ constitutes a forceful means to bring about a change in that Member State's behaviour.

The comparison between public international law and Community law in respect of

---

[1] Case 294/83 *Parti Ecologique 'Les Verts'* [1986] ECR 1339; Case C–2/88 *Zwartveld* [1990] ECR I–3365; Case C–314/91 *Beate Weber* [1993] ECR I–1093; Cases C–181 and 248/91 *EP* v *Council and Commission* [1993] ECR 3685.

[2] Under art 170 EC Member States are also empowered to bring an action against another Member State for an alleged breach of Community law but only after the matter has been laid before the Commission.

State responsibility for the infringement of its international obligation demonstrates that there are a number of features which enhance the originality of Community law. First, in Case 7/71 *Commission v France*[3] the ECJ held that the liability of a Member State is not conditional upon the existence of loss suffered by another Member State for the purposes of the enforcement procedures. Second, the principle of public international law under which no liability is placed upon the State unless it is at fault is rejected by Community law. Indeed, as the ECJ held in Case 25/59 *The Netherlands v High Authority*[4] an action for failure to fulfil an obligation under the Treaties aims at ensuring that the interests of the Community prevail over the inertia and resistance of the Member States. Also, some defences which a State may plead under public international law in order to exonerate itself from liability have been rejected by the ECJ as incompatible with the Community legal order.[5] Finally, an action for failure to fulfil a Treaty obligation has also a broader context: the judgment of the ECJ is not only rendered against the defaulting State but often it determines the exact scope of obligations imposed upon the Member States in the case of divergency in their interpretation.[6] As a result, the uniformity in the application of Community law constitutes one of the main objectives in its enforcement.

The EC Treaty provides for administrative and judicial procedures aimed at ensuring the observance of Community law. They are contained in arts 169, 170, 93(2), 100a(4) and 225 EC. This Chapter focuses on the most important and most often used procedure provided for in art 169 EC.[7] Also, art 170 EC and the procedures which are in derogation from arts 169 and apply in special circumstances will be discussed. They are defined in arts 90(2) EC which concerns State aid, art 100a(4) EC which concerns harmonisation of national laws, and art 225 EC which concerns measures necessary in matters of public security and in the time of war, international tension and internal disturbance.

9.1 Action under art 169 EC

Article 169 EC states:

'If the Commission considers that a Member State has failed to fulfil an obligation under this Treaty, it shall deliver a reasoned opinion on the Matter after giving the State concerned the opportunity to submit its observation.

If the State concerned does not comply with the opinion within the period laid down by the Commission, the latter may bring the matter before the Court of Justice [ECJ].'

In the examination of art 169 EC the following questions should be analysed:

---

[3] [1971] ECR 1003.
[4] [1960] ECR 723.
[5] For example, the defence of necessity in Case 7/61 *Commission v Italy* [1961] ECR 317, or based on reciprocity in Joined Cases 90 and 91/63 *Commission v Luxembourg and Belgium* [1964] ECR 1217; Case 232/78 *Commission v France* [1979] ECR 2729.
[6] Case 7/71 *Commission v France* [1971] ECR 1003.
[7] There are important differences between arts 169 EC and 88 ECSC which concerns actions against Member States for failure to fulfil their obligations under the Treaty, although they share some common features. This question will not be examined in this book. However, arts 169 EC and 141 Euratom are identical.

1. the definition of the failure of a Member State to fulfil an obligation under the Treaty;
2. the determination of the kind of obligation which is likely to give rise to an action under art 169 EC;
3. the procedure which the Commission must observe in the pursuance of its tasks under art 169 EC;
4. the procedure before the ECJ including the legal effect of its judgment; and
5. sanctions which the Commission is empowered to impose on a Member State refusing to comply with the judgment of the ECJ rendered in the proceedings under art 169 EC.

Definition of a failure of a Member State to fulfil its obligation under the Treaty

The failure to fulfil an obligation under the Treaty entails that there is an obligation imposed by the Treaty. However, this obligation must be well determined, that is, art 169 EC requires that a Member State is in breach of a specific, precise obligation.[8] The failure under art 169 EC may consist of some action taken by a Member State, such as the application of national law incompatible with Community law, the adoption of a legislative act contrary to EC law,[9] the express refusal to fulfil an obligation imposed by EC law, or it may derive from its failure to act. In many cases under art 169 EC the Commission initiates proceedings against a Member State for the non-implementation of EC directives within the prescribed time-limit. When a Member State does not take all necessary measures required under Community law it is also liable under art 169 EC. Therefore, the failure to fulfil an obligation by a Member State is assessed in the light of the nature and scope of that obligation,[10] and may result from an action or from an omission or a failure to act. However, in Case 301/81 *Commission v Belgium*[11] the ECJ held that in order to constitute a failure to fulfil an obligation it is not necessary to prove the opposition or the inertia on the part of a Member State.

The failure within the meaning of art 169 EC arises regardless of the national body which is the origin of the action or inaction. In Case 77/69 *Commission v Belgium*[12] the ECJ held that this principle applies even to a constitutional, independent body. In this case the Belgian government tried to plead in its defence the independence of the Belgian Parliament, which could not be forced by the government to adopt a required legislative act. The ECJ answered that:

'... the liability of a Member State under art 169 arises whatever the agency of the State whose action or inaction is the cause of the failure to fulfil its obligations, even in the case of a constitutional independent institution'.

In Cases 227–230/85 *Commission v Belgium*[13] the ECJ emphasised that national division of competences between central and regional authorities which, especially in the context of

---

[8] Case 7/71 *Commission v France* [1971] ECR 1003.
[9] Case C–157/89 *Commission v Italy* [1991] ECR I–57.
[10] Case 31/69 *Commission v Italy* [1970] ECR 25.
[11] [1983] ECR 467.
[12] [1970] ECR 244; also Case 8/70 *Commission v Italy* [1970] ECR 961.
[13] [1988] ECR 1; also Case C–57/89 *Commission v Germany* [1991] ECR 924.

a federal State, may result in a large measure of autonomy being conferred on the local or regional authorities, would not constitute a sufficient defence for a Member State if the local authorities solely empowered to implement the necessary local legislation failed to do so. Also, the failure to fulfil the obligations under the Treaty by any private or semi-public body which is controlled by a Member State is imputable to that Member State. In Case 249/81 *Commission v Ireland (Re Buy Irish Campaign)*,[14] Ireland was held liable under art 169 EC for financing, through the Irish Goods Council, a government-sponsored body, a campaign to 'Buy Irish' which promoted Irish products to the disadvantage of imports, although the Irish Goods Council could not adopt binding measures and the campaign itself was a failure.

It results from the case law of the ECJ that a Member State is liable under art 169 EC if the failure is imputable to a national government, or a national parliament or even a court or a tribunal. In this respect, the Commission had initiated proceedings against the French Cour de Cassation,[15] as well as the German Bundesfinanhof (the highest court in financial matters),[16] although in the context of the traditional independence of judiciary the Commission exercised its discretion and is likely to settled such cases. Also in Case 9/75 *Meyer-Buckhardt*[17] Advocate-General Werner suggested that an action under art 169 EC should be taken if a national court of last resort fails to refer a question on the interpretation of Community law to the ECJ for a preliminary ruling under art 177(3) EC. Once again, this is a very delicate matter and the Commission would certainly prefer to settle such cases if possible. The ECJ itself, in the context of the procedure under art 177 EC, especially in Case C–93/92 *Motorradcenter*,[18] recognised the possibility that judgments of national courts may infringe Community law. It is important to note that whichever body is at the origin of the failure to fulfil an obligation under the Treaty the action under art 169 EC is always taken against the Member State.

Determination of an obligation which is likely to give rise to an action under art 169 EC

The term 'an obligation under this Treaty' is widely interpreted. In comprises not only the obligations imposes by the founding Treaties as amended over the years, protocols, annexes and all other primary sources, but also the Community secondary legislation – regulations,[19] decisions[20] and directives.[21] Also included are binding acts not expressly mentioned in art 189 EC[22] adopted by the Community institutions, and obligations arising out of international agreements concluded between the Community and third countries which by virtue of art 228(7) EC are 'binding on the institutions of the Community and on Member

---

[14] [1982] ECR 4005.
[15] S Weatherill and P Beaumont, *EC Law*, 2nd ed, London: Penguin Books, 1995, p202.
[16] See question no 1907/85 (OJ C137 4.6.86 p7).
[17] [1975] ECR 1171.
[18] [1993] ECR I–5009; also Case C–217/91 *Deutsche Renault* [1993] ECR I–6227.
[19] Case 33/69 *Commission v Italy* [1970] ECR 103; Case 8/70 *Commission v Italy* [1970] ECR 961.
[20] Cases 6 and 11/69 *Commission v France* [1969] ECR 539.
[21] The majority of proceedings under art 169 EC concern Community directives.
[22] Case 141/78 *France v United Kingdom (Re Fishing Mesh)* [1979] ECR 2923.

States'.[23] It is still uncertain whether the infringement of complementary sources gives rise to an action under art 169 EC. As to the rulings of the ECJ, under art 169 EC the non-compliance of the Member State concerned constitutes a new breach of Community law by that Member State which is dealt with under art 171 EC.

It is submitted that the failure of a Member State to fulfil its obligations deriving from the general principle of Community law may also give rise to the liability of a Member State under art 169 EC. First, the ECJ has underlined in many cases that the general principles of Community law form an integral part of Community law. Second, the general principles may be invoked in the proceedings against the Community institutions under arts 173, 175 and 215(2) EC, *a fortiori* this solution should also be applied to the Member States in breach of Community law. Furthermore, in Case C–260/89 *ERT*[24] the ECJ held that the general principles of Community law are binding on the Community institutions and on the Member States when they act within the scope of Community law. Finally, the combined effect of art 164 EC, which provides that the Court of Justice (ECJ) shall ensure that in the interpretation and application of this Treaty the law is observed, and art F(2) of the TEU which states that:

'The Union shall respect fundamental rights, as guaranteed by the European Convention for the Protection of Human Rights and Fundamental Freedoms signed in Rome on 4 November 1950 and as they result from the constitutional traditions common to the Member States, as general principles of Community law'

clearly indicates that the general principles of Community law are of such importance for the proper functioning of the Community that their breach by a Member State should be subject to sanctions under art 169 EC.

In the context of obligations likely to give rise to the liability of a Member State under art 169 EC, it is interesting to examine art 5 EC which provides that:

'Member States shall take all appropriate measures, whether general or particular, to ensure fulfilment of the obligations arising out of this Treaty or resulting from action taken by the institutions of the Community.
    They shall facilitate the achievement of the Community's tasks. They shall abstain from any measure which could jeopardise the attainment of the objectives of this Treaty.'

This provision was considered for a long time as an interpretive device requiring Member States to act in good faith. Gradually, its scope of application has been extended. First, art 5 EC has served to strengthen the binding effect of the Community obligations imposed upon the Member States. Second, the ECJ has imposed, by virtue of art 5 EC, the obligation on national courts to interpret national law in conformity with Community law. And, finally, art 5 EC has become an independent and autonomous source of obligation. As a result, a breach of art 5 EC gives rise to the liability of the Member States under art 169 EC. In Case C–137/91 *Commission* v *Greece (Re Electronic Cash Registers)*[25] the ECJ has explained the autonomous function of art 5 EC.

---

[23] Case 104/81 *Kaupferberg* [1982] ECR 3662; Cases 194 and 241/85 *Commission* v *Greece* [1988] ECR 1037; Case C–228/91 *Commission* v *Italy* [1993] ECR I–2701.
[24] [1991] ECR I–2925.
[25] [1992] 3 CMLR 117.

In this case Greek law, enacted in 1988, required the use of electronic cash registers by certain retailers. However, the approval of such registers was conducted by national authorities which refused to certify any register containing less than 35 per cent add-on value from Greece. Other Member States complained to the Commission that this policy was contrary to art 30 EC. During the investigation the Commission sent two faxes to the Greek Permanent Representation in Brussels asking for more information. None came. The Commission considered that the lack of response constituted an infringement of art 5 EC. In those circumstances, the Commission issued a formal notice under art 169 EC against Greece, but the latter did not submit its observation on the alleged incompatibility of Greek law with Community law. Finally, the Commission delivered the reasoned opinion which is required as a part of the proceedings under art 169(1) EC prior to its judicial part which takes place before the ECJ. No reply was received by the Commission in response, and the Commission decided to bring proceedings before the ECJ.

The government of Greece challenged the Commission proceedings. It claimed that it gave the Commission all necessary information concerning the legislation in question at a meeting in Athens in September 1990, and a year later sent the Commission the text of a new Act. According to the Greek government there was no reason for providing additional information required by the Commission as the latter was fully aware of the situation before the action under art 169 EC was brought. The Commission argued that the Greek government provided the required information two years after it was requested, and that at that stage the time-limit fixed by the reasoned opinion had elapsed.

The ECJ held that Greece had violated art 5 EC. The ECJ stated that 'the failure to reply to the Commission's questions within a reasonable period made the task which it has to perform more difficult and therefore amounts to a violation of the obligation of co-operation laid down in art 5 EEC.'

It results from the case law of the ECJ in relation to art 5 that the latter imposes a positive duty on Member States to co-operate with the Commission in its investigations into alleged violations of Community law. Failure to do so is in itself sufficient reason to give rise to the liability of a Member State under art 169 EC,[26] regardless of whether a Member State refuses or simply ignores the request of the Commission for information,[27] or omits to forward necessary indications allowing the Commission to exercise its control of the observance by the Member States of Community law.[28]

Procedure under art 169 EC

The procedure itself reflects the philosophy of art 169 EC, that is, that the action should not be brought unless there is no other possibility of enforcing Community law. The use of non-contentious means in the proceedings under art 169 EC constitutes one of its dominant features. Furthermore, the Commission plays a central role in any action against a Member State for the failure to fulfil its obligation stemming from the Treaty. Under art 88 of the

---

[26] See also Case C–33/90 *Commission* v *Italy* [1991] ECR I–5987; Case C–65/91 *Commission* v *Greece* [1992] ECR I–5245.

[27] Case 272/86 *Commission* v *Greece* [1988] ECR 4875; Case C–375/92 *Commission* v *Spain* [1994] ECR I–923.

[28] For example, Case C–40/92 *Commission* v *The United Kingdom* [1994] ECR I–989.

Treaty of Paris the Commission/High Authority has an exclusive competence in initiating proceedings, and the Member States may only invite the High Authority to act. Also, under the ECSC Treaty the High Authority has jurisdiction to give a binding decision confirming the failure of a Member State to fulfil its obligation under this Treaty and the ECJ may only intervene in its appellate capacity.[29] Under the Treaties of Rome the Commission does not enjoy the monopoly in initiating the proceedings but it plays a predominant role in this respect, as well as in deciding whether or not proceedings should be brought against a Member State in breach of Community law.

In the proceedings under art 169 EC three stages can be distinguished: the informal stage prior to the formal procedure; and the formal procedure itself which comprises the administrative and the judicial stage.

Informal stage

In the informal stage the Commission enjoys a double discretion: first, it decides whether or not a Member State is in breach of art 169 EC; and, second, it assesses various aspects of the situation in question, especially by placing it in the political context in order to determine whether or not to commence proceedings against the defaulting State. Indeed, in many cases the Commission decided not to act when faced with sensitive political issues. For example, the United Kingdom was in breach of Community law for more than 20 years by not introducing national legislation required by the ECJ under its ruling in *Van Duyn*.[30] Advocate-General Roemer in Case 7/71 *Commission* v *France*[31] suggested that in certain circumstances the Commission should abstain from initiating proceedings under art 169 EC: when there is a possibility to reach a settlement; when the effect of the breach of Community law is minor; when the proceedings of the Commission would exacerbate a major political crisis in the defaulting Member State, especially in the context of a minor violation of Community law by that Member State; or when there is a possibility that the provision in question would be modified or annulled in the near future. The corollary of the discretion recognised as held by the Commission is that the latter cannot be forced to act under art 169 EC. As a result, the Commission's refusal to initiate proceedings under art 169 EC cannot be challenged under art 173 EC. Also, because the Commission enjoys a large measure of discretion under art 169 EC, as the ECJ emphasised in Case 48/65 *Alfons Lütticke*,[32] it has no obligation to state its position as required under art 175 EC since there is no legal obligation imposed on the Commission by the EC Treaty to act. The reasoned opinion issued by the Commission, which terminates the administrative stage of the proceedings under art 169 EC, is not legally binding and, in any event, this is always addressed to a Member State and not to the person who lodged complaint under art 169 EC.[33]

---

[29] Under art 88(2) ECSC a Member State has two months to appeal to the ECJ after it was notified of the decision of the High Authority.

[30] The violation was finally rectified by the Immigration (European Economic Area) Order 1994 (SI 1895/1994).

[31] [1971] ECR 1003.

[32] [1966] ECR 28. This is compensated by the possibility for individuals to bring proceedings before a national court. This was also the manner in which Alfons Lütticke proceeded. He obtained a ruling under art 177 EC from the ECJ stating that art 95 EC was directly effective and thus it could be applied in his favour by the German court.

[33] Case C–97/94 *Schultz* [1994] ECR I–1701; Cases T–479 and 559/93 *Bernardi* [1994] ECR II–1115 Ord.

Usually, the violation of Community law by a Member State is brought to the attention of the Commission as a result of its own inquiries, the complaints of individuals or undertakings affected by the breach, although all sources of information are taken into consideration, such as articles in the newspapers, documentaries presented by TV stations, etc. In this respect, the role of national press and information offices in each Member State is particularly useful. They not only provide information to EC nationals concerning their individual and collective rights but also their complaints concerning the violations of Community law by national authorities. All complaints are registered by the General Secretariat of the Commission and are the subject of reports concerning the situation of the presumed violations of the Treaties. These reports are periodically examined by the Chief of private office or *Cabinet* of each Commissioner and their observations are forwarded to the Commission. Once there is sufficient evidence that a Member State is in breach of Community law the appropriate Directorate-General initiates proceedings. At this stage the Commission invites the Member State concerned to provide some explanations and that Member State is reminded that it has an obligation to co-operate under arts 5 and 155 EC.[34] The request for information takes a form of a 'letter pre-169' proceedings which fixes a time-limit for the reply. Usually, the Commission and representatives of that Member State discuss the matter. Sometimes, the negotiations between them take a considerable amount of time, sometimes both parties will settle the matter immediately. The length of time spent during the informal stage is of some importance, especially when the Commission decides to take formal proceedings against the defaulting Member State. In that case, usually, the longer the period of time spent on the informal proceedings the more easily the ECJ will accept a short time period in the formal proceedings. The informal proceedings emphasises the non-punitive nature of art 169 EC. The objective of the provision is to terminate the violation of Community law and not to exacerbate the dispute. It is uncertain how many disputes are resolved by the Commission in the informal stage.[35] However, if no settlement is possible, the Commission will start the formal proceedings.

Administrative stage

The administrative stage can be analysed from the point of view of the subsequent acts which the Commission is under a duty to adopt vis-à-vis the defaulting Member State: the letter of formal notice and the reasoned opinion.

Letter of formal notice In Case 51/83 *Commission* v *Italy*[36] the ECJ held that the letter of formal notice constitutes an essential formal requirement under art 169 EC, and its omission would result in the inadmissibility of an action under art 169 EC. The letter of formal notice determines the scope of the case and cannot be widened even at the stage of the reasoned opinion.[37] According to art 169(4) EC the letter of formal notice invites a defaulting Member State to submit its observation on the disputed matters. It guarantees

---

[34] Case 147/77 *Commission* v *Italy* [1978] ECR 1307.
[35] See S Weatherill and P Beaumont, supra note 15, p194, note 7. According to them between 10 and 40 per cent; in 1993 the Commission investigated 1,340 cases and issued 1,209 letters.
[36] [1984] ECR 2793.
[37] Case 51/83 *Commission* v *Italy* [1984] ECR 2793.

the right of defence to the Member State concerned, although the latter is not obliged to reply. Usually, the Commission gives a defaulting Member State two months to reply, but in urgent matters the time may be shorter. At this stage the procedure may be terminated if the Commission is convinced that in the light of the explanations provided by the Member State concerned there is no violation of Community law, or if the latter rectifies the failure immediately. Otherwise, after the expiry of the time-limit fixed in the letter of formal notice, the Commission issues the reasoned opinion.

Reasoned opinion The main difference between the letter of formal notice and the reasoned opinion is that the former 'is intended to define the subject-matter of the dispute and to indicate to the Member State ... the factors enabling it to prepare its defence',[38] while in the reasoned opinion the Commission must established the legal arguments in respect of the alleged failure of a Member State to fulfil its obligation under the Treaty.[39] The reasoned opinion invites the defaulting Member State to cease the infringement and indicates the appropriate measures that should be taken to end the breach.[40] It also fixes a time-limit for the Member State concerned to comply; this is usually two months, but in urgent cases this period may be shortened. The time-limit cannot be changed by the ECJ,[41] although it will be taken into account when the ECJ determines whether the Commission had given a 'reasonable time' to comply with the reasoned opinion. In Case 74/82 *Commission* v *Ireland*[42] the ECJ viewed with disapproval the period of five days given in the reasoned opinion to Ireland to amend its legislation which had applied for more than forty years. There was no urgency and this period was considered by the ECJ as unreasonable, although the action was not dismissed. The ECJ took into consideration the fact that the Commission issued its reasoned opinion on 9 November 1981 and referred to the ECJ on 19 February 1982.

In Cases 142 and 143/80 *Amministrazione delle Finanze dello Stato* v *Essevi and Salongo*,[43] in proceedings under art 177 EC, the ECJ held that the Commission is not the final arbiter as to the determination of the rights and obligations of the Member States. Where a Member State has complied with the Commission's reasoned opinion this does not mean that it may invoke that opinion to prevent future parties from claiming that the Member State is still in violation of Community law. However, if the Member State concerned complies with the reasoned opinion within the prescribed time-limit the Commission is barred from bringing proceedings before the ECJ.[44] Otherwise, the Commission may commence the next step in the proceedings under art 169 EC, that is bring the matter before the ECJ.

The discretion that the Commission enjoys under art 169 EC applies throughout the proceedings. The Commission may decide at any stage to set aside the proceedings, even after the time-limit for the compliance with the reasoned opinion elapses. The wide

---

[38] Ibid.

[39] In Case 7/61 *Commission* v *Italy (Re Pigmeat)* [1961] ECR 317 the ECJ held that 'the opinion referred to in art 169 of the Treaty must ... contain a sufficient statement of reasons to satisfy the law'.

[40] Case 7/61 *Commission* v *Italy* [1961] ECR 317; Case 70/72 *Commission* v *Germany* [1973] ECR 813.

[41] Case 28/81 *Commission* v *Italy* [1981] ECR 2577; Case 29/81 *Commission* v *Italy* [1981] ECR 2585.

[42] [1984] ECR 317.

[43] [1981] ECR 1413.

[44] Case C–200/88 *Commission* v *Greece* [1990] ECR I–4299.

discretion of the Commission is justified by the fact that under art 169 EC the Commission has no obligation to act. The ECJ in Case 7/71 *Commission v France*[45] held that the proceedings under art 169 EC are not enclosed in the pre-established time-limit 'since, by reason of its nature and its purpose, this procedure involves a power on the part of the Commission to consider the most appropriate means and time-limits for the purposes of putting an end to any contravention of the Treaty'. Thus, the Commission is the master of proceedings under art 169 EC and as such empowered to decide about their desirability. This aspect of the Commission's discretion is enhanced by the possibility of bringing proceedings against a defaulting Member State even when the latter complied with the reasoned decision but after the expiry of the time-limit specified in it. The Commission may decide to bring proceedings before the ECJ many years after the expiry to the time-limit fixed in the reasoned opinion.[46] In Case 7/61 *Commission v Italy*[47] the ECJ recognised that the Commission may have an interest to determine whether a violation of Community law occurred. Furthermore, in Case 39/72 *Commission v Italy*[48] the ECJ held that its ruling in such a case may be useful, especially in order to established the basis of that Member State's liability vis-à-vis other Member States, the Community and the individuals concerned.

It is also necessary to note that neither the formal letter of notice nor the reasoned opinion have binding legal effect. For that reason they cannot be challenged under art 173 EC. In Case 48/65 *Alfons Lütticke*[49] the ECJ stated that the reasoned opinion was merely a step in the proceedings.

Judicial proceedings

The ECJ has gradually developed its own conditions for the admissibility of actions under art 169 EC which aim at ensuring that a defaulting Member State's rights to a defence are protected. The ECJ will dismiss an application under art 169 EC in the following circumstances:

1. *If the time-limit fixed by the Commission, either in the letter of the formal notice or in the reasoned opinion, is not reasonable.* In Case 293/85 *Commission v Belgium (Re University Fees)*,[50] which concerned the compliance of Belgium with the ECJ ruling in *Gravier*, Belgium had only eight days to reply to the letter of formal notice and 15 days to comply with the reasoned opinion. The ECJ held that the prescribed time-limit was insufficient for Belgium, taking into account the complexity of the matter.[51] The ECJ will examine many factors in deciding whether or not the time-limit fixed by the Commission may be considered as reasonable. In Case 85/85 *Commission v Belgium*[52]

---

[45] [1971] ECR 1003.
[46] In Case C–422/92 *Commission v Germany* [1995] ECR I–1097 there was a delay of six years; in Case C–317/92 *Commission v Germany* [1994] ECR I–2039 the delay was two years.
[47] [1961] ECR 633.
[48] [1973] ECR 101.
[49] [1966] ECR 28.
[50] [1988] ECR 305.
[51] In Case 293/83 *Gravier v City of Liège* [1989] ECR 593, the ECJ held that the fees (so-called minerval) imposed upon EC nationals studying in Belgium were discriminatory and in breach of art 59 EC which ensures the free movement of services throughout the Community.
[52] [1986] ECR 1149; see also Case 74/82 *Commission v Ireland* [1984] ECR 317 already examined in this chapter.

the ECJ held that a period of 15 days was reasonable in the light of the considerable length of time taken by the informal proceedings.

2. *If the complaints and legal arguments in the application under art 169 EC are not identical to those invoked in the letter of formal notice and the reasoned opinion.*[53] The case law of the ECJ demonstrates that the Court has rigorously applied this requirement which, on the one hand, protects the defaulting Member State against new complaints and legal arguments of the Commission and, on the other hand, is necessary as a counterbalance to the discretion which the Commission enjoys under art 169 EC. However, it seems that the ECJ which was excessively strict with regard to this formal requirement has changed its position. Indeed, in some cases the Member States invoke this argument in order to avoid proceedings under art 169 EC. In Case C–96/95 *Commission v Germany*[54] the ECJ declared the application admissible despite the fact that the government of Germany considered that the Commission had modified the legal grounds as compared to the previous submission presented in the letter of formal notice and in the reasoned opinion.

In this case, the Commission did not receive any information from Germany concerning the implementation measures in relation to Council Directive 90/364, on the right of residence for persons who have sufficient resources to avoid having to rely on the social security system in the host State (the so-called Playboy Directive), and Directive 90/365, on the right of residence for employees and self-employed persons who have ceased their occupational activity. As a result, the Commission decided to issue a letter of formal notice. The German government replied that the authorities of Länder had been informed by means of a circular of the obligation to grant a residence permit to the beneficiaries of both Directives. However, later the government of Germany informed the Commission that the principle of supremacy of Community law which is incorporated into the German law on immigration (Auslandergesetz) guaranteed the proper application of both Directives in Germany and that, in addition, EC directives would be incorporated in new legislation which was being prepared (Aufenthaltgesetz/EWG). The Commission considered that Germany did not implement both Directives correctly and delivered a reasoned opinion. The German government repeated its previous arguments. At that stage the Commission brought proceedings before the ECJ. The German authorities argued that the application was inadmissible since the complaints in the administrative stage and in the judicial stage were not identical. The Commission responded that in all proceedings the complaints were identical, that is, they concerned the non-implementation of EC directives. The ECJ confirmed that the Commission did not modify the essence of its complaints.

It seems that the ECJ is now more concerned with the essence of the complaints than with the actual terms used in the letter of formal notice and the reasoned opinion.[55]

---

[53] For example, in Case C–210/91 *Commission v Greece* [1994] ECR I–6735; Case C–157/91 *Commission v The Netherlands* [1994] ECR I–5899; Case C–296/92 *Commission v Italy* [1994] ECR I–1.

[54] Judgment of 20 March 1997 [1997] Europe (May), no 143, comm D Simon.

[55] In Case 274/83 *Commission v Italy* [1985] ECR 1090, the ECJ permitted the Commission to make certain modifications in support of its arguments.

The Commission's application must state precisely the grounds on which it is based, as well as providing some legal and factual indications. It cannot simply refer to the letter of formal notice and the reasoned opinion.[56]

The burden of proof is placed on the Commission. Recently, in Case 300/95 *Commission v United Kingdom*[57] the ECJ provided clarification in respect of the Commission's obligation to prove its allegation that a Member State is in breach of art 169 EC. In this case the Commission argued that the United Kingdom was in violation of art 7 of Council Directive 85/375 on product liability, as it was implemented without transposing its text verbatim. However, the form and methods of implementation of directives are left at the discretion of the Member State; what is important is that the objectives of the directive are attained. The Commission considered that this was not the case since the British courts have to interpreted art 7 of Directive 85/375 *contra legem* in order to achieve the objectives of that Directive. The ECJ reminded the Commission that in order to establish the failure of a Member State to fulfil its obligations the Commission could not base its application under art 169 EC on a presumption or a simple allegation.[58] As a result, the ECJ rejected the application submitted by the Commission. The ECJ held that in order to assess the scope of national legislative or administrative provision the Commission must take into account the way that national court interprets that provision. Thus, the Commission must not only establish that a Member State is in breach of Community law, but also prove that national courts in practice interpret the provision in question contrary to Community law. It seems therefore, that the ECJ has set out a presumption in favour of the interpretation of national law in conformity with Community law by national courts which is, in any event, required under Community law.[59] It is submitted that this solution, which confers on national courts the role of the guardian of Community law, is contrary to the principle of legal certainty, especially when national courts have to interpret the provision of national law which implements Community law *contra legem* in order to attain the objectives required by the directive.

Also, in the judicial stage, the ECJ fully investigates the merits of the case. Thus, it decides the matter *ab novo* taking into consideration the situation as it was at the expiry of the time-limit fixed in the reasoned opinion.[60] However, in certain circumstances, especially in the light of the interests of the Community, the ECJ may take into account any changes that occurred after the deadline.[61] The ECJ may also give an interlocutory ruling inviting the Commission and the Member State concerned to find a solution ensuring the effective application of Community law in the light of the legal arguments submitted by both parties during the proceedings under art 169 EC, but, as with any interlocutory decision, the proceedings can be reopened if necessary[62] and the Commission is entitled to request

---

[56] Case C–347/88 *Commission v Greece* [1990] ECR I–4747; Case C–52/90 *Commission v Denmark* [1992] ECR I–2187.

[57] Judgment of 29 May 1997.

[58] Case C–62/89 *Commission v France* [1990] ECR I–925.

[59] See Case 14/83 *Von Colson and Kamann* [1984] ECR 1891; Case C–91/92 *Faccini Dori* [1994] ECR I–3325.

[60] Case C–200/88 *Commission v Greece* [1990] ECR I–4299, especially if the implementation of a directive was not notified to the Commission; Case C–133/94 *Commission v Belgium*, Judgment of 2 May 1996.

[61] Case C–105/91 *Commission v Greece* [1992] ECR I–5871; Case C–422/92 *Commission v Germany* [1995] ECR I–1097.

proceedings can be reopened if necessary[62] and the Commission is entitled to request interim measures.

Defence

The ECJ has strictly interpreted the defences available to the Member States under art 169 EC. This restrictive approach is the corollary of the definition of 'the failure to fulfil an obligation under the Treaty' provided by the ECJ. Indeed, the philosophy of art 169 EC requires that the defaulting Member State puts an end to the violation of Community law as soon as possible and thus some traditional defences recognised under public international law are not appropriate to the peculiar nature of the Community legal order.

Successful defences

Josephine Steiner has rightly pointed out: 'Many defences to an action under art 169 have been attempted; few have succeeded.'[63] She added that the best defence for a defaulting Member State it to deny the obligation. Also, the claim of a procedural irregularity in the adoption of a Community measure constitutes an excellent defence. Indeed, the strict interpretation of defence offers little hope for a defaulting Member State. Obviously, the fact that the time-limit prescribed in the secondary legislation, or in the reasoned opinion, has not yet expired is one possibility but in practice it is hard to imagine that the ECJ will accept an application under art 169 EC in those circumstances. The are a few defences which are recognised as valid under art 169 EC.

Unlawful obligation The best defence for the Member State concerned is to bring an action for annulment under art 173 against the challenged measure. However, the ECJ has permitted the defaulting Member State to call into question the validity of the Community act directly in the art 169 EC proceedings. It seems quite strange that a defaulting Member State may challenge the validity of Community acts in the proceedings under art 169 EC in view of its privileged *locus standi* under art 173 EC. Indeed, that was the initial case.[64] There is still no clear justification for the change of attitude of the ECJ in this respect, but it seems that the reason is provided by art 184 EC which permits indirect action for annulment of Community measures and thus, at least theoretically, to escape the strict deadline of art 173 EC. In general, the ECJ excludes the possibility for a Member State to invoke the illegality of a decision addressed to it[65] or any other individual act.[66] However, there are two exceptions to the principle. The first was discussed by the ECJ in Case 226/87 *Commission v Greece*[67] in which the ECJ stated that a Member State may call into question the legality of a decision if the latter is affected by evident and serious vices which rendered it 'non-existent'. The

---

[62] Case 170/78 *Commission v United Kingdom* [1980] ECR 415; Case 149/79 *Commission v Belgium* [1980] ECR 3881.

[63] J Steiner, *EC Law*, 4th ed, London: Blackstone, 1994, p347.

[64] For example, Case 20/59 *Italy v High Authority* [1960] ECR 663.

[65] Case 226/87 *Commission v Greece* [1988] ECR 3620.

[66] Case C–183/91 *Commission v Greece* [1993] ECR I–3131 in relation to EC regulations and Case C–74/91 *Commission v Germany* [1992] ECR I–5437 in relation to EC directives.

[67] [1988] ECR 3620.

second exception was established in Case 6/69 *Commission v France*[68] in which the French government successfully proved that the decision in question was adopted in the area in which the Member State had exclusive competence. With regulations, in Case 116/82 *Commission v Germany*[69] the ECJ accepted that the illegality of EC regulations may be invoked as a defence in the proceedings under art 169 EC. This solution is in conformity with the requirements laid down in art 184 EC.

Force majeure Another possibility for a Member State is to invoke *force majeure*, although so far this defence has not been successfully pleaded. Indeed, the ECJ has, once again, strictly interpreted this concept. As a result, what are considered under national law as exonerating circumstances, such as unforeseeable and irresistible political events – namely the dissolution of national parliaments, political difficulties, governmental crises, delays in the legislative procedure, social and economic disorders, etc – were rejected by the ECJ.[70] The only circumstance in which *force majeure* may be successfully pleaded is in the case of an absolute impossibility to perform its obligation. In Case 101/84 *Commission v Italy (Re Traffic Statistics)*[71] the government of Italy was close to succeeding in that case; it argued that it was impossible to comply with EC Directive 78/546 which required the Member State to forward statistical data in respect of the carriage of goods by road because a bomb attack conducted by the Red Brigade on the Ministry of Transport's data-processing centre destroyed its vehicle register. However, the delay of four-and-a-half years in the implementation of the Directive was considered to be too long to exonerate Italy. In this respect the ECJ held that:

> '… although it is true that the bomb attack, which took place before 18 January 1979, may have constituted a case of *force majeure* and created insurmountable difficulties, its effect could only have lasted a certain time, namely the time which would in fact be necessary for an administration showing a normal degree of diligence to replace the equipment destroyed and to collect and prepare the data'.

The definition of *force majeure* was provided in Case 296/86 *McNicholl v Ministry of Agriculture*[72] in proceedings under art 177 EC, but it can be transposed to proceedings under art 169 EC. The ECJ held that:

> '… whilst the concept of *force majeure* does not presuppose an absolute impossibility of performance, it nevertheless requires that non-performance of the act in question be due to circumstances beyond the control of persons pleading *force majeure*, that the circumstances be abnormal and unforeseeable and that the consequences could not have been avoided through the exercise of all due care'.

Uncertainty as to the exact meaning of the obligation Under art 169 EC the Commission must determine with precision, or at least sufficiently from a legal point of view, the

---

[68] [1969] ECR 923.
[69] [1986] ECR 2519; also Case C–258/89 *Commission v Spain* [1991] ECR I–3977.
[70] See Magliveras, 'Force Majeure in Community Law' (1990) 15 ELR 460.
[71] [1985] ECR 2629.
[72] [1988] ECR 1491.

obligation which a Member State has violated.[73] This requirement has been used by the Member States as a defence under art 169 EC. At first, the ECJ recognised this defence, however, in limited circumstances, that is only if ambiguity concerned the essential aspect of the obligation.[74] Gradually the ECJ has accepted that even in proceedings under art 169 EC the Member States are still entitled that the ECJ elucidates the exact scope of the obligations they are supposed to fulfil, especially in the event of divergent interpretations.[75] However, the extent of the ECJ acceptance of this defence is still difficult to determine, apart from the above-mentioned case. In this respect, in Case C–133/94 *Commission v Belgium*,[76] the government of Belgium pleaded, *inter alia*, the obscurity and ambiguity of a provision concerning the concept of 'chemical installation' under Council Directive 85/337/EEC on environmental impact assessment. The Commission implicitly agreed with Belgium as it had undertaken to define later the precise meaning of that concept. The ECJ held Belgium in breach of art 169 EC.

Unsuccessful defences

The ingeniousness of the Member States in constructing defences to art 169 EC is astonishing. Over the years, they have attempted to plead every justification imaginable for their failure to fulfil their obligations under the Treaty. One of the most interesting cases concerned the defence which is recognised under public international law but rejected by Community law as contrary to the spirit and objectives of the Community legal order. In Cases 90 and 91/63 *Commission v Luxembourg and Belgium (Re Import of Powdered Milk Products)*[77] the ECJ rejected a defence based on reciprocity. In that case Luxembourg and Belgium were in breach of art 12 EC. They argued that their action would have been legal if the Commission had introduced certain measures which the latter was authorised to enact, and that under public international law if one party fails to perform its obligation the other is entitled to withhold its own performance. The ECJ held that:

'In fact the Treaty is not limited to creating reciprocal obligations between the different natural and legal persons to whom it is applicable, but establishes a new legal order which governs the powers, rights and obligations of the said persons, as well as the necessary procedures for taking cognisance of and penalising any breach of it. Therefore, except where otherwise expressly provided, the basic concept of the Treaty requires that the Member State shall not take the law into their own hands. Therefore, the fact that the Council failed to carry out its obligations cannot relieve the defendants from carrying out theirs.'

This is the straightforward rejection of the defence based on reciprocity. It this context it is interesting to note that art 60 of the 1969 Vienna Convention on the Law of Treaties, as well the constitutions of some Member States, for example art 55 of the French Constitution, recognised the *exceptio inadempleti contractus*. However, the decision of the ECJ is fully justified, taking into account that in the international legal order there is no international court which exercises permanent and mandatory jurisdiction in respect of disputes between

---

[73] Case 20/59 *Italy v High Authority* [1960] ECR 663.
[74] Case 26/69 *Commission v France* [1970] ECR 565; Case 70/72 *Commission v Germany* [1973] ECR 813.
[75] Case 7/71 *Commission v France* [1971] ECR 1003.
[76] Judgment of 2 May 1996.
[77] [1964] ECR 1217.

sovereign States. The situation is different in the Community: first, the objectives of the Treaty require that unilateral actions on the part of a Member State are prohibited; and, second, under the Treaty the unlawful actions or omissions either of other Member States or the Community institutions are investigated and sanctioned. Thus, there is neither the need nor any justification for permitting the Member States to 'take the law into their own hands'. The strict application of this principle by the ECJ entails that any unilateral action of a Member State aiming at correcting the effect of a violation of Community law by another Member State is prohibited. In Case 232/78 *Commission v France*[78] the ECJ held that:

> 'A Member State cannot under any circumstances unilaterally adopt, on its own authority, corrective measure or measures to protect trade designed to prevent any failure on the part of another Member State to comply with the rules laid down by the Treaty.'

This statement has been recently repeated almost verbatim by the ECJ in Case C–14/96 *Paul Denuit*[79] in which a Belgian judge, although under art 177 EC proceedings, asked the ECJ whether Belgium was entitled to take unilateral measures against the Member States in breach of Council Directive 89/552 establishing a single audio-visual area in the Community, especially to oppose the re-transmissions in the territory of Belgium of programmes broadcast by the national broadcasting body of another Member State which did not conform to certain provisions of the Directive.[80]

The ECJ held that, in such a case, if a Member State considers that another Member State has failed to fulfil its obligations under the Community law that State may bring an action under art 170 EC against the defaulting State or ask the Commission to act under art 169 EC. It is worth noting that:

1. A Member State cannot invoke in its defence in proceedings under art 169 EC that another Member State is also in breach of the same obligation, even though the Commission has not initiated proceedings against that State.[81] Also neither the Member State which is an alleged victim of the violation of Community law by another Member State nor any other Member State is allowed to plead that violation in its defence to art 169 EC.[82]

2. As already noted in Cases 90 and 91/63 *Commission v Luxembourg and Belgium*, a Member State cannot rely in its defence under art 169 EC on the fact that a Community institution has acted unlawfully or failed to act when it was under a duty to act. Articles 173 and 175 EC ensure in such a case an appropriate procedure for the very purpose of rectifying those problems. In Case C–359/93 *Commission v The Netherlands*[83] the ECJ held that this solution also applies when a Community institution fails to comply with its own obligations under the Treaty subsequent to a failure by a Member State.

Another defence recognised under public international law is based on necessity. The criteria for such a claim are very stringent: there must be exceptional circumstances of

---

[78] [1979] ECR 2729.
[79] Judgment of 29 May 1997.
[80] Another recent case which confirms this principle is Case C–11/95 *Commission v Belgium* [1996] ECR I–4115.
[81] Case 232/78 *Commission v France (Re Restrictions on Imports of Lamb)* [1979] ECR 2729.
[82] Case 52/75 *Commission v Italy* [1976] ECR 277.
[83] [1995] ECR I–157.

extreme urgency; the *status quo ante* must be re-established as soon as possible; and the State concerned must act in good faith.[84] In Case 7/61 *Commission v Italy (Re Pigmeat)*[85] Italy banned all imports of pork into Italy from other Member States in order to avert an economic crisis. The ECJ held that in emergency situations the appropriate remedy is laid down in art 226 and, for reasons similar to those under the principle of reciprocity, declared the unilateral action by Italy in breach of Community law.

A defence based on the peculiarity of national systems, especially their constitutional, administrative and institutional organisation, was rejected by the ECJ. In Case 77/69 *Commission v Belgium*[86] the government of Belgium claimed *force majeure* in order to exonerate its responsibility for breach of art 95 EC. It argued that its attempts to pass the necessary legislation were fettered by the Belgian Parliament, a body which the government had no power to compel to act. Indeed, a draft to amend the discriminatory tax scheme on wood was submitted to the Belgian Parliament but had fallen with the dissolution of Parliament. The ECJ firmly held that the Member State is liable under art 169 EC whenever an agency of the Member State, including a constitutionally independent institution, fails to fulfil its obligation arising from Community law.

Another rejected defence was one which tried to justify a failure to comply with obligations arising from Community law on the division of powers between central and regional authorities based on the Belgian Constitution. In Case C–225/86 *Commission v Belgium (Re Failure to Implement Directives)*[87] the Belgian government stated that it was constitutionally unable to compel some of its regions to comply with a decision of the ECJ.

The ECJ delivered a ruling in February 1982 against Belgium for failure to implement a number of EC directives within the prescribed time-limit. In July 1985 Belgium was still in breach of the decision the ECJ as the directives in question were not implemented in certain constituent parts of its territory, namely in the Wallon and Brussels regions. The Commission brought another action under art 169 EC against Belgium. The Belgian government claimed that its failure resulted from constitutional limitations imposed upon the central government by the Belgian Constitution. At the national level the Royal Decree on the discharge of waste water into surface water was adopted in 1986 which implemented Directive 78/176. However, the central government had no power to compel regional authorities, in this case in the Wallon and Brussels regions, to wholly implement Directive 78/176. The central government could not implement it or substitute Community legislation for local legislation. The ECJ rejected the arguments submitted by the government of Belgium. The ECJ held that:

> '... each Member State is free to delegate powers to its domestic authorities as it considers fit
> and to implement directives by means of measures adopted by regional or local authorities.
> That division of powers does not however release it from the obligation to ensure that the
> provisions of the directive are properly implemented in national law ... a Member State may

---

[84] The defence of necessity was successfully invoked by the United Kingdom when it bombed the *Torrey Canyon*, a ship flying the Liberian flag, which was grounded outside the British territorial waters, as it represented a threat of an ecological disaster, but France failed in the *Rainbow Warrior Case* (1990) 82 ILR 499.

[85] [1961] ECR 317.

[86] [1970] ECR 237; see also Case C–133/94 *Commission v Belgium*, Judgment of 2 May 1996.

[87] [1988] ECR 579.

not plead provisions, practices or circumstances existing in its internal legal system in order to justify failure to comply with its obligations under Community law'.

In this category of defence, the following were rejected by the ECJ: the dissolution of the national Parliament,[88] the mandatory deadline imposed by a national constitution for the accomplishment of necessary formalities,[89] and administrative difficulties.[90]

Political difficulties cannot be pleaded in order to justify a failure to comply with obligations resulting from Community law. In Case 8/70 *Commission v Italy*[91] the defence based on the ministerial crises in Italy was rejected. Indeed, in the light of the political turbulence in Italy after World War II, the acceptance of this defence would paralyse the operation of Community law in that country. Interesting arguments relating to political difficulties were submitted by the United Kingdom in Case 128/78 *Commission v UK (Re Tachographs).*[92]

In this case the Commission brought an action under art 169 EC against the UK for failure to comply with Regulation 1463/70 relating to the introduction of tachographs in commercial vehicles. Tachographs were made compulsory and had to replace the use of individual control books in the UK. They were strongly opposed by the trade unions ('the spy in the cab'). The government of the UK suggested the installation and use of tachographs on a voluntary basis. It argued that the resistance from the trade unions would result in strikes in the transport sector and thus seriously damage the whole economy of the UK.

The ECJ held that Regulation 1463/70, as any other regulation, is binding in its entirety in the Member State and thus its incomplete or selective application would breach Community law. In addition, the ECJ stated that it is inadmissible that a Member State disapplies those provisions of the Regulation which it considers contrary to national interests. Practical difficulties in the implementation of a Community measure cannot permit a Member State unilaterally to opt out of fulfilling its obligations, since the Community's institutional system ensures that due consideration is given to them in the light of the principles of the common market and the legitimate interests of the other Member States. As a result, the ECJ rejected the possible political difficulties as a justification for non-compliance with Regulation 1463/70.

Also, defences based on economic difficulties,[93] or the threat of social troubles or specific local conditions,[94] were rejected by the ECJ. In Case C–45/91 *Commission v Greece*[95] the Greek government tried to justify its failure to implement the Directive on the safe disposal of toxic waste upon the 'opposition by the local population'. This argument was rejected and the ECJ repeated, once again, that a Member State cannot rely on an internal situation to justify its failure to fulfil its obligations under the Treaty.

Furthermore, the ECJ rejected a defence based on the minimal effect of the violation of

---

[88] Case 7/68 *Commission v Italy* [1968] ECR 617.
[89] Case 30/72 *Commission v Italy* [1973] ECR 171.
[90] Case 5/86 *Commission v Belgium* [1987] ECR 1777.
[91] [1970] ECR 961.
[92] [1979] ECR 419.
[93] Case 70/86 *Commission v Greece* [1987] ECR 3558.
[94] Case C–56/90 *Commission v United Kingdom (Re Bathing Water Directive)* [1994] 1 CMLR 769; Case 339/87 *Commission v The Netherlands (Re Protection of Wild Birds)* [1990] ECR I–851.
[95] [1992] ECR I–2509.

Community law. There is no *de minimis rule* under art 169 EC. The scale or the frequency of the infringement cannot justify the failure of the Member State to fulfil is obligations under the Treaty. In Case C–105/91 *Commission v Greece*[96] the Greek government admitted that its tax scheme on foreign vehicles was unlawful and discriminatory, but argued that the Greek vehicles concerned represented no more than 10 per cent of internal demand and thus there was no manifest discrimination. This argument was rejected.

Another defence pleaded under art 169 EC was based on the argument that administrative practices ensure that national law in breach of Community law is not applied in fact. In Case 167/73 *Commission v France (Re French Merchant Seamen)*[97] the French government attempted to justify the existence of national law, the French Code Maritime enacted in 1926, which was in breach of Community law on the basis that it was no longer enforced in practice. The Code required a ratio of three Frenchmen to one foreigner for certain jobs on French merchant ships. This provision was in breach of art 48 EC and EC Regulation 1612/68. The ECJ held that although according to the French government this provision was a secondary hindrance, since it was not applied in practice by the French Administration and that there was, in addition, a ministerial circular to this effect, the uncertainty resulting from its continued existence constituted itself a hindrance incompatible with the requirements of the free movement of workers. It is interesting to mention that France did not comply with the decision of the ECJ. As a result, the Commission after more than twenty years brought proceedings against France. In Case C–334/94 *Commission v France*[98] the French government repeated the same arguments as 20 years before with the knowledge that since 1973 the ECJ has confirmed in many cases that neither a ministerial circular nor an administrative practice, even long established, are adequate measures to ensure the proper application of Community law.[99] It was probably proof of the famous French sense of humour which certainly did not amuse the ECJ, when the French government declared that new French legislation aimed at replacing the Maritime Code, which should be adopted in the near future, was in preparation.

Another defence which was invoked in Case 167/73 *Commission v France,* and which failed for the reason of confusing EC nationals and creating legal uncertainty, was based on direct effect of Community law. This is, indeed, an interesting defence under which, on the one hand, the supremacy of EC law ensures that in the case of a conflict between Community law and national law the former will prevail and, on the other, hand that an individual may rely on directly effective provisions of Community law in proceedings brought before a national court. After some hesitation[100] the ECJ in Case C–433/93 *Commission v Germany*[101] held that under art 189(3) EC the application of a directive must

---

[96] [1992] ECR I–5871.
[97] [1974] ECR 359.
[98] Judgment of 7 March 1996.
[99] For example, Case 168/85 *Commission v Italy* [1986] ECR 2945.
[100] Case 29/84 *Commission v Germany (Re Nursing Directive)* [1985] ECR 1661 in which the ECJ held that the defence based on direct effect of Community law might be accepted provided that three conditions were satisfied: administrative practice must fully ensure the application of Community law; there must be no legal uncertainty concerning the legal situation which the directive regulates; and individuals concerned must be aware of their rights. In this case those conditions were not satisfied.
[101] [1995] ECR I–2303.

be ensured by implementing measures adopted by a Member State independently of the possible direct effect of its provisions. In Case C–253/95 *Commission* v *Germany*[102] the ECJ added that the direct effect is invoked only in special circumstances, especially when a Member State did not take the necessary implementing measures as required under the directive or if it has adopted implementing measures but they have not conformed with the directive. The ECJ emphasised that direct effect constitutes only a minimum guarantee resulting from the binding nature of the obligation imposed upon the Member State by the directive and is insufficient in itself to ensure its full and complete application.

9.2 Action against a Member State by another Member State under art 170 EC

For the Member States an alternative to proceedings under art 169 EC is provided in art 170 EC which states that:

'A Member State which considers that another Member State has failed to fulfil an obligation under this Treaty may bring the matter before the Court of Justice [ECJ].

Before a Member State brings an action against another Member State for alleged infringement of an obligation under this Treaty, it shall bring the matter before the Commission.

The Commission shall deliver a reasoned opinion after each of the States concerned has been given the opportunity to submit its own case and its observations on the other party's case both orally and in writing.

If the Commission has not delivered an opinion within three months of the date on which the matter was brought before it, the absence of such opinion shall not prevent the matter from being brought before the Court of Justice.'

The Treaties of Rome, arts 170 EC and 142 Euratom, recognise the autonomous right for the Member States to act against a Member State that has failed to fulfil its obligations arising from Community law. A Member State is not required to justify its interest to act and thus may bring an action against the defaulting State if it believes that the general interests of the Community necessitates such action, or if it considers that the illegal conduct of another Member State affected its vital interests. However, the Commission is very much involved in those proceedings: first, before a Member State brings an action against another Member State, the Commission must be seised; second, the Commission must proceed in the exactly same manner as under art 169 EC, that is, it investigates the matter, and gives both parties an opportunity to submit their arguments orally and in writing; and, finally, the Commission delivers a reasoned opinion within three months of the date on which the matter was brought.

The involvement of the Commission serves two purposes. On the one hand the Commission during the period of three months acts as an intermediary between the Member States concerned, and it attempts to settle the case and find an acceptable solution to the crisis. Indeed, hostility between two Member States undermines the unity of the

---

[102] [1996] ECR I–2423.

Community as a whole and may even paralyse its proper functioning. Therefore, the period of three months is in reality the 'cooling-off' period during which the Commission endeavours to resolve the matter in the light of the Community interest. On the other hand, the participation of the Commission in proceedings under art 170 EC emphasises its privileged role as 'guardian of the Treaty', as well as the exceptional nature of an action against a Member State by another Member State. The case law in respect of art 170 EC confirms this point. Actions under art 170 EC are extremely rare and in general never reach the ECJ. So far the ECJ has delivered only one judgment under art 170 EC in Case 141/78 *France v United Kingdom (Re Fishing Mesh)*.[103]

In this case the United Kingdom enacted an Order in Council concerning the size of the mesh of fishing nets. Fishing policy is within the exclusive competence of the Community but under the Resolution adopted by the Council at The Hague meeting in 1976, and pending the implementation of the appropriate measures by the Community, the Member States were permitted to take unilateral interim measures to ensure the protection of fishery resources. Annex VI to the Council Resolution requires that the Member State which intends to take conservation measures notifies the other Member States. Furthermore, those measures must be approved by the Commission and the latter must be consulted at all stages of the procedure. The United Kingdom failed to do so. The United Kingdom argued that the measures taken to conserve fishing stocks were not unilateral as they were adopted under the North-East Atlantic Fisheries Convention and thus there was no need to consult the Commission and the other Member States. The Commission delivered a reasoned opinion in favour of France. It stated that the United Kingdom failed in its obligation arising from art 5 EC and that in the light of divergencies of interest, which made it impossible for the Community to establish a common policy in the area of the conservation of the biological resources of the sea, the consultations with the other Member States and the Commission were even more necessary. France decided to bring the matter before the ECJ because the Commission did not assume responsibility for continuing the action.

The ECJ held that the United Kingdom was in breach of art 5 EC, Annex VI to the Hague Resolution and arts 2 and 3 of Regulation 101/76 which set out a common structural policy for the fishing industry and which require Member States to notify any alterations to fishery rules. The ECJ held that:

> 'Annex VI to the Hague Resolution, in the words of which "the Member States will not take any unilateral measures in respect of the conservation of resources" except in certain circumstances and with due observance of the requirements set out above, must be understood as referring to any measure of conservation emanating from the Member State and not from the Community authorities. The duty of consultation arising under that resolution thus also covers measures adopted by a Member State to comply with one of its international obligations in this matter. Such consultation was all the more necessary in this case since it is common ground, as has been emphasised by the French government and the Commission and accepted by the government of the United Kingdom itself, that the order in question, although carrying out certain recommendations of the North-East Atlantic Fisheries Convention, nevertheless in some respects goes beyond the requirements flowing from those recommendations.'

---

[103] [1979] ECR 2923.

Disputes between Member States concerning the application of the Treaty, for political reasons, are settled under art 169 EC. This solution is advantageous to the Member States for two reasons. The Member State concerned avoids unnecessary confrontations with another Member State while achieving the objectives sought, that is, to compel the defaulting Member State to comply with Community law. The Commission bears the burden of proof and conducts the investigations. Furthermore, under art 37 of the Statute of the ECJ the Member State, or the other Community institutions, may intervene to support or reject the application of the Commission in the case brought before the ECJ.[104]

9.3 Effect of a ruling confirming a failure of a Member State to fulfil its obligations under the Treaty

There is no express provision in the EC Treaty regarding the legal effect of the ECJ rulings under art 169 EC. However, it results from art 171 EC that they are declaratory in nature. In this respect art 171(1) EC provides that:

> 'If the Court of Justice finds that a Member State has failed to fulfil an obligation under this Treaty, that State shall be required to take the necessary measures to comply with the judgment of the Court of Justice.'

Thus, the defaulting Member State must take all necessary measures in order to remedy the failure and its consequences both in the past and in the future.[105] Furthermore, national courts and national authorities of the defaulting Member State are required to disapply any national law declared incompatible with Community law, and to take all appropriate measures to ensure the effective application of the latter.[106] If the judgment concerns the interpretation of Community law, its effect under art 169 EC is similar to ECJ rulings rendered under art 177 EC.[107] For individuals there are two aspects of a ruling under art 169 EC. In Joined Cases 314–316/81 and 83/82 *Procureur de la Republique* v *Waterkeyn*[108] the ECJ held that:

> '... if the Court finds in proceedings under arts 169 to 171 of the EEC Treaty that a Member State's legislation is incompatible with the obligations which it has under the Treaty the courts of that State are bound by virtue of art 171 to draw the necessary inferences from the judgment of the Court. However, it should be understood that the rights accruing to individuals derive, not from that judgment, but from the actual provisions of Community law having direct effect in the internal legal order.'

---

[104] In such cases the ECJ grants or refuses to grant leave to intervene in support of the order sought by the Commission or the Member State concerned. For example, in Case C–80/92 *Commission* v *Belgium* [1994] ECR I–1019, the ECJ granted the United Kingdom leave to intervene in support of the form of order sought by the Commission. In Case C–246/89 *Commission* v *United Kingdom (Re Nationality of Fishermen)* [1991] ECR 3125 the ECJ granted leave to Spain to intervene in support of the form of order sought by the Commission and to Ireland to intervene in support of the form of order sought by the United Kingdom. However, private parties are not permitted to intervene.
[105] Case 70/72 *Commission* v *Germany* [1973] ECR 813.
[106] Case 48/71 *Commission* v *Italy* [1972] ECR 536.
[107] See chapter 11.
[108] [1982] ECR 4337.

It means that if the provision in question of the Community law is not directly effective, an individual cannot invoke it in the proceedings before a national court. The latter will apply a national provision contrary to Community law even though the ECJ has expressly recognised that this provision is in breach of EC law. Second, for individuals who have suffered loss resulting from the infringement of Community law by the Member State, the ruling of the ECJ confirming the failure of the Member State to fulfil that particular obligation provides sufficient evidence for national courts to award them pecuniary compensation.[109]

However, the ECJ is not a federal court and thus it is not empowered to annul national law incompatible with Community law,[110] or to compel the defaulting Member State to comply with its judgment by granting an injunction or to impose pecuniary penalty.

In the context of judgments rendered by the ECJ under art 169 EC, it is interesting to mention Case 274/93 *Commission v Luxembourg*.[111] In this case the ECJ gave the judgment in default of appearance. Indeed, Luxembourg neither replied to the letter of formal notice, nor to the reasoned opinion, nor submitted its arguments during the proceedings before the ECJ. The default of appearance is very unusual,[112] although this case has many peculiarities: the ECJ accepted the application from the Commission even though the complaint in the judicial stage concerned the incorrect implementation of a directive, while in the administrative stage the Commission submitted that Luxembourg did not implement the directive in question and failed to provide information as to the implementing measure. As already discussed, failure of the Commission to ensure that the complaint remains the same in all stages of the proceedings under art 169 EC results in the rejection by the ECJ of the application. Probably, the attitude of Luxembourg incited the ECJ to accept the application as it stood, although the ECJ might have limited the complaint to the provisions which were incontestably non-implemented,[113] or invoked art 5 EC to sanction the failure of Luxembourg to co-operate in the proceedings.[114]

Failure to comply with a ruling under art 169 EC

The Treaties of Rome do not specify a time-limit for compliance with a judgment rendered under art 169 EC. However, the ECJ has imposed strict conditions in this respect. In Case 69/86 *Commission v Italy*[115] the ECJ held that:

'Article 171 of the EEC Treaty does not specify the period within which a judgment must be complied with. However, it is beyond dispute that the action required to give effect to a

---

[109] Case C–6/90 *Francovich* [1991] ECR I–5403.
[110] For example, Case 6/60 *Humblot* [1960] ECR 1125.
[111] [1996] ECR I–2019.
[112] Also Case 68/88 *Commission v Greece* [1989] ECR 2965.
[113] As suggested by Advocate-General Jacobs. This possibility was recognised in Case C–257/94 *Commission v Ireland* [1995] ECR I–3041.
[114] It seems that the government of Luxembourg has a habit of ignoring the letters of formal notice and the reasoned opinion delivered by the Commission: see conclusions of Advocate-General Elmer in Case C–46/95 *Commission v Luxembourg* [1997] ECR I–1279 concerning Directive 89/618/ Euratom [1996] Europe (June), no 235, comm D Simon.
[115] [1987] ECR 773. See also Case 169/87 *Commission v France* [1988] ECR 4093 and Case C–334/94 *Commission v France* [1996] ECR I–1307, which has probably set a record – more than 20 years of non-compliance (that is, between the judgment of the ECJ in the original infringement proceedings rendered on 4 April 1974 and the subsequent proceedings based on art 171 EC).

judgment must be set in motion immediately and be completed in the shortest possible period.'

The non-compliance with judgments rendered under art 169 EC became a serious problem in the late 1980s when the Commission started to pursue the defaulting Member States more vigorously and discovered that Member States were more than reluctant to co-operate with the Commission on many matters. Until the entry into force of the Treaty of Maastricht the excessive delays and flagrant refusals on the part of the defaulting Member States to comply with the judgments of the ECJ were not sanctioned. The Commission as a guardian of the Treaty was bound to take the necessary steps to compel the defaulting Member State to remedy the breach,[116] which consisted of introducing second proceedings based on art 169 EC for the breach of art 171 EC.[117] In those circumstances a more radical approach was necessary. The Treaty of Maastricht has addressed this situation.

Pecuniary sanctions under art 171(2) EC

The TEU added a new para 2 to art 171 which provides that:

> 'If the Commission considers that the Member State concerned has not taken such measures it shall, after giving that State the opportunity to submit its observations, issue a reasoned opinion specifying the points on which the Member State concerned has not complied with the judgment of the Court of Justice.
>
> If the Member State concerned failed to take the necessary measures to comply with the Court's judgment within the time-limit laid down by the Commission, the latter may bring the case before the Court of Justice. In so doing it shall specify the amount of the lump sum or penalty to be paid by the Member State concerned which it considers appropriate in the circumstances.
>
> If the Court of Justice finds that the Member State concerned has not complied with its judgment it may impose a lump sum or penalty payment on it.
>
> This procedure shall be without prejudice to art 170.'

In the Memorandum of 5 June 1996 on applying art 171 EC,[118] the Commission submitted its view on the actual amount of the lump sum or penalty payment. It stated the criteria it meant to apply in asking the ECJ to impose monetary penalties. The Commission emphasised that:

1. It has a discretion in deciding whether to refer the case to the ECJ, which means that in some cases the Commission will not ask for a penalty to be imposed, for example where the infringement is minor or there is no risk of the offence being repeated.
2. Although art 171(2) EC refers to two types of pecuniary sanction, a lump sum or a penalty payment, the Commission considers that a penalty payment is the most appropriate taking into account the objective of art 171(2) EC, that is to secure compliance as rapidly as possible.
3. In the determination of the amount of the penalty the Commission considers that three

---

[116] Case 281/83 *Commission v Italy* [1985] ECR 3397.
[117] Case 48/71 *Commission v Italy* [1972] ECR 529.
[118] OJ C242 21.8.96 p6.

factors are fundamental: the seriousness of the infringement; its duration; and the need to ensure that the penalty itself is a deterrent to further infringement.

These criteria were further elaborated in the Commission Communication of 8 January 1997, which contained the detailed mode of calculation of penalty payments applicable to all types of non-compliance with the original judgment.[119]

The Commission fixed the 'basic uniform flat-rate amount' at ECU 500 per day of delay which is affected by two coefficients: one relating to the seriousness of the infringement; and the second relating to the duration of the infringement. For example, the Commission considers as very serious the breach of the principle of non-discrimination, and also the infringement of EC Treaty provisions ensuring the four freedoms of movement and the proper resources of the European Union. Furthermore, a Member State which contravenes a clear rule or well-established case law of the ECJ is committing a more serious infringement than one which incorrectly applies a vague and complex community rule which has never been interpreted by the ECJ. The effect of the infringement on general interests of the EU and particular interests of individuals will be assessed on a case-by-case basis in order to determine the seriousness of the infringement. In this respect the loss of own resources suffered by the Community, the impact of the infringement on the functioning of the Community, its damage to human health or the environment, the financial advantage the Member State might gain as a result of non-compliance with the ECJ judgment, and the number of people affected by the infringement will be taken into account. Depending on the seriousness of the infringement the flat-rate amount will be multiplied by a co-efficient of at least one and no more than 20.

In relation to the duration of the infringement, it runs from the date of the first ECJ judgment, and in its assessment the Commission will take into account the Member State's refusal to respond or its delay in doing so. Depending on the duration of the infringement, the flat-rate amount will be multiplied by a co-efficient of at least one and no more than three.

In order to make the penalty a real deterrent to non-compliance with the judgment, the Commission will apply a special factor 'n' which is a geometric mean based on the Member State's gross domestic product (GDP), and the weighting of votes in the Council of the European Union. It reflects the ability of each Member State to pay (measured by its GDP) and the number of votes it has in the Council. The special factor is within the scale of one to 26.4. The amount of the daily penalty is arrived at by multiplying the flat rate by the co-efficients for the seriousness and duration of the infringement and by the special (invariable) factor 'n'.

Examples of financial implications of the daily penalty and the invariable factor 'n' for each Member State follow:[120]

---

[119] Method of calculating the penalty payments provided for pursuant to art 171 of the EC Treaty: OJ C63 28.2.97 p2.
[120] The European Commission, IP/97/5, 8 January 1997 (OJ C63 28.2.97).

Member State	Invariable Factor (n)	Example of penalty with minimum duration and severity	Example of penalty with maximum duration and severity
Belgium	6.2	3,115	186,888
Denmark	3.9	1,935	116,130
Germany	26.4	13,188	791,293
Greece	4.1	2,030	121,786
Spain	11.4	5,682	340,903
France	21.1	10,530	631,771
Eire	2.4	1,180	70,783
Italy	17.7	8,852	531,150
Luxembourg	1.0	500	30,000
Netherlands	7.6	3,776	226,567
Austria	5.1	2,549	152,961
Portugal	3.9	1,933	115,972
Finland	3.9	1,644	98,652
Sweden	5.2	2,578	154,683
United Kingdom	17.8	8,906	534,344

The Commission favours the penalty payment which is more appropriate that the imposition of the lump sum.

The Commission announced its intention to apply the penalty payments envisaged in art 171 EC. For non-compliance with original judgments of the ECJ rendered in relation to non-implementation or incorrect implementation of EC directives in environmental matters the Commission suggested, for example, against Germany the penalty of ECU 26,400 per day (Directive 'Wild Birds'), ECU 264,000 per day (Directive 'Underground Water'), ECU 158,400 per day (Directive 'Surface Water'); and against Italy ECU 123,900 per day (Directive 'Waste'), ECU 159,300 per day (Directive 'Radiation').[121]

The ECJ is not bound by the figure suggested by the Commission. It may increase or reduce the fine or may decide not to impose any penalty at all. It remain to be seen to what extent the imposition of penalty payments encourage, if at all, defaulting Member States to honour their obligations under the Treaty.

In respect of art 171 EC an interesting point was raised by Advocate-General Fenelly in Case C–334/94 *Commission v France (Re the French Maritime Code II)*.[122] He argued that if the defaulting Member State has failed to comply with the original judgment under art 169 EC, the Commission should bring the second proceedings under art 171(2) EC instead of art 169 EC. He considered that art 171(2) EC contains a specific procedure which applies only to the cases of non-compliance with original judgments. According to him, art 171(2) EC presents an imperative character and excludes an action against a defaulting Member State under art 169 EC taking into account that the failure was already declared in the original proceedings on the same basis. Although Advocate-General Fenelly submitted his

---

[121] [1997] Europe (April), no 104.
[122] [1996] ECR I–1307.

suggestion on 15 of his 22 pages of conclusions, the ECJ declined to reply. Thus, the relationship between arts 169 and 171 EC, and especially its para 2, is still unclear.

9.4 Simplified procedures

Under certain provisions of the EC Treaty the proceedings against the defaulting Member State are simplified. The common point of those procedure is the possibility for the Commission or the Member States to bring the matter directly before the ECJ in a much shorter period of time than under arts 169 or 170 EC. Usually, the administrative stage takes a different, simplified form and the Commission is not bound to deliver the reasoned opinion.

Procedure under art 93(2) EC

Under art 93(1) EC the Commission, in co-operation with Member States, must keep under constant review all systems of State aid existing in those States, while under art 93(3) 'any plans to grant or alter aid' intended to modify or establish new ones must be notified to the Commission with a view to assessing their compatibility with the common market. Thus, there are two simplified procedures under art 93 EC, but the differences between them are not substantial. In both cases, if a Member State fails to notify new aid or substantially alters the existing aids the Commission may bring proceedings under art 169 EC, especially if the legality of the aid must be assessed in the light of other provisions of the Treaty.[123] However, if the Commission is not certain whether the aid in question conforms to the objectives of the common market it may act on its own initiative, or on the basis of the complaint from a Member State, or an undertaking affected by the aid under art 93(2) EC. The Commission gives notice to the parties concerned – the Member State in question, other Member States, the undertaking[124] – to submit their comments, and on the basis of these it decides whether the aid granted by a State, or through State resources, is compatible or not with the common market. Under art 169 EC the Commission has a large measure of discretion in commencing proceedings under art 90(3) EC. The procedural guarantees, such the right to a hearing for all concerned, etc, as well as the formal requirements under art 93(2), must be respected. If the Commission considers that the aid in question in incompatible with the common market, it issues a decision fixing the time-limit for the Member State concerned to abolish or alter such aid. If the Commission fails to impose a time-limit for compliance with its decision in the case of the abolition or amendment of existing aid the ECJ decided in Case 120/73 *Lorenz* v *Germany*[125] that a two-month period would normally be appropriate. This decision is reviewable under art 173 EC.[126] Once, the time-limit elapses, the Commission or any Member State may bring the matter directly before the ECJ without

---

[123] Case 70/72 *Commission* v *Germany* [1973] ECR 813; Case 177/78 *Pigs and Bacon Commission* v *McCarren* [1979] ECR 2161.
[124] Case 60/79 *Producteur de vins de table et vin de pays* v *Commission* [1979] ECR 2429.
[125] [1973] ECR 1471.
[126] For example, Case C–312/90 *Spain* v *Commission* [1992] ECR I–4117.

satisfying the procedural requirements laid down in art 169 EC. There is a possibility for a Member State in exceptional circumstances to apply to the Council to have the existing or the intended aid authorised. The latter must decide unanimously. In such event, the Commission suspends proceedings under art 93(2) EC until a decision is reached by the Council.

It is interesting to note that under art 93(2) EC some Member States succeeded in invoking *force majeure* in their defence, although within the limit determined by the ECJ.[127] In order to comply with the decision, under art 93(3) EC the Member State concerned must not only abolish the offending aid but also recover it from recipients.

Procedure under arts 100a(4) and 100b(2) EC

The SEA introduced majority voting in matters necessary for the completion of the common market. As a counterpart, a simplified procedure was introduced in art 100a(4) EC which allows the Member States to apply national provisions incompatible with the harmonisation measures adopted by the Council on the grounds of major needs defined in art 36 EC, that is: public policy, public morality, public security, the protection of health and life of humans and animals, protection of national treasures possessing artistic, historic or archaeological value and protection of intellectual property, or relating to protection of the environment or the working conditions. Those national measures must be notified to the Commission which decides whether or not to authorise them. Under art 100a(4), by way of derogation from the procedure of arts 169 and 170 EC, the Commission or any Member State may bring proceedings directly before the ECJ if it considers that a Member State is abusing or making improper use of art 100a(4) EC, that is, it applies national rules incompatible with the establishment and functioning of the internal market without prior authorisation from the Commission.

An identical procedure is provided in art 100b(2) EC. It applies when a Member State refuses to accept that the national provisions in force are equivalent to those applied by another Member State despite the decision of the Council recognising their identity.

Procedure under art 225 EC

Similarly, under art 225 EC in the circumstances described in art 223 EC, that is, in matters relating to national security, especially connected with the production of, or trade in, arms, ammunition and war material, or under art 224 in the event of war, serious internal disturbances and international tension, a Member State is not permitted to adopt abusive measures distorting the conditions of competition in the common market. If it does, the Commission or any Member State may bring the matter directly before the ECJ.[128]

---

[127] Case 52/84 *Commission v Belgium* [1986] ECR 89; Case C–183/91 *Commission v Greece* [1993] ECR I–3131; Case C–349/93 *Commission v Italy* [1995] ECR I–343.

[128] So far this procedure has been used once in Case C–120/94R *Commission v Greece* [1994] ECR I–3037, Ord of the ECJ of 29 June 1994, and concerned the imposition by Greece of restriction on the movement of goods from the former Yugoslav Republic of Macedonia.

10 Action against Community Institutions

10.1 Direct action for annulment: art 173 EC

10.2 Indirect action: plea of illegibility under art 184 EC

10.3 Direct action for failure to act: art 175 EC

10.4 Action for damages: non-contractual liability of the Community

---

Under art 3b(1) EC all Community institutions are required to act within the limits of the powers conferred upon them by the Treaties. Community law provides for a number of mechanisms intended to ensure that EC institutions function properly and do not exceed their powers. The protection of the interests of all subjects of Community law against illegal acts of Community institutions is conferred upon the Community courts: the ECJ and the Court of First Instance. In this respect, they exercise jurisdiction similar to administrative courts in the Member States and the role of the ECJ is very similar to the French *Conseil d'Etat* (the highest administrative court in France).

Community law recognises three direct actions against Community institutions – action for annulment of Community acts under art 173 EC; action for failure to act against Community institutions under art 175 EC; and action for damages caused by the Community to individuals involving non-contractual liability of the former under arts 178 and 215(2) EC – and one indirect action, the so-called plea of illegality under art 184 EC.

10.1 Direct action for annulment: art 173 EC

Actions for annulment are provided in arts 33 and 38 ECSC, 146 Euratom and 173 EC and, although regulated by different procedural rules, they present a certain substantive homogeneity because they are all inspired by the French administrative procedure. However, they reflect the peculiarity of the Community legal order, especially in relation to conditions of admissibility, which tend to restrict access to the Community courts for certain categories of applicants. The main features of an action of annulment concern: conditions of admissibility which are set out in art 173 EC; the grounds for annulment provided in art 173(2) EC; and the effect of annulment which is regulated in arts 174 and 176 EC. Article 173 EC was substantially altered in order to incorporate changes introduced by the TEU to the EEC Treaty, or already recognised by the ECJ, mainly to include the European Parliament as a possible applicant and to add the European Central Bank (ECB), a new EC institution, to the list of applicants. Furthermore, it has extended the category of acts capable of review to acts adopted jointly by the European Parliament and the Council, acts of the European Parliament and acts of the ECB.

The new version of art 173 EC provides:

> 'The Court of Justice shall review the legality of acts adopted jointly by the European Parliament and the Council, of acts of the Council, of the Commission and the ECB, other than recommendations and opinions, and of acts of the European Parliament intended to produce legal effects vis-à-vis third parties.
>
> It shall for this purpose have jurisdiction in actions brought by a Member State, the Council or the Commission on grounds of lack of competence, infringement of an essential legal requirement, infringement of this Treaty or any rule of law relating to its application, or misuse of powers.
>
> The Court shall have jurisdiction under the same conditions in actions brought by the European Parliament and by the ECB for the purpose of protecting their prerogatives.
>
> Any natural or legal person may, under the same conditions, institute proceedings against a decision addressed to that person or against a decision which, although in the form of a regulation or a decision addressed to another person, is of direct and individual concern to the former.
>
> The proceedings provided for in this article shall be instituted within two months of the publication of the measure, or of its notification to the plaintiff, or, in the absence thereof, of the day on which it came to the knowledge of the latter as the case may be.'

An action for annulment is similar to what is known under English law (and also recognised in Scottish law) as an application for judicial review.

Conditions of admissibility of Community acts

The conditions of admissibility of Community acts concern: the time-limit for bringing an action for annulment; the category of acts susceptible to be reviewed; and the category of applicants permitted to act on the basis of art 173 EC.

Time-limit

The time-limit is different for each Community: one month under the ECSC Treaty and two months under the EC and Euratom Treaties. It is regrettable from the point of view of legal certainty that the subsequent amendments to the founding Treaties have omitted to provide the same the time-limit for bringing an action for annulment.

The time-limit begins to run from the date of publication of an act in the Official Journal of the European Communities, or from its notification to the applicant.[1] If the act was published, by virtue of art 81 of the Rules of Procedure of the ECJ and the CFI, the commencement of the time-limit is extended by 15 days, and further extension is granted to take into consideration the distance of the applicant from the Community courts.[2] In the case of an applicant from the United Kingdom the extension amounts to an additional ten days. Therefore, the time-limit is two months, plus 15 days, plus ten days. In the absence of

---

[1] In Case 76/79 *Konecke* [1980] ECR 665 the ECJ held that the time-limit starts to run the day after the notification took place, which should permit the applicant to identify the adopted decision, and take notice of its exact content in order to exercise his right of appeal.

[2] Article 42 of the Statute of the ECJ and arts 80–82 of the Rules of Procedure of the ECJ and the CFI.

publication or notification the time-limit starts at the day when the act came to the knowledge of the applicant.[3]

The time-limit is rigorously enforced by the Community courts. Once it elapses, the application is deemed inadmissible *d'office*,[4] that is the act is immune from annulment. This is justified by the principle of legal certainty and equality in the administration of justice.[5] However, in Cases 25 and 26/65 *Simet* the ECJ accepted an exception to the strict observance of the time-limit based on *force majeure*.[6]

Reviewable acts

Under the terms of art 173 EC the following acts adopted by Community institutions are reviewable: acts of the Council and the Commission other than recommendations and opinions; acts adopted jointly by the European Parliament and the Council, that is, acts adopted within the framework of the procedure laid out in art 189b EC; acts of the ECB other than recommendations and opinions; and acts of the European Parliament intended to produce legal effects vis-à-vis a third party. As a result, acts capable of review must be examined from two perspectives: the author of the act and the nature of the act.

Author of the Act. Only acts adopted by EC institutions are reviewable. As a result, acts adopted by a particular Member State or Member States are excluded from the scope of art 173 EC. This principle is self-evident, but in practice it is not always easy to determine whether a particular act should be considered as adopted by a Community institution or a Member State. For example, in Case C–97/91 *Oleificio Borelli*[7] the ECJ held as inadmissible an act adopted by a Member State within the framework of a very complex Community procedure concerning the granting of aid from Community structural funds. Therefore, if an act constitutes an element of the Community procedure it is not within the scope of art 173 EC. Second, sometimes Member States act within the Council but outside its competence as a Community institution. The question of how to determine whether an act, irrespective of its form and name, adopted by the Council is considered as an act of the Council, or as an act adopted by the Member States meeting within the framework of the Council as a international conference, was resolved in Case 22/70 *Commission v Council (ERTA)*.[8] In this case the ECJ had to decide, *inter alia*, whether deliberations concerning the European Road Transport Agreement (ERTA) were reviewable under art 173 EC. The ECJ held that the qualification of an act depends upon the determination as to who, at the envisaged time, has competence to negotiate and conclude an agreement. The legal effect of the deliberations varies depending whether they are considered as an act within the competence of the Community or an expression of the policy co-ordination between the

---

[3] Case 59/84 *Tezi Textiel* [1986] ECR 887. However, in the absence of a formal notification, and provided that the applicant knew the content of the final position adopted by an EC institution, the time-limit starts to run at the time the definite decision came into his knowledge: Case T–452 and 453/93R *Pesqueria Vasco-Montanesa Ord* [1994] ECR II–229 Ord.

[4] For example, Case 108/79 *Belfiore* [1980] ECR 1769.

[5] Case 209/83 *Valsabbia* [1984] ECR 3089.

[6] [1967] ECR 40. See also Case C–195/91P *Bayer* [1994] ECR I–5619.

[7] [1992] ECR I–6332, recently confirmed in Case T–271/94 *Branco* [1996] ECR II–749.

[8] [1971] ECR 263.

Member States in a specific area. The ECJ decided that these deliberations belonged to the first category since the Community had competence to negotiate and conclude the ERTA and as such it was reviewable under art 173 EC. The opposite decision was rendered by the ECJ in Cases C–181/91 *Parliament v Council* and C–248/91 *Parliament v Commission* in which the ECJ held inadmissible for the purposes of art 173 EC an act adopted on the proposal of the Commission by 'the Member States meeting within the Council' granting emergency aid to Bangladesh,[9] in so far as there is no exclusive competence of the Community in the area of humanitarian aid.

It is submitted that an act adopted by the European Council should not be excluded from being reviewable under art 173 EC if that act was intended to produce legal effects.[10] Nevertheless, the Community courts, so far, seem to be reluctant to accept it.[11]

Where one EC institution delegates certain powers to another EC institution, the question arises as to who is the author of the act. The case law of the ECJ is well established in this respect: the author of the act is the institution which has delegated its competences.[12] This solution is justified for two reasons. First, the delegate institution may adopt an act which would not be reviewable and thus the applicants would be prevented from challenging that act under art 173 EC and, second, the delegate institution is empowered to implement the measure but on its own has no competence to adopt it. Also, if a certain task is delegated to a particular person, for example the Commission empowers one of the Commissioners to inform the addressee that an act has been adopted by the Commission, that act is deemed to emanate from the Commission.[13]

Acts adopted by the European Parliament were not reviewable under art 173 EC. The ECJ has, however, in a number of decisions, recognised that acts of the EP may be challenged. In Case 230/81 *Luxembourg v Parliament*[14] the deliberations of the European Parliament concerning the change of its seat were challenged by Luxembourg under art 173. The ECJ held the action was admissible since those deliberations concerned all three Communities, and based its decision on art 38 ECSC Treaty which permits a challenge to acts of the Parliament. The full recognition of acts of Parliament, as reviewable by the ECJ, constitutes one of the cases of judicial revision of the Treaty and was necessary taking into account the evolution of the EP from an advisory and supervisory body to a body involved in the decision-making procedures. It was also necessary in the light of the doctrine of *effet utile* in relation to the control of the legality of acts of EC institutions in cases of acts adopted by the European Parliament intended to produce a legal effect vis-à-vis a third party. In Case 294/83 *Les Verts v Parliament*[15] the ECJ could not make reference to art 38 ECSC as in Case 230/81 *Luxembourg v Parliament* since this provision rules out the possibility of natural and legal persons commencing an action for annulment. As a result, the ECJ recognised the reviewability of acts emanating from the Parliament and explained

---

[9] Cases C–181 *Parliament v Council* and C–248/91 *Parliament v Commission* [1993] ECR I–3685.
[10] Answers of the Council to Certain Parliamentary Questions, Q no 293/76 (OJ C269 15.11.76 p6) and Q no 294/76 (OJ C294 13.12.76 p4).
[11] Case C–253/94P *Roujanski* [1995] ECR I–7.
[12] Cases 32 and 33/58 *SNUPAT* [1959] ECR 275.
[13] Case 48/69 *ICI* [1972] ECR 652. The ECJ has accepted the validity of the delegation of signature.
[14] [1983] ECR 255.
[15] [1986] ECR 1339.

that since the EEC is a Community based on the rule of law, neither the Member States nor Community institutions can escape the control of the conformity of their acts with the basic constitutional charter, that is the EEC Treaty. It further added that:

'... Measures adopted by the European Parliament in the context of the EEC Treaty could encroach on the powers of the Member States or of the other institutions, or exceed the limits which have been set to the Parliament's powers, without its being possible to refer them for review by the Court. It must therefore be concluded that an action for annulment may lie against measures adopted by the European Parliament intended to have legal effects vis-à-vis third parties'.

The last sentence was incorporated into art 173 EC by the Treaty on European Union.

The case law of the ECJ demonstrates that reviewable acts of the EP comprise not only acts adopted by the EP as an institution but also by its organs such as its Bureau for the allocation of funds amongst political parties,[16] or the Declaration of the President of the European Parliament regarding the adoption of the Community budget.[17] Acts which are not considered as reviewable under art 173 EC include: the act establishing a Parliamentary Commission of inquiry,[18] the waiver of immunity,[19] or acts emanating from the EP's political parties or political groups.[20]

Acts adopted by the Court of Auditors are also reviewable. While the Treaty of Maastricht is silent in this respect, in Cases 193 and 194/87 *Maurissen*[21] the ECJ accepted an action for annulment brought by a union against the Court of Auditors. All uncertainty was further dissipated by the ECJ in Case C–416/92 *H* v *Court of Auditors*.[22]

On the basis of the TEU acts of other EC Institutions are reviewable and these include: acts of the European Investment Bank under art 180 EC,[23] and the European Monetary Institute under art 109f(9) EC; the European Investment Fund under art 30(6) of the Protocol on Statute of the EIB; the Board of Appeal of the Community Trade Mark Office under art 63 of Council Regulation 40/94;[24] and the Community Plant Variety Office and its Board of Appeal under art 73 and 74 of Council Regulation 2100/94.[25]

Finally, international agreements concluded between the Community and third countries cannot be considered as acts emanating from the EC institutions. Since a Member State or Member States and third countries participate in their adoption they cannot be classified as Community acts. It is submitted that the ruling of the ECJ in Case 181/73 *Haegeman*,[26] in which the Court decided otherwise, should be rejected. Indeed, the reviewability of international agreements between the Community and third countries

---

[16] Ibid.

[17] Case 34/86 *Council* v *Parliament* [1986] ECR 2155; Case C–284/90 *Council* v *Parliament* [1992] ECR I–2328.

[18] Case 78/85 *Groupe des Droites Européennes* [1986] ECR 1754.

[19] Case 149/85 *Wybot* [1986] ECR 2403.

[20] Case C–210/89 *Le Pen* [1990] ECR I–1183.

[21] [1989] ECR 1045.

[22] [1994] ECR I–1741.

[23] In Case T–460/93E *Tete* v *EIB* [1993] ECR II–1257 the CFI specified that acts of the EIB are reviewable within the limits defined by art 180 EC.

[24] OJ L11 14.1.94 p1.

[25] OJ L227 1.9.94 p1.

[26] [1974] ECR 449.

ignores the distinction between international agreements themselves and acts adopted by EC institutions regarding the conclusion or application of such agreements. In the first case, the ECJ should not exercise jurisdiction under art 173 EC because international agreements are not acts of EC institutions, they are international treaties within the meaning of public international law. However, in the second case, the ECJ should be empowered to annul, for example, a decision of the Commission concerning the conclusion an agreement with a third country,[27] or a decision regarding the application of an international agreement,[28] because those acts emanate from EC institutions and as such are reviewable under art 173 EC.

Nature of the act. The ECJ has considerably extended the category of reviewable acts. In Case 22/70 *Commission v Council (ERTA)*[29] it held that not only acts listed in art 189 EC can be challenged under art 173 EC but also any act which has binding legal effects whatever their nature and form. This means all acts adopted by EC institutions which produce legal effects vis-à-vis third parties are reviewable, which considerably modifies the legal position of the applicant. The content and scope of application are the determinant factors, not the form and name of the act. The case law of the ECJ has clarified this point in relation to borderline cases since, in practice, it is not difficult to determine whether an act produces binding legal effect vis-à-vis the applicant.

The following acts have been held to be as reviewable under art 173 EC:

1. Deliberations of the Council in ERTA.[30]
2. A Communication of the Commission which by means of interpretation of a directive has introduced new obligations.[31]
3. A Code of Conduct adopted with a view of co-ordinating management of structural funds but published in the 'Communication and information' section of the Official Journal.[32]
4. A letter from the Commission.[33]
5. A decision orally communicated to the applicant.[34]
6. An official declaration made by the Commissioner in charge of competition matters declaring the EC Merger rules inapplicable to the acquisition of Dan Air by British Airways.[35]
7. A letter from the Commission stating reasons for rejecting a complaint under competition law.[36]

---

[27] Case C–327/91 *France v Commission* [1994] ECR I–3641.
[28] Case 30/88 *Greece v Commission* [1989] ECR 374.
[29] [1971] ECR 263.
[30] [1971] ECR 263.
[31] Case C–325/91 *France v Commission* [1993] ECR I–3283.
[32] Case C–303/90 *France and Belgium v Commission* [1991] ECR I–5315.
[33] Case 1/57 *Usines à Tubes de la Sarre* [1957] ECR 201.
[34] Cases 316/82 and 40/83 *Kohler* [1984] ECR 641; Case T–3/93 *Air France* [1994] ECR II–121.
[35] Case T–3/93 *Air France*, ibid.
[36] Case T–37/92 *BEUC* [1994] ECR II–285.

The ECJ held that the following acts are not reviewable under art 173 EC:

1. All acts which only confirm an existing situation since they do not modify a legal position of the applicant.[37]
2. All acts which set up a global policy of the Community in a specific area, that is establishing programmes of the Community since they envisage future measures and thus do not change the current legal situation of the applicant.[38]
3. All internal measures adopted by an EC institution which produce legal effects only vis-à-vis that institution, such as instructions, internal rules, circulars, etc.[39] However, they may be challenged indirectly, provided they produce binding legal effect, if an individual decision was based on such internal measures.[40]
4. All preparatory acts of EC institutions, since the challengeable act must be a final statement of an institution's position, not merely an interim position. In Case 60/81 *IBM v Commission*[41] the Commission's decision to commence proceedings against IBM and a statement of objections to its marketing practices as being incompatible with arts 85 and 86 EC (which was annexed to the decision) was considered as a step in the proceedings. The idea behind this rule is that work of EC institutions would be paralysed if preparatory acts were susceptible to challenge. However, an action of annulment against such acts is allowed if they produce binding effects, or if they constitute a final position in ancillary proceedings which would result in the adoption of a final decision. This distinction is difficult to determine in practice, especially in cases concerning competition law, State aid, and anti-dumping measures. For example, a decision to forward documents to the complaining undertaking,[42] a decision to deny access to a dossier in an anti-dumping case,[43] a decision to refuse to initiate proceedings under art 90(2) EC[44] and art 93(2) EC[45] were considered as reviewable, but not a letter refusing to protect confidentiality of documents forwarded to the Commission by the applicant.[46]
5. The decision of the Commission to refuse to initiate proceedings against a Member State in breach of Community law under art 169 EC. In Case 48/65 *Lütticke*[47] the ECJ held that the stage of proceedings under art 169 EC when the Commission states its position by issuing a reasoned opinion cannot be considered as producing binding legal effect. This has been confirmed in many cases.[48]

---

[37] Cases 42 and 49/59 SNUPAT [1961] ECR 105.
[38] Case 94/71 *Schlüter* [1973] ECR 307.
[39] Case 20/58 *Phoenix Rheinrohr* [1959] ECR 153; Case C–322/91 *TAO AFI* [1992] ECR 6373 (Ord).
[40] Cases 32 and 33/58 *SNUPAT* [1958] ECR 45.
[41] [1981] ECR 2639. See also Case C–282/95P *Guerin Automobiles*, Judgment of the ECJ of 18 March 1997, *Europe*, May 1997, note 162, comm L Idot.
[42] Case 53/85 *AKZO* [1986] ECR 1965; Case T–46/92 *The Scottish Football Association* [1994] ECR II–1039.
[43] Case C–170/89 *BEUC* [1991] ECR I–5709.
[44] Case C–313/90 *CIRFS* [1993] ECR I–1125
[45] Case C–312/90 *Spain v Commission* [1992] ECR I–4117; Case C–47/91 *Italy v Commission* [1992] ECR I–4145.
[46] Cases T–90 and T–136/96 *Automobiles Peugeot SA*, CFI Ord of 2 May 1997, *Europe*, July 1997, no 226, comm D Ritleng.
[47] [1966] ECR 28.
[48] Case C–87/89 *Sonito v Commission* [1990] ECR I–1981; Case C–247/90 *Emrich* [1990] ECR I–3914; Cases T–479 and 559/93 *Giorgio Bernardi v Commission* [1994] ECR II–1115.

6. Regulation 2187/93 which was adopted by the Council in order to comply with ECJ rulings concerning the illegality of Council regulations allocating milk quotas.[49] In those cases the ECJ held that the applicants (approximately 12,000 farmers) were entitled to damages by virtue of art 215(2) EC. Council Regulation 2187/93 contained a proposal for their compensation. In Case T–541/93 *Connaughton, Fitzsimons and Griffin* and Case T–554/93 *Murray*[50] the applicants brought an action for annulment of art 8 and 14 of Regulation 2187/93 which provided that the acceptance of compensation by a farmer precludes him from any other action, irrespective of its nature, against any Community institutions. The CFI held that the Regulation in question was only a proposal and as such did not produce legal effects. Consequently, it was not considered as a reviewable act within the meaning of art 173 EC. The CFI emphasised that once the proposal was accepted it would produce legal effects vis-à-vis the applicant, but not before.

Applicants under art 173 EC

Article 173 EC establishes three categories of applicants: privileged applicants who may bring an action for annulment against all reviewable acts and are not required to justify their interest to act; semi-privileged applicants, such as the European Parliament and the ECB which may only challenge acts in order to defend their prerogatives; and non-privileged applicants who have a reduced legal ability to bring an action under art 173 EC, in the sense that they may only challenge certain reviewable acts provided they demonstrate their particular position vis-à-vis the act they wish to challenge.

Privileged applicants

Under arts 33 and 38 ECSC the High Authority, the Council and the Member States and under arts 173 EC and 144 Euratom the Council, the Commission and the Member States are privileged applicants. They may challenge any reviewable acts and have unrestricted *locus standi*.[51] In relation to the Commission it is justified on the basis that the Commission is 'guardian of the Treaty' as specifically provided in art 155 EC. The extension of this facility to the Council is a logical consequence of its position within the institutional framework of the Community. The Member States as contracting parties to the Treaty are particularly interested in defending their rights affected by unlawful measures adopted by the Community institutions. A Member State under its unrestricted *locus standi* may challenge an act addressed to another Member State,[52] or even an act which was adopted with its consent.[53] The only condition for privileged applicants is that they must challenge an act within a time-limit set out in art 173(5) EC.

---

[49] For example, Case 104/89 *Mulder II* [1992] ECR I–3061; see section 10.4 of this Chapter.
[50] CFI, 16 April 1997 [1997] Europe (June) no 187, comm F Lagondet.
[51] *Locus standi* means literally recognised position, right to intervene, right to appear in court.
[52] Case 6/54 *The Netherlands* v *High Authority* [1956] ECR 201.
[53] Case 166/78 *Italy* v *Council* [1979] ECR 2575, that is, it voted in favour of the measure in the Council.

Semi-privileged applicants

Until the TEU only two categories of applicants were mentioned in art 173 EC: privileged and non-privileged, which referred to any natural or legal person. The European Parliament was denied the status of applicant under art 173 EC. It was logical in the sense that acts adopted by the EP were not reviewable under art 173 EC. However, once the ECJ permitted challenge of the acts of the EP,[54] the EP argued that its position as an applicant should also be recognised. In Case 302/87 *Parliament v Council (Comitology)*[55] the ECJ had refused to confer to the EP even limited *locus standi* under art 173 EC and held, *inter alia*, that the Commission as a guardian of the Treaty could introduce an action for annulment of acts which would endanger the prerogatives of the EP. In this case Advocate-General Darmon suggested that the EP should have limited *locus standi* to maintain the institutional balance of power, especially in cases where its interests or rights were directly affected by acts of the Commission or the Council, since in such circumstances the position of the EP would be worse than that of a non-privileged applicant. Nevertheless, it took the ECJ two years to reverse its position. In Case 70/88 *Parliament v Chernobyl*[56] the ECJ conferred the EP with the status of a semi-privileged applicant. In this case, the EP challenged Council Regulation 3954/87 concerning the permitted levels of radioactive contamination in food and feeding stuffs after the nuclear accident at Chernobyl. The EP argued that the Regulation should be adopted under art 100a EC, which requires the opening of the co-operation procedure, instead of art 31 Euratom, which imposes upon the Council the mere obligation to consult the EP. As a result, the EP claimed that its prerogatives were infringed by Council Regulation 3954/87.

The ECJ held that the mechanisms provided under the Treaties did not always allow censure of an act adopted by the Council or the Commission in violation of competences of the EP. The ECJ referred to the suggestions of A-G Darmon made in the *Comitology* case and decided that the action of the EP was admissible under art 173 EC since its prerogatives, which in this case concerned the right of the EP to influence the legislative process leading to the adoption of a measure, were infringed. This is also a restriction imposed upon the EP: the admissibility of an action for annulment submitted by the EP is limited, it must be intended to protect its prerogatives and be based solely on the violation of its prerogatives.

The ECJ has consolidated this approach by rejecting any supplementary restrictions which the Council tried to impose on the EP in cases when the latter was acting to defend its prerogatives. In Case C–295/90 *European Parliament v Council*[57] the EP, supported by the Commission, the Council, the United Kingdom and The Netherlands, argued that Directive 90/366 on the right of residence of students was wrongly based, *inter alia*, on art 235 EC which requires only consultation of the EP instead of art 7(2) EEC (now art 6(2) EC) which specifies that the co-operation procedure should be used. The Council claimed that the Commission should have initiated an action under art 173 EC to safeguard the prerogatives of the EP. The ECJ disagreed with the Council and annulled Directive 90/366.

---

[54] Case 294/83 *Parti Ecologiste 'Les Verts' v European Parliament* [1986] ECR 1339 and Case 34/86 *Council v Parliament (Budget)* [1986] ECR 2155.
[55] [1988] ECR 5615.
[56] [1990] ECR I–2041.
[57] [1992] ECR I–4193.

In Case C–316/91 *European Parliament* v *Council*[58] the ECJ held that the EP was entitled to invoke the infringement of its prerogatives when the Council used a legal base for a particular piece of legislation which did not require mandatory consultation of the EP, although the latter was optionally consulted during the preparation of the measure. Also, when the Council, within the consultation procedure, did not reconsult the EP and adopted a measure substantially modifying the original proposal, the EP successfully challenged that measure.[59]

The Treaty of Maastricht has recognised the European Parliament as a semi-privileged applicant under art 173 EC. Both the European Central Bank (on the grounds of art 173(3) EC) and the European Monetary Institute (on the basis of art 109f(9) EC in the second stage of EMU) have been added to the list of applicants which may bring an action for annulment for the purpose of protecting their prerogatives.

Non-privileged applicants

Non-privileged applicants under art 173 EC are natural or legal persons. They must justify their interests to act. Thus, they have to demonstrate that they have an interest protected under the Community law which exists at present. As a result, interests regarding a future legal situation which might happen, is uncertain or subject to changes of circumstances in law or in fact are excluded from the scope of art 173 EC.[60] It also means that an applicant cannot challenge a decision which is favourable to his interests, such as a decision of exemption, negative clearance, etc, under competition law.[61] Furthermore, he must prove that the measure has affected his personal situation which would have improved if the act was annulled.[62]

The ECJ has been very liberal in the assessment of the interest to act under art 173 EC. The ECJ considered admissible an application against an act which was no longer applied due to its alleged illegality,[63] or an act which was abrogated or already performed and thus its annulment was devoid of legal effects.[64] However, very strict requirements as to the admissibility of applications in relation to the nature of the act and the situation of applicants vis-à-vis the act has more than compensated for the favourable approach of the Community courts to the concept of the interest to act.

In Case T–117/95 *Corman SA*[65] the CFI has confirmed the importance of the interest to act under art 173 EC which is often underestimated as a condition of admissibility of an action for annulment. The latter held that an applicant had no interest to challenge

---

[58] [1994] ECR I–625.

[59] Case C–21/94 *European Parliament* v *Council* [1995] ECR I–1827.

[60] For example, Case T–138/89 *NBV and NVB* [1992] ECR II–2181.

[61] Ibid.

[62] This is assessed favourably to the applicants: Case 77/77 *BP* [1978] ECR 1513; see also Case 88/76 *SES* [1977] ECR 709 in which the challenged measure had no influence on the situation of the applicant.

[63] Case 201/86 *APESCO* [1988] ECR 2151.

[64] Case T–46/92 *The Scottish Football Association* [1994] ECR II–1039; Cases T–480 and 483/93 *Antillean Rice Mills* [1995] ECR II–2305.

[65] Judgment of 30 January 1997. Although the facts of the case indicated that the subsequent legislation had in fact modified the legal situation of the applicant, *Europe*, March 1997, no 70, comm D Ritleng.

Regulation 455/95 as it confirmed previous Regulation 570/88 both concerning granting of aid to undertakings producing 'industrial butter technologically adopted'. The CFI emphasised that when subsequent legislation only confirms the legislation in force, and thus the legal situation of the applicant is not modified, an applicant cannot invoke an interest in the first act in order to challenge the subsequent act.

Reviewable acts

Under the terms of art 173(4) EC a non-privileged applicant may challenge:

1. A decision addressed to the applicant.
2. A decision in the form of regulation which is, however, of direct and individual concern to the applicant.

The first situation constitutes a classical case of judicial review. A decision addressed to the applicant is *ipso facto* of direct and individual concern to him. His *locus standi* under art 173 EC is obvious. The second situation is more complex as the applicant must prove direct and individual concern by challenging an act which, although in the form of regulation, is in fact a decision.

The difference between a regulation and a decision was explained by the ECJ in Cases 41–44/70 *International Fruit Co v Commission*.[66] The ECJ held that essential features of a Decision result from the limitation of its addressees, while a regulation has essentially a normative character, and is applicable not to a limited number of addressees, named or otherwise individually identified as in the case of a decision, but to the category of persons envisaged in their entirety since a regulation is of general application.

The case law of the ECJ has evolved as to the determination of circumstances in which a decision is disguised under the form of regulation. At first, the ECJ considered that it may happen in the situation in which the entire regulation is in fact a decision which an EC institution adopted with the exclusive or main purpose of evading a procedure specifically prescribed by the Treaty for dealing with the applicant, that is an EC institution misusing its powers.[67] In the next stage the ECJ accepted that a true regulation may also be addressed to determined persons.[68] Finally, the ECJ recognised that a regulation may be in fact a bundle of decisions addressed to each applicant.[69] However, the ECJ considered that a provision of a regulation cannot have at the same time general and individual scope of application.[70] Under the influence of the so-called theory of 'hybrid regulations' developed by certain Advocates-General such as Verloren Van Themaat in Cases 239 and 275/82 *Allied Corporation*,[71] and which applied mostly to anti-dumping cases, the ECJ has softened its position. In Case C–309/89 *Codorniu*[72] the ECJ recognised that a provision may have at the same time general and individual scope of application. In this case the ECJ held that the regulation was 'by nature and by virtue of its sphere of application of a legislative nature', which did not

---

[66] [1971] ECR 411.
[67] Cases 16 and 17/62 *Confédération Nationale des Producteurs de Fruits et Légumes* [1962] ECR 901.
[68] Case 30/67 *Molitaria Immolese* [1968] ECR 171.
[69] Cases 41–44/70 *International Fruit Co v Commission* [1971] ECR 411.
[70] Case 45/81 *Moksel* [1982] ECR 1129.
[71] [1984] ECR 1005.
[72] [1994] ECR I–1853.

prevent it from being of individual concern to some of those who were affected. Thus, it seems that the ECJ accepts that an act of general application may also affect the interests of an individual. However, as the ECJ emphasised in Case 6/68 *Zuckerfabrik Watenstedt*[73] the fact that a provision of a regulation may, in practice, differently affect its addressees does not call into question its nature as a regulation when the situation to which it applies is objectively determined. The case law of the ECJ suggests that the criterion which is essential in the determination of the nature of an act is whether the group of the potential addressees of the act is open, which means that the act has no limitation *ratione tempore*, or closed, that is, an act which applies retroactively or immediately by creating rights and obligations for a limited and easily definable group of persons, unless the membership of that fixed and ascertainable group is determined by an objective situation connected with the objective of that act.[74]

Very often, the ECJ avoids making a distinction between a decision and a regulation by declaring that the act in question is not of direct and individual concern to the applicant. Article 173 EC requires that the ECJ decides first whether the act in question is a decision or a regulation before examining the subjective situation of an applicant vis-à-vis that act.

Decision addressed to another person which is of direct and individual concern to the applicant. The ECJ has broadly interpreted the notion of a decision addressed to another person. Such a person may be not only an individual, that is any natural or legal person, but also a Member State[75] or a third country.[76] As to EC directives, the ECJ seems to accept the possibility that an action for annulment of a directive can be admissible provided a directive contains a provision which could be assimilated into a decision and that the applicant is directly and individually concerned by that measure.[77]

Individual concern

The most confusing and complicated question under art 173 EC is the issue of individual concern, mostly because of inconsistency in the decisions of Community courts in this area. Individual concern was defined by the ECJ in Case 25/62 *Plaumann* v *Commission*.[78] Plaumann was an importer of clementines. Under the Common Customs Tariff he paid 13 per cent customs duty, as did any importer of clementines from outside the Community. The government of Germany asked the Commission for authorisation under art 25(3) EEC to suspend this duty. The Commission refused and issued a decision in this respect. Plaumann challenged this decision.

The ECJ held that Plaumann was not individually and directly concerned by the Commission's decision, although he was affected like any importer of clementines by the

---

[73] [1968] ECR 595.
[74] Case 101/76 *KSH NV* v *Council and Commission* [1977] ECR 797.
[75] In most cases an individual applicant challenges a decision addressed to the Member State, for example, Case 25/62 *Plaumann* [1963] ECR 95. See case law on individual and direct concern.
[76] Case C–135/92 *Fiscano* [1994] ECR I–2885 in which the ECJ considered that a Swedish company was individually and directly concerned by a decision addressed by the Commission to the government of Sweden.
[77] Case C–298/89 *Government of Gibraltar* [1993] ECR I–3605; Case C–10/95P *Asocarne* [1995] ECR I–4149, *Europe*, January 1996, no 3, comm D Simon.
[78] [1963] ECR 95.

decision. His commercial activity (import of clementies) was such that may be practised at any time by anyone, and thus he did not distinguish himself from all other persons. Individual concern may only be invoked if persons other than the addressees of the decision demonstrate that 'that decision affects them by reason of certain attributes which are peculiar to them or by reason of circumstances in which they are differentiated from all other persons by virtue of these factors distinguishing them individually just as in the case of the person addressed'.[79]

The ECJ has restrictively interpreted 'certain peculiar attributes' or 'circumstances which differentiate' a person from others in view of challenging a decision addressed to another person or a regulation in the form of a decision. As a result, the ECJ refused to recognise that a person was individually concerned in the following situations: in the *Plaumann* case when the decision concerned specific activities, that is the importation of clementines; when a number of the affected persons was limited;[80] when an undertaking was the only one concerned by a measure in a particular Member State;[81] when an undertaking operated in a defined zone and the regulation expressly applied to that geographically delimited zone;[82] when an undertaking was a direct competitor of another undertaking to which the decision was addressed;[83] and when the number of undertakings concerned was limited to three undertakings in a Member State but potential producers would not be in a position to enter the market for at least two years taking into account the technological requirements involving the production of isoglucose.[84]

In all those cases the applicants were considered as being members of the 'open class', that is, anyone may at any time practice the commercial activity in question and potentially join the group of producers of particular goods. The case law of the ECJ indicates that in order to be individually concerned a person must prove that at the time the measure was passed it was possible to identify all potential applicants. This only happens if the membership of that class was fixed at that time which means, in practice, that only in respect of retrospective measures is it possible to invoke individual concern, as was confirmed in Cases 106 and 107/63 *Toepfer* v *Commission*.[85] Toepfer applied for an import licence for maize on 1 October 1962 when the German authority mistakenly reduced the levy for imports of maize from France to zero. The German intervention agency realised the mistake and refuse to grant licences from 2 October 1962. Three days later the Commission confirmed the ban and authorised German authorities to impose the levy. Toepfer challenged the Commission's decision on the grounds that he was individually and directly concerned.

The ECJ held that he was individually concerned because the number and identity of those individually concerned 'had become fixed and ascertainable' before the contested decision was made. They were a 'closed group': the decision affected their interests and

---

[79] Ibid, at 107.
[80] In *Plaumann* there were 30 importers of clementines.
[81] Case 231/82 *Spijker Kwasten BV* v *Commission* [1983] ECR 2559; Case 97/85 *Union Deutsche Lebensmittelwerke* [1987] ECR 2265.
[82] Case 30/67 *Molitaria Immolese* [1968] ECR 172.
[83] Case 10 and 18/68 *Eridania* [1969] ECR 459.
[84] Case 101/76 *Koninklijke Scholten-Honig NV* v *Council and Commission* [1977] ECR 797.
[85] [1965] ECR 525.

position in a significantly different way from other importers who might wish to apply for a licence after the decision but during the remaining period of the ban. Therefore, only those who applied on 1 October were individually concerned since from 2 to 4 October applications were refused, and on 4 October the Commission issued its decision. As a result, Toepfer was within the closed group who applied on 1 October; the larger group – those who applied between 2 and 4 October – was open since they were refused licences and could reapply thereafter without loss to them as the levy would be the same after 2 October.

Similarly in Case 62/70 *Bock v Commission*[86] the ECJ held that Bock was individually concerned by a decision adopted by the Commission because when he applied for a licence to import Chinese mushrooms the German authorities refused to grant it, and asked the Commission to confirm their decision, which the latter did. Not only was the decision issued to deal with his application but Bock belonged to the ascertainable and fixed group of importers at the time of the passing of that decision. However, the ECJ has gradually attenuated the requirements necessary to demonstrate individual concern.

First, in the various areas characterised by the existence of non-contentious procedures which involve more or less direct participation of undertakings in the adoption of the measures. If an applicant assists the Commission in the preparation of the measure then his association with the adoption of the measure differentiates him from others and his individual concern is self-evident. This is mostly used in competition, anti-dumping and State-aid cases. For example, if a complaint was lodged against a competitor for an alleged breach of art 85 and 86 EC which led to a decision of the Commission exempting the latter, or confirming that there was no breach of competition rules on its part, then the complaining undertaking is individually concerned by the decision addressed to another undertaking,[87] not because it is in competition with the other undertaking but because it initiated the proceedings which resulted in the adoption of the measure. Similarly, a decision of the Commission to refuse the opening of proceedings under art 93(2) EC concerning aid granted to an undertaking by a Member State may be challenged by the undertaking which made the original complaint to the Commission.[88]

In the context of the common market, dumping occurs when a non-EC undertaking sells its products below domestic market prices which is at the same time a price below the real cost of goods. This strategy is used to penetrate the market and eliminate the existing competitors. The undertaking affected by such dumping conduct of a foreign undertaking can complain to the Commission, which may adopt a provisional regulation and request the Council to issue a definite regulation imposing an anti-dumping duty to counterbalance the competitive advantage of the foreign undertaking – this is determined in the light of the effect of the dumping on EC undertakings, especially the one that lodged a complaint. In Case 264/82 *Timex Corporation v Council*[89] the applicant challenged a regulation which was adopted because of Timex complaints concerning cheap mechanical watches coming from

---

[86] [1971] ECR 897.
[87] Case 26/76 *Metro* [1977] ECR 1875; Cases 142 and 156/84 *British American Tobacco* [1987] ECR 4487.
[88] Case 169/84 *Cofaz* [1986] ECR 391; Case C–198/91 *William Cook* [1993] ECR I–2487; Case C–225/91 *Matra* [1993] ECR I–3203.
[89] [1985] ECR 861. There are many similar cases, for example Case 239/82 *Allied Corporation* [1984] ECR 1005; Case C–313/90 *CIRFS* [1993] ECR I–1125.

the Soviet Union. The regulation imposed an anti-dumping duty taking into account information forwarded by Timex. However, Timex also claimed that the new duty was too low. The ECJ held that because the regulation was based on the situation of Timex, the latter was individually concerned. It is interesting to mention that in Cases T–528, 542, 543 and 546/93 *Métropole Télévision*[90] the Commission argued that the applicant was not individually concerned as it did not participate in the preparation of the measure. The CFI replied that effective participation in the adoption of a measure cannot be required in order to establish an individual concern as it would amount to the introduction of an additional requirement which is not provided for in art 173 EC. Therefore, the CFI has rightly indicated that the participation in the adoption of a measure constitutes solely a factor facilitating the recognition of an individual concern, but it is not a necessary requirement.

The relaxation of strict requirements for *locus standi* in the above-mentioned areas has also extended to potential applicants. As a result, professional associations,[91] and even representatives of workers,[92] have been permitted to bring an action for annulment.

Second, the restrictive interpretation of requirements relating to individual concern has been relaxed in respect to cases in other areas. It may be said they are a harbinger of a new approach.

The Community courts have demonstrated such a new approach toward the concept of individual concern based on the assessment of the economic situation of the applicant vis-à-vis the measure in question. The unrealistic approach, based on the assumption that as long as any person at any time may practise a particular activity or join a particular class of producers in order to determine *locus standi* of individuals, has been slowly abandoned by the Community Courts. In Case C–152/88 *Sofrimport SARL v Commission*[93] the ECJ for the first time assessed the influence of a regulation on the economic interests of the applicant. Sofrimport shipped apples from Chile prior to the regulation suspending import licences for Chilean apples. When the regulation came into force the apples imported by Sofrimport were in transit. The French authorities refused to issue an import licence to Sofrimport and the latter challenged the regulation. The ECJ held that a previous regulation imposed upon the Community authorities to take into consideration the case of goods in transit while adopting new legislation. Consequently importers with goods in transit constituted a fixed and ascertainable group, and thus could be considered as individually concerned. The only logical explanation of the ECJ decision was that Sofrimport's economic interests were affected to a such degree that they were successful in their action for annulment. Later case law of the ECJ maintains this approach, although the context of those cases was slightly different from *Sofrimport*.[94]

---

[90] [1996] ECR II–649.

[91] Case 191/82 *Fediol* [1983] ECR 2913; Cases T–448 and 449/93 *Associazion Italiana Technico Economica del Cemento* [1995] ECR II–1971; [1995] Europe (September), no 317, comm L Idot.

[92] Case T–96/92 *Perrier* [1995] ECR II–1213.

[93] [1990] ECR I–2477.

[94] Case T–489/93 *Unifruit Hellas* [1994] ECR II–1201; Cases T–480 and 483/93 *Antillean Rice Mills* [1995] ECR II–2305, [1995] Europe (November), no 375, comm D Simon; Cases T–481 and 483/93 *Vereiniging van Exporters* [1995] ECR II–2941; Case C–209/94P *Buralux* [1996] ECR I–615. However, it was rejected in recent Case T–47/95 *Terres Rouges Consultant SA v Commission supported by the Council, Spain and France* [1997] ECR II–481, in which the largest importer of bananas from Cote d'Ivoire (70 per cent of the market) was denied an individual concern in respect of a regulation adopted by the Commission in order to comply with the requirement of GATT and international agreements concluded between the Community and certain South American countries.

This approach has also been applied to anti-dumping cases. In Case C–358/89 *Extramet*[95] the economic analysis of the situation of an undertaking, its degree of dependence vis-à-vis the effect that the regulation in question had on the market differentiated and individualised the applicant from other undertakings so as to allow him to claim individual concern.[96] The real breakthrough came in Case C–309/89 *Codorniu*,[97] in which the fact that the applicant was prevented from using a trade mark placed him, from a point of view of his economic interests, in such a disadvantageous position that he was differentiated from other undertakings and thus was individually concerned by the regulation in question.

Codorniu, a Spanish producer of quality sparkling wines, had been a holder of a graphic trade mark since 1924 in relation to one of its wines styled as 'Gran Cremant de Codorniu'. In certain regions of France and Luxembourg the word 'cremant' was also used for certain quality wine. The producers in those countries asked the Community to adopt a regulation which would reserve the word 'cremant' only for their sparkling wine. Council Regulation 2045/89 restricted the use of word 'cremant' to wines originated in France and Luxembourg in order to protect the traditional description used in those areas. Codorniu challenged the Regulation.

The ECJ held that Codorniu was differentiated from other producers of wine since it had registered and used the word 'cremant' since 1924. Although Regulation 2045/89 was a true Regulation it did not prevent it from being of individual concern to Codorniu which was badly affected by the Regulation. Also the restriction of word 'cremant' to wine originating from a certain region of France and Luxembourg could not be objectively justified and, in addition, was contrary to art 7(1) EC which prohibits discrimination based on nationality.

This approach has been confirmed in some later cases[98] and rejected in others.[99]

The ECJ expressed the necessity for the amendment of art 173 EC,[100] however this was not taken into consideration by the draft Treaty of Amsterdam.

Direct concern

An applicant under art 173 EC must demonstrate both individual and direct concern as they apply cumulatively, although as the ECJ stated in *Plaumann* the requirement of direct concern is superfluous, if the applicant is not individually concerned by a decision. Indeed, in the majority of cases the question of individual concern is examined by the Community courts and if the applicant cannot establish this first requirement then the second is not investigated. Direct concern means that a Member State has no discretion in implementing a Community act. The best way to illustrate this point is to examine Case 123/77 *UNICME*[101] in which the ECJ rejected an application under art 173 EC on the grounds of lack of direct concern because a Member State retained a discretion, that is, there was an imposition of

---

[95] [1991] ECR I–2501.

[96] See A Arnull, 'Challenging EC Anti-dumping Regulations, the Problem of Admissibility' [1992] European Competition Law Review 73.

[97] [1994] ECR I–1853.

[98] Cases T–481 and 484/93 *Exporteurs in Levende Varkens* [1995] ECR II– 2941.

[99] For example, in Case T–482/93 *Weber* [1996] ECR II–609; Case T–47/95 *Terres Rouges Consultant SA* v *Commission supported by the Council, Spain and France* [1997] ECR II–481.

[100] EC Bull Suppl 9/75, 15.7.74, p18.

[101] [1978] ECR 845.

the autonomous will of the Member State between the decision and its effect on the applicant.

In this case under a Council regulation importation of Japanese motor cycles was allowed only by holders of an import licence issued by the Italian government. The applicants, Italian importers of such motor cycles and their trade association, UNICME, challenged the regulation. The ECJ held that the applicants were not directly concerned since the Italian government had a discretion as to the grant of an import licence. As a result, they were concerned not by the regulation but the subsequent refusal of import licences by the Italian authorities.

If a Member State has no discretion as to the application of a Community measure, the applicant can claim that he is directly concerned. For example, in Cases 41–44/70 *International Fruit Co v Commission*[102] the granting of import licences for dessert apples, which was based on a Community rule, was modified by a Commission regulation. The latter imposed on the Member States specific rules for dealing with such applications. As a result, national authorities had no discretion in this matter. Similarly, if a Member State decides first how to deal with a particular issue and then asks the Commission to confirm its decision, as happened in Cases 106 and 107/63 *Toepfer*,[103] an applicant is directly concerned by the Community measure because a Member State has no discretion in its implementation. It must do exactly as required by the Community measure. Furthermore, the requirements regarding direct concern have been weakened by the Community courts. In Case 11/82 *Piraïki-Patraïki*[104] the ECJ held that the possibility for a Member State of taking further measures than provided by a Community act itself does not prevent an applicant from invoking direct concern, since the link between the applicant and a Community act has not been severed by a mere possibility that a Member State may take authorised measures, which in this case was highly unlikely.

In *Piraïki-Patraïki* the Commission permitted the French government to impose quotas on imports of yarn from Greece. Although the French authorities had discretion as to whether or not to impose new quotas, in the light of previous restrictions imposed on such imports and the request to use new quotas submitted to the Commission by the French government, it was highly unlikely, or as the ECJ held 'purely theoretical', that the French authorities would not exercise their discretion. As, in addition, Greek producers of yarn, on the basis of an express provision of the Greek Accession Act, had concluded export contracts prior to the decision, they were also individually concerned and thus successfully challenged the decision.

It is submitted that the requirements under art 173 EC regarding both direct and individual concern are too restrictive. The need of the Community courts not to be flooded with applications under art 173 EC should not prevent individuals from exercising their rights, especially the right to due process. Even though they have other means at their disposal to enforce their rights, such as through art 184(4) EC or national courts under art 177 EC, the basic point is that the case law of the ECJ on individual concern applies regardless of the way they choose to claim their rights. The situation of the applicants

---

[102] [1971] ECR 411.
[103] [1965] ECR 405.
[104] [1985] ECR 207; see also Case 62/70 *Bock* [1971] ECR 897 and Case 29/75 *Kaufhof* [1976] ECR 431.

should be assessed realistically in the light of the true effect of a Community measure to their particular situation. Although the ECJ seems to have softened its approach towards the determination of individual concern, it is still not sufficient. It is submitted that anyone who can demonstrate his legal interest to act should have *locus standi* under art 173 EC.

Grounds for annulment

Article 173 EC enumerates the grounds for annulment which are: lack of competence, infringement of an essential procedural requirement; infringement of the Treaty or any rule of law relating to its application; and misuse of powers. The Community courts have to apply the first two grounds *ex officio*,[105] the last two must be invoked by the applicant. It is very important to claim all grounds, as under French administrative law, since new grounds introduced after the expiry of the time-limit are inadmissible under art 42(2) of the Rules of Procedure of the ECJ and art 42(2) of the Rules of Procedure of the CFI. Also, the reference to all possible or probable grounds which is permitted under art 173 EC is highly recommended because, on the one hand, the Community courts are empowered to specify and further crystallise the grounds invoked by the applicant,[106] and on the other hand the courts do not necessarily state upon which grounds they have decided the matter.

Lack of competence

This ground is similar to substantive *ultra vires* in British administrative law, which occurs when an administrative organisation exceeds its powers. Under arts 3b and 4 EC the EC institutions have only powers conferred upon them by the Treaty. It was considered that this ground would be invoked often, especially by the Member States for the encroachment of the Community law upon the national competences of the Member States. This has not materialised. As a result, this ground is rarely used, mostly because the applicants prefer to based their claims on the infringement of the Treaty.[107] This ground has been invoked in cases challenging the legal basis of Community measures,[108] as already examined in Chapter 4, in two cases concerning the principle of subsidiarity the Member States invoked lack of competence.

Infringement of an essential procedural requirement

Infringement of an essential procedural requirement is analogous to procedural *ultra vires*. It occurs when an EC institution fails to comply with a mandatory procedural requirement in the adoption of the measure, for example if the Council fails to consult the EP when the Treaty requires mandatory consultation of the European Parliament prior to the adoption of a measure. The ECJ has annulled acts which provided for optional consultation of the EP where the Council did not give enough time to the EP to issue its opinion,[109] or when the EP was not reconsulted when an act of the Council substantially altered an original proposal

---

[105] Case 1/54 *France v High Authority* [1954] ECR 7; Case C–29/89 *Interhotel* [1991] ECR I–2276.
[106] Case 4/73 *Nold* [1974] ECR 491.
[107] For example, see Cases 3–18, 25– 26/58 *Erzberbau* [1960] ECR 367.
[108] Case C–350/92 *Spain (supported by Greece) v Council (supported by France and the Commission)* [1995] ECR I–1985; Case C–84/94 *UK v Council (Working Time Directive)* [1996] ECR I–5758.
[109] Case 138/79 *Roquette Frères v Council* [1980] ECR 3333.

submitted to the EP.[110] When an EC institution fails to comply with its own internal Rules of Procedure, the ECJ will annul the act in question.[111]

The failure to provide proper justification for an act required by art 190 EC is most often invoked under this ground.[112]

Infringement of the Treaty or any rule of law relating to its application

This is the most frequently invoked ground. It comprises not only the provisions of the Treaty but all sources of Community law including the general principles of Community law,[113] and infringements of an international agreement concluded between the Community and third countries.[114]

Misuse of powers

The ECJ has adopted the same definition of misuse of powers as under French administrative law (*detournement de pouvoir*).[115] Misuse of powers takes place when Community institutions have used their powers for objectives other than those provided by the Treaty: a legitimate power is used for an illegal end or in an illegal way. This ground is often invoked but rarely successfully because of the burden of proof it imposes on the applicant, as well as the fact that in the case of a number of objectives which an EC institution may legitimately pursue the ECJ will annul an act only if it was adopted with the exclusive aim of achieving objectives other than those prescribed by the Treaty, or evading a procedure specifically provided by the Treaty for dealing with the circumstances of the case.[116] Misuse of powers was successfully invoked in the context of a dispute between the Community and its staff when the Community servants proved that an EC institution had acted in bad faith.[117]

Effect of annulment

The effect of annulment of a Community act is described in art 174 EC which provides:

> '(1) If the action is well founded, the Court of Justice shall declare the act concerned to be void.
>
> (2) In the case of a regulation, however, the Court of Justice shall, if it considers this necessary, state which of the effects of the regulation which it has declared void shall be considered as definitive.'

---

[110] Case 41/69 *Chemiefarma* [1970] ECR 661; Case C–388/92 *EP* v *Council* [1994] ECR I–2067.

[111] Case C–137/92P *Commission* v *BASF (PCV)* [1994] ECR I–2555.

[112] Case 24/62 *Germany* v *Commission (Brennwein)* [1963] ECR 63.

[113] Case 62/70 *Bock* [1971] ECR 897; Case 17/74 *Transocean Marine Paint* [1974] ECR 1063; Directive–Case C–212/91 *Angelopharm GmbH* [1994] ECR I–171; implementing measures based on secondary legislation but in breach of the latter: Case 25/70 *Köster* [1970] ECR 1161; Case 30/70 *Sheer* [1970] ECR 1197.

[114] Cases 21–24/72 *International Fruit* [1972] ECR 1219.

[115] Case 2/57 *Hauts Fourneaux de Chasse* [1958] ECR 129.

[116] Case C–331/88 *Fedesa* [1990] ECR I–4023.

[117] In Cases 18 and 35/65 *Gutmann* [1966] ECR 149 a Community official was transferred to Brussels in the interest of the service but in fact it was a disciplinary transfer; Case 105/75 *Giuffrida* [1976] ECR 1395.

As a result, the effect of annulment is that an act is void. The decision of the ECJ applies *erga omnes*.[118] The successfully challenged act is void immediately, from the day on which the ECJ renders its decision, and it means the act in question is devoid of past, present and future legal effects. In the case of the Court of First Instance, under art 53 of its Statute the act is void from the expiry of the time-limit for appeal, or from the time the appeal was rejected. In principle, as already been stated, a decision of annulment has a retroactive effect subject to art 174(2) regarding annulment of a regulation. In that case, the ECJ, if it considers it necessary, indicates which of the effects of the regulation should be considered as definitive. Therefore, the ECJ may declare some or all of its provisions to be operative. Also, acts other than regulations may be declared void *ex nunc*, for example budgetary provisions[119] or directives.[120] The justification for this use of declaratory power of the ECJ may be based on a number of reasons, such as legal certainty,[121] legitimate expectation, or the suspension of the effects of annulment until a competent institution adopts an act which will replace the one struck down by the ECJ.[122]

Under art 176 EC the decision of annulment imposes upon the Community institution whose act has been declared void an obligation 'to take the necessary measures to comply with the judgment of the Court of Justice'. If that institution refuses to comply with the decision of the ECJ the applicant may bring an action under art 175 EC, and, if appropriate, commence an action for damages under art 215(2).

10.2 Indirect action: plea of illegality under art 184 EC

Article 184 EC provides:

> 'Notwithstanding the expiry of the period laid down in the fifth paragraph of art 173, any party may, in proceedings in which a regulation adopted jointly by the European Parliament and the Council, or a regulation of the Council, of the Commission, or the ECB is at issue, plead the grounds specified in the second paragraph of art 173 in order to invoke before the Court of Justice the inapplicability of that regulation'.

The indirect action contained in arts 184 EC, 156 Euratom and 36 ECSC originates from French administrative law where it is known as the exception of illegality. Unlike actions under art 173 EC, the plea of illegality is not time-barred but it requires a direct relationship between the challenged act and the allegedly invalid regulation.[123] The grounds for an action under art 184 EC are the same as an action for annulment under art 173 EC, that is lack of competence, infringement of an essential procedural requirement, infringement of the Treaty or any rule of law relating to its application, and misuse of powers.

---

[118] Case 3/54 *Assider* [1955] ECR 123.
[119] Case 34/86 *Council v Parliament* [1986] ECR 2155; Case C–284/90 *Council v Parliament* [1992] ECR I–2322.
[120] Case C–295/90 *Parliament v Council (Student Directive)* [1992] ECR I–4193
[121] Case C–21/94 *Parliament v Council* [1995] ECR I–1827.
[122] Case C–65/90 *EP v Council* [1992] ECR 4616; Case 275/87 *Commission v Council* [1989] ECR 259.
[123] Cases 25 and 26 /65 *Simet* [1967] ECR 39.

The procedure under arts 184 EC, 156 Euratom and 36 ECSC[124] does not provide for an independent form of action. The plea of illegality can only be invoked as an ancillary plea, as a means by which an applicant, in support of an action challenging implementing measures addressed to him or to a third person, or in the case of direct and individual concern to the applicant, pleads the illegality of the general measure upon which the implementing measures are based. In practice, the plea of illegality is mostly used to challenge individual decisions based on EC regulations whose validity is called into question.[125]

The main feature of the plea of illegality is that it allows, subject to certain conditions, softening of the stringent requirements imposed under art 173 EC as to access to the ECJ in terms of *locus standi* and the time-limit. The ECJ held in Case 92/78 *Simmenthal*[126] that 'the need to provide those persons who are precluded ... from instituting proceedings directly in respect of general acts with the benefit of a judicial review of them at the time when they are affected by implementing decisions which are of direct and individual concern to them.' Thus, the plea of illegality constitutes an alternative way of judicial review of Community acts, permitting any person to raise indirectly the question of validity of a Community act.

This point is well illustrated by Case 92/78 *Simmenthal*. Simmenthal, an Italian meat importer, claimed that the fees for health and sanitary inspection carried out at the Italian border were unlawful on a number of bases. *Inter alia*, he challenged under art 173 EC a Decision adopted by the Commission and, in support of his action, indirectly under art 184 EC a number of regulations and notices, especially the notices of invitation to tender of 13 January 1978, upon which that decision was based and which he could not challenge directly due to the elapse of a two-month time-limit.

The ECJ held that the notices of invitation to tender are general acts 'which determine in advance, and objectively, the rights and obligations of the traders who wish to participate' and as acts of general application could not be challenged under art 173 EC. Only the challenged decision which was adopted in consequence of the tender could be of direct and individual concern to Simmenthal and thus reviewable under art 173 EC. As a result, Simmenthal was allowed to challenge indirectly under art 184 EC the regulations and the notices of invitation to tender of 13 January 1978, although as the ECJ stated the latter were not *senso stricto* measures laid down by regulation.

Requirement imposed by art 184 EC

Article 184 EC is subject to certain conditions regarding the applicants and acts susceptible of being subject to the plea of illegality.

---

[124] Article 36 ECSC is formulated in more restrictive terms under which it is open to undertakings wishing to challenge pecuniary sanctions imposed by the High Authority, but was in Case 9/56 *Meroni* [1958] ECR 11 considered by the ECJ as being of general scope of application due to the fact that the plea of illegality is based on general principles of law ensuring the respect of legality of Community acts.
[125] Cases 275/80 and 24/81 *Krupp* [1981] ECR 2489.
[126] [1979] ECR 777.

Acts susceptible to be subject to the plea of illegality

Article 184 EC was amended by the TEU. In its new version it provides that a regulation adopted jointly by the European Parliament and the Council, and a regulation of the Council, the Commission or the ECB may be challenged under art 184 EC. However, the ECJ has widely interpreted this requirement. As a result, the plea of illegality may be invoked not only against regulations adopted by the above-mentioned institutions but also against any act of general application susceptible to produce legal effects similar to Community regulations.

Applicants

Article 184 EC cannot be used to circumvent the requirements of art 173 EC. For that reason the addressees of individual acts who have not challenged them within the time-limit prescribed by art 173(5) EC are not permitted to rely on the plea of illegality,[127] apart from the case of an individual decision being null and void, that is non-existent,[128] or being a part of a 'complex procedure comprising a number of interdependent acts' as, for example, in Case 16/64 *G Rauch*[129] concerning the recruitment of a Community official.

The Commission and certain Advocates-General suggested a restrictive interpretation of art 184 EC in relation to the Member States in order to compensate the stringent requirements for *locus standi* under art 173 EC in relation to individuals.[130] However, the ECJ reluctantly permits the Member States to invoke the plea of illegality for a different reason. The reason for its reluctance is that the exception of illegality may encourage the Member States to ignore certain regulations and thus not challenge them within the time-limit. This would jeopardise the principle of legal certainty. The ECJ recognised that a Member State may rely on the plea of illegality in order to challenge a regulation which served as a legal foundation for another regulation which implemented the former.[131] It is still uncertain, although in general the ECJ seems rather unenthusiastic, whether a Member State may invoke the plea of illegality within the framework of enforcement proceedings under art 169 EC.[132]

Community institutions, contrary to the Member States and individuals, are not required to prove their interest while invoking the plea of illegality.

Exclusive jurisdiction of the Community courts under art 184 EC

The ancillary nature of the plea of illegality requires, as the ECJ emphasised in Case 31/62 *Milchwerke*,[133] that non-application of a regulation may only be invoked in procedures brought before the ECJ itself – now also before the CFI – on the basis of other provisions of the Treaty. This statement needs to be examined more closely. First, the plea of illegality

---

[127] Case 156/77 *Commission v Belgium* [1978] ECR 3707.
[128] Cases 1/57 and 14/57 *Usines à Tubes de la Sarre* [1957] ECR 201.
[129] [1965] ECR 179.
[130] See G Bebr, 'Judicial Remedy of Private Parties against Normative Acts of the EEC, the Role of the Exception of Illegality' [1966–67] CMLR esp 11–13.
[131] Case 32/65 *Italian Republic* [1966] ECR 563.
[132] Cases 6 and 11/69 *Commission v France* [1969] ECR 522; Case 156/77 *Commission v Belgium* [1978] ECR 1881.
[133] [1962] ECR 971.

cannot be invoked in proceedings before national courts. There is, however, an indirect possibility for an applicant to rely on the plea of illegality in national proceedings based on art 177 EC and not on art 184 as such. An applicant who challenges national measures introduced to implement a Community act is allowed to invoke the plea of illegality.[134] As national courts have no jurisdiction to declare void a Community act, and provided they have reason to believe that the Community act is invalid, they will under art 177 EC ask the ECJ to determine the validity of such an act. However, its ancillary nature is still preserved under art 177 EC, that is the plea of illegality cannot be invoked on its own. Furthermore, the ECJ has introduced two important limitations in this respect. In Case C–188/92 *TWD Textilwerke*,[135] as recently confirmed in Case C–178/95 *Wiljo*,[136] the ECJ established a firm principle that once the time-limit for a direct action under art 173 EC elapses, the Community courts would consider as inadmissible proceedings under art 177 EC in relation to the applicant who had *locus standi* to bring a direct action under art 173 EC but neglected to do so within the time-limit prescribed under art 173(5) EC. The ECJ justified its decision on the basis of the principle of legal certainty. In this case, TWD was individually and directly concerned by a decision addressed to a third party. *A fortiori*, this solution is even more obvious vis-à-vis the addressees of a decision. It results from the case law of the ECJ that national courts may only refer the question of the pleas of illegality under art 173 EC in two situations after the expiry of the time-limit prescribed in art 173(5) EC: when the applicant challenges the validity of a regulation; or, in the case of a decision, only if the decision was neither addressed to the applicant nor of a direct and individual concern to him.

Effect of a successful action under art 184 EC

If the applicant is successful, the general act, which may be called a parent act, is rendered inapplicable only to his case, that is it produces binding legal effect only between parties. The implementing measure is annulled in respect of the applicant, but the parent act is still in force – it cannot be declared void as it was 'perfected' or rendered immune from direct challenge under art 173 EC by lapse of time, although in practice the institution which adopted the parent act will amend or repeal that act, as under art 176(1) EC the institution in question is under a legal obligation to comply which the ECJ's judgment.

10.3 Direct action for failure to act: art 175 EC

The Community courts have also jurisdiction to sanction omissions or failures to act of the Community institutions where the latter have a duty to act. This possibility in contained in Article 175 EC which provides:

'(1) Should the European Parliament, the Council or the Commission, in infringement of this

---

[134] Case 216/82 *Universität Hamburg* [1983] ECR 2771.
[135] [1994] ECR I–846.
[136] Judgment of 30 January 1997 [1997] Europe (March), note 72, comm D Ritleng.

Treaty, fail to act, the Member States and the other institutions of the Community may bring an action before the Court of Justice to have the infringement established.

(2) The action shall be admissible only if the Institution concerned has first been called upon to act. If, within two months of being so called upon, the Institution concerned has not defined its position, the action may be brought within a further period of two months.

(3) Any natural or legal person may, under the conditions laid down in the preceding paragraphs, complain to the Court of Justice that an institution of the Community has failed to address to that person any act other than a recommendation or an opinion.'

The action under art 175 EC is similar to the English writ of mandamus or, in Scotland, to the petition for an order requiring the specific performance of a statutory duty.

An action for failure to act is common to the three Communities. The procedure is respectively governed by arts 35 ECSC, 175 EC and 148 Euratom. Under art 35 ECSC an action for failure to act may be brought only against the High Authority when the latter is legally bound to adopt a decision or a recommendation, but fails to conform to this duty. However, in Cases 7 and 9/54 *Groupement des Industries Sidérurgiques Luxembourgeoises*,[137] the ECJ held that this action should be assimilated to an action for annulment. As a result, there are the same requirements as to *locus standi*, interest to act and the same grounds as in an action for annulment. Under the Treaties of Rome an action for failure to act is separate from an action for annulment and has its own specific requirements, even though in Case 15/70 *Chevalley*[138] the ECJ held that an action under art 175 EC provides an applicant with a method of recourse parallel to that of art 173 EC. The relationship between arts 175 and 173 EC was explained by the ECJ in Case 10 and 18/68 *Eridania*.[139]

In this case the Commission had granted aid to three Italian sugar refineries which was contested by other sugar producers before the Commission. The latter refused to annul its decision. It resulted in an action both for annulment under art 173 EC and for failure to act under art 175 EC brought by the other producers.

The ECJ held that the applicants could not succeed under art 175 EC since the refusal of the Commission to annul its decision was tantamount to an act rather than to a failure to act. Also, the applicants were prevented from bringing an action under art 173 EC as they were not able to prove that they were directly and individually concerned by the decision. The ECJ emphasised that art 175 EC should not to used to circumvent the requirement set out in art 173 EC.

Article 175 EC imposes its own conditions as to the applicant, the defaulting institution and the procedure.

Defaulting institution

Article 175 EC states that the EP, the Council and the Commission are the EC institutions against whom an action for failure to act may be brought. To this list other institutions

---

[137] [1956] ECR 55.
[138] [1970] ECR 975.
[139] [1969] ECR 459.

should be added, such as the European Central Bank on the basis of art 175(4) EC and the European Monetary Institute in the second stage of EMU under art 109f(9) EC.

The main contribution of the Treaty of Maastricht is the recognition of the European Parliament as an institution against whom the proceedings may be brought under art 175 EC. In the Treaty of Rome only the Council and the Commission were mentioned. Until the amendment of art 175 EC by the TEU there was no clear answer from the ECJ in this respect. In Case C–41/92 *The Liberal Democrats*[140] this political party brought an action against the EP for failure to submit a proposal to the Council under art 138(1) EEC concerning the adoption of a uniform Community procedure for the election of Members of the European Parliament. In the meantime the EP adopted a resolution in this respect. As a result, the ECJ held that the EP had defined its position and, therefore, the ECJ avoided answering the question whether or not an action under art 175 EC could be brought against the EP, although Advocate-General Darmon was in favour of this solution provided the omission or the failure to act of the EP concerned an act which was susceptible to produce binding legal effects.

Applicants

There are three category of applicants: privileged, semi-privileged and non-privileged.

As to the privileged applicants, art 175 EC states that the Member States and the other institutions of the Community may bring an action before the Court of Justice. This group of applicants is not required to justify their interest in the act. They may bring an action against any failure or omission of any act: regulations, directives, decisions, recommendations, opinions, or even a proposal concerning the Community budget[141] provided the Community law imposes a duty to act. The EP, which was initially excluded from bringing an action for annulment under art 173 EC, has always been included in the list of privileged applicants. The ECJ in Case 13/83 *EP v Council*[142] has formally recognised the right of the EP to bring an action under art 175 EC.

The ECB and the EMI are considered as semi-privileged applicants, that is, they would have *locus standi* to raise an action for failure to act in respect of areas within their fields of competence.

Non-privileged applicants are any natural or legal person complaining that 'an institution of the Community has failed to address to that person any act other than a recommendation or an opinion'. The literal interpretation of this formula implies that an applicant may only challenge the failure of an institution to adopt an act addressed to him, that is an individual decision. This would *a priori* limit his *locus standi* under art 175 EC even more than under art 173 EC. Fortunately, the ECJ has given a liberal interpretation of art 175 EC, assimilating actions for annulment with actions for failure to act in respect of *locus standi* of non-privileged applicants. In Case 134/73 *Holtz and Willemsen*[143] the ECJ rejected the application submitted under art 175 EC because the applicant was not directly

---

[140] [1993] ECR I–3153.
[141] Case 302/87 *EP v Council* [1988] ECR 5637.
[142] [1985] ECR 1513.
[143] [1974] ECR 1.

and individually concerned, and not because he brought an action against the EC institution failing to adopt a regulation. This was clearly confirmed in Case 246/81 *Lord Bethell*.[144]

Lord Bethell, a Member of the EP and Chairman of the Freedom of the Skies Committee, complained to the Commission about anti-competitive practices of a number of European airlines in relation to passenger fares. He argued that the Commission was under a duty to submit proposals under art 89 EC in order to curtail those practices. Dissatisfied with the answer from the Commission he brought an action for failure to act against the latter under art 175 EC, claiming that the Commission's reply amounted in fact to a failure to act and alternatively under art 173 EC arguing that this answer should be annulled.

The ECJ held that the application of Lord Bethell would be admissible only if the Commission 'having been duly called upon … has failed to adopt in relation to him a measure which he was legally entitled to claim by virtue of the rules of Community law'. Lord Bethell, although indirectly concerned by the measure as a user of the airlines and Chairman of the Freedom of the Skies Committee which represented users, was nevertheless not in the legal position of the potential addressee of a decision which the Commission has a duty to adopt with regard to him. His application under art 173 EC was rejected for the same reason. The analogy between *locus standi* of non-privileged applicants under arts 173 and 175 EC was thus confirmed by the ECJ.

The similarity between arts 173 and 175 EC means that an application under art 175 EC is admissible if the applicant is directly and individually concerned by a measure which an EC institution failed to adopt, including a decision addressed to a third party but of individual and direct concern to the applicant.[145] It is still uncertain whether a non-privileged applicant is entitled to force the Community institution to adopt a normative measure of a general application.[146]

Procedure

The procedure under art 175 EC comprises two stages: a preliminary administrative stage and a judicial stage which takes place before the Community Courts.

Administrative stage

An action for failure to act may be brought before the Community courts only if the institution concerned has been called upon to act by the applicant who notified it of the complaint and indicated what precise measures he wished that institution to take in his respect.[147] There is no time-limit for the submission of a complaint but in Case 59/70 *The Netherlands v Commission*[148] the ECJ held that the right to notify the Commission of its omission or a failure to act should not be delayed indefinitely and that the complaint should

---

[144] [1982] ECR 2277.

[145] In Case C–107/91 *ENU* [1993] ECR I–599 the ECJ recognised this possibility within the framework of the Euratom Treaty, and in Case T–32/93 *Ladbroke Racing Ltd* [1994] ECR II–1015 the CFI extended it to the EC Treaty.

[146] In Case 134/73 *Holtz and Willemsen* [1974] ECR 1 the ECJ rejected this possibility but Case 65/87 *Pfizer* [1987] ECR 1691 confirms rather the uncertainty than a firm rejection.

[147] Cases 114–117/79 *Maziere* [1980] ECR 1529.

[148] [1971] ECR 639.

be lodged within a 'reasonable time'. This decision was rendered in relation to the ECSC Treaty, but it seems that this solution can also be transposed to the Treaties of Rome. Once the institution concerned is notified of the complaint it has two months to define its position. The main problem is to determine what is meant by the notion 'define the position'. The ECJ has gradually elucidated this notion. In the early cases under art 175 EC the Court held that the institution defined its position if it had adopted any act, apart from a reply asking the applicant to wait which could not be considered as an answer[149] or refers to the position previously adopted. For example, when the Commission sends a letter refusing to start proceedings against a competitor undertaking, it defines its position.[150] However, the refusal to take measures which are required under a specific procedure amounts to a failure to act, for example, an applicant is entitled to an answer, even stating the refusal of the Commission to act.[151] Gradually, it has become clear that art 175 EC aims at failures caused by an abstention to define the position, or the adoption of a measure, but not the adoption of a different act from that which was requested by the applicant.[152]

The result is that an institution defines its position by issuing a statement of its views on a particular matter, its proposal for action or, in the case of refusal, the reason for not taking a particular action.

Silence or refusal to act by the institution concerned are not necessarily tantamount to a failure to act. The institution concerned must be legally bound under the Community law to act. Conversely, if it has a discretion in this respect, an action for failure to act is not admissible. This point is illustrated by Case 48/65 *Alfons Lütticke*.[153]

Lütticke argued that a German tax on import of powder milk was contrary to art 95 EC. He asked the Commission to take an enforcement action against Germany under art 169 EC. The Commission replied that the tax was not contrary to Community law and, as a result, it did not intend to take action under art 169 EC. The ECJ held that by refusing to act the Commission defined its position and, second, under art 169 EC the Commission enjoyed a large measure of discretion whether or not to start proceedings under art 169 EC.

As a result, an applicant cannot force the Commission to act since he is not legally entitled to a particular measure. The Commission has no duty to act in respect of him. For that reason successful actions are rare under art 175 EC.

Once the institution concerned defines its position the proceedings under art 175 EC are *ipso facto* terminated. The applicant, provided he is legally entitled to a specific measure and unhappy about the answer he obtained from a particular institution, may bring proceedings against that institution under art 173 EC to annul the decision adopted in his case. In this context it is interesting to note that often unsuccessful applicants under art 175 EC – when the ECJ decided that the institution in question did define its position – asked the ECJ to transform their action under art 175 EC into an action under art 173 EC. The ECJ has always refused. Its refusal may have serious consequences for the applicant if the time-limit

---

[149] It happens usually when the Commission conducts further investigations concerning that matter: Cases 42 and 49/59 *SNUPAT* [1961] ECR 101.

[150] Case 125/78 *GEMMA* [1979] ECR 3117.

[151] Case T–28/90 *Asia Motor France* [1992] ECR II–2285; Case T–32/93 *Ladbroke Racing Ltd* [1994] ECR II–1015.

[152] Case C–107/91 *ENU* [1993] ECR I–599; Case C–25/91 *Pasqueras Echebaster SA* [1993] ECR I–1719.

[153] [1966] ECR 19.

of two months provided under art 175 EC had expired, since it would also mean that the time-limit for bringing an action under art 173 has also expired.[154]

Judicial stage

If the institution concerned does not define its position within two months the applicant has another two months to bring proceedings before the Community courts under the Treaties of Rome, but only one month under the ECSC Treaty. The applicant is required to submit an application limited to the points he raised in the original complaint.[155] The time-limit is strictly enforced by the ECJ.[156] If after the introduction of an action under art 175 EC, but before the judgment of the Community courts, the institution in question defines its position, the application is considered as admissible but 'without object'.[157] This solution seems unfair to the applicant, especially if he envisages bringing an action under art 215(2) EC against the institution concerned. The ECJ justified its position by stating that the decision in such circumstances would have no effect in respect to the defaulting institution.

The consequence of a successful action under art 175 EC is that the ECJ declares the failure to act of the institution concerned, which under art 176 EC 'shall ... take the necessary measures to comply with the judgment of the Court of Justice ...' within a reasonable period of time.[158]

10.4 Action for damages: non-contractual liability of the Community

Exclusive jurisdiction of Community courts regarding non-contractual liability of the Community is based on art 178 EC which provides:

> 'The Court of Justice shall have jurisdiction in disputes relating to the compensation for damage provided for in the second paragraph of art 215.'

The CFI has jurisdiction in actions for damages brought by individuals while the ECJ exercises its jurisdiction in actions commenced by the Member States.

Article 215(2) states:

> 'In the case of non-contractual liability, the Community shall, in accordance with the general principles common to the laws of the Member States, make good any damage caused by its institutions or by its servants in the performance of their duties.'

Non-contractual liability of the Community is a corollary of the transfer of certain powers to the Community institutions by Member States which requires that individuals are protected against unlawful conduct of the Community.

In Joined Cases C–46 and 48/93 *Brasserie du Pêcheur SA* v *Germany* and *R* v *Secretary*

---

[154] Case T–28/90 *Asia Motor France* [1992] ECR II–2285.

[155] Cases 24 and 34/58 *Chambre Syndicale Sidérurgique de la France* [1960] ECR 609; Cases 41 and 50/59 *Hamborner Bergbau* [1960] ECR 1016.

[156] Cases 5–11 and 13–15/62 *San Michele* [1962] ECR 859; Case C–25/91 *Pesqueras Echebastar* [1993] ECR I–1719

[157] In Case 302/87 *EP* v *Council* [1988] ECR 5615, the Council submitted a draft of the Community budget after the EP lodged its application under art 175 EC.

[158] Case 13/83 *EP* v *Council* [1985] ECR 1513.

of State for Transport, ex parte Factortame (No 3),[159] concerning a Member State's liability for acts and omissions of the national legislature contrary to Community law, the ECJ held the principle that public authorities must make good any damage caused in the performance of their duties contained in art 215(2) EC: '... holds good in any case in which a Member State breaches Community law, whatever be the organ of the State whose act or omission was responsible for the breach'.

Autonomous nature of an action under art 215(2) EC

In the majority of cases an action for damages is based on illegality of a Community act. For that reason, an action under art 215(2) EC may 'reopen' the time-limit imposed by arts 173 and 175 EC, and especially allows natural and legal persons to challenge Community acts without satisfying the very strict requirements of art 173 EC. In Case 25/62 *Plaumann*[160] the ECJ seemed to adopt a restrictive approach by refusing to award damages for the reason that the action in damages intended in reality to nullify the decision in question against which the applicant had also brought an action for annulment which was declared inadmissible by the ECJ. However, in later cases the ECJ has clearly established that an action for damages under art 215(2) EC is independent.[161] In Case 5/71 *Zuckerfabrik Schöppenstedt*[162] the ECJ held that an action in damages under arts 178 and 215(2) of the Treaty is autonomous as it has a peculiar function within the system of remedies. The difference between an action for annulment and an action for damages is that the latter is intended not to nullify a particular measure but to make good damage caused by the EC institution in the exercise of its functions. For that reason the autonomous nature of an action under art 215(2) EC is subject to one exception. Where an action for damages would have the same effects as an action for annulment, but the applicant did not institute the latter within the prescribed time-limit, the former will be inadmissible. As the ECJ emphasised in Case 175/84 *Krohn*[163] this happens only in exceptional situations when the action for damages would result in the payment of an amount corresponding to the sum already paid by the applicant in the performance of an individual decision. Therefore, if an application under art 215(2) EC is intended in reality to nullify an individual decision which has become definitive, that is immune from annulment due to the expiry of the time-limit provided for in art 173(5) EC or otherwise designed to provide a means of escaping the restrictions imposed by art 173 EC, it will be rejected.[164] The CFI in Case T–485/93 *Louis Dreyfus* and Case T–491/93 *Richco Commodities*[165] confirmed the exception and emphasised that the burden of proof is placed upon the party who alleged that the claim was in essence for the annulment.

---

[159] [1996] ECR I–1029.

[160] [1963] ECR 95.

[161] Case 175/84 *Krohn* [1986] ECR 753.

[162] [1971] ECR 975. See also Conclusions of Advocate–General Roemer who analyses case law of the Community courts in relation to art 215(2) EC, ibid, p992–93.

[163] [1986] ECR 753.

[164] Case 175/84 *Krohn* [1986] ECR 753; Case T–514/93 *Cobrecaf* [1995] ECR II– 621.

[165] [1996] ECR II–1101 and 1131; [1996] Europe (November), no 389, comm FG.

In addition, a decision under art 215(2) EC produces binding legal effects solely vis-à-vis the applicant, as opposed to a decision under art 173 EC which is valid *erga omnes*.[166]

An action for damages is also independent from an action for failure to act under art 175 EC.[167]

Parties to the proceedings under art 215(2) EC

Any natural or legal person, as well as a Member State, may bring an action under art 215(2) EC provided they have suffered loss resulting from unlawful conduct of the Community or its servants in the performance of their duties.

An action may be brought against the Community institution or institutions responsible for causing damage.[168] In practice the plaintiff is either the Commission or the Council, or both when an act was adopted by the Council acting on the proposal submitted by the Commission. An action may also be brought against the European Investment Bank,[169] the European Central Bank[170] or the European Monetary Institute.[171] The European Parliament and the ECJ or the CFI can only became defendants in actions brought by its staff,[172] although if the EP and the Council adopt jointly an act within the co-decision procedure set out in art 189b EC the EP may became a defendant. However, the EP cannot be liable for conduct of its political groups.[173]

Time-limit

Actions for damages are also subject to the time-limit. Under art 43 of the Statute of the ECJ an applicant may bring an action within five years from the event giving rise to the claim. However, the ECJ has interpreted this provision broadly. The *dies a quo* is considered to be the time when the damage has materialised, not the time of the occurrence of the event or fact giving rise to damage.[174]

Distinction between liability of the Community and liability of its servants

The Community must make good any damage caused by its institutions and by its servants in the performance of their duties. A vicarious liability principle applies and the Community is liable if a servant acted in the course of his duty. In Case 9/69 *Sayag*[175] the ECJ held that the Community is only liable for those acts of its servants which by virtue of an internal and

---

[166] See also Case T–489/93 *Unifrut Hellas EPE* [1994] ECR II–1201.

[167] Case 4/69 *Lütticke* [1971] ECR 325; Case 134/73 *Holtz and Willemsen* [1974] ECR 1.

[168] Case 63 and 69/72 *Werhahn* [1973] ECR 1229.

[169] Case 370/89 *SGEEM* [1992] ECR I–6211.

[170] As provided in art 215(3) EC.

[171] Article 109f(9) EC.

[172] In theory, in practice the ECJ cannot be a judge and a party in the same proceedings.

[173] Case 210/89 *Le Pen* [1990] ECR I–1183. It was an action for defamatory statement contained in a brochure.

[174] Case 256/80 *Birra Wuhrer* [1982] ECR 85. However, the *dies a quo* is postponed if the damage come to knowledge of the applicant after the expiry of five-year time-limit: Case 145/83 *Adams* [1985] ECR 3539. This period will also be suspended by any other ECJ proceedings.

[175] [1969] ECR 336.

direct relationship constituted the necessary extension of the tasks conferred on the Community institutions. This very restrictive approach requires that if the conduct of a servant which gave rise to damage was performed outside the course of his duties, that is on a 'frolic of his own', the action should be brought against him before the national court which has jurisdiction *ratione loci*, and the conditions of liability will be determined under the administrative law of the forum. Conversely, if a wrongful act or omission was committed by a particular employee acting in the course of his duties, the victim should commence proceedings before the Community courts, that is the CFI, and the conditions of liability will be determined according to Community law. By virtue of art 22(1) of the Statute of the ECJ, if there is joint liability then the Community, after compensating the victim, may bring an action against a servant in order to recover all or part of money paid to the victim.

Distinction between liability of the Community and liability of the Member States

Very often the Community institutions confer upon national authorities the task of applying or implementing Community measures. When the conduct of the latter causes damage to individuals the question arises: who is liable, the Member State or the Community? The best solution for the applicant would be to permit him to claim compensation for his loss at his option: before national courts or before the ECJ. Unfortunately, this option is rejected by Community law for many reasons, the most important being that neither a Community judge has jurisdiction to decide cases against the Member States in tort nor do national judges have jurisdiction to decide cases against the Community institutions in this area. Second, the division of competences between the Community and the Member States in general, and in relation to a disputed matter in particular, prohibits encroachment on each other's sphere of competence. Three situations can be distinguished.

Liability of national authorities for wrongful or negligent implementation or application of lawful Community acts

In this case, an action for damages should be brought against national authorities before national courts according to national procedure, and the conditions of liability should be determined by national administrative law. In Case 101/78 *Granaria*[176] the ECJ held that the question of compensation for loss incurred by individuals caused by a national body or agents of the Member States, resulting from either their infringement of Community law or an act or omission contrary to national law while applying Community law, is not covered by art 215(2) and has to be assessed by national courts according to the national law of the Member State concerned.

Liability of national authorities in the case of application or implementation of unlawful Community acts

When national authorities have correctly applied or implemented a Community measure, there is no fault on the part of a Member State concerned. As a result, the Community is

---

[176] [1979] ECR 623.

liable. In this case the ECJ has determined that national courts have exclusive jurisdiction if the action is for payment of money – reimbursement of a sum of money unlawfully paid and payments due. The question of validity of a Community act is subject to proceedings under art 177 EC since only the ECJ has jurisdiction to declare a Community act void. Once a measure is declared void by the ECJ a national court may award compensation for the damage suffered by the applicant.[177] The exclusive jurisdiction of national courts in actions for payments means that such actions will be declared inadmissible by the Community courts, unless the applicant has exhausted all avenues to obtain a remedy in his national courts and still has not obtained compensation. There are also other exceptions to this rule: first, the applicant may bring an action directly before the Community courts if it is impossible for national courts to order payments in the absence of Community provisions authorising national authorities to pay in the claimed amount;[178] and, second, if an action before national courts is for procedural or other reasons not susceptible to result in the compensation of the alleged damages.[179]

In all actions which do not involve payments of money the Community courts have jurisdiction.[180]

Joint liability of the Community and a Member State

In Cases 5, 7 and 13/66 *Kampffmeyer*[181] the ECJ held that the applicant must first bring an action before national courts. As a result, a national court must refer the case under art 177 to the ECJ which will decide whether or not the measure in question is valid. If invalid, then the measure will be annulled by the ECJ. At that time, the national court will assess solely the liability of the Member State and will award damages corresponding to the damage caused by national authorities. The next step for the applicant is to bring an action before the CFI for the latter to determine liability of the Community and award appropriate damages.

It is submitted that the solution adopted in relation to the division of responsibility between the Community and the Member State is too complex, time-consuming and confusing. In some cases it may lead to a denial of justice where both the national courts and the Community courts have no jurisdiction to decide a particular case.[182]

Conditions of Community liability under art 215(2) EC

Article 215(2) EC contains a general guideline concerning non-contractual liability of the Community and leaves it to the ECJ to determine specific rules in this area. Indeed, art 215(2) EC is unique as it requires the ECJ to establish the conditions of liability based on

---

[177] Case 96/71 *Haegeman* [1972] ECR 1005; Case C–282/90 *Vreugdenhil* [1992] ECR I–1962.
[178] For example, Case 64/76 *Dumortier* [1979] ECR 3091; Case 5/71 *Zuckerfabrik Schöppenstedt* v *Council* [1971] ECR 975.
[179] Case 281/82 *Unifrex* [1984] ECR 1969; Case 81/86 *De Boer Buizen* [1987] ECR 3677; Case T–167/94 *Nolle* [1995] ECR II–2589.
[180] Case 126/76 *Dietz* [1977] ECR 2431; Case C–282/90 *Vreugdenhil*, ibid; Case C– 104/89 and C–37/90 *Mulder* [1992] ECR I–3126.
[181] [1967] ECR 317.
[182] The best illustration is provided by Case C–55/90 *Cato* [1992] ECR I–2533

'general principles of the laws of the Member States'. It means that general principles of laws of Member States regarding liability of public authorities are relevant. Furthermore, it is not necessary for a particular rule to be recognised in all Member States, since this would lead to a lowest common denominator and thus ensure only the minimum protection for victims of wrongful conduct of the Community. The ECJ approach is more selective and based on a comparative study of national legal systems in the context of the specific requirement of Community law. This approach leaves the ECJ a considerable margin of appreciation in the selection of general principles appropriate to the particular needs of the Community. This is necessary taking into account the complexity of action for damages based on art 215(2) EC. On the one hand, the ECJ exercises its jurisdiction in relation to non-contractual liability in the context of disputes involving economic policies of the Community and thus must take into account its legal implications when assessing damage to the applicant, or determining the unlawful conduct on the part of the Community institutions; on the other hand, the ECJ must often resolve the delicate question of delimitation of competences between the Community and the Member States.

In Case 4/69 *Lütticke* v *Commission*[183] the ECJ held that general principles common to certain Member States concerning the conditions of liability are:

1. unlawful conduct on the part of the Community;
2. damage to the applicant; and
3. a causal link between the conduct of the Community institution and the alleged damage.

These three conditions have been constantly applied and recently confirmed in Case C–55/90 *Cato*.[184]

At the first glance these conditions appear very generous to the applicants, but in practice successful actions under art 215(2) EC are rare.

Unlawful conduct on the part of the Community

The determination of unlawful conduct on the part of the Community and its servants is based on the concept of fault which is explicitly mentioned in arts 34 and 40 ECSC. The fault of the system or the 'faute de service' refers to the Community institutions and in the case of its servants, liability is based on 'faute personnelle', which is the personal wrongful act or omission of a servant of the Community acting in the course of his duty. The case law of the ECJ has gradually determined the meaning of 'fault of the system', which is referred to in art 40 ECSC. First, liability can only be based on fault. As a result liability without fault, that is based on risks or stemming from the duty of guarantee, was rejected.[185] Second, art 40 ECSC has been interpreted restrictively: the concept of fault in the conduct of economic policies was rejected.[186] Third, the ECJ has refused to determine the different degrees of the gravity of fault and has instead used such formulas as 'inexplicable bad management' or 'inexcusable mistakes',[187] or 'manifest lack of diligence'[188] which amount to

---

[183] [1971] ECR 325.
[184] [1992] ECR 2533 at 2564.
[185] Case 23/59 *FERAM* [1959] ECR 501; Case 33/59 *Hauts Fourneaux de Chasse* [1962] ECR 719.
[186] Case 33/59, ibid, conclusions of M Lagrange.
[187] Case 14/60 *Meroni* [1961] ECR 319.
[188] Case 29/63 *Usines de la Providence* [1965] ECR 1123.

serious fault. Article 215(2) EC doe not mention fault but makes reference to the general principle of the national laws of the Member States. However, the ECJ has interpreted art 215(2) EC in the light of its previous case law regarding the ECSC Treaty. While this approach ensured homogeneity of the Community legal system, and coherence of its solutions, it lacked originality and required some adjustments – these have been made, for example, establishing the liability of the Community for legislative acts.[189] The concept of the fault of the system was recognised under the EC Treaty,[190] although the ECJ has since preferred to use different formulas such as 'illegality of the conduct of the institutions',[191] and 'manifest and grave disregard of the limits on the exercise of [the Institution's] power'.[192] Under the cover of those formulas, the ECJ has sought to determine a wrongful conduct of a Community institution. Lasok explained that the fault of the system '… occurs where damage results from the malfunctioning of Community institutions or Community servants'.[193] The Community exercises both administrative and legislative functions, and its system may fall occasionally below the standard of sound and efficient administration.

The fault of the system comprises all defects in the organisation and the functioning of the service, such as defaulting organisations of the service,[194] negligence in the management,[195] inappropriate supervision,[196] breach of the principle of confidentiality of information obtained by the Commission,[197] forwarding of erroneous information by a Community institution,[198] and breach of the provisions relating to hygiene and security at work.[199] The case law of the ECJ makes no distinction in the degree of fault unlike, for example, under French law where there is a difference between simple and serious *faute*. The Community will be liable in damages in cases of inexcusable errors or manifest and grave lack of diligence. However, the solution is very different in liability for legislative acts.

Liability for legislative acts

The ECJ has taken into account the fact that the activities of Community institutions concern less pure administration and more and more economic administration, which is characterised by the exercise of a wide discretion by the Community institutions as they have to make choices of economic policies. Such factors as the complexity inherent to

---

[189] When the CIF in Case T–120/89 *Stahlwerke Peine-Salzgitter* [1991] ECR II–366 tried to transpose the solution under the EC Treaty regarding liability for legislative acts which requires the choice of economic policy, the ECJ rejected this approach and held that fault should be assessed in the light of the criteria proper to arts 34 and 40 ECSC: Case C–220/91 *Commission* [1993] ECR 2393.

[190] Case 5/66 *Kampffmeyer* [1967] ECR 317.

[191] Case 4/69 *Lütticke* [1971] ECR 325.

[192] Case 83/76 *Bayerische HNL v Council and Commission* [1978] ECR 1209.

[193] D Lasok, Lasok and Bridge, *Law and Institutions of the European Union*, 6th ed, London: Butterworths, 1994, p273.

[194] Case 23/59 *FERAM* [1959] ECR 501.

[195] Cases 14, 16, 17, 20, 24, 26, 27/60 *Meroni* [1961] ECR 321.

[196] Cases 2 and 3 /61 *Fives Lille Cail* [1961] ECR 501.

[197] Case 145/83 *Adams* [1985] ECR 3539.

[198] Cases 19, 20, 25 and 30/69 *Richez-Parise* [1970] ECR 325; Case 169/73 *Compagnie Continentale France* [1975] ECR 117.

[199] Case 308/87 *Grifoni* [1990] ECR I–1203.

economic choices, difficulties in the application and interpretation of legislative measures in this area, and the wide margin of discretion exercised by the EC institutions have led the ECJ to interpret the concept of fault restrictively. Indeed, in Case 83/76 *Bayerische HNL* the ECJ emphasised that '... exercise of the legislative function must not be hindered by the prospect of [an] action for damages whenever the general interest of the Community requires legislative measures to be adopted which may adversely affect individual interests', and that 'in a legislative context ... the Community cannot incur liability unless the institution concerned has manifestly and gravely disregarded the limits on the exercise of its powers'.[200]

The case law of the ECJ has dissociated the concept of illegality and fault, thus the validity of an act does not exclude liability of the Community by reason of its adoption. In Case 74/74 *CNTA*[201] the ECJ held that the violation of the principle of legitimate expectation caused damage to the applicants since the adoption of an act which withdrew compensatory payments was valid but nevertheless entered into force immediately without transitional measures. Conversely, an illegal act may not give rise to liability. This was expressed in Case 5/71 *Zuckerfabrik Schöppenstedt* v *Council* in the following terms:

> 'When legislative action involving measures of economic policy is concerned, the Community does not incur non-contractual liability for damage suffered by individuals as a consequence of that action, by virtue of the provisions contained in art 215, second para, of the Treaty, unless a sufficiently flagrant violation of a superior rule of law for the protection of the individual has occurred.'[202]

This formula is taken from German concept of *Schutznortheorie*. It is referred to under EC law as the Schöppenstedt formula. It requires proof of the three conditions relating to non-contractual liability in general – unlawful conduct on the part of the Community, damage to the applicant and a causal link between the conduct of the Community institution and the alleged damage. In addition, another three conditions must be also satisfied: there must be a breach of a superior rule of law; the breach must be sufficiently serious; and the superior rule must be one for the protection of the individual.

The Schöppenstedt formula requires some comments. First, it is important to highlight that in Case 169/73 *Compagnie Continentale* the ECJ held that non-contractual liability of the Community institutions is excluded in cases when a provision of the Treaty causes damages to the applicant.[203] Thus, the Community institutions are liable in damages resulting from the adoption of a legislative measure. Second, this formula enhances the fact that EC institutions are particularly protected against actions in damages under art 215(2) EC for the very simple reason that all legislative acts imply that their authors enjoy a large margin of discretion. Indeed, it is not important whether a legislative act concerns economic policies *senso stricto* or other areas such as transport, social policy etc. What is important is that an institution has a wide discretion and must exercise it in the interest of the Community. It must make choices in conducting the Community policies in the areas of

---

[200] [1978] ECR 1229.
[201] [1975] ECR 533.
[202] [1971] ECR 975.
[203] [1975] ECR 117.

Community competences in order to attain the objectives which are essential for integration of national policies, and especially to harmonise national laws in specific areas,[204] regardless of the fact that those legislative measures may adversely affect individual interests. The prospect of continual applications for damages must not hinder the Community in its policy-making. For that reason the requirements contained in the Schöppenstedt formula are very restrictive and rigorous. The applicant has to demonstrate the following:

Breach of a superior rule of law

This requirement has as its objective the exclusion of claims founded upon minor illegality. The rule in question must occupy a fundamental place in the Community legal order. This comprises, *inter alia*, provisions of the Treaty and general principles of Community law. In Case 74/74 *CNTA v Commission*[205] a regulation, which entered into force immediately after its publication, did not provide for a transitional period and abolished compensation for the effect of exchange-rate fluctuations in trade in colza and rape seeds, was held legal but contrary to the principle of a legitimate expectation in relation to undertakings which had already obtained export licences fixing the amount of compensation in advance and concluded contracts prior to the abolition of the compensation scheme. In the second *Skimmed Milk Powder* case[206] the ECJ held that the regulation concerning the compulsory purchase of Community stocks of skimmed milk powder was contrary to the principle of non-discrimination.[207] In Case 114/76 *Bela-Mühler*,[208] which concerned the same regulation, the ECJ held that it was also disproportionate to the objective to be achieved. Among others principles recognised by the ECJ are: the principle of the protection of acquired rights in Cases 95–98/74, 15 and 100/75 *Union Nationale des Co-operative Agricoles de Céréales*;[209] the principle of proportionality in Cases 63–69/72 *Werhahn*;[210] and the principle of non-retroactivity in Case 71/74R *Nederlande Vereniging voor de Fruit en Groentenimport-handel.*[211]

Superior rule must be one for the protection of the individual

Not only must the rule have the protection of rights of individuals as an object, but it must also have the *effect* of providing such protection. It excludes rules such as those regarding the decision-making procedure, for example, non-consultation of the EP in the adoption of a measure which was required by that procedure or absence of a proposal from the Commission or non-respect of the division of competences between the Community institutions.[212] However, it is not necessary that the rule has exclusively as its object the

---

[204] Case C–63/89 *Les Assurances du Credit* [1991] ECR I–1799.
[205] [1975] ECR 533; also Case 97/76 *Merkur* [1977] ECR 1063 and Case C–104/89 *Mulder* [1992] ECR I–3061.
[206] Cases 83 and 94/76 and 4, 15, 40/77 *Bayerische HNL* [1978] ECR 1209
[207] There are many cases concerning the principle of non-discrimination and equality: Case 238/78 *Ireks-Arkady* [1979] ECR 2955; Cases 116 and 124/77 *Amylum* [1979] ECR 3497; Cases 64 and 113/76, 167 and 239/78, 27, 28 and 45/79 *Dumortier* [1979] ECR 3091.
[208] [1977] ECR 1211.
[209] [1975] ECR 1615.
[210] [1973] ECR 1246.
[211] [1975] ECR 563.
[212] Case C–282/90 *Vreugdenhil* [1992] ECR I–1937.

protection of individuals. It is sufficient that it also has an effect on the protection of individuals, in general. In Cases 5, 7 and 13–24/66 *Kampffmeyer*[213] which concerned similar circumstances as in Cases 106 and 107/63 *Toepfer v Commission*[214] the ECJ held that the failure of the Commission to investigate fully the protective measures concerning the imposition of a levy on maize had infringed a rule of law which was of a general nature as it referred to the free trade in maize, and the support of this market was, nevertheless, for the protection of individuals.

Breach must be sufficiently serious

The ECJ has interpreted this requirement in a very restrictive manner. The case law demonstrates that even a serious fault is not sufficient. It must be more than that. A bad or wrong manner of exercising a discretion by an EC institution will only give a right to reparation if the institution 'manifestly and gravely disregarded the limits on the exercise of its powers'.[215] In this particular case – *Bayerische HNL* – the ECJ explained that the manifest and grave disregard was one which has an obvious (manifest) and serious (grave) effect on the applicant undertaking. It held that in *Bayerische HNL* this requirement was not satisfied, since the measure affected a wide range of undertakings, had a small effect on the price of feed as compared to other factors, and thus was within the inherent economic risks of that particular trade. As a result, the Community did not manifestly and gravely disregard the limits of its powers. This restrictive interpretation reached its apogee in Cases 116 and 124/77 *GR Amylum VN and Tunnel Refineries Limited v Council and Commission*[216] and Case 143/77 *Koninklijke Scholten-Honig NV v Council and Commission*,[217] the so-called *Isoglucose* cases, in which a regulation imposing levies on the production of isoglucose, successfully challenged under art 173 EC[218] prior to the application for damages, had such effect on the remaining three or four isoglucose undertakings in the Community that, for example, Koninklijke had to close down its business. The ECJ held that only if the conduct of an EC institution was 'verging on the arbitrary', which was not the case here, would it be considered as a sufficiently serious breach. The ECJ refused to award damages. The interest of the Community prevailed, it was entitled to limit the production of isoglucose and stabilise the market, although some mistakes were made which resulted in the annulment of the regulation. This much criticised approach led to the rejection of most applications under art 215(2) EC but seems to be softening in recent cases. In Case C–220/91P *Stahlwerke Peine-Salzgitter*,[219] which concerned liability of the ECSC, the ECJ held that conduct 'verging on the arbitrary' is not a necessary requirement. Also, in Cases C–104/89 and 37/90 *Mulder*[220] the Court held that in the absence of 'the peremptory public interest' the Community cannot justify a measure which is gravely illegal and thus, the Community would incur liability in such circumstances.

---

[213] [1967] ECR 317.
[214] [1965] ECR 525.
[215] Cases 83 and 94/76 and 4, 15, 40/77 *Bayerische HNL* [1978] ECR 1209.
[216] [1979] ECR 3497.
[217] [1979] ECR 3583.
[218] Cases 103 and 145/77 *RSH and Tunnel Refineries* [1978] ECR 2037.
[219] [1993] ECR I–2393.
[220] [1992] ECR I–3126. See also Cases 120/86 *Mulder* [1988] ECR 2321, 170/86 *Von Deetzen* [1988] ECR 2355, C–189/89 *Spagl* [1990] ECR I–4539 and C–217/89 *Pastatter* [1990] ECR I–4858 (below).

In this case, Mulder and other farmers submitted an application under art 215(2) claiming that they had suffered loss as a result of various Community regulations dealing with the over-production of dairy products. Under one regulation they were paid a premium for five years for not selling milk and milk products. At the end of this five-year period they could apply for 'special reference quantities' which would have allowed them to come back on the market. They failed to obtain the 'special reference quantities' but successfully challenged this regulation under art 173 EC (Cases 120/86 *Mulder* and 170/86 *Von Deetzen*). Later they were allocated quantities tantamount to 60 per cent of their marketing capacities prior to the five-year period. This regulation was also successfully challenged in Case C–189/89 *Spagl* and Case C–217/89 *Pastatter*.

The ECJ confirmed the Schöppenstedt formula and returned to its old statement that in relation to legislative acts involving choices in economic policy the Community institutions enjoyed a wide discretion and thus they were liable only if they had manifestly and gravely disregarded the limits of the exercise of their powers. Also, as previously stated, the ECJ held that in order to incur non-contractual liability the damage must go beyond the bounds of normal economic risks inherent in the activities relevant to a particular sector. As result, the ECJ decided the Community incurred liability in relation to the regulation allocating 'special reference quantities' but not the one which imposed the 60 per cent rule. However, the case of the regulation concerning the allocation of 'special reference quantities' although the ECJ held that the group of people affected was clearly defined, it comprised more than 12,000 farmers which were entitled to claim approximately of ECU 250 million.

Nevertheless, the change of approach of the Community courts in the application of the Schöppenstedt formula has not eliminated the requirement that only grave illegality in the absence of the peremptory public interest of the Community would permit the applicants to successfully claim damages under art 215(2) EC.[221]

In relation to damages in the case of liability for legislative acts the requirements are more stringent. In addition to conditions relating to damage which apply to all cases under art 215(2) EC in this area the damage must be abnormal and special. In Cases 83 and 94/76 and 4, 15, 40/77 *Bayerische HNL*[222] the ECJ also held that consequences stemming from the annulment of the act must be taken into consideration, which in fact introduced two new requirements in relation to damage. It must be special, which means that the measure must affect a limited and clearly defined group – this was not the case in *Bayerische* since the measure applied to a large number of people, producers of cattle, poultry and pork. In Case 238/78 *Ireks-Akady*[223] the measure concerned a limited and clearly defined group, the producers of quellmehl (a product used in the bakery industry). Also, in this case the ECJ held that a second requirement relating to abnormal or grave damage was satisfied since '... the damage alleged by the applicants goes beyond the bounds of the economic risks inherent in the activities in the sector concerned', unlike the situation in *Bayerische* where an increase of 2 per cent in the price of animal feedstuffs was deemed to be within the inherent economic risks of that sector of business.

---

[221] Case T–572/93 *Odigitria* [1995] ECR II–2025, [1995] Europe (August/September), no 290, comm D Simon and F Gazin.
[222] [1978] ECR 1209.
[223] [1979] ECR 2955.

These requirements contributed to the limitation of successful applications under art 215(2) EC. So far, the ECJ has awarded damages for the effects of regulations in two series of cases: *Ireks-Arkady* and three other decisions rendered the same day, and *Mulder* in which the economic operators were considered to be a clearly defined group of economic agents (producers who had marketed no milk in the reference year upon which 'reference quantities' were based), although it comprised a large number of people.

Damage

The damage suffered must be real and certain regardless whether it is present or future.[224] However, it must not be purely hypothetical[225] or speculative.[226] The compensation may be obtained for all damage suffered which comprises *damnum emergens* (the actual loss) and *lucrum cessans* (the income which would have been earned). Advocate-General Capatori said in Case 238/78 *Ireks-Arkady*[227] that damage 'covers both a material loss ... a reduction in a person's assets and also the loss of an increase in those assets which would have occurred if the harmful act had not taken place'.

As to the actual amount of damages, it is generally negotiated between the parties. Where there is a large number of applicants, the Commission and the Council submit a collective offer of indemnification as happened in *Mulder*.[228]

There is also a duty to mitigate loss. In *Mulder* the ECJ reduced the damages awarded by the amount of profit which the producers could have reasonably earned from alternative activities. Although the ECJ made no suggestion as to alternative activities, the term 'reasonable' implies that fundamentally different activities from their previous business would not be considered as alternatives.

Community law also recognises contributory negligence. If the applicant has contributed through his own negligence to the resulting damage, the amount of damages will be reduced proportionally to the loss he has brought upon himself. In Case 145/83 *Adams*[229] the ECJ held that Adams contributed through his negligence to the resulting damage and reduced by half the awarded amount.

Adams was employed by the Swiss-based multinational Hoffman-La Roche. He forwarded confidential information to the Commission concerning breaches of art 86 by his employer for which the latter was heavily fined. During the proceedings Hoffman-La Roche asked the Commission to disclose the name of the informant. The Commission refused but, contrary to the duty of confidentiality contained in art 214 EC, forwarded to Hoffman-La Roche certain documents which enabled them to identify Adams as the source of the information. In the meantime Adams moved to Italy where he set up his own business. Hoffman-La Roche, due to its international connections, destroyed Adam's Italian business. The

---

[224] Case 33/59 *Hauts Fourneaux de Chasse* [1962] ECR 748.

[225] Case 54/65 *Châtillon Commentry & Neuves-Maisons* [1966] ECR 265; Case 4/65 *Hainaut-Sambre* [1965] ECR 1363.

[226] Cases 54–60 /76 *Compagnie Industrielle et Agricole* [1977] ECR 645; Case 74/74 *CNTA* [1975] ECR 533.

[227] [1979] ECR 2955.

[228] The Council and the Commission adopted a Regulation regarding the modality of indemnification: Communication from the Council and Commission delivered by the ECJ in Joined Cases C–104/89 *Mulder* and C–37/90 *Heineman* (OJ C198 5.8.92 p4).

[229] [1985] ECR 3539.

Commission failed to inform Adams that his former employer was planning to persecute him. On his return to Switzerland Adams was arrested by the Swiss police for economic espionage and held in solitary confinement. His wife committed suicide. Adams brought proceedings before the ECJ against the Commission for loss of earnings and loss of reputation as a result of his conviction and imprisonment.

The ECJ held that the Commission was liable for the breach of duty of confidentiality as it allowed Adams to be identified as an informer and awarded Adams £200,000 in damages for his mental anguish and lost earnings and £176,000 for costs, half the amount he had demanded. The reason for the reduction was Adams' contributory negligence. The ECJ held that Adams contributed to the resulting damage by failing to warn the Commission that he could be identified from the confidential documents, and by failing to inquire about progress of proceedings especially before returning to Switzerland.

Causation

A direct causal link must be established between the damage suffered and the unlawful conduct.[230] The burden of proof is on the applicant.[231] In Cases 64/76 and 113/76, 239/78, 27, 28 and 45/79 *Dumortier Frères*[232] the ECJ held that there is no obligation to compensate all prejudicial consequences, however remote, resulting from an unlawful legislative act. In this case a regulation which abolished production refunds for maize grits but not for maize starch, both used in brewing and baking and thus in direct competition, was successfully challenged by the producers of maize grits. The ECJ held that the regulation was contrary to the principle of non-discrimination and equality, affected a limited and clearly defined group, that is, the producers of maize grits, and the damage exceeded the bounds of the inherent economic risks in this sector of business. In addition, when adopting the regulation, the Council disregarded the advice of the Commission to re-introduce the refunds. As a result of the successful action under art 173 EC, the producers of maize grits brought an action under art 215(2) EC. They claimed compensation in relation to loss of refunds prior to this date, lost sales and the closure of factories by two producers and bankruptcy of a third one. The ECJ awarded damages only in relation to the loss of refunds. The reduction in sales was not considered as resulting from the abolition of refunds since the producers decided not to increase prices of maize grits and thus passed the loss to their purchasers. The closing of factories and the bankruptcy were not a sufficiently direct result of the withdrawal of refunds. Therefore, too remote a damage will not give rise to the right of reparation. This question was also examined by the ECJ in Cases 5, 7 and 13–24/66 *Kampffmeyer*[233] in which the facts were identical to Cases 106 and 107/63 *Toepfer*[234] already discussed as a result of a mistake made by German authorities the import levy for maize from France was fixed at zero. When the mistake was discovered, the German authorities refused to grant licences for imports of maize and asked the Commission to raise the levy

---

[230] Case 18/60 *Worms* [1962] ECR 401.
[231] Case 40/75 *Produits Bertrand* [1976] ECR 1.
[232] [1979] ECR 3091.
[233] [1967] ECR 317.
[234] [1965] ECR 525.

and confirm the ban which the latter did three days later. The Commission decision was successfully challenged under art 173 EC but the German importers asked for compensation under art 215(2) EC. The ECJ held that only those importers who had concluded contracts to buy French maize before their applications for import licences had been rejected were entitled to claim damages. As a result, those who performed their contracts were awarded damages in respect to the higher levies which they had to pay. The importers who cancelled their contracts were awarded damages in respect of penalties payable for breach of contract. However, they were only entitled to 10 per cent of the profits which might have been made, taking into account that the expected profit was of a purely speculative nature. The importers who did not enter into contracts before applying for import licences had no right to compensation.

11 Preliminary Rulings: art 177 EC

11.1 General jurisdiction of the ECJ under art 177 EC

11.2 Interpretation of Community law by the ECJ under art 177 EC

11.3 Validity of Community law

Article 177 EC provides:

'(1) The Court of Justice shall have jurisdiction to give preliminary rulings concerning:
(a) the interpretation of this Treaty;
(b) the validity and interpretation of acts of the institutions of the Community and of the ECB;
(c) the interpretation of the statutes of bodies established by an act of the Council, where those statutes so provide.
(2) Where such a question is raised before any court or tribunal of a Member State that court or tribunal may, if it considers that a decision on the question is necessary to enable it to give judgment, request the Court of Justice to give a ruling thereon.
(3) Where any such question is raised in a case pending before a court or tribunal of a Member State, against whose decisions there is no judicial remedy under national law, the court or tribunal shall bring the matter before the Court of Justice.'

Preliminary rulings are common to all three Communities and respectively defined in arts 41 ECSC,[1] 150 Euratom[2] and 177 EC. They constitute the main form of co-operation between national courts and the ECJ. In Case 16/65 *Schwarze*[3] the ECJ emphasised this aspect of preliminary rulings by stating that on the basis of the mechanism of co-operation established in art 177 EC, national courts and the ECJ, within their respective competences, are called to contribute directly and reciprocally to render a judgment. Indeed, the ECJ under art 177 EC is not a court of appeal. It assists national courts to reach a correct decision from the point of view of Community law. Article 177 EC allows national courts when applying Community law to adjourn the proceedings pending before them and to seek advice from the ECJ on the interpretation or validity of EC law. The contribution of the ECJ to a final judgment is incidental since it only elucidates referred issues, and it is the national court that delivers judgment. It may be said that there are four stages of the procedure under art 177 EC. First, there is a dispute before a national court involving EC law; second, the latter refers the question concerning the interpretation or validity of Community law to the ECJ; third, the ECJ gives its decision on a specific issue which was the subject-matter of the referral; and, finally, it is the task of a national judge to draw conclusions from the

---

[1] Under art 41 ECSC the jurisdiction of the ECJ is limited to the validity of Community law, but the latter by analogy to art 177 EC extended its jurisdiction to interpretation of Community law in Case C–221/88 *Busseni* [1990] ECR I–493.
[2] Article 150 Euratom has never been invoked.
[3] [1965] ECR 1081.

decision of the ECJ in relation to the dispute at hand. Thus, the procedure under art 177 provides for a prior ruling by the ECJ on the question of interpretation or validity of EC law before a decision on the principal issue, which must take into consideration the ruling of the ECJ, is delivered by the national court.

Proceedings under art 177 EC are not adversarial, and parties to the original proceedings are not involved, although art 20 of the Statute of the ECJ offers them the opportunity to make written and oral observations. Also, the Member States, the Commission and the Council, which must be notified upon receipt of a reference, are invited to make their positions known on a specific issue if they so wish.

The main reason for preliminary rulings lies in the peculiarity of Community law. The principle of supremacy requires that Community law is uniformly applied in all Member States, that is, that EC law has the same meaning and effect throughout the Community. Thus, the main objective of art 177 EC is to ensure that irrespective of the Member State, national courts when applying EC law – which they do independently from one another and are always more or less influenced by their own legal system – will reach the same solution on a point concerning EC law. In Case 166/73 *Rheinmühlen*[4] the ECJ held that:

'Article 177 is essential for the preservation of the Community character of the law established by the Treaty and has the object of ensuring that in all circumstances this law is the same in all States of the Community.'

At the same time the mechanism under art 177 EC ensures that national courts are not placed in a position of subordination vis-à-vis the ECJ, since in a certain sense it is a dialogue between a Community judge and a national judge. They must co-operate, and not encroach upon one another's jurisdiction, as national law and Community law are still two separate legal systems.

Article 177 EC greatly contributes to the legal protection of individuals, and it allows them, via national courts, to have access to the ECJ. The stringent requirements concerning *locus standi* for non-privileged applicants under Community law are to a certain extent alleviated by the possibility provided by preliminary rulings. The importance of preliminary rulings to homogeneity and uniformity of Community law is enhanced by the fact that only the ECJ is empowered to give them. The Court of First Instance has no jurisdiction under art 177 EC.

This chapter focuses on the main features of the procedure under art 177 EC.

11.1 General jurisdiction of the ECJ under art 177 EC

The ECJ has jurisdiction to interpret Community law and to assess the validity of Community acts adopted by its institutions. As a result, the ECJ exercises two different functions under art 177 EC – although both contribute to define the scope of application of Community law, the interpretation of Community law under art 177 EC has become the main activity of the ECJ. However, the importance of the ECJ in the review of the validity of Community measures to ensure uniform application of EC law is strengthened by the fact

---

[4] [1974] ECR 33.

that national courts have no jurisdiction to declare a Community act invalid. Only the ECJ may make a declaration of its invalidity; national courts must refer to the ECJ whenever they have serious doubts as to the validity of Community acts. There are, however, certain conditions under art 177 EC common to the exercise of both functions which must be satisfied before the ECJ accepts a reference. They concern the provisions of Community law which are liable to be referred to the ECJ, the status of the body allowed to refer, and the territorial jurisdiction of the ECJ under art 177 EC.

Community law susceptible to be referred to the ECJ

National courts may ask the ECJ to rule on the interpretation of primary sources of Community law: the founding Treaties as amended,[5] Protocols and Annexes to the Treaties, and the Acts of Accession to the Communities.[6] In this respect it has to be noted that art 31 of the SEA restricts jurisdiction of the ECJ to Title II of the Single European Act and art 32. This has resulted in General Provisions of the SEA and its Title III concerning political co-operation being excluded from the scope of art 177 EC. Further limitations were introduced by the Treaty of Maastricht. Under art L TEU the ECJ cannot give preliminary rulings in the matters regulated by Common Provisions of Title I (arts A–F), Pillar 2 apart from art K3(2)(c) TEU and Pillar 3. Because of their constitutional nature, the validity of primary sources cannot be determined by the ECJ.

The ECJ has jurisdiction to both interpret and determine the validity of secondary legislation. In Case 9/70 *Franz Grad*[7] the ECJ held that all acts of the Community institutions, without distinction, may be referred under art 177 EC. This includes not only acts expressly mentioned in art 189 EC, or in the Treaty, but all other acts adopted outside its framework such as, for example, resolutions of the Council.[8] National courts may also refer a question concerning Community law which is not directly effective since the exact meaning of national law which they have to apply and which implement Community directives or decisions addressed to a Member State may pose difficult interpretation problems,[9] or may give rise to doubts as to their validity.[10] Furthermore, the ECJ has jurisdiction to interpret non-binding acts such as recommendations[11] and opinions. It is clear that the validity of non-binding acts is decided by national courts.

Under the EC and Euratom Treaties not only acts emanating from the Council and the Commission but also the EP[12] and the ECJ are included within the scope of art 197 EC for interpretive purposes. This also applies to a decision of the ECJ.[13] However, the validity of

---

[5] Article 8 of the 1965 Merger Treaty provides for its interpretation by the ECJ which includes the Protocol on the Privileges and Immunities of the European Communities annexed to that Treaty: Case 23/68 *Klomp* [1969] ECR 43.
[6] Case 812/79 *Burgoa* [1980] ECR 2787.
[7] [1970] ECR 91.
[8] Case 59/75 *Manghera* [1976] ECR 91.
[9] Case 111/75 *Mazzalaï* [1976] ECR 657.
[10] Case 5/77 *Tedeschi* [1977] ECR 1555.
[11] Case 113/75 *Giordano Frecassetti* v *Amministrazione delle Finanze dello Stato* [1976] ECR 983; Case C–322/88 *Grimaldi* [1989] ECR 4407.
[12] Case 208/80 *Lord Bruce of Donington* v *Aspden* [1981] ECR 2205.

interpretive purposes. This also applies to a decision of the ECJ.[13] However, the validity of judgments of the ECJ cannot be challenged.[14]

As to international agreements concluded between the Community and third countries, in Case 181/73 *Haegemann II*[15] the ECJ held they were considered to be acts adopted by the Community institutions within the meaning of art 177 EC. The assimilation of international agreements into Community acts is very important. In this manner the ECJ ensures uniformity in their interpretation and application throughout the Community, although national courts or tribunals of third countries, and contracting parties to those agreements are neither allowed to refer to the ECJ under art 177 EC nor bound by its judgments. The jurisdiction of the ECJ to give preliminary rulings is also extended to the decisions adopted by bodies created by such international agreements in order to ensure their proper application.[16]

Complementary sources of Community law are concluded between the Member States and as such are excluded from the scope of art 177 EC. In Case 130/73 *Vandeweghe*[17] the ECJ ruled out the possibility that the interpretation or the validity of such agreements might be referred under art 177 EC even if they were concluded under art 220 EC. For that reason, international agreements concluded among the Member States often expressly confer upon the ECJ the task of interpreting their provisions and thus ensure their uniform application throughout the Community. The agreement itself may contain a provision conferring an interpretative role to the ECJ such as arts 2 and 3 of the Community Patent Convention,[18] or more often a protocol is annexed to the convention relating to its interpretation, as in the case of the 1968 Brussels Convention on Jurisdiction and the Enforcement of Judgments in Civil and Commercial Matters, or the 1968 Convention on the Mutual Recognition of Companies and Legal Persons, or the 1980 Rome Convention on the Law Applicable to Contractual Obligations.

Courts and tribunals which can refer to the ECJ

Article 177 EC specifies that only courts and tribunals may ask for preliminary rulings. This formula excludes the parties to a dispute referring directly to the ECJ, and rules out any possibility for them to insert a clause into their contract, providing that in the case of a dispute on a point of Community law the ECJ will have jurisdiction to settle the matter as it would impose jurisdiction upon the ECJ under art 177 EC.[19]

In most cases the question whether or not a particular body is a court or a tribunal is

---

[13] Case 135/77 *Bosch* [1978] ECR 855.

[14] Case 69/85 *Wünsche* [1986] ECR 947.

[15] [1974] ECR 449, which concerned an association agreement between EEC and Greece and the position has been confirmed in many cases, for example, in Case 52/77 *Cayrol* [1977] ECR 2261 concerning the association agreement between the EEC and Spain and Case 65/77 *Razamatsimbo* [1977] ECR 2229 concerning the Lomé Convention.

[16] Case C–192/89 *Sevince* [1990] ECR I–3461; it also includes non-binding recommendation of such bodies: Case C–188/91 *Deutsche Shell* [1993] ECR I–363.

[17] [1973] ECR 1329; see also Case 44/84 *Hurd* [1986] ECR 29.

[18] OJ L401, 31.12.89 p1.

[19] Case 44/65 *Hessische Knappschaft* [1965] ECR 965; Case 93/78 *Mattheus* [1978] ECR 2203.

referring body in the context of art 177 EC. Indeed, uniformity in the application of Community law throughout the Community requires that the definition of a court or a tribunal for the purposes of art 177 EC is independent from national concepts, which vary from one Member State to another. It has to have an autonomous, Community meaning. The case law of the ECJ has gradually determined the criteria permitting to identify a body which is considered as 'a court or a tribunal' under art 177 EC. Apart from all judicial bodies expressly recognised as such under national law of a Member State, the ECJ held that other bodies can refer under art 177 EC provided they meet certain requirements. In Case 61/65 *Vassen-Göbbels*[20] the ECJ held that technical factors, such as whether the type of procedure is adversarial or not,[21] the involvement of national authorities in the appointments of the members of that body, and the mandatory jurisdiction of that body imposed by national law upon the parties to the dispute, were all relevant for the purpose of art 177 EC. In *Vassen-Göbbels* the ECJ confirmed that a Dutch social security arbitration tribunal could refer under art 177 EC since:

1. its members and the chairman were appointed by the Dutch Minister for Social Affairs and Public Health who also laid down the rules of procedure;
2. it was a permanent body which settled disputes under art 89 of the RBFM;[22]
3. the procedure was adversarial;
4. the jurisdiction of the social security arbitration tribunal was compulsory in all disputes involving social security and the insurer; and
5. this body was bound to apply rules of law and not equity.

In Case C–24/92 *Corbiau*[23] the ECJ examined the relationship between a body in question and the person that took the decision being challenged in the proceedings before that body in order to determine whether the latter is a court or tribunal for the purposes of art 177 EC. In *Corbiau*, the Director of Taxation (Directeur des Contributions) in Luxembourg was not considered as a court or tribunal in the context of art 177 EC and could not refer to the ECJ because there was an institutional link between the Luxembourg tax authorities which made a decision challenged by Corbiau and the Director of those authorities. As a result, he was not a third party to the proceedings. Further indications regarding 'functional' aspects of competences of a national body were provided in Case 138/80 *Borker*[24] in which the Paris Conseil de l'Ordre des Avocats à la Cour (Paris Bar Council) was not considered to be a court or tribunal within the meaning of art 177 EC because that body was not exercising any judicial function but in fact 'made a request for a declaration relating to a dispute between a member of the Bar and the courts or tribunals of another Member State'. In Case 246/80 *Broekmeulen*[25] the reference from the Appeals Committee for General Medicine, which was

---

[20] [1966] ECR 377.
[21] The ECJ has never rejected a referral on the sole ground that the proceedings before a natural body are not adversarial: Case C–13 and 113/91 *Debus* [1992] ECR I–3617; Case C–10/92 *Balocchi* [1993] ECR I–5105; Case C–18/93 *Corsica Ferries Italia* [1994] ECR I–1783.
[22] Reglement van het Beamtenfonds voor het Mijenbedriff, the regulation governing the relations between social security and those insured by it.
[23] [1993] ECR I–1277.
[24] [1980] ECR 1975.
[25] [1981] ECR 2311.

established by the Royal Netherlands Society for the Promotion of Medicine and not considered as a court or tribunal under Dutch law, was accepted by the ECJ for the following reasons: the national authorities appointed the chairman and one-third of the members of the Society's body which constituted, according to the ECJ, a significant degree of involvement of The Netherlands public authorities in its composition; the procedure was adversarial; there was no appeal from the Appeals Committee to the courts; and, most importantly, any Dutch general practitioner, or a practitioner from any other Member State intending to establish himself in The Netherlands was compelled to have his status recognised by the Society, and in the case of refusal the Appeals Committee was competent in the last resort to decide the question of his registration as a doctor. The protection of the right of establishment for doctors from another Member State was emphasised by the ECJ which stated that if a professional body, acting under a certain degree of governmental supervision, was assigned a task of implementing Community law and which together with the public authorities:

> 'creates appeal procedures which may affect the exercise of rights granted by Community law, it is imperative, in order to ensure the proper functioning of Community law, that the Court should have an opportunity of ruling on issues of interpretation and validity arising out of such proceedings.'

The question whether a body which exercises not only a judicial function but also other tasks may be considered as a court or tribunal within the meaning of art 177 EC was addressed in Case 14/86 *Pretore di Salo* v *Persons Unknown*.[26] A referral from an Italian pretore, a magistrate who initially acts as a public prosecutor and then as an examining magistrate, concerning the interpretation of an EC directive was accepted by the ECJ on the ground that the request emanated from a body that acted in the general framework of its task of judging, independently and in accordance with the law, despite the fact that certain functions performed by that body were not *senso stricto* of a judicial nature.[27] However, a referral from an Italian public prosecutor was rejected by the ECJ in Cases C–74 and 129/95 *Criminal Procedures against X*,[28] in which Advocate-General Ruiz Jarabo Colomer stressed that the main task of the Procura della Repubblica is to submit evidence during the trial and thus it is a party to the proceedings. Further, it does not exercise judicial functions and consequently should not be considered as a court of tribunal under art 177 EC.

Private arbitration

The issue of private arbitration has also been examined by the ECJ. In Case 102/81 *Nordsee Deutsche Hochsefischerei GmbH* v *Reederei Mond*[29] the parties to the disputed contract inserted an arbitration clause in the original contract providing that any disagreement between them on any question arising out of the contract would be resolved by an arbitrator and that all recourse to the ordinary courts was excluded. When a problem concerning the performance of that contract by a number of German shipbuilders arose an arbitrator was

---

[26] [1987] ECR 2545. See also Case C–338/85 *Fratelli Pardini* [1988] ECR 2041.
[27] Confirmed in Case 318/86 *Greis Unterweger* [1986] ECR 955; Case C–393/92 *Almelo* [1994] ECR 1477.
[28] [1996] ECR I–6609.
[29] [1982] ECR 1095.

appointed by the Chamber of Commerce of Bremen in accordance with the contract, but the parties could not agree on his appointment. The arbitrator asked the ECJ to give a preliminary ruling, but the latter refused to recognise the arbitrator as a court or tribunal within the meaning of art 177 EC for two reasons. First, that the parties to the dispute freely selected arbitration as a way of resolving any dispute between them; and, second, that neither were German public authorities involved in the choice of arbitration by the parties nor were they 'called to intervene automatically in the proceedings before the arbitrator'. The ECJ emphasised that if private arbitration raises questions concerning Community law, national courts may have jurisdiction to examine them, either in the framework of assistance they provide for arbitral tribunals (especially in the context of certain judicial measures which are not available to the arbitrator), or in the interpretation of the law applicable to that contract, or within the framework of control which they exercise in relation to arbitration awards.[30]

It is submitted that the refusal to recognise an arbitration tribunal as a court or tribunal under art 177 EC will be subject to further development since the advantages that arbitration offers to businessmen – choice of their own arbitrator, confidentiality of proceedings, more speedy and less expensive proceedings as compared to those conducted before national courts, although the last two points are subject to a certain degree of scepticism – will be seriously undermined if arbitration tribunals, which are bound to settle more and more disputes involving Community law, are not allowed to refer to the ECJ. Furthermore, arbitration as an extrajudicial method of settling disputes is well recognised in all Member States.

If public authorities are involved in arbitration, for example as in Case 109/88 *Handels-og Kontorfunktionaererernes Forbund i Danmark* v *Dansk Arbejdsgiverforening*[31] the situation is very different. In that case a Danish Industrial Arbitration Board was recognised as a court or tribunal within the scope of art 177 EC, since its jurisdiction was imposed upon the parties if they could not agree on the application of a collective agreement, its composition and procedure was governed by Danish law, and its award was final.

Territorial jurisdiction of the ECJ

Article 177 EC provides that only courts and tribunals of the Member States may ask for preliminary rulings. As a result, courts located in third countries or international courts are not permitted to refer to the ECJ under art 177 EC. It also excludes courts common to certain Member States such as the Benelux Court. Nevertheless, the ECJ has given a wide interpretation to the territorial scope of application of art 177 EC. It accepted a reference from the court situated in the Isle of Man which is outside the system of British courts[32] on the ground that the United Kingdom under its Act of Accession is responsible for its external relations. Also an administrative court of Papeete in Polynesia was allowed to make referral to the ECJ under art 177 EC. The government of the United Kingdom argued that the court of Papeete was not within the jurisdiction of France as it was situated in a French overseas

---

[30] Case C–393/92 *Almelo* [1994] ECR I–1477.
[31] [1989] ECR 3199.
[32] Case C–355/89 *Barr* [1991] ECR I–3479.

department, and that under art 227(3) EC it was outside the territorial scope of application of Community law. The ECJ held that this court under French law was considered as a French administrative court and that the question referred was within the jurisdiction of the ECJ as it concerned the application of the special conditions on association of overseas territories which includes French Polynesia.[33]

References in interlocutory proceedings

In Case 107/76 *Hoffman-La Roche* v *Centrafarm*[34] the ECJ held that preliminary references can be made in the course of interlocutory proceedings. It is, however, very unusual for a national court to do so because of the nature of interlocutory proceedings, which requires prompt resolution of the submitted matters, and the fact that the interlocutory issue can be examined again during the main proceedings.

11.2 Interpretation of Community law by the ECJ under art 177 EC

The ECJ has jurisdiction to interpret Community law aiming at its uniform application throughout the Community and has given a wide meaning to this function. As a result, the interpretation comprises:

1. The determination of the exact meaning and scope of application of the provisions of Community law, as well as the concepts which those provisions expressly or implicitly describe,[35] such as for example the concept of non-discrimination.
2. The determination as to whether or not EC regulations need to be further completed or specified by national legislation.[36]
3. The determination of the application of the provisions of Community law *(ratione materiae, ratione personae, ratione temporis)*, the legal effect they produce and, especially, whether or not they are directly effective.
4. The determination of the meaning and legal implications of the principle of supremacy of Community law vis-à-vis national laws of the Member States.

Furthermore, art 177(1)(c) EC provides that the ECJ has jurisdiction to interpret the statutes of bodies established by an act of the Council, where those statutes so provide.

The role of the ECJ under art 177 EC is to interpret Community law not national law. Therefore, the question of interpretation and the validity of national law is outside the jurisdiction of the ECJ,[37] although in some cases when national law was at issue national courts, by formulating the questions in a manner that make them Community questions, or the ECJ by selecting specific aspects relevant to Community law, had in fact interpreted

---

[33] Cases C–100 and 101/89 *Kaefer and Procacci* v *France* [1990] ECR I–4647; also Case C–260/90 *Leplat* [1992] ECR I–643.

[34] [1977] ECR 957.

[35] Case 10/69 *Portelange* [1969] ECR 309.

[36] Case 94/71 *Schlüter* [1972] ECR 307.

[37] For example, Case 75/63 *Unger* [1964] ECR 347; Case 188/86 *Lefebre* [1987] ECR 2963; Case 20/87 *Gauchard* [1987] ECR 4879; Case 152/83 *Demouche* [1987] ECR 3833; Case C–347/89 *Euripharm* [1991] ECR I–1717.

national law. In Case 112/75 *Directeur Régional de la Securité Sociale de Nancy* v *August Hirardin*[38] the ECJ has justified this interference in the following terms:

'Although the Court when giving a ruling under art 177, has no jurisdiction ... to pronounce upon a provision of national law, it may however provide the national court with the factors of interpretation depending on Community law which might be useful to it in evaluating the effects of such provision.'

There is also another exception to this principle that the ECJ has no jurisdiction to give preliminary rulings upon questions relating to national law which, fortunately, seems to have declined in use. It occurs when national law expressly refers to Community law, and the interpretation of the latter is necessary for a national court in order to give a judgment. The ECJ in Cases C–297/88 and 197/89 *Dzodzi*[39] and Case C–231/89 *Gmurzynska*[40] accepted the referral and thus, in fact, interpreted national law. While it certainly ensures uniformity in the application of Community law, this approach of the ECJ was rightly criticised by Advocate-General Dermon in his conclusions in the above-mentioned cases, and it seems that the practice has been gradually abandoned by the ECJ. In Case C–37/92 *Jose Vanacker*[41] the ECJ held that national courts should interpret national law.

Another problem with the interpretation of Community law by the ECJ under art 177 EC is that it is not easy to draw a line between the interpretation and the actual application of EC law. Under art 177 EC the ECJ has jurisdiction to interpret Community law *in abstratio* and objectively. However, the necessity to assist national courts in rendering a judgment in a particular case requires that the Community judges give their decision within the context of law and facts of that case.

The essence of art 177 EC is to create a spirit of co-operation between national courts and the ECJ. For that reason it is important that each court acts within its jurisdiction. The ECJ must only interpret Community law, while the national court must apply it in the context of a particular dispute. However, in practice the boundary between interpretation and application is fluid and varies depending upon the degree of precision of the question asked by national courts, the complexity of the factual and legal context of the dispute, etc. For that reason the ECJ is in a difficult position. On the one hand, if its decision is too concrete and too precise, it pre-determines the outcome of the dispute and a national judge has no discretion at all but must follow the preliminary ruling given by the ECJ. In these circumstances, instead of interpreting Community law, the ECJ is applying it – this encroaches upon the jurisdiction of national courts and undermines the division of competences between national courts and the ECJ, which is contrary to the spirit and the terms of art 177 EC. On the other hand, if the preliminary ruling is too general, and the interpretation of a provision of Community law is too abstract, the national judge has a large measure of discretion and thus the preliminary ruling instead of clarifying a particular question may obscure it even more. This approach calls into question the main objective of

---

[38] [1976] ECR 553; also Case 97/83 *Melkunie* [1984] ECR 2367.

[39] [1991] ECR I–3783.

[40] [1990] ECR I–4003.

[41] [1993] ECR I–4947; also confirmed in Case C–346/93 *Kleinwort Benson* [1995] ECR I–615 which concerned the interpretation of the 1968 Brussels Convention on Recognition and the Enforcement of Judgments in Civil and Commercial Matters, but this solution is transposable to art 177 EC: [1995] Europe (May), no 192, comm DS and AR.

art 177 EC, that is the uniformity of application of Community law throughout the Community. Indeed, it is not easy for the ECJ to reach a decision which is neither too precise nor too general, and in relation to the validity of national law in the light of the principle of supremacy of Community law some decisions of the ECJ under art 177 EC have left no doubts as to the outcome of the case.[42]

In the context of preliminary rulings on the interpretation of Community law it is important to underline that the ECJ refuses to consider its rulings as irrevocable. As a result, the ECJ may modify its interpretation of Community law and thus national courts are entitled to bring the same or a similar matter (although based on different facts or supported by new legal arguments[43]) before the ECJ by way of a reference for a preliminary ruling under art 177 EC. For that reason a new referral, or a referral concerning the same or similar question, cannot be easily dismissed by the ECJ. For example, in Case 28/67 *Molkerei-Zentrale*[44] the ECJ examined at length new arguments invoked against its previous interpretation. If the referred question is identical to the one already decided the ECJ accepts the preliminary question but refers to its previous ruling.[45]

Distinction between discretionary and compulsory reference by national courts to the ECJ

There are two possible approaches aimed at ensuring the uniformity in the application of Community law. One is the compulsory referral to the ECJ each time a national court or tribunal has difficulties with the interpretation or the validity of Community law. This would be inconvenient in terms of the duration of proceedings and the heavy workload imposed upon the ECJ. The alternative is to grant an unlimited discretion to national courts, whatever their position in the hierarchy of their national judicial systems, as to whether or not to refer to the ECJ, which would jeopardise the homogeneity of the Community law. Article 177 EC represents a compromise between these two approaches. Thus, national courts or tribunals against whose decisions there is no judicial remedy under national law 'shall bring' a question of interpretation of Community law before the ECJ, while other national courts or tribunals will have unfettered discretion in matters of referrals. The idea behind this compromise is that in the case of obviously wrong decisions of lower courts on the point of Community law an appeal to a superior court would rectify that mistake, especially in the light of a mandatory referral to the ECJ by the court of last resort.

Discretion of national courts and tribunals to refer: art 177(2) EC

The lower courts within the meaning of art 177(2) EC have an unfettered discretion to refer to the ECJ. Article 177 EC recognises the exclusive jurisdiction of a national court which hears the principal issue to decide whether or not to refer a question to the ECJ. As a result,

---

[42] Case 33/65 *Dekker* [1965] ECR 1116; Case 82/71 *Sail* [1972] ECR 136; Case C–213/89 *R v Secretary of State for Transport, ex parte Factortame (No 2)* [1991] ECR I–2433; Case 222/84 *Johnson* [1986] ECR 1651.

[43] In Case 22/78 *ICAC* [1979] ECR 1168 the ECJ upheld its previous ruling on the ground that the new referral did not demonstrate any new factual or legal circumstances which would lead to a different interpretation.

[44] [1968] ECR 229.

[45] Case 44/65 *Hessische Knappschaft* [1965] ECR 965 at 1200.

a national judge has the sole discretion as to whether to refer. Neither the parties to the dispute, nor their legal representatives, nor any other public authorities which under certain national legal systems may interfere in the proceedings, can force a national court to refer to the ECJ under art 177 EC. To the contrary, a national judge may decide to refer even if the parties to the dispute have not raised the issue,[46] or not to refer even if so requested by one of them,[47] or both as in Case 31/62 *Wöhrman*.[48] In Case C–85/95 *J Reisdorf*[49] the ECJ held that parties cannot challenge a question referred by a national judge to the ECJ as irrelevant to the dispute, and in Case 5/72 *Fratelli Grassi*[50] ruled out the possibility for the parties to the dispute to change the content of a referred question. National procedural rules cannot impose restrictions on the court's discretion in this respect. In Case 166/73 *Rheinmühlen*[51] the ECJ emphasised that 'a rule of national law whereby a court is bound on points of law by the rulings of a superior court cannot deprive the inferior courts of their power to refer to the Court questions of interpretation of Community law involving such rulings'. National courts may refer the question at any stage of proceedings.[52] The ECJ in Case 70/77 *Simmenthal*[53] held that the proper administration of justice requires that the question should not be referred prematurely although it is outside the jurisdiction of the ECJ to specify at which particular point of the proceedings the national courts should ask for preliminary rulings.[54] The ECJ has emphasised many times that national courts have the best knowledge of the case, and that taking into account their responsibility for rendering correct judgments they, alone, are competent to assess the relevance of the question of Community law raised in the dispute and the necessity of obtaining a preliminary ruling.[55]

In order to facilitate the tasks of national courts and tribunals the ECJ issued a Note containing recommendations on the technical aspects of the referral under art 177 EC.[56] The Note is very useful since the initial liberal approach has changed over the years and, although the ECJ maintains a strict policy of non-interference vis-à-vis national courts and tribunals over matters of what to refer, when to refer and how to refer, it has introduced certain requirements, especially concerning the existence of a genuine dispute, the relevance of the referred question to the dispute at issue and the determination of the factual and legal context of the dispute.

Existence of a genuine dispute
In Case 104/79 *Foglia* v *Novello*[57] the ECJ refused to give a preliminary ruling on the ground that there was no genuine dispute between the parties to national proceedings. In this case

---

[46] Case 126/80 *Salonia* v *Poidomani and Giglio* [1981] ECR 1563.
[47] Case C–152/94 *Van Buynder* [1995] ECR I–3981.
[48] [1962] ECR 501.
[49] [1996] ECR I–6257.
[50] [1972] ECR 443.
[51] [1974] ECR 33; see also Case C–312/93 *Peterbroeck* [1996] 1 CMLR 793.
[52] Case 43/71 *Politi* [1971] ECR II–1039; Case 162/73 *Birra Dreher* [1974] ECR 201.
[53] [1978] ECR 1453.
[54] Cases 36 and 71/80 *Irish Creamery Milk Suppliers Association* [1981] ECR 735; Case 72/83 *Campus Oil* [1984] ECR 2727.
[55] For example, in Case 53/79 *ONPTS* v *Damiani* [1980] ECR 273 and Case 26/62 *Van Gend en Loos* [1963] ECR 1.
[56] Note informative sur l'introduction de procédure préjudicielles par les juridictions nationales: Activités de la Cour de justice et du Tribunal de première instance, no 31/96, [1997] Europe (January), no 8, comm DR.
[57] [1980] ECR 745.

Foglia, an Italian wine merchant, entered into a contract with Novello, an Italian national, for the delivery of liqueur wine to a person residing in France. They inserted an express clause providing that Novello would not pay any unlawfully levied taxes. The French authorities imposed a tax on the importation of the wine to France which Foglia paid, although his contract with a shipper also provided that he should not be liable for any charges imposed in breach of the free movement of goods. Foglia brought proceedings against Novello who refused to reimburse the French tax levied on wine.

The ECJ declined to exercise jurisdiction under art 177 EC on the ground that there was no real dispute in the case. It held that:

> 'It … appears that the parties to the main action are concerned to obtain a ruling that the French tax system is invalid for liqueur wine by the expedient of proceedings before an Italian court between two private individuals who are in agreement as to the result to be obtained and who have inserted a clause in their contract in order to induce the Italian court to give a ruling on the point. The artificial nature of this expedient is underlined by the fact that Foglia did not exercise its rights under French law to institute proceedings over the consumption tax although it undoubtedly has an interest in doing so in view of the clause in the contract by which it was bound and moreover by the fact that Foglia paid the duty without protest'.

Both parties had the same interest in the outcome of the dispute which was to obtain a ruling on the invalidity of the French legislation since under their contracts they were not liable to for any unlawful charges imposed by France; their action was a collusive and artificial device aimed at obtaining a ruling and not a genuine dispute which the ECJ could settle.

When the Italian court asked the ECJ to provide clarification on its preliminary judgment in Case 104/79 *Foglia v Novello*, the ECJ accepted the second reference in the case but once again declined its jurisdiction to give a preliminary ruling on the same grounds.[58] The existence of a real dispute in the proceedings before a national court is determined from the point of view of art 177 EC. Thus, neither the fact that the parties challenge national legislation of one Member State before a court of another Member State, nor their agreement to 'organise' the proceedings before a national court leading to the preliminary ruling, is sufficient to exclude a real dispute from the scope of art 177 EC.[59] In Case C–150/88 *Eau de Cologne v Provide*[60] a German manufacturer of Eau de Cologne brought an action against an Italian company, Provide, when the latter refuse to accept the products and make payments on the ground that the packaging of the products was incompatible with Italian law and could not be marketed in Italy, even though it was in conformity with Community law. The ECJ accepted the referral from a German court even though the compatibility of Italian law with Community law was at issue.

The decision of the ECJ in *Foglia v Novello* has been much criticised[61] but the ECJ has reaffirmed its position in a number of cases.[62] In addition, the ECJ has provided further specifications as to the existence of a genuine dispute. In Case 93/78 *Mattheus*[63] the ECJ

---

[58] Case 244/80 *Foglia v Novello (No 2)* [1981] ECR 3045.

[59] Case C–412/93 *Société d'Importation E Leclerc-SIPLEC and TF1 Publicité SA and M6 Publicité SA* [1995] ECR I–179; Case C–141/93 *Bosman* [1995] ECR I–4921, Europe, February 1996, no 56, comm FG and DS.

[60] [1989] ECR 3891.

[61] See E Bebr, 'The Possible Implications of *Foglia v Novello (No 2)*' (1982) 19 CMLR 421.

[62] Case 98/85 *Bertini* [1986] ECR 1885; Case C–231/89 *Gmurzynska* [1990] ECR I–4003.

[63] [1978] ECR 2203.

declined to exercise its jurisdiction under art 177 EC because the referred question concerned not the interpretation of Community law in force but the opinion of the Court on the enactment of future laws. Also, the ECJ refuses to answer general or hypothetical questions.[64] In Case C–83/91 *Meilicke v ADV/ORGA FA Meyer*[65] the question of compatibility of the German legal theory of disguised non-cash subscription of capital with the Second Company Law Directive was considered hypothetical as it was irrelevant to the dispute in question.

In this context it is interesting to note that when referred questions do not concern a genuine dispute and have no real connection with Community law, the ECJ has developed a new manner in which to deal with them. Instead of declaring them inadmissible under art 177 EC, the ECJ under art 92 of its Rules of Procedure issues an order which declares them manifestly inadmissible.[66]

Another aspect concerning the existence of an actual dispute was examined by the ECJ in Case 159/90 *Society for the Protection of Unborn Children (Ireland) v Grogan.*[67] In this case the plaintiff asked the Irish High Court for an injunction prohibiting Irish student organisations distributing information concerning abortion clinics in the United Kingdom as contrary to the Irish Constitution. During the interlocutory proceedings, the High Court referred the question on merits to the ECJ. In the meantime the decision to refer was appealed to the Irish Supreme Court which granted the injunction, but did not quash the part of the High Court referral regarding the issue whether the defendants were entitled under the Community provision on the freedom to provide services to distribute the information on abortion clinics in the United Kingdom.

The ECJ found a very diplomatic solution to the highly sensitive issue. The ECJ refused to give a preliminary ruling on the ground that it had no jurisdiction to hear a referral when the proceedings before the referring court were already terminated.

Because in the event that a higher court had already ruled on the matter and there was no dispute pending before the referring lower court, the ECJ declined to exercise its jurisdiction under art 177 EC.

Relevance of a referred question to the main dispute

The relevance of a referred question to the actual dispute was for the first time clearly assessed in Case 126/80 *Salonia v Poidomani and Giglio*,[68] in which the ECJ held that it could reject a reference since the national court was seeking to obtain a preliminary ruling on the interpretation of Community law quite clearly not relevant to the actual case. As a result, the ECJ has declined its jurisdiction under art 177 EC to answer a question which had no connection with the subject matter of the main action,[69] or, as the ECJ held in Case C–18/93 *Corsica Ferries*,[70] which 'does not respond to the objective need to resolve the main

---

[64] Case C–343/90 *Dias* [1992] ECR I–4673; Case C–412/93 *Leclerc-Siplec* [1995] ECR I–179; Cases C–422–424/93 *Teresa Zabala Erasun* [1995] ECR I–1567.

[65] [1992] ECR I–4871.

[66] Case C–428/93 *Monin Automobiles* [1994] ECR I–1707 Ord; Case C–378/93 *La Pyramide SARL* [1994] ECR I–3999 Ord.

[67] [1991] ECR I–4685.

[68] [1981] ECR 1563.

[69] Case C–343/90 *Dias* [1992] ECR I–4673; Cases C–332, 333 and 335/92 *Eurico Italia* [1994] ECR I–711.

[70] [1994] ECR I–1783.

action', or to assess the validity of Community acts which do not apply to a particular dispute.[71] However, this new approach is attenuated by the possibility of the ECJ reformulating the question referred by a national court,[72] or taking into consideration provisions of Community law which the national court did not mention in its referral.[73]

Determination of factual and legal context of the dispute

In the Note containing recommendations on the technical aspects of the referral under art 177 EC[74] the ECJ emphasised that the request for a preliminary ruling should state all the relevant facts with clarity and precision, the legal context of the dispute, the reasons which compelled the judge to ask for a referral and the arguments submitted by the parties to the dispute. The ECJ has underlined that a well-drafted referral contributes to a better comprehension of the factual and legal context of the dispute and thus permits the Member States and the Community institutions to submit their observations and the ECJ to give a useful reply. The more stringent formal requirements have been gradually introduced by the ECJ. In the early case law the ECJ held that it was not a task of the ECJ to verify the facts and the qualification of the legal nature of the referred question.[75] In later cases the ECJ declined to exercise its jurisdiction under art 177 EC for lack of relevant information,[76] while recent cases demonstrate that the insufficient contextualisation of a dispute may lead to the ECJ rejecting the referral as manifestly inadmissible.[77] However, the strict requirement of contextualisation of a dispute is of lesser importance in areas in which the facts are not that essential, for example if the referred question concerned the validity of the Community acts. In Case C–295/94 *Hüpeden* and Case C–296/94 *Bernard Pietsch* a national court formulated the referred question in very lucid terms – Is the provision X of Regulation Y valid? – and the ECJ accepted the referral.[78] In Case C–316/93 *Vaneetveld*[79] the ECJ held that despite insufficient information having been submitted by the national court on the legal and factual context of the dispute it was able to formulate a useful reply because the insufficient contextualisation was less important in this case as its subject-matter covered technical points.

It is worth noting in this context that the factual situation as described by a national court will be accepted by the ECJ although it may be inexact or even erroneous. In Case C–352/95 *Phytheron International SA*[80] the national court submitted not only insufficient information, as it did not mention the holder of the disputed trade mark in France and in Germany, but also provided the ECJ with erroneous factual and legal information as it

---

[71] Case C–297/93 *Grau Hupka* [1994] ECR I–5535.

[72] Case 35/85 *Tissier* [1986] ECR 1207; Case C–315/92 *Clinique* [1994] ECR I–317.

[73] Case C–151/93 *Voogd Vleesimport en Export BV* [1994] ECR I–4915.

[74] Supra note 56.

[75] Case 20/64 *Albatros* [1965] ECR 41; Case 5/77 *Tedeschi* [1977] ECR 1555.

[76] Cases C–320–322/90 *Telemarsicabruzzo* [1993] ECR I–393.

[77] The ECJ issued an order of manifest inadmissibility of referrals for lack of information in Case C–378/93 *La Pyramide SARL* [1994] ECR I–3999; Case C–458/93 *Mostafa Saddik* [1995] ECR I–511; Case C–165/94 *Juan Carlos Grau Gomis* [1995] ECR I–1023; Case C–307/95 *Max Mara* [1995] ECR I–5083; and more recently in three cases: Case C–101/96 *Italia Testa*, Order of 25 June 1996; Case C–191/96 *M Modesti* [1996] ECR I–3937 Ord; and Case C–196/96 *Lahlou Hassa* [1996] ECR I–3945 Ord.

[78] Case C–295/94 *Hüpeden* [1996] ECR I–3375; Case C–296/94 *Bernard Pietsch* [1996] ECR I–3409.

[79] [1994] ECR I–763.

[80] [1997] ECR I–1729.

stated that the place where the product was manufactured was in Turkey while in fact it was Germany. The ECJ gave a preliminary ruling which in the light of new facts was irrelevant to the main dispute, and justified its decision on the ground of legal certainty and the right to defence. In particular, the Court highlighted the fact that the holder of the disputed trade mark was not a party to the main dispute and therefore could not submit his arguments to the ECJ, and that by taking into account new facts the ECJ would deprive the Member States and the Community institutions of their right to present their observations within the framework of the preliminary ruling.[81] This approach was confirmed in Case C–233/95 *A Moksel* in which a German court erroneously described the factual situation of the dispute. The ECJ held that the separation of functions between national courts and the ECJ within the framework of art 177 EC requires that the national court determine the particular factual circumstances of each case, and the ECJ has jurisdiction solely to give a ruling on the interpretation and the validity of Community law on the basis of the facts submitted by the national court.[82]

Mandatory referral of national courts of last resort: art 177(3) EC

The exact meaning of art 177(3) EC, which states that if a question of interpretation of Community law 'is raised in a case pending before a court or tribunal of a Member State, against whose decision there is no judicial remedy under national law, the court or tribunal shall bring the matter before the Court of Justice', has been clarified by the ECJ.

The first point elucidated by the ECJ was the determination of courts or tribunals within the scope of art 177(3) EC. In this respect the ECJ held that courts against whose decision there is no judicial remedy under national law, that is no right of appeal against their decisions under national law, are within the scope of art 177(3) EC.[83] This formula, however, comprises not only final appellate courts in each Member State but also all courts which decide a case in the last instance. In Case 6/64 *Costa* v *ENEL*[84] the Giudice Conciliatore in Milan was the court of last instance because of the sum of money involved in the dispute, £1, which Costa refused to pay. As a result, any court or tribunal against whose decision there is no judicial remedy in a given case falls within art 177(3) EC, although in other cases an appeal would be possible against decisions of that court and tribunal. In the United Kingdom there is still uncertainty whether the Court of Appeal should be considered as a final appellate court if leave to appeal to the House of Lords is unobtainable.[85] In *Generics (UK) Ltd* v *Smith, Kline and French Laboratories Ltd*[86] the Court of Appeal held that:

> 'We are not ... the final appellate court for the purposes of art 177 of the Treaty even though an appeal to the House of Lords lies only with leave ... So we are not obliged to refer the question to the EEC Court of Justice. But we have discretion.'

---

[81] Cases 141–143/81 *Holdijk* [1982] ECR 1299.

[82] Judgment of 7 May 1997 [1997] Europe (July), no 229, comm A Rigaux.

[83] There are the final appellate courts in each Member States such as the House of Lords in the United Kingdom or the Cour de Cassation or Conseil d'Etat in France

[84] [1964] ECR 585.

[85] The question was addressed in *Chiron Corporation* v *Murex Diagnostic* [1995] All ER (EC) 88 (CA, HL) but not settled.

[86] [1990] 1 CMLR 416.

It is submitted that in cases where the right of appeal or judicial review is conditional upon the granting of leave the best solution is to impose upon the lower courts the obligation of granting such leave or to refer to the ECJ. Once the proceedings are no longer pending before that court the principle of legal security requires that the proceedings will not be reopened before that court. If leave to appeal to the House of Lords is denied it seems that the parties would still have the possibility of complaining to the Commission under art 169 EC. According to Weatherill and Beaumont, on one occasion the Commission brought proceedings against France under art 169 EC 'for an allegedly manifest error of application of Community law by the Cour de Cassation in failing to overturn the decision of a lower court in favour of the French prosecuting authorities'.[87]

The second point which the ECJ has clarified in respect of art 177(3) EC concerns the requirements of mandatory references by national courts of last resort. At first glance it seems that the terms of art 177(3) EC are imperative and that they impose an obligation upon the courts of last instance to ask for a preliminary ruling each time the interpretation of Community law is at issue. In addition, the formula used in art 177(2) EC, which provides that national courts or tribunals may refer to the ECJ if they consider that a preliminary ruling is necessary to enable them to give judgments, is absent in art 177(3) EC. This is not, however, the case. In Joined Cases 28–30/62 *Da Costa en Schaake* v *Nederlandse Belasting-administratie*[88] the ECJ held that art 177(3) EC 'unreservedly' requires the courts of last resort to refer, but it recognised one exception. It is not necessary to refer if the ECJ had already interpreted the same question in an earlier case since '... the authority of an interpretation under art 177 already given by the Court may deprive the obligation [to refer] from its purpose and thus empty it of its substance'. This is so, especially when the question raised is materially identical with a question which has already been the subject of a preliminary ruling in a similar case. In *Da Costa* the question asked was identical to that raised in Case 26/62 *Van Gend en Loos*.[89] In Case 83/78 *Pigs Marketing Board*[90] the ECJ held that the court should assess the relevance of the question raised before it in the light of the necessity to obtain the preliminary ruling. Those two exceptions were restated and further developed in Case 283/81 *CILFIT* v *Ministro della Sanita*[91] in which the extent of the discretion of courts of last resort was fully explained. Here, the Italian Ministry of Health imposed an inspection levy on imports of wool coming from other Member States. An Italian importer of wool challenged the levy. The Italian court considered that the case law on this matter was reasonably clear, but as a court of final instance it was uncertain whether or not it should refer the question of legality of this fixed health inspection levy to the ECJ. The Italian court asked the ECJ whether it was obliged to refer under art 177(3) EC when the Community law was sufficiently clear and precise and there was no doubt as to its interpretation.

The ECJ held that the courts of last resort, like any other courts or tribunals, have the discretion to assess whether a referral is necessary to enable them to give judgment. They are not obliged to refer if a question concerning the interpretation of Community law raised

---

[87] *EC Law*, 2nd ed, London: Penguin Books, 1995, p202.
[88] [1963] ECR 31.
[89] [1963] ECR 1.
[90] [1978] ECR 2347.
[91] [1982] ECR 3415.

before them is not relevant to the dispute, that is, if it can in no way affect the outcome of the case. The ECJ confirmed the principle of *Da Costa* by stating that if the ECJ had already dealt with a point of law in question, even though the questions were not strictly identical, the court of last resort is not obliged to refer. Finally, the ECJ held that there is no obligation to refer if 'the correct application of Community law may be so obvious as to leave no scope for any reasonable doubt as to the manner in which the question raised is to be resolved. Before it comes to the conclusion that such is the case, the national court or tribunal must be convinced that the matter is equally obvious to the Courts of the other Member States and to the Court of Justice (ECJ)'.

In *CILFIT* the ECJ endorsed the French doctrine of *acte clair*, according to which the court before which the *exception prejudicielle* is raised concerning the interpretation or validity of a particular provision must refer it to a competent court in order to resolve that question, but only if there is real difficulty concerning its interpretation or validity or if there is a serious doubt in this respect. However, if this provision is clear, if its validity is obvious, the court may apply it immediately. It stems from *CILFIT* that it is not necessary for a court of last resort to refer if:

1. The question of Community law is irrelevant to the dispute.
2. The question of Community law has already been interpreted by the ECJ, even though it may not be identical. However, it does not mean that national courts, whatever their position in the hierarchy of national courts, are prevented from referring an identical or a similar question to the ECJ. In *CILFIT* the ECJ clearly stated that all courts remained entirely at liberty to refer a matter before them if they consider it appropriate to do so.
3. The correct application of Community law is so obvious as to leave no scope for reasonable doubt. This incorporates the French theory of *acte clair*. However, the ECJ added that before a national court concludes that such is the case it must be convinced that the question is equally obvious to courts in other Member States and to the ECJ itself. Furthermore, the ECJ added that there were three requirements which a national court must take into consideration when deciding that the matter is clear and free of doubts. First, it must assess such possibility in the light of the characteristic features of Community law and especially the difficulties that its interpretation raise, that is that it is drafted in several languages and all versions are equally authentic. Second, it must be aware that Community law uses peculiar terminology and has legal concepts which have different meanings in different Member States. And, finally, a national court must bear in mind that every provision of Community law must be placed in its context and interpreted in the light of the provisions of Community law as a whole, its objectives and the state of its evolution at the date on which that provision is to be applied.

The ruling in *CILFIT* has also explained the circumstances in which any court or tribunal as mentioned under art 177(2) should refer to the ECJ for a preliminary ruling. As a result it applies to any courts or tribunals of a Member State if they consider that a preliminary ruling on the question of interpretation of Community law is necessary in order to enable them to give judgment (art 177(2) EC), and to a court or tribunal of a Member State against whose decision there is no judicial remedy under national law (art 177(3) EC). In the case of courts within the scope of art 177(2) EC, the ruling in *CILFIT* assists them in deciding whether or not to refer, while under art 177(3) EC it should be interpreted more strictly, that is, the court of last resort must refer to the ECJ if there are any reasonable doubts as to the meaning of a provision of Community law. However, in practice the endorsement by the ECJ of the doctrine of *acte clair* has sensibly extended the discretion of the courts of last resort. It has also increased the risk of conflicting decisions being rendered by the highest courts in each Member States. On many occasions national courts decided not to refer to the ECJ on the basis of this doctrine and imposed their own interpretation of Community law, and thus prevented the ECJ from expressing its views. In the United Kingdom in *R v Secretary of State for the Home Department, ex parte Sandhu*[92] the House of Lords refused to refer to the ECJ, although the question whether a divorced Indian husband of an EC national who was threatened with deportation from the UK was entitled to stay on the basis of Directive 68/360 was far from being clear and free of doubts. The House of Lords decided that certain statements delivered *obiter* by the ECJ in Case 267/83 *Diatta v Land Berlin*[93] were applicable to this case. However, in *Diatta* the spouses were separated and the matter was examined in the light of Regulation 1612/68 regarding rights of residence of members of the family of workers, while in *Sandhu* they were divorced and he based his claim on Directive 68/360.[94] Mr Sandhu was deported despite the fact that he had been previously married to a German national, he and his wife had established their domicile in the UK, his son whom he often visited in Germany where his former wife returned after their divorce had been born in the UK, and Mr Sandhu had permanent employment in the UK which allowed him to financially support his son. Also in *Magnavision NV v General Optical Council*[95] the Divisional Court on the basis of the ruling in *CILFIT* refused to give leave for certain points of law to be examined by the House of Lords, without which no appeal could be made to the ECJ. In this case the defendant raised the question of Community law, more precisely the application of art 30 EC concerning the free movement of goods in relation to his conviction for breach of s21 of the Opticians Act 1958 which prohibited the sale of optical appliances without the supervision of a registered medical practitioner or optician. The Divisional Court decided that there was no infringement of art 30 EC by s21 of the Opticians Act 1958, although this point was very controversial, and thus refused to refer to the ECJ. The defendant was left without a remedy.

Sometimes the Court of Appeal and the House of Lords disagree on the interpretation of Community law as in *Freight Transport Association and Others v London Boroughs Transport Committee*.[96] In this case the Court of Appeal held that the local regulations restricting vehicle noise emissions were in breach of Community law, while the House of Lords based on the ruling in *CILFIT* decided the contrary and refused to refer the question to the ECJ.[97]

---

[92] [1982] 2 CMLR 553.

[93] [1985] ECR 567.

[94] For detailed examination of this case see P Beaumont and Campbell, 'Preliminary Rulings' (1985) 53 SLG 62–64.

[95] [1987] 1 CMLR 716.

[96] [1991] ECR I–5403.

[97] In *R v Secretary of State for Environment, ex parte RSPB* [1995] JPL 842 the House of Lords referred to the ECJ. It was faced with conflicting views on the interpretation of the EC Birds Directive which was clear and obvious for all concerned, but the Divisional Court and the majority of the Court of Appeal held that under this Directive the Secretary of State could take into consideration economic factors in determining whether a particular area should be excluded from a Special Protection Area for Birds, while the dissenting judge in the Court of Appeal argued that economic factors should not be taken into account by the Secretary of State.

Also, in other Member States national courts of last resort may abuse the doctrine of *acte clair*. For example in France the Conseil d'Etat refused to refer to the ECJ the question of interpretation of art 37 EC despite the fact that its exact meaning was uncertain.[98] Probably the best example of abuse of the doctrine of *acte clair* is provided by *Cohn-Bendit* in which the French *Conseil d'Etat* imposed its own interpretation of art 189 EC upon all administrative courts in France, contrary to the case law of the ECJ.[99] However, the French *Conseil d'Etat* is not the only superior court in this position.[100]

This kind of infringement of art 177(3) EC threatens the very existence of Community law and for the individual concerned results in a denial of justice. For that reason the Commission considers that proceedings under art 169 EC may be brought against national courts in the case of patent abuse of art 177(3) EC.[101] As already noted, the first proceedings against the French Cour de Cassation have already been initiated by the Commission under art 169 EC.

Procedure before the ECJ under art 177 EC

The procedure under art 177 EC is not adversarial and constitutes in reality a dialogue between national courts or tribunals and the ECJ. In the Note to national courts the ECJ emphasised that until its preliminary ruling is given the ECJ would stay in touch with the referring court to which it would send copies of subsequent documents, such as observations, conclusions of Advocate-General, etc. Also, the ECJ expressed a wish to be informed by the sending court of the actual application of the preliminary ruling to the main action and to obtain a copy of the final decision rendered by that court.[102]

The reference can only be made by national courts or tribunals within the meaning of art 177 EC. The procedure for reference in England is provided in the ordinary rules of proceedings for that court.[103] The information that a referring court must provide is very similar to that specified in the ECJ Note, that is the names of the parties, the factual and legal context of the dispute including the domestic law and relevant provisions of the Community law, and the contentions of the parties. The ECJ held in Case 13/61 *Bosch*[104] that no particular form is required for reference, but emphasised in Case 101/63 *Wagner*[105] that the referring court is free to formulate it in direct and simple form.

---

[98] Judgment of 19 June 1964, *Shell-Berre* [1964] RDP 134, concl N Questiaux [1964] AJDA, note Laubadere; see also the decision of the Conseil d'Etat of 12 October 1979, *Société Nationale des Importateurs de Vetements* [1989] AJDA 95.

[99] This case is fully discussed in Chapter 7.

[100] In The Netherlands the *Hoge Raad*, Judgment of 22 December 1965 [1967] CDE 84; in Germany the *Bundesfinanzhof* (the German Federal Fiscal Court), Judgment of 23 July 1968 [1969] AWD 203; also the rejection by that court of the direct effect of directives in *Re VAT Directives* [1982] 1 CMLR 525 and in a decision of 25 April 1985 in *Kloppenburg* [1989] 1 CMLR 873. See G Bebr, 'Article 177 of the EEC Treaty in the Practice of National Courts' [1977] ICLQ 264.

[101] See the answers of the Commission to the parliamentary questions: OJ C71 17.7.68 p1; OJ C161 17.7.75 p12; OJ C137 4.7.86 p7.

[102] Supra note 56.

[103] Reference for the High Court is contained in RSC O.114 r l, the form is governed by O.114 r2 which is Form 109 in the Supreme Court Practice.

[104] [1962] ECR 89.

[105] [1964] ECR 383.

As to an appeal against a decision to refer, in Case 166/73 *Rheinmühlen*[106] the ECJ held that an order for reference is subject to the remedies normally available under national law. In England RSC O.114 r1 provides that a reference to the ECJ is a final order and thus an appeal lies to the Court of Appeal without leave. An appeal against an order for reference made by the Court of Appeal is subject to the leave of the House of Lords. Usually the order is not sent to Luxembourg before the expiry of the time for appealing, but discretion lies with the referring court. In *R v Stock Exchange of the United Kingdom and the Republic of Ireland*[107] the Court of Appeal overturned the decision of a lower court to refer to the ECJ and held that when the criteria of the ruling in *CILFIT* are satisfied and the referring court could have resolved the matter itself with complete confidence there was no need for reference. In Case 72/83 *Campus Oil v Minister for Industry and Energy*[108] it was recognised that national rules of procedure in this area should not inhibit lower courts which have unfettered discretion under art 177(2) EC to refer. However, it is outside the jurisdiction of the ECJ to verify whether the decision to refer was taken in conformity with national procedural rules.[109]

Usually, the ECJ is seised by the Registrar of the referring court which addresses the referral to the Registrar of the ECJ, in cases coming from the UK to the Registrar in charge of British referrals. The procedure for the ECJ is set out in the Protocol on the Statute of the ECJ annexed to each founding Treaty and in the Rules of Procedure of the ECJ. Article 177 proceedings are very similar to proceedings before French courts. The emphasis is on written pleadings more than on oral procedure. Once the Registry of the ECJ has formally acknowledged the referral it is translated into the other official languages of the Community. The Registrar notifies the referral to the Community institutions, especially the Commission which is a guardian of the Treaties and as such is almost always involved in the proceedings, the Council if the disputed act was adopted by the latter, the Member States, and the parties to the original proceedings which have two months to submit their written observations. Under art 20 of the Statute of the ECJ only notified parties are entitled to submit observations. The text of the referral in published in the 'C' series of the Official Journal. At this stage the ECJ designates one of its judges as the 'judge rapporteur'. He prepares a preliminary assessment of the referral for the exclusive use of the ECJ and decides whether any procedural measures are necessary, such as reports from expert witnesses, etc. Once the ECJ is seised by the referring court it has jurisdiction to give a preliminary ruling until the withdrawal of the reference by the sending court.[110] In Case C–194/94 *CIA Security International SA, Signalson SA and Securitel SA*[111] the ECJ rejected the argument of the original parties that the modification of national law applicable to the dispute subsequent to the referral rendered the preliminary ruling unnecessary. The ECJ held that this question should be assessed by the referring court, which is solely competent

---

[106] [1974] ECR 33.

[107] [1993] 1 All ER 420.

[108] [1984] 1 CMLR 479.

[109] Case 65/81 *Reina* [1982] ECR 33; Case C–10/92 *Balocchi* [1993] ECR I–5105, recently confirmed in Case C–39/94 *Syndicat Français de l'Express International* [1996] ECR I–3547.

[110] Case 106/77 *Simmenthal* [1978] ECR 629.

[111] Judgment of 30 April [1996] Europe (June) no 233.

to decide whether or not the preliminary ruling is still required in order to enable it to give judgment. In Case 31/68 *Chanel*[112] the ECJ held that when it is informed by the referring court, or the superior court, that an appeal has been lodged against a national decision under consideration then proceedings before the ECJ would be postponed until the decision of the referring court is confirmed by a superior court, and if it is overturned the ECJ would set aside the proceedings under art 177 EC.

The next stage is the oral procedure which commences with a report submitted by the judge rapporteur stating the facts of the referral and the contentions of the parties. It is followed by a very short hearing, approximately 30 minutes for each party to present their arguments as well as the Commission or the Council or any other EC institution or a Member State which submitted written pleadings. The oral and written pleadings of the parties must be limited to the legal context as determined by the referring court.[113] The parties are not allowed to change the content of the question formulated by a national judge nor to add their own questions,[114] or to declare the referral without object.[115] Furthermore, the original parties are not entitled to challenge the jurisdiction of the ECJ[116] or to involve in the proceedings persons other than those specified in art 20 of the Protocol of the ECJ.[117] This rule also applies to the Community institutions and the Member States participating in the proceedings.[118] The original parties' involvement in the proceedings under art 177 EC seems to have increased. In this respect Case C–66/95 *Eunice Sutton*[119] is especially instructive. In this case the ECJ, instead of answering the question asked by the referring court, actually replied to questions submitted by the original party to the proceedings, Mrs Sutton. The ECJ examined two possibilities presented in her pleadings, ignoring the fact that the referring jurisdiction as well as Advocate-General Leger expressly excluded the possibility of assessing the dispute in the light of non-contractual liability of a Member State for breach of EC law. As a result, the referring court obtained an answer to a question it did not ask. This attitude of the ECJ is contrary to its position taken since 1965 and often expressed in the formula used in Case 44/65 *Hessische Knappschaft*,[120] according to which it is solely for national courts to determine the questions referred to the ECJ and the parties to a main action are neither entitled to change their content nor to declare them without object. The oral procedure ends when the Advocate-General gives his opinion on the case.

The procedure under art 177 is still time-consuming as it takes at least 18 months. For that reason in some cases the preliminary rulings have been used as tactical devices. The best example is provided by the Sunday trading cases[121] in which the referral to the ECJ permitted the defendant companies to trade on Sundays while awaiting the preliminary rulings. Over a

---

[112] [1969] ECR 403.

[113] Case 62/72 *Bollman* [1973] ECR 269.

[114] Case 247/86 *Alsatel* [1988] ECR 5987.

[115] Case 5/72 *Fratelli Grassi* [1972] ECR 443.

[116] Case C–364/92 *SAT* [1994] ECR I–43.

[117] Case 19/68 *De Sicco* [1968] ECR 699.

[118] Case 39/75 *Coenen* [1975] ECR 1547.

[119] Judgment of 22 April 1997, *Europe*, June 1997, no 191, comm A Rigaux.

[120] [1965] ECR 1192.

[121] Case 145/88 [1989] ECR 765; also A Arnull, 'What Shall We Do on Sunday' 16 ELR 112. See also *Torfaen Borough Council v B & Q plc* (1990) 57 CMLR 337 and *Wellingborough Council v Payless DIY Ltd* (1990) 57 CMLR 773.

number of years the defendants who were in breach of the Shops Act 1950 argued that the latter was contrary to the Community provisions on the free movement of goods.

The costs of the proceedings under art 177 EC are incidental to the national proceedings and as such the referring court decides this question.[122] Nevertheless in some cases under art 104 of the ECJ's Rules of Procedure the ECJ may itself grant legal aid to the original parties.

Effect of preliminary rulings concerning the interpretation of Community law

The Treaties are silent on the legal effect of preliminary rulings concerning the interpretation of Community law. In Cases 28–30/62 *Da Costa*[123] the ECJ defined the legal effects of preliminary rulings: the referring court is bound by the interpretation given by the ECJ either in reply to its question or when it decides an identical question. The *ratio legis* of the proceedings under art 177 EC requires that the preliminary rulings rendered by the ECJ are taken into consideration by the referring court. However, the obligation to take into account the reply from the ECJ is limited. Only if the latter permits the referring court to resolve the dispute at issue is such a ruling binding on it. Otherwise, the referring court may seise the ECJ with the same question in a second referral as it happened in *Foglia* v *Novello (No 2)*. The situation is different if the ECJ not only replies to the referred question but also defines temporal effects of the preliminary ruling. In Case 52/76 *Benedetti* v *Munari*[124] the ECJ held that: '… the rule as … interpreted may, and must, be applied by the courts even to legal relationships arising and established before the judgment ruling on the request for interpretation'.

This retroactive effect of the preliminary ruling – it applies from the entry into force of the provision in question – has many drawbacks. On the one hand, national rules on the limitation period differ from one Member State to another and, on the other hand, the *ex nunc* effect of the preliminary ruling is contrary to the principle of legal certainty. For these reasons in some cases the ECJ has decided to take into consideration the fact that the *ex nunc* effect may cause serious problems in respect of *bona fide* legal relationships established before the preliminary ruling[125] and has restricted its temporal effects. Only the ECJ may limit it *ex nunc* and only in the case in which the ruling was given, not in any subsequent case. For example in Case 309/85 *Barra* v *Belgium*[126] the ECJ refused to restrict the temporal effect of its ruling in Case 293/83 *Gravier* v *Belgium*.[127] As a result, illegal fees charged by the Belgian authorities for vocational training courses for nationals from other Member States were reimbursed to those who claimed them before the ruling in *Gravier* since the ECJ did not impose any temporal restriction. However, in Case 24/86 *Blaizot*[128] or

---

[122] Case 13/61 *Bosch* [1962] ECR 107.

[123] [1963] ECR 59.

[124] [1977] ECR 163.

[125] For example Case 43/75 *Defrenne* [1976] ECR 455; Cases 66, 127 and 128/79 *Salumi* [1980] ECR 1258; Case 61/79 *Denkavit Italiana* [1980] ECR 1205; Case 24/86 *Blaizot* [1988] ECR 379; Case C–262/88 *Barber* [1990] ECR I–1889; Cases C–197 *Société Francaise Maritime* and 252/94 *Société Bautiaa* [1996] ECR I–505.

[126] [1988] ECR 355.

[127] [1985] ECR 593.

[128] [1988] ECR 379.

Case 43/75 *Defrenne*[129] the ECJ decided to limit *ex nunc* the temporal effect of the rulings. It meant that the rulings applied only to those who had started proceedings before the ruling and those who in future may have similar claims. In *Blaizot* the ECJ held that university education was within the scope of the Treaty as it constituted vocational training. As a result the illegal fees charged for those courses by Belgium were only reimbursed to students who had already brought proceedings before Belgian courts and would not be charged to future students. In *Defrenne* claims for backdated pay could only be made by those who had already started legal proceedings or submitted an equivalent claim prior to the date of the ruling. The differences in salary between male stewards and female air hostesses were to be abolished *ex nunc*.

11.3 Validity of Community law

The question of validity of acts adopted by EC institutions may also be referred to the ECJ under art 177 EC.[130] However, as already noted the ECJ cannot rule on the validity of the founding Treaties because of their constitutional nature, or on the statutes of bodies established by an act of the Council mentioned in art 177(1)(c) EC. The ECJ does not permit preliminary references concerning the validity of its own decisions.[131]

Requirements in referrals on validity of Community acts

There is no distinction between national courts in matters relating to validity. Lower courts and the courts of final resort must refer to the ECJ if there are some doubts as to the validity of a Community measure. In Case 314/85 *Foto-Frost v Hauptzollamt Lübeck-Ost*[132] the ECJ has provided a guideline to national courts as to the preliminary rulings on the validity of Community acts. In this case Frost applied to a German municipal court to declare a decision issued by the Commission invalid on the grounds that it was in breach of the requirements set out in the Council regulation which delegated authority to the Commission to adopt decisions. The German court requested a preliminary ruling as to whether it could review the validity of the decision in question.

The ECJ held that for the uniformity of Community law it was especially important that there was no divergence between Member States as to the validity of Community acts since this would jeopardise the very unity of the Community legal order, as well as detracting from the fundamental requirement of legal certainty. The ECJ drew a comparison between its exclusive jurisdiction under art 173 EC and the preliminary ruling on validity of Community acts. It stated that the coherence of the system required that where the validity of Community measures was challenged before a national courts the jurisdiction to declare the act invalid must also be reserved to the ECJ. As a result the ECJ held that 'national courts have no jurisdiction themselves to declare the acts of Community Institutions invalid'.

---

[129] [1976] ECR 455.
[130] For more details see the introduction to this chapter.
[131] Case 69/85 *Wünsche* [1986] ECR 947.
[132] [1987] ECR 4199.

This case confirmed that the ECJ has an exclusive jurisdiction to declare an act of a Community institution invalid. National courts may consider the validity of Community acts and may declare them valid. However, if they have doubts as to their validity they must make reference to the ECJ under art 177 EC.

In a recent decision the ECJ has excluded the possibility of referring a question of validity in certain circumstances. In Case C–188/92 *TWD Textilwerke Deggendorf GmbH*[133] the ECJ held that the possibility was excluded for the beneficiary of aid, who was the subject of a decision adopted on the ground of art 93 EC, and who could have challenged its validity by virtue of art 173 EC but had let the prescribed time-limit elapse, to call into question the validity of measures implementing this decision adopted by national authorities in proceedings under art 177 EC. It means that when the applicant does not bring an action for annulment under art 173 EC within the prescribed time-limit national courts are precluded from making a reference to the ECJ under art 177 EC in respect of validity of such an act.

It is submitted that the solution in *TWD Textilwerke* is contrary to the spirit of co-operation between national judges and the ECJ which art 177 EC aims to foster. The procedure of the preliminary ruling has as one of its main objectives the alleviation of the stringent requirements for *locus standi* under art 173 EC by permitting the challenge in national proceedings of the validity of Community acts without imposing any particular time-limit. Furthermore, the objective nature of the procedure under art 177 EC has been called into question by the introduction of the subjective assessment of the situation of the applicant by a national court which is alien to the philosophy of art 177 EC. The interdependence and similarity between actions for annulment under art 173 EC and the preliminary reference in respect of the validity of Community acts by national courts under art 177 EC is not a sufficient reason to justify the decision of the ECJ in *TWD*. Indeed, there is an important and substantial difference between judicial review of Community acts contained in art 173 EC and a request for assistance from national courts to the ECJ under art 177 EC. Furthermore, it seems that, in principle, preliminary rulings in respect of the validity of individual acts were within the scope of art 177 EC until the decision in *TWD*.[134]

Effect of a preliminary ruling on validity

The peculiarity of the legal effects of preliminary rulings on the validity of Community acts derives from the close connection with actions for annulment under art 174, as well as the distinction between a preliminary ruling confirming the validity of the act concerned and a ruling declaring that act invalid. In the first case, the referring court, as well as all other courts and tribunals within the meaning of art 177 EC, may apply the act, or if it considers that it is invalid, the referring court may refer again to the ECJ under art 177 EC.

However, if the ECJ declares the challenged act invalid the situation is different. In Case 66/80 *International Chemical Company*[135] the ECJ held that although the preliminary ruling declaring a Community act invalid is addressed to the referring national court it

---

[133] [1994] ECR I–833.
[134] Case 156/77 *Commission* v *Belgium* [1978] ECR 1881; Case 216/82 *Universität Hamburg* [1983] ECR 2771; Cases 113–136/86 *Rau* [1987] ECR 2344.
[135] [1981] ECR 1191.

constitutes at the same time sufficient justification for all other national judges to consider the act in question invalid in respect of judgments they may render. However, the ECJ added that its declaration in respect of invalidity of a Community act should not prevent national courts from referring again the question already decided by the ECJ if there are problems regarding the scope or possible legal implications of the act previously declared invalid. The extent of the ECJ liberal approach in this area is illustrated in Case 32/77 *Giuliani*[136] in which the ECJ accepted a request for preliminary ruling asking whether it upheld its position in respect of the act previously declared invalid. This approach is justified by the fact that a Community act declared invalid under art 177 EC is still in force. Only the Community institution which adopted the act in question is empowered to annul or modify it, as well as compensating for the damage it caused. In addition, only national authorities are entitled to nullify a national provision which was adopted in order to implement or to apply the invalid act.[137] In this context it is important to mention that the ECJ may declare only a part of the act invalid.[138] The analogy with the effect of a successful action for annulment is obvious. For that reason, the ECJ decided that it was empowered to specify the consequences deriving from invalidity of the act in question, although it has always maintained that it had jurisdiction to draw the conclusions from its preliminary ruling declaring a Community act invalid, that is to decide the main action. First, the ECJ held that it had jurisdiction to limit the temporal effect of such preliminary rulings. In principal, all preliminary rulings have retroactive effect, including those confirming or denying the validity of Community acts.[139] The ECJ has applied art 174(2) EC by analogy in the context of art 177 EC. In Case 112/83 *Produits de Maïs*[140] the ECJ held that the coherence of the Community legal order provides sufficient justification for the application of art 174 EC, which concerns legal effects of a successful action for annulment, in the context of art 177 EC. When the ECJ decides that a regulation is question is invalid *ex nunc* (in the future), under art 177 EC the referring court is barred from drawing any consequences from the ECJ declaration on invalidity of the act, even for the parties to the main action in which the question of validity arose.[141] This solution was strongly criticised by national courts which considered that the ECJ had encroached upon their jurisdiction since under art 177 EC national courts have to apply Community law to the main dispute.[142] The justification provided by the ECJ was based on the principle of legal certainty. The strong opposition of national courts was taken into account by the ECJ in Case C–228/92 *Roquette*[143] in which it held that the exceptional effect *ex nunc* should not deprive those who had already commenced proceedings or made an equivalent claim of the rights stemming from the recognition of invalidity of Community acts. For that reason in many cases the ECJ applies

---

[136] [1977] ECR 1863.

[137] Case 23/75 *Rey-Soda* [1975] ECR 1279.

[138] Case 130/79 *Express Dairy Food* [1980] ECR 1887.

[139] Cases 117/76 and 16/77 *Rückdeschel* [1977] ECR 1753.

[140] [1985] ECR 742.

[141] Case 4/79 *Providence Agricole de Champagne* [1980] ECR 2823.

[142] For example, the judgment of 26 June 1985 of the French Conseil d'Etat in *ONIC* v *Société Maïseries de Beauce* [1985] AJDA 615, concl Genevois; or the judgment of 21 April 1989 of the Italian Constitutional Court in *Fragd* [1989] RDI 103.

[143] [1994] ECR I–1445.

the solution in *Defrenne*, that is, the temporal limitations are not imposed upon the parties to the main action and those who have already brought legal proceedings or made an equivalent claim prior to the date of the judgment.[144] Second, the ECJ has authorised itself to replace the invalidated provisions by ones applicable while awaiting the adoption of appropriated measures by the institution concerned.[145] Finally, it reserves to the Community institution concerned the exclusive right to draw conclusions from the invalidity of its act and take the necessary measures to remedy the situation.[146]

Interim relief

In the context of validity of Community acts the question of interim measures arises with a particular intensity, although it may also have some importance in relation to the interpretation of Community law. Indeed, sometimes the question of interim relief is vital for a party to the proceedings if his rights under Community law are to have any substance. The ECJ in Cases C–143/88 and 92/89 *Zuckerfabrik Süderdithmarschen* v *Hauptzollamt Itzehoe*[147] established the conditions for obtaining interim relief. The referring court asked the ECJ to assess the validity of a regulation and to determine whether it had jurisdiction to suspend a national administrative act based on that regulation. The ECJ replied that a national court could suspend the application of a national measure implementing a Community act until the ruling of the ECJ, providing that a ruling had been sought from the ECJ. Where a national court had not yet made reference to the ECJ it must do it. The suspension of the operation of a national measure is permitted only if certain stringent conditions are satisfied:

1. there is a serious doubt as to the validity of the Community act;
2. the matter must be urgent;
3. there is a risk to the applicant of serious and irreparable harm, that is, pecuniary compensation would not be an adequate remedy;
4. the interests of the Community must be duly taken into account by the national court concerned.

The conditions for the suspension of national legislation implementing a Community act are the same as in an application for interim relief under art 173 EC. In Case C–213/89 *R* v *Secretary of State for Transport, ex parte Factortame*[148] the ECJ held that if national law prevented the court from granting interim relief such rule should be set aside, which in that case led to the interim suspension of the operation of a statute.

In Case C–465/93 *Atlanta Fruchthandelsgesellschaft* v *BEF*[149] the ECJ held that a national court in certain circumstances may grant interim relief from the application of a Community act. In this case Council Regulation 404/93 provided for a revised system of import quotas for bananas from non-ACP countries. The German Federal Food Office (BEF)

---

[144] Case 41/84 *Pinna* [1986] ECR 1.
[145] Case 300/86 *Van Landshoot* [1988] ECR 3443.
[146] Case 124/76 *Moulins et huileries de Point-à-Mousson* [1977] ECR 1795.
[147] [1991] ECR I–415.
[148] [1990] ECR I–2433.
[149] [1995] ECR I–3761.

granted Atlanta such reduced quotas. Atlanta challenged the Regulation and asked for interim relief. The German court asked the ECJ whether it could, while awaiting a preliminary ruling, by an interim order temporary resolve the disputed legal positions and, if so, under what conditions and whether a distinction should be made between an interim order designated to preserve an existing legal position and one which was intended to create a new legal position.

The ECJ confirmed its reasoning in *Zuckerfabrik* as well as its jurisdiction under art 186 EC to order any necessary interim measure. In relation to the first question the ECJ held that:

> 'The interim legal protection which the national courts must afford to individuals under Community law must be the same, whether they seek suspension of enforcement of a national administrative measure adopted on the basis of a Community regulation or the grant of interim measures settling or regulating the disputed legal positions or relationships for their benefit.'

As a result, a Community act may be suspended by a national court, provided the latter has made reference to the ECJ under art 177 EC. The conditions are very stringent. Indeed to those laid down in *Zuckerfabrik* the ECJ added the following:

1. the national court must justify why it considers that the ECJ should find the Community measure invalid;
2. the national court must take into consideration the extent of the discretion allowed to the Community institutions resulting from the ECJ's case law;
3. the national court must assess the Community interest in the light of the impact of suspension on the Community legal regime and the appropriateness of financial guarantees or security;
4. the national court must take into account any previous art 173 judgments concerning the disputed legislation.

In the context of *Atlanta* it is interesting to note that under the strict conditions for an interim order set out in this case, *Atlanta* would have never obtained interim relief as Regulation 404/93 had been challenged unsuccessfully in two previous actions under art 173, once by *Atlanta*, which could not satisfy the requirements for *locus standi,* and once by Germany.

Index